P9-BID-295

Investments

Investments:
A Practical Approach

Ben Branch

LONGMAN FINANCIAL SERVICES PUBLISHING, INC./CHICAGO
a Longman Group USA company

While a great deal of care has been taken to provide
accurate and current information, the ideas, suggestions,
general principles, and conclusions presented in this book
are subject to local, state, and federal laws and regulations,
court cases, and any revisions of same. The reader is thus
urged to consult legal counsel regarding any points of
law—this publication should not be used as a substitute
for competent legal advice.

© 1985 by Longman Group USA Inc.

Published by Longman Financial Services Publishing, Inc.
a Longman Group USA company

Printed in the United States of America.
85 86 87 10 9 8 7 6 5 4 3 2 1

Acquisitions Editor: Ivy Lester
Project Editor: David Walker
Cover/internal design: Cameron Poulter
Cover photo: James L. Ballard

Library of Congress Cataloging in Publication Data

Branch, Ben, 1943–
    Investments : a practical approach.

    Includes index.
    1. Investments. I. Title.
HG4521.B6463   1985   332.6'78   84-26237
ISBN 0-88462-520-6

Contents

Preface

Investments: A Practical Approach is, as the title suggests, designed to help people become successful investors. The book addresses readers with a few thousand dollars to invest, as well as those with larger portfolios already established. Though the text offers no get-rich-quick approaches, those who study it seriously should benefit from its stress on the practical aspects of investing. Abstract theoretical considerations are introduced, but only when they shed light on real-world investment decisions.

Much of what we know about investing relates to how difficult it is to outperform the market; much of the history of the markets confirms the ubiquity of techniques that have not lived up to their advocates' expectations. One thing is certain, however: investors who want maximum returns consistent with the degree of risk they accept need a close working knowledge of the markets, investment vehicles, financial planning, and a host of other topics. This text provides broad and detailed coverage of subjects essential to the rational investor. The traditional finance/investment topics are treated in depth, including investment theory, fundamental analysis, market timing, mutual funds, bonds, and option securities. Going beyond those traditional themes, the book discusses such additional investor opportunities as life insurance, pensions, estate planning, collectibles, commodities, and real estate.

In order to consider a similarly wide range of perspectives and information, *Investments: A Practical Approach* draws extensively on both the academic and the professional investment literature. Material from such academic journals as the *Journal of Finance* and *Financial Management*, translated for the non-expert, add theoretical background and academic reliability to articles from such non-academic sources as *Forbes* or *Barron's*, which often introduce testable hypotheses for academicians to explore. To extract maximum value from these multitudinous sources, the text includes extensive citations, which most readers will simply pass by. For the student writing a term paper, however, or the professor working on a journal article, the notes following each chapter constitute a very useful bibliography.

Text Organization and Its Alternatives

The text is divided into six sections, as follows:

- I (Chapters 1–3): *overview*. Short- and long-term personal financial management; investment characteristics and types; the mechanics, regulation, and economic functions of the securities markets.
- II (Chapters 4–6): *investment theory and valuation*. Valuing and forecasting expected income streams; risk and diversification; empirical evidence on predictions of investment valuation.
- III (Chapters 7–10): *fundamental approaches*. Traditional analysis: economic, industry, firm; accounting statements and the misuse of accounting discretion; operational approaches; sources of investment information.
- IV (Chapters 11–13): *market timing*. The stock market and the business cycle; emotional aspects of the stock market; the timing of individual security trades.
- V (Chapters 14–18): *stock-related investment types*. Mutual funds; short- and long-term debt securities; determinants of debt security yields; pure option securities; convertibles and other combination securities.
- VI (Chapters 19–20): *often-neglected investment areas*. Commodity futures and related areas; real estate and real estate-related stock.

As arranged, the text presents a logical progression and groups topics in a manner designed to clarify the relationships between them. For readers with different needs and preferences, however, other orderings may also prove effective. Chapters 14–20, for example, are largely self contained, and so may be taken up in any order. Chapter 10, on sources of investment information, may be read earlier in the fundamental analysis section, and some readers may want to take up Chapters 7 and 11 together, as both deal with economic analysis.

Readers with specific interests may find the text useful as a source for those topics, and skip other parts. Those interested in stocks and bonds, for example, might pass up the chapters on commodities and real estate. Chapter 2 surveys the material treated in depth in Chapters 14–20, so some readers may choose only one or the other. Those particularly interested in investment timing and selection may want to concentrate on Sections III and IV and skim lightly over the rest of the book.

Acknowledgements

During the years of its creation this text has benefitted from a wide and diverse set of reviews many by people whose anonymity precludes my thanking them by name. Every review offered useful ideas, however, many of which helped to shape the book into its present form. The publishers of this text and my previous one retained a number of reviewers, including Donald Chambers and Randall Woolridge of Penn State; Adrian Edwards, Western Michigan; Larry Guin, Murray

State; Carl Schweser, University of Iowa; Peter Williamson, Dartmouth; Howard Van Auken, Iowa State; Harold Stevenson, Arizona State; Eugene Drzycimski, University of Wisconsin, Oshkosh; Seth Anderson, Wake Forest University; and Thomas Johnson, William Rainey Harper College.

In addition, several of my past and present colleagues read and commented on various chapters: Joanne Hill, Thomas Schneeweis, and Joseph Finnerty.

I would like to thank all the people at Longman who helped in the production of this book—specifically Libby McGreevy, who took care of rights and permissions; and David Walker, who edited the manuscript and managed the product. Special thanks to acquiring editor Ivy Lester for her efforts in development and promotion. Thanks, too, to Candlin Dobbs and Anita Constant for their participation.

Last but not least I must mention the help that I received from those who typed the many drafts of the manuscript. In many ways Elaine Fydenkevez had the most difficult job, as she typed the early drafts with an ordinary typewriter. In light of the quality of my handwriting and my propensity to revise and edit, her patience was amazing. Eventually the manuscript's typing was moved to the University of Massachusetts Word Processing Center under the direction of Vesta Powers. In addition to Mrs. Powers, the word processing staff includes Deborah Misterka, Rebecca Baldwin, Denise Lessard, Joyce Sicard and Lynda Vassallo. Without their constant high-quality work, the manuscript would never have evolved into a finished product, at least not in our lifetimes.

Section I:
Basic Investment Concepts

This beginning section lays the groundwork for a practical approach to investment and money management. The following hypothetical case raises many of the issues that are dealt with in the three chapters of this section:

The Newleys: A Young Couple's Finances

Dick and Jane Newley have decided to take a careful look at their finances. They got married immediately after their college graduation five years ago and now have two children ages 3 and 1 1/2. Dick earns $17,000 per year as a history teacher at Metropolis High School. While he expects modest salary increases if he remains a teacher, he may move into school administration, in which case his income should rise somewhat faster. Jane is an Earnest Anderson CPA earning $26,500. She seems on a fast track and may become a partner in ten to fifteen years. Even junior partners of her firm earn in excess of $150,000 per year.

The Newley's principal assets are a home ($60,000 mortgage), $15,000 in savings and a tract of land left to them by Jane's parents. Jane's father was a real estate developer who died three years ago. Jane's mother, who is in ill health, is supported from a large trust whose principal asset is her father's development firm. The principal of the trust will be divided between Jane and her two brothers upon her mother's death. Dick's parents are in good health and have relatively modest assets. Dick and Jane both have small amounts of life insurance through their respective employers. They are currently adding about $4,000 per year to their savings.

While the Newleys seem relatively well off financially, they believe that a careful examination of their situation will reveal a variety of ways of preparing better for the future. Since their combined income puts the Newleys in a relatively high tax bracket, they would like to reduce that tax burden. They also want to protect their children should anything happen to them. Finally, they expect their financial situation to improve over time. Accordingly, they want their personal financial management skills to grow as their professional careers progress. Consider each of the following questions which relate to their situation:

1) They maintain a balance of about $2,000 in their NOW checking account. Should they switch to a superNOW, Money Market, or Cash Management Account?
2) Their life insurance coverage may be inadequate. How should they determine how much and what kind to buy?
3) Their income is substantial and provides a surplus relative to their spending needs. Should they consider a tax-sheltered pension plan? If so, what type?
4) Their children will probably go to college some day. How can they begin now to prepare financially for that day? Can they save taxes in the process?
5) Their $15,000 in savings is currently in a passbook savings account at their bank. That money serves as an emergency reserve but they could also borrow against the equity in

1

their house (its market value is at least $100,000). Thus they are now ready to begin investing this sum for growth and are willing to take some risks. What might they do?

6) Since Jane's share of her parents' estate will probably exceed $300,000, she would like to learn more about investment opportunities. What are the various types of invest-ment media for her to consider?

7) Dick has been a stamp collector since he was eight. While he has a large collection, most of his stamps are relatively inexpensive. Thus, the entire collection has only a modest value. He is, however, thinking of becoming more serious and using the hobby as an investment vehicle. Should he? Why or why not?

8) After some thought the Newleys concluded that they should begin investing some of their savings in the stock market. How should they go about selecting a broker? Should they use a discounter or full service broker?

9) Having selected a brokerage firm, they now would like to buy stock in a company rec-ommended to one of Jane's colleagues. What orders should they give their broker? Should they try to diversify? What about mutual funds?

10) The Newleys have heard about such aspects of stock market trading as short-selling, margin-trading, the over-the-counter markets and tender offers. What do they need to know about each of these issues?

While many of these questions do not have single simple answers, the basic issues are dealt with extensively in the first three chapters of this book. The first chapter treats various aspects of personal finance, beginning with such short-term topics as managing personal debt, shopping for a loan and handling cash and other transaction balances. Then long-term financial issues such as life in-surance, pensions and estate planning are explored. Clearly these topics have immediate applicability for many readers. Chapter 2 provides an overview of the investment scene including a discussion of generalizable investment-char-acteristics such as return, risk, liquidity, marketability, investment effort, min-imum investment size and tax-treatment. Then a variety of specific investment-types are introduced: short-term debt securities; long-term debt securities; com-mon stock; preferred stock; pure option securities; convertibles; mutual funds, small firm ownership; venture capital; real estate; commodities; collectibles; noncollectible offbeat investments and Ponzi schemes. Most of these topics are covered in greater detail in later chapters. The current coverage is designed to give readers a framework in which to evaluate specific investment-types. Chap-ter 3 explores security market mechanics in considerable detail, beginning with such topics as brokers, investment advisors, stock exchanges, commissions, types of orders, specialists, floor traders, the over-the-counter market, short selling, margin trading, secondary offerings, block trades and tender offers. Then secu-rities market regulation is examined with principal emphasis placed on the de-veloping central market. Chapter 3 primarily focuses on how security trades of various sizes may be executed. While often neglected, effective security market executions is an extremely important aspect of successful investing. The chapter concludes with a discussion of the economic role of the securities market. The capital allocation, management allocation and use in implementing economic policy roles are all considered.

1 Personal Financial Management

Rational individuals allocate their resources (wealth and income) between savings and current expenditures to maximize the resulting benefits. Thus, one should reallocate expenditures (say less on current consumption and more on savings for retirement) whenever the derived benefits would be increased.

Any asset that is expected to confer benefits over time is an investment. One's investment portfolio includes not only stocks, bonds and real estate but other assets such as durable goods and an education. Everyone who manages his or her own personal finances is an active investor. Personal financial management involves many current investment-type decisions that may have long-term implications. This chapter discusses the major investment-related aspects of short- and long-term personal financial management:

- Immediate concerns: managing transactions/balances and debts
- Long-term personal finance
- Life insurance: who needs it, how much, what kind, how to find the best rates
- Pensions; tax-sheltered plans
- Estate planning; shifting income to dependent children

THE PERSONAL BALANCE SHEET

Generating and analyzing a personal balance sheet is an important starting point in developing a lifetime financial plan. Table 1.1 illustrates a typical household's financial situation (personal balance sheet). The left side lists assets (tangible or intangible property) at their estimated values. Liabilities (debts) and the difference between assets and liabilities—"net worth"—appear on the right. The *before* and *after* columns will be explained shortly.

The family's house is normally its most valuable tangible asset. An assortment of personal and consumer items such as furniture, appliances, motor vehicles, jewelry, silverware and clothing are also listed along with such financial assets as bank deposits, a life insurance policy's cash value, and perhaps some cash. Human capital (value of education and experience), often the household's most valuable intangible asset, does not generally appear on the balance sheet. This can, however, be one of the most important assets to consider.

Table 1.1   Personal Balance Sheet Example Before and After Debt Repayment

	Assets			Liabilities and Net Worth	
	Before	After		Before	After
Short-Term			Short-Term		
Cash	$ 35	$ 35	Installment credit	$ 1,600	$ 600
Checking Acct.	300	300			
S&L Assoc.	4,700	400	Intermediate-Term Liabilities		
Intermediate-Term Assets			Auto Loan	3,300	0
Automobile	5,000	5,000	Long-Term		
Furniture & personal items	8,000	8,000	Mortgage on house	46,000	46,000
			Net Worth	39,735	39,735
Long-Term Assets					
House	67,000	67,000	Total Liabilities		
Life Insurance			and Net Worth	$90,035	$86,335
cash value	5,000	5,000			
Total	$90,035	$86,335			

Consumer and mortgage loans are the most common types of individual liabilities. Personal loans, credit card and charge account debt balances all represent consumer credit. Most home purchases are financed with long-term mortgages.

Assets and liabilities are usually grouped by maturity. Short-term assets and liabilities are due within a year, intermediate-term in one to five years, and long-term in six or more years.

Personal Debt Management

Sound debt management is one of the most important goals in personal financial management. One seeks to limit borrowing to the amounts needed and to minimize interest charges without unduly sacrificing other needs. Even modest consumer credit balances require careful attention. Interest is not generally charged on credit card and charge account balances paid before the end of the billing-period, but stores offering this "free" credit may pass on the extra cost in higher prices. Moreover, once a payment is missed, at least 18% per year compounded monthly is charged on the balance including the "free" first 30 days. Borrowing at high rates while earning low yields on available funds is clearly undesirable, so low-interest savings account funds might be better used to repay high-rate consumer loans.

Though some people maintain a modest emergency reserve in low-interest accounts, a bank line of credit (check/loan account, automatic overdraft privilege, etc.) can provide an alternative reserve. Similar lines of credit are available through some banks and brokerage firms using house equity as collateral. An individual with such a creditline (prior permission to borrow up to some previously agreed-upon sum) may obtain a short-term loan by simply writing a check. The loan may cost 1% to 2% per month and may be repaid under relatively flexible terms. Such borrowing potential can provide a cheaper source of short-term funds than continuously tying up funds in a low-interest account. To remain available as a reserve, however, such a line of credit should be used only for temporary borrowing.

A critical examination of the balance sheet in Table 1.1 suggests that the emergency reserve now provided by the $4,700 savings account might be replaced with a $5,000 line of credit. Repaying the $3,300 auto loan and $1,000 in installment credit would still leave a $400 balance to meet minor unexpected expenses. Savings earmarked for a vacation, addition to the house, or other soon-to-be-executed purpose should not be used to repay other loans, however.

Mortgage Debt

Using this technique to reduce mortgages may not offer the same benefits as in the case of consumer loans. Long-term mortgage loans often carry lower interest rates than short-term consumer loans because of a house's collateral value and the spreading of administrative cost over a large sum and long term. Moreover, previously negotiated low mortgage rates (1982–84 mortgage rates have been 12% to 20%) are a bargain worth retaining. For example, an "8% mortgage" only requires an annual interest payment of $80 per $1,000 owed plus a principal payment sufficient to amortize (pay off) the debt over the life of the loan. Prepaying any part of this 8% debt with funds that might otherwise earn 10% or more is usually unwise. A person with a high mortgage rate could, in contrast, profitably apply savings to the mortgage balance. For example, several thousand dollars earning 12% could effectively be used to reduce an outstanding 18% mortgage balance. Similarly, a substantial down payment on a new mortgage might lower the interest rate and would certainly reduce the monthly payments. Moreover, the points (lenders' fees for granting the loan) charged, if any, may vary with the size of the down payment. Minimizing the mortgage principal has a number of advantages, particularly when interest rates are high. One should consider the entire picture, however: a large down payment taken from high-yielding investments might not be worth the modest interest savings and/or flexibility-loss.

Shopping for a Loan

Borrowers should always shop for the most attractive loan rates. Consumer loans include auto loans, home-improvement loans, student loans, credit card advances, personal loans, passbook loans and cash-value loans from insurance companies (discussed later). Financial institutions that make consumer loans include commercial banks, savings and loan associations, credit unions, savings banks, consumer finance companies and insurance companies. With this wide array of lenders and loan types, careful comparison shopping is clearly in order.

While effective loan shopping generally requires calling around for the best rates, a few suggestions may help focus one's search. First, government-subsidized student loan rates are so attractive that borrowers can often reinvest any otherwise-unneeded funds at a higher rate. Second, credit unions typically offer their members such attractive rates that some people join specifically to obtain loans. Third, companies that specialize in consumer loans generally charge higher rates than banks and savings institutions. Fourth, passbook loans, cash-value loans, margin loans, auto loans and other collateralized loans are usually less expensive than uncollateralized loans. Fifth, even within each loan category, different lenders charge different rates. Thus investors should first determine the most attractive loan type for their needs and then shop for the best rate within that type.

Tax Impacts

Both borrowing and investing can affect one's tax liability. Most interest income is taxable, while interest paid is only deductible from the taxable income of those who itemize. Thus differential tax effects should be carefully considered. One who does not itemize expenses can, for example, reduce nondeductible interest payments by paying off loans with funds that would otherwise generate taxable income. For example, an investor/borrower might earn 14% on a high-yield investment while paying 12% on consumer credit. The 14% return is fully taxable while the 12% interest expense is only deductible for one who itemizes. A non-itemizing individual in the 30% marginal tax-bracket has a 14% before-tax return reduced to a 9.8% return (70% of 14%) after taxes. Thus paying off a 12% consumer credit loan may provide a higher return than earning 14% before tax (only 9.8% after taxes).

Handling Liquid Assets

Cash and near-cash accounts (largely deposits in financial institutions) should be managed both to provide ready funds and to earn a high return on otherwise-unneeded resources. Cash and checking account balances earn no interest while savings and other types of noncash accounts may be more difficult to spend. Thus resources should be carefully distributed among checking, savings and higher-yielding deposits to achieve an attractive balance between convenience and yield.

Since increasing costs have led many banks to raise their fees, choosing the appropriate type of account is increasingly important. Traditional passbook-type savings accounts pay a modest interest rate and require only a small minimum balance but do not allow check-writing. Savings accounts with check-writing privileges called "negotiable orders of withdrawal" or NOW accounts generally require a relatively large minimum balance ($500 to $1,500). Those with very large average balances ($5,000 or more) may find a cash-management account at a brokerage firm most attractive. Such accounts pay competitive money market rates on large balances (over a minimum) compared with 5 1/4% on NOW account balances. A superNOW account ($2,500 minimum) also pays money market rates but usually coupled with an extensive fee schedule for services (checks, deposits, etc.). Regular checking accounts, which earn no interest, require a service fee only if the balance falls below the minimum (e.g., $300). Special checking accounts impose no monthly minimum fees (or a much lower fee) but charge 10¢ to 25¢ for each check written. People with large sums passing through their account should use NOW accounts. Those with very large balances may do still better with a cash-management or superNOW account. The regular checking account is usually least expensive for those who only write a few checks per month and maintain modest balances. One with a relatively inactive small account may find a special checking account most attractive. To determine which account is least costly for a specific situation, one needs to assess the differential service charges and interest earned or forgone.

Money market mutual funds offer attractive yields on short-term assets. These mutual funds purchase high denomination short-term securities with the pooled funds of their investors. The portfolio's net return is passed on to the fundholders. While returns have varied substantially over time, rates of 8% to 18% have been common in the period 1979–1984. Moreover, such facilities as wire-transfers and check-writing privileges ($500 minimum) ensure easy access to deposited funds. The money funds normally require a minimum initial deposit of $1,000.

Bank money market accounts offered by banks provide many of the same advantages as money market mutual funds. Their minimum balance is $2,500 and depositors are restricted to six withdrawals per month, only three of which may be by check. FDIC (Federal Deposit Insurance Corporation) insurance is an advantage of the bank funds relative to the money market mutual funds. Table 1.2 summarizes the various types of depository accounts.

Table 1.2 Types of Depository Accounts

	Non interest bearing	
Special checking accounts	Low minimum balance	Charge for each check
Regular checking accounts	Modest minimum balance	No fees
	Low interest rates (5 1/2% typically)	
NOW accounts	Modest minimum balance	No fees
Savings accounts	Modest minimum balance	No check-writing privileges
	Money-market-based interest rates	
SuperNOW accounts	$2,500 minimum balance	Extensive fees
Cash-management account	Extensive combination of financial accounts	
Money market accounts	$2,500 minimum	Limited withdrawal-rights
Money market mutual funds	$1,000 minimum	Not usually government-insured

LONG-TERM FINANCIAL PLANNING

All too often, otherwise-talented people mismanage their long-term finances.[1] One prepares for future financial needs either actively or by default. Inaction involves as much choice as action. The wealthy have long had access to financial help. More recently, however, many financial consultants have begun serving the middle-income group.[2] While experts may be helpful, most people still prefer to do most of their long-term planning (with or without occasional ad hoc advice from financial salespeople).[3] Life insurance, pension plans, social security, estate planning, paying off the house mortgage, acquiring consumer assets (furniture, appliances, automobiles, etc.) and long-term investing all affect a family's future financial security.

Life Insurance

Obtaining adequate life insurance protection at minimum cost contributes to long-term financial security. Most life insurance policies are sold by agents who receive sales commissions and so frequently try to sell people more protection than they need at relatively high cost. A consumer who understands the essentials of life insurance will be able to structure a plan offering essential protection at minimum cost.

Who Needs Life Insurance?

Life insurance protects the beneficiary from financial hardship if the insured's income is lost. Anyone with dependents and limited resources probably needs life insurance. Anyone without a family or other dependents, or with a sufficiently large estate, probably does not need life insurance: in the first instance no one needs protecting and in the second the protection is already available.

For businesses, "key-person life insurance" compensates for the sudden loss of important employees, providing a potential financial cushion that makes for more comfortable relationships with creditors, customers, suppliers and employees. As a management technique, key-person insurance is tax-deductible.

When to Purchase?

Agents may advise life insurance purchases at an early age to avoid the risk of later failing the physical examination. Historically, however, only about 3% of those who take insurance physicals fail, while another 5% are put into a higher-risk pool.[1] Moreover, many of these people would have been uninsurable or risks at an earlier age. Thus one's chance of becoming uninsurable is relatively small.

Perhaps the least persuasive argument for pre-need life insurance purchases is to obtain a lower rate. Since the reduced premiums for insurance purchased at an earlier age must be paid over a longer period, the total outlay may well be higher. Moreover, the initial incomes of young people are also likely to be lower. Thus, even at higher rates, life insurance may be more affordable if purchased later in life. Finally, the entire argument presupposes that whole-life insurance is purchased even though term insurance is often more attractive. The pros and cons of these two insurance types will be discussed shortly.

How Much Insurance Is Needed?

Ideally, life insurance should fully protect the household from loss of income or household service that would otherwise result from the insured's death or disability.[5] Thus estimating life insurance needs requires determining the desired family income. Since a household member's death would also eliminate his or her support-cost, approximately 75% of the previous income level should be sufficient to maintain a family of four's lifestyle. Taking account of inflation, differential tax-effects and different family sizes might alter the percentage somewhat.

Next, the family's residual income before considering any life insurance proceeds should be determined. How much could the spouse make (after allowing for added expenses such as babysitter costs) if he or she were to begin (or continue) working? What would Social Security and survivorship payments be? How much would investment income contribute? Deducting the continuing-income total from the needed income reveals the gap that life insurance should fill. The capital required to produce income equal to this amount is the desired level of insurance.

An example: Consider John Q. Insurance, whose annual income of $24,000 supports a family of four. Approximately $18,000 (75% of $24,000) would be needed annually to support the remaining three family members. Widows or widowers covered by Social Security qualify for benefits until their children reach age 18. Depending on past payments into the Social Security system and the number of qualifying dependents, a family might receive as much as $1,200 per month. Perhaps $400 per month, or $4,800 of the needed $18,000, is closer to the actual benefit amount in this case. John's wife could, after allowing for babysitter-costs and other job-related expenses, net $5,000 from a part-time job. Survivorship rights under the husband's company pension plan would provide another $3,500 per year. Finally, the family's small $4,000 savings account provides an 8% return or $320 per year. These various income sources total $13,620, leaving a gap of $4,380. If the insurance principal is invested at 10%, $45,000 would earn the needed sum. Purchasing more than $45,000 in protection would provide an inflation cushion. Moreover, the household's other adult member might be insured for the economic loss resulting from his or her death.

Note that the above analysis' detail could easily be expanded to take account of specific family expenses and differences in tax-liability before and after the primary wage-earner's death. Increased detail should not greatly alter the figures, however, as many of the additional considerations are offsetting. Basically one estimates needed household income and subtracts the remaining family income to determine the difference that insurance should fill. The amount of needed insurance depends upon the return on the insurance proceeds. While determining reasonable return expectations is a complicated topic, current long-term rate estimates can be obtained from an insurance agent, banker, or broker.

Term and Whole Life Insurance

The two principal types of life insurance are whole life and term. Whole life combines insurance with a savings element. Premiums are set at a constant annual rate based on the insured's age when the policy is purchased. Mortality tables report the life expectancies for men and women of different ages. For example, at age 25, a male has one chance in 560 of dying within the next year and can, on the average, expect to live 48 more years (to age 73). For a 65-year-old female, the chance of dying in the next year is 1 in 58 and her future life expectancy is 17 years (to age 82). The premium rates set on whole life policies initially far exceed what is required to satisfy claims for their age groups. The excess in the premiums, plus the return on that surplus, is accumulated in a fund. Once the age group's mortality rate rises to a level where premium income is no longer sufficient, the fund is called upon to cover the gap. Figure 1.1 illustrates this relationship.

Figure 1.1   Whole Life Premium versus Risk of Dying at Various Ages

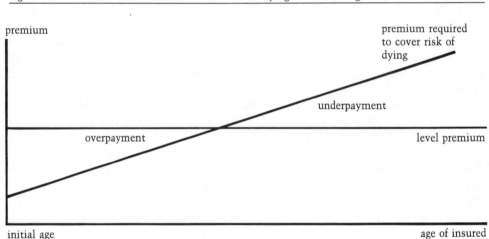

Term insurance, in contrast, has no savings feature. Term insurance premiums reflect actual mortality rates and thus rise with the insured's age. Since commissions are much higher on whole life than for an equivalent-dollar term policy, agents have an incentive to recommend whole life. Term, however, is usually the better value—especially for a younger person. Since incomes are often relatively low for young people while their expenses (particularly for setting up a household) may be abnormally high,[6] obtaining equivalent protection at a lower cost is especially attractive. Moreover the returns on the insurance companies' surplus have been unimpressive (5 to 7% is typical).[7] Most alternative investments offer higher returns.

One may be able to borrow most or all of a whole life policy's cash value (accumulated surplus) at a relatively low (6% or so) rate. Such seemingly attractive borrowing privileges only allow access to what would otherwise be available interest-free with equivalent term. Moreover, an increasing number of states are allowing policy-loan rates to be raised.[8]

On the other hand, earnings on the accumulated surplus of whole life is not subject to current tax; any investment income earned on the money saved by buying term is taxed in the ordinary way. Thus one should compare the policy's before-tax return with the expected after-tax return on the fund's alternative uses.

Participating versus Nonparticipating Insurance

Both whole life and term insurance are available in participating and nonparticipating forms. Nonparticipating insurance premiums are set in the policy. Such policies' profits accrue to the nonparticipating company's stockholders. Participating insurance (sold by a mutual life insurance company) is, in contrast, owned by its policyholders who share what would otherwise have been the insurance company's income.[9] Participating premiums are generally set somewhat higher than those of nonparticipating policies. Dividends are then declared to reflect the firm's recent expense, investment, and claims experience. Net costs to holders of participating policies are usually a bit below those of nonparticipating policies, which have established rates typically reflecting the relatively low interest rates of the 1960s. Poor investment and claims experience can cause net premium cost to be higher for participating companies, however.

Universal and Variable Life Insurance

Rapid inflation, tight budgets, high interest rates, and relatively low imputed returns on cash values have reduced traditional life insurance sales.[10] The insurance companies' inability to pay high market rates on existing policies (caused by low returns earned on their own investment portfolios) has discouraged whole life sales. The industry responded with a flexible variable-return product tied to current market yields.[11] Universal policies permit the insured to vary the premium payments. The insurance company simply adjusts the cash-value and death-benefits to correspond to the actual payment. Variable policies are similar to whole life except that their cash value's growth depends on the policy's portfolio return. Both types' abilities to flow market interest rates through to their policyholders make them superior to most whole life policies. Given the favorable tax treatment (no tax liability on the imputed return), they also claim to be competitive with alternative investments. *Consumer Reports*, however, calculates that their relatively high fees and selling-costs make universal life less attractive to most people than term-plus-investing-the-difference.[12] Table 1.3 summarizes the various types of life insurance.

Table 1.3   Types of Life Insurance

Principal Types	
Whole Life	Insurance plus savings feature with constant annual premiums determined by the insured's age at purchase.
Term	Pure insurance with premiums rising with the insured's age.
Variable-Value Types	
Decreasing Term	Amount of coverage declines as the insured gets older.
Universal Life	Cash value varies with the policyholder's premium payments and return on the accumulated surplus.
Variable Life	Cash value varies with the return on the accumulated surplus.
Type of Sellers	
Participating	Sold by mutual insurance company, which flows through its "profits" to policyholders.
Nonparticipating	Sold by stock company, which retains any profits for its shareholders.
Individual	Sold separately by an agent who receives a substantial fee.
Group	Sold without an agent, thereby eliminating the agent's fee.

Should an Agent Be Used?

Some experts strongly advocate selecting an agent to tailor an individualized life insurance program. A talented insurance agent should offer any needed assistance rapidly and effectively and be able to explain the available options clearly and fully. A careful reader of this chapter should, however, be able to save about a year's premium by avoiding the agent's commission. One might, for example, purchase group plan insurance either at work or through a professional, alumni, or civic association. Mutual savings banks in New York, Massachusetts, and Connecticut also sell low-cost group-rate insurance. Many mutual funds offer group-rate insurance to their fundholders. One can become a policyholder by investing as little as $1,000 into a money market or other type of mutual fund. Some insurance companies also sell policies through the mail or by phone.

Pensions

Most retirees living on Social Security and perhaps a company pension are unable to maintain their preretirement living standards. Rapid inflation and longer life expectancies have heightened the need for early retirement planning. As with life insurance planning, one should compare estimated retirement income with anticipated needs. Since many post-retirement expenses decline (taxes, business related expenses, etc.), one's living standard can usually be maintained with less income than was required before retiring (Table 1.4). On the other hand, an

Table 1.4   Equivalent Retirement Income
The last column of the table below shows the income required after retirement to maintain preretirement living standards. These figures were calculated by the President's Commission on Pension Policy in 1980 for people at various income levels.

Gross preretirement income	Taxes ①	Work-related expenses ②	Savings and investments ③	Net pre-retirement income ④	Post-retirement income taxes ⑤	Equivalent retirement income ⑥
			Single people			
$10,000	$ 2008	$ 480	$ 240 (3%)	$ 7272	—	$ 7272 (73%)
15,000	3703	678	678 (6%)	9941	—	9941 (66%)
20,000	5783	853	1280 (9%)	12,084	$ 198	12,282 (61%)
30,000	10,355	1179	2357 (12%)	16,109	1282	17,391 (58%)
50,000	22,249	1665	4163 (15%)	21,923	3752	25,675 (51%)
			Married couples			
$10,000	$ 1444	$ 513	$ 257 (3%)	$ 7786	—	$ 7786 (78%)
15,000	2860	728	728 (6%)	10,684	—	10,684 (71%)
20,000	4488	931	1396 (9%)	13,185	—	13,185 (66%)
30,000	8047	1317	2634 (12%)	17,999	$ 63	18,062 (60%)
50,000	17,824	1931	4826 (15%)	25,419	1965	27,384 (55%)

① Includes Federal income tax, Social Security taxes, state and local income taxes (calculated at 19% of Federal income taxes). Does not include property taxes.
② Estimated at 6% of income after taxes.
③ Estimated at a percentage (shown) of income after taxes.
④ Gross preretirement income less taxes, work-related expenses, and savings and investments.
⑤ Post-retirement taxes are on income in excess of Social Security benefits, which are not taxable. Retirees without Social Security benefits would need higher retirement income.
⑥ Equivalent retirement income as a percentage of preretirement gross income shown in parentheses.

Reprinted by permission from "Will You Ever Collect a Pension?" *Consumer Reports*, March 1982. Copyright 1982 by Consumers Union of United States, Inc., Mount Vernon, NY 10553.

inflation-cushion is advisable. Needed retirement income often substantially exceeds that provided by Social Security and employee pension plans. While savings can be used to fill the gap, specific pension preparation receives much more attractive tax-treatment than generalized savings.

The Advantage of Tax-Deferral

Table 1.5 illustrates the advantage of tax-deferred savings. An investor in the 40% tax bracket is assumed to set aside $1,000 annually and earn a conservative 8%. Clearly the tax-deferred sum grows at a much faster rate. While the sum is taxable at withdrawal, the extra return more than offsets the tax.

Company Pensions

Many people believe their pension income is solely determined by their place of employment, length of service, preretirement income and retirement age. A number of other parameters may also be relevant, however. Employees may be

Table 1.5   Tax-Deferred versus Taxable Savings: $1,000 a year taxable at 40% (8% return)

Term	Tax-Deferred*	Taxable
1	$ 1,080	$ 620
5	6,335	3,461
10	15,645	7,835
15	29,323	13,366
20	49,421	20,356
25	78,951	29,195
30	113,080	40,369
35	186,097	54,494
40	279,774	72,351
45	417,417	94,925

* Taxable when withdrawn

able to influence their pension-levels by varying the size of their own contributions, for example. Contributions to and subsequent income on most pension plans are tax-sheltered (federal) until retirement, when reduced post-retirement income usually puts them in a lower bracket. High interest rates have allowed many plans to increase the amounts and flexibility of their benefit packages,[13] so increasing one's contribution to the limit is often advisable.

Qualifying for Several Pensions

Some people may be able to qualify for so many pensions that retirement increases their income. In an extreme case, a couple might qualify for a military or civil service pension, several company pensions and Social Security on both members. Qualifying for a pension requires a specified minimum employment, so moving from job to job can be costly. Several separate pensions may be no greater than a single pension from longer service at one place. Indeed, many people lose most or all pension rights because of especially stringent qualifying requirements. An effective multiple-pension strategy requires that a substantial minimum pension be relatively easy to obtain, in order to qualify for at least one primary employer pension. Since such pension-protection is common in government and uncommon elsewhere, relatively young retirees from government service are best positioned to play the pension game. One should always try to qualify for Social Security. Modest earnings for forty quarters entitle one to some monthly Social Security benefits.

IRA and Keogh Accounts

Until 1982, most employees covered by company pension plans had no other tax-sheltered pension options. Uncovered employees could put up to $1,500 of tax-sheltered income per year into an Individual Retirement Account (IRA). Since 1982, however, any employee (covered or uncovered) has been able to contribute a tax deductible $2,000 per year to such an account. A married couple can contribute $2,250 if only one spouse is employed and $4,000 if both are employed.

Self-employed or partially self-employed individuals can contribute up to $30,000 or 20% of their net self-employment income (whichever is less) to a tax-sheltered Keogh plan. Withdrawals from both Keoghs and IRAs may begin as early as age 59 1/2 and must begin at 70 1/2 but can continue to be withdrawn for another 20 years. Withdrawals prior to age 59 1/2 incur a 10% penalty tax and all income is taxed as ordinary income. Since no taxes are paid until such a withdrawal, however, one may still come out ahead.[14] Note that these provisions have changed in the past and will undoubtedly change again.

Retirement Account Managers

Banks, thrift institutions, mutual funds, insurance companies, brokerage firms and other types of financial institutions offer qualified Keogh and IRA plans.[15] Retirement funds may be invested in most types of securities including short- and long-term bonds, common and preferred stocks, mutual funds, and bank deposits. One can even set up self-managed investment accounts. IRA and Keogh funds may not be invested in collectibles, mortgaged real estate or margined commodities or securities, however. Fees for setting up and managing IRA and Keogh accounts are generally rather modest unless one uses an agent.[16] Table 1.6 summarizes the available options.

Professional Corporation Pension Plans

Self-employed people who are constrained by the Keogh plan's maximum may set up a professional corporation and its own in-house pension plan. The 1982 tax act has largely eliminated the pension advantage of professional corporations, however.[17]

Employee Stock Ownership Plans

Employee Stock Ownership Plans (ESOPs) allow a corporation to contribute up to 15% of employee payrolls into what amounts to a profit sharing or stock plan. Employers may offer ESOPs in place of higher salaries or other benefits. The ESOP funds are invested in the company's stock. Often the firm issues new shares and thus in effect uses the ESOP to raise additional equity capital. An employee's share of the ESOP holdings may be repurchased at retirement. Thus the firm sells its shares to its employees for tax-sheltered income. Such plans are particularly attractive to small capital-poor companies.[18] Companies with an ESOP may or may not also have an employee pension plan.

Deferred Compensation (401k Plans)

Deferred compensation schemes (401k plans) provide an additional way of accumulating tax-sheltered savings.[19] Under the 1978 tax reform act as interpreted in a 1982 IRS ruling, companies may allow their employees to place a portion of their current income into a tax-sheltered fund much like a pension plan. The

Table 1.6   Retirement Management Accounts

	Investment Choices	Initial Charges to Open Account	Annual Maintenance or Management Fees	Early Withdrawal Penalties
Banks and Thrift Institutions	Certificates of deposit Savings accounts	Usually none	$10 or less	Minimum six months interest None
⌐ Self-Directed Brokerage Firms	Stocks, bonds, Ginnie Maes, real estate, oil and gas	None to $30	$25-$50, plus any brokerage commissions	None
└ "Load" Funds	Money-market, stocks, bonds, stocks and options	8 1/2% of investment	$2-$9, $5 to switch funds	None
Credit Unions	Certificates of deposit Savings accounts	None	Usually none	Minimum six months interest None
⌐ "Front-Load" Insurance Cos.	Fixed-premium annuities	8 3/4% of investment	About $8-$10	Usually none
└ "Back-Load"	Variable-premium annuities	None	About $25-$30	7%-8% first year
"No-Load" Mutual Fund "Families"	Money-market, stocks, bonds, stocks and options	$5 or less	$10 or less Free switching	None

Source: J. Bettner, "To Decide Where to Put Your IRA Dollars Look at Risks, Management and all the Fees," *Wall Street Journal*, December 14, 1981. Reprinted by permission of *Wall Street Journal*, © Dow Jones & Company, Inc., 1981. All Rights Reserved.

sum is in addition to any company or IRA pension (perhaps as much as 10% of salary, depending on relative participation of low- versus high-salary people) and unlike IRAs and Keoghs, the funds may be withdrawn in hardship cases (e.g. a major illness) penalty-free before age 59 1/2. Tax treatment of lump-sum withdrawals after age 59 1/2 is more favorable than with the tax-sheltered pension plans. Under so-called "ten-year forward-averaging," one computes the tax on one-tenth of the sum accumulated as if it were the only income to be received. This sum is then multiplied by 10. As a result the total tax on a $100,000 distribution would be about 15% compared with about 40% on a similar sum of ordinary income. Table 1.7 summarizes the various types of retirement funds.

The Role of Long-Term Investing

The tax shelter of most pension contributions provides a strong incentive to contribute the maximum allowed. Three factors reduce the attractiveness of

Table 1.7   Types of Retirement Funds

IRAs	Allows any employee to set aside up to $2,000 per year into a tax-sheltered fund.
Keoghs	Allows the self-employed to set aside up to 20% of their self-employed income ($30,000 maximum) into a tax-sheltered fund.
Professional Corporation Pension Plans	Allows the self-employed greater flexibility in setting up pension plans than with Keoghs but the two plans have similar restrictions.
ESOPs	Allows corporations to contribute up to 15% of employee payrolls into what is in effect a profit-sharing stock-purchase plan.
Deferred Compensation	Allows employees to set aside up to 10% of their salaries into a tax-sheltered fund if their employer establishes such a plan.

pension-plan savings, however. First, the shelterable amount is limited. Second, pension fund contributions are largely untouchable until retirement. Third, pension funds cannot be invested in collectibles or assets that are partially financed by borrowing. Accordingly, most investors will want to have both tax-sheltered pension plans and less restricted but taxed private investment portfolios. These latter funds can supplement retirement income, be used for preretirement purposes (vacation home, children's college fund, buying a business to start a career, major medical expenses, etc.) and may be invested more flexibly than pension funds.

Obviously investors should try to maximize the risk-adjusted returns on their pension and nonpension portfolios. While investment management is a very complicated topic, three general points can now be made. First, only surplus funds should be committed to long-term investing. The market seldom cooperates when the investor needs funds in an emergency. Second, a relatively modest sum accumulated over a sufficiently long period can grow to a considerable amount. Third, the accumulated total and resulting income will vary substantially with the yield. Table 1.8 shows the value and income produced from $1,000 invested at various interest rates annually for 30 years.

Table 1.8   Value and Income from $1,000 Invested Annually for 30 Years at Various Interest Rates

Interest Rate	End-Period Value	Annual Income at That Date
4%	$ 51,080	$ 2,044
6%	79,060	4,744
8%	113,080	9,061
10%	165,080	16,508
12%	244,090	34,290
14%	356,786	49,950
16%	530,311	84,849
18%	790,948	142,371

We see that $1,000 set aside annually at rates from 4% to 18%, would grow to between $51,080 and $790,948 in 30 years and produce annual incomes varying from about $2,000 to $142,000. While the resulting amounts are substantial even for modest yields, they vary greatly with the assumed rate.

Estate Planning

Those with the foresight to purchase life insurance, set up a pension plan and accumulate a non-pension portfolio should also plan for their estates' disposition. Since estate planning is a complicated and detailed task, only the bare outlines are presented here.

Effective estate planning minimizes estate taxes and distributes assets according to the estateholder's wishes. Under the 1981 tax law, no federal estate taxes are assessed on bequests to one's spouse or estates of up to $400,000 (in 1985) regardless of the beneficiaries.[20] The maximum untaxed estate is scheduled to rise to $500,000 in 1986 and $600,000 in 1987. Thus the large untaxed sums that can now be passed on greatly reduce the need for death-tax protection. Since larger estates are still taxed up to 50% at the federal level and most states have either estate or inheritance taxes, the wealthy continue to need careful estate distribution planning. An able lawyer specializing in estate planning should be consulted for such a task.

Writing a Will

Regardless of their estate's size, most people prefer to have their property distributed according to their stated wishes rather than by some long, costly and arbitrary legal proceeding. While a lawyer will generally be needed, the individual can reduce the legal bill and increase the plan's suitability by doing much of the preparatory work. One should first list and value his or her assets and liabilities. Many people are surprised at how large the difference—their net worth —has become. Moreover, its value is likely to continue growing. Asset-disposal programs often utilize gifts, wills and trusts.

Those with significant estates should have a will to specify how they want their assets distributed. While a will may be drawn up without a lawyer, most people prefer legal help. A simple will can usually be assembled for less than $200.

Assets given away prior to one's death are removed from the estate (avoiding estate taxes), permit the recipient to use the asset sooner, avoid potential misunderstandings when the estate is probated, and allow the giver to present the assets personally. Gifts to charity can yield substantial tax savings.[21] Thus many people distribute assets that they no longer want or need. Up to $10,000 ($20,000 for a couple) may be given per recipient annually without any gift or estate tax implications.

Trusts

Trusts are portfolios of assets administered for one or more individual's benefit. A trustee such as a bank trust department often administers the trust for a fee. Investment principal is usually retained by the trust and income is periodically distributed to the beneficiaries. All trusts must eventually distribute their principal but may skip a generation before doing so. Some trusts distribute both income and principal once the beneficiaries reach a certain age. Trusts may be funded either during the giver's lifetime or at his or her death. As with wills, most people use a lawyer to establish a trust. Indeed, trusts are often set up along with the will.

The Clifford Trust

Most trusts are employed in estate planning. People wishing to establish an education fund for their children may find the Clifford trust particularly useful, however. A fund accumulated in the parent's personal savings would be fully taxed, while an account established in each child's name would shift the income's tax liability to the children's typically lower tax bracket. Establishing a fund in the child's name transfers both principal and income, but only the income's tax liability is shifted. By only transferring investment income, the Clifford trust achieves much greater tax savings per dollar transferred. An example should help clarify this point. An investor could, over the next ten years, accumulate a $50,000 education fund in three different ways: (a) save the full amount in the investor's name, (b) contribute principal and allow income to accumulate in a fund in the child's name, (c) establish a Clifford trust in the child's name and transfer earning assets to it that will revert to the investor at the end of ten years (the minimum duration for a Clifford Trust). Assume that the fund yields 10%, the investor is in the 35% tax-bracket, and the child with no other income would incur about a 10% tax rate.

Setting aside $3,137 per year for ten years compounded at 10% will produce an end value of $50,000. If all of this money comes from the investor's taxable income (option a), a $17,500 tax liability is incurred. Should the fund's income be taxed at the child's rate while the initial contributions come from the investor's taxable income (option b), the tax liability is reduced to $12,542.50 (35% of the $31,370 contribution and 10% of the $18,630 in income). If a Clifford trust is used (option c), the entire $50,000 would be taxed as income to the child's trust. With allowable deductions and no other income, the rate should be less than 10% ($5,000). Thus taxes would be $17,500 on savings, $12,500 with a regular trust, and $5,000 with a Clifford trust.

While the Clifford trust is a useful device, some important limitations should be noted. First, one may only transfer income-producing assets to the trust. Personal service income may not be shifted in this way. Second, transfers to the trust must be irrevocable for at least ten years. Third, the fund's proceeds may not be used to satisfy the legal obligation of the parent or guardian. Thus trust income could not pay for a minor child's food, shelter, or clothing. Fourth, a lawyer is usually needed to draw up the trust agreement. Still, for those who are able to use it, the Clifford trust is a particularly attractive way of reducing one's taxable income while setting aside funds for a dependent child.

Interest-Free Loans to Dependents (Crown Loans)

While IRS frowns on the practice, increasing numbers of parents are loaning money to their children interest-free.[22] The income on these so-called Crown loans are then taxed at the child's low rate. Funds may be derived either from existing resources or by borrowing. In the former instance, the parent's income tax liability is reduced by the foregone income, while in the latter the loan interest is a deductible expense. A parent in the 40% tax bracket, for example, who pays 17% for the loan while the child is in the 14% tax bracket and earns 15% on the funds has an after-tax cost of 10.2% compared with an after-tax return of 12.9% to the child. Since such a maneuver may be challenged by IRS, one contemplating making a Crown loan should carefully explore the matter with an able lawyer. Indeed, the 1984 Tax Reform Act largely eliminated the tax advantage for loans above $10,000 as the interest income is imputed to the lender.

SUMMARY AND CONCLUSIONS

Personal finance is a useful starting point for novice investors. Sound personal financial management is a part of investing, involves principles similar to those of traditional investing, and can help fund long-term investments. One's financial affairs should be managed to provide funds for unexpected needs, the protection of one's dependents, and for one's long-term financial security. Debts and short-term liquid assets should be managed to minimize the financing cost of debts and maximize the yield on liquid assets, while maintaining resources for unexpected needs and keeping risk to manageable levels. Checking, NOW, cash-management, superNOW and/or money market accounts should be selected on the basis of flexibility, convenience, safety and yield. Life insurance should be purchased to protect the household from income loss. One should first determine how much (if any) protection is needed and then shop for the most attractive policy (generally a term policy purchased without an agent). Keoghs, IRAs, ESOPs and deferred compensation plans allow individuals to postpone taxes on the funds contributed until benefits are paid, normally when one is in a lower tax bracket. Long-term investments may also be used to provide long-term financial security. Tax and estate-planning considerations (asset disposals, wills and trusts) should also be considered in investment decisions. Indeed Clifford trusts and Crown loans are two particularly attractive devices for reducing the investor's tax liability by shifting income into the name of a dependent child.

REVIEW QUESTIONS

1. Discuss the goals of sound personal financial management.
2. Under what circumstances should personal and mortgage debts be reduced?
3. What steps should be followed in obtaining a loan?
4. Compare the various types of checking accounts (regular, cash-management, superNOW, special and NOW) and discuss the advantages and disadvantages of each.
5. Compare the various ways of handling an emergency reserve.
6. Discuss the factors determining who does and does not need life insurance. Explore the various arguments sometimes advanced by insurance agents.
7. Why might one want to supplement pension savings with non-pension savings?
8. Consider the role of long-term investing in personal financial planning.
9. Why do middle-income people seldom have to worry very much about estate taxes? What aspects of estate planning remain important?
10. Discuss the role of gifts, wills, and trusts in asset disposal.
11. Compare the Clifford trust and interest-free loan devices with other methods of establishing a college education fund.

REVIEW PROBLEMS

1. Analyze the following family balance sheet and recommend improvements.

Assets		Liabilities	
Short-term Assets		Short-term	
Cash	$ 150	Installment Credit	$ 450
Checking Account	300		
Savings Account	5,000		
Intermediate-term		Intermediate-term	
Auto	7,000	Auto Loan	$ 5,000
Personal Items	12,000		
Long-term		Long-term	
House	90,000	Mortgage	$ 65,000
Life Insurance		Total Liabilities	70,450
Cash Value	8,000	Net Worth	62,000
Mutual Fund	10,000		
TOTAL	$132,450	TOTAL	$132,450

Savings Account yields 5.5%
Life Insurance Cash Value may be borrowed on at 6%
Mutual Fund owns a diversified portfolio of low-risk stocks with a current dividend yield of 7%
Installment Credit costs 18%
Auto Loan costs 16%
Mortgage costs 14% and is being amortized over a 25-year period
Money Market Mutual Funds are yielding 12%

2. Go to three local banks and ask for rates on their various types of checking, NOW, and superNOW accounts. Make up a table of the charges. Now for each type of account determine the annual cost for each of the following situations.
   a) 10 checks per month; $50 average balance
   b) 25 checks per month; $300 average balance
   c) 40 checks per month; $2,000 average balance
   d) 20 checks per month; $10,000 average balance
3. Determine the needed insurance protection for the following situation:
   Family consisting of father, mother, and three children
   Family income: $26,000 per year
   Social Security survivor's benefits: $6,900 per year
   Survivor's pension: $3,000 per year
   Investment income: $2,000 per year
   Assumed interest rate for insurance principal: 8%
4. Write for rates on life insurance from several companies that do not use agents and make a table. Now ask several insurance agents for their rates and compare. Write a report.
5. Assume you are in the 25% tax bracket and can save $500 per year, which can be invested at 10%. Make a table of the value of your savings after 5, 10, 20, 30 and 40 years, assuming it is taxed and that it is untaxed.
6. Assume that over a 16-year period you wish to accumulate $100,000 for a child's college education and that you can earn 12% on whatever funds you decide to commit. You are in the 30% tax bracket and your child will pay an average tax of 12% on any income earned. Compute the cost of accumulating $100,000 under each of the following plans:
   a) Set up a fund in your own name with annual contributions.
   b) Set up a fund in your child's name with annual contributions.
   c) Set up a Clifford trust in your child's name and place assets in it.
   d) Make an interest-free loan to your child that is reinvested.

NOTES

1. R. Ricklefs, "Doctors and Other Professionals Often Err in Money Planning: Ten Mistakes Listed," *Wall Street Journal*, May 22, 1978, p. 42.
2. D. Cuff, "Peddling Advice to the Middle Class," *New York Times*, November 7, 1982, p. 14F; M. Williams, "Financial Planners Come in a Lot of Varieties; Be Careful that Yours Isn't Mainly a Salesman," *Wall Street Journal*, July 11, 1983, p. 42.
3. *Business Week*, "A Midyear Review of Your Personal Finances," *Business Week*, July 19, 1982, pp. 188–191; R. Gable, *Investments and Financial Planning: The Complete Picture*, Reston Publishing Co., Reston, VA, 1983.
4. Consumer's Union, "A Guide to Life Insurance: Parts 1, 2 and 3," *Consumer Reports*, January, February and March, 1981.
5. R. Campbell, "The Demand for Life Insurance: An Application of the Economics of Uncertainty," *Journal of Finance*, December 1980, pp. 1155–1172; H. Shapiro, "Life Insurance

Needs: Ignore the Rules," *New York Times*, May 22, 1983, p. 11F; K. Slater, "Changing Life-Insurance Needs Require Periodic Look at Your Family's Coverage," *Wall Street Journal*, April 2, 1984, p. 33.

6. R. Ferber and L. Lee, "Asset Accumulation in Early Married Life," *Journal of Finance*, December 1980, pp. 1173–1188.

7. *Business Week*, "Promising Richer Yields to Revive Sales," *Business Week*, December 28, 1981, p. 153.

8. L. Sloane, "Insurance Loan Rates," *New York Times*, November 6, 1982, p. 38.

9. R. Kamath and C. Lin, "Factors Affecting the Cost of Participating Whole Life Insurance," *Nebraska Journal of Economics and Business*, Summer 1981, pp. 55–69.

10. E. McDowell, "The Appeal of Life Insurance Fades, But Most Families Still Buy It," *New York Times*, September 30, 1979, p. 9.

11. D. Hertzberg, "Life Insurers Start Offering Policies That Look More Like Investments," *Wall Street Journal*, February 23, 1983, p. 31.

12. Consumers Union, "Universal Life Insurance: It's Billed as the 'New Improved' Insurance Product, but Is It Really as Good as It Sounds?" *Consumer Reports*, January 1982, pp. 42–44.

13. T. O'Donnell and A. Field, "More Than Enough Money in the Pot," *Forbes*, December 21, 1981; *Business Week*, "Pension Plans Get More Flexible," *Business Week*, November 8, 1982, pp. 82–87.

14. W. Flannagan, "Whose Nest Egg is it, Anyway?," *Forbes*, February 14, 1983, pp. 131–132; D. Smith, "IRAs and Breakeven Point," *American Association of Judicial Investors*, March 1984, pp. 13–16.

15. E. Finn, "Growing Interest in IRAs Prompts Big Marketing Bottle for Investors," *Wall Street Journal*, April 13, 1984, p. 35.

16. T. Friedman, "Where to Open a Retirement Account," *New York Times*, December 6, 1981, p. 3E; L. Asinof, "Now You Can Hire a Money Manager to Move Your IRA Account to Investments He Prefers," *Wall Street Journal*, November 7, 1983, p. 60.

17. S. Schmedel, "Professionals are Urged to Stay Incorporated Despite Loss of Some Benefits Under 1982 Law," *Wall Street Journal*, November 14, 1983, p. 60; C. Gould, "Should Professionals Incorporate?" *New York Times*, April 15, 1984, p. F11.

18. R. Johnson, R. Pratt and S. Stewart Jr., "The Economic Consequences of ESOPS," *Journal of Financial Research*, Spring 1982, pp. 75–84; L. Rohmann, "An ESOP Fable," *Forbes*, February 14, 1983.

19. L. Asinof, "If Your Firm Offers a Salary-Reduction Plan, You Can Cut Your Taxes and Ease Retirement," *Wall Street Journal*, March 14, 1983, p. 56; D. Dunn, "An Investment that is One up on the IRA," *Business Week*, September 26, 1983, pp. 147–148; M. Brody, "Better Than a Gold Watch," *Barron's*, November 7, 1983, pp. 11, 24, 26 & 30.

20. *Business Week*, "Estate Tax Law is Changing Again," *Business Week*, May 7, 1984, pp. 156–160.

21. K. Slater, "How You Structure Your Gifts to Charity Can Have a Big Effect On Your Tax Status," *Wall Street Journal*, May 14, 1984, p. 29.

22. J. Bettner, "Interest-Free Loan to Poorer Relation Can Cut Income Taxes If He Invests More in His Name," *Wall Street Journal*, December 20, 1982, p. 42.

2 Investment Types and Characteristics

Many different types of investments appeal to a diverse array of investor interests. Some assets promise nearly certain short- or long-term yields. More risky investments offer less certain but potentially much higher returns. Some investment areas require detailed management while others are virtually troublefree. "Liquid" investments can be quickly converted into spendable form at little cost or risk, while relatively large amounts of "marketable" assets can usually be bought and sold at the "market price." Some investment areas are open to those of modest means, while others require large minimum commitments. Finally, tax treatment of investment returns varies substantially.

This chapter describes the relevant characteristics of a wide range of investments, and their implications for portfolio assembly:

- Risk/return
- Liquidity and marketability
- Tax considerations
- Psychological aspects of investing
- Categories of investments: debt securities, equity securities, real estate, commodities, collectibles, the far-out and the fraudulent

INVESTMENT CONSIDERATIONS

Return

Most investments yield some form of cash flow and may increase in value over time. The return over a particular period is defined as the per-period cash flow plus price appreciation as a percentage of the asset's first-of-period price:

$$\text{Return} = \frac{\text{cash flow} + \text{price change}}{\text{beginning price}}$$

For example: a stock bought a year ago for $100 per share paid a $5 dividend and now trades for $108. Its annual return is calculated as follows:

$$\frac{\$5 + \$8}{\$100} = 13\%$$

24

Returns can be either positive or negative. If, for example, the above-mentioned stock's price had declined by $10, the result would have been:

$$\frac{\$5 - \$10}{\$100} = -5\%$$

These two examples represent simple one-year returns. Returns for longer or shorter holding periods are usually expressed on an annualized basis and reflect the impact of compounding, particularly for longer holding periods. Compounding is the result of earning interest on interest. Thus an investment that earned 10% during the first year and another 10% the second would have appreciated to 21% of its starting value (1.10 × 1.10). Similarly an investment which appreciated by 21% over a two-year period would be said to have generated a 10% annual return compounded annually.

Returns can be compounded more frequently than once a year. For example, 10% compounded semi-annually (5% per six months or .05) appreciates to 121.55% after two years (1.05 × 1.05 × 1.05 × 1.05). Thus to be fully descriptive, a stated return needs to include both the per-period return and the frequency of compounding.

Risk

The term *risk* is generally used to refer to the probability of some undesirable and unexpected event. In finance and economics, however, the term relates to the likelihood that returns will differ from those expected. The expected return is the average of the possible returns weighted by their likelihoods. Thus the probabilities of below-expectation and above-expectation returns balance out. An asset whose actual return is likely to approximate its expected return closely is less risky than one where the likely difference is larger. Risky assets often yield returns that are well above or well below their expectations. Thus the owner of an asset expected to earn 10% with a range of 2 to 18%, bears the risk that the actual return will differ from the expected. Low-risk assets' actual returns are, in contrast, generally very close to their expected values.

The Risk-Return Trade-Off

The insurance industry illustrates the demand for risk reduction. The insurer and insuree in effect wager on the possibility of a significant casualty loss. Most homeowners realize that the expected loss from fire or some other covered event is smaller than the corresponding insurance premium. Since administrative costs, commissions, profits, and benefit claims must be met out of premiums, the insured must pay extra for the peace of mind that the protection offers.

Like those who purchase insurance, most investors are willing to sacrifice some potential return to reduce risk.[1] Accordingly, risky assets must normally be priced to yield a high expected return to be saleable. Note, however, that risky assets do not automatically offer a high expected return. For example, a company organized to exploit the moon's mineral resources would certainly be risky but would, with current technology, have little chance of yielding a positive return. On the other hand, a company organized to mine the nodules on the ocean floor might very well offer an expected return high enough to justify the risk. Thus the nodule company could probably raise capital in spite of its high risks. The moon company, in contrast, probably could not offer a sufficient expected return to attract adequate starting capital.

Liquidity

Liquid assets may be converted into spendable form quickly, easily, and with little or no risk of principal loss. Paper money, coin, and checking account deposits can be spent in their present forms. Similarly, savings deposits in banks, savings and loan associations, credit unions, and money market mutual funds may be readily converted to spendable form at little or no cost, inconvenience or danger of receiving less than purchase-price-plus-accrued-interest. Bonds with short maturities or the right to be redeemed upon demand are also quite liquid. The more distant the redemption, however (i.e., the longer until maturity), the less liquid the investment. Thus long-term debt securities and non-debt investments like stocks and real estate (no maturity date) tend to be very illiquid.

Marketability

Marketability, the ease or difficulty of buying or selling an asset at its market value, is related to but distinct from liquidity. The *market value* is the price that a willing buyer and willing seller would reach if neither were under pressure to trade quickly. Thus shares in very large firms like Exxon or General Motors are very marketable since they trade nearly continuously at prices which vary little from transaction to transaction. Most assets exchanged in active high-volume markets sell at market prices even though such prices may vary appreciably over time. On the other hand a house, rare painting, or other one-of-a-kind asset comes on the market so infrequently that one must either be patient or be willing to trade at a substantial sacrifice.

 While marketable assets tend to be liquid and vice versa, some exceptions exist. A widely held company's stock can generally be sold for the current market price (marketable) but that price may vary substantially from the purchase price (illiquid). Similarly, U.S. government savings bonds and small bank CDs may be cashed in early with an interest penalty (liquid), but are not negotiable (unmarketable).

Investment Effort

Selecting and managing some types of portfolios requires little or no special knowledge, facilities or time commitment. For example, non-experts can easily understand the relevant characteristics of Treasury bills and other short-term debt securities including their risk, expected return, liquidity, marketability and tax-treatment; the certificates of ownership can be conveniently held by a brokerage firm or in a safe deposit box. Investors in other assets such as real estate, collectibles, soybean futures or mink farms need very special knowledge, talent, and/or storage facilities. Similarly, some asset types may be maintained with little or no effort (bonds) while others require constant management (an apartment complex). Accordingly, would-be investors need to consider carefully the expertise, talent, facilities and time required to assemble and manage the particular type of investment portfolio properly.

Minimum Investment Size

Some types of portfolios may be assembled with small sums while others require a much larger minimum commitment. For example, a savings account can be opened for as little as $100 and some higher-yielding bank certificates are available in $500 units. Most mutual funds will accept initial deposits of $1,000. Many collectibles sell for a few hundred dollars or less. On the other hand, assembling a diversified stock portfolio would require several thousand dollars and a diversified bond portfolio somewhat more. A single real estate purchase (to say nothing of a real estate portfolio) is likely to incur a down payment of thousands of dollars and most brokers will not accept commodity accounts of less than $20,000 to $50,000. Obviously the capital requirements of different investment areas differ appreciably. Those beginning with relatively small sums are restricted to investments available in modest sizes. Over time, however, such individuals may be able to shift into investment areas having higher minimums.

TAXES

Investors may keep only the after-tax component of their returns. Since different types of incomes are subject to very different levels of taxation, tax considerations are extremely important to investors, particularly those in high tax brackets.

To understand how investment income is taxed we need to examine our tax system's basic structure. Most personal income is taxed as ordinary income. Total income from wages, salaries and most other sources are added to compute adjusted gross income. Adjusted gross income is then reduced by $1,000 per dependent and itemized deductions or the zero-bracket amount to arrive at taxable income. Itemizing is advantageous if one's personal deductions exceed the zero-bracket amount. Such allowable deductions include certain business expenses, interest payments, a portion of high medical expenses, and casualty losses and most state and local taxes.

Extra Income is Taxed at the Marginal Rate

Additions to adjusted gross income almost always increase taxable income. Extra income is taxed at a rate higher than the average rate on pre-addition income. An example should help to clarify this point.

Jan Q. Investor's $35,000 per year income is sole support for her family of four. The three dependents and her personal exemption permit her to exclude $4,000, while deductions of another $6,000 (primarily interest and taxes on the family house and state sales and income taxes) reduce her taxable income to $25,000. The tax table (Table 2.1) shows that taxable incomes between $24,600 and $29,900 pay (1984 rates) $3,465 plus 25% of the excess over $24,600. This implies a tax of $3,565 ($3,465 + $100) which is equivalent to an *average* tax on gross income of 10.2% ($3,565/35,000), or 14.3% ($3,565/25,000) on taxable income. Any additional income would be taxed at the *marginal* tax rate, however. If Mrs. Investor's income increased to $36,000 without changing deductions, her taxable income would increase to $26,000 and her tax would rise by $250 or 25% of the income increase. A taxable income rise to $30,000 would move her to a marginal tax bracket of 28%, however. The marginal tax rate is always higher than the average rate on taxable income. Since investment income is added to other income to produce taxable income, the marginal rate is the relevant rate for most investment decisions.

Table 2.1   1984 Tax Rate Schedules

Taxable Income	Marginal Tax on base	Rate (Percent)
$ 20,200 to 24,600	$ 2,497	22%
24,600 to 29,900	3,465	25
29,900 to 34,200	4,790	28
35,200 to 45,800	6,274	33
45,800 to 60,000	9,772	38
60,000 to 85,600	15,168	42
85,600 to 109,400	25,920	45
109,400 to 162,400	36,630	49
162,400 and up	62,600	50

While Congress may change the tax rates from time to time, each investor's marginal rate (whatever its current level) remains the relevant rate for most investment decisions.

Tax Treatment of Investment Income

Since investment income may be fully taxable, partially tax-sheltered or fully tax-sheltered, effective tax planning is an important aspect of both investing and personal finance. The following discussion reports the relevant tax laws as this is written (1984). Periodic revisions increase both the complexity and the desirability of tax planning. Serious investors need to stay abreast of the tax laws.[2]

The form of an investment's income determines how it is taxed. Interest income on savings accounts, corporate bonds and federal government bonds is taxed as ordinary income (like wages and salaries), while state and local government bond interest is untaxed at the federal level. Net income from rents, royalties and most dividends is fully taxed. A single taxpayer can (in 1984) exclude $100 in dividends (from U.S. corporations) each year while married couples filing jointly can exclude $200.

Through 1985, up to $750 ($1,500 per couple) in dividends of qualifying public utilities is untaxed if reinvested in the company's stock. Dividends not covered by current profits considered "capital distributions" are untaxed. Both reinvested public utility dividends and capital distributions do, however, affect the taxable capital gains or losses on such assets when they are sold.

Capital Gains and Losses

Capital gains and *capital losses* arise whenever capital assets such as stocks and bonds are bought and sold for different amounts. Normally the taxable gain equals the sale price (minus commissions) less the purchase price (plus commissions). Any capital distributions must, however, be subtracted from the purchase price to determine the "basis," which in turn is subtracted from the sale price to produce the taxable gain. Suppose 100 shares of the BDC Company are purchased for $25 per share and sold for $35 per share. The taxable gain (ignoring commissions) would normally be $1,000 ($3,500 − $2,500). Prior capital distribution dividends of $500 would, however, reduce the basis from $2,500 to $2,000, increasing the taxable gain to $1,500 ($3,500 − $2,000).

Only 40% of the realized gain on any capital asset held more than six months is added to the investor's taxable income. Capital losses are netted against capital gains. First, short-term gains are netted against short-term losses and long-term gains against long-term losses. Then for losses the net short- and long-term positions are netted against each other. One-half of any resulting long-term loss may then be subtracted from taxable income. When the holding period is twelve months or less, the full amount of the net gain or loss is added to or subtracted from taxable income. A maximum of $3,000 per year in income may be offset by capital losses, but any additional sums may be carried over to the next year. Capital gains distributions of mutual funds are taxed in the same way as capital gains on assets in an investor-managed portfolio.

Individuals with large amounts of long-term capital gains and certain other types of tax-sheltered income (accelerated depreciation, non-mortgage interest deductions, etc.) may be subject to the alternative minimum tax. One first computes tax liability in the ordinary way. Then after adding back all of the includable tax-sheltered items, the alternative minimum tax is computed (essentially 20% of the sum after certain allowable deductions are subtracted). The individual pays the higher of the two tax figures.

State and Local Taxes

Investment income may also be subject to state and local taxes. Provisions vary with the locality; all U.S. Treasury issues as well as state and local securities in the state of issue are exempt from state and local taxes. State and local bonds issued by other jurisdictions are, in contrast, fully taxed in the owner's own residence jurisdiction.

Tax Treatment Summary

In summary, the three basic types of investment income for federal tax purposes are: (1) the first $100 of dividends and reinvested public utility dividends up to $750; capital distributions and the interest on state and local government bonds— these are tax free; (2) capital gains and capital gains distributions for assets held over six months—40% of these are taxed; and (3) dividends beyond the exclusion, non-municipal interest income, net rents, royalties, other investment income, and capital gains on assets held less than six months—these are taxed as ordinary income. Table 2.2 illustrates these tax categories.

Table 2.2   Tax Treatment of Investment Income

Not subject to federal income tax.	1. First $100 of dividends received annually ($200 if joint) 2. Reinvested public utility dividends (to $750) 3. Capital distributions 4. Interest on state and local bonds
40% of total subject to tax	1. Capital gains on assets held more than six months 2. Capital gains distributions arising from assets held more than six months
Taxed as ordinary income	1. Dividend and interest income (other than municipal interest) in excess of the excludable amount 2. Rents, royalties and any other investment income payments (less relevant deductions) 3. Capital gains on assets held less than six months

Implications of Investment Tax Treatment

Those in higher tax brackets should prefer assets with special tax treatment, even at an appreciably lower before-tax return. Table 2.3 illustrates the relative attractiveness of a 10% tax-free yield for investors in various tax brackets at 1984 rates. This table shows the fully taxable yield necessary to produce a 10% after-tax return. Regardless of the tax-free rate, however, the basic point remains— a given tax-free yield is worth more to people in higher tax brackets.

The market prices assets on an after-tax basis, thereby producing a trade-off between before-tax return and tax treatment. Thus tax-free bonds generally yield well below otherwise-equivalent taxable bond returns. Similarly, investments expected to produce capital gains may be evaluated more favorably than otherwise-similar investments whose principal expected income sources are fully taxed (dividends, rents, etc.). The market-determined tradeoff between fully taxed

Table 2.3   Tax-Equivalent Yield for Joint Return 1984 Rates

If Your Taxable Income is Over:	Your Marginal Tax Bracket is:	And at 10% the Tax-Equivalent Yield is:
20,200	22%	12.8%
24,600	25%	13.3%
29,900	28%	13.9%
35,200	33%	14.9%
45,800	38%	16.1%
60,000	42%	17.2%
85,600	45%	18.2%
109.400	49%	19.6%
162,400	50%	20.0%

and tax-preferred income reflects the average tax impact on the relevant investors. As a result, tax-sheltered investments normally offer those in very high tax brackets relatively higher after-tax returns, while those in below-average tax brackets will find fully-taxed investments more attractive.

Table 2.4 lists principal investment characteristics and high and low examples for each.

Table 2.4   Investment Characteristics

High Example	Characteristic	Low Example
Oil Well	Expected Return	Savings Account
Futures Contract	Risk	Treasury Bill
Money Market Account	Liquidity	Small Business
Actively Traded Stock	Marketability	Collectibles
Real Estate	Investment Effort	Mutual Fund
Commercial Paper	Minimum Investment Size	Savings Bonds
Municipal Bonds	Favorable Tax Treatment	Corporate Bonds

PSYCHOLOGICAL ASPECTS OF INVESTING

Along with the objective factors just discussed psychological factors may influence investment decisions as well. Investors are subject to all the shortcomings and biases inherent in human judgment, and so will profit by evaluating their own tendencies to detect the ones that could lead them astray. A tendency to buy and sell too frequently, for example, might be reduced by taking a day to think over each trade. The market as a whole may also have psychological tendencies that individual investors can exploit in their own trading decisions.[3]

Paul Slovic and his co-workers at the Oregon Research Institute have pioneered the study of human judgment biases and their impacts on investor decisions. His classic work, "Psychological Study of Human Judgment:

Implications for Investment Decision Making,[4] synthesizes a number of psychological studies' investment implications. Slovic observes that the human mind frequently makes random judgmental errors. This trait may be overcome by programming individual decision processes with mathematical models of the considerations, weights, and estimates involved. The programmed and unprogrammed approaches often yield different results because of random human error.

Slovic also reported that in the light of new evidence, people usually revise their opinions in the correct direction—but more conservatively than is warranted by the new data. On the other hand, people tend to extrapolate from a small nonrandom sample to an unsupportable generalization.

Complex decisions may be divided into a series of smaller subquestions with the judgments on each combined into an answer for the initial major problem. Systematic biases in the smaller decisions may lead to a biased decision on the larger question, however.

Bias Sources

Selective recall is one typical human bias. Some events are more easily remembered than others. People also tend to see patterns where none exist and to ascribe causation to spurious correlation. The claimed success of many chartists may be due to such tendencies.

Individuals also sometimes respond differently to the same question asked in different ways. For example, an individual might simultaneously predict a 10% and $5 price rise on a $40 stock (10% of $40 is $4, not $5). Thus questions should be phrased to elicit the most accurate approach to answering them. If available data are in percentages, for example, a question phrased in percentage terms may ellicit a more reliable response.

Apparently the degree of risk aversion is not a universally generalizable characteristic. People may be very risk averse in their investment decisions but much less so in their driving or vice versa. Moreover, decisions made by a group tend to be riskier than individual decisions. Finally, people tend to overrate the reliability of their own judgments.[5] A related set of common psychological errors was adapted from a list compiled by Pines[6] (Table 2.5).

INVESTMENT TYPES AND THEIR CHARACTERISTICS

The remainder of this chapter explores a number of specific investment types in light of the basic characteristics already examined. This discussion is divided into four parts: short-term debt securities, bonds, equity investments, and a catch-all category including real estate, commodities, collectors' items, and "noncollectible" nontraditional investments.

Table 2.5   Sources of Common Errors in Investor Judgment

Judgmental Bias or Error	Source of Error
1. Being bearish at market bottoms and bullish at market tops	Failing to consider a "contrarian," causal scenario
2. Selling winners and holding losers	Inconsistent risk preference and the biasing effects of decision frames
3. Over-optimistic appraisal of a security	Believing that special factors will allow your stock to do better than historical experience would suggest
4. Acting on unreliable "tips"	Vivid, "personal" information is more memorable than statistical data
5. Indecision and/or inconsistency	Effect of emotion on information availability and probability
6. "It's the 1960s again!": misleading market metaphors	Selective recall
7. The "sure thing" that wasn't	Overreliance on one available scenario

Short-Term Debt Securities

Aside from money itself, the most liquid assets available are savings deposits in banks and thrift institutions. Funds can normally be deposited or withdrawn at any time during office hours; most accounts are guaranteed up to a maximum of $100,000 by a United States government agency. Accordingly, depositors should select a convenient deposit institution offering good service and attractive rates (including premiums). Banks and savings institutions have generally paid the maximum allowed rates. Compared with other savings institutions, credit unions generally offer a slightly higher (allowed) government-insured return coupled with valuable borrowing privileges.

The maximum rates paid on traditional savings accounts have generally been well below those allowed on other highly liquid assets. However, rates have now been deregulated on a number of account types. These include savings certificates of $500 or more having maturities of 31 days or greater. While pre-maturity redemption is permitted, a savings certificate redeemed early must be assessed an interest penalty.

Money market funds, sponsored by non-bank financial institutions, generally offer small investors attractive yields on liquid investments. Market interest rates on high-denomination ($10,000 or more) money market securities have often been well above the rates that banks and savings institutions were permitted to pay small depositors. Money funds purchase these instruments with their fundholders' pooled resources and (after administrative expenses) yield slightly less than the rates on the money market instruments themselves. If, for example, money market returns are 9%, a $1,000 money fund account would earn about 8.5%. Money fund deposits are readily accessible by check or wire transfer. Most funds' concentration on high quality short-term securities minimizes their risks.

Banks for a time watched helplessly as their depositors moved capital into the high-paying funds. Then they obtained government permission to market an account that competes directly with the money market funds. These money market accounts have a minimum of $2,500 and maximum of six withdrawals (three by check) per month. The banks may pay whatever interest rates they want in order to be competitive.

U.S. government savings bonds are also designed to compete for small investors' funds. In 1982 their yield structure was set to float at 85% of the government bond rate on five-year-or-longer bonds with a fixed minimum of 7.5%. While not really short-term securities, their early-redemption feature provides an analogous degree of liquidity. Early redemption leads to a yield sacrifice, however. The option of deferring taxes until cashing in the bonds is one major advantage of savings bonds.

A number of other types of securities also compete in the short-term market. Virtually all of these (Treasury bills, banker's acceptances, Eurodollar deposits, commercial paper and short-term municipals) are only available in large denominations and must either be held to maturity or sold at a market price which may differ somewhat from their cost. A variety of different types of bank savings certificates also pay competitive returns.

Highly liquid investments generally offer a very secure (often government-guaranteed) return. Savings accounts are highly liquid, while savings certificates and money market instruments are somewhat less so depending on maturity. Marketing these securities is seldom difficult or costly. Indeed the issuer will redeem some types before maturity. Little or no time commitment or special expertise is required to purchase or manage portfolios of many types of short-term debt securities. On the other hand, most of these investments' interest income is fully taxable. Moreover the returns are often below those available on less liquid investments and only the high-denomination ($10,000 to $100,000) securities offer the highest short-term returns.

Bonds and Similar Long-Term Debt Instruments

"Bonds" are obligations to pay interest periodically and principal at the end of a specified period. Bond investors face two types of risk: default and interest rate. An issuer failing to fulfill (defaulting on) its interest and/or principal obligation risks bankruptcy and possibly liquidation. Even in a bankruptcy, however, the bondholder will often receive a portion of the promised principal and accrued interest. Relatively few bonds default and those that do are almost always rated "speculative" prior to their default. Thus one can largely avoid default risk by investing in nonspeculative bonds.

The issuer's "guarantee" makes most bonds less risky than most stocks. Corporate bonds are at least as secure as the financial conditions of the issuing company. Similarly extensive taxing power minimizes the default risk on federal and many state and local government bonds. The bonds of some smaller governmental units and cities in shaky financial condition (New York and

Cleveland) are considered rather risky, however.

Potentially adverse interest rate fluctuations are the primary risk for long-term bond investors. As market interest rates rise, the price of bonds (which yield a fixed dollar amount) declines and vice versa. Although a bond with a market price below its purchase price will repay its full face value at maturity, such a hold-to-maturity strategy does not take advantage of the higher yields that become available when rates rise. The gain from a favorable interest rate move, on the other hand, may be limited by the "call feature" that permits the issuer to repurchase its bonds prior to maturity, usually for slightly more than face.

A bond's vulnerability to interest rate fluctuations varies directly with its maturity. The prices of debt instruments that will soon mature are unlikely to fluctuate greatly as they will soon be redeemed at face value. While shorter-term debt instruments are less sensitive to adverse interest rate moves, their yields are often lower than those on longer-term bonds.

Most of a bond's return is fully-taxed interest, as compared with the larger proportion of tax-sheltered capital gains in the returns on most other investments. Corporate bonds are issued at $1,000 face values (with market prices typically $600 to $1,200). Current bond commissions are about $5 per bond with a $50 minimum (ten bonds). A minimum of five different companies' bonds is required for effective diversification.[7] Thus a diversified portfolio would require $30,000 or more, putting serious bond investing beyond the reach of small investors.

Most bonds are riskier and less liquid than most short-term debt securities, but are typically less risky and more liquid than most equity instruments. Individual bonds differ substantially in risk, yield and liquidity, however. Since United States government bonds have very low default risks, their yields are almost always below those of similar-maturity corporates. Moreover corporate bond yields vary appreciably with their respective risks.

Bond liquidity varies greatly with maturity: short-term bonds are more liquid than longer-term issues. Bonds of well-known issuers are generally quite marketable, while those of small corporations and governmental units often trade in rather thin markets. Inexperienced investors can rely on bond ratings to select bonds matching their own risk preferences. Realtively little time or effort is required to manage most bond portfolios. Table 2.6 lists the principal types of short- and long-term debt securities.

Equity Instruments

Equity-related investments include publicly traded common stock, preferred stock, options, convertibles, and mutual funds as well as ownership positions in small firms and venture capital investments. Each of these assets represents direct or indirect ownership in a profit-seeking enterprise. Equityholders' claims are junior to all debtors' but encompass all residual value and income after the senior claims are satisfied.

Table 2.6   Types of Debt Securities

Short-Term

Deposits in Banks and Thrift Institutions
Money Market Mutual Funds
Money Market Accounts
U.S. Savings Bonds
Money Market Securities: T-bills, Acceptances, Eurodollars, Commercial Paper, Short-term Municipals

Long-Term

Corporate Bonds
Federal Government Bonds
State and Local Bonds (Municipals)

Common Stock

By far the most important type of equity-related security is common stock. Approximately 42 million U.S. investors own stock directly, while several times that many have an indirect ownership through such vehicles as mutual funds, trust funds, insurance company portfolios, and the invested reserves of their pension funds.[8] As the residual owners, shareholders participate in their firm's profits through dividends and capital appreciation. Stockholders theoretically control the firm by electing its board of directors, which in turn selects upper-level management and makes major policy decisions. The widely dispersed and unorganized nature of most stock ownership groups, however, generally creates a vacuum that existing management fills by nominating and electing friendly slates of directors.

According to one frequently cited study covering the 1926–65 period, long-run stock returns averaged 8 to 9%.[9] In general, stock returns compare favorably with those of most bonds and savings deposits.[10] Table 2.7, taken from a detailed study by Ibbotson and Sinquefield, reports the average returns of various securities for the 1926-1981 period. Clearly average stock returns were highest for this period. On the other hand, returns on particular stocks over particular periods have differed greatly from the average. Furthermore, most stocks' returns were well below these long-term averages during much of the 1960s and 1970s (see Tables 2.9 and 2.10).

Since dividends are not assured and common stock never matures, shareholders are particularly dependent on the firm's future profitability and market acceptance. Thus investors in loss-plagued firms usually experience both a reduction or elimination of dividends and a dramatic decline in the stocks' values. Bond prices generally fluctuate much less and promised interest must be paid regardless of the firm's profit picture. Although a very weak company's bonds may be riskier than a very strong company's stock, bonds almost always have less downside risk than the stocks of the same- or similar-risk firms.

Table 2.7   Average Security Returns 1926–1981

SERIES	MEAN RETURN	DISTRIBUTION
COMMON STOCKS	9.1%	
SMALL STOCKS	12.1	
LONG TERM CORPORATE BONDS	3.6	
LONG TERM GOVERNMENT BONDS	3.0	
U.S. TREASURY BILLS	3.0	
INFLATION	3.0	

−90×   0×   +90×

Source: R. Ibbotson and R. Sinquefield, *Stocks, Bonds and Inflation: The Past and the Future*, p. 15, *Financial Analysts Research Foundation*, 1982. Reprinted with permission.

Stocks can be bought and sold effectively for as little as a few thousand dollars making them relatively accessible to small investors. Commissions are disproportionately high on very small transactions (less than about $1,000 and/ or less than 100 shares), however. The average (median) stockholder's portfolio was worth around $5,100 in 1983.[11]

In summary, common stock offers somewhat higher but more risky expected returns than bonds. Stocks are not especially liquid but those of most large- and medium-sized firms are quite marketable. Small investors can begin assembling a stock portfolio with relatively modest sums. Moreover, the capital gains derived from common stock ownership are partially tax-sheltered. Informed stock-selection requires considerable skill and time, however.

Preferred Stock

Preferred stocks vary greatly in risk, but as a class tend to be more risky than bonds and less risky than common stocks. While "preferred stock" also represents ownership, it is generally less risky than common stock because common dividends are paid only after the preferred dividend requirement is satisfied. In any liquidation the preferred's par value must be redeemed before the common stockholders receive anything. While preferred is senior to common, bondholders are assured of interest income and principal payments before preferred stockholders receive any dividends or liquidation payments.

The dividend yield on preferreds is usually below the average long-term total return (dividend plus capital gains) on common stocks. The preferred of a weak company may, however, be riskier and have a higher expected yield than the common of a stronger company. Preferreds' prices vary inversely with interest rates. Preferred dividends paid to individuals (in excess of the exclusion) are fully taxed. Only 15% of the dividends paid to corporations are subject to federal tax, however. Moreover, a firm owning 80% or more of the dividend-payer's stock incurs no tax liability on the dividends. This special tax treatment also applies to common dividends but is particularly attractive for preferreds where dividends constitute most of the return. Like common, preferred stock is not particularly liquid although it is generally marketable. Assembling a diversified portfolio of preferreds requires a modest amount of time, funds and effort.

Options: Calls, Puts, Warrants and Rights

A *call* is a contract between two parties in which the writer sells an option to purchase some asset (usually 100 shares of stock) at a specified price during a particular period. Similarly, a *put* is a sell-option contract for a particular security, price, quantity and period. Exercising the option privilege is solely at the owner's (not the seller's) discretion. A call buyer hopes that the associated asset's price will rise sufficiently to make exercising the option profitable. Suppose an investor pays $200 for an option to buy 100 shares of stock at 20 ($20 per share). If the price subsequently rises to 30, he or she can exercise (utilize the option) at 20 and sell at 30, yielding a profit of $800 (before commissions) over the $200 cost. A similar profit would be made on a $200 put if the price fell from 20 to 10. The same $200 could, in contrast, have only purchased 10 shares at 20, producing a $100 gain for a similar price rise. An adverse stock-price move can, however, lead to a total loss of the option investment for the optionholder. The shareholder's potential loss is, in percentage terms, generally much less.

Standardized option trading began with the 1973 opening of the Chicago Board Option Exchange. Soon thereafter other exchanges began listed option trading. By 1984, approximately 400 different stocks had listed options. Since most options have relatively short lives (nine months or less) which are dominated by random price fluctuations, option trading is ill-suited to novice investors.

Warrants, like calls, permit a particular stock to be purchased at a prespecified price over a certain period. Unlike calls, warrants are generally exercisable over relatively long periods. Furthermore, when warrants are exercised, the issuing company simply creates more shares, while a call's exercise is satisfied with existing shares. Thus warrants are company-issued securities whose exercise generates cash for the issuer. Calls, in contrast, are contracts between individual investors which do not involve the underlying company.

Rights, like warrants, are company-issued options to buy stock. Unlike warrants, however, rights are very short-run options that can be exercised for substantially less than the stock's current market price. Rights are normally given to existing shareholders on the basis of their existing holdings.

Returns on warrants and rights, like those of calls, tend to be a magnification of the underlying stock's price fluctuations. Because warrants' lives are generally longer, investors who believe that they can forecast long-term price moves may find them attractive.

Since option returns tend to magnify the price fluctuations of the underlying common stocks, options are relatively risky securities. On the other hand, option writing may reduce a portfolio's risk. Listed options tend to be quite marketable, while unlisted options are generally traded in thin markets. The expertise and time commitment required for profitable option trading are at least as great as with common stock. Since options eventually expire and are generally short-run vehicles, gains are much more likely to be short term than are gains on common stock.

Convertible Bonds

Convertible bonds can be exchanged for the issuing company's stock at a preassigned ratio. They are technically debt instruments, but their conversion feature gives them an equity-related component. Such securities offer a compromise between the relatively assured income of bonds and the speculative appeal of stock. Convertible prices tend to rise with their conversion values, but are somewhat insulated from price falls by their values as income securities. Since convertibles generally sell for more than their conversion value, direct stock ownership is normally more profitable in a rising market. Moreover, since their conversion feature allows convertibles to be sold for lower yields than otherwise-similar nonconvertible bonds, straight bonds are generally more attractive in declining markets.

Convertible bonds tend to be less risky than common stock but somewhat more risky than straight bonds. Their liquidity, marketability and minimum investment requirements are similar to those of straight bonds. The expertise and time-commitment required of convertible investors is similar to that of common stock investors. Tax advantages with convertibles that are eventually converted are similar to those of common stocks. Convertible interest is taxed like that of other bonds.

Mutual Funds and Closed-End Investment Companies

Investors can leave most of the investment selection work to a mutual fund whose shares represent proportional ownership of its managed investment portfolio. A change in the portfolio's value (relative to the number of shares outstanding) will, after subtracting expenses and management fees, change the per-share net asset value (value of the fund's portfolio divided by the number of its shares). Most funds will redeem their shares at their net asset values. Funds also transfer portfolio income to their fundholders by declaring dividends and capital gains distributions periodically.

A large but shrinking percentage of mutual funds (load funds) are sold by agents who receive a fee—typically 8.5% of the purchase price. No-load funds, in contrast, sell and redeem their shares through the mail, thereby eliminating the need for a sales force and load fee. No-load fund portfolios generally offer about the same average risk-adjusted returns as those of load funds.

Unlike mutual funds, which are open ended (more shares will be sold to the public if demanded), closed-end investment companies do not redeem their shares. Such shares are usually listed on an exchange, although some are traded over-the-counter. Closed-end share prices can vary substantially from their net asset values.

Mutual funds differ widely in investment goals and portfolio composition. Portfolios may be made up of low-risk or speculative bonds or stocks; tax-exempt securities; short-term highly liquid securities; combinations of stocks and bonds, etc. Still other mutual funds invest in such assets as options, commodities, and collectibles. Thus mutual fund investors can choose from a wide array of risk, liquidity and tax-treatment characteristics. The ability to assemble a diversified portfolio from the pooled resources of many small investors is a major advantage of mutual funds. Average mutual fund performance does not differ appreciably from average market performance, however.[12]

Overall, mutual fund risks, liquidities and tax treatments vary greatly. One can invest in a mutual fund for as little as $500 or $1,000. Most diversified mutual funds are considerably less risky than most individual common stocks, but individual portfolios can also be diversified. No-load funds are at least as liquid and marketable as common stocks. Load funds are costly to trade, however. While mutual funds require less expertise and time-commitment than individually managed portfolios, selecting a suitable fund does require some effort.

Small Firm Ownership

Those who take an active role in their small sole proprietorship, partnership, or closely held corporation are much more managers than investors.[13] The commitment may cut deeply into their other activities. Moreover, joint ownership can lead to troublesome policy disputes and non-expert part-time owner-managers may be at a disadvantage relative to specialist competitors; valuing and ultimately selling can become especially difficult.[14]

Silent-partner-type owners have different problems. A suitable manager may be difficult to find. Managers may misuse their positions (legally or illegally) and may have less incentive than the owners to operate the business profitably. The manager may have to be given a share in the firm's profits as an inducement. The owners remain personally liable for a partnership's or sole proprietorship's unpaid debts, and many creditors require a small corporation's owners to cosign its loans.

Venture Capital

Venture capitalists provide risk capital to otherwise-undercapitalized companies with attractive growth prospects. In exchange, the venture capitalist receives a ground-floor equity position in what may become a highly lucrative venture. For example, Georges Doriot invested $70,000 of the American Research and Development's (ARD) money into what eventually grew into several hundred million dollars worth of Digital Equipment common stock when Textron acquired ARD in 1972.[15] Venture capital may be used to help fund both start-up firms and going concerns with insufficient capital.

Direct venture capital investing is largely closed to all but institutions and wealthy individuals who can invest $500,000 or more. Indirect participation is available, however, through public venture capital funds, mutual funds that specialize in venturing, small business investment companies (SBICs) geared toward venture-capital investing, newly public companies needing venture capital, commercial banks with venture capital components, and private venture capital funds.[16] Regardless of how one participates, venture capital investing is a risky business. Martin and Petty, however, found that while they were quite risky, publicly traded venture capital companies tended to outperform the S&P 500.[17]

Table 2.8 summarizes various types of equity-related investments and their main characteristics.

Table 2.8   Equity-Related Securities

Common Stock	Residual ownership of corporations
Preferred Stock	Preferred to common in dividends and liquidation
Options	
Call	Private option-to-buy contract
Put	Private option-to-sell contract
Warrant	Company-issued option-to-buy
Right	Short-term company-issued option-to-buy
Convertible Bonds	Debt securities that may be exchanged for a prespecified amount of stock
Mutual Funds and Closed-End Investment Companies	Pooled portfolios of securities
Small-Firm Ownership	May be organized as corporation, partnership, or sole proprietorship
Venture Capital	Risk capital provided to start-up companies

Other Investments

The two most important investment types (in dollar value outstanding and traded) remaining to be considered are real estate and commodity futures contracts. Several other "investments," including collectibles, noncollectibles and Ponzi schemes, will also be discussed briefly.

The Shift Toward Other Investments

Rather poor stock and bond performance during the 1970s heightened interest in other types of investments, as reflected in a 1980 *Forbes* summary (Table 2.9). By 1983, however, Barron's showed that the relative performances had changed appreciably (Table 2.10). While the ten-year rankings were relatively similar over the 1971–80, 1974–83 periods, the one-year performance differed markedly. Bond performance, for example, ranked low in 1980 but ranked near the top in 1983. Both tables reveal the relative strength of collectibles, however.

Real Estate

Real estate investing can be quite profitable and offers a number of tax advantages. On the other hand, many small investors' life savings have been wiped out by

Table 2.9   A Dreary Decade for Stocks and Bonds

Gold and oil were the best investments during the 1970s. Both posted a compounded annual rate of return of 31.6%. Stocks with a 6.8% gain and bonds with a 6.4% increase failed even to match the CPI, which rose by 7.7%.

	10 years	Rank	5 years	Rank	1 year	Rank
Gold	31.6%	1	28.4%	3	104.0%	1
Oil	31.6	2	17.7	7	92.4	2
Silver	23.7	3	27.3	4	76.8	3
US stamps	21.8	4	31.0	2	43.2	4
Chinese ceramics	18.8	5	38.7	1	13.1	11
Rare books	16.1	6	12.7	10	14.0	10
US coins	16.0	7	21.9	5	25.3	5
Diamonds	15.1	8	18.3	6	25.0	6
Old masters	13.4	9	15.2	8	17.4	7
US farmland	12.6	10	13.4	9	14.3	9
Housing	10.2	11	11.6	11	10.4	13
Consumer Price Index	7.7	12	8.9	12	14.5	8
Foreign currency*	7.5	13	8.4	13	4.5	14
Stocks	6.8	14	6.4	14	12.5	12
Bonds	6.4	15	5.8	15	–3.1	15

*West German mark, Japanese yen, Swiss franc and Dutch guilder.   *Source: Salomon Brothers*

Source: Salomon Brothers, in T. O'Donnell, "Stocks or Collectibles?" *Forbes*, September 15, 1980. Reprinted by permission of *Forbes* Magazine, September 15, 1980, © Forbes Inc., 1980.

Table 2.10 Investment Performance

One-Year Rankings, 1983 vs. 1982

	This Year* Return	Rank	Last Year Return	Rank
Silver	109.5%	1	−44.5%	15
Stocks	51.8	2	−10.5	11
Bonds	39.0	3	11.4	2
Gold	28.6	4	−34.0	14
U.S. Coins	16.8	5	−27.8	13
Treasury Bills	10.8	6	16.2	1
CPI	3.9	7	6.6	3
Housing	2.1	8	3.4	5
Old Masters	1.7	9	−22.0	12
Diamonds	0.0	10	0.0	6
Chinese Ceramics	0.0	11	−0.5	7
Foreign Exchange	−4.3	12	−1.9	9
Farmland	−5.7	13	−0.9	8
U.S. Stamps	−6.2	14	−3.0	10
Oil	−14.7	15	6.3	4

*Period ended June 1.   Source: Salomon Brothers Inc.

Compounded Annual Rates of Return

	15 Years*	Rank	10 Years	Rank	5 Years	Rank	1 Year	Rank
Oil	20.4%	1	25.4%	2	16.2%	4	−14.7%	15
U.S. Coins	17.9	2	25.7	1	13.2	6	16.8	5
U.S. Stamps	16.8	3	19.2	3	21.8	1	−6.2	14
Gold	16.6	4	15.5	5	17.5	3	28.6	4
Chinese Ceramics	14.2	5	4.0	14	13.1	7	0.0	11
Silver	12.6	6	17.3	4	19.7	2	109.5	1
Diamonds	10.1	7	10.3	7	5.4	13	0.0	10
Farmland	10.0	8	11.7	6	7.0	12	−5.7	13
Treasury Bills	8.8	9	10.1	8	12.8	8	10.8	6
Housing	8.6	10	9.2	9	7.4	10	2.1	8
Old Masters	7.8	11	8.4	10	4.1	14	1.7	9
CPI	7.3	12	8.5	11	9.1	9	3.9	7
Bonds	6.4	13	6.6	13	7.2	11	39.0	3
Stocks	5.7	14	7.5	12	14.8	5	51.8	2
Foreign Exchange	3.1	15	1.4	15	−2.8	15	−4.3	12

*All returns are for the period ended June 1.

Source: L. Rubin, "Smashing Return: Stocks and Bonds Come Roaring Back in the Investment Sweepstakes," *Barron's*, June 20, 1983. Reprinted by permission of *Barron's*, © Dow Jones & Company, Inc., 1984. All Rights Reserved.

the Florida land boom-bust in the 1920s and other less spectacular market collapses. Potential real estate investors have good reasons to be cautious. First, real estate purchases are usually levered, thereby increasing the risk. Second, the one-of-a-kind nature of real estate creates a relatively illiquid market. Selling real estate on short notice can involve a substantial sacrifice. Third, determining an asking price's fairness requires considerable expertise. Fourth, managing improved property is a time-consuming task. Fifth, real estate commissions are considerably higher than those of securities. Sixth, most real estate purchases require a relatively large initial investment (down payment). Finally, those who move often or travel frequently may have difficulty properly managing their property. Thus, real estate may offer attractive returns to investors with the required talents, but the securities markets demand less time and expertise and offer greater liquidity and lower risk. The stock of real estate-related companies offers an interesting compromise, however.

Commodity Futures Contracts

Commodity speculators and hedgers buy and sell contracts for future delivery of a prespecified amount of some commodity—so many ounces of silver, bushels of corn, or thousands of dollars worth of T-bills. Standardized commodities contracts are traded on the various commodity exchanges. Since traders typically must deposit only 5 to 15% of the contract's value, price fluctuations are magnified 8 to 20 times. Thus a contract valued at $100,000 might require a 10% margin ($10,000 in earnest money). A 20% increase in the contract's value (to $120,000) would produce a profit of $20,000 (less commissions) or 200% of the original $10,000 investment. A 10% reduction would wipe out the original $10,000 investment. Most brokerage firms require a relatively large beginning balance and net worth position to open an individual commodity account. Commissions on commodity trades are only a tiny fraction of the potential gains or losses.

Predicting future price movements involves outguessing the commodity market's expectations of weather conditions, government intervention, consumer and producer attitudes, and other factors that may influence the supply and demand for the underlying commodity. Thus its risky nature and the need for a very special understanding of a complex market makes commodity speculation unattractive to most individual investors. Some traders, however, use the commodity futures markets to hedge their risks. For example, a farmer might in effect tie down a price for his or her expected soybean harvest by selling bean futures.

Commodity speculation is generally quite risky. Futures contracts are marketable but illiquid. Substantial expertise, time and resources are required. Also, since commodity trades seldom qualify as long-term capital gains, tax advantages are limited.

Collectibles

Compared with securities, real estate and commodities, collectibles constitute a minor investment medium. Nonetheless their popularity has grown substantially and their market coverage increased in the past few years, to the extent that

Table 2.11   The Sotheby Index

Category	Weights	1975	1976	1977	1978	1979	1980	1981	1982	1983	1984
Old Master Paintings	17	100	105	131	173	224	255	199	199	217	242
19th Century European Paintings	12	100	99	118	160	215	225	176	183	197	209
Impressionist & Post-Impressionist Paintings	18	100	107	114	133	175	206	239	255	298	317
Modern Paintings (1900–1950)	10	100	105	108	132	178	204	232	245	275	301
American Paintings (1800–pre-WW II)	3	100	129	171	255	315	350	424	459	501	589
Continental Ceramics	3	100	121	154	213	261	336	299	266	272	284
Chinese Ceramics	10	100	159	181	241	353	462	459	460	445	459
English Silver	5	100	89	95	124	165	205	160	183	219	237
Continental Silver	5	100	89	92	113	146	179	143	134	156	161
American Furniture	3	100	109	120	134	150	172	209	213	239	241
Continental Furniture	7	100	104	121	148	197	232	218	234	254	270
English Furniture	7	100	125	156	195	244	256	270	263	309	342
AGGREGATE		100	111	128	164	217	253	244	251	275	295

The figures are based on a year ending September 1975 = 100.

Source: Sotheby Parke Bernet as reported in various issues of *Barron's*. © 1984 Sotheby Parke Bernet Inc. Reprinted with permission.
The dates reflected in the Sotheby Index are based on results of auction sales by affiliated companies of the Sotheby Parke Bernet Group and other information deemed relevant by Sotheby's. Sotheby's does not warrant the accuracy of the data reflected therein. Nothing in the commentary furnished by Sotheby's nor any of Sotheby's Indices is intended or should be relied upon as investment advice or as a prediction, warranty or guaranty as to future performance or otherwise. All individual prices quoted in this review are aggregate prices, inclusive of the buyer's premium

Barron's now reports the Sotheby Index of prices on various types of art, ceramic, silver, and furniture collectibles (Table 2.11).[18]

Investors should recognize collectibles' substantial risks and drawbacks. A bewildering assortment of collectibles are now considered investable. Such assets are usually relatively illiquid, very speculative, sold with a high markup, subject to a substantial fraud risk, and involve all of the uncertainties present in the more traditional types of investing. Still, success stories abound. Investors should enter the collectibles market very slowly (if at all), so that mistakes are made with smaller sums before a major commitment is undertaken.

Covering all the various collectible types would be impossible, but the following discussion should give some idea of the flavor. Coins, stamps, art, and antiques have long been collected. For almost as long, investors have sought to profit from the price appreciation which must "certainly" follow the "inevitable" growth of the hobby. As prices have risen for established collectibles, many newer hobbies have sprung up to take advantage of the lower prices on what had until recently been thought of as out-of-date junk. Among the more unusual recently recognized collectibles are manhole covers and the insulators off old telephone poles—the collection of which has caused problems for public works departments and telephone companies.

New collectible areas seem to go through a relatively predictable cycle. First, everything is very cheap and most collectors are amateur hobbyists. As time passes the hobby becomes more commercial. The entry of professional dealers and serious investors causes prices to rise. For a while everyone is happy as increased interest raises the value of everyone's material. New investors attracted by the sharp increase in values drive prices still higher. Eventually, however, the hobby begins to attract unscrupulous promoters who increase the likelihood of fraud, unconscionable markups, and unfairly graded material. Many unaware novices are taken in by these people, which dampens their interest. Once those most likely to enter the collectible areas have been attracted, the hobby's growth rate slows. Some collectors eventually become bored and drop out. Higher prices further discourage potential interest. Without growing numbers of hobbyists, prices soften. Some who entered the hobby for its profit potential try to sell, only to find that the market will absorb their collections only at appreciably lower prices. Declining prices lead others to sell or stop buying. The area may even experience a temporary panic.

Toy collecting is an example of a relatively young hobby. The nostalgia fad has greatly increased interest in old toys. Model trains of the 1920s and 1930s have long been collected, but now even relatively recent windup toys of the 1950s are collectible. Many an attic or cellar contains a gold mine of broken-down old toys if prices hold.[19] No doubt many unaware souls can be persuaded to part with such junk for a song. This, too, is a common experience for a young hobby. The 1976 bicentennial gave 19th century Americana collecting a big boost that continued into the 1980s.[20] With collectibles from the 18th century garnering ever-higher prices, interest inevitably shifted forward—indeed flea markets abound with material from the first half of this century. No doubt the pinball machines and neon signs of the 1960s and 1970s will soon be collectors' items.

Another type of collectible is a subject close to the heart of many people: automobiles. Antique cars have long been collected, though many can remember when such items were available for next to nothing. More recently classic cars of the 1920s and 1930s and even milestone cars of the 1940s, 1950s and 1960s have become collectible. Old cars are an expensive but interesting hobby.

Numerous other items are now collectibles, including the following subjects of popular articles: antiques, prints, young artists, literary collectibles, porcelain, Oriental rugs, photographs, diamonds, Christmas plates, colored gems, old stock certificates, Oriental art, antique maps, antique jewelry, tin cans, and even old clothes.[21] Taylor has even written an academic article on stamp auction returns.[22]

Selling is one of the most difficult aspects of collectibles investing. Investors may, of course, use the same outlets to sell as they used to buy, but this may not always be the best approach. One set of guidelines adapted from a *Business Week* article appears as Table 2.12.

Table 2.12 How to Sell What You Have Collected

Item	Percent appreciation 1969–79	Selling advice
Americana (19th century paintings, furniture, folk art)	100 to 150%	Use regional and country auctions, paying a 10% to 25% commission. Breaking up sets can trim 20% or more from the total selling price.
Automobiles (antique and classic)	100 to 200	Use antique car dealers, selling on consignment for a 30% commission. Small pre-1920 cars and cars costing over $20,000 are hard to sell today.
Coins (government issue, collector quality)	200 to 400	Use a numismatic auction house, paying a 15% to 20% commission. Pre-1915 issues sell the best.
Commemorative coins and medals (private issue)	Appreciation in the intrinsic value of the metal but no gain in numismatic value	Try coin dealers, or advertising in newspapers or numismatic publications. But you will seldom get what you paid, and you may have to settle for the "melt" or intrinsic price of the metal.
Diamonds	100 to 400	Use jewelers of established reputation, trying an outright sale first, then consignment. But expect only 40% to 60% of the current retail price.
Fine jewelry	100 to 200	Use a reputable auctioneer, who will charge a 10% to 25% commission. But you will seldom get what you paid.
Prints	100 to 500	Art auctioneers in major cities run special print auctions. The commission is 10% to 25%.
Rare books	50 to 100	Use book auction houses, waiting for a sale fitting your item. The commission is 20%. For highest prices, sell in complete sets.
Rugs	150 to 200	Persian rug market is unsettled because of uncertainty over the supply of new rugs from Iran. Sell at rug auctions, setting a minimum bid 20% below the price you hope to get.
Stamps	250 for pre-1940 issues	Use a stamp dealer-auctioneer, paying 25% of the value for appraisal and 10% to 20% in commission. The market for pre-1940 issues is strong; the market for later issues is weak.
Western art	100 to 200—and more for top names	Use major auction houses, but wait for special sales of Western art. The commission is 20%. Inflated prices of a few years ago have sagged, and profits will be hard to come by.

Table 2.12   Continued

Item	Percent appreciation 1969–79	Selling advice
Works of young artists	0 to 500	Use a dealer in contemporary art, selling on consignment, with a 50% commission common. It's a long-shot market, and the work may take a long time to sell, if it sells at all.
Wine	200 and more, depending on vintage	Advertise for a private sale. The major auction is in London. You pay shipping and a 20% commission.

Source: "How to Sell What You Have Collected," *Business Week*, June 11, 1979. Reprinted by permission of McGraw-Hill, Inc.

Noncollectibles

Many nontraditional investments do not involve collectibles. The possibilities include Broadway shows, movies, California vineyards, discos, coal mines, computerized home delivery of groceries, racehorses, baseball clubs, freight cars, and the list goes on and on.[23] Some of these investment-media may be worth pursuing, while others should be avoided entirely. One example of the former is Lloyd's of London, which takes on partners to bear its insurance risks. While the risk exposure is technically unlimited, the likelihood of losses beyond the initial investment is relatively small. This type of investment may offer those with substantial resources an attractive return. Moreover, only a letter of credit is required to back up the potential loss.[24]

Many others have, however, been taken in by promoters of such "investments" as Scotch whiskey and farm co-ops. The Scotch whiskey warehouse receipts case reveals a familiar pattern.[25] Investors are attracted to a potentially legitimate investment medium by a rapid price runup. For example, new Scotch available for $1.40 per gallon in 1961 was selling for $4.76 in 1964. Soon, unscrupulous promoters are pushing sales at inflated prices with stories of very attractive returns. By the time the uninformed investor is ready to sell, the promoters have long since departed for greener pastures, and the investor discovers that reselling Scotch whiskey warehouse receipts from this side of the Atlantic is not easy even in the best of times. Investors who in 1969–74 paid between $3.25 and $5 per gallon were lucky to get out at 92¢ in 1976.

Similar experiences occurred more recently in strategic metals, and the "New Farm Co-op" took the life's savings of many "investors" who did not believe that "Bible City" (a theme park with Biblical attractions such as Noah's Ark, the Tower of Babel, and a tour inside a fiberglass whale led by Jonah) could be a fraud.[26]

Dozens of similar examples of offbeat investments with disastrous results could be cited.[27] Gross mismanagement, highly inflated prices, and totally unrealistic profit forecasts are all too common. Anyone considering a nontraditional investment outlet should exercise extreme caution. While most traditional investments (securities, real estate, and commodities) are risky, at least one has a better idea of past history and a modicum of regulatory protection. All too often offbeat investment investors have almost no knowledge of the subject—a nearly certain recipe for disaster.

Ponzi Schemes

The Ponzi scheme is a classic investment fraud. Ponzis attract purchasers by promising high "yields" that are secretly financed from capital. Such schemes are inverted pyramids that need ever larger new "investments" to pay returns on earlier "investments." Eventually the fraud is exposed or not enough new money is brought in and the scheme collapses. In either case, those holding such "investments" are left with little or nothing. The scheme was named after Charles Ponzi who, in 1919, promised $1.40 in 90 days for each dollar "invested." Ten million was taken in before the fraud was discovered and Ponzi sent to jail. He later died in impoverished Brazilian obscurity. Since Ponzi's time, numerous imitators have appeared, one of the largest of which was an oil hoax that took in over $100 million.[28] A visit to the supposed oil fields revealed sewer pipes painted black to look like they carried oil. Anyone with any experience in legitimate oil operations would have detected the fraud. Some of the biggest names in the business and entertainment world were purchasers, each apparently believing that the others must have checked it out. More recently a securities firm named J. David appears to have cost its "investors" around $125 million. It was paying "returns" of 30 to 40 percent per year that it claimed to be earning in foreign currency transactions.[29]

Ponzi schemes can utilize almost any type of investment. A number have involved chain letter applied to whiskey, savings bonds, and gold. Investors should therefore, be wary whenever unrealistically high returns are offered. By the time the scheme is revealed, usually almost nothing is left for the "investors." Table 2.13 summarizes the various types of other (not debt or equity securities) investments.

Table 2.13   Other Investments

Real Estate	Huge market with many risks
Commodity Futures	Contracts calling for deferred delivery of some physical commodity
Collectibles	Diverse array of tangible assets
Noncollectibles	Diverse array of investments including Broadway shows, coal mines, race horses, sports clubs, freight cars, etc.
Ponzi Schemes	Frauds which secretly pay out high returns from principal

SUMMARY AND CONCLUSIONS

Expected return and its associated risk are key factors in most investment decisions. Other relevant characteristics include liquidity (the ease of converting the asset into spendable form without sacrificing return), marketability (the likelihood of trading at the market price without waiting), effort (the time and expertise required of a serious investor), capital requirements (the minimum sum needed to purchase one unit and/or a diversified portfolio), and tax treatment.

Generalizing about the various types of investments is difficult, as each type offers advantages and disadvantages. While an assortment of the more popular investment vehicles have been discussed, the list is by no means complete. Such diverse investments as wildcat oil wells, equipment leases, and currency speculation were not covered.[30]

Very conservative investors may prefer fixed-income investments such as savings accounts, bonds, and preferred stock. Commodities or options may be attractive to more speculative investors. Investors with the time and special expertise may find real estate, collector's items, or small businesses appealing. Investors with limited time, funds, expertise, and willingness to take risks may find common stock and related securities (convertible bonds, convertible preferreds, warrants, mutual funds) an attractive compromise. Whenever an unrealistically high return is offered, the investor should be wary of Ponzi scheme. Table 2.14 describes the general characteristics of the types of investments considered.

Table 2.14   Characteristics of Various Types of Investments

	Risk	Return	Liquidity	Market-ability	Expertise Required	Time Commit-ment	Tax Advan-tage
Short-term Debt Securities							
Passbook Accounts	None	Low	Excellent	Exc	None	None	None
Savings Bonds	None	Low	Good	Exc	None	None	Min
Money Market Mutual Funds	Min	Var	Excellent	Exc	Little	Little	None
Other Money Market							
Securities	Little	Var	Var	Exc	None	Little	Min
			Var	Var	Var	Var	Sub
Long-Term Debt Securities							
U.S. Government Bonds	None	Var	Var	Var	Var	Var	Min
State/Local Bonds	Var	Var					
Corporate Bonds	Var	Var	Excellent	Exc	Little	Modest	Min
Equity-related							
Securities							
Common Stock	Sub	Var	Average	Usu exc	Sub	Sub	Var
Preferred Stock	Var	Var	Average	Usu exc	Var	Var	Small
Listed Options	Sub	Var	Poor	Exc	Sub	Sub	Min
Warrants	Sub	Var	Poor	Varies	Sub	Sub	Small
Unlisted Options	Sub	Var	Poor	Poor	Sub	Sub	Min
Convertible Bonds	Var	Var	Varies	Varies	Var	Sub	Var

Table 2.14   Continued

	Risk	Return	Liquidity	Market-ability	Expertise Required	Time Commit-ment	Tax Advan-tage
No-load Mutual Funds	Var	Var	Average	Exc	Little	Small	Var
Load Mutual Funds	Var	Var	Average	Good	Little	Small	Var
Ownership Position							
of Small Firm	Sub	Var	Poor	Poor	Very Sub	Very Sub	Var
Other:							
Real Estate	Sub	Var	Poor	Poor	Sub	Very Sub	Sub
Commodities	V Sub	Var	Poor	Exc	Very Sub	Sub	Min
Collectors Items	Sub	Var	Poor	Poor	Sub	Sub	Var
Noncollectibles	Sub	Var	Poor	Poor	Sub	Sub	Var

Var = varies
Sub = substantial
Min = minimum
Exc = excellent

REVIEW QUESTIONS

1. Define return and risk.
2. Discuss the risk/return trade-off.
3. Define and compare liquidity and marketability.
4. Discuss the various aspects of investment effort. Illustrate your discussion with specific examples.
5. Outline the various ways investment income may be taxed.
6. Discuss the advantages and disadvantages of the following types of fixed-income securities: savings deposits, savings bonds, money market mutual funds, Treasury bonds, corporate bonds, and municipal bonds.
7. Equity or ownership may be acquired directly with common or preferred stock, or indirectly with warrants, options, convertible bonds, and mutual funds. Compare these types of investments.
8. Real estate, commodity futures, a small firm ownership position, and a portfolio of collectors' items offer investment opportunities attractive to certain types of investors. Discuss the characteristics of these instruments that determine their popularity.
9. How should one seek to spot Ponzi schemes?

REVIEW PROBLEMS

1. Compute the appreciated value of an investment held for two years with a 10% return compounded annually, semi-annually, quarterly and monthly.
2. Compute the average and marginal tax rates for the Jan Q. Investor example (p. 28) using current tax rates.

3. Obtain the most recent year's tax forms and compute the tax liability for the following information:
   Wages: $29,000
   Dividends: $750 (jointly held)
   Municipal Bond interest: $500
   Savings Account interest: $500
   Long-Term Gain on stock: $1,200
   Insufficient deductions to itemize
   3 dependents, married filing jointly

4. Evaluate your own approach to investing (if you do not have an investment portfolio per se, refer your portfolio of longer-term consumer assets) in light of the psychological errors that are frequently made. Make a list of pitfalls to which you tend to be subject. What can you do to avoid these pitfalls?

5. Ask three local banks for their terms on all of their various savings/investment vehicles. Do the same for a local credit union and savings and loan association. Also ask about rates on U.S. government savings bonds. Then make a table of the various alternatives and indicate which offers the most attractive terms for the following:
   a) $500 available for one year
   b) $5,000 available for six months
   c) $20,000 available for three years
   d) $1,000,000 available for three months
   Now go through *Wall Street Journal* and find comparable rates in their advertisements. Add these to your table.

6. Go to a local coin dealer and record the asking prices and description of five high-priced (over $100) coins. Now ask a second coin dealer what he or she would pay for these coins. Compute the percentage markup. Realize that the first coin dealer would probably take less for the coins and that the second dealer would need to see the coins to give a firm offer. Write a report.

Notes

1. P. Slovic, B. Fischloff and S. Lichtenstein, "Rating and Risks," *Environment*, #21, April 1979, pp. 14–39.

2. M. Cox, "Accent is on Growth as Tax Law Changes Many Investor Ways," *Wall Street Journal*, January 12, 1982, p. 1, 18; M. Williams, "Advent of Alternative Minimum Tax Suggests Rechecking of Tax Shelters and Capital Gains," *Wall Street Journal*, August 15, 1983, p. 36.

3. S. Lohr, "The Stock Market's Puzzling Psychology," *New York Times*, January 13, 1981, pp. 1D, 13D.

4. P. Slovic, "Psychological Study of Human Judgment: Implications for Investment Decision Making," *Journal of Finance*, September 1972, pp. 779–799.

5. B. Fischoff, P. Slovic and S. Lichenstein, "Knowing with Certainty: The Appropriateness of Extreme Confidence," *Journal of Experimental Psychology*, 1977, No. 4, pp. 552–564.

6. H. Pines, "A New Psychological Perspective on Investor Decision Making," *American Association of Individual Investing Journal*, September 1983, pp. 10–21.

7. R. McEnally and C. Boardman, "Aspects of Corporate Bond Portfolio Diversification," *Journal of Financial Research*, Spring 1979, pp. 27–36.

8. New York Stock Exchange, *Shareownership 1984*, New York Stock Exchange, 1984.

9. L. Fisher and J. Lorie, "Rates of Return on Investment in Common Stocks: The Year-by-Year Record, 1926–65," *Journal of Business*, July 1968, pp. 291–316.

10. R. Norgaard, "An Examination of the Yields of Corporate Bonds and Stocks," *Journal of Finance*, September 1974, pp. 1275–1286.

11. New York Stock Exchange, op. cit.

12. W. Sharp, "Mutual Fund Performance," *Journal of Business*, January 1966, pp. 119–138; J. Traynor and K. Mazuy, "Can Mutual Funds Outguess the Market?" *Harvard Business Review*, July–August 1966, pp. 131–136; M. Jensen, "Problems in Selection of Security Portfolios." *Journal of Finance*, May 1968, pp. 389–416. H. Shawky, "An Update on Mutual Funds: Better Grades," *Journal of Portfolio Management*, Winter 1982, pp. 29–34.

13. S. Jacobs, "For New Small-Firm Owners, Reality, Plans Tend to Differ," *Wall Street Journal*, June 28, 1982, p. 17.

14. S. Jacobs, "Venture Capital Has its Price: Conflicts Over Firm's Control," *Wall Street Journal*, October 18, 1982, p. 37; D. Moffitt, "Why You Should Set Value on Your Business; Professionals Tell How to Make an Appraisal," *Wall Street Journal*, June 25, 1977, p. 28.

15. R. Phalon, "Getting a Little Crowded: The Venture Capital Businesses Booming—A Mixed Blessing for Venture Capitalists," *Forbes*, February 15, 1982, pp. 51–52; V. Zonana, "Despite Greater Risks, More Banks Turn to Venture-Capital Business," *Wall Street Journal*, November 28, 1983, p. 83.

16. A. Friedman, "The Small Investor as Venture Capitalists," *New York Times*, February 28, 1982, p. 14F; S. Jacobs, "Limited Partnerships Offered for Venture-Capital Investing," *Wall Street Journal*, August 2, 1981, p. 17; *Business Week*, "Venturing into Venture Capitalism," *Business Week*, September 13, 1982, pp. 126–129; V. Zonana, "Despite Greater Risks, More Banks Turn to Venture-Capital Business," *Wall Street Journal*, November 28, 1983, p. 83; *Business Week*, "Now Anyone can be a Venture Capitalist," *Business Week* March 26, 1984, pp. 114–115.

17. J. Martin and J. Petly, "An Analysis of the Performance of Publicly Traded Venture Capital Companies," *Journal of Financial and Quantitative Analysis*, September 1983, pp. 401–410.

18. G. Mahon, "Unveiling Sotheby's Art Index," *Barron's*, November 9, 1981, pp. 4, 59 and 28; G. Mahon, "The Sotheby Index: What is It?" *Barron's*, February 15, 1982, pp. 59–62.

19. S. Sansweet, "Toys in the Attic Find New Owners: Antique Collectors," *Wall Street Journal*, December 15, 1977, p. 1.

20. *Business Week*, "From Oils to Antiques Americana is In," *Business Week*, December 28, 1981, pp. 155–158.

21. *Business Week*, "A Summer's Lust for Country Antiques," *Business Week*, May 10, 1982, pp. 168–172; R. Penn, "The Economics of the Market in Modern Prints," *Journal of Portfolio Management*, Fall 1980, pp. 25–35; *Business Week*, "Investing in Young Artists," *Business Week*, May 3, 1976, pp. 127–134; N. McInnis, "Bulls in a China Shop," *Barron's* August 2, 1972, p. 9; J. Powell, "Flying Carpets," *Barron's*, August 16, 1976, p. 9; J. Powell, "Think Positive," *Barron's*, July 12, 1976, p. 12; *Business Week*, "Adding New Facets to Investing in Diamonds" *Business Week*, June 13, 1983, pp. 119–120; B. Donnelly, "Blue-Plate 'Specials' Turn into Highfliers for Some Collectors," *Wall Street Journal*, December 22, 1978, p. 1; J. Powell, "More Precious Than Rubies," *Barron's*, September 3, 1979, pp. 11, 12, 27; J. Bettner, "Old Securities You Thought Were Losers Might Still Be Winners in New Collector Market," *Wall Street Journal*, January 5, 1981, p. 82; *Business Week*, "A Guide to Collecting Oriental Art," *Business Week*, August 20, 1979, pp. 122–126; C. Salzberg, "The Road to Treasure in Antique Maps," *Fact*, May 1983, pp. 60–63; J. McQuown, "Antique Jewelry:

Steady Gains in An Overlooked Market," *Fact*, April 1983, pp. 61–63; N. Marx, "Have Any Old Tin Cans at Home? They Might be Collector's Items," *Wall Street Journal*, July 18, 1983, p. 21; J. Greenberg, "Rags to Riches," *Forbes*, January 17, 1983, pp. 57–60.

22. W. Taylor, "The Estimation of Quality-adjusted Rates of Return in Stamp Auctions," *Journal of Finance*, September 1983, pp. 1095–1110.

23. J. Andresky, "So You Want to be an Angel," *Forbes*, January 31, 1983, pp. 92–97; L. Landro, "Movie-Investment Venture Finds Film Financing Can be Treacherous," *Wall Street Journal*, April 8, 1983; p. 41; L. Landro, "If You Have Wanted to Be in Pictures, Partnerships Offer the Chances, but with Risks," *Wall Street Journal*, May 23, 1983, p. 60; J. Madrick, "A Fresh Look at California Vineyards," *Business Week*, June 14, 1976, pp. 41; *Forbes*, "Discomania," June 1, 1976, pp. 47–48; D. Conperet, "Bottomless Pits? Offering Big Returns Coal-Mine Promoters Seek Investor Money," *Wall Street Journal*, August 8, 1977, p. 1; R. Welling, "Get-Rich-Quick Scheme? At Futuristic Foods it Only Works for Some," *Barron's*, December 28, 1976, p. 3; K. Gilpin, "Betting on the Ponies: Before or After the Race," *New York Times*, July 31, 1983, p. 10 F. *Business Week*, "Now Small Investors Can Play the Ponies," *Business Week*, March 7, 1983, p. 91; A Block, "So, You Want to Own a Ball Club," *Forbes*, April 1, 1977, pp. 37–40; S. Andreder, "The Short Haul: Investors Have Made Loads of Money Leasing Freight Cars," *Barron's*, April 30, 1979, p. 11, 14, 16, 118.

24. *Forbes*, "Ye Olde Negative Sell," *Forbes*, November 15, 1977, pp. 31–32.

25. P. DuBois, "Over a Barrel," *Barron's*, December 11, 1976, pp. 9, 16, and 17.

26. J. Winski, "Rural Missourians Lose Millions in Investment in 'New' Farmer Co-op," *Wall Street Journal*, November 10, 1977, p. 30.

27. J. Cooney and S. Penn, "Illusory Profits: How Theater Producer Induced Investments in her Foreign Deals," *Wall Street Journal*, April 8, 1977, p. 1; J. Drinkhall, "Top Con Men of the '70s and Still in Business Court Records Disclosure," *Wall Street Journal*, June 25, 1982, p. 1, 8; R. D. Lowenstein, "Dealing in Diamonds Hasn't Lost Its Luster for Bernie Dohrman," *Wall Street Journal*, January 11, 1983, pp. 1, 20; R. Stern, "Now You See It, Now You Don't," *Forbes*, June 20, 1983, pp. 33–34; J. Drinkhall, "How Farm Town Bore Brunt of Alleged Fraud by a Factoring Outfit," *Wall Street Journal*, November 28, 1983, pp. 1, 14.

28. D. McClintick, "Rich Investors' Losses in New 'Ponzi Scheme' Could Hit $100 Million," *Wall Street Journal*, June 26, 1974, p. 1.

29. D. Bander, "Scam or Snafu? The Strange Story of J. David," *Barron's* February 20, 1984, pp. 14, 28.

30. *Business Week*, Money Starts Flowing to the Oil Drillers," *Business Week*, April 26, 1976, p. 71; M. Farrell, "Equipment Leasing," *American Association of Individual Investors Journal*, May 1984, pp. 11–16; W. Shepherd, "Playing Currency Rates," *Business Week*, May 25, 1974, p. 99.

3 The Securities Markets

This chapter explores the mechanics, regulation, and economic functions of the securities markets. While common stocks are the principal focus, preferred stocks and warrants are traded in virtually identical fashions. The listed option, mutual fund, and bond markets also have much in common with the stock market, unlike futures and real estate.

Most of this chapter deals with security market mechanics. The broker's role is explored, followed by a discussion of investment managers, exchanges, and the over-the-counter market. Then we examine commissions, bid-ask spreads, and types of orders in the context of how to minimize transactions costs. This is followed by a discussion of short selling and margin trading. Then various specialized institutional arrangements for trading stock are considered: third and fourth markets, new issues, private placements, rights offerings, secondary distributions, block trades, and tender offers. Security market regulation is discussed next, first in its historical context and then in terms of progress toward a competitive central market. The third and final topic of this survey is the security market's place in the economy, especially in its role in capital allocation. Other functions considered include the security market's effect on allocating managerial talent and its use by the Federal Reserve Board in implementing monetary policy.

THE MECHANICS OF THE SECURITIES MARKETS

Most investors are far more interested in the practical aspects of trading securities than in economic and regulatory topics. Buying and selling stocks and bonds usually involves dealing with some or all of the following: brokers, exchanges, limit orders, specialists, margin borrowing, stock certificates, commissions, underwritings, tenders, and other special entities. Understanding these aspects of everyday market operations may prevent costly mistakes.

Brokers and Brokerage Firms

Somewhat confusingly, the term *broker* is used for both the individual employee and the employing firm. In this text the term *broker* refers to the employee and *brokerage firm* or *brokerage house* refers to the employer. Essentially, brokers

55

and their firms link investors to the securities markets. Like real estate agents, stockbrokers implement their customers' trading instructions. Dealers, in contrast, make markets by buying, selling, and holding an inventory of securities.

In addition to facilitating trades, most full-service brokerage firms engage in a variety of other activities such as offering investment advice, maintaining customer's securities, sending out periodic statements, lending money on the collateral value of certain securities (margin loans), and acting as investment bankers by marketing new security issues and large blocks of already-outstanding securities called secondary offerings. Many brokerage firms also manage and sell mutual funds, make a market in unlisted securities, sell insurance, offer and manage various types of pension plans, manage some customer accounts individually, provide access to commodity exchanges, deal in government securities, sell tax-sheltered annuities, etc. As brokerage firms have expanded their activities, however, many nonfinancial firms such as retailers and manufacturers have entered the securities field, mainly through acquisitions. Such diverse companies as Sears, RCA, Gulf and Western, National Steel, Greyhound, General Electric, Controlled Data, American Express, Merrill Lynch, Prudential, Beneficial, and Transamerica now have financial services components. Some of these firms offer an entire array of financial services including checking, credit cards, travelers checks, personal loans, insurance, pension packages, real estate trading and management, as well as the traditional brokerage functions.[1]

What Should Be Expected of a Broker?

Brokers should implement orders and quickly correct their firm's errors. Brokers also provide investment ideas, for which customers pay in the form of commissions. Brokers' recommendations generally prove no more useful than the notoriously unreliable advice of investment analysts, but discussing prospective trades with one's broker may provide perspective.

If brokers could produce the dramatic results many investors expect, they would have no need to earn their livings as brokers. Moreover, since a single broker can closely follow only about 30 of the roughly 5,000 actively traded issues, individual brokers are often unfamiliar with the specific stocks that interest particular investors. Accordingly, investors should either assume full responsibility for their portfolio management or hire a mutual fund or investment manager. Increasing numbers of investors are switching to discount brokers who offer minimal service and low cost executions.

While seeking investment miracles from one's broker is unrealistic, investors have every right to expect financial soundness and integrity. Even these modest expectations are sometimes unfulfilled, however.

Bankruptcy of Brokerage Firms

The failure in 1973 of Weis Securities, Inc., a member of the New York Stock Exchange (NYSE or Big Board) with 43,000 customers, prompted a reevaluation of provisions protecting the customers of bankrupt brokerage firms. Prior to 1971, customers of failed Big Board firms were compensated by the NYSE through membership assessments. While no customer ever lost money as a result of a NYSE member's failure, by late 1970 the trust fund was exhausted and the solvent NYSE members opposed further assessments. Congress then set up the Security Investors Protection Corporation (SIPC) to liquidate troubled firms upon an SEC request. Customers are insured up to $500,000, but not more than $100,000 in cash, with any claims above those sums applied against the firm's assets. Some brokerage firms carry additional insurance.

The SIPC may take several months to complete a liquidation, thereby tending to lock in the affected investors. Furthermore, the securities of bankrupt brokerage firms' margin customers are sold to pay their loans. Such investors must incur commissions on the sale and repurchase (perhaps at higher prices) if they are to restore their positions. The 1981 failure of John Muir again illustrated SIPC's inability to cope quickly with a large failure.[2] Some investors had to wait months to reclaim their accounts.

Integrity of Brokerage Houses

Most brokers and brokerage firms are honest. The exchanges and Securities and Exchange Commission (SEC) try to monitor their industry closely. Those found guilty of serious wrongdoing soon lose their right to work in the industry. Still, improprieties such as the following are uncovered with some frequency:

1. Conflicts of interest: Potential conflicts are raised by managing mutual funds, underwriting securities, making a market in some stocks, and advising customers. Most firms do take great pains to avoid even the appearance of a conflict, however.
2. Kickbacks: Order clerks may receive kickbacks to steer over-the-counter (OTC) orders to particular market makers. The customer usually pays the kickback in the form of higher prices.
3. Misuse of customer assets: Brokerage firms sometimes use customers' money and the collateral value of their securities for positioning stocks and operating expenses. As long as the firm remains solvent, the customer may not be harmed, but the practice is questionable and dangerous.
4. Embezzlement: Alert customers should quickly detect misappropriation of their assets by carefully monitoring their monthly statements. Since the brokerage firm is responsible for any employee's fraud, the stolen property should be easy to recover, if detected.
5. Improper use of discretionary authority: Sometimes brokers trade without specific customer approval. Customers who give their broker limited or complete money management powers may encourage churning. Brokers who actively buy and sell generate substantial commissions but few profits.

Investment Managers

Some investors retain professionals to manage their investments. Individuals with $100,000 or more have long been able to hire a portfolio manager for a fee equal to a percentage of the portfolio's asset value. Many investment advising firms and banks will handle portfolios as small as $10,000, making professional advice available to modest investors. Accounts of less than $100,000 are generally managed as part of a pool with a pro rata return assigned to each account. Accounts of $100,000 or more may be individually managed.

Most mutual funds earn risk-adjusted returns no higher than those of the market averages, and the advice of investment analysts is about as likely to be inaccurate as accurate. Investment managers combine the random performance and advice of mutual funds and investment analysts. Most such advisors charge a management fee of up to 2% (small accounts) compared with 1/2 of 1% for most mutual funds.[3] No-load mutual funds, however, offer small investors greater diversification, lower cost, and more specialized attention than do most investment advisors. Those who do decide to use an investment advisor may find the following rules useful.

Eight Questions to Ask in Choosing an Investment Advisor

1. How does the firm make its money? Some base their fee on the account's assets. Others charge commissions for the work done, which can prove more costly.
2. Is financial counseling the only service offered? One should at least know in advance if the firm also sells insurance, tax shelters, pension-packages or mutual funds.
3. Is the firm independently owned? If it is owned by a bank or a brokerage house, how independent is it? Does it do its own research, for instance?
4. Will the firm provide at least three reliable business references such as a top local banker? One should not expect an advisor to supply client names, however.
5. What is the firm's track record? Will it list its recent market selections and fully explain its investment philosophy?
6. How many accounts are handled by one portfolio manager? The high-quality firms assign each manager no more than 20 to 60 accounts. Some firms hesitate to answer, but one should press the point.
7. Does the firm use a limited power of attorney? Otherwise, ask how it would handle a situation requiring quick attention when the owner is unavailable.
8. Will the firm contact clients, if necessary, while they are traveling? If the account is large and service personalized, a conscientious firm should even be willing to phone overseas.

Whether to manage one's own investments, hire an investment manager, or purchase mutual fund shares is an individual decision involving such considerations as the sum to be invested, time available, and investor's goals. Presumably most people interested enough in investing to read this book intend to manage their own investments.

TYPES OF SECURITIES MARKETS

Regardless of how one's portfolio is managed, securities must be bought and sold. Potential buyers could try to find sellers themselves, but relatively few people wish to trade any one stock at a particular time. The need to bring buyers and sellers together efficiently led to centralized facilities (exchanges) for trading stocks, bonds, commodities, and options. Other trading takes place in somewhat less organized over-the-counter markets.

The Stock Exchanges

NYSE-listed companies produce about half of the economy's gross national product. NYSE rules tend to be followed by most other exchanges. Only members can transact business on the exchange, and only listed securities may be traded. Since large firms are generally traded on the Big Board, a certain amount of prestige attaches to such listings.[4] Smaller firms may be listed on the American Stock Exchange (AMEX), which is the second largest in terms of primary listings. Still smaller firms trade on the regional exchanges. Table 3.1 reports NYSE and AMEX listing requirements. Some exchanges permit trading other exchanges' listings, and many stocks are listed on more than one exchange (dual listings).

Table 3.1 NYSE and AMEX Listing Requirements

	NYSE	AMEX
Pre-Tax Income Last Year	$2,500,000	$750,000
Pre-Tax Income Last Two Years	$2,000,000	—
Net Income Last Year	—	$400,000
Net Tangible Assets	$16,000,000	$4,000,000
Shares Publicly Held	1,000,000	400,000
Market Value Publicly Held Shares	$16,000,000	$3,000,000
Number of Round Lot Holdings	2,000	1,200

In addition to meeting these requirements, a firm must apply for listing, pay a fee, and not engage in any practice prohibited by the exchange. The exchanges have much less stringent delisting criteria and may choose not to apply them in specific cases.

The Over-the-Counter Market

While large firms are generally listed on a stock exchange, numerous small publicly owned firms are traded in the over-the-counter (OTC) market. Moreover, 500 to 600 NYSE-eligible companies choose to remain unlisted and many listed companies are also traded OTC in the so-called third market. The OTC is an informal network of market-makers who offer to buy and sell. To trade an OTC stock one would have his or her broker contact an OTC dealer handling the stock.

NASDAQ

As recently as 1971, brokers had to call each relevant market-maker to determine the best OTC price. Since few brokers were willing to contact what could be as many as fifteen market makers, customers often traded at unfavorable prices. To overcome this problem, the National Association of Securities Dealers (NASD) set up the National Association of Securities Dealers Automatic Quotation System (NASDAQ) to connect the quoting dealers and brokers and report the best available OTC prices.

The NASDAQ Lists

Most small companies' securities trade OTC. NASD assembles three lists of OTC companies and their price quotations for newspaper distribution. The largest and most actively traded issues are reported in their National Market System list. Its quotations report the same information categories as for the NYSE and AMEX quotations. The second tier of OTC issues appear on the NASDAQ National List, which contains firms with financial characteristics similar to those for AMEX listing. Together, the two lists have about 2,500 firms. About 1,000 of the next largest OTC issues are included on their Supplemental List. In addition many newspapers maintain their own list of local stocks. All actively traded OTC issues are reported in the "Pink Sheets" available at most brokerage firms. These Pink Sheets contain recent price quotes and list market-makers on the 10,000 or more issues that actively trade in the OTC market.

Size of the Stock Markets

Figure 3.1 reports the size and recent growth of the three principal stock markets: NYSE, AMEX and NASDAQ. Regional exchange volumes are relatively small and much of that is for NYSE and AMEX primary listings. In 1983 total NYSE volume was about 24 billion shares (26 billion including third market and regional trading of its listings). The AMEX volume, in contrast, was around 2.1 billion (2.4. billion with other trading). NASDAQ 1983 volume was almost 16 billion. These numbers are not directly comparable, however. Average NYSE share prices are two to three times those of AMEX issues while the NASDAQ average price is even lower than the AMEX's. The frequency with which a given share is traded also varies from market to market, and institutional trading makes up a much larger part of NYSE volume than that of the AMEX or NASDAQ.

Figure 3.1   Recent NYSE, AMEX and NASDAQ Volume

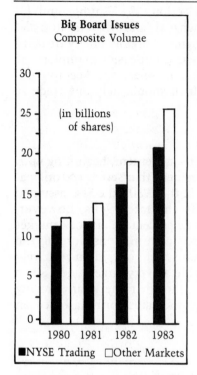

Big Board Issues
Composite Volume

(in billions
of shares)

1980 1981 1982 1983
■NYSE Trading □Other Markets

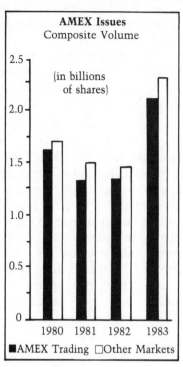

AMEX Issues
Composite Volume

(in billions
of shares)

1980 1981 1982 1983
■AMEX Trading □Other Markets

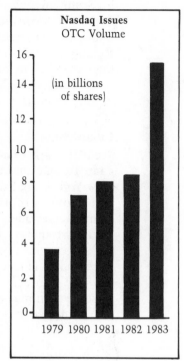

Nasdaq Issues
OTC Volume

(in billions
of shares)

1979 1980 1981 1982 1983

Source: *Wall Street Journal.* Reprinted by permission of *Wall Street Journal,* © Dow Jones & Company, Inc., 1983. All rights reserved.

Other Securities Markets

Preferred stocks, warrants and rights are traded on the same exchanges and OTC markets as common stocks. Corporate bonds may also be listed on exchanges but most are traded OTC. The commission structure for bonds differs from that of stocks, and trading on an exchange is generally physically separated from equity trading. While exchanges handle some United States government bond trading, the vast majority of trades are made with a small number of OTC government bond dealers. Commercial paper, large CDs, municipal bonds and other money market instruments principally trade in similar OTC markets. Puts and calls were initially exchanged in a rather thin OTC market. In 1973, however, the Chicago Board Option Exchange (CBOE) demonstrated that options could be effectively traded on an exchange. In addition to the CBOE, standardized (price, delivery date, etc.) stock options are now listed on the American, Philadelphia and Pacific Coast exchanges. While also traded on exchanges, the institutional features of commodities markets are quite different from those of stock exchanges.

TRANSACTIONS COSTS

Investing involves three basic processes: (1) Selection, (2) Timing, and (3) Execution. Most literature on investing deals with what (1) and when (2) to trade. Though how to trade at the lowest costs (3) is often ignored or only briefly treated,[5] techniques exist that are not only relatively worthwhile but easier to implement than the various approaches to successful timing and selection. Accordingly, stock market mechanics, the understanding of which should help one trade at minimum costs, is discussed in detail herein.

Commissions

Security market commission rates were long fixed by agreement, beginning with a rate-fixing clause in the so-called Buttonwood agreement that set up the original New York Stock Exchange in the late 18th century. In the 1930s, the SEC assumed regulatory authority over the rate structure. By the late 1960s, however, institutional traders, who made up a large and growing percentage of stock market volume, found various ways around the high fixed commissions, forcing the brokerage industry to respond. First quantity discounts were offered on relatively large trades. Then commissions were made negotiable on very large trades. Since May 1, 1975, each brokerage firm must set its own schedule rather than agreeing to some common formula. Table 3.2 contains a commission formula based on one from a large retail brokerage firm.

Table 3.2   A Hypothetical Retail Commission Schedule

Principal Value (Stocks, Rights and Warrants Selling for more than $1.00)

$ 0– 300	11% of principal
301– 800	$ 9 + 2.75% of principal
801– 2,500	$18 + 1.75% of principal
2,501– 20,000	$30 + 1.25% of principal
20,001– 30,000	$125 + .90% of principal
30,001–300,000	$210 + .60% of principal
300,000 and over	$1,300 + .25% of principal

Lot Charges

100 shares or less	No Charge
101–1,000 shares	8.00 per lot
1,001 or more	80.00 plus 5.50 per lot

Maximum Commission charge per share $ 1.00

Minimum Commission for principal value exceeding $300 $35.00

Principal Value (Stocks, Rights and Warrants Selling for less than $1.00)

$ 0– 1,000	11% of principal
1,001–10,000	$ 50 + 7% of principal
10,001 and over	$200 + 5.5% of principal

Commissions average about 2% to 3% of a trade's dollar value, although larger transactions receive quantity discounts and smaller trades tend to pay proportionately more. For a 200-share trade of a $15 stock, the money involved is $3,000. Thus, from Table 3.2, the commission on the principal value would be $30 + 1.25% of $3,000. In addition, a lot charge of $8 per round lot, or $16, applies. The total commission of $83.50 is equivalent to 2.78% of the $3,000 principal.

Discount Commissions

The end of fixed commissions greatly expanded potential competition among brokerage firms, primarily benefitting institutional customers such as mutual funds, insurance companies, and bank trust departments.[6] While the full service firms do offer discounts to their large individual customers, most do not compete openly on a price basis. A few firms (Merrill Lynch's share builder program, for example) offer special plans for trades of less than $2,000 but the cash or certificate must be delivered in advance and the trade executed at the opening. Small investors generally find the most attractive rates at discount brokers. Some discounters' rates are a specific percentage below the old fixed rates while other schedules are based on the dollar value of the trade, the number of shares traded or a combination of factors.

Table 3.3 illustrates some comparative rates for three retail brokers (Merrill Lynch, Shearson, and Bache) and five discounters (Ovest, Schwab, Quick and Reilly, Rose & Company and Fidelity/Source.) These discounts range from 40 to 70% below the average retail rate. Most discounters only execute trades, although a few offer services similar to retail houses. Investors should shop for the combination of discounts and services (including the quality and quantity of investment information) that best suits their needs.

Table 3.3   Representative Retail and Discount Commissions

Shares/Price	200 @ 15	500 @ 25	1000 @ 25	Options 10 @ 15/16	10 @ 5
Merrill Lynch	86.00	235.00	419.00	108.00	154.00
Shearson	88.25	237.87	423.50	86.62	165.27
Bache	87.00	235.00	420.00	76.25	150.00
OVEST	35.00	65.00	102.50	32.00	70.98
Schwab	54.00	94.50	132.00	35.00	78.00
Quick & Reilly	43.48	122.58	217.60	42.50	75.44
Rose & Co.	46.97	110.00	200.00	56.30	90.81
Fidelity/Source	49.00	96.00	147.50	37.19	72.00

Source: Ovest advertisement appearing in various financial publications. Reprinted by permission of Ovest Financial Services.

Spreads

Spreads represent the second major component of transactions costs. OTC dealers and their stock exchange equivalent, the specialist, quote both a "bid price," at which they will buy, and the "asked price," at which they will sell. The difference or spread between the buy and sell prices is the dealer's markup. Higher priced and more actively traded stocks tend to have lower percentage spreads than other stocks. OTC spreads average 4% to 5% for the national list but sometimes exceed 10% of the dollar value of the trade.[7] To understand how the spread's impact may be reduced, we need to explore the ways of placing purchase and sale orders.

THE MECHANICS OF THE MARKET

The Ticker Tape

Actual transactions for listed securities are reported on the ticker tape most brokerage houses display on large screens. Each stock has an identifying ticker symbol. For example, the symbol "T" is for telephone (American Telephone and Telegraph) , and "XRX" is for Xerox. Each transaction's volume and price follows and appears below the company ticker symbol. Figure 3.2 illustrates a typical ticker tape reading:

Figure 3.2   Ticker Tape Reading

C	SOH	G
6 3/4	2s 49	2700 17 1/2

The first entry, C with 6 3/4 below and behind it, reports a single round lot sale of Chrysler corporation at $6.75 per share. The second entry, SOH followed by 2s 49 reports a trade of 200 shares (2s) of Sohio at $49 per share. The entry G, with 2700 17 1/2 following it, reports that 2,700 shares of Greyhound traded at $17.50 each. The full number of shares are displayed for trades of 1,000 shares or more. Ticker symbols are contained in some investment references such as the *S & P Stock Guide*, and most brokerage houses keep booklets that list stocks and their symbols.

Market and Limit Orders

One initiates security trades with an order. A market order leads to an immediate execution at the highest unexercised bid for a sell and at the lowest unexercised ask for a buy. A limit order, in contrast, is only executable at the limit price (or better). Thus a market order ensures a transaction, while a limit order transaction must await an acceptable price.

Brokerage firm representatives take limit orders to the section of the exchange where the stocks are traded (trading stations or "posts") and attempt to execute them. A representative may seek to purchase 100 shares of XYZ at 23, for example. If the stock is available at 23 or less, the trade will be executed forthwith. Indeed the order will be filled at less than 23 if possible. A limit order only stipulates the least favorable price that will be accepted. Limit order prices are normally set at levels more favorable to the initiator than the current price, however. Thus the order to buy XYZ at 23 might be entered when the stock was offered at 23 3/4 (asked) and others were willing to pay 23 1/4 (bid). After waiting a short time, the representative will leave any unexecuted orders with the specialist (explained later).

Stop-Loss and Stop-Limit Orders

Stop-orders limit one's loss exposure. A stop-loss sell order implements a sale at market if the price falls to the prespecified level, thereby protecting the investor from a further fall. Since the stock must be traded immediately after the stop price is reached, the realized price is usually relatively close to the stop-loss price. A stop-limit order, in contrast, activates a limit order when the market reaches the stop-level. Thus with a stop-limit order, hitting the stop-level may or may not liquidate the position. While the vast majority of stop orders lead to sales if the price drops, buy stop-orders are triggered by a price rise. Thus a stop-loss buy order at 30 might be placed on a stock trading at 25. As long as the price stays below 30 nothing is done. Once it touches 30, the stock is bought.

Good 'Til Cancelled, Day, Fill-or-Kill and All-or-Nothing Orders

Limit, stop-loss, and stop-limit orders may be entered either as "Good 'Til Cancelled" (GTC) or as executable for a specified period. Thus an order can be placed to remain on the books for a day or week or some other period or until it is executed—whichever comes first. Day orders are cancelled automatically; the broker must cancel other orders on the prespecified day. Fill-or-kill orders must either be executed immediately or cancelled.

One who wishes to trade more than one round lot may either allow the order to be filled a bit at a time or stipulate an all-or-nothing trade. Commissions are computed on daily trades of the same security. Thus an order to sell 1,500 shares could involve as many as fifteen 100-share-a-day trades. The total commission on such a stretched-out trade would appreciably exceed that on a single 1,500-share trade. An all-or-nothing order must trade as a unit incurring a single commission (with any volume discount applying) but can only be executed when sufficient volume is simultaneously available. A regular order might be filled pieces at a time even though insufficient volume existed for a single fill. Moreover, all-or-nothing orders are automatically superceded by any other limit orders at the same price. Thus those who would use all-or-nothing orders need to compare the potentially lower commission with the reduced likelihood of execution.

Versus Purchase Orders

Investors frequently sell only a portion of their holdings of a particular issue. Normally the shares which were purchased earliest are recorded as the ones sold (First in First Out, FIFO). The seller may, however, prefer to sell different certificates. Selling securities that were purchased at a later date than would be required by FIFO may produce a higher basis (thereby reducing the profit or increasing the loss for tax purposes) or allow the investor to realize a short-term loss (thereby allowing a greater deduction against short-term gains or ordinary income). Making the order "versus purchases" allows the seller to specify which block of shares within his or her holdings of that company's stock are to be identified as the ones sold. Table 3.4 summarizes the various types of orders.

Table 3.4   The Various Types of Orders

	Principal Types of Orders
Market Order	Requires an immediate execution at the best available price
Limit Order	Stipulates the minimum (sell) or maximum (buy) price acceptable for a trade to take place
Stop-Loss Order	Requires an immediate trade if the specified price is reached
Stop-Limit Order	Activates a limit order if a specified price is reached
	Period for Which an Order Is Executable
GTC (Good Till Canceled)	Executable until filled or canceled
Day	Executable only during the day it is placed
Fill-or-Kill	Canceled if not immediately executed
	Orders for More Than One Round Lot
All-or-Nothing	Must be executed as a block
If Not Specified	May be executed in pieces of as small as one round lot
	Sales of a Portion of Holdings of a Particular Issue
Versus Purchase	Allows the seller to specify which block of stock within his or her holdings are to be sold
If Not Specified	The shares which were purchased earliest are identified as sold (FIFO)

The Specialist

Like OTC market makers, specialists quote bid and asked prices on assigned stocks. Most securities are handled by a single specialist, although a given specialist may make markets in a dozen or so securities, and a few actively traded securities are handled by more than one specialist. Specialists record limit and stop orders in their order books and are responsible for their execution whenever the prespecified limit prices are reached.[8] If the bid dropped from 23 1/4 to 23 1/8 for example, a limit order at 23 would still be superceded by all orders at 23 1/8. Once all orders to buy at 23 1/8 are filled, the bid will fall to the next highest unexercised order level—in this case 23. Until higher bids arrive, orders at 23 will be executed chronologically. For example, a particular order to purchase 100 shares at 23 may be preceded by other buy orders at 23 for 500 shares and another 300 shares at 23 may follow. Once the 500 shares at 23 are purchased, our 100-share order will be crossed with any incoming market sell order or limit order to sell at 23 or lower. On the other hand, any offer to pay more than 23 would immediately supercede our order.

Floor Traders or Registered Competitive Market Makers (RCMM)

Stock prices are influenced both by specialists, who make markets, and unexecuted limit orders, which represent potential demand and supply. Individuals called floor traders or RCMMs, who own exchange seats and trade for their own account, also have modest price impacts. The advantages of floor trading include quick access to the market, very low incremental trading costs (coupled with the high fixed cost of exchange membership), and the information derived from the feel of being where the action is. As recently as the 1960s, a substantial fraction of NYSE members were floor traders. Since that time, however, various restrictions have reduced their ranks substantially. By 1982, only 23 were registered and only 10 of them were active on the NYSE.[9] The options and commodity exchanges continue to have many floor traders, however.

TRADING AT THE MOST ATTRACTIVE PRICE

Investors should always seek to trade at the best available price. Why pay 23 1/4 for a stock that can be bought at 23? Since future prices are very likely to be both higher and lower, the current level is seldom the best obtainable price. Nonetheless between 75 and 85% of all transactions involve market orders that require immediate execution at the current level. Limit orders, in contrast, are structured to take advantage of short-run imbalances in supply and demand. Buy limit orders usually seek slightly lower prices and sell limit orders normally await somewhat higher prices. While saving a fraction of a point on a single small trade will not make one rich, enough small savings could easily be the difference between outperforming and underperforming the market.

If limit orders are so useful, why are they not more widely employed? First, brokers may be reluctant to explain their more complicated mechanics when a commission is certain on a market order trade. Second, one may prefer a certain execution to a possible fraction-of-a-point savings. Their greater complexity and nonexecution risk notwithstanding, limit orders generally work to the trader's advantage.

Unlike a limit order, a market order can result in an appreciably less favorable price than the investor expects. With a current bid of 23 1/4 and an asked of 23 3/4 for example, a buy market order on 100 shares would normally be executed at the quoted asked of 23 3/4. The price could move above 23 3/4 between the time the quote is obtained and the order reaches the floor, however. Prices seldom change markedly in the short time required for an order to reach the post, but an eighth or quarter of a point move is not uncommon. A dramatic news event such as an assassination rumor could cause a much greater change. A GTC buy limit order at 23 3/4 would, in contrast, either be executed at the current asked price (if it is less than or equal to 23 3/4), or be held for possible later execution. Thus a limit order set at or near the market price protects the trader from a temporary price change, but in ordinary circumstances is executed at the same price as a market order.

Setting the Limit Price

A limit order placed close to the current price incurs little nonexecution risk and offers more protection than a market order. Setting a more favorable limit than the current quote increases both the nonexecution risk and the potential gain from a more attractive price. Elsewhere I have suggested three rules for striking a favorable balance between the probability of execution and the possibility of a better price.[10]

First, if an imminent development is expected to affect the price, the limit should be set to assure quick execution. For example, if the price is temporarily depressed by year-end tax-loss selling, a limit price might be set very close to or equal to the current level.

Second, where the trade is not dictated by imminent developments, the limit price should be set near the expected forthcoming low for a buy or expected high for a sale. Past trading ranges may help identify the expected highs and lows. A stock with a two-week high and low of 24 5/8 and 22 1/2 and a last trade of 23 1/2, would seem to be trading in a range a point above and a point below the current price. Thus one might try to buy close to 22 1/2 and sell close to 24 1/2. To reduce the nonexecution risk, the limit price could be set closer to the current level.

Third, the investor should take advantage of the tendency for prices to cluster at focal points. Whole number prices occur more frequently than halves, which are more common than quarters which, in turn, are more common that eighths. Orders entered at the same price are executed on a first-come-first-serve basis. If, for example, the bid drops from 23 1/4 to 23, each buy order at 23 will be executed when its turn comes. The bid could easily move above 23 before all orders at 23 are filled. The tendency of prices to cluster at round numbers implies that far fewer unexecuted limit orders will be entered at 23 1/8 or 22 7/8 than at 23. Thus a buy at 23 1/8 or sell at 22 7/8 is considerably more likely to be executed than an end-of-the-line order at 23. Accordingly, one should normally set limit orders to buy at 1/8 and sell at 7/8.

A large trade might effectively utilize several limit orders placed at varying prices. Some near the current quote would be very likely to be executed while orders entered further away would produce a lower average price if the stock reaches their level. Only round-lot orders should be used, however. The total commission on below round-lot (odd lot) orders would generally be too large to justify the price savings.

OTC Limit Orders

While properly placed limit orders can help one avoid the spread on a listed stock, most OTC transactions are executed against a dealer's quote. Were market makers to substitute superior outside limit orders for their own quotes, spreads might narrow and many outside orders would be crossed against each other. Since OTC spreads average 4 to 5% or more (compared to 1 to 2% on the NYSE),[11] a significant narrowing of OTC spreads would make OTC stocks appreciably more attractive to trade. OTC market makers would probably be paid for handling limit orders much as specialists receive a fee (floor brokerage) for processing limit orders on an exchange. Limit orders would also reduce the market maker's need for inventories and provide useful information on potential supply and demand.[12] Commission money would have to be shared with the market maker, but an increase in OTC volume might offset this loss. Permitting exchange trading of unlisted OTC stocks might also improve the market's efficiency. The more efficient markets arising from effective OTC limit order mechanics would clearly benefit society with modest costs to brokers and market-makers. Such a change could come through competitive pressure, SEC action, an antitrust suit, or Congressional legislation.

OTC versus Listed Stocks

While listed stocks are generally more marketable than those traded OTC, the local issues that interest many investors are usually unlisted. Furthermore, a disproportionate percentage of the numerous small companies traded OTC may be misvalued.[13] A market is likely to be most efficient where the greatest attention is paid to each stock. Jessup and Upson, however, (1973) concluded that average risk-adjusted returns on OTC stocks were significantly below those of NYSE stocks.[14] Senchack and Beedles (1979), in contrast, found that a group of Southwest OTC stocks exhibited higher returns and higher risks than the national markets' stocks. This finding may reflect 1970s Sunbelt stock performance rather than that of the entire OTC. Both studies reveal appreciably different return patterns for OTC and listed stocks, however. Investors must balance the OTC's poorer marketability and different returns pattern against the potential advantages of greater familiarity and higher percentage of misvalued situations.

The Third and Fourth Markets

OTC trading of listed stocks takes place in the "third market," while the "fourth market" is an informal arrangement for direct trading between institutions. The third market grew up in response to the exchanges' then-fixed commission schedules, which on a large institutional transaction (over $500,000 for example) could exceed $10,000, even though no more paperwork was required than a single round lot trade. Third market dealers, not bound by exchange-set commissions, usually charged high-volume institutional traders much less. By the time the exchanges stopped setting commissions, the third market had established itself. Third market dealers often offer a more attractive overall price (price and commission) than the exchanges. Since fourth market trades are directly between institutions, no commission is incurred. Sometimes a finder's fee is paid to those who help put the two sides of the trade together, however.

Dually Traded Securities

Many high-volume stocks trade simultaneously on the NYSE, several regional exchanges and OTC. Each market's bid and asked prices may differ somewhat. While "arbitragers" who seek profits from price disparities tend to drive the different markets' prices together, fractions permit some disparities. Thus shopping around may be worthwhile for large orders.

Short-Selling

Most trades involve the purchase and sale of stock that the seller had owned. Unlike offering to sell the Brooklyn Bridge, however, selling stock that is not owned—"short-selling"—is perfectly legal. The short-seller's broker simply borrows and sells someone else's shares. The short-seller then owes the lender the shorted shares. The customer whose stock is borrowed is as secure as a bank depositor whose funds are loaned. Should the lender wish to sell the loaned stock, the brokerage firm will borrow from another customer or brokerage firm.

Short-selling is not supposed to be used to drive down the price of the shorted stock. Accordingly one may not sell short immediately after a negative price change (downtick) in the stock. Thus if the last two or more transactions in the stock have been at successively lower prices, a would-be short-seller must wait until the price stabilizes (two or more successive trades at the same price— a zerotick) or begins to rise again (two or more successive trades at rising prices— an uptick) before implementing a short sale.

The short-seller hopes the price will fall enough for the stock to be repurchased at a profit. Shorting 100 shares at 50 and then repurchasing them at 35 produces a gross profit of $1,500 [100 × (50 − 35)] reduced somewhat by commissions on the short sale and covering (repurchase) transactions. Furthermore, the short-seller must pay any dividends accruing on the borrowed stock. Should the stock price increase to 65, however, the seller would incur a loss of $1,500 plus commissions and accrued dividends. The short-sale proceeds and an additional percentage (margin) of the sale price must be left in a non-interest-bearing account at the brokerage house. A further adverse price move may increase the margin required still more. Finally, losses are technically unlimited on a short sale, as stock prices have no ceiling. The short-seller may legally remain short as long as he or she chooses, but the dividend payment and margin deposit requirements make such positions costly to maintain. Given its risks, short-selling is a relatively sophisticated device that is ill-suited to amateurs.

Buying on Margin

The Federal Reserve Board allows almost all listed and many OTC securities to be used as collateral for margin loans. A margin requirement of x% permits marginable stock to be purchased with x% cash and the remainder with borrowed funds (initial margin). Thus a 60% margin requirement allows the purchase of $10,000 worth of stock with as little as $6,000 in cash. The margin requirement has typically been set at between 50 and 90% (1984, 50%).

To be marginable, an OTC stock must have at least 1,200 shareholders and a market value of $5 million or more. Listed companies are marginable unless specifically excluded by the SEC. Most brokerage firms will not extend margin loans on low-priced shares (below $5), however. An individual's equity holdings must be worth at least $2,000 to open a margin account.

Margin loans may remain outstanding as long as the borrower's equity position does not fall below 30% or so of the market value of the securities in the account (the maintenance margin position set by the listing exchange). Thus a 50% margin rate allows $10,000 in marginable stocks to be purchased with $5,000 in cash and $5,000 in credit. Any fluctuation in the portfolio's value will be reflected in a change in the equity position (equity = portfolio value − margin debt). If such margined stock's value falls to $7,150 (equity position = $2,150 or 30%), however, the investor will receive a margin call. Unless the loan value is reduced or additional collateral deposited, the brokerage firm must sell some of the borrower's stock. In the above example, a $1,000 stock sale would reduce the loan from $5,000 to $4,000, increasing the equity position to 35% ($2,150 ÷ $6,150).

Preferreds, warrants and convertibles are subject to the same margin requirements as common stocks. Margin restrictions also apply to bond purchases, although their proportional collateral value is typically higher (35% margin rate in 1984). While brokerage houses specialize in margin loans, banks and other financial intermediaries also accept securities as collateral. If such loans finance other security purchases, the Fed's margin restrictions apply. Otherwise the lender can determine the maximum loan value.

Margin loans are normally used to purchase more stock than could be bought with cash alone. Such loans tend to magnify both gains and losses. With $5,000 one could buy 50 shares of a marginable stock outright or (with a 50% margin rate) 100 shares by borrowing the additional $5,000. Table 3.5 illustrates some possible results (neglecting the impact of dividend payments and interest charges) from a cash versus margin purchase.

Table 3.5   Margin Example: $5,000 Available to Invest in Stock Selling for $100 Per Share

Stock Price Moves to	Purchase 100 Shares Using 50% Margin		Purchase 50 Shares for Cash	
	Change in Holding's Value	Change Relative to Equity	Change in Holding's Value	Change Relative to Equity
70	−$3,000	−60%	−$1,500	−30%
80	− 2,000	−40%	− 1,070	−20%
90	− 1,000	−20%	− 500	−10%
100	0	0	0	0
110	+ 1,000	+20%	+ 500	+10%
120	+ 2,000	+40%	+ 1,000	+20%
130	+ 3,000	+60%	+ 1,500	+30%

To examine the impact of margin interest, assume that the loan costs 9 1/2%. If a year later the stock illustrated in Table 3.5 had risen to 120, the cash purchase would have generated a $1,000 profit ($20 × 50), compared with a $1,525 ($20 × 100 = $2,000; 9.5% × $5,000 = $475; $2,000 − $475 = $1,525) profit with margin. Should the stock fall to 80, the losses would be $1,000 and $2,475 respectively. Interest costs may be at least partially offset by dividend payments, however. Considering commissions and taxes also changes the amounts modestly but leaves the basic point unaffected. Margin credit tends to magnify both gains and losses. If the stock's return exceeds the cost of the loan, leverage will enhance the overall return. Using margin may also have some tax advantages. Interest costs are fully deductible as incurred, while any price appreciation is only taxable when the asset is sold. Long-term gains are partially tax sheltered.

Interest Rates on Margin Loans

Brokerage firms finance some of their margin lending by borrowing from commercial banks at the broker call-loan rate. Additional loan funds are obtained from other customers' credit balances such as those generated through short sales. A positive balance in a customer's account is said to be a credit balance, while a negative one (i.e., a margin loan) is called a debit balance. Interest is applied to the exact length of each part of the margin loan. If, for example, one borrows $10,000 and then repays $750 a week later, interest will be calculated on $10,000 for a week and on $9,250 thereafter. Margin-loan interest rates are usually determined by a sliding scale added to the broker call-loan rate:

Table 3.6   Typical Margin-Loan Rates

Net Debit Balance	Call Rate Plus
$ 0– 9,999	2 1/4%
$10,000–29,999	1 3/4%
$30,000–49,999	1 1/4%
$50,000 and over	3/4%

The call-loan rate is generally lower than the prime rate (the lowest advertised business rate). Thus margin-loan rates are normally no more than 2% above the prime business rate. Relatively favorable interest rates and flexible payment schedules make margin loans an attractive credit source.

MANAGING EQUITIES

Cash-Management Accounts

Beginning with Merrill Lynch, a number of brokerage firms now offer a special service called the cash-management account.[15] Such accounts combine checking, credit card, money fund, and margin accounts into a single framework. Funds are transferred back and forth to minimize interest costs and/or maximize short-term yields. When a cash-management accountholder writes a large check, his or her checking account is first drained of funds. Then, if necessary, the money fund is tapped. If more funds are needed, a margin loan is extended. Credit card balances are handled in a similar fashion. Alternatively, a large deposit will first be applied to loans and then put into the money fund. Such accounts relieve the investor/money manager of some cash-management burdens.

Street-Name Accounts vs. Stock Certificates

Securities used as collateral must, and unmargined securities may, be left on deposit with the shareholder's brokerage house. Broker-held securities are generally registered in the "street-name" (name of the brokerage house), although the customer retains beneficial ownership. Street-name registration offers secure storage and allows securities to be traded without handling the certificates. On the other hand, street-name assets may be tied up during a bankrupt brokerage firm's reorganization. Moreover, dividends and interest on street-name securities may be credited to an improper account, and the customer must spot and report the error before it is likely to be corrected. Even a properly credited dividend may be retained by the broker in a non-interest bearing account for a month before being sent to the shareholder. Furthermore, all company reports (annual reports, quarterly reports, proxy materials, class-action suit notices, etc.) for street-name securities are sent initially to the brokerage firm, which may prove lax about forwarding it. While they usually claim the report-issuing companies sent insufficient copies, they seldom request additional reports. Customers who want to be sure of receiving all company mailings may retain a small portion (say ten shares) of each security in their own names.[16]

The Stock Certificate

In this day of computerized accounting and electronic transfers, using stock certificates to prove ownership is akin to a payment system without checks or credit cards. Stock certificates must be issued whenever a stock is registered in an individual's name. Since the certificates require a great deal of paperwork and may be stolen or forged, many experts have advocated substituting computer cards or bookkeeping entries. Individuals might still receive a stock certificate upon request or at least be given some proof of ownership such as a receipt or bill of sale.

A large percentage of securities transactions involve institutions where appropriately safeguarded bookkeeping entries largely eliminate the need for stock certificates. Stock certificate reissues are minimized by the National Securities Clearing Corporation (NSCC) which records each member's transactions, verifies the consistency of their accounts, and reports net positions daily. NSCC members settle within the clearing house rather than between individual brokerage firms. Moreover, the Depository Trust Company immobilizes many certificates by holding member firms' securities. Securities traded between members can be handled internally by simply debiting one account and crediting another. While institutional and street-name accounts benefit from these facilities, investors with non-street-name securities continue to experience all the inconveniences inherent in a stock certificate transfer system.

OTHER TRADING MECHANISMS

The vast majority of security trades take place in modest-sized lots on an exchange or OTC (including the third and fourth markets). Special mechanisms have, however, been devised both for newly issued securities and trades whose size would strain everyday market facilities.

The Primary Market

The primary or new issues market handles initial sales of securities, while subsequent exchange and OTC trading takes place in the secondary market. Some shares of a primary distribution may already be actively traded in the secondary market, or the issuing firm may have heretofore been privately held. A private firm that creates a more active and diverse ownership for its stock is said to *go public* (Table 3.7). Normally an *investment banker,* usually also a broker, is retained to assemble a syndicate to *underwrite* the issue. Investment bankers facilitate new-issue sales of debt and equity by agreeing to buy the securities for resale (underwriting). Together, the firm and its investment banker compose a registration statement and a *prospectus* detailing all of the relevant material information. These statements must be filed with the SEC and supplied to every buyer. The investment banker deducts its underwriting fee from the offering price. Approximately 8% of NYSE member revenues come from underwriting fees.[17] The investment-banking syndicate generally guarantees to sell the issue, although the job might be taken on a best-effort" basis.

Table 3.7   Going Public

	Number of Offerings	Total Dollar Value in millions
1971	391	$1,655
1972	568	2,724
1973	100	330
1974	15	51
1975	15	265
1976	34	234
1977	40	153
1978	45	249
1979	81	506
1980	237	1,397
1981	551	3,162
1982	317	1,588
1983	854	7,568

Source: SCC Monthly Statistical Review

While most primary sales are marketed quickly, *shelf-registration* is now permitted by the SEC's Rule 415. Under this authority a firm can file one registration statement for a relatively large block of stock and then sell parts of it over a two-year period. The shelf-registration option tends to reduce red tape and (because the stock can be sold directly to institutional investors) often eliminates the underwriting fee.

Private Placements

New issues are sometimes sold in large lots to a small group of buyers in what is called a *private placement*. New issues may be privately placed initially, with additional shares subsequently marketed though an underwriter. Such a private placement allows the firm to demonstrate viability by successfully raising some capital on its own. The private placements are usually sold below the new-issue price. In exchange for a favorable price, the initial investors may agree to accept *lettered stock*. Under SEC Rule 144, such securities can be resold only after a reasonable holding period, and in a manner that does not disrupt trading markets. Osborne, however, argues that disrupting the market with a sale would not generally be in the seller's own interests.[18] Debt issues are frequently placed privately with large buyers such as insurance companies.

Rights Offerings

Publicly owned firms may raise additional equity by selling shares through an underwriting syndicate, private placement, the ordinary channels of trade (exchange or OTC), or through a *rights* offering. Any sale that increases shares outstanding beyond the number authorized must first receive the stockholders' approval. Thus a sale of 200,000 shares when 400,000 are authorized and 300,000 issued would require an additional 100,000-share authorization. Indeed a preemptive-rights clause, if part of the corporate bylaws, insures shareholders of the right to maintain their proportion of the company. In a 5% stock sale, stockholders with preemptive rights would have first refusal on one new share for each twenty shares that they owned. The rights offering price would generally be set sufficiently below the market price to make the purchase attractive. Normally stockholders may sell their rights for a price that reflects the savings offered. If twenty rights are required to buy one share of a $50 stock at 40, rights will sell for about 50¢ each: (50-40) ÷ 20. Some companies still use rights offerings, but many others have persuaded shareholders to give up their preemptive rights.

Indirect Stock Sales: Warrants and Convertibles

Stock is sometimes sold indirectly through warrants and convertibles (bonds and preferred stock). Warrants are frequently attached as "sweeteners" to packages whose principal components are other securities. Firms requiring capital often sell warrants or convertibles when they consider the current stock price too low. A direct sale, which immediately increases shares outstanding, dilutes ownership. An indirect sale of similar magnitude causes less dilution since immediate exercise (convert or purchase stock at a prespecified price) is unattractive to the holder. The issuing company hopes that the stock's price will rise sufficiently to make exercise worthwhile. If the exercise does eventually take place, fewer shares will be issued than had the same sum been raised through an immediate stock sale.

Clearly the stock's price must rise above the exercise level or the warrants will not be exercised and the convertibles will not be converted. Thus an indirect stock sale is an uncertain way for the issuing company to raise equity.

LARGE SECONDARY MARKET TRADES

The vast majority of secondary market trades can be handled comfortably by the specialists or OTC market makers who earn their livings positioning the stock. Other institutional arrangements have, however, arisen to handle trades that would strain the specialist's or market maker's capital resources. Very large amounts of stock usually require a secondary-distribution (sale) or tender-offer (buy) while intermediate-size trades may go through a block trader or be handled as a special offering.

Block Trades

Since buying or selling 10,000 shares or more in the ordinary channels might result in a very unfavorable price to the initiator, large traders often use a block trade. For a large sell order, the block trader first obtains buyer commitments for part or all of the shares and then offers to buy and resell the lot at a bit below the current price, charging commissions to both sides. To facilitate the transaction, the block trader may purchase some of the lot and then may ultimately have to sell it at a loss. While block traders are usually given large quantities to sell, they sometimes are asked to assemble large blocks for single buyers.

Special Offerings
Special offerings or spot secondaries are also sometimes used to sell relatively large blocks of stock.[19] Such offerings pay brokers a special incentive fee for buying the securities for their clients. The exchange must approve the offering, which is then announced on the ticker and must remain open for at least fifteen minutes. The offering price must generally equal or exceed the current bid and not exceed either the last sale price or the current ask.

Secondary Distributions
Block traders do not want to hold a large position long enough for an adverse price movement to offset their commission profit, and very large blocks generally require relatively long periods to be sold at reasonable (non-distress-level) prices. These *secondary distributions* are handled in much the same way as new issues. A syndicate or the original seller directly markets the issue over time at a price somewhat below the pre-offering level. The offering price includes a discount to the selling syndicate. No direct commission is charged.

Tender Offers
Large buyers sometimes seek to control a particular firm; make a substantial investment; or buy stock in their own firm or buy out most of the smaller shareholders in order to "go private" (SEC disclosure-requirements are greatly reduced when shareholder numbers fall below 600). A *tender offer*, or reverse secondary offering, is normally used for such large purchases. For a limited period, the buyer offers to purchase a substantial block of stock, normally at a premium price. The tenderer usually pays an additional fee to brokers who handle their customer's trades. The buyer may purchase only the amount of the original offer or agree to take the excess. If the offer is oversubscribed and not fully purchased, stock may be bought on a pro rata basis. If too little is tendered, the buyer may reject all bids or purchase what is offered. Table 3.8 summarizes the various ways stock may be traded.

SECURITY MARKET REGULATION
Because it is "clothed with the public interest," aspects of the securities markets are regulated. Investors need to understand the nature and direction of this regulation in order to take maximum advantage of any resulting opportunities.

Historical Background
For many years the security markets were operated largely in the interests of the Big Board's members. Typical of a rational monopolist, the NYSE responded

Table 3.8   The Various Ways Stock Is Traded

Initial Stock Sales (Primary Market)

New Issues (Public Sale)	Sold through a syndicate of investment bankers organized to underwrite the issue
New Issue (Private Placement)	Sold to one or a few buyers who may agree to take lettered stock
Rights Offerings	Gives existing shareholders the opportunity to maintain their proportional ownership by purchasing stock from the company at below-market prices
Warrants and Convertibles	Indirect, uncertain, and delayed stock sales depending on exercise by holders

Trading in Already-Issued Stock (Secondary Market)

Small to Moderate Size Blocks

Exchanges	Organized trading in shares of large to medium size firms
OTC	Informal hookup of market makers trading small and medium size companies
Third Market	OTC trading in listed securities
Fourth Market	Direct trading between institutional investors

Large Blocks of Stock

Block Trade	Trades of 10,000 shares or more with the passive side assembled by a block trader
Special Offerings	Offerings pay special incentive commissions to brokers who buy for their customers
Secondary Distributions	Offerings of very large blocks of stock through a syndicate of investment bankers
Tender Offers	Offers to purchase large amounts of stock almost always at a premium over the preoffer market price

to potential competition by seeking to: combine with, destroy, or limit the power of the rival exchange.[20] Responding to its first serious threat, the NYSE merged with the Open Board and Government Bond Department in 1869. In the late nineteenth and early twentieth century, the Consolidated Board (or "Little Board") provided a challenge. After the NYSE responded by forbidding its members to deal with the rival exchange's members, disreputable elements took control and the Consolidated withered away. The outdoor traders of the New York Curb Exchange only traded unlisted stocks. When the Curb went indoors in 1921 and eventually changed its name to the American Stock Exchange in 1953, it did so with NYSE's blessing.

More recent forces have, however, been draining the NYSE of its power and authority. Institutional investors have used their newly acquired power to force some changes.[21] Its presumed turf has been invaded by commodity exchanges who now trade listed options and financial futures. The Securities and Exchange Commission, under pressure from the Justice Department's Antitrust Division, has taken an increasingly hard line against the Exchange. Finally, competition from the third and fourth markets and the regional exchanges is being felt over, under, around, and through the exchange's regulations.

Current State of Security Regulation

The exchanges, led by the NYSE, engage in a great deal of self-interest self-regulation. The NYSE maintained three monopolistic rules into the mid-1970s: fixing commissions, prohibiting exchange members from off-exchange trading of listed shares, and prohibiting the AMEX from trading NYSE-listed securities. After a long struggle, fixed commision rates were ended in 1975. While the AMEX now trades NYSE listings, only a relative handful are dually traded, and most of that volume takes place on the NYSE. Thus the two New York exchanges still do not compete head-on. Off-exchange member trading of listed securities is no longer prohibited per se, but effective restrictions still discourage such activity. Some NYSE regulations help both the exchange and its customers. For example, protecting customers from fraud or bankruptcy of member firms inspires public confidence.

Government influence over the industry is felt primarily through the SEC's broad powers of oversight. This commission's sympathies, however, like those of most regulatory commissions, often lies with the industry rather than the investors.[22] The Antitrust Division may, however, prod the commission when its industry orientation appears too cozy. Furthermore, other groups (institutional investors, for example) can sometimes foster reforms.

The SEC has been diligent in protecting investors from fraud, mis-representation, financial manipulation, and trading on inside information. The SEC has very strict regulations requiring full disclosure of relevant information. Public security offerings must be accompanied by a prospectus that fully discloses all pertinent information. Publicly owned firms must file periodic financial statements with the SEC, the exchanges where they are traded, and their stockholders. Trading by insiders must be reported to the SEC. In spite of the SEC's efforts, however, substantial insider-informed trading continues. Any attempt to manipulate security prices runs afoul of both SEC regulations and the antitrust laws. The SEC has also extended its jurisdiction to many non-stock investments and has pushed for greater corporate disclosure. The major remaining security-regulation controversy involves the development of a central market for security trading.

THE DEVELOPMENT OF A CENTRAL MARKET

Congress has mandated that all of the various exchanges and other securities markets (third and fourth) be fully linked. If and when that mandate is realized, buyers and sellers in all submarkets can trade directly with each other. The more numerous alternatives should move buying and selling prices closer together (narrower spreads) and the greater diversity of reachable markets should allow larger blocks to be absorbed. Not surprisingly, this vision requires a number of difficult changes.

Consolidated Reporting

Until the mid-1970s, security trading was highly segmented. To obtain the best price, each market had to be checked separately and NYSE members could not trade in the third market. Most NYSE brokers simply funneled their orders to the market with the greatest volume. In 1974, consolidated trades began to be reported on a common ticker tape. The financial press initiated consolidated quotation reporting in 1976. Consolidated reporting without fully consolidated trading is confusing, however. One expects a buy (sell) limit order to be executed if the subsequent low falls below (rises above) the limit price. If, however, the limit order is entered on the Big Board, and the low (high) occurs on the third market or another exchange, the trade may not take place. Two related reforms could help solve this problem. First, the quotation machines could be programmed to display the prevailing bid and asked prices in each market where a given security is traded. This reform is already partially accomplished. Second, a Composite Limit Order Book (CLOB) and free order flow would allow all orders to be executed in any market where the security is traded. The NYSE specialists do not want to lose their quasi-monopoly position, however, and regional specialists and third market dealers do not want to give their local markets to the NYSE specialists. Since the various submarkets cannot be linked without exposing the participants to some risks, such conflicts, coupled with the SEC's unwillingness to impose a solution, has slowed the pace of reform.[23]

Seven years after Congress mandated a central market (1975), the SEC finally ordered as a first step that on May 17, 1982, that trading in 30 stocks be linked. This number was later expanded, but the linking of the entire list still seems a long way off.

Rule 390

As with the CLOB and market-link controversy, rules barring member off-exchange trading of listed securities have been fiercely defended by the securities profession. NYSE Rule 394, which prohibited such trading, was replaced with Rule 390, which restricts such trading. In mid-1977, the SEC announced that it intended to require the repeal of Rule 390 by January 1, 1978, a deadline that it subsequently moved forward a number of times. Some industry sources argued that if Rule 390 were repealed prior to the complete establishment of a central market, off-exchange markets made by the larger brokerage houses would cause some exchanges to close and others to shrink.[24] Brokerage houses too small to make markets for their customers would, according to this argument, be unable to obtain competitive prices because of the reduced exchange volume. Cohen, Maier, Schwartz and Whitcomb go so far as to advocate concentrating trading on a single exchange.[25] Similar self-serving arguments were used to oppose the end of fixed commissions which in fact left the overall security trading system largely intact.[26] Easy access to the third and fourth markets should increase competition, leading to more efficient pricing.

The intermarket information system, which facilitates an exchange of price quotations, is a small step toward centralized trading. Ultimately, however, trading on and off the exchanges should, as Congress has mandated, be unrestricted and orders should be allowed to flow freely from market to market. If the industry fails to devise such a system, the SEC may exert more pressure or impose a solution.

THE ECONOMIC FUNCTIONS OF THE SECURITIES MARKETS

Securities markets for stocks and bonds play an important, but not all-important, role in assisting with capital and managerial allocation and providing a vehicle for the Fed to transmit monetary policy to the economy.

Capital Allocation

Shifting technology, evolving tastes and preferences, and the introduction of new and improved products lead to changes in consumer spending patterns. Increasing demand outstrips existing capacity and bids up prices in some areas, while overcapacity tends to drive prices down elsewhere. Profits increase where demand is strong at the expense of firms with excess capacity. The securities markets are supposed to allocate capital toward firms with bright prospects and away from firms where the outlook is poorer.[27] Let us consider how well they perform this task.

Sources and Uses of Funds

Plant, equipment, and working capital can be financed with debt or equity. Corporate debt sources include bonds, notes, trade credit, bank loans, accrued expenses, and all other firm borrowings. Stock sales and earnings retention (profit after taxes and dividends) are the two primary ways of raising equity capital. Retained earnings supply most equity capital for most firms over most time periods. Stock sales generate only a modest portion of total new equity funds (Figure 3.3). The stock market's capital-availability impact is, however, much greater than the relatively modest amount of capital raised through stock sales might suggest.

Firms have several reasons for keeping the equity portion of their total assets (debt + equity) near or above some preassigned level. First, principal and interest must be paid, while equity is permanent capital and the company may

Figure 3.3   Equity Capital Sources

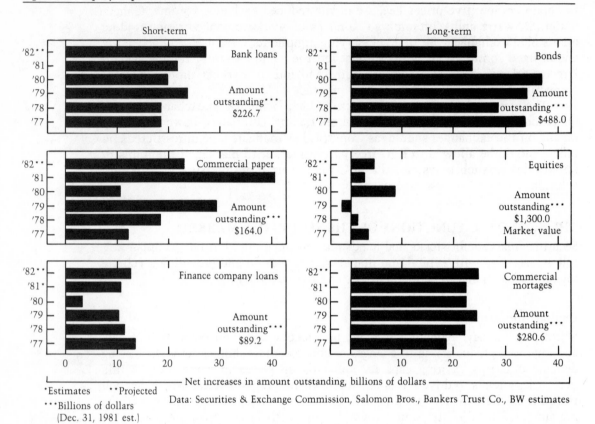

Source: "The Perilous Hunt for Financing," *Business Week*, March 1, 1982. Reprinted by permission of McGraw-Hill, Inc.

suspend, reduce, or freeze its dividend. Second, a high debt ratio tends to increase the interest cost of all of the company's borrowings. Third, if management fails to earn a higher return on assets than its borrowing cost, a high debt percentage will depress earnings. Thus even though the target may vary with the industry, firm, and over time, efforts to stay within the desired debt/equity range still limit borrowing and encourage equity sales.

The Securities Markets' Role in Allocating Capital Funds

The higher a stock's price relative to its per-share book value (accounting value of equity), the easier equity capital is to raise. A high relative share price allows a given sum to be raised with less dilution. Suppose the BCD company, with a total accounting equity value of $5,000,000, has one million shares outstanding selling at ten. To raise $1,000,000 (ignoring underwriting costs) it could sell 100,000 shares, which would increase shares outstanding by 10%. Its per-share book value would rise from $5 ($5,000,000 ÷ 1,000,000) to $5.45 ($6,000,000 ÷ 1,100,000). Now contrast this with the CDE corporation, also having a total accounting equity value of $5,000,000, but with its stock selling for $2.50. To raise $1,000,000, CDE would need to sell 400,000 shares. As a result, shares outstanding would increase 40% and per share book value would fall to $4.29 ($6,000,000 ÷ 1,400,000). Thus companies like BCD, with high stock prices relative to book values, are much better positioned to raise additional equity than those like CDE with lower relative stock prices. Moreover, since debt is considered less risky when the capital structure contains proportionately more equity, a high relative stock price indirectly contributes to a debt offering's success. Thus both debt and equity capital tend to be more available to firms with the greatest perceived potential.

The stock market also influences a firm's ability to retain earnings. The stock prices of rapidly growing firms are unlikely to be affected adversely by a large retention ratio. Increased per-share earnings, which are generally associated with rapid growth, tend to raise stock prices sufficiently to offset the foregone dividends. Other firms may maintain a higher payout to compensate for their slower growth, however. Alternatively, companies with otherwise-unneeded funds may purchase their own stock, thereby channeling funds toward firms with greater potentials.

Allocating Management Talent

The stock market also helps allocate managerial talent. Poorly managed firms often sell for prices that do not fully reflect their potential. Such undervalued situations attract investors who may try to take control, put in more effective managements, and profit from the improved operation. For example, the Hunts (a very wealthy Texas family) took control of Great Western United (later renamed Hunt International Resources) in large part to remove an ineffective management. Similarly, such investors as J.B. Fuqua of Fuqua Industries, Saul Steinberger of Reliance and Leasco and Carl Icahn of Carl Icahn and Company specialize in what are called *leveraged buy-outs*. Such investors use the acquisition targets' own asset values to finance much of the acquisition costs. Once in control, the acquirer may replace ineffective management and sell company assets in order to increase profitability and generate cash. Mobil Oil's unsuccessful attempts to acquire CONOCO (acquired by Dupont) and Marathon Oil (acquired by U.S. Steel), and Texas International's takeover of Continental Airlines all envisioned some mangement turnover. Otherwise, why do the targets resist so vigorously?[28] While takeovers have many motivations, almost all stem at least in part from a belief by the acquirer that the acquisition is undervalued relative to its potential.[29] Such potential can best be exploited (even in a friendly takeover) by bringing in fresh ideas, resources and faces. Thus takeovers and potential takeovers help weed out deadwood and keep managers on their toes.[30] While such acquisitions are often accomplished through tender offers, proxy fights have become increasingly popular because they are generally cheaper.[31] Similarly, since the value of stock-option packages tend to increase with the firm's growth potential, promising firms' options may attract talent that other firms could only hire with higher salaries.

Criteria for Efficient Capital Allocation

To distribute capital and management talent effectively, the stock market needs to reflect each firm's potential earnings accurately. Otherwise funds and talent may flow toward overvalued firms and away from undervalued firms. Moreover, high transactions costs would raise barriers to resource flows.

Friend carefully considered pricing efficiency and transaction costs.[32] He concluded that the stock market has been markedly unsuccessful in forecasting firm performance, although its record has improved since the 1920s. He also found that while underwriting fees have declined since the 1920s, commission rates have tended to increase. More recently, the end of fixed commissions has reduced trading costs for some while raising them for others. Friend also felt that increased security regulation contributed to improved market performance although he offered no suggestions for facilitating further improvement. Bentson, in contrast, contended that the Securities Exchange Act of 1934 did not improve market efficiency. He found no evidence that trading on fraudulent and misleading reports decreased with the Act's passage.[33]

OTHER ROLES OF THE MARKET

Consumers' spending is influenced by both their current income and their financial resources, including their stockholdings. Thus a rising stock market tends to increase investor wealth and spending.[34] The Federal Reserve Board (Fed) relies on the stock market-induced wealth-effect when it implements monetary policy changes. The Fed may also lower the margin rate to encourage speculation and thereby increase stock prices. The rise in consumer wealth should then induce greater consumption spending. On the other hand, the Fed may decide to restrain consumer demand by raising the margin rate. Figure 3.4 illustrates the relationship between stock prices and consumer spending.

SUMMARY AND CONCLUSIONS

This chapter considered the trading mechanics, regulation, and economic functions of the securities markets. A wide array of mechanisms may be used to buy and sell securities. Most trading involves the larger companies listed on an exchange. Smaller companies are generally traded OTC. Newly issued securities may be

Figure 3.4   How Stock Values Move Consumer Spending

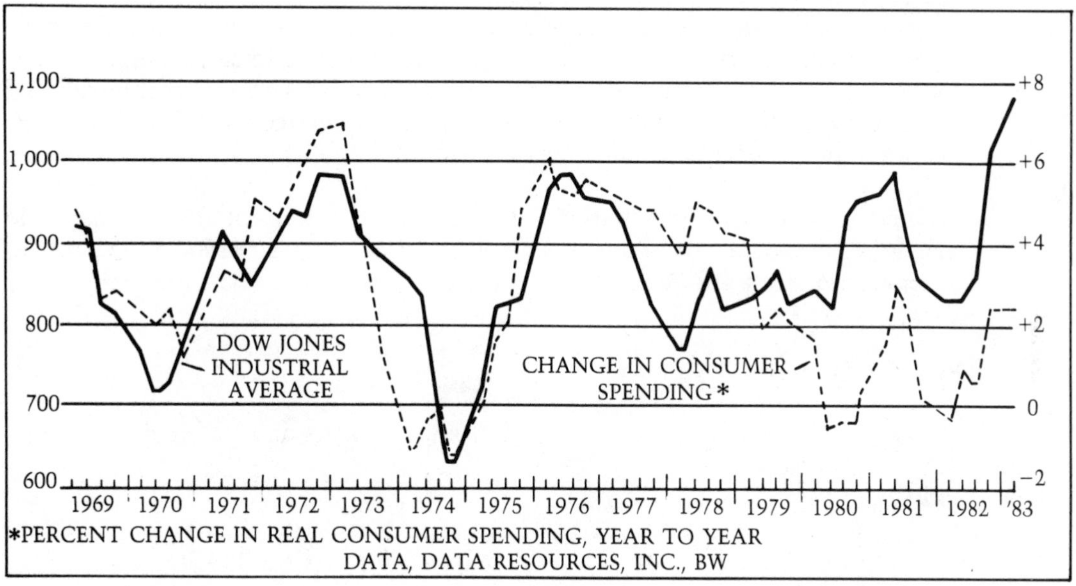

*PERCENT CHANGE IN REAL CONSUMER SPENDING, YEAR TO YEAR
DATA, DATA RESOURCES, INC., BW

sold through a rights offering, underwriting-syndicate, or private placement. Large blocks of already-issued securities are normally marketed through a block trader, special-offering, or in a secondary offering. A tender offer is generally used for a large purchase. Short sales are employed by those who expect a price decline, while margin purchases lever one's equity position. A variety of types of orders are used in securities trading. Market orders require immediate execution, while limit orders await an acceptable price. Stop orders offer protection from adverse price moves.

The following stock-trading rules are discussed in this chapter: First, for a large transaction, shop for the best price on the third market, regional exchanges and principal exchange. Second, use discount brokerage firms to obtain reduced commissions. Third, take careful account of the advantages and disadvantages of the OTC market. To yield a profit, an OTC stock's price must rise sufficiently to offset the spread which is usually wider than on listed stocks. Furthermore, many unlisted stocks are not marginable. On the other hand, some OTC stocks are more familiar and more likely to be undervalued. Fourth, limit orders, which offer much greater flexibility and protection, should generally be used rather than market orders. Fifth, margin credit, a flexible source of funds available at relatively low interest costs, may be used to magnify profit potential. Sixth, if a stock is held in a street name, a portion should be retained in the customer's name to ensure receiving company reports.

As for the development of the central market, reform forces are quite powerful; much progress has been made; opposition to additional reform is intense; further reforms are needed and will probably be enacted. The principal unresolved issues involve the consolidation of trading, limit-order access, and repeal of off-board trading restrictions. The question is not whether but when these reforms will take place.

Finally, the securities markets play an important but not all-important role in allocating capital and managerial talent, as well as facilitating Fed implementation of economic policy.

REVIEW QUESTIONS

1. Discuss the expanding functions of brokerage firms and financial services companies.
2. Explain the role of SIPC.
3. Consider the pros, cons, and selection of investment advisors.
4. Compare exchanges with the OTC market. What is the NASD?
5. Discuss commissions and discount brokers.
6. Explain the various types of orders.
7. Discuss Branch's three rules for setting a limit price.
8. Why are limit orders on regional exchanges and the OTC relatively ineffective?
9. How has the NYSE acted in the past to maintain its dominance?
10. What forces have led to the decline of the NYSE's power?
11. In the past how have the exchanges regulated themselves and how has the SEC regulated the industry?
12. What would the institution of a central market accomplish? What further reforms are needed?
13. Discuss street-name securities, the elimination of the stock certificate, and unlisted trading.
14. How do the securities markets affect a firm's ability to raise funds?
15. What role do the securities markets play in allocating management talent?
16. What factors are necessary for the securities markets to be able to allocate capital and management talent efficiently?
17. How do the securities markets affect the economy? How does the Fed use this relationship?

REVIEW PROBLEMS

1. Compute the commissions for the following, using the schedule in Table 3.2:
   a) 300 shares selling at $21
   b) 5,000 shares selling at $3 3/4
   c) 50 shares selling at $250

2. Ask two retail and two discount brokers for their rate schedules. From these schedules compute the rates for the following:
   100-share order for stock at 5, 10, 20, 40 and 80
   300-share order for stock at 5, 10, 20, 40 and 80
   1,000-share order for stock at 5, 10, 20, 40 and 80
   2,000-share order for stock at 1, 2, 5, 10 and 50
   Compare the rates and write a report.

3. Select four groups of five OTC stocks: (1) priced under $5 per share; (2) priced at $5 to $15 per share; (3) priced at $15 to $25 per share; (4) priced at more than $25 per share. Compute the average spread on each and display the results graphically.

4. Ask a broker to compile a list of 5 OTC stocks selling for 10¢ a share or less. Ask for a current bid-ask quote on each. The pink sheets should list them. Compute the percentage spread. Do the same thing for 5 OTC stocks selling for approximately $10 per share. Do the same thing for 5 NYSE stocks selling for over $50 per share. Write a report.

5. Using Table 3.2, compute the commission on a single trade of 1,500 shares at $7 per share. Now compute the commission on fifteen separate 100-share trades at $7 per share. Compare the two commissions.

6. Plot a stock's price for two weeks. Now select a level to place a limit order to buy the stock. Monitor the security for the next two weeks to see if you would have bought it and, if so, how much lower it went. Now repeat the process for a sell order. Write a report.

7. Select a stock to sell short. Determine how much margin would be required to sell 100 shares. Assuming you maintain the short position for one year, determine the price to which the stock must fall for you to break even. Realize that you must cover commissions on the sale and repurchase, the opportunity cost of foregone interest on the margin deposit (assume 12%), plus any dividends on the shorted stock.

8. Compute the percentage gains and losses on a margined and unmargined investment assuming the following:
   purchase stock at 100
   hold for a year
   margin rate = 50%
   margin borrowing cost = 10%
   At the end of year stock sells for:
   50, 60, 70, 80, 90, 100, 110, 120, 130, 140, 150, 200

9. Assume the broker call loan rate is 10 1/2% and that Table 3.6 applies. Compute the cost of margin for each of the following using monthly compounding:
    a) $53,000 borrowed for six months
    b) $27,000 borrowed for three months
    c) $7,000 borrowed for ten months.

NOTES

1. G. Putka, "Merrill Lynch and Company Bankers," *New York Times*, April 27, 1980, pp. 1–4D; February 7, 1982, p. 1F; *Business Week*, "How They Manage the New Financial Supermarkets," *Business Week*, December 20, 1982, pp. 50–54; W. Flanagan and J. Bauford, "A Buyer's Guide to the Financial Supermarkets," *Forbes*, August 1, 1982, pp. 144–152.

2. P. Brimelow, "SPIC Falls Short," *Barron's*, April 19, 1982, p. 12; *Wall Street Journal*, "Panel Recommends Congress Broader SIPC's Authority," *Wall Street Journal*, May 10, 1982, p. 20; M. Brody, "When Brokers Go Bust," *Barron's*, May 16, 1983, pp. 8, 9, 38.

3. J. Briggs, "Check the Middle of the List," *Forbes*, July 5, 1982, p. 166.

4. N. Kleinfield, "Getting a Big Board Listing," *New York Times*, June 23, 1982, p. D1; *Business Week*, "Why the Big Board is Fishing for Smaller Fry," *Business Week*, September 26, 1983, p. 132.

5. T. Loeb, "Trading Cost: The Critical Link Between Investment Information and Results," *Financial Analysts Journal*, May/June 1983, pp. 39–45.

6. B. Branch, "Deregulation and Price Competition in the Securities Industry: It Takes More than Benign Neglect," *Antitrust Law and Economics Review*, Vol. 10, No. 1, 1978, pp. 67–73; G. Blum and W. Lewellen, "Negotiated Brokerage Commissions and the Individual Investor," *Journal of Financial and Quantitative Analysis*, September 1983, pp. 331–343; L. Demeria, "How to Pick a Stockbroker," *New York Times*, February 21, 1982, p. F14; M. Coler, "How to Choose a Discount Broker," *Barron's*, October 17, 1983, pp. 28, 30, 31, 34, 36.

7. B. Branch, "The Determinants of Bid Asked Spreads on the OTC Market," *Industrial Organization Review*, Vol. 4, No. 2, pp. 69–74; B. Branch and S. Grady, "Making OTC Limit Orders Effective," Paper presented to 1982 Financial Management Association Meetings.

8. J. Boland, "Going by the Book: How Jud Kaplan Handles the Action at Post 10," *Barron's*, January 18, 1982, pp. 10–11; T. Carrington, "Big Board Tinkers with Specialist System, But Some Fear Major Changes are Needed," *Wall Street Journal*, January 14, 1983, p. 33; Y. Eason, "Stock Market Specialists," *New York Times*, May 10, 1983, pp. D1, D2.

9. J. Pearl, "Smart Money?," *Forbes*, October 11, 1982, pp. 132–137.

10. B. Branch, "The Optimal Price to Trade," *Journal of Financial and Quantitative Analysis*, September 1975, pp. 497–514.

11. B. Branch, "The Determinants of Bid Asked Spreads on the OTC Market," *op. cit.*

12. R. Conroy and R. Winkler, "Information Difference Between Limit and Market Orders for a Market Maker," *Journal of Financial and Quantitative Analysis*, December 1981, pp. 703–724.

13. A. Senchack and W. Beedles, "Price Behavior in a Regional Over-the-Counter Securities Market," *The Journal of Financial Research*, Fall 1979, pp. 119–131.

14. Jessup and R. Upson, *Returns in Over-the-Counter Stock Markets*, University of Minnesota Press, Minneapolis, 1973.

15. D. Hilder, "New One-Step Financial Accounts are Growing in Popularity, But it Pays You to Shop Around," *Wall Street Journal*, September 19, 1983, p. 60.

16. *Business Week*, "The SEC Looks at Curbing Street Name," *Business Week*, January 25, 1982, p. 34; K. McManus, "Stock Options," *Forbes*, February 28, 1983, pp. 114–115.

17. J. Carrington, "Investment Bankers Enter a Different Era, and Many are Uneasy," *Wall Street Journal*, June 21, 1982, pp. 1, 10.

18. A. Osborne, "Rule 144 Volume Limitations and the Sale of Restricted Stock in the Over-the-Counter Market," *Journal of Finance*, May 1982, pp. 505–517.

19. B. Branch, "Special Offerings and Market Efficiency," *Financial Review*, March 1984, pp. 26–35.

20. R. Sobel, *The Curbstone Brokers*, Macmillan and Company, New York, 1970.

21. *New York Times*, "Institutions Dominate the Big Board," *New York Times*, November 27, 1982, pp. D1–D2.

22. C. Wilcox, *Public Policy Toward Business*, 4th Edition, R.D. Irwin, Homewood, Ill., 1971, pp. 275–480; *Business Week*, "The SEC Under Shad: Can a Deregulation Protect the Public?," *Business Week*, June 13, 1983, pp. 135–142; R. Hudson, "With Shad as Chief, SEC Eases many Rules and Stirs a Big Outcry," *Wall Street Journal*, Jan. 12, 1984, pp. 1, 12.

23. *Business Week*, "A Step Backward for a National Market," *Business Week*, August 8, 1983, pp. 27–31.

24. E. Block and R. Schwartz, "The Battle over Rule 390," *Wall Street Journal*, September 11, 1978; W. Batten, "The National Market System," *Wall Street Journal*, June 18, 1982, p. 16.

25. K. Cohen, S. Mair, R. Schqartz and D. Whitcomb, "An Analysis of the Economic Justification for Consolidation in a Secondary Security Market," *Journal of Banking and Finance*, #6, 1982, pp. 117–136.

26. H. Stoll, *Regulation of Securities Markets: An Examination of the Effects of Increased Competition*, New York University Mongraph Series in Finance and Economics, #1979–2.

27. J. Steglitz, "Parato Optimality and Competition," *Journal of Finance*, May 1981, pp. 235–251.

28. T. Metz, "To Forestall Takeovers Many Concerns Move to Shore Up Defenses," *Wall Street Journal*, March 17, 1983, p.1, 17; R. Vilkin, "Tales of the Proxy Wars," *The National Law Journal*, March 21, 1983, pp. 1, 23, 33; P. Blustein, "Measures to Discourage Takeovers Stin Controversy at Annual Meetings," *Wall Street Journal*, April 18, 1983, pp. 24, 41.

29. P. Durker, "Why Some Mergers Work and Many More Don't," *Forbes*, January 18, 1982, pp. 34–36; S. Grossman and D. Hart, "The Allocational Role of Takeover Bids in Situations of Asymmetric Information," *Journal of Finance*, May 1981, pp. 253–270.

30. R. Tomasson, "The Trauma in a Takeover," *New York Times*, January 9, 1982, pp. 31–41.

31. *Business Week*, "Stockholders Go On the Attack," *Business Week*, June 13, 1983, pp. 32–34; J. Williams, "More Holders Use Proxy Weapon to Obtain Control of Companies," *Wall Street Journal*, January 5, 1984, p. 26.

32. I. Friend, "The Stock Market and the Economy," *American Economic Review*, May 1972, pp. 212–219.

33. E. G. Benston, "Required Disclosures and the Stock Market: An Evaluation of the Securities Act of 1934," *American Economic Review*, March 1973, pp. 133–135.

34. R. Rache, "Importance of the Stock Market on Private Demand," *American Economic Review*, May 1972, pp. 220–228; Also in the same issue, F. Modigliani, "Stock Market and Economy—Discussion." L. Rosen, *Stock Market Capital Gains and Consumption Expenditures*, Dissertation, Yale University, 1971; T. Carrington, "Bull Market Begins to Induce Investors to Spend More Freely," *Wall Street Journal*, May 26, 1983, pp. 1, 21.

Section II:
Investment Theory

Section II explores the theoretical foundation of investment valuation. While much of this material is relatively abstract, it does provide a workable format for evaluating investment opportunities. The following hypothetical case raises many of the issues that are dealt with in this section.

Evaluating Cash Flows: Three Investments

Your grandmother, who is a smart lady but knows little about investing, is considering three different investment ideas that a family friend/broker suggested to her. Since your grandfather recently died leaving her a relatively large sum of money, she is quite at a loss as to her future course. You, a business school major and her favorite grandchild, are the one she asks first for advice.

The first investment is a long-term (20 year) corporate bond in a local electric utility (no nuclear exposure). It has a 12% coupon and currently sells for 90. Its yield-to-maturity is 1.5% above that of otherwise similar government bonds. The broker says it is quite safe (AA rating).

The second investment is stock in a newly formed company that claims to be close to discovering a practical way of generating electricity from the lightning in thunderstorms. The broker acknowledges that the risks are substantial but claims that this investment offers the potential for spectacular gains. If the technology is successful, it could be supplying 5% of our energy needs by the year 2000. While the firm's founders and managers are keeping most of the stock for themselves, they need risk capital. Accordingly they recently sold stock to outside investors through a new issue (prospectus available). The broker estimates that 100 shares of this stock (now trading for about $10 per share) could be worth one to ten million dollars in 10 to 20 years. Alternatively, it could be worth nothing. The current technological problems may not be overcome and the firm has no other types of operations. Moreover, because of continuing capital needs, no dividends are likely to be paid for at least ten years.

The final investment option is a common stock mutual fund. In the past this fund's price has tended to move in approximately the same pattern as the S&P 500 index. It pays a dividend plus capital gains distribution of around 8% and its per share price has tended to rise an average of 6% per year over the past five years. It is part of a family of funds which allow investors to switch into different types of investments without extra charge. The other funds in the family are: 1) money market mutual fund; 2) international fund; 3) tax-free bond fund; 4) long-term government bond fund; 5) social responsibility stock fund; and 6) option fund.

Buying any of these investments will incur commissions. Bond trades will cost $5 per $1,000 face amount of the bonds. The stock is subject to a 3% commission and trades at $10 bid, $10.50 asked. The mutual fund is subject to an 8.5% load, but this is reduced to 6% for purchases over $20,000.

Your job is to explore the pros and cons of each of these investment opportunities, both for your grandmother's specific circumstances and more generally. You should first analyze the projected cash flows of each investment and then relate the expected returns to the risks associated with each. Finally you should recommend a strategy. Realize that you may recommend only one investment or a combination. Also note that as one of her heirs, you have a personal interest in the performance of your grandmother's portfolio.

Once your own analysis is complete, write a report on your findings. Make sure your case is convincing. While your grandmother has confidence in you, she will want to understand clearly not only what you advise but why you have made that particular recommendation. Be sure and explain all of your assumptions and the relevant risks to each investment.

While you would need considerably more information to analyze these investments thoroughly, the descriptions contained herein do illustrate some of the commonly encountered issues in cash flow evaluation. Section II explores the theory of such valuations. Chapter 4 examines the discounted-expected-income-stream approach to valuation. Both stock and bond applications are used to illustrate this method of valuing assets. The chapter ends with a discussion of various approaches to forecasting income streams. Chapter 5 explores risk and portfolio theory's role in investment valuation. Several simplified ways of estimating portfolio risk are given particular attention. Tests of three major implications of portfolio theory are discussed in Chapter 6: (1) Markets are efficient; (2) Discount rates are only related to market risk; and (3) Realized returns are linearly related to risk.

4 The Valuation of Investments

Understanding the implications of market prices is an important step in any comparative-valuation process. Since investments trade on the basis of their expected income and price appreciation, we shall examine how such expectations influence market values. First-time value is introduced and its investment-valuation role assessed. Both bond and stock valuations are explored in the context of their expected income-stream values. Risk's role in establishing the appropriate discount rate is also discussed. The remainder of this chapter deals with various approaches to forecasting stocks' income streams.

TIME VALUE

To understand time value's role in expected income stream valuations, consider the value of a commitment to pay $5,000 a year for 20 years. While $100,000 in payments are promised, the value is considerably less. Even at 5% annual interest, a $100,000 savings account would yield $5,000 a year forever. A current dollar that can earn interest should be worth more than a promise to pay an identical sum in the future. In other words, money has time value. Since most investments yield a series of payments through time, the expected payment streams provide the basis for determining the investment's value.

Discounting to Take Account of Time Value

Future dollars can be compared to present dollars by discounting the sums to what are called *present value equivalents*. Using a 6% discount rate, one dollar received today is equivalent to $1.06 a year from now, or $1.1236 two years hence. In contrast, a promise to pay a dollar next year is worth $.944 today (.944 × 1.06 = 1.00). Discounting an asset promising three annual payments of $100 at 6% yields:

$$PV = \frac{\$100}{1.06} + \frac{\$100}{(1.06)^2} + \frac{\$100}{(1.06)^3} = \$267.30$$

where: PV = present value of the income stream

Discounting the first year's payment at 6% is equivalent to dividing it by

93

1.06. The second year's payment is discounted at 6% twice, which corresponds to dividing it by (1.06×1.06) or $(1.06)^2$. Similarly, the third year's payment is divided by $1.06 \times 1.06 \times 1.06$ or $(1.06)^3$.

Valuing an asset yielding successive annual payments of $100, $300, $50, $100, and $300 and a sale price of $1,000 involves a little more complicated arithmetic but the principle is the same:

$$PV = \frac{\$100}{(1.06)} + \frac{\$300}{(1.06)^2} + \frac{\$50}{(1.06)^3} + \frac{\$100}{(1.06)^4} + \frac{\$1,300}{(1.06)^5}$$

or $\$94.34 + \$267.00 + \$41.98 + \$79.21 + \$971.45 = \$1,453.98$

Note that the sale price and final payment are both discounted by $(1.06)^5$, as both are to be paid five years hence. Present-value tables (Appendix A) or an electronic calculator with financial functions are often employed to simplify present-value computations. How the discount rate is determined will be discussed in a later section.

Present Value Applied to Bonds

Now let us see how time value relates to the income stream of a bond. Clearly the discount rate plays a central role in bond valuation. A given income stream will have a higher computed value the lower the discount rate and vice versa. Where a constant amount is to be paid forever, a very simple formula relates the market price to the discount rate:

$$PV = \frac{CF}{r} \tag{1}$$

where: PV = present value of the income stream
CF = each period's cash flow
r = appropriate discount rate

Thus a perpetual $50 annual payment rate divided by 5% has a present value of $1,000. Dividing $50 by 10% produces a $500 value. While Britain has issued some infinite-maturity bonds called "Consols," the vast majority of debt obligations promise to repay principal at some future date. When the income stream is variable and/or principal is to be repaid, a more complicated present value formula [Equation (2)] is used:

$$PV = \frac{CF_1}{1 + r} + \frac{CF_2}{(1 + r)^2} + \cdots \frac{CF_n}{(1 + r)^n} \cdots \tag{2}$$

where: CF_i = cash flow received in period i

r = appropriate discount rate

Regardless of which equation applies, a given income stream will always have a lower value the higher the discount rate, and vice versa. For example, a $1,000 (face value) bond paying $50 per year and maturing in seven years is, assuming a discount rate of 8%, worth:

$$\text{Present Value} = \frac{\$50}{1.08} + \frac{\$50}{(1.08)^2} + \frac{\$50}{(1.08)^3} + \frac{\$50}{(1.08)^4} +$$

$$\frac{\$50}{(1.08)^5} + \frac{\$50}{(1.08)^6} + \frac{\$50}{(1.08)^7} + \frac{\$1,000}{(1.08)^7}$$

$$= \$50 \ (.926 + .857 + .794 + .735 + .681 + .630 + .583)$$
$$+ \$1,000 \ (.583)$$

$$= \$843$$

Note that this bond's present value is less than its $1,000 face value. Indeed any bond with a coupon rate below the discount rate sells for less than face. In this instance the promised coupon rate is $50 on $1,000 or 5% (50 ÷ 1,000 = .05), which is below the assumed discount rate of 8%.

Why Do Bond Prices Vary from Their Face Values?

While most bonds are initially sold for a price close to their par or face values, their price seldom stays very close to that level. A 5% bond might have been issued when 5% was a competitive (market) rate for similar bonds. Such a bond will pay $50 per year and return $1,000 of principal at maturity regardless of future market rates. If otherwise-similar newly issued 8% bonds ($80 per year coupon) sell at their face values, the 5% bond must also be priced to return 8%. No one will pay $1,000 for a bond yielding $50 per year when equally safe bonds yielding $80 per year can be bought at the same price. The 5% coupon bond must be priced to produce a yield to maturity equivalent to the 8% bond. The yield to maturity is the discount rate that makes the present value of the coupon and principal payments equal to the bond's market price. Thus a bond whose present value at 9% is $950 will have a 9% yield to maturity if it sells for $950. While the yield to maturity can be computed by hand, most people prefer to use a bond book[1] or financial calculator.

Thus bond prices, and indeed most security prices, move inversely with market interest rates. If interest rates rise, bond prices will decline and vice versa, so that the face value of a seasoned bond may bear no more resemblance to its market value than a car's when-new sticker price does to its value as a used or antique car.

DETERMINANTS OF THE DISCOUNT RATE

Since discount rates play such an important role in valuation, we shall now explore their determination. In general, the more certain the expected outcome,

Table 4.1   Present Value of $1

Years hence	1%	2%	4%	6%	8%	10%	12%	14%	15%	16%	18%	20%	22%	24%	25%	26%	28%	30%	35%	40%	45%	50%
1	0.990	0.980	0.962	0.943	0.926	0.909	0.893	0.877	0.870	0.862	0.847	0.833	0.820	0.806	0.800	0.794	0.781	0.769	0.741	0.714	0.690	0.667
2	0.980	0.961	0.925	0.890	0.857	0.806	0.797	0.769	0.756	0.743	0.718	0.694	0.672	0.650	0.640	0.630	0.610	0.592	0.549	0.510	0.476	0.444
3	0.971	0.942	0.889	0.840	0.794	0.751	0.712	0.675	0.658	0.641	0.609	0.579	0.551	0.524	0.512	0.500	0.477	0.455	0.406	0.364	0.328	0.296
4	0.961	0.924	0.855	0.792	0.735	0.683	0.636	0.592	0.572	0.552	0.516	0.482	0.451	0.423	0.410	0.397	0.373	0.350	0.301	0.260	0.226	0.198
5	0.951	0.906	0.822	0.747	0.681	0.621	0.567	0.519	0.497	0.476	0.437	0.402	0.370	0.341	0.328	0.315	0.291	0.269	0.223	0.186	0.156	0.132
6	0.942	0.888	0.790	0.705	0.630	0.564	0.507	0.456	0.432	0.410	0.370	0.335	0.303	0.275	0.262	0.250	0.227	0.207	0.165	0.133	0.108	0.088
7	0.933	0.871	0.760	0.665	0.583	0.513	0.452	0.400	0.376	0.354	0.314	0.279	0.249	0.222	0.210	0.198	0.178	0.159	0.122	0.095	0.074	0.059
8	0.923	0.853	0.731	0.627	0.540	0.467	0.404	0.351	0.327	0.305	0.266	0.233	0.204	0.179	0.168	0.157	0.139	0.123	0.091	0.068	0.051	0.039
9	0.914	0.837	0.703	0.592	0.500	0.424	0.361	0.308	0.284	0.263	0.225	0.194	0.167	0.144	0.134	0.125	0.108	0.094	0.067	0.048	0.035	0.026
10	0.905	0.820	0.676	0.558	0.463	0.386	0.322	0.270	0.247	0.227	0.191	0.162	0.137	0.116	0.107	0.099	0.085	0.073	0.050	0.035	0.024	0.017
11	0.896	0.804	0.650	0.527	0.429	0.350	0.287	0.237	0.215	0.195	0.162	0.135	0.112	0.094	0.086	0.079	0.066	0.056	0.037	0.025	0.017	0.012
12	0.887	0.788	0.625	0.497	0.397	0.319	0.257	0.208	0.187	0.168	0.137	0.112	0.092	0.076	0.069	0.062	0.052	0.043	0.027	0.018	0.012	0.008
13	0.879	0.773	0.601	0.469	0.368	0.290	0.229	0.182	0.163	0.145	0.116	0.093	0.075	0.061	0.055	0.050	0.040	0.033	0.020	0.013	0.008	0.005
14	0.870	0.758	0.577	0.442	0.340	0.263	0.205	0.160	0.141	0.125	0.099	0.078	0.062	0.049	0.044	0.039	0.032	0.025	0.015	0.009	0.006	0.003
15	0.861	0.743	0.555	0.417	0.315	0.239	0.183	0.140	0.123	0.108	0.084	0.065	0.051	0.040	0.035	0.031	0.025	0.020	0.011	0.006	0.004	0.002
16	0.853	0.728	0.534	0.394	0.292	0.218	0.163	0.123	0.107	0.093	0.071	0.054	0.042	0.032	0.028	0.025	0.019	0.015	0.008	0.005	0.003	0.002
17	0.844	0.714	0.513	0.371	0.270	0.198	0.146	0.108	0.093	0.080	0.060	0.045	0.034	0.026	0.023	0.020	0.015	0.012	0.006	0.003	0.002	0.001
18	0.836	0.700	0.494	0.350	0.250	0.180	0.130	0.095	0.081	0.069	0.051	0.038	0.028	0.021	0.018	0.016	0.012	0.009	0.005	0.002	0.001	0.001
19	0.828	0.686	0.475	0.331	0.232	0.164	0.116	0.083	0.070	0.060	0.043	0.031	0.023	0.017	0.014	0.012	0.009	0.007	0.003	0.002	0.001	
20	0.820	0.673	0.456	0.312	0.215	0.149	0.104	0.073	0.061	0.051	0.037	0.026	0.019	0.014	0.012	0.010	0.007	0.005	0.002	0.001	0.001	
21	0.811	0.660	0.439	0.294	0.199	0.135	0.093	0.064	0.053	0.044	0.031	0.022	0.015	0.011	0.009	0.008	0.006	0.004	0.002	0.001		
22	0.803	0.647	0.422	0.278	0.184	0.123	0.083	0.056	0.046	0.038	0.026	0.018	0.013	0.009	0.007	0.006	0.004	0.003	0.001	0.001		
23	0.795	0.634	0.406	0.262	0.170	0.112	0.074	0.049	0.040	0.033	0.022	0.015	0.010	0.007	0.006	0.005	0.003	0.002	0.001			
24	0.788	0.622	0.390	0.247	0.158	0.102	0.066	0.043	0.035	0.028	0.019	0.013	0.008	0.006	0.005	0.004	0.003	0.002	0.001			
25	0.780	0.610	0.375	0.233	0.146	0.092	0.059	0.038	0.030	0.024	0.016	0.010	0.007	0.005	0.004	0.003	0.002	0.001	0.001			
26	0.772	0.598	0.361	0.220	0.135	0.084	0.053	0.033	0.026	0.021	0.014	0.009	0.006	0.004	0.003	0.002	0.002	0.001				
27	0.764	0.586	0.347	0.207	0.125	0.076	0.047	0.029	0.023	0.018	0.011	0.007	0.005	0.003	0.002	0.002	0.001	0.001				
28	0.757	0.574	0.333	0.196	0.116	0.069	0.042	0.026	0.020	0.016	0.010	0.006	0.004	0.002	0.002	0.002	0.001	0.001				
29	0.749	0.563	0.321	0.185	0.107	0.063	0.037	0.022	0.017	0.014	0.008	0.005	0.003	0.002	0.002	0.001	0.001	0.001				
30	0.742	0.552	0.308	0.174	0.099	0.057	0.033	0.020	0.015	0.012	0.007	0.004	0.003	0.002	0.001	0.001	0.001					
40	0.672	0.453	0.208	0.097	0.046	0.022	0.011	0.005	0.004	0.003	0.001	0.001										
50	0.608	0.372	0.141	0.054	0.021	0.009	0.003	0.001	0.001	0.001												

PRESENT VALUE TABLES AND THEIR USES

Present value tables facilitate a comparison of present and future sums. For example: to determine the value of $150 to be paid eleven years hence, discounted at 12%, one could either calculate:

$$\$150 \times \left(\frac{1}{1 + .12}\right)^{11}$$

or look in a present value table for the equivalent of

$$\left(\frac{1}{1 + .12}\right)^{11}.$$

Table 4.1 shows the expression to be .287. Thus the present value of $150 discounted at 12% for eleven years is .287 × $150 = $43.05. Turn the problem around. What is the value of $150 growing at 12% per year for eleven years?

Now the expression to be evaluated is $150 $(1 + .12)^{11}$. Since $(1 + .12)^{11}$ is the reciprocal of the equivalent of .287,

$$\$150\left(\frac{1}{.287}\right) = \$522.65$$

Thus Table 4.1 may be used both to discount future income and determine compound values.

A second form for a present value table helps value assets which periodically pay a constant amount for a prespecified time. While Table 4.1 could be used by multiplying the present value factor for each payment and then summing, Table 4.2 has summed the factors to that point in Table 4.2. Thus the 4% five-year

Table 4.2 Present Value of $1 Received Annually for N Years

Years (N)	1%	2%	4%	6%	8%	10%	12%	14%	15%	16%	18%	20%	22%	24%	25%	26%	28%	30%	35%	40%	45%	50%
1	0.990	0.980	0.962	0.943	0.926	0.909	0.893	0.877	0.870	0.862	0.847	0.833	0.820	0.806	0.800	0.794	0.781	0.769	0.741	0.714	0.690	0.667
2	1.970	1.942	1.886	1.833	1.783	1.736	1.690	1.647	1.626	1.605	1.566	1.528	1.492	1.457	1.440	1.424	1.392	1.361	1.289	1.224	1.165	1.111
3	2.941	2.884	2.775	2.673	2.577	2.487	2.402	2.322	2.283	2.246	2.174	2.106	2.042	1.981	1.952	1.923	1.868	1.816	1.696	1.589	1.493	1.407
4	3.902	3.808	3.630	3.465	3.312	3.170	3.037	2.914	2.855	2.798	2.690	2.589	2.494	2.404	2.362	2.320	2.241	2.166	1.997	1.849	1.720	1.605
5	4.853	4.713	4.452	4.212	3.993	3.791	3.605	3.433	3.352	3.274	3.127	2.991	2.864	2.745	2.689	2.635	2.532	2.436	2.220	2.035	1.876	1.737
6	5.795	5.601	5.242	4.917	4.623	4.355	4.111	3.889	3.784	3.685	3.498	3.326	3.167	3.020	2.951	2.885	2.759	2.643	2.385	2.168	1.983	1.824
7	6.728	6.472	6.002	5.582	5.206	4.868	4.564	4.288	4.160	4.039	3.812	3.605	3.416	3.242	3.161	3.083	2.937	2.802	2.508	2.263	2.057	1.883
8	7.652	7.325	6.733	6.210	5.747	5.335	4.968	4.639	4.487	4.344	4.078	3.837	3.619	3.421	3.329	3.241	3.076	2.925	2.598	2.331	2.108	1.922
9	8.566	8.162	7.435	6.802	6.247	5.759	5.328	4.946	4.772	4.607	4.303	4.031	3.786	3.566	3.463	3.366	3.184	3.019	2.665	2.379	2.144	1.948
10	9.471	8.983	8.111	7.360	6.710	6.145	5.650	5.216	5.019	4.833	4.494	4.192	3.923	3.682	3.571	3.465	3.269	3.092	2.715	2.414	2.168	1.965
11	10.368	9.787	8.760	7.887	7.139	6.495	5.988	5.453	5.234	5.029	4.656	4.327	4.035	3.776	3.656	3.544	3.335	3.147	2.752	2.438	2.185	1.977
12	11.255	10.575	9.385	8.384	7.536	6.814	6.194	5.660	5.421	5.197	4.793	4.439	4.127	3.851	3.725	3.606	3.387	3.190	2.779	2.456	2.196	1.985
13	12.134	11.343	9.986	8.853	7.904	7.103	6.424	5.842	5.583	5.342	4.910	4.533	4.203	3.912	3.780	3.656	3.427	3.223	2.799	2.468	2.204	1.990
14	13.004	12.106	10.563	9.295	8.244	7.367	6.628	6.002	5.724	5.468	5.008	4.611	4.265	3.962	3.824	3.695	3.459	3.249	2.814	2.477	2.210	1.993
15	13.865	12.849	11.118	9.712	8.559	7.606	6.811	6.142	5.847	5.575	5.092	4.675	4.315	4.001	3.859	3.726	3.483	3.268	2.825	2.484	2.214	1.995
16	14.718	13.578	11.652	10.106	8.851	7.824	6.974	6.265	5.954	5.669	5.162	4.730	4.357	4.033	3.887	3.751	3.503	3.283	2.834	2.489	2.216	1.997
17	15.562	14.292	12.166	10.477	9.122	8.022	7.120	6.373	6.047	5.749	5.222	4.775	4.391	4.059	3.910	3.771	3.518	3.295	2.840	2.492	2.218	1.998
18	16.398	14.992	12.659	10.828	9.372	8.201	7.250	6.467	6.128	5.818	5.273	4.812	4.419	4.080	3.928	3.786	3.529	3.304	2.844	2.494	2.219	1.999
19	17.226	15.678	13.134	11.158	9.604	8.365	7.366	6.550	6.198	5.877	5.316	4.844	4.442	4.097	3.942	3.799	3.539	3.311	2.848	2.496	2.220	1.999
20	18.046	16.351	13.590	11.470	9.818	8.514	7.469	6.623	6.259	5.929	5.353	4.870	4.460	4.110	3.954	3.808	3.546	3.316	2.850	2.497	2.221	1.999
21	18.857	17.011	14.029	11.764	10.017	8.649	7.562	6.687	6.312	5.973	5.384	4.891	4.476	4.121	3.963	3.816	3.551	3.320	2.852	2.498	2.221	2.000
22	19.660	17.658	14.451	12.042	10.201	8.772	7.645	6.743	6.359	6.011	5.410	4.909	4.488	4.130	3.970	3.822	3.556	3.323	2.853	2.498	2.222	2.000
23	20.456	18.292	14.857	12.303	10.371	8.883	7.718	6.792	6.399	6.044	5.432	4.925	4.499	4.137	3.976	3.827	3.559	3.325	2.854	2.498	2.222	2.000
24	21.243	18.914	15.247	12.550	10.529	8.985	7.784	6.835	6.434	6.073	5.451	4.937	4.507	4.143	3.981	3.831	3.562	3.327	2.855	2.499	2.222	2.000
25	22.023	19.523	15.622	12.783	10.675	9.077	7.843	6.873	6.464	6.097	5.467	4.948	4.514	4.147	3.985	3.834	3.564	3.329	2.856	2.499	2.222	2.000
26	22.795	20.121	15.983	13.003	10.810	9.161	7.896	6.906	6.491	6.118	5.480	4.956	4.520	4.151	3.988	3.837	3.566	3.330	2.856	2.500	2.222	2.000
27	23.560	20.707	16.330	13.211	10.935	9.237	7.943	6.935	6.514	6.136	5.492	4.964	4.524	4.154	3.990	3.839	3.567	3.331	2.856	2.500	2.222	2.000
28	24.316	21.281	16.663	13.406	11.051	9.307	7.984	6.961	6.534	6.152	5.502	4.970	4.528	4.157	3.992	3.840	3.568	3.331	2.857	2.500	2.222	2.000
29	25.066	21.844	16.984	13.591	11.158	9.370	8.022	6.983	6.551	6.166	5.510	4.975	4.531	4.159	3.994	3.841	3.569	3.332	2.857	2.500	2.222	2.000
30	25.808	22.396	17.292	13.765	11.258	9.427	8.055	7.003	6.566	6.177	5.517	4.979	4.534	4.160	3.995	3.842	3.569	3.332	2.857	2.500	2.222	2.000
40	32.835	27.355	19.793	15.046	11.925	9.779	8.244	7.105	6.642	6.234	5.548	4.997	4.544	4.166	3.999	3.846	3.571	3.333	2.857	2.500	2.222	2.000
50	39.196	31.424	21.482	15.762	12.234	9.915	8.304	7.133	6.661	6.246	5.554	4.999	4.545	4.167	4.000	3.846	3.571	3.333	2.857	2.500	2.222	2.000

entry in Table 4.2 is 4.452, which is the sum of .962, .925, .889, .855, and .822 (rounding accounts for slight differences). A payment of $100 a year for five years discounted at 4% is worth $445.20.

Table 4.2 may be used to compute a bond's yield to maturity. Suppose a bond has a coupon of 6 1/2%, matures in 16 years, and is currently selling at 85. The yield to maturity may be approximated in various ways. Dividing the coupon rate by the price of $65 ÷ $850 = 7.65% provides a crude estimate. This so-called current yield neglects the appreciation from holding the bond to maturity, however. Allocating the straight-line appreciation to the coupon yields a less crude approximation. Since the bond matures in 16 years at $150 more than the current price, $9.38 ($150/16) could be added to the coupon for a coupon-plus-appreciation of $74.38 per year. Dividing

by the $850 price produces an estimate of 8.75%. This return estimate is, however, too high, as the end-period appreciation is not discounted to reflect the wait for payment. Calculating the present value of the appreciation factor, subtracting it from the purchase price and proceeding as before produces a somewhat closer approximation. Discounting the $150 gain ($1,000 − $850 = $150) to be received in 16 years requires the selection of an approximate discount rate, however. The proper rate to discount the appreciation is that rate which makes the entire repayment and income stream equal to the market price. Since this is the rate we are seeking, it must be approximated. Our previous efforts suggest a value between 7.65% and 8.75%. Thus 8% can be taken as an approximation. The discount factor for 8% for 16 years is .292, so the present value of the appreciation is approximately

$43.80 (.292 × $150). Subtracting $43.80 from the $850.00 purchase price produces a cost-less-present-value-of-appreciation of $806.80. Dividing this amount into the coupon rate provides a rate estimate of: $65 ÷ $806.80 = 8.06%. This value is probably sufficiently close to the 8% estimate to require no further work. If greater accuracy were required, the 8.06% rate could be used to discount the bond's return.

The procedure for determining a bond's rate of return may be summarized as follows:

(1) Determine the approximate yield by dividing the coupon by the current price. If the market price is near par, this approximation may be close enough. If par and market differ substantially, further work is required.

(2) Using an approximation of the appropriate rate, the difference between market and par is discounted to the present.

(3) This present value of the difference between market and par is then applied to the current price.

(4) The result is divided into the coupon and this estimate is compared with the rate used to discount the difference between market and par.

(5) If the rates are close, no further work is required. If not, the new estimate is used to discount the difference, and the present value is subtracted from the market price.

(6) This result is then divided into the coupon.

(7) The procedure is repeated until the rates are approximately equal.

An even easier way to find a bond's yield to maturity is to use a computer or finance calculator.

the lower the appropriate discount rate. Since a lower discount rate increases an income stream's value, low-risk expected income streams are valued more highly than equivalent-magnitude high-risk expected streams. Accordingly, bonds of very secure companies should be discounted at lower rates than those of less secure companies. Similarly, a stock with a stable or steadily increasing dividend should be evaluated with a lower discount rate (and thus have a higher market price) than an otherwise-similar stock whose dividends are expected to be less stable.

Interest Fluctuation Risk and Default Risk

A bond's risk may be decomposed into interest fluctuation and default risk components. The likelihood that the issuer's obligation will not be fulfilled (e.g., bankruptcy or repudiation) is called default risk. Interest fluctuation risk, in contrast, stems from sensitivity to changing market rates.

Each of these risks finds its lowest level—zero—in government-guaranteed savings accounts. The guarantee eliminates default risk, while the ability to withdraw part or all of the account eliminates interest fluctuation risk. Similarly, short-maturity Treasury bills have very little default and interest fluctuation risk. Indeed all government-guaranteed investments have minimal default risk because the market trusts its guarantee, it has extensive taxing power, and because the Fed can facilitate its debt sales.

The default risk of municipal and corporate debt securities is always considered greater than that of Treasury issues. How much greater depends on the income-producing capacity and/or liquidation value of the issuers. Some issues with strong financial positions are only slightly more risky than federal government securities, while default is much more likely for others.

Interest fluctuation risks also vary substantially. The price of longer maturity debt issues and all equity securities are much more sensitive to interest rate shifts than are shorter-term debt issues. Thus we might well expect that their greater interest fluctuation risk would generally lead to higher discount rates for longer-term issues. While the so-called term structure of interest rates often has this pattern (higher rates for longer maturities), the relationships are more complex. We shall return to this topic in a later chapter.

The Discount Rate for a Risky Asset

The discount rates applied to risky investments are scaled up from the current market rate on riskless assets such as government bonds. A riskless rate of 9% and risk premium (inducement required to attract risk-averse investors) of 2% would imply an 11% (nine percent plus two percent) discount rate. Should the riskless rate fall to 7%, the appropriate rate for this risky asset would become 9% (assuming the 2% risk premium remains unchanged). The appropriate rate for discounting any income stream is the riskless rate plus a specific risk premium associated with the asset's risk.

The Risk Premium

Different bonds can have very different risk premiums. The difference between a bond's promised yield and the yield on an otherwise-similar riskless bond is relatively easy to observe. A bond's coupon and principal-repayment terms are fixed by the indenture encompassing all of the commitments the company makes to its bondholders. If a bond does default, the trustee (usually a bank identified in the bond's indenture) is obligated to take legal action to force compliance with the indenture provisions or force the firm into bankruptcy and then represent the bondholders' interests in the reorganization or disposition of the firm's assets.

With the income stream fixed in the indenture, the risk premium set by the market is directly observable as the difference between the bond's stated yield-to-maturity and the riskless rate. For example, a medium-grade corporate bond yielding 11% has a risk premium of 3% when similar-maturity government bonds yield 8%. Table 4.3 illustrates some estimated risk premiums.

The risk premium as it is commonly understood reflects both the expected loss from default and a pure risk premium.[2] Thus the market might estimate that a particular bond's probability of default is 1% and the expected default loss is 50% of the payment stream's present value. The corresponding expected loss from default would equal .5% (.01 x .5) of the principal. If the total risk premium is 3%, the pure risk premium needed to induce risk-averse investors to purchase this risky security must be 2.5%. While these two risk-premium components cannot be observed directly, inferences can be drawn from historical default experience. For the vast majority of bonds (particularly those rated medium-risk or better), the default loss has, since the end of World War II, been

Table 4.3   Yield-to-Maturities for Selected Bonds, January 4, 1982

Issuer	Coupon Rate (%)	Maturity	Price ($)	Yield (%)	Risk Premium (%)
U.S. Treasury	13 1/4	1991	94 7/16	13.8	0
AT&T	13	1990	94	14.1	.3
Citicorp	14 3/8	1986	97 1/4	14.5	.7
Pacific Telephone	15 1/8	1988	100	15.0	1.2
Alabama Power	14 3/4	1995	95	15.5	1.7
Montgomery Ward	16	1986	98 1/4	16.3	2.5
Georgia Pacific	16.9	1987	97 1/4	17.3	3.5
Eastern Airlines	17 1/2	1998	96 7/8	18.1	4.3

*Note that the computed risk premiums are approximations that ignore the impacts of differential tax rates and maturity differences.

very much lower than the risk premiums of the various risk classes.[3] Thus either the market does not trust the forecast value of past default experience or expected default losses are a relatively small component of risk premiums.

Other Factors Affecting the Discount Rate

We have already seen that the risk of default plays a large role in determining the appropriate rate for discounting a bond's (or other asset's) expected income stream, as do the term structure and the riskless rate. More broadly, general market conditions largely determine the riskless rate and thus all other interest rates that are scaled up from it. Relations between rates for different maturities (the term structure) are also determined by the market. A particular bond's characteristics, such as whether or not it can be called (repurchased at a specified price prior to maturity), may further affect its price, and thus its discount rate.

DETERMINING THE APPROPRIATE DISCOUNT RATE

This exploration of discount rate determinants has only shifted our focus. To ascertain the appropriate rate one must still identify the riskless rate, assess the asset's risk, and estimate the appropriate risk premium. The market rate on government securities approximates the riskless rate. Assessing risk and determining the appropriate risk premium (pure and default) are, however, rather complicated topics requiring more detailed treatment.

Applying Present Values to Stocks

Stocks can be valued with the same basic approach as is used for bonds. A share of stock represents fractional ownership of a corporation. Shareholders participate in the firm's profits through dividends. Profits not paid out as dividends (retained earnings) are plowed back into the company, and may increase future earnings and dividends. Stockholders can also sell shares at a profit if the price rises. Thus stock returns may result both from dividends and price appreciation. In principle, discounting a stock's dividend stream and future market value should yield its present value:

$$S_o = \frac{d_1}{(1 + r)} + \frac{d_2}{(1 + r)^2} + \frac{d_3}{(1 + r)^3} + \frac{d_n + S_n}{(1 + r)^n} \qquad (3)$$

where S_o = present value of share
d_t = expected dividend for year t
r = appropriate discount rate
S_n = expected stock price for year n

Moreover S_n can be evaluated by discounting subsequent dividends. Note that S_n's value stems entirely from the future dividends that its owners expect to receive. That is:

$$S_n = \frac{d_n + 1}{(1 + r)^1} + \frac{d_n + 2}{(1 + r)^2} + \ldots$$

Thus:

$$S_o = \frac{d_1}{(1 + r)} + \frac{d_2}{(1 + r)^2} + \ldots \frac{d_n}{(1 + r)^n} + \ldots \qquad (4)$$

Note that formula (4) merely restates formula (2).

The Market Price of an Investment

Investment prices implicitly reflect their discounted expected income streams. While very few potential traders discount expected incomes explicitly, an implicit future-returns estimate and risk evaluation is an integral part of the pricing process. The more efficient the market, the more accurately the price will reflect available risk/returns information.

The "promised" future income stream of bonds (coupon plus principal) is directly observable; for those who hold to maturity, it generally differs little from the "expected" future income stream (coupon plus interest less expected default loss). Similarly, preferred stocks normally have observable promised future income streams (indicated dividends) close to their expected values (expected dividends). In addition, some preferreds mature and most are callable.

Common stocks, in contrast, do not promise a future income stream or redemption and are not callable. Thus expected income streams are much more difficult to observe in common stock than in fixed-income securities. While one may use market analysts' forecasts or historical extrapolations to estimate expectations, the market's true expectations may differ.[4] Nonetheless, the market does always generate a price.

Implications of the Market Price

The market's weighted-average opinion (as reflected by its price) of a particular investment is, by itself, of little help in investment selection. Market expectations may or may not be accurate. The investment-selection process can be viewed largely as a search for assets that the market has improperly valued. In other words, investment analysis generally involves an attempt to understand and find errors in the market's evaluation. Investors can compare their own discounted dividend forecasts with the market's or compare their assessments of the appropriate rates with the discount rate that equates the present value of their income stream expectations to the market price. The two approaches are mathematically equivalent. With either, investors identify "undervalued" and "overvalued" securities by contrasting their valuations with the market's. Selections based on such analysis can fail in a number of ways, however: (1) The income stream forecasts can be inaccurate; (2) Even if the income forecasts are on target, errors in the assumed discount rates can account for the apparent difference between the investor's and the market's evaluations; (3) The anticipated earnings increase can be offset by an increase in risk; (4) The investor may sell the asset before the market reevaluates it; (5) The investor may correctly identify undervalued securities whose subsequent revaluations are offset by a general market decline. Clearly a security identified as undervalued may not necessarily produce profits for its owners.

If the analysis proves to be both timely and more accurate than the market, the selections should show superior risk-adjusted returns. Where the market's expectations are essentially correct, the selections will tend neither to outperform nor underperform the market. Frequently, however, both the market's and the investor's analysis are too optimistic and the selections underperform the market. Equally frequently, a general market decline pulls down the prices of even many "undervalued" securities. Investment analysts hope that their evaluations are more accurate than the market's often enough to outweigh the times that they are either both too optimistic or the market declines. Since, however, average market performance reflects the weighted-average performance of all participants, the average investor/analyst cannot outperform the market average. This zero-sum-game nature of stock market analysis illustrates the difficulty of successful investing. Only a minority of stock market participants can outperform the market averages, and only a still smaller minority can do so consistently. Nonetheless most investors continue to try. Investing is a game which may not be worth playing but it is certainly a game worth winning.

FORECASTING THE INCOME STREAM

Evaluating an investment involves forecasting its income stream and assessing its risk. While more detailed risk analysis is beyond this chapter's scope, we shall discuss efforts to forecast the income streams of stocks.

The Relationship Between Dividends and Earnings

Most valuation equations call for dividend forecasts. In practice, however, earnings per share are usually forecast instead. This is an imperfect substitution at best. The value of the expected dividend stream only equals the value of that firm's expected earnings stream precisely when the payout equals 100%, (or retained earnings raise future dividends enough to offset precisely the lower current payout). Since this very rarely happens in practice, values based on earnings streams are at best only an approximation. The appropriateness of such an approach depends upon the relationship between expected dividends and earnings, called the *payout ratio*, which firms usually try to keep a stable over the long term.[5] Payouts tend to vary inversely with growth, risk, and earnings volatility. Thus a company with rapidly growing, volatile, and uncertain earnings, tends to set a lower payout rate than a slower-growth firm with a more dependable earnings stream. Most mature companies have a relatively high, stable long-run payout ratio, however. Typically, between 50 and 60% of corporate after-tax earnings are paid out as dividends. While the short-run relationship between dividends and earnings is variable and uncertain, the longer-run relationship is relatively stable and certain.[6] Moreover, because dividends are often only adjusted after a lag, a given year's dividend rate may less accurately reflect the firm's long-term ability to pay dividends than do that year's earnings. That portion of profits not paid out as dividends (retained earnings) is plowed back into the company with the intention of enhancing growth, future profits, and future dividends. Accordingly, security evaluation often begins with earnings predictions. Accurate earnings predictions should facilitate similarly reliable dividend forecasts, which should, when appropriately discounted, yield meaningful value estimates. The relationship between earnings and stock prices is illustrated in Figure 4.1.

The Value of Accurate Earnings Predictions

One extensive study covering the 1962–63 period found that stocks with above-average earnings growth outperformed Standard and Poor's 500 stock average by 4.3%, while stocks with below-average earnings growth underperformed the S&P index by 12%. Similar results have been found for many different samples and

Figure 4.1   Earnings, Dividends and Stock Prices

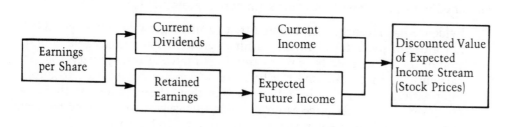

time periods.[7] The key question, however, is not whether accurate earnings forecasts be useful, but how accurate most earnings forecasts are.

Types of Earnings Forecasts

Investment analysts base their earnings predictions on relevant available data (usually public). Management forecasts generally utilize at least some nonpublic information. In addition, annual earnings predictions can be based on already-reported quarterly earnings. Past earnings can be extrapolated mechanically.

Investment Analysts

Investment analysts' predictions and recommendations are notoriously uneven. For example,[8] in July 1972, Wertheim and Company said: "Equity Funding's inherently conservative approach to business may be viewed as a strong defensive weapon in the hands of a group of uncommonly able executives aggressively seeking and obtaining a growing share of the financial service market." In April 1973, Equity Funding was exposed in a two billion dollar phony insurance scheme. Similarly, Jas. H. Oliphant and Company had been recommending Levitz Furniture since it was at 5. After the stock reached a high of 60 1/2 in 1972, Oliphant recommended Levitz at 41, and again at 26. The stock fell to 1 5/8 in December 1974. The nation's largest brokerage firm, Merrill Lynch, Pierce, Fenner and Smith issued favorable reports on Scientific Controls between March 1, 1968, and November 14, 1969—just one week before the firm filed for bankruptcy. An SEC suit alleged that Merrill Lynch either knew or should have known that its recommendation was based on false and misleading information. Merrill Lynch eventually paid 1.6 million dollars to customers who lost money by following the firm's misguided recommendation.[9] Many similarly disastrous recommendations could be cited.

Two basic problems with most investment analysts are their tendency to utilize similar approaches and their reluctance to recommend sales. Thus those rare analysts who do not follow the herd and do sometimes recommend selling may deserve close attention.[10]

While not all analysts' recommendations and forecasts are disastrous, many are ill-advised. Cragg and Malkiel studied five financial institutions covering 185 companies over the 1962–63 period. They found predicted growth highly correlated with past growth but not with actual growth:

> Evidence has recently accumulated that earnings growth in past periods is not a useful predictor of future earnings growth. The remarkable conclusion of the present study is that careful estimates of the security analysts participating in our survey, the bases of which are not limited to public information, perform only a little better than these past growth rates. Moreover, the market price-earnings ratios themselves were not better than either analysts' forecasts or the past growth rates in forecasting future earnings growth.[11]

Similar conclusions emerged from a series of studies appearing in the early 1970s.[12] More recently, however, Richards, Benjamin and Strawser[13] (RBS) studied 92 firms over the 1972–76 period and another 50 for 1969–1972. They reported that security analysts' forecasts had relative absolute errors of 24.1% compared with 28.9% for the best mechanical rule that they tested. Brown and Rozeff[14] (BR) found that *Value Line's* 1972–1975 earnings predictions for 50 randomly selected firms were superior to the best forecasts that they could generate by mechanical means. A follow-up study of 11 *Value Line* analysts' 1973–75 performance produced equivalent results.[15] Thus the earlier studies emphasized the forecasts' shortcomings and the more recent work stressed their superiority over naive prediction methods. BR's samples were, however, restricted to a small number of *Value Line* company forecasts and RBS's sample includes only firms having forecasts for every year from 1972–1976. Thus both studies were based on small and possibly biased samples.

Branch and Berkowitz, in contrast, examined a much larger and broader-based sample of forecasts that appeared annually in *Business Week* over the 1973–77 period.[16] They concluded that these *Business Week* earnings forecasts tended to outperform their trend estimates and were significantly more accurate than random chance. The forecasts were biased, however, and except for 1976 explained substantially less than 10% of the interfirm variation in per-share earnings changes.

The Branch-Berkowitz findings shed light on the apparent conflict between the first and second generation of earnings-forecast papers. According to BR, ". . . past comparisons of analysts' forecasts are not more accurate than time series forecasts" while their own results ". . . overwhelmingly favor the superiority of analysts over time series models."[17] In fact, however, Craig and Malkiel (whom they cite as one source of their statement on past research) actually stated ". . . that careful estimates of the security analysts participating in our survey, the bases of which are not limited to public information, perform only a little better than these past growth rates."[18] "[O]nly a little better than" does not translate into ". . . not more accurate than." Thus the two sets of studies largely disagree in emphasis and interpretation while agreeing on substance.

Corporate Forecasts

For a number of years, the SEC has encouraged corporations to make their internal earnings predictions public. Since corporate officials have direct access to nonpublic corporate information and special expertise in analyzing expected profit impacts, they have the means to make high quality forecasts. Stockholder demands provide a strong incentive to make productive use of that advantage. In spite of SEC encouragement, however, relatively few corporations have made public earnings forecasts. Moreover, the firms that disclose their forecasts tend to be those with more stable and therefore more predictable earnings streams.[19]

Apparently stockholders use dividend changes to assess management's confidence in future earnings. Both Pettit and Watts reported that unexpected dividend changes accompany stock price changes.[20] Both authors also found dividend changes tended to forecast earnings changes. Somewhat more to the point, Copeland and Marioni found executive forecasts superior to naive forecasts (trend extrapolation).[21] Basi, Carey and Twark reported that management forecasts were slightly more accurate than analyst forecasts, while Ruland found no significant difference between the two groups.[22] Porter found both that management's ability to forecast depended upon past earnings variability and that utilities' earnings were easier to forecast than manufacturers' earnings.[23] Penman reported that both dividend change announcements and management's earnings forecasts reflected management's expectations.[24]

Quarterly Earnings Extrapolations

Since investors often try to extrapolate interim earnings, the reliability of such inferences should be tested. Green and Segall found almost no relationship, while Brown and Niederhoffer reported a very modest relationship between first-quarter and annual earnings growth.[25] Apparently year-end adjustments dominate the first-quarter results. Boyle and Hogarty did find that firms tend to delay releasing unfavorable earnings, perhaps to prepare their position once the poor results are reported.[26] Thus delay in an earnings report may forecast unfavorable results.

Past Earnings Growth

One might well expect a high correlation between past and future growth. Able management should generate consistently above-average performance, and vice versa. "Not so," said Little in "Higgledy Piggledy Growth."[27] While Little's work was confined to British corporations, subsequent work with United States firms supported his conclusion.[28] Lintner and Glauber did find that firms with the most stable relationship (first quintile) between growth, income, and production showed a significant positive correlation (.40) between successive growth rates.[29] Subsequent work has, however, found somewhat greater association between future earnings growth and more sophisticated extrapolations of past growth.[30]

An Integrated Forecasting Approach

The largely unsuccessful results of past forecasting efforts suggests the need for a more comprehensive approach. While simple extrapolations of past earnings may not produce especially realiable forecasts, perhaps a more insightful use of past earnings data could facilitate superior predictions. Chant, for example, reasons that past business cycle sensitivity of earnings reflects future earnings relationships.[31] That is, earnings may be more accurately forecast when the firms' relations to their economic environments are considered. Preliminary work utilizing leading indicators has produced encouraging results. As yet, however, such leading indicator-based forecasts are not publicly available.

Implications for Investment Analysis

Analyst's forecasts are of modest value; corporate forecasts are largely unobtainable and when available, may not be appreciably more reliable; interim earnings have very little explanatory power; past growth rates are poor forecasters except when the growth rates have been stable; and leading indicator-based forecasts are not publicly available. The relative inaccuracy and/or unavailability of most types of year-ahead earnings predictions suggest that longer-term forecasts may be especially unreliable. While year-to-year fluctuations may be smoothed, the uncertainties of the more distant future tend to compound the inaccuracies of long-term forecasts.[32] Indeed, few analysts even make such forecasts.

The shortcomings of earnings forecasts should be put in perspective, however. Anyone seeking to analyze investment opportunities encounters substantial difficulties and uncertainties. Success relative to others may lead to satisfactory results even when everyone must rely on rather inaccurate forecasts. Furthermore, other aspects of fundamental analysis may help investors form useful expectations of the future income streams which do not presuppose the accuracy implicit in the present value approach.

SUMMARY AND CONCLUSIONS

An investment's price represents the market's assessment of the present value of its expected future income stream. Observing the expected income streams and implied discount rates of bonds is relatively straightforward. The expected income streams and discount rates for stocks are, in contrast, appreciably more difficult to observe. Investment analysis seeks to generate superior (to the market's) estimates of the future income stream and appropriate discount rate. Thus investor/analysts compare the present value implied by their estimates of an asset's future income stream and appropriate discount rate with its market price. An undervalued asset is a buy—particularly if it is more undervalued than the available alternatives. Such an analysis is, however, only as reliable as the inputs on which it is based. The approach may be useful when the estimates are relatively accurate (bonds). For stocks, however, forecasting difficulties make a straightforward application of present value estimates very nearly useless. Valuing assets on the basis of their discounted expected income streams provides a useful framework, but identifying undervalued securities requires much more.

REVIEW QUESTIONS

1. Discuss the meaning of time value.
2. Explain how a 20-year bond with a $1,000 face value could sell for $600 or $1,200.
3. How is the present value of the expected future income stream approach used to value investment assets?

4. Discuss the various components of risk: default, liquidity, pure-risk premium.
5. Describe how the market's evaluation and one's own evaluation may be used to identify misvalued securities.
6. Discuss what can go wrong with investment analysis.
7. Why do investment analysts concentrate on earnings predictions rather than dividend predictions?
8. Compare earnings forecasts based on analysts' predictions, current earnings growth, management forecasts, interim earnings, and an integrated approach.

REVIEW PROBLEMS

1. Compute the present value for the following income streams:
   a) $50 annually forever discounted at 10%
   b) $200 annually for 20 years discounted at 20%
   c) bond with $150 coupon for 12 years, maturing at $1,070 discounted at 16%
   d) payment stream of
      year 1 $200
      year 2 $300
      year 3 $400
      year 4 $500
      subsequent years   0
      discount at 8%
2. Compute the price of a 20-year bond with a 10% coupon when comparable market interest rates are
   a)   7%
   b)   9%
   c)   10%
   d)   11%
   e)   13%
3. Select eight bonds with various yields and make a table similar to Table 4.2. Write a report.
4. The American Pig Company (ticker symbol PORK) currently pays a dividend of $3 per share, which is expected to rise annually by 25¢ per share for the next five years. The stock currently sells for $36 per share per year, a ratio of twelve times its current dividends. At the end of five years that ratio of dividends to price is also expected to obtain. Compute the present value of PORK's expected income stream for discount rates of 8%, 10%, 12%, 15%, 18%. Repeat the computations for a stable dividend of $3.

5. Evaluate a stock using the following information:
   a) Current dividend rate—$1
   b) Dividend rate over next 5 years—$1.10, $1.20, $1.30, $1.40, $1.50
   c) Current market discount rate—16%
   d) Current market price/dividend rate—6.5
      Repeat the analyses for discount rates of 10% and 20%
6. Select ten large companies at random and record the earnings forecast from the previous year's *Business Week* annual year-end investment issue. Compare these forecasts with the actual earnings for that year. What was the average percentage error? Write a report.

NOTES

1. *Expanded Bond Value Tables,* Financial Publishing Company, Boston, Massachusetts, 1970.

2. T. Lawler, "Default, Risk and Yield Spreads," *Journal of Portfolio Management,* Summer 1982, pp. 65–66.

3. G. Pye, "Gauging the Default Premium," *Financial Analysts Journal,* January/February 1974, pp. 49–52.

4. B. Deschamps and D. Mechta, "Predictive Ability and Descriptive Validity of Earnings Forecasting Models," *Journal of Finance,* September 1980, pp. 933–950.

5. A. Kalay, "Signaling, Information Content and the Reluctance to Cut Dividends," *Journal of Financial and Quantitative Analysis,* November 1980, pp. 555–870; L. Senbet, "Discussion of Kalay Paper" *Journal of Financial and Quantitative Analysis,* November 1980, pp. 871–873.

6. R. Kolb, "Predicting Dividend Changes," *Journal of Economics and Business,* Spring/Summer 1981, pp. 218–230.

7. M. Kosor and V. Messner, "The Filter Approach and Earning Forecasts—Part One," unpublished manuscript cited in J. Lorie and M. Hamilton, *The Stock Market Theory and Evidence,* Homewood, IL, Irwin, 1973, p. 157; R. Brealey, *An Introduction to Risk and Return from Common Stocks,* MIT Press, Cambridge, 1969; H. Latane and D. Tuttle, "An Analysis of Common Stock Price Ratios," *Southern Economic Journal,* January 1967, pp. 343–354; C. Lee and K. Zummalt, "Associations Between Alternative Accounting Profitability Measures and Security Returns," *Journal of Financial and Quantitative Analysis,* March 1981, pp. 71–94.

8. M. Connor, "Wall Street Analysts Give Lots of Bad Advice Along with Good," *Wall Street Journal,* May 25, 1973, p. 1.

9. *Wall Street Journal,* "SEC Charges that Merrill Lynch Pushed Investors into Buying Ailing Firm's Stock," *Wall Street Journal,* March 12, 1974, p. 3; *New York Times,* "SEC Fines Merrill $1.6 Million," *New York Times,* November 11, 1977, p. D 1.

10. M. Barofather, "Cottage Money Men," *Forbes,* August 30, 1982, pp. 158–160; B. Rudolph, "Three Brave Men," *Forbes,* August 30, 1982, pp. 154–157.

11. J. Cragg and B. Malkiel, "The Consensus and Accuracy of Some Predictions of the Growth of Corporate Earnings," *Journal of Finance,* March 1969, pp. 67–84.

12. M. Richards, "Analysts' Performance and the Accuracy of Corporate Earnings Forecasts," *Journal of Business,* July 1973, pp. 350–357; E. Elton and J. Gruber, "Earnings Estimates and the Accuracy of Expectational Data," *Management Science,* April 1972, pp. 409–424.

13. M. Richards, T. Benjamin and R. Strawser, "An Examination of the Accuracy of Earnings Forecasts," *Financial Management,* Fall 1977, pp. 78–86.

14. L. Brown and M. Rozeff, "The Superiority of Analysts' Forecasts as Measures of Expectations: Evidence from Earnings," *Journal of Finance*, March 1978, pp. 1–16.

15. L. Brown and M. Rozeff, "Analysts Can Forecast Accurately," *Journal of Portfolio Management*, Spring 1980, pp. 31–35.

16. B. Branch and B. Berkowitz, "The Predictive Accuracy of the *Business Week* Earnings to Forecasts," *Journal of Accounting Auditing and Finance*, Spring 1981, pp. 215–219.

17. Brown and Roseff, *op. cit.*, p. 1.

18. Craig and Malkie, *op. cit.*, p. 83.

19. B. Jaggi and P. Grier, "A Comparative Analysis of Forecast Disclosing and Non-disclosing Firms," *Financial Management*, Summer 1980, pp. 38–46.

20. R. Pettit, "Dividend Announcements, Security Performance, and Capital Market Efficiency," *Journal of Finance*, December 1972, pp. 993–1007; R. Watts, "The Information Content of Dividends," *Journal of Business*, April 1973, pp. 199–211.

21. R. Copeland and R. Marioni, "Executive Forecasts of Earnings Per Share versus Forecasts of Naive Models," *Journal of Business*, October 1972, pp. 497–511.

22. B. Basi, K. Carey and R. Twark, "A Comparison of the Accuracy of Corporate and Security Analyst's Forecasts of Earnings," *The Accounting Review*, April 1976, pp. 244–254; W. Ruland, "The Accuracy of Forecasts by Management and by Financial Analysts," *The Accounting Review*, April 1978, pp. 439–447.

23. G. Porter, "Determinants of the Accuracy of Management Forecasts of Earnings," *Review of Business and Economic Research*, Spring 1982, pp. 1–13.

24. S. Penman, "The Predictive Content of Earnings Forecasts and Dividends," *Journal of Finance*, September 1983, pp. 1181–1199.

25. D. Green and J. Segall, "The Prediction Power of First Quarter Earnings Reports," *Journal of Business*, January 1967, pp. 44–55; R. Brown and V. Niederhoffer, "The Prediction Power of Quarterly Earnings," *Journal of Business*, October 1968, pp. 488–497; D. Green and J. Segall, "Brickbats and Strawmen: A Reply to Brown and Niederhoffer," *Journal of Business*, October 1968, pp. 498–502; V. Niederhoffer, "The Predictive Content of First Quarter Earnings Reports," *Journal of Business*, January 1970, pp. 60–62.

26. S. Boyle and T. Hogarty " 'Good' News vs. 'Bad' News: Another Aspect of the Controversy Between Manager and Owner," *Industrial Organization Review*, Vol. 1, 1973, pp. 1–14.

27. I. Little, "Higgledy Piggledy Growth," *Journal of Statistics*, Oxford, November 1962; I. Little and A. Rayman, *Higgledy Piggledy Growth Again*, Basil Blackwell, Oxford, 1966.

28. J. Murphy, "Relative Growth in Earnings Per Share—Past and Future," *Financial Analysts Journal*, November/December 1966, pp. 73–76.

29. J. Lintner and R. Glauber, "Higgledy Piggledy Growth in America?" Paper presented to the seminar on the Analysis of Security Prices, University of Chicago, May 1967; "Further Observations on Higgledy Piggledy Growth" presented to same seminar; R. Brealey, "The Character of Earnings Changes," Paper presented to the same seminar.

30. W. Ruland, "On Choice of Simple Extrapolative Model Forecasts of Annual Earnings," *Financial Management*, Summer 1980, pp. 30–37; Deschamps and Mehta, *op. cit.*

31. P. Chant, "On the Predictability of Corporate Earnings Per Share Behavior," *Journal of Finance*, March 1980, pp. 13–21.

32. Deschamps and Mehta, *op. cit.*

5 Risk and Modern Portfolio Theory

Most investors realize that: (1) risk is related to the confidence placed in return expectations; (2) investors will generally trade off some expected return for a reduction in risk; and (3) the discount rate applied to any expected income stream's valuation should vary directly with its risk. This chapter expands on that base with a focus on risk in its primary forms and its role in investment analysis and portfolio management. Portfolio risk is analyzed and a simplified approach introduced.

A SIMPLE EXAMPLE OF INVESTMENT RISK

Suppose investment A guarantees a return of precisely 5% while investment B offers a 90% chance of returning 5% and one chance in ten of a 0% return. Since A always returns 5%, its mean, average or expected return must be 5%. B's expected return is 4.5% $[(.90 \times .05) + (.10 \times .00) = .045]$. Therefore, not only will B on the average return less than A, but B's uncertain yield also makes it more risky. Now consider investment C with a 90% chance of a 5% return, a 5% chance of a 0% return and a 5% chance of a 10% return. While C's expected return of 5% $[(.90 \times .05) + (.05 \times .00) + (.05 \times .10) = .05]$ is the same as A's, C's actual return is less likely to equal its expected return than is A's. Thus risk-averting investors would prefer A.

Now consider asset D with a 90% chance of a 5% return, a 5% chance of a 3% return, and a 5% chance of a 7% return. Like A and C, D offers an expected return of 5% $[(.90 \times .05) + (.05 \times .03) + (.05 \times .07) = .05]$. Since D's actual return is uncertain, risk-averters would prefer A. On the other hand, since D's return-variation is less than that of C, D seems the less risky asset. That is, the possible returns for C are 0%, 5%, and 10%, while D's are 3%, 5%, and 7%. C's actual return could be 5% above or below its expected value while D's can differ only 2% from its mean. Histograms of these various return possibilities are illustrated in Figure 5.1.

THE RISK OF A DISTRIBUTION OF POSSIBLE RETURNS

Determining the expected value of a returns distribution is rather straightforward; measuring its risk is more complex. That C's possible returns varied from 0%

Figure 5.1   Histograms of Return Possibilities for Four Investments

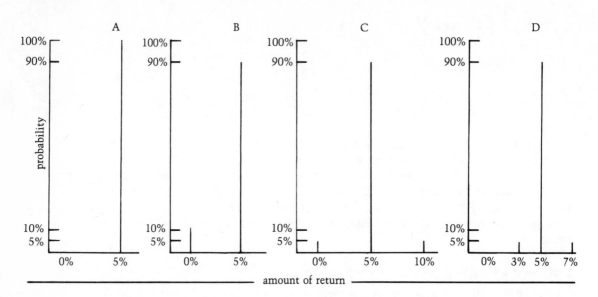

to 10% compared with 3% to 7% for D suggests that C is riskier. Measuring risk as the difference between the maximum and minimum possible returns would, however, ignore the shape of the distribution between the extremes. While a risk measure might be based on the average deviation from the expected return, the simple average deviation from the mean is precisely zero (the negative differences exactly offset the positive differences). The absolute value of the deviation from the mean measures the average distance of the actual return from the expected return. Since this mean-absolute deviation statistic is difficult to work with, the deviations are generally first squared (producing non-negative values) and then averaged to form the "variance." The variance and its square root, the standard deviation, are frequently employed descriptive statistics. To understand how the standard deviation serves as a risk measure, we first need to explore its relationship to probability distributions.

Probability Distributions

Histograms (Figure 5.1) relate possible discrete events to their likelihoods or frequencies; probability distributions are used for continuous phenomena. Figure 5.2, a probability distribution, illustrates the relation between a large number of expected returns and their probabilities.

The probabilities rise to a peak at return r_m and decline symmetrically thereafter. With a symmetrical distribution, the probabilities for returns equidis-

Figure 5.2   A Probability Distribution of Returns

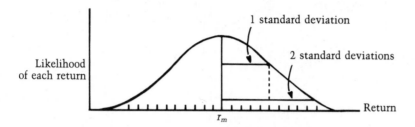

tant from r_m are equal. Since the simple average of such paired returns is r_m, the weighted average of all of these averages must also be r_m.

Figure 5.2 also illustrates one and two standard deviations from the average. For most commonly encountered distributions, the actual value will be within one standard deviation of the mean approximately two-thirds of the time, while about 95% of the time it will be within two standard deviations. Thus, the standard deviation of the return distribution may be used as an index of the degree of confidence (or risk) in the expected return (expected return variability).

A Simple Probability Distribution

Suppose we had N equally likely returns denoted by R_t where t ranges from 1 to N. The mean or expected return for R_t is given by the formula:

$$E(R) = \sum_{t=1}^{N} R_t/N$$

Similarly, the variance would be:

$$\sigma^2 = \sum_{t=1}^{N} \frac{[R_t - E(R_t)]^2}{N}$$

The standard deviation is, of course, the square root of the variance.

For unequal weights the mean and standard deviation computations are a bit more complex. Rather than taking the simple (unweighted) average of returns, a weighted average is computed. Thus:

$$E(R) = \sum_{t=1}^{N} P(R_t)R_t$$

where $P(R_t)$ = probability of return R_t

Similarly:

$$\sigma_r^2 = \sum_{t=0}^{N} P(R_t)[R_t - E(R_t)]^2$$

In a simple example we might have:

$$\frac{R_1 \quad R_2 \quad R_3 \quad R_4}{.00 \quad .04 \quad .10 \quad .14} \quad P(R_1) = P(R_2) = P(R_3) = P(R_t) = .25$$

$$E(R) = \left(\frac{.00 + .04 + .10 + .14}{4}\right) = \frac{.28}{4} = .07$$

Similarly:

$$R_t - E(R) \frac{X_1 \quad X_2 \quad X_3 \quad X_4}{-.07 \quad -.03 \quad .03 \quad .07}$$
$$[R_t - E(R)]^2 \quad .0049 \quad .0009 \quad .0009 \quad .0049$$
$$\sigma_r^2 = .0116/4 = .0029$$
$$\sigma_r = \sqrt{.0029} = .054$$

Thus investment R has an expected return of 7% and standard deviation of 5.4%. In words, this means that the best guess for R's return is 7%. Two-thirds of the time R should yield between 1.6% and 12.4%—a relatively large (i.e., risky) variation. Suppose investment Y had an expected return of 6.5% with a 2% standard deviation. Two-thirds of the time Y's investors could expect to earn between 4.5% and 8.5%. In spite of its slightly lower expected yield, many investors might prefer Y to R because of its more certain return. Let us now explore why.

RISK AVERSION

We have already seen that risk may be measured in terms of the standard deviation from the mean. If two assets have the same expected return but different risk levels, the riskier asset will have a higher probability of achieving both a lower and a higher return. Mathematically, the upside potential and downside risk cancel out, producing the same expected return as the lower-risk asset. And yet risk-averse investors will prefer the asset with the return that is expected to be less variable.

Risk aversion in the marketplace results from the tendency of most people to dislike an unexpectedly low (perhaps negative) return more than they like a favorable return of similar magnitude above the mean. For example: if the mean return is 10%, the pain resulting from a minus 10% return (20% below the mean) is viewed psychologically as of greater magnitude than the pleasure of a return of plus 30% (20% above the mean). To avoid the risk of possibly experiencing the pain of an unexpectedly low return, risk-averse investors prefer assets with less variable expected returns.

In spite of the general risk-averse nature of most investors, many assets do offer expected payment streams that have a wide range of possible outcomes. To attract risk-averse investors, such investments must be priced attractively.

In practice this means that more risky assets tend to have higher discount rates applied to their expected income streams.

INDIVIDUAL RISK VERSUS PORTFOLIO RISK

Standard deviation is useful for measuring an individual investment's risk, but less so for measuring the risk contribution of an asset to a larger portfolio. For example: an investment with an expected return of 12% and a standard deviation of 3% will on the average earn between 9 and 15% two-thirds of the time and between 6 and 18% 95% of the time. Such dimensions indicate that particular investment's downside risk and upside potential. The standard deviation of an individual asset's expected return does not reflect diversification impacts, however. Since one's wealth stems from his or her entire portfolio, investors should be primarily concerned with portfolio risk rather than the risks of their portfolio's components. If two investments' values fluctuate by offsetting amounts, the owner is no poorer or richer than if neither had varied. Since component-return variabilities are usually somewhat offsetting, portfolio return variability is almost always below the components' average variabilities. Moreover, different assets may contribute disproportionately to a portfolio's total risk. Risk measures of a multi-asset portfolio's components should reflect these considerations.

TWO-ASSET PORTFOLIO RISK

The formula for a two-asset portfolio's risk (σ_p^2) is:

$$\sigma_p^2 = X^2\sigma_x^2 + 2XYC_{xy} + Y^2\sigma_y^2 \qquad (1)$$

where:

X = portfolio weight of asset x
Y = portfolio weight of asset y
σ_x^2 = variance of asset x
σ_y^2 = variance of asset y
C_{xy} = covariance of asset x with y

For simplicity, the weights X and Y are restricted to the zero-one range (ruling out short-selling and borrowing). The terms $X^2\sigma_x^2$ and $Y^2\sigma_y^2$ are the squares of each component's weight times its respective variance. The remaining term, $2XYC_{xy}$ requires further explanation. Its key part, and indeed a central aspect of portfolio risk in general, is the covariance C_{xy}.

The Covariance

The covariance of two assets' returns is a measure of their movement relative to each other. To understand how the covariance statistic is defined, consider first the difference between asset x's period t return (x_t) and its mean value $(\bar{x})$.

Since a mean value is generally located near the center of the distribution, this difference $(x_t - \bar{x})$ should be equally likely to be positive or negative. Now consider the product $(x_t - \bar{x})(y_t - \bar{y})$. When the two asset returns are either both above or both below their means together, the product is positive. The product is negative when one deviation is above its mean and the other below. The covariance is defined as the average of the product $(y_t - \bar{y})(x_t - \bar{x})$ and reflects the relatedness of the assets' returns. An analogous statistic, the correlation coefficient of x and y (ρ_{xy}), is their covariance divided by the product of their standard deviations. The division scales the correlation coefficient between a maximum of $+1$ and a minimum of -1. What follows will utilize the covariance, but it could all be recast in correlation terms with the substitution:

$$\rho_{xy} = C_{xy}/\sigma_x\sigma_y$$

Figure 5.3 helps illustrate the meaning of the covariance. Suppose we are interested in the comovements of assets x and y. We might explore this relation by plotting $(x_t - \bar{x})$ and $(y_t - \bar{y})$ over time. Whenever investments x and y are above their averages together, we would place the observation in the upper right-hand quadrant. When they are simultaneously below their means, the point will plot in the lower left-hand quadrant. Investments that tend to vary together will largely plot in an area concentrated in those two quadrants (Figure 5.3A). Indeed, most asset pairs exhibit this so-called positive covariance. One investment may, however, experience above-average returns while another is below average (upper left and lower right quadrants). If the returns move in opposite directions more than they move together, the covariance will be negative (Figure 5.3B). Finally, if the returns move in a totally independent fashion, a zero covariance will result (Figure 5.3C).

Computing a Covariance

To explore how the covariance of two variables is computed, suppose we have the following five observations on variables x and y:

$(x_1, y_1) = (1, 3)$
$(x_2, y_2) = (2, 7)$
$(x_3, y_3) = (3, 8)$
$(x_4, y_4) = (4, 10)$
$(x_5, y_5) = (5, 12)$

First we must compute $\bar{x}$ and $\bar{y}$:

$\bar{x} = (1 + 2 + 3 + 4 + 5)/5 = 15/5 = 3$
$\bar{y} = (3 + 7 + 8 + 10 + 12)/5 = 40/5 = 8$

Next we must compute $(x - \bar{x})(y - \bar{y})$ for each pair of values:

Figure 5.3   Covariance for Different Types of Relatedness

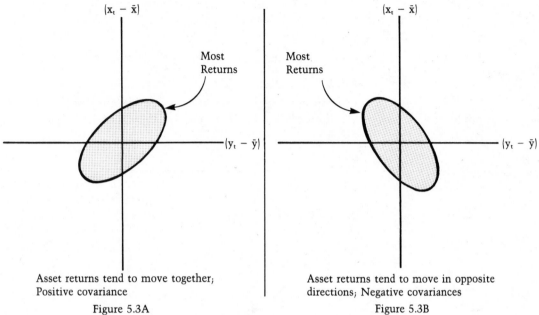

$(x_t - \bar{x})$

Most
Returns

$(y_t - \bar{y})$

$(x_t - \bar{x})$

Most
Returns

$(y_t - \bar{y})$

Asset returns tend to move together;
Positive covariance

Figure 5.3A

Asset returns tend to move in opposite
directions; Negative covariances

Figure 5.3B

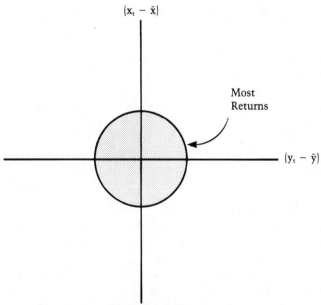

$(x_t - \bar{x})$

Most
Returns

$(y_t - \bar{y})$

Asset returns are unrelated; Zero covariance

Figure 5.3c

$$(1 - 3)(3 - 8) = -2 \times -5 = 10$$
$$(2 - 3)(7 - 8) = -1 \times -1 = 1$$
$$(3 - 3)(8 - 8) = 0 \times 0 = 0$$
$$(4 - 3)(10 - 8) = 1 \times 2 = 1$$
$$(5 - 3)(12 - 8) = 2 \times 4 = 8$$

Finally we obtain the covariance by averaging these values:

$$(10 + 1 + 0 + 2 + 8)/5 = 4.2$$

Note that in this example the x and y values tended to move together, producing a positive covariance. The result, Figure 5.4 shows a relationship similar to that of Figure 5.3A.

Figure 5.4   Covariance Example

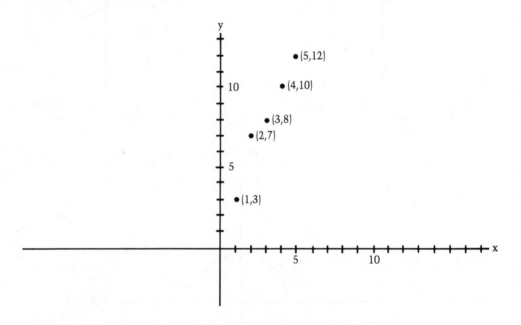

An Example of a Two-Asset Portfolio's Risk

Now returning to equation (1), consider a simple example: suppose x and y have standard deviations of .10 and .15 respectively, and a covariance of .01, and we form a portfolio of half x and half y. If the expected returns of x and y are .09 and .11, the portfolio's expected return would be .10, a weighted average of the component returns. One might think that the portfolio's standard deviation would also be a weighted average of .10 and .15 (.125). The formula reveals a different result, however:

$$\sigma_p^2 = X^2\sigma_x^2 + 2XYC_{xy} + Y^2\sigma_y^2$$
$$\sigma_x = .10$$
$$\sigma_y = .15$$
$$X = .5$$
$$Y = .5$$
$$C_{xy} = .01$$

Thus:

$$\sigma_p^2 = (.5)^2(.10)^2 + 2(.5)^2(.01) + (.5)^2(.15)^2$$
$$\sigma_p^2 = .25(.01) \times .5(.01) + .25(.0225)$$
$$\sigma_p^2 = 0.013125$$
$$\sigma_p = \sqrt{0.013125} = .115$$

In this case, diversifying the portfolio has reduced the risk below the two components' average risk of .125.

Two-Asset Portfolio with Equal Weights and Variances

The two-variable portfolio variance depends upon each asset's variance and the covariance between them. If weights X and Y are equal and variance σ_x^2 and σ_y^2 are equal, equation 1 reduces to:

$$\sigma_p^2 = (1/2)^2 \sigma_x^2 + (1/2) C_{xy} + (1/2)^2\sigma_y^2 \qquad \text{(1a)}$$
$$= 1/4 (\sigma_x^2 + 2C_{xy} + \sigma_y^2)$$
$$= 1/4 (2\sigma_x^2 + 2C_{xy})$$
$$= 1/2 (\sigma_x^2 + C_{xy})$$

The reader will not be burdened with a proof,[1] but C_{xy} can in this example be no larger than σ_x^2 and no smaller than $-\sigma_x^2$. If $C_{xy} = \sigma_x^2$, the two assets' returns x and y move in precise lockstep. Stocks of two merging firms might approach this degree of relatedness. In this extreme case:

$$\sigma_p^2 = 1/2 (\sigma_x^2 + \sigma_x^2) = \sigma_x^2 \qquad \text{(1b)}$$

If $C_{xy} = -\sigma_x^2$, the two assets' returns always vary inversely by precisely proportional magnitudes. Few, if any, such asset pairs exist, but otherwise-equivalent (underlying stock, maturity, terms to exercise, etc.) puts and calls would come close. As the underlying stock fluctuated, the puts and calls would move in opposite directions.

When $C_{xy} = -\sigma_x^2$, equation 1a becomes:

$$\sigma_p^2 = 1/2(\sigma_x^2 - \sigma_x^2) = 0 \qquad \text{(1c)}$$

When the two risky assets' returns move precisely inversely, portfolio risk can be eliminated by appropriate choice of weights. A covariance of zero (the assets' return fluctuations are unrelated) is another interesting special case:

$$\sigma_p^2 = 1/4 \,(2\sigma_x^2 + 0) = \sigma_x^2 \div 2 \tag{1d}$$

Where the assets are unrelated, the portfolio's variance is equal to half of the components' variance. Most two-asset portfolios' variances will lie between zero and $+\sigma_x^2$, in which case the portfolio variance will be between $\sigma_x^2 \div 2$ and σ_x^2.

Some examples of portfolio risk for equal weights and variances:
Suppose $\sigma_x^2 = \sigma_y^2 = .1$ and $C_{xy} = .06$ Formula 1a reveals σ_p^2 as:

$$\begin{aligned} \sigma_p^2 &= 1/2(\sigma_x^2 + C_{xy}) \\ &= 1/2(.1 + .06) \\ &= 1/2(.16) \\ &= .08 \end{aligned}$$

Now suppose $\sigma_x^2 = \sigma_y^2 = C_{xy} = .1$ Then from formula 1b we have:

$$\sigma_p^2 = 1/2(\sigma_x^2 + \sigma_y^2) = \sigma_x^2 = .1$$

If $\sigma_x^2 = .1$ and $C_{xy} = -.1$ then from formula 1c we have:

$$\begin{aligned} \sigma_p^2 &= 1/2 \,(\sigma_x^2 - \sigma_x^2) = 0 \\ &= 1/2 \,(.1 - .1) = 0 \end{aligned}$$

The reader may wish to verify these formulas by computing portfolio risk for the above examples from formula 1:

$$(\sigma_p^2 = X^2\sigma_x^2 + 2XYC_{xy} + Y^2\sigma_y^2).$$

Two-Asset Portfolios with Unequal Weights and Variances

Relationships are similar to those described above when the equal weights and equal component-variance assumptions are modified. Whenever C_{xy} is at a maximum, the portfolio variance equals the weighted average variance of the components. If C_{xy} is at its minimum value, an appropriate choice of weights can eliminate the portfolio's variance. If C_{xy} equals zero, the portfolio variance equals one-half the weighted average variance of the components. Figure 5.5 illustrates this relationship. Table 5.1 summarizes the various possibilities for the two-asset case.

For C_{xy} at its maximum possible value, a portfolio of x and y will have expected returns and standard deviations that are a simple weighted average of those of x and y separately (straight line from x to y). The relative proportions of x and y will determine where on line xy the portfolio lies. For C_{xy} at its minimum value, the portfolio risk/expected return levels lie on lines xf-fy. Note that $\sigma_p = 0$ at point f. Thus for that particular combination of x and y, the portfolio's risk is totally eliminated. When $C_{xy} = 0$, the portfolios of x and y lie on a curved line connecting x and y that lies partway between that for C_{xy} at its maximum and C_{xy} at its minimum. For every other value of C_{xy}, a curved

Figure 5.5   Two-Asset-Portfolio Risks for Different Values of C_{xy}

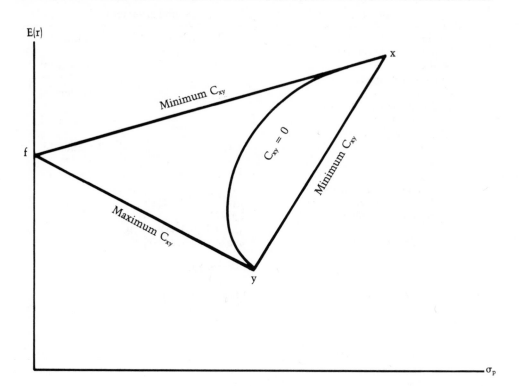

line between x and y represents the possible risk/expected return levels. The closer C_{xy} is to its maximum value, the closer the curve approaches line xy.

N-ASSET PORTFOLIO RISK

The N-asset equivalent of Equation 1 contains variance and covariance terms for every asset and asset pair in the portfolio. While a thorough analysis is beyond the scope of this book, Figure 5.6 does illustrate the fact that risk declines as the number of portfolio components increases. Note, however, that portfolio risk only declines asymptotically toward the average covariance t of the components.

Estimating Variances and Covariances

While covariance and variance statistics can be estimated from past data, such estimates should, where possible, utilize future-oriented information. For example: the stock of a firm whose future environment is expected to be similar to its

Table 5.1   Portfolio Variances for Two-Asset Cases

Case	Portfolio Variance	
General Formula	$X^2\sigma_x^2 + 2XYC_{xy} + Y^2\sigma_y^2$	(Equation 1)
Equal Variances and Weights		
General Case	$1/2\,(\sigma_x^2 + C_{xy})$	(Equation 1a)
Perfectly Related Assets		
$(C_{xy} = \sigma_x^2)$	σ_x^2	(Equation 1b)
Perfectly Inversely-Related Assets		
$(C_{xy} = -\sigma_x^2)$	0	(Equation 1c)
Unrelated Assets		
$(C_{xy} = 0)$	$\sigma_x^2 \div 2$	(Equation 1d)
Normal Case		
$(0 \leqq C_{xy} \leqq \sigma_x^2)$	$\sigma_x^2 \div 2 \leqq \sigma_p^2 \leqq \sigma_x^2$	
Unequal Variances and Weights		
Perfectly Related Assets		
$(C_{xy}$ at maximum value$)$	$X\sigma_x^2 + Y\sigma_y^2$	
Perfectly Inversely-Related Assets	0 (possible to choose weights to	
$(C_{xy}$ at minimum level$)$	make variance $= 0$)	
Unrelated Assets		
$(C_{xy} = 0)$	$1/2\,(X\sigma_x^2 + Y\sigma_y^2)$	
Normal Case		
$0 \leqq C_{xy} \leqq (X\sigma_x^2 + Y\sigma_y^2)$	$1/2\,(X\sigma_x^2 + Y\sigma_y^2) \leqq \sigma_p^2 \leqq (X\sigma_x^2 + Y\sigma_y^2)$	

Figure 5.6   Portfolio Risk Declines as N Increases

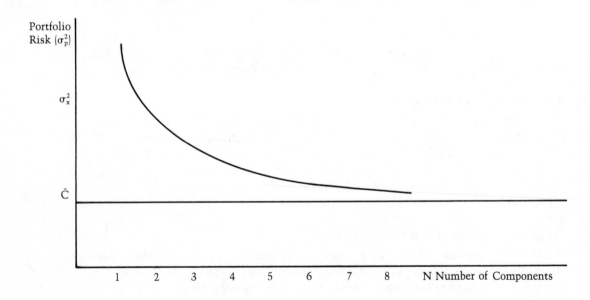

past is likely to behave much as its historically estimated variance and covariance statistics imply. On the other hand, a firm that has recently experienced a major change (merger, new product introduction, changed regulatory environment, large capital infusion, etc.) is more likely to behave differently. If the change has tended to increase risk, historically based risk measures should be adjusted upward.

SIMPLIFYING PORTFOLIO-RISK DETERMINATION

We could estimate a portfolio's risk by applying all the relevant weights, variances, and covariances to the N-asset equivalent of Equation 1. Possible composition shifts could be assessed by reapplying the formula. Mutual funds and other institutional investors, those best situated to utilize the methodology, rarely evaluate portfolio risk in this way, however. First, the required data (N variances and $N(N - 1) \div 2$ covariances) grow exponentially with N. Since most institutional investors consider large sets of securities, making and continually updating the required estimates would be costly and time consuming. Second, like earnings forecasts, historically based variance and covariance estimates are rather unreliable—adjusting them to reflect future-oriented information is an uncertain process at best. Third, several simplified approaches provide risk estimates that are about as reliable as those of Equation 2, particularly for a large N.

Applying the full equation to a portfolio with many components requires numerous covariance estimates. For large N, the variances' impacts on σ_p^2 are small enough to ignore. Rather than using each component return's estimated covariability with every other component return, one could restrict the analysis to covariability with the market as a whole. Generalizable factors (business cycle, interest rates, energy availability, inflation, war scare, etc.) tend to affect the market and most firms similarly. Since they are nonrandom, such influences cannot be diversified away. Random firm-specific and industry-specific influences, in contrast, (strikes, weather impacts, competitor moves, etc.) will largely offset each other in a sizable portfolio.

Estimating Market Covariability: Betas

Since all portfolio-risk-assessment methods depend on the estimated relatedness of the component returns, we need a way of estimating such relatedness. Asset-return variability may be divided into two components: that which is associated with the general market and that which is not. To this end, we may plot an individual security's returns, S_{it}, relative to the market, M_t (Figure 5.7).

Most securities' returns are positive when the market rises and negative when it falls (positive covariance). A line centered through the data illustrates the average tendency of the security to move with the market (Figure 5.8). The slope of that line, called the β, measures the degree of proportionality between the security's returns and the market's. An asset with returns that tend to be proportional to the market will have a β close to unity. A β greater than one

Figure 5.7   Asset Return versus The Market

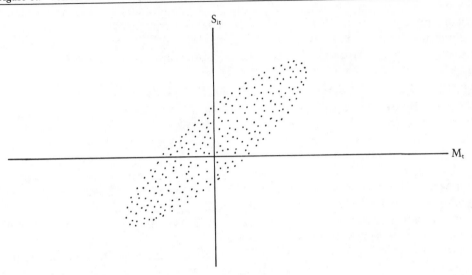

indicates the asset's returns tend to exceed the market's when the market's return is positive and be lower when the market's return is negative. Similarly, a β between zero and one indicates a tendency for the asset's returns to fluctuate proportionately less than the market. Negative βs reflect a tendency for such assets' returns to move inversely with the market. Table 5.2 summarizes these probabilities.

Table 5.2   Expected Asset Returns for Different β's and Market Returns

Range	Expected Asset Return for Positive Market Return	Expected Asset Return for Negative Market Return
$\beta \geqq 1$	above market	below market
$\beta = 1$	market	market
$0 < \beta < 1$	below market	above market
$\beta < 0$	negative	positive

Estimating the Market Model for Stocks

Although a β may be estimated for any investment, most applications have been to stocks. If future relationships are like the past, a given stock's β may appropriately be estimated from past data (daily, weekly, or monthly stock and market index returns). The following type of equation called the market model is often used in the estimation:

$$S_t = \alpha + \beta M_t + e_t \tag{2}$$

where:

S_t = percentage return of stock for period t
M_t = percentage return of market for period t
β = beta ratio (to be estimated)
α = intercept (to be estimated)
e_t = random error term (to be minimized in estimation process)

The generalized form of Equation 2 is called the *market model*. Each stock's equation is called its *characteristic line*. A separate α and β can be estimated for each relevant stock. The resulting α forecasts the stock's return for a 0% market return, while β reflects the tendency of the stock's returns to vary with the market. A technique called "regression analysis" finds α and β estimates that explain the historical data as efficiently as possible. The regression of Equation 2 is illustrated graphically by a straight line through a scatter diagram of S_{it} and associated M_t values (Figure 5.8). The regression line estimated by ordinary least squares minimizes the squares of the distance of the data points to the regression line. The line's α is its intercept and β its slope coefficient.

Figure 5.8   Regression Line for Fitting α and β

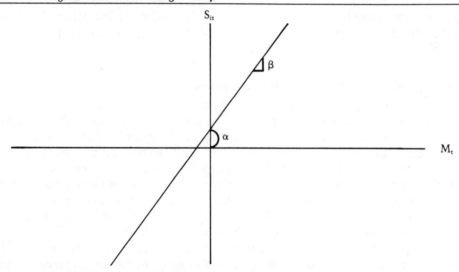

The Capital Asset Pricing Model

An alternative formulation of the security return/market return relationship, called the capital asset pricing model (CAPM), brings the riskfree return (R_{ft}) explicit into the model:

$$S_t = R_{ft} + \beta(M_t - R_{ft}) + e_t \qquad (4)$$

Thus, the CAPM intercept equals the riskfree return and the market return variable $(M_t - R_{ft})$ is measured in deviations from the riskfree rate since the expected value of e_t is zero:

$$E(S_t) = R_{ft} + \beta(M_t - R_{ft}) \tag{4a}$$

The market model and CAPM, while conceptually similar, do have some significant differences. CAPM may be derived precisely from theoretical specifications, while the market model includes the CAPM as a special case $\alpha = (1 - \beta) R_{ft}$. Because the more general market model is easier to work with and understand, we shall use it exclusively herein. The discussion could be recast in CAPM terms, however.

Market versus Nonmarket Risk

Return fluctuations peculiar to one security tend to be offset by unrelated return fluctuations of other securities. As a result, the substantial nonmarket component of most asset's risks can be largely eliminated through diversification. A component's market-related return fluctuations cannot be so simply diversified away, however. Thus portfolio-risk analysis is particularly concerned with market risk or β. Since a portfolio's β equals the components' weighted average β values, the only way to reduce a portfolio's β is to select lower-β securities. Moreover, since expected returns tend to vary inversely with β, reducing a portfolio's β tends to sacrifice potential return.

Four Approaches to Portfolio-Risk Estimation

Now that the simplification facilitated by the market model has been introduced, we can discuss four specific approaches to estimating portfolio risk. A classic 1952 article by Markowitz proposed an extensive analysis of each asset's estimated mean return and its variance and covariance with the other component returns.[2] Each possible two-security combination in a 100-stock-choice set would require 4,950 unique covariance estimates. Indeed, a 1,000-stock universe would call for 501,500 separate estimates. Since estimating thousands of such parameters is time-consuming, expensive, and likely to produce unreliable inputs, techniques requiring less information and effort have been developed.

Sharpe's single-index model[3] is much simpler than the full Markowitz model. Each portfolio asset's estimated α, β and corresponding characteristic line's goodness-of-fit (or R^2) are used to analyze each relevant portfolio's risk. For a 100-stock universe, the Markowitz model requires more than 5,000 estimates, while Sharpe's model needs only 300. Furthermore, the Sharpe estimates, being conditional forecasts (the model implies different return forecasts for each possible market return), may well be more meaningful than the absolute forecasts needed for the full-covariance model.

The multi-index model's complexity lies between that of the single-index

Sharpe model and the full-covariance Markowitz model. This model uses separate indexes for estimating the α and β values of related assets such as stocks in the same industry. Then a covariance matrix between the indexes is formed and used in the portfolio-risk computation. According to Cohen and Pogue, industry-index portfolio-risk estimates offer little improvement over the single-index model.[4] Farrell suggests, however, that improved multi-index model results are obtained by grouping stocks on the basis of such characteristics as growth, stability, and other factors.[5]

Sharpe's linear model,[6] the simplest of the four approaches, only requires α and β estimates. If each security represents only a small proportion of the portfolio (less than 5%, for example), the linear model is a close approximation of the single-index model and can easily be applied without a computer.[7] Table 5.3 summarizes the four approaches.

Table 5.3   Approaches to Portfolio-Risk Estimation

Markowitz's Full Model	Utilizes full complement of estimated returns, variances and covariances for each component
Sharp's Single-Index Model	Only requires α, β and R^2 for each component
Multi-Index Model	Uses separate indexes for groups of stocks to estimate their α and β values
Sharp Linear Model	Only requires α and β for each component

Price Impact of Market and Nonmarket Risk

Note that the linear model computes portfolio risks with only component α and β values. Since α values should average close to zero (and thus not affect the portfolio's return) and have no impact on portfolio risk, they can be largely ignored in portfolio work. Nonmarket risk, which is fully diversifiable, should be irrelevant to those who can diversify effectively. Accordingly, a well-diversified portfolio's risk should depend exclusively on its component's market risks (β values). If separating risk into market and nonmarket components and then ignoring the nonmarket portion is justified, an asset's risk would be fully reflected in its β. Thus, the risk premium contained in market discount rates should be based only on market risk (β). In other words, nonmarket risk should not affect asset prices.

CHOOSING AN EFFICIENT PORTFOLIO

Thus far we have seen that: (1) a security's total risk can be defined as the standard deviation (or variance) of its expected income stream; (2) risk can be broken down into market and nonmarket components; (3) β measures market risk; (4) a diversified portfolio's risk is largely a function of its component's β values; and (5) if most market participants can diversify effectively, nonmarket risk should not deserve a risk premium.

Assume that portfolios may be assembled from a group of risky securities; short-selling and borrowing are not allowed, and risks and expected returns (for any given market return) may be estimated from historical data. How should these data be used to assemble the most attractive portfolio? In principle, the expected returns and risks could be plotted for every possible combination of securities. Since the number of possible portfolio combinations is infinite, an efficient search requires some shortcuts.

The Market Portfolio

The so-called *market portfolio,* which represents each investment in the relevant universe of possible investments in proportion to its share of the value of that universe, offers a useful starting point. For example, the relevant investment universe might be divided as follows: Real estate 50%, stocks 25%, bonds 15%, other 10%. The market portfolio would then represent each category in these proportions. Moreover, within each category the proportions assignable to each specific asset would be so allocated. The market portfolio is the appropriate index to apply to the market model, and as such, has a β of precisely unity. Moreover, the market portfolio, which is fully diversified, contains no nonmarket risk. Finally, if securities have been accurately priced relative to their expected performances, the market portfolio will be "efficient" in the sense that all other portfolios will offer either a lower expected return, a higher risk or both. Figure 5.9 illustrates an efficient market portfolio in risk-return space. Portfolio M, the market portfolio, has a β of one and an expected return of *m*. All portfolios with lower β's also have lower expected returns while all portfolios with higher returns also have higher β's.

Figure 5.9   An Efficient Market Portfolio

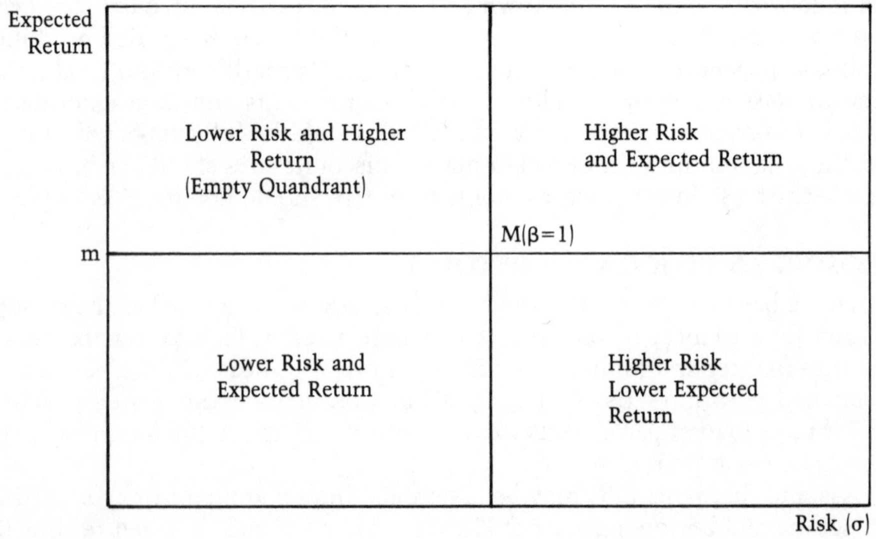

The Efficient Frontier

A given universe of assets contains many portfolios that are efficient in the sense that each offers the highest expected return for its risk. Mathematical procedures can identify all such efficient portfolios from any given set of assets. Figure 5.10 illustrates a typical set of efficient portfolios called the *efficient frontier*. All other portfolios are inefficient, since a more attractive risk/expected return tradeoff is available at the frontier. The concave (bowed downward) shape of the efficient frontier indicates that increasing risk increments must be sacrificed to gain additional expected return increments.

Figure 5.10   The Efficient Frontier (No Lending or Borrowing)

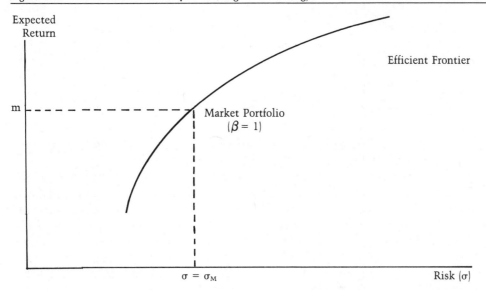

Choosing the Most Attractive Risk/Return Tradeoff

Each efficient portfolio offers the highest expected return for its risk level. Rational risk-averse investors might, depending on their degrees of risk aversion, legitimately choose any efficient portfolio. A very risk-averse investor would select a low-risk point; the less risk-averse would accept greater risk to achieve a higher expected return. The rational investor should choose a portfolio whose risk/expected return tradeoff equals his or her own willingness to trade off expected return for risk.

The Efficient Frontier with Lending

Thus far we have assumed that investors assemble portfolios by purchasing risky securities. Borrowing, selling short, and purchasing a riskfree asset have not been allowed. If one or more of these restrictions is relaxed, however, the efficient

Figure 5.11 The Efficient Frontier with Lending and Borrowing at the Risk-Free Rate

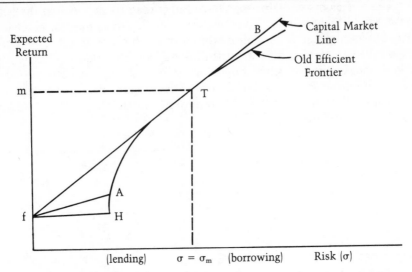

frontier takes on a different shape. The effect of lending risklessly (for example investing in riskless government bonds) is illustrated in Figure 5.11.

Asset F yields a riskless return f, which is below the expected market return m. A horizontal line from f to the efficient frontier (fH) contains portfolios that offer an equal expected return and higher risk than F. Clearly fH is superior to all portfolios below it. Still more attractive risk/return tradeoffs are possible with asset F, however. Riskfree return f has a zero covariance with all other returns. Thus, the risk of a portfolio containing F equals the weighted average risk of the risky components and its own zero-risk level. Similarly, the portfolio's expected return equals the weighted average of the expected returns of the risky and riskless components. In fact, the risk-expected return combinations of any portfolio that combines F with risky portfolios lie on a straight line between the two portfolios (fA). A derivation of these relationships can be found in more advanced textbooks. Only combinations of F and efficient portfolios (on the old efficient frontier) should be considered. A line from f to a tangency-point on the efficient frontier could be found by rotating a ray beginning at f. The risk/expected return combinations along that ray from f to the tangency-point are superior to those of any lines below it. Moreover, because fT is tangent to the efficient frontier, no line above fT intersects the efficient frontier.

The Efficient Frontier with Borrowing

Suppose we could borrow at rate f (for example margin borrowing at riskless rate) to invest in some efficient portfolio G. In effect, asset F is sold short and the proceeds invested in G. How does allowing such borrowing or short-selling affect the efficient frontier? Clearly only otherwise-efficient portfolios should be used. As with permitting riskless lending, the risks and expected returns of the combination portfolios equal a linear combination of the risks and expected returns of its components. With borrowing or short-selling, however, the weight on the risky component is greater than unity while the riskless-component's weight is negative. In fact, financing additional investments (at rate f) in a risky portfolio simply extends the line of risk/expected return combinations of F and the risky portfolio. Again, an infinite number of lines begin at f and pass through the efficient frontier. The one passing through the tangency point (fTB) reflects the most attractive available set of risk/expected return combinations. Accordingly, the efficient frontier, when lending and borrowing at the riskless rate are allowed, is formed by drawing a line from point f through the tangency-point T on what would have been the efficient frontier had lending and borrowing not been allowed.

The Capital Market Line

When all marketable assets are considered part of the choice set, the just-derived relationship (fTB) is called the *capital market line*. Given the assumptions used to derive it, the capital market line identifies the market's optimal risk/expected return combinations. Thus, one should invest in the tangency portfolio and F in the proportions (either positively or negatively) that produce the desired risk/ expected return tradeoff. Investors will maximize their expected returns by levering the tangency portfolio to the desired risk level and should, regardless of their risk preferences, hold risky assets in the proportions of the tangency portfolio. Only if the weights are the same as those of the market portfolio will the market clear. Indeed, asset prices would adjust so that investors would hold assets in proportion to their relative market values. If, for example, investors wished to hold too much (relative to supply) of some assets and too little of others, the prices of the former would be bid up and the latter bid down until the prices reached the level where the quantity demanded precisely equaled the quantity available (the market would clear). Indeed this is generally how markets work. Prices move up or down to bring supply and demand into balance. Therefore the market portfolio is the only sustainable tangency portfolio consistent with the above-stated assumptions.

The capital market line can be expressed in equation form as:

$$E(R_p) = W_f(f) + (1 - W_f) E(R_m) \tag{3}$$

where

$\quad E(R_p)$ = expected return on portfolio
$\quad W_f$ = percentage of portfolio invested in risk free asset
$\qquad\quad$ (negative if investor is a borrower)
$\quad f$ = riskfree return
$\quad E(R_m)$ = expected return of market

The above analysis allows us to divide the investment from the financing decision. Investors are assumed to invest in the market portfolio (the investment decision) and choose their desired risk level by levering (lending or borrowing) that portfolio to the desired risk/expected return level (the financing decision). Particularly risk-averse investors will choose risk/return tradeoffs lying on the lower portion of the capital market line. More risk-oriented investors will choose a financing level which offers a higher expected return coupled with a higher risk. This division of the investment and financing decision is called the *separation theorem*.

In practical terms, the separation theorem or two-mutual-fund theorem implies that investors can achieve optimal efficient diversification with just two assets. Thus an investor who can buy into a government-only fund (money market mutual fund that buys only T-bills) and a well-diversified common stock mutual fund (including the right to buy on margin) can construct a series of risk/expected-return-efficient portfolios from varying combinations of these two assets. In theory, any risk/expected return combination on the efficient frontier can be reached with these two assets. Since the two assets already allow one to reach the efficient frontier, no other portfolio (even one constructed from a larger number of securities) can produce a more attractive risk-expected return tradeoff.

The Security Market Line

The security market line takes the analysis a bit further. If individual assets are priced efficiently, their expected returns should be linearly related to their market risk or beta (Figure 5.12). Since the expected return for a zero-beta asset is the

Figure 5.12 The Security Market Line

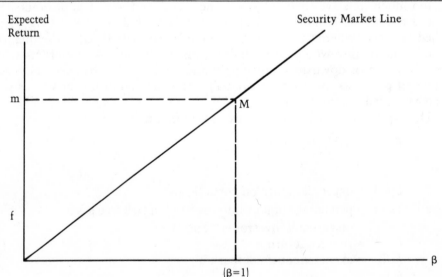

riskfree rate, the equation of the security market line may be expressed as:

$$E(R_i) = f + \beta_i[E(R_m) - f]$$

where:

$E(R_i)$ = expected return of asset i
f = riskfree return
$E(R_m)$ = expected return of market

Assumptions

Let us now state explicitly the assumptions that were used to derive the capital market and security market line relationships:

(1) **Market-equivalent portfolios are easy to assemble.** Market-equivalent portfolios may be assembled, bought, and sold as easily as any other investment asset. That is, all investment assets are available in very small units; transaction costs (commissions, bid-asked spreads) can be ignored; no individual investor or group of investors can appreciably affect market prices; and no institutional or psychological barriers retard the free flow of investable funds.

(2) **Investors seek to maximize expected return and minimize its standard deviation.** Investors are rational risk-averters who want to maximize their expected return and minimize its standard deviation. Moreover, they are unconcerned with any other properties of expected returns.

(3) **Differential tax-treatments are in the aggregate irrelevant to investment decisions.**

(4) **Investors have identical asset/return expectations.** Investors have access to the same body of public information and analyze it in identical fashions so that they have equivalent asset/return expectations.

(5) **Investors may borrow and lend without limit at the riskless rate.**

If the market behaves at the margin as assumed, the model will precisely explain its actions. This is too much to ask, however. All models are built on assumptions that depart from reality, even at the margin. The best test of a model's value is not its assumptions' realism, but its predictions' reliability.[9] A model whose assumptions are severely violated may still yield useful predictions. For example, Kepler's model of planetary motion which (heroically) assumes all masses are concentrated in a single point and that the universe is frictionless, accurately explains planetary motions. In like manner, the security market line might accurately explain asset prices in spite of its unrealistic assumptions. Thus we need to examine the empirical evidence relating to the model's predictions.

SUMMARY AND CONCLUSIONS

Total risk is defined as the standard deviation of the expected return distribution. Portfolio risk depends crucially on the covariance (covariability between component returns). The market model offers a simplified way of analyzing portfolio risk and expected return. This model assumes that market risk (return variability with the market portfolio) justifies a risk premium, while nonmarket risk (return variability unrelated to market-return variability) is fully diversifiable and therefore irrelevant to asset pricing. The efficient frontier of portfolios each offer the highest expected return for a given risk level. When borrowing and lending at the riskfree rate are allowed, the efficient frontier becomes a line from the riskfree rate through the tangency position at the market portfolio and beyond. This *capital market line* implies that investors should obtain the highest risk-adjusted expected return for their risk-preferences by levering the market portfolio to the desired risk/expected return level. The *security market line* implies that expected asset returns are a linear function of β. The real world should behave as the model implies if at the margin investors act according to the assumptions used to develop this framework.

REVIEW QUESTIONS

1. How is an individual asset's risk generally defined?
2. State and explain the two-asset portfolio risk formula. When is risk zero and at a maximum? How does the covariance enter the picture?
3. Discuss the N-asset portfolio risk case.
4. Why is portfolio risk normally analyzed in a simpler fashion than the full variance/covariance approach?
5. Discuss the three simplified approaches to estimating portfolio risk.
6. Compare the market model and capital asset pricing model.
7. Define and discuss market and non-market risk.
8. Discuss the concept of risk, indicating how it may be measured and what role it plays in the investment selection process.
9. What is a beta? What is an alpha?
10. Define the efficient frontier, first without and then with a riskless lending and borrowing rate.
11. What is the capital market line and what does it imply?

REVIEW PROBLEMS

1. Compute the expected return and standard deviation for the following:
   a) Equally probable returns of: -5%, 0%, 5%, 10%
   b) 10% chance of a 0% return
      15% chance of a 5% return
      25% chance of a 10% return

      25% chance of a 15% return
      15% chance of a 20% return
      10% chance of a 25% return
   c) 100% chance of a 10% return
Now plot the risk and expected return for each investment.

2. Compute the portfolio variance for the following:
   a) $X = Y = .5$
      $\sigma_x^2 = \sigma_y^2 = .05$
      $C_{xy} = 0$
   b) $X = .3 \quad Y = .7$
      $\sigma_x^2 = .03 \quad \sigma_y^2 = .05$
      $C_{xy} = .8$
   c) $X = .1 \quad Y = .9$
      $\sigma_x^2 = .08 \quad \sigma_y^2 = .06$
      $C_{xy} = -.05$

3. Compute the covariance estimate for the following observations:
   $(X_1, Y_1) = (.03, .05)$
   $(X_2, Y_2) = (.05, .03)$
   $(X_3, Y_3) = (-.01, -.05)$
   $(X_4, Y_4) = (.10, .08)$
   $(X_5, Y_5) = (0, 0)$
   $(X_6, Y_6) = (.01, -.01)$

4. Use the following data to plot a scatter diagram and draw a characteristic line (using a straightedge to center a line through the dots). (Market
   return, stock return)
   (9%, 9%)
   (3%, 2%)
   (5%, 6%)
   (-2%, 0%)
   (-5%,-8%)
   (12%,14%)
   (-7%,-9%)
   From your line-of-sight estimate of the characteristic line estimate the
   α and β.

5. For three separate stocks having respectively αs and βs of .01, .7; .05,
   1.1; and $-.02$, 1.5 compute their expected returns for market returns of
   .05, .10, .15, $-.05$ and $-.10$.

6. Plot an efficient frontier for the following portfolio risk, expected return
   combinations (.03, .10); (.05, .11); (.06, .14); (.07, .16). Now assume a
   riskless rate of .08 and extend the frontier.

NOTES

1. W. Sharpe, *Investments*, Prentice-Hall, Englewood Cliffs, N.J, 1978, pp. 80–82.

2. H. Markowitz, "Portfolio Selection," *Journal of Finance*, March 1952, pp. 77–91.

3. W. Sharpe, "A Simplified Model for Portfolio Analysis," *Management Science*, January 1963, pp. 277–293.

4. K. Cohen and J. Pogue, "A Compound Evaluation of Alternative Portfolio Selection Models," *Journal of Business*, April 1967, pp. 166–193; B. Wallingford, "A Sum and Comparison of Portfolio Selection Models," *Journal of Financial and Quantitative Analysis*, June 1967, pp. 85–106.

5. J. Farrell, "Analysis of Covariance of Returns to Determine Homogeneous Stock Groupings," *Journal of Business*, April 1974, pp. 186–207.

6. W. Sharpe, "A Linear Programming Algorithm for Mutual Fund Portfolio Selecting," *Management Science*, March 1967, pp. 499–510.

7. J. Williamson, *Investments: New Analytic Techniques*, Praeger, New York, 1971, p. 114.

8. E. Elton and M. Gruber, *Modern Portfolio Theory and Investment Analysis*, Wiley, New York, 1981, pp. 70–103.

9. M. Friedman, *Essays in Positive Economics*, University of Chicago Press, Chicago, 1953.

6 Empirical Tests of Modern Portfolio Theory

The Sharp-Lintner Capital Asset Pricing Model[1] is an elegant theoretical framework derivable from a short list of admittedly heroic assumptions. Since a theory is best judged by the accuracy of its predictions,[2] this chapter considers three interesting implications of modern portfolio theory: (1) no trading method can consistently generate risk-adjusted returns that exceed those implied by the model (market efficiency). While a capital market theory could be derived for inefficient markets, the resulting market portfolio would not necessarily be efficient and nonmarket risk would not necessarily be irrelevant. (2) Nonmarket risk does not affect the discount rate applied to risky assets. (3) Returns tend to vary linearly (the security market line) with (nondiversifiable) market risk. Thus most returns should approximate their corresponding market-model simulated estimates.

Types of Investment Analysis

Meaningful discussion of the efficient market hypothesis, requires some understanding of fundamental and technical analysis. Fundamental analysts forecast returns by analyzing the factors affecting the worth of expected future income streams. Thus fundamental security analysts assess a firm's earnings and dividend prospects by evaluating its sales, costs and capital requirements. Fundamental commodity analysts base their futures forecasts on the relevant demand and supply factors. Fundamental real estate analysts generate price and rental-value expectations from future construction costs and demand-growth estimates.

Technical analysts, in contrast, concentrate on past price and volume relationships (narrow form) or technical market indicators (broad form). Both types claim to be able to identify evolving investor sentiment, but neither possesses a very sound theoretical base. Technical analysts argue, however, that results are what ultimately matter. In other words, if witchcraft produces attractive returns, one should follow the advice of talented witches. A wealth of available data facilitates technical analysis' application to the security and commodity markets while the lack of such data has prevented any extensive application to most nonsecurity investment types such as real estate or collectibles.

THE EFFICIENT MARKET HYPOTHESIS

Market efficiency, or as it was once known, the "random walk hypothesis," questions the usefulness of technical analysis and in some versions fundamental analysis as well. Many natural phenomena follow a random walk or what the physical sciences call Brownian motion. A drunk in the middle of a large field who is as likely to move in one direction as another follows a random walk. Similarly, the next price change of a randomly moving stock is unrelated to past price behavior. Obviously if prices move randomly, the repeating price patterns that technical analysts claim to observe do not exist.

Price movements need not be precisely random for past price data to be useless. Marginally associated relations between past and future price changes may be either too small or unreliable to generate gross returns that consistently exceed transaction costs. Indeed commissions, search costs, and bid/ask spreads would generally offset any expected price change of less than two or three percent.

The Weak Forms of the Efficient Market Hypothesis

The random walk or weak form of the efficient market hypothesis implies that past price behavior cannot be used to outperform the market on a risk-adjusted basis. Weak form adherents argue that if prices moved in dependable patterns, alert market participants' reactions would rapidly destroy any resulting profit opportunities. Thus if a price pattern forecasts a rise, some market participants might react before most investors could take advantage of the move. Indeed, premature actions by some traders would often destroy the full pattern. The weak form of the efficient market hypothesis may also be extended to imply that future movements in market prices are unrelated to the past performance of any technical market indicators. This as yet unnamed form of hypothesis might be called the "semiweak form."

The Semistrong Form of the Efficient Market Hypothesis

The weak and semiweak forms of the efficient market hypothesis imply that narrow and broadly based technical analysis are useless, but neither form addresses the effectiveness of fundamental analysis. The semistrong form, in constrast, asserts that the market quickly and correctly evaluates all relevant publicly available technical and fundamental information. Thus market prices should accurately reflect the relevant public information.

The efficient market hypothesis' semistrong form sees only two ways for risk-adjusted returns to exceed those of the market. Investments may be affected by unexpected developments. Thus some (lucky) investors may do the right things for the wrong reasons while other (unlucky) investors suffer from unexpectedly unfavorable developments. Second, nonpublic knowledge may facilitate superior analysis. For example, a corporate insider, lender, supplier, or a friend of such individuals may know and be able to trade profitably (but illegally) on relevant knowledge prior to its public release.

The Strong Form of the Efficient Market Hypothesis

According to the strong form of the efficient market hypothesis, the market anticipates inside information so effectively that those with such knowledge are rarely able to react quickly enough to use it profitably. Table 6.1 summarizes the various forms of the efficient market hypothesis.

Table 6.1   Forms of the Efficient Market Hypothesis

Weak Form	Future returns are unrelated to past return patterns (Charting does not work)
Semiweak Form	Future market moves are unrelated to current or past economic and noneconomic data series (Technical market indicators are useless)
Semistrong Form	Future returns are unrelated to any analysis restricted to public data (Fundamental analysis does not work)
Strong Form	Future returns are unrelated to any analysis based on public or nonpublic data (Inside information is useless)

Outperforming the Market

Now that the various forms of market efficiency have been introduced, we can turn to the empirical tests of them. Both technical and fundamental analysis are judged by the returns they produce as compared to those of the market. To be considered successful, a trading rule must generate returns that in the aggregate exceed the corresponding periods' market returns. In order to compare returns on a risk-adjusted basis, the results of technical and fundamental analysis must be tested with real world data. A market index such as the New York Stock Exchange Composite (a weighted average of all NYSE listings) is ordinarily used to represent the market. If the technique to be tested generates a portfolio whose average market risk differs appreciably from the market's—produces a beta appreciably different from one—the market-return benchmark should be adjusted accordingly.

Weak- and Semiweak-Form Tests

Technical market influences have been explored empirically in two basic ways. First, the relationship between past and future price changes have been tested for statistical dependence (relatedness) or independence (unrelatedness). Second, filter rules analogous to technical trading rules have been tested on historical data. If past price patterns help forecast future price change, past and future price changes should be related, and technically inspired filter rules should help identify profitable trading opportunities.

Some studies have examined serial correlation (relationship between past and present price changes); others have investigated runs of prices. A run is an uninterrupted series of price increases or price decreases. Many studies such as Granger and Morgenstern's exhaustive application of spectral analysis have consistently failed to find any important dependences (relation in price changes).[2] Thus past price patterns do not appear to forecast future price movements. Chartists contend that these statistical tests, which look largely for linear relations, are much too crude to capture their subtleties. They assert that their "craft" is as much art as science, heavily dependent on such unquantifiables as judgment, interpretation and experience. Even so, most nonlinear dependencies that they claim to observe should show up in the tests as linear approximations, but chartists have offered no convincing evidence that this occurs.

A second set of tests has explored technical analysis using so-called filter rules. Filter rules mechanically identify supposed buy and sell situations. One such rule flashes a buy signal whenever a stock increases by $x\%$. After an $x\%$ decline from a subsequent high, a sell signal emerges. Thus a 5% filter would signal "buy" whenever a stock rose 5% from the preceding high. A second type of filter rule, Levy's so-called relative strength criterion, identifies stocks that have recently outperformed the market as buys and those that have underperformed as sells. For example, a stock rising 10% when the market rose only 5% has outperformed the market and thereby exhibited relative strength. Filters attempt to reflect the momentum/resistance-level factors that technical analysts consider important. When transactions costs are included, none has been shown to outperform a buy-and-hold strategy.[3] On the other hand, the available evidence on the semiweak form suggests that some market indicators may have some predictive value.[4]

Semistrong- and Strong-Form Tests

While general semistrong- and strong-form tests are virtually impossible to perform, various subhypotheses have been examined. Many studies claim to have found specific types of fundamental analysis useful. Some suggest that stocks with low price/earnings ratios tend to outperform the market.[5] One now-classic study found that the market reacts rather efficiently[6] to stock splits: prior to the announcement, stocks tended to outperform the market, but after the announcement performance was random. Some academicians suggest that since institutional investors, with all their professional expertise, rarely outperform the market on a risk-adjusted basis, individual investors are unlikely to do better.[7] Others claim to see enough market imperfections to permit talented investment analysts to outperform the market.[8] Even if the market eventually evaluates public information accurately, the nimble investor/analyst may be able to take advantage of lags in the price-adjustment process. With so much conflicting evidence, the extent of semistrong-form efficiency remains controversial.

Most strong-form supporters would concede that insider information is on rare occasions useful. However, several studies have found insider trading to be generally quite profitable: insiders tend to earn above-market returns when they buy and sell their own companies' stock. Indeed those who derive signals from the SEC's insider trading reports tend to outperform the market.[9]

The Emerging Consensus on the Market Efficiency Debate

While some continue to hold extreme positions, the market efficiency debate's dimensions have narrowed appreciably. Few academicians who have examined the issue now believe that the market is strong-form efficient or always semistrong-form efficient. On the other hand, virtually all serious finance scholars agree that the weak form is essentially correct. The principal disagreements relate to the importance, extent, and causes of the semistrong-form imperfections. Thus far, however, little or no theoretical work has been done on portfolio models that allow for market imperfections. Such imperfections are largely viewed as departures or exceptions to normal behavior.

Causes of Persistent Market Imperfections

Why, if the market contains many talented, rational investors, do imperfections persist? One informed speculation suggests that since a market imperfection exists whenever any group of investors can consistently earn above-market risk-adjusted returns, imperfections have numerous causes. Brokers, investment advisors and the financial press continually tug investors in many directions. Most investors have difficulty discriminating between valid and invalid analysis—why else do so many newsletters prosper in spite of the random and often conflicting nature of their advice? Eliminating market imperfections requires a sufficient reaction to an observed mispricing to force prices back in line. If the transactions of investors acting on valid mispricing evidence are swamped by trading based on incorrect analysis, observable mispricings will persist. For example, investors who erroneously project past earnings growth into the future may pay too much for "growth stocks," allowing others to outperform the market by avoiding or shorting such issues (contrary opinion). Subsequent growth rates that differ from those expected should lead to price "corrections." Such scenarios could occur frequently enough for some to profit from their ability to "predict" the resulting price moves. Mispricings will continue as long as trading by those who recognize them is insufficient to bid prices back into line. Investors who do recognize such misvaluing tendencies, of course, have an incentive to keep quiet.

Modern portfolio theory generally assumes that market prices are formed by a homogeneous group of investors analyzing the same sources of information in identical fashions. While market efficiency does not require perfect homogeneity of investor expectations, marginal investors must behave as if they accurately analyze all relevant public information and are unaffected (or identically affected) by such matters as tax status, costs of trading, risk orientation, borrowing power, liquidity preference, familiarity with local markets, total available funds, etc. In the real world, however, those positioned to profit may have insufficient resources to eliminate some mispricings. Since investment analysts and periodicals concentrate on the larger, better-known firms, many smaller firms' security prices may depart from the values that a careful analysis would yield.[10] Because such firms generally trade in localized markets, few investors are positioned to observe the mispricings.

Other types of mispricings can be exploited only by those who purchase control. An investor acquiring control of a firm worth more dead than alive could liquidate its assets for more than the firm's current market value. Takeover efforts, however, tend to bid up prices and provoke vigorous defensive efforts by those whose interests are threatened. Thus investors with the necessary resources may frequently have inadequate incentives to eliminate the mispricing. Still other imperfections (arbitrage opportunities) may require very quick and low-cost access to several markets. Only if enough investors are able to take advantage of such imperfections will their actions right the price imbalances.

Market efficiency assumes that investors rationally pursue the highest available risk-adjusted returns. In a broader context, however, investors are not merely maximizers of risk-adjusted returns, but complex individuals who may choose to maximize their total welfares by devoting more resources to leisure time, education, or other non-market activities. As a result, some apparent market imperfections may be overlooked or ignored by those best positioned to take advantage of them.

Three major reasons emerge, then, as contributors to a persistently imperfect market:

- Difficulty in discriminating between valid evidence and useless advice
- Differing investor circumstances: tax status, trading costs, risk orientation, borrowing power, liquidity preferences, wealth level, familarity with local markets
- Investors maximizing a broad range of personal resources rather than just their portfolios' risk-adjusted return.

THE RISK PREMIUM ON NONMARKET RISK

Portfolio theory implies that risk premiums should be solely determined by each asset's market risk. A number of studies have found, however, that risk premiums are also related to nonmarket risk. This apparent contradiction has spawned a number of hypotheses. A high relative cost for effective diversification, for example, would encourage many investors to diversify incompletely.[11] Since nonmarket risk contributes to such investors' overall portfolio risks, they might consider it relevant.

Practical Diversification

Risk-neutral investors maximize expected returns without regard to risk. While few investors are truly risk-neutral, those with adequate financial protection (insurance, retirement benefits, appreciable low-risk investments, etc.) may view their remaining portfolio through approximately risk-neutral eyes. Thus some investors may put part of their wealth in less-risky assets such as mutual funds, preferred stocks, or convertible bonds, and manage the remainder for maximum nominal return.

Investors with long time-horizons may try to maximize their portfolio values 10 or 20 years hence while being relatively unconcerned with their interim values.[12] They may start with small positions in one or two stocks and periodically expand their portfolios' size and diversity. Such investors might initially opt for high-risk, high-expected-return securities in the hopes that the "winners" will eventually make the strategy pay off. Such an approach, however, risks what is called "gambler's ruin": a streak of bad luck may wipe out the investor's limited resources even though the chosen strategy might pay off with unlimited resources.

Investors who are neither risk neutral nor on long time-horizons may either diversify their own portfolios or let mutual funds or other institutional investors do the job. Efficient portfolio diversification requires purchasing a number of different securities. While commission and search costs may not be justified by the resulting risk reduction for a small portfolio, a rather modest number of stocks may yield substantial diversification. Evans and Archer concluded: "Much of the unsystematic variation (of returns) is reduced by the time the eighth security is added to a portfolio."[13]

Other researchers also found that effective bond-diversification requires few issues.[14] On the other hand, Frankfurter argues that even efficiently diversified portfolios will contain a substantial amount of nonmarket risk,[15] and Tole shows that when portfolios are assembled nonrandomly, for example, by following brokerage firm recommendations, eliminating most nonmarket risk requires substantially more than eight to ten stocks.[16]

Effective diversification is not easy or automatic. While risk declines, administrative costs increase appreciably with portfolio size. Furthermore, portfolios whose components are likely to be affected by similar factors (GM and Ford) may not be effectively diversified. While all firms are affected by economic fluctuations, industry-specific and firm-specific impacts are averaged over the securities represented in the portfolio. Beedles, Joy and Ruland report that conglomerate firms tend to offer greater diversification value than single-industry firms.[17]

Diversification difficulty for some might not by itself account for nonmarket risk's price effect. If small investors' aversion to nonmarket risk caused some securities to be underpriced (vis a vis their market risk), large investors could exploit that aversion by constructing well-diversified portfolios of such securities. Indeed the market might well contain enough such large investors to keep security prices in line with their market risks. Since, however, the empirical evidence points to a nonmarket risk effect, we need to search further.

Additional Reasons for a Nonmarket Risk Effect

Miller and Scholes found that various possible sources of estimation error were unlikely to account for nonmarket risk's price effect.[18] Their results did suggest that inefficiently estimated betas and a positive correlation between estimated betas and nonmarket risk may account for nonmarket risk's apparent price impact.

Black, Jensen, and Scholes reasoned that if investors cannot borrow and lend at the same riskless rate, effective diversification of nonmarket risk may be impossible.[19] Non-normal potential return distributions provide yet another possible explanation. The mean and variance completely specify the shape of normal distributions. Nonsymmetric or skewed distributions, in contrast, may have identical means and variances and yet have very different shapes.

Portfolio theory generally assumes that expected returns are normally distributed. When expected returns are not normally distributed, the model's implications may not apply. For example, distributions A and B in Figure 6.1 have the same mean and standard deviation, yet offer markedly different return possibilities. Distribution A's returns have some probability of being very large, coupled with almost no chance of being more than one standard deviation below the mean. Distribution B's return could well be more than one standard deviation below but is unlikely to be even one standard deviation above its mean. The mode of B exceeds the mode of A, however. While individual preferences vary,

Figure 6.1   Skew Distributions

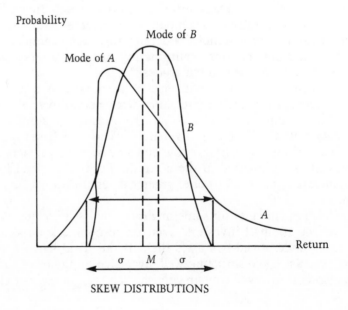

SKEW DISTRIBUTIONS

most investors seem to prefer some possibility of a very large gain.[20] McEnally found that stocks with highly variable returns also tended to have highly skewed returns that on average were lower than those of less risky stocks.[21]

An investor preference for skewness may cause very high-risk stocks to be priced to offer a lower expected return than less risky stocks. Moreover, Duvall and Quinn found that to achieve their desired skewness level, investors must hold too few securities to be fully diversified.[22]

Real-world distributions may differ from the normal form in several respects. All normal distributions have the same probability associated with each distance (scaled in standard deviations) from the mean: approximately two-thirds within one standard deviation; 95% within two; and 99% within three. Compared with the normal, leptokurtic distributions are relatively more dense in the peaks and the tails and relatively less dense in the intermediate zones. Platakurtic distribution reverses that characteristic.

The longer the holding period, the more nearly actual returns tend to approach the normal.[23] The normal is a reasonably accurate working hypothesis for the monthly returns of both portfolios and individual securities. Daily returns tend to be somewhat leptokurtic and skewed, however.[24]

Assessment: Nonmarket Risk's Price-Impact

Most empirical studies find that nonmarket risk affects security prices. A variety of explanations have been offered, each of which may contribute to the effect: (1) Evans and Archer's results notwithstanding, most investors' portfolios contain significant amounts of nonmarket risk; (2) errors in estimated betas may be correlated with nonmarket risk, thereby contributing to an apparent empirical relationship; (3) investors who are unable to lend and borrow risklessly may find inefficient portfolios the most effective way of achieving their desired risk levels; (4) non-normal expected return distributions coupled with an investor preference for skewness may further compound the difficulty of assembling efficient portfolios and thus increase the relevance of nonmarket risk.

ESTIMATED BETAS AND SUBSEQUENT PERFORMANCE

A security's performance can be simulated by adding its estimated α to the product of its estimated β and the corresponding period's market return. The accuracy of individual security return simulations is related to both random nonmarket influences and the appropriateness of the simulation process. A sufficiently large sample should, however, largely eliminate individual random influences and reveal any biases and inefficiencies in the β estimation process. Thus let us consider some properties of estimated βs.

A large number of investment firms sell their beta-estimate lists to investors and portfolio managers. *Value Line* for example, publishes estimates for the more than 1700 stocks it analyzes. Similarly Barr Rosenberg, the "guru" of modern portfolio theory, and Bill Fouse of the Wells Fargo Bank, are two among a number in the same business. Betas are normally estimated by regressions of historical security returns on market returns.

Most beta estimates are relatively close to unity. Less than 10% have values greater than two, and less than 2% have negative values.[25] Betas estimated from historical data are generally similar to risk estimates based on fundamental analysis (financial ratios, etc.).[26] While individual beta estimates tend to be relatively unreliable, portfolio betas are much more dependable.[27] Thus Farrar found that mutual fund portfolios are usually near both the efficient frontier and the risk/return tradeoff indicated in their prospectuses.[28] Growth-oriented funds had high risk-efficient portfolios, while more conservative funds were less risky and had lower expected returns. Such funds tended to perform as their betas implied. Moreover, hypothetically constructed portfolios generally performed close to their predicted levels. Apparently errors inherent in individual company beta estimates are largely offsetting.

The inconsistency between actual returns and those implied by individually estimated betas could be due to instability in the underlying betas[29] and/or errors in the estimation process. A number of different phenomena, including beta estimates, exhibit a tendency for extreme-value estimates to move toward the grand mean (regression toward the mean): individual high and low first-month batting averages, for example, generally move toward the overall average. Note, however, that such phenomena describe the behavior of extreme values, not the entire population. Thus batting averages and betas near the mean tend to move randomly away from the mean with sufficient frequency to repopulate the extremes as the prior-period extremes move in. Several estimation techniques called Stein estimators take account of the regression-toward-the-mean phenomena.[30]

Blume suggests that the β for next year = .35 + .68 (average unadjusted β estimate from last three years).[31] Vasicek advocated using historically estimated beta estimation errors compared with the variability of the estimate to adjust the values.[32] Extensive study of the three beta estimation techniques (unadjusted, Blume adjustment and Vasicek adjustment) show the Blume and Vasicek approaches to be clearly superior both in explaining future betas and future security return correlation matrices.[33] On the other hand, beta adjustments appear unnecessary for large portfolios.[34] Further efforts to generate more reliable beta estimates include either substituting or combining fundamental factors with historically estimated betas.[35] While such efforts may have improved the resulting beta estimates, the best estimates are still not especially reliable.[36] This undependability is probably due both to instability in the underlying betas and to other factors.

The Market Index

The proxy chosen for the market index may also introduce estimation error. The theoretical model assumes that betas are estimated with an index reflecting all capital assets in proportion to their relative contribution to investor wealth. Practitioners, however, usually employ the NYSE composite or an even less-broad index. The NYSE index is an acceptable measure of U.S. stock movements as NYSE-listed securities are a large part of the total U.S. stock market and NYSE, AMEX, regional and OTC stocks tend to move together. Option, warrant, and convertible prices also tend to vary with the NYSE index. Its acceptability declines, however, as the relevant universe expands to include U.S. debt securities, real estate, futures contracts, foreign securities, collectibles, precious metals, etc. While many of these assets are influenced by the U.S. equity market, the correlations are relatively weak for most and essentially zero for others.[37] Since non-U.S. stock investments represent an appreciable part of U.S. investors' total wealth,[38] excluding them from the market index may bias the resulting beta estimates. Indexes of varying quality do exist for debt securities, foreign securities, commodities, some collector's items, real estate and non-NYSE equities.[39] While Ibbotson and Siegel come reasonably close, no one has yet dared to make all the arbitrary assumptions needed to assemble a complete broad-based market index.[40] Stambaugh has, however, investigated the impact of an expanded index for U.S. assets. His results were relatively insensitive to the inclusion or exclusion of a particular asset class.[41]

Figure 6.2   Risk and Portfolio Size

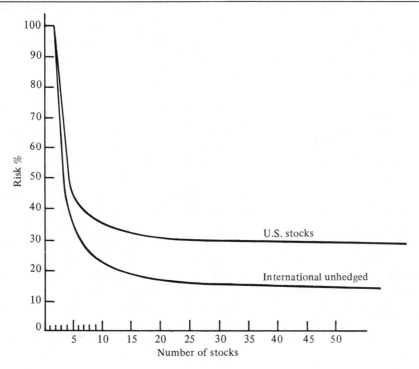

International Diversification

Different countries' stock markets appear to have a large component of independent variability that can be used to reduce the impact of the home country's market cycle.[42] Hill and Schneeweis found that an international portfolio of debt and equity securities offers even greater diversification gains.[43] The risk-reduction potential of international diversification is illustrated in Figure 6.2.

Investors can diversify internationally by purchasing shares in an international mutual fund, a U.S.-based multinational company, a foreign company's stock, or American Depository Receipts (ADRs) representing ownership of such securities. Approximately 550 foreign firms are tradable as ADRs. Table 6.2 lists the principal foreign firms with stocks traded in the U.S. U.S.-based multinational firms' securities continue to fluctuate with other domestic firms, but may offer slightly higher risk-adjusted returns.[44] While brokerage houses now pay closer attention to foreign investment opportunities and foreign business news, data on most foreign firms are still not readily available or easy to interpret. Furthermore, offshore mutual funds are less closely regulated than United States funds, and investing in foreign securities exposes one to exchange-rate risk.

Diversification Across Types of Investments

Buying international assets is not the only way of diversifying stock market risk. Robichek, Cohn, and Pringle find that nonsecurity assets such as commodities and real estate have considerable diversification appeal.[45] McEnally suggests that government bonds can be effectively used to diversify a stock portfolio.[46] Thus international stocks and bonds and domestic non-stock assets may all be useful diversification vehicles.

Implications of Modern Portfolio Theory Tests

The preceding discussion implies that: (1) the markets are not as efficient as assumed; (2) nonmarket risk may affect prices; and (3) market-model-based relative return forecasts are unreliable. In view of these shortcomings, why is so much time devoted to modern portfolio theory?

First, just as the Mandarins of China clung tenaciously to their complicated many-character alphabet, the Mandarins of portfolio theory have a huge human capital investment they prefer to preserve.

Second, for all its shortcomings, modern portfolio theory's only meaningful competitor is the arbitrage pricing model. It expands the number of return-generating factors from traditional portfolio theory's one (the market index) to several (e.g., market index, interest sensitivity, business cycle sensitivity, etc.).[47] This alternative model does not, however, seem much better able to explain security returns than modern portfolio theory.[48]

Third, modern portfolio theory offers a useful point of departure. Economists

Table 6.2   Overseas Opportunities Over Here

Not all these 74 foreign securities listed on U.S. exchanges are blue chip stocks, but some might prove to be good investments. About half of the firms have dollar-converted sales over $1 billion, so they can't be considered fly-by-night. Currency fluctuations offer additional leverage, but this can work both ways.

Company*	Industry	ADRs in $US (mil)	Recent price	Revenues (mil)†	Earnings per share†	P/E	Indicated yield	Country
Broken Hill Proprie-tary	energy	$2,365	7 1/8	$ 4,635	$1.00	7	2.5%	Australia
Santos	energy	891	5 7/8	57	0.16	37	0.7	Australia
Minerals & Resources	copper mining	2,228	14	1,445	0.61	23	1.5	Bermuda
Novo Industries A/S	med research, drugs	1,159	59	317	2.44	24	0.5	Denmark
Bank Leumi le-Israel	banking	832	1 1/8	7,331	0.05	24	0.0	Israel
Teva Pharmaceutical Inds	drugs	707	6	47	0.04	150	0.3	Israel
IDB Bankholding	bank	396	1 1/8	NA	0.14	8	0.0	Israel
Elscint	med instruments	362‡	22 3/4	103	0.92	25	0.0	Israel
Elron Electronic Inds	computers	135	17 1/4	77	0.64	27	0.0	Israel
Scitex	computer graphics	126‡	25 3/4	51	0.81	32	0.0	Israel
Matsushita Electric Indl	electrical equip	9,685	62 1/2	14,771	4.23	15	0.6	Japan
Hitachi	electrical equip	9,142	33 1/8	15,799	1.87	18	0.8	Japan
NEC	electrical equip	4,760	22 1/2	4,760	0.54	42	0.5	Japan
Nissan Motor	automotive	4,011	6 1/8	15,289	0.61	10	0.7	Japan
Sony	electrical equip	3,605‡	15 5/8	4,446	0.53	29	1.0	Japan
Ito-Yokado	retailer	3,393	19 3/4	3,817	1.01	20	1.3%	Japan
Fuji Photo Film	photo equip	3,117	16 7/8	2,554	1.36	12	0.1	Japan
Honda Motor	automotive	2,956‡	34 3/8	8,926	3.57	10	1.0	Japan
Tokio Marine & Fire Ins	insurance	2,706	99 1/2	2,322	5.72	17	0.9	Japan
TDK	electrical equip	2,407	44	1,292	2.30	19	0.6	Japan
Canon	photo equip	2,145	31 1/8	2,418	1.36	23	0.6	Japan
Kyocera	electrical equip	2,090	50	638	1.57	32	0.6	Japan
Kubota	farm machinery	1,862	28	2,406	0.84	33	1.9	Japan
Mitsui & Co	wholesaler	1,506	30 7/8	68,184	0.36	86	0.9	Japan
Pioneer Electronic	electronic equip	1,354	23	1,255	−0.43	NM	0.7	Japan
Kirin Brewery	consumer goods	1,144	17 3/4	4,306	1.22	15	1.3	Japan
Shiseido	consumer goods	833	20	1,362	1.14	18	0.8	Japan
Makita Electric Works	electrical equip	452	24 3/8	278	1.35	18	1.2	Japan
Daiei	retailer	127	4 7/8	5,440	−0.11	NM	1.8	Japan
Telefonos de Mexico	utility	233	3/4	NA	0.44	2	28.3	Mexico
Tubos de Acero de Mexico	steel piping	105	1 7/8	276	0.62	3	0.0	Mexico
Royal Dutch Petro-leum	energy	11,224‡	41 7/8	43,866	8.08	5	6.9	Netherlands
Philips Lamp	electrical equip	2,935‡	16 1/4	16,100	0.91	18	3.5	Netherlands
Unilever	consumer goods	2,225‡	69 1/2	23,134	10.03	7	6.3	Netherlands
KLM Royal Dutch Airlines	airline	197‡	49 3/8	1,698	−0.14	NM	0.0	Netherlands

Table 6.2   Continued

Company*	Industry	ADRs in $US (mil)	Recent price	Revenues (mil)†	Earnings per share†	P/E	Indicated yield	Country
Advanced Semicond Matls	electrical equip	164	28 1/4	55	0.30	94	0.0	Netherlands
Atlas Cons Mng & Dev B	copper mining	293‡	3 1/2	222	−0.24	NM	0.0	Philippines
Benguet Cl B	gold mining	110‡	9	233	0.59	15	0.0	Philippines
Anglo American S Africa	gold mining	4,859	21 1/2	953	2.64	8	4.0	S Africa
Driefontein Consolidated	gold mining	3,455	33 7/8	830	3.15	11	5.5	S Africa
De Beers Consol Mines	precious metals	3,125	8 5/8	1,468	1.14	8	3.2	S Africa
Anglo Amer Gold Inv	invests gold mining	2,640	120 1/4	187	8.02	15	5.6	S Africa
Gold Fields S Africa	gold mining	2,300	141	163	7.26	19	2.7	S Africa
Vaal Reefs Explor & Mng	gold mining	2,266	119 1/4	993	14.63	8	6.3	S Africa
Western Deep Levels	gold mining	1,513	60 1/2	527	7.27	8	5.3	S Africa
Kloof Gold Mining	gold mining	1,504	49 3/4	305	4.02	12	4.5	S Africa
President Steyn GM	gold mining	816	56	273	6.19	9	7.3	S Africa
Western Holdings	gold mining	778	54 1/4	478	9.50	6	9.8	S Africa
Buffelsfontein GM	gold mining	718	65 1/4	331	7.23	9	6.5	S Africa
President Brand GM	gold mining	695	49 1/2	278	6.98	7	8.7	S Africa
Free State Geduld Mines	gold mining	532	51	280	11.06	5	6.4	S Africa
Palabora Mining	copper mining	481	17	232	0.92	18	1.8	S Africa
St Helena Gold Mines	gold mining	436	45 1/4	275	10.58	4	7.8	S Africa
Blyvooruitzicht GM	gold mining	405	16 7/8	211	2.70	6	9.5	S Africa
Highveld Steel & Vanadium	steel prod	374	5 1/2	325	0.57	10	5.0	S Africa
Welkom Gold Mining	gold mining	372	14 1/8	NA	NA	NA	9.3	S Africa
LM Ericsson Tel	telecom	2,002	61 1/4	2,972	2.39	26	1.3	Sweden
AB Fortia	drugs	1,535	79 3/4	264	1.73	46	0.2	Sweden
Biogen	drugs	306‡	16 1/2	20	−0.31	NM	0.0	Switzerland
British Petroleum	energy	10,900‡	24	51,353	2.18	11	6.5	UK
Shell Transport & Trdg	energy	9,115‡	33	29,244	4.29	8	5.8	UK
Glaxo Holding	drugs	4,599	13 3/8	1,533	0.48	28	0.9	UK
Imperial Chemical Inds	chemicals	4,381	7 3/8	12,880	0.48	15	4.5	UK
Beecham Group	drugs	3,803	5 7/8	2,701	0.36	16	2.4	UK
B.A.T Industries	multicompany	3,078	9 1/8	11,300	2.07	4	5.0	UK
Plessey	telecom	2,670	110	1,665	5.26	21	1.6	UK
Imperial Group	consumer goods	1,386	2	7,145	0.25	8	6.0	UK
Bowater	paper, paper prods	533	3 3/8	2,302	0.28	12	4.1	UK
Rank Organisation	office equip	486	2 3/8	1,038	0.20	12	5.5	UK
Courtaulds	chemicals	410	1 1/2	2,966	0.18	8	3.5	UK
Fisons	agrichemical	373	10	526	0.58	17	2.1	UK

Table 6.2   Continued

Company*	Industry	ADRs in $US (mil)	Recent price	Revenues (mil)†	Earnings per share†	P/E	Indicated yield	Country
Tricentrol	energy	259	6 3/4	151	0.51	13	4.4	UK
Dunlop Holdings	tire & rubber	163	1 1/4	2,705	−0.33	NM	0.0	UK
Dresdner Bank	bank	1,164	68 1/2	NA	NA	NA	1.7	Germany

*All figures are converted into U.S. dollars as of the latest reporting period. Market value, recent price and earnings per share reflect ADR or U.S. shares. †Latest available figures. ‡Actual shares, not ADRs. NA: Not available. NM: Not meaningful. Source: *William O'Neil & Co.; Forbes; International Investors*

Source: P. Bornstein, "Over There," *Forbes*, July 4, 1983. Reprinted by permission of *Forbes* Magazine, July 4, 1983, © Forbes Inc., 1983.

study the competitive model in a world nearly devoid of truly competitive markets just as most physicists are quite familiar with the properties of a frictionless world and perfect gas. These idealized models yield interesting insights and testable predictions. A particular non-idealized effect may be observed in the difference between the model forecast and the actual event. Finance theorists and empiricists are expected to know modern portfolio theory's implications even though the real world often behaves differently.

Fourth, while the model's predictions are not uniformly accurate, some of the evidence is approximately consistent and the theory's insights may be useful. Indeed: (1) Individual inefficiencies notwithstanding, the market appears to be relatively efficient. (2) While market prices may take nonmarket risk into account, the rational investor may be able to profit from the observed price effects. (3) Some market model relative-return forecast inaccuracies may result from inadequate estimation techniques and data errors rather than model shortcomings. Thus until a demonstrably superior theory is devised, modern portfolio theory will continue to provide the foundation for the study of finance.

SUMMARY AND CONCLUSIONS

We have explored predictions of modern portfolio theory dealing with market efficiency, nonmarket risk, and the properties of estimated betas. Much of the evidence conflicts with the theory's predictions: various inefficiencies are observed; nonmarket risk does appear to affect prices and the market risk/expected return relationship for securities is not demonstrably linear. A number of real-world violations of the model's assumptions were considered. Too few may be appropriately situated to eliminate some mispricings; different investors borrow and lend at differing rates; return distributions may be nonnormal; some investors may be concerned with skewness; most empirical work with the market portfolio utilizes an index that excludes everything but U.S. equity securities; and imperfections such as taxes and transactions costs influence market prices.

In spite of the drawbacks, modern portfolio theory continues to be studied and utilized. Most researchers have a substantial human capital stake in the theory; the current model seems appreciably ahead of whatever is in second place; it offers a useful point of departure; and it fits some aspects of the real world reasonably well.

REVIEW QUESTIONS

1. Compare the two principal types of investment analysis.
2. Discuss the four forms of the efficient market hypothesis and summarize the relevant evidence on each.
3. Discuss the possible causes of persisting market imperfections.
4. Compare the theoretical price impact of nonmarket risk with real world experience. Discuss the possible explanations for the apparent inconsistency.
5. Discuss the practical approaches to diversification.
6. What does portfolio theory usually assume for return distributions? How are actual returns distributed? How do investors seem to react to skewness?
7. How are betas estimated? What problems arise? How may betas be adjusted? What problems remain?
8. What is the impact of international diversification? How might a portfolio be diversified internationally and what are the advantages and disadvantages?
9. Summarize the problems of traditional portfolio theory.
10. Why, in spite of its shortcomings, is standard portfolio theory still studied?

REVIEW PROBLEMS

1. Interview three brokers and three serious investors on market efficiency. What form or forms of investment analysis do they utilize? What has been their experience? Ask them for counter examples of market efficiency if they assert the market is inefficient. Write a report.
2. Survey the investors you know. Ask each about his or her tax status, cost of trading, risk orientation, borrowing power, liquidity preference, familiarity with local markets, and portfolio size. Also ask each how long they have been investors and what their average return (preferably relative to the market) has been. Look for patterns. For example, do the more risk-oriented investors report higher returns?
3. Construct a list of five investment opportunities. Describe each so that a reader would conclude that they have equivalent expected returns and market-risk levels. Give one positive skewness and one negative skewness while the others have symmetrical distributions. Now ask a sample of investors (or potential investors) to choose the investments that

they find most and least attractive. Write a report.

4. Plot monthly returns on ten stocks for six months. Obtain beta estimates for these stocks and compute their expected returns with the market index (use NYSE composite). Correlate expected returns with actual returns. Repeat the process using the Dow Jones Industrial Average and S&P 500. Write a report.

5. Identify five major foreign companies and study their investment attractiveness. Explore how one would go about buying their stocks and following their performances. Repeat the process for five U.S. mutual funds that invest in foreign stocks. Write a report.

6. Construct a list of five hypothetical companies and describe their return possibilities. They should correspond to the following types:

   a) low risk, low expected return
   b) moderate risk, moderate expected return
   c) high risk, high expected return
   d) moderate risk, moderate expected return, positive skewness
   e) high risk, high expected return, positive skewness

Now choose ten people at random and ask them to rank the investment opportunities. Write a report.

NOTES

1. W. Sharp, "Capital Asset Prices: A Theory of Market Equilibrium Under Conditions of Risk," *Journal of Finance*, September 1965, pp. 425–442; John Lintner, "The Valuation of Risk Assets and The Selection of Risky Investments in Stock Portfolios and Capital Budgets," *Review of Economics and Statistics*, February 1965, pp. 13–37.

2. W. Granger and O. Morgenstern, *Predictability of Stock Market Prices*, Heath, Lexington, MA, 1970; E. Fama, "Random Walks in Stock Market Prices," *Financial Analysts Journal*, September/October 1965, pp. 55–59.

3. R. Levy, "Random Walks: Reality or Myth," *Financial Analysts Journal*, November/December 1967; E. Fama and M. Blume, "Filter Rules and Stock Market Trading," *Journal of Business*, January 1966, pp. 226–241; M. Jensen and G. Benington, "Random Walks and Technical Theories: Some Additional Evidence," *Journal of Finance*, May 1970, pp. 469–482.

4. B. Branch, "The Predictive Power of Market Indicators," *Journal of Financial and Quantitative Analysis*, June 1976, pp. 269–285; R. Daigler and B. Fielitz," A Multiple Discriminate Analysis of Technical Indicators on the New York Stock Exchange," *Journal of Financial Research*, Fall 1981, pp. 169–182; M. Landingham, "The Day Trader: Some Additional Evidence," *Journal of Financial and Quantitative Analysis*, June 1980, pp. 341–356.

5. S. Basu, "The Investment Performance of Common Stocks in Relation to Their Price Earnings Ratios: A Test of the Efficient Market Hypothesis," *Journal of Finance*, June 1977, pp. 665–682; H. Oppenheimer and G. Schlarbaum, "Investing with Ben Grahan, A Test of the Efficient Market Hypothesis," *Journal of Financial and Quantitative Analysis*, September 1981, pp. 341–360; G. Smith, "A Simple Model for Estimating Intrinsic Value," *Journal of Portfolio Management*, Summer 1982, pp. 46–49.

6. E. Fama, L. Fisher, M. Jensen and R. Roll, "The Adjustment of Stock Prices to New Information," *International Economic Review*, February 1969, pp. 1–21.

7. M. Jensen, "The Performance of Mutual Funds in the Period 1954–64," *Journal of Finance*, May 1968, pp. 389–416.

8. K. Welling, "Stock Picker Extraordinary," *Barron's*, July 27, 1981, pp. 4, 5, 16; K. Welling, "Maria's Midas Touch," *Barron's*, October 25, 1982, pp. 14, 24, 34, 35.

9. J. Finnerty, "Insiders and Market Efficiency," *Journal of Finance*, September 1976, pp. 1141–1148; J. Jaffe, "Special Information and Insider Trading," *Journal of Business*, July 1974, pp. 410–428.

10. A. Arbel and P. Strebel, "The Neglected Small Firm Effect," *Financial Review*, November 1982, pp. 201–218.

11. B. Douglas, *Risk in the Equity Markets: An Empirical Appraisal of Market Efficiency*, University Microfilm, Ann Arbor, Michigan, 1968; B. Gouldy, "Evidence of Nonmarket Risk Premiums in Common Stock Returns," *Journal of Financial Research*, Fall 1980, pp. 243–260.

12. W. Lloyd and R. Haney, "Time Diversification: Surest Route to Lower Risk," *Journal of Portfolio Management*, Spring 1980, pp. 5–9; W. Lloyd and N. Modani, "Stocks, Bonds, Bills and Time Diversification," *Journal of Portfolio Management*, Spring 1983, pp. 7–10.

13. Evans and S. Archer, "Diversification and the Reduction of Dispersion," *The Journal of Finance*, December 1968, pp. 761–767.

14. R. McEnally and C. Boardman, "Aspects of Corporate Bond Portfolio Diversification," *Journal of Financial Research*, Spring 1979, pp. 27–36.

15. G. Frankfurter, "Efficient Portfolios and Non-Systematic Risks," *Financial Review*, Fall 1981, pp. 1–11.

16. T. Tole, "You Can't Diversify Without Diversifying," *Journal of Portfolio Management*, Winter 1982, pp. 5–11.

17. W. Beedles, O. Joy and W. Ruland, "Conglomeration and Diversification," *Financial Review*, Winter 1981, pp. 1–13.

18. M. Miller and M. Scholes, "Rates of Return in Relation to Risk: A Reexamination of Some Recent Findings" in M. Jensen (ed.), *Studies in the Theory of Capital Markets*, Praeger, New York, 1972.

19. F. Black, M. Jensen, and M. Scholes, "The Capital Asset Pricing Model: Some Empirical Tests," in M. Jensen (ed.) *Studies in the Theory of Capital Markets*, Praeger, New York, 1972, pp. 79–121.

20. F. Mosteller and P. Nogee, "An Experimental Measure of Utility," *Journal of Political Economy*, October 1959, pp. 371–404; F. Arditti, "Risk and the Required Return of Equity," *Journal of Finance*, March 1967, pp. 19–36; F. Arditti and H. Levy, "Portfolio Efficiency Analysis Three Moments: The Multiperiod Case," *Journal of Finance*, June 1979, pp. 797–809; R. Duvall and J. Quinn, "Skewness Preference in Stable Markets," *Journal of Financial Research*, Fall 1981, pp. 249–264.

21. R. McEnally, "A Note on the Return Behavior of High Risk Common Stocks," *Journal of Finance*, March 1974, pp. 199–202.

22. Duvall and Quinn, *op. cit.*; A. Kane, "Skewness Preference and Portfolio Choice" *Journal of Financial and Quantitative Analysis*, March 1982, pp. 15–25; R. Sears, and G. Trennepohl, "Diversification and Skewness in Option Portfolios, *Journal of Financial Research*, Fall 1983, pp. 199–213.

23. E. Fama, *Foundations of Finance*, Basic Books, 1976.

24. J. Rozelle and B. Fielitz, "Skewness in Common Stock Returns," *Financial Review*, Fall 1980, pp. 1–23.

25. R. A. Levy, "On the Short-Term Stationarity of Beta Coefficients," *Financial Analysts Journal*, November/December 1971, pp. 55–62.

26. M. Scholes, "The Association Between Market Determined and Accounting Determined Risk Measures," *The Accounting Review*, October 1970, pp. 654–682; B. Rosenberg and W. McKibben, "The Prediction of Systematic and Specific Risk in Common Stocks," *Journal of Financial and Quantitative Analysis*, March 1973, pp. 317–333; and R. Melicher, "Financial Factors Which Influence Beta Variations Within a Homogeneous Industry Environment," *Journal of Financial and Quantitative Analysis*, March 1974, pp. 231–241.

27. S. Chen, "Beta Nonstationarity, Portfolio Residual Risk and Diversification," *Journal of Financial and Quantitative Analysis*, March 1981, pp. 95–112; D. Harrington, "Whose Beta is Best?," *Financial Analysts Journal*, July/August 1983, pp. 67–73; M. Schneller, "Are Better Betas Worth the Trouble?," *Financial Analysts Journal*, July/August 1983, pp. 74–77; G. Hawawini and A. Vora "Investment Horizon, Diversification, and the Efficiency of Alternative Beta Forecasts," *Journal of Financial Research*, Spring 1982, pp. 1–16; S. Chen and J. Martin, "Beta Nonstationarity and Pure Extra-Market Covariance Efforts as Portfolio Risk," *Journal of Financial Research*, Fall 1980, pp. 267–282.

28. D. Farrar, *The Investment Decision Under Uncertainty*, Prentice-Hall, Englewood Cliffs, N.J., 1965; T. Bos and P. Newbold, "An Empirical Investigation of the Possibility of Stochastic Systematic Risk in the Market Model," *Journal of Business*, January 1984, pp. 35–42.

29. E. Scott and S. Brown, "Biased Estimaters and Unstable Betas," *Journal of Finance*, March 1980, pp. 49–56; S. Sunder, "Stationarity of Market Risk: Random Coefficients Tests for Individual Stocks," *Journal of Finance*, September 1980, pp. 883–896; B. McDonald, "Beta Non-Stationarity: An Empirical Test of Stochastic Forms," *Financial Review*, May 1983, pp. 175–183.

30. B. Efron and S. Morris, "Stein's Paradox in Statistics," *Scientific American*, May 1977, pp. 119–127; J. Lavely, G. Wakefield and B. Barrett, "Toward Enhancing Beta Estimates," *Journal of Portfolio Management*, Summer 1980, pp. 43–46.

31. M. E. Blume, "On the Assessment of Risk," *Journal of Finance*, March 1971, pp. 1–10.

32. O. Vasicek, "A Note on Using Cross-Sectional Information in Bayesian Estimation of Security Betas," *Journal of Finance*, December 1973, pp. 1233–1239.

33. R. Klemkosky and J. Martin, "The Effect of Market Risk on Portfolio Diversification," *Journal of Finance*, March 1975, pp. 147–153; E. Elton, M. Gruber, and T. Urich, "Are Betas Best?," *Journal of Finance*, December 1978, pp. 1375–1384.

34. Hawawini and Vora, *op. cit*; Schneller, *op. cit.*

35. W. Beaver, P. Kettler and M. Scholes, "The Association Between Market Determined and Accounting, Determined Risk Measures," *The Accounting Review*, October 1970, pp. 654–682; B. Rosenberg and J. Buy, "Predictor of Beta From Investment Fundamentals," *Financial Analysts Journal*, May/June 1976, pp. 60–72.

36. Wallace, *op. cit*; Harrington, *op. cit.*

37. A. Robichek, R. Cohn, and J. Pringle, "Returns of Alternative Investment Media and Implications for Portfolio Construction," *Journal of Business*, July 1972, pp. 427–443.

38. R. Ibbotson, R. Carr and A. Robinson, "International Equity and Bond Returns," *Financial Analysts Journal*, July/August 1982, pp. 61–84.

39. G. Mahon, "The Southby Index: What is it?," *Barron's*, Feb. 15, 1982, pp. 59–62; J. Hoag, "Towards Indices of Real Estate Value and Return," *Journal of Finance*, May 1980, pp. 569–580.

40. R. Ibbotson and L. Siegel, "The World Market Wealth Portfolio," *Journal of Portfolio Management*, Winter 1983, pp. 5–17

41. R. Stambaugh, "On the Exclusion of Assets from Tests of the Two-Parameter Models," *Journal of Financial Economics*, November 1982, pp. 237–269.

42. T. Agnon, "The Relation Among Equity Markets: A Study of Share Price Movements in the United States, United Kingdom, Germany, and Japan," *Journal of Finance*, September 1972, pp. 839–856; B. Solnik, "The International Pricing of Risk: An Empirical Investigation of the World Capital Market Structure," *Journal of Finance*, May 1974, pp. 365–378; D. Lessard, "International Portfolio Diversification: A Multivariate Analysis for a Group of Latin American Countries," *Journal of Finance*, June 1973, pp. 619–634; B. Solnik, "Why Not Diversify Internationally?," *Financial Analysts Journal*, July/August 1974, pp. 48–59; D. Lessard, "World, National and Industry Factors in Equity Returns," *Journal of Finance*, May 1974, pp. 379–391; M. Joy, D. Pastor, F. Reilly and S. Martin, "Co-Movements of International Equity Markets," *Financial Review*, 1976, pp. 1–20; J. McDonald, "French Mutual Fund Performance: Evaluation of Internationally-Diversified Portfolios," *Journal of Finance*, December

1973, pp. 1161–1180; R. Maldonado and A. Saunders, "International Portfolio Diversification and the Future-Tempored Stability of International Stock Market Relationships, 1957–1978," *Financial Management*, Autumn 1981, pp. 54–63; B. Horn, "International Investing Strategies," *American Association of Individual Investors Journal*, November 1983, pp. 11–23; G. Philipputos, A. Christofi and P. Christofi, "The Inter-Temporal Stability of International Stock Market Relationships: Another View," *Financial Management*, Winter 1983, pp. 63–69.

43. J. Hill and T. Schneeweis, "Efficient International Diversification of Equities and Fixed Income Securities," *Journal of Financial Research*, Winter 1983, pp. 333–344; M. Adler, "Global Fixed-Income Portfolio Management," *Financial Analysts Journal*, September/October 1983, pp. 41.

44. B. Jacquillat and B. Solnik, "Multinationals are Poor Tools for Diversification," *Journal of Portfolio Management*, Winter 1978, pp. 8–11. H. Brewer, "Investor Benefits from Corporate International Diversification", *Journal of Financial and Quantitative Analysis*, March 1981, pp. 113–126; Errunza and L. Senbet, "The Effect of International Operations on the Market Value of The Firm: Theory and Evidence," *Journal of Finance*, May 1981, pp. 401–418.

45. Robichek, *et. al., op. cit.*

46. R. McEnally, "Some Portfolio-Relevant Risk Characteristics of Long-Term Marketable Securities," *Journal of Financial and Quantitative Analysis*, September 1973, pp. 565–585; W. Sharpe, "Bonds Versus Stocks: Some Lessons from Capital Market Theory," *Financial Analysts Journal*, November/December 1973, pp. 74–80.

47. S. Ross, "The Arbitrage Theory of Capital Asset Pricing," *Journal of Economic Theory*, 1976, pp. 341–360; R. Rall and S. Ross, "An Empirical Investigation of the Arbitrage Pricing Theory," December 1980, pp. 1073–1104; H. Fogler, K. John and J. Tipton, "Three Factors, Interest Rate Differentials and Stock Groups," *Journal of Finance*, May 1981, pp. 323–335; G. Oldfield and R. Rogalski, "Treasury Bill Factors and Common Stock Returns," *Journal of Finance*, May 1981, pp. 337–350.

48. M. Reinganum, "The Arbitrage Pricing Theory: Some Empirical Results," *Journal of Finance*, May 1981, pp. 313–322. (also see others in session); J. Shanken, "The Arbitrage Pricing Theory: Is it Testable?," *Journal of Finance*, December 1982, pp. 1129–1140; R. Folger, "Common Sense on CAPM, APT and Correlated Residuals," *Journal of Portfolio Management*, Summer 1982, pp. 20–29; N. Chen, "Some Empirical Tests of the Theory of Arbitrage Pricing," *Journal of Finance*, December 1983, pp. 1393–1414; P. Dhrymes, I. Friend and B. Gultskin, "A Critical Reexamination of the Empirical Evidence on the Arbitrage Pricing Theory," *Journal of Finance*, June 1984, pp. 323–346; R. Roll and S. Ross, "A Critical Reexamination of the Empirical Evidence on the Arbitrage Pricing Theory: A Reply," *Journal of Finance*, June 1984, pp. 347–350.

Section III:
Fundamental Analysis:
Security Selection

Fundamental analysis is the principal method by which investors evaluate and select investments. This section explores various approaches to fundamental analysis/stock selection that is practical and potentially usable. In a sense this section and the one which follows (Investment Timing) are the heart of the book. The following case illustrates many of the issues that are encountered in fundamental analysis.

Demonstrating Your Skills as an Investment Analyst

You are given a golden opportunity but you must show that you are worthy of it. A small midwestern brokerage firm is looking for a junior securities analyst. While their starting salaries are not at New York levels, they are willing to consider applicants who have had no direct securities market experience. They are looking for a person with a keen mind and sufficient background to begin producing meaningful analyses immediately. Because you are one of the top finance majors in this year's graduating class, the placement director has recommended you.

The brokerage firm has asked each applicant to demonstrate their analytical skills by completing the following assignment: You are to choose two firms from the 30 companies of the Dow Jones Industrial Average and two smaller (AMEX or OTC) issues to analyze. For each selected company you must write an extensive report on its investment potential. In each case conduct relevant economy, industry, and firm analyses. Examine each firm's financial statements for its strengths and weaknesses, hidden assets, accounting gimmicks and future potential. Obtain as much background material as you can to back up your analysis. Assemble a file of your sources. Come up with an investment recommendation on each company.

The section covers the topics that are needed to complete such an assignment. Chapter 7 takes up traditional methods of the fundamentalists, beginning with economic analysis. Then industry analysis is explored with particular attention devoted to assessing the developmental stage. Most of the chapter, however, deals with firm analysis. While scale economics, competitive position, and management quality are each considered, the analysis of financial strengths and weaknesses is stressed. Chapter 8 explores accounting discretion and the problems caused by its abuse. Examples of misleading accounting are discussed along with methods for spotting accounting gimmickry. Chapter 9 considers a variety of operational approaches to fundamental analysis: *Forbes* lists, low PE stocks, small and neglected firms, R&D-intensive firms, takeover candidates, bankruptcy stocks, contrary opinion, specialized advisory services, and management-oriented firms. This is followed by a discussion of PE ratio models. Chapter 10 explores investment-information sources. Company-issued reports, business- and investor-oriented periodicals, systematic coverage of companies, and investor-oriented computer data and manipulative systems are all discussed.

7 Traditional Approaches to Fundamental Analysis

The theory supporting expected-income-stream-based valuations is unimpeachable. Since, however, the required input estimates are generally unreliable, most practical fundamental analysis deals with more qualitative factors. While any type of investment analysis can generate explicit income-stream forecasts, most analysts do not go that far.

Fundamental analysis is traditionally divided into three subcategories: (1) economic analysis, (2) industry analysis, and (3) firm analysis. Economic analysis seeks to evaluate the current economic setting and its effect on industry and firm fundamentals. Industry analysis assesses the outlook for particular industries, while firm analysis examines a firm's relative strengths and weaknesses within its industry or industries.

These three subcategories correspond to the three principal influences on stock performances. Clearly each is important. According to Brown and Ball, 30 to 40% of a firm's annual earnings variability can be ascribed to economy-wide influences.[1] Another 10 to 15% result from industry factors. This leaves about half of the variability to be accounted for by firm-specific factors. Similarly, the stock market's aggregate moves appear to account for between a third and a half of an individual stock's returns; industry factors account for about 10%.[2] Thus in terms of both firm profits and stock returns (dividends plus price changes), market/economy and firm-specific factors are the dominant influences; industry factors account for only around 10% of the variability.

This chapter examines the three traditional categories of fundamental analysis, and how each relates to investment selection. The relevance of these techniques to market price and the efficient market hypothesis is then explored.

ECONOMIC ANALYSIS

Publicly held firms make up a large part of the economy. Profit rates, a major determinant of share prices, are closely tied to the nation's economic health. When the economy is depressed (a "recession") most firms operate well below their capacities. Companies can lay off workers, reduce raw material orders, work down inventories and reduce expansion and modernization spending but are unlikely in the short run to scrap fixed plant and equipment and can do little to reduce property taxes and interest payments. As output declines, these so-called fixed costs absorb a larger proportion of revenues, thereby squeezing profits. In the 1982 recession, John Deere's sales fell by 14% while its profits declined by 97%. At the same time many of its competitors (International Harvester, Allis Chalmers, Massey Ferguson) were losing money and in Harvester's case threatened with bankruptcy. Table 7.1 illustrates the general tendency for profits to drop more than economic activity in a recession.

Table 7.1   Percentage Change Economic Activity for Postwar Recessions

Recession	Change in Civilian Nonfarm Employment	Change in Personal Consumption Expenditures	Change in Profits
1948–49	−.66%	+.01%	−18.4%
1953–54	−2.47	+3.16	−1.8
1957–58	−1.91	+1.27	−22.3
1960–61	−.96	−.64	−12.2
1970–71	+.08	+8.27	−11.4
1973–75	+.71	+12.60	−34.2
1979–80	−.83	+6.38	−17.8
1981–82	−1.40	+7.05	−24.3

Source: Economic data obtained from the *Economic Report of the President* for various years.

During these recessions personal consumption generally increased, employment dropped modestly, while profits fell appreciably. Rapidly growing GNP (Gross National Product, a measure of the nation's output of final goods and services), in contrast, leads to above-average employment, sales and profit increases.

While investors may fare better in booms than recessions, the relationships are complex. The economy's primary stock price impact relates to its effect on expected income streams. Firms' dividend decisions tend to reflect long-term (not annual) earnings trends. Investors do, however, expect earnings increases to lead to higher dividends eventually. Thus an earnings increase is still a favorable sign even if the dividend-response is slow. Profitably employed retained earnings should produce still higher earnings and eventually lead to both increased dividends and a higher stock price. Figure 7.1 illustrates these linkages.

Relations Between the Stock Market and the Economic Outlook

Since economic activity affects company sales, profits and dividends, the investment community pays close attention to the business cycle. According to conventional Wall Street wisdom, stock values reflect the economy's expected status six months hence. Thus the economy and stock market often move together, but just before a turning point they may move in opposite directions. At still other times the market may incorrectly forecast business behavior and

Figure 7.1   Links Between the Stock Market and the Economy

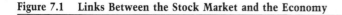
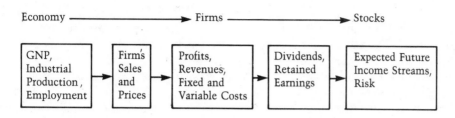

move perversely until its mistake is realized. Moreover the market sometimes responds to emotional influences that are largely unrelated to any change in the economic outlook. For example unfavorable news such as the fall of France in 1940, President Eisenhower's heart attack in 1955, the Cambodian invasion in 1970, the Watergate disclosures of 1973–74, the energy crises of 1974 and 1978, and the Iranian hostage crisis of 1980 were each a shock to the stock market. Such noneconomic influences are, however, superimposed on the basic stock market/economy relationship.

Forecasting Economic Performance

While accurate business cycle forecasts might well facilitate profitable investment decisions, only economic forecasts that are superior to the market's (six months ahead) view offer any real advantage. Thus an ability to foresee a business downturn one year in advance might afford six months' prior notice of a market move. Accurately forecasting economic behavior is very difficult, however. Indeed the market itself would probably anticipate the economic outlook by more than the traditionally assumed six months if more reliable forecasts were available.

The various methods of predicting economic activity are taken up in Chapter 11 (the first of three chapters on market timing). Assuming one can construct or obtain a usable forecast of the economic outlook, it should be employed to analyze how the industries and firms of interest are likely to be affected. That is, one should analyze past economy/industry/firm relationships to determine how sensitive particular investments are to such matters as economic activity, interest rates, inflation, etc. Then one's economic forecast should be employed to assess the investment's likely profit/dividend performance. Finally, this estimated performance can be compared with the market's view as reflected in its price. One should, however, always bear in mind that investment values are relative. Thus an economic outlook that is quite favorable for a particular firm only makes the firm's stock an attractive investment if its price is not inflated. Similarly, a very poor economic outlook may so depress the market that many stocks are underpriced relative to their potentials.

INDUSTRY ANALYSIS

Economic analysis assesses the general environment in which firms operate. Industry analysis, in contrast, examines the specific environment. One might begin a search for attractive investments by either evaluating the component firms of a selected industry or analyzing a particular firm first and then its industry and competitors. With either scenario both firm and industry analysis are undertaken. What follows assumes the process begins with industry analysis.

Before proceeding very far we ought to establish industry analysis' relevance to investors. The evidence is rather clear on one point: individual industries have experienced very different investment returns. Latane and Tuttle's extensive study of industry returns found an average market value increase of 500% over 1950–67. The least successful industry (brewing) actually declined while the most successful (office and business equipment) exhibited a 4,000% gain.[4] Thus, over specific periods, some industries show much higher returns than others. Within particular industries, however, the performance of individual firms may vary widely.

Their independent movements notwithstanding, attractively performing industries contain a disproportionate number of profitable investments.[6] Therefore we would like to know how to identify the industries that will show the highest future returns. One could select industries with strong recent records. Projecting past industry performance, however, involves uncertainties similar to those of extrapolating past earnings growth.[7] Past growth may imply some momentum but also establishes a higher base. The central issue is whether past growth reflects the industry's stage of development or isolated circumstances. Thus identifying an industry's development stage may help assess its growth prospects.

Stages of Industry Development

Industries typically pass through several developmental stages (Figure 7.2). Initially many new firms enter (startup stage) and growth is rapid. Then a shakeout reduces firm numbers (consolidation stage). After the adjustment, growth slows to that of the economy (mature stage). Finally, new industries grow at the existing industry's expense (declining stage). Predicting evolution from one stage to another is not easy. In fact, some industries follow different schemes from the normal one outlined above. For example, the solid waste disposal industry experienced modest performance until the ecology movement brought it to life. In spite of the difficulties, industry prospects need to be assessed. A firm moving from one stage to another usually experiences substantial stock price volatility. For example, firms and industries introducing new products or concepts (startup stage) will eventually see growth slow (mature stage) to the level of replacement demand: automobiles in the 1920s; black and white TV in the 1950s; bowling equipment in the early 1960s; color TV in the mid-1960s; fast food restaurants (McDonalds); retailing concepts (Levitz Furniture); rest homes, mobile homes, campers and

Figure 7.2   The Life Cycle of an Industry

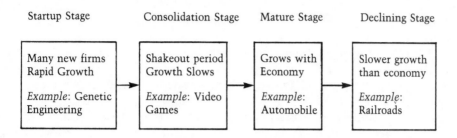

motor homes, and camping equipment in the early 1970s; and gambling stocks in the early 1980s. Future candidates include personal computers, proprietary hospitals and genetic engineering. Rapid growth should never be projected beyond a reasonable saturation point! Stock prices usually suffer when the market realizes that growth is slowing.

While past industry growth offers little guide to the future, several studies found not only that individual industries exhibited rather different risk levels but that their risks were relatively stable over time.[8]

Industry Analysis: Assessment

We could discuss industry analysis in much greater detail. Ideally one would like to be able to forecast future levels of industry sales, costs, and profitabilities. Relevant governmental policies should be assessed. Competing, complementary, supplier, and customer industries should all be considered. While relatively little is known about how to perform such analysis effectively, only industry analysis that is superior to the market's assessment is helpful.

As with economic analysis, one should bear in mind the relative nature of the process. While an industry's prospects need to be evaluated, the most attractive industries to invest in are not necessarily the ones with the brightest prospects. Rather one seeks investments with greater potentials than the market recognizes. Thus an industry with bleak prospects may contain attractive investments if the market is even more pessimistic than is justified by the true outlook.

FIRM ANALYSIS

Once a potentially attractive (for investment) industry has been identified, the firms within that industry need to be evaluated. Three important characteristics are the firm's competitive position, management quality, and financial soundness. Each relates to how successful a firm is likely to be within its industry or industries.

Competitive Position

While somewhat more difficult to evaluate than its financial strengths and weaknesses, the firm's competitive position is an important performance determinant. How able is the firm to withstand competitive pressures? How vigorous are its rivals? What is the government's attitude?

A firm's ability to compete within its industry depends on how its resources compare to those of its rivals. Scale economies in production, distribution, and advertising generally give larger firms an advantage.[9] On the other hand, control problems increase with size. U.S. Steel, for example, has since its inception been described as a lumbering dinosaur too large for effective control.[10] Antitrust vulnerability is yet another disadvantage of size. Every competitive move of high-market-share firms such as Kodak, IBM, Xerox, General Motors, and AT&T risks antitrust action. While mere size does not constitute an offense, a firm with a very large percentage of its market has difficulty avoiding illegal actions. Kodak, for example, has sought to avoid antitrust suits by sharing new-product technology with its competitors. Similarly, IBM's chairman ordered his salespeople not to solicit RCA customers after Sperry Rand bought out RCA's customer base.[11] Antitrust pressure led AT&T to spin off its operating companies. Even when within-market expansion is legal, a dominant firm has little opportunity to grow other than with its industry or by diversifying. For the giants, even diversification-inspired mergers may provoke an antitrust suit. Procter & Gamble's Clorox acquisition and General Food's S.O.S. acquisition were both undone by government action. Thus, some firms may be too small to compete effectively, while the existing size of others may limit further growth. Within a wide range of viable sizes, however, other factors have greater impacts on performance.

Management Quality

Management quality is another important performance characteristic. A perceptive, aggressive, forward-looking management improves the odds of realizing most firms' full potentials. Cohen, Zinbarg, and Zeikel[12] list the following as relevant: motivation, R&D activity, willingness to take risks, success in integrating merged firms, effectiveness in delegating authority, information systems, use of board of directors, relations with financial analysts, and social responsibility. Others have noted that managers who are especially interested in stockholder welfare generally outperform those more concerned with their own well-being.[13] While a broad array of information on managerial quality is probably relevant, few investor/analysts have the resources to evaluate most of these factors effectively. Past performance is one useful guide, although of less help when needed most—when leadership shifts. Investors can normally do little more than read the financial press. A few may contact some managers directly (particularly those of small local firms), however.

Analyzing a Firm's Financial Position

While an attractive industry environment, strong competitive position, and effective management are all important components of a firm's fundamental position, only companies with adequate financial resources can fully exploit their opportunities. Accordingly, much of fundamental analysis involves assessing the firm's financial strengths and weaknesses.

Basic Accounting Concepts Used in Fundamental Analysis

Since accounting data are utilized extensively in financial analysis, we shall briefly review the principal types of financial statements. A *balance sheet* provides an instantaneous picture of a firm's resources and obligations. A classified listing of assets appears on the left. Plant and equipment are valued at cost-less-depreciation; most other assets are valued at the lower of either cost-less-depreciation or market value. Liabilities (both long- and short-term debts) and net worth (the stockholder's residual ownership position) appear on the right. Since net worth equals assets minus liabilities, the two sides of the balance sheet are always equal—hence the name "balance sheet."

The income statement begins with total revenues. Various expenses are then subtracted until only the firm's earnings remain. The income statement helps answer questions such as: How much did the firm make or lose in the recent period? How much went to its stockholders? How do current earnings compare with past results? Every year the firm's net worth will change by that year's retained earnings (profit after taxes and dividends). Thereby are the income statement and balance sheet connected.

The change in financial position statement, the third of the principal statements, helps one analyse the firm's liquidity/cash flow position. Figure 7.3 summarizes these three types of statements.

Accounting statement preparation is sufficiently subjective that permissible accounting conventions are frequently misused to alter a firm's financial appearance. Accounting gimmickery notwithstanding, the vast majority of accounting statements probably reflect a consistent and meaningful financial picture.

Figure 7.3   Types of Accounting Statements

Balance Sheet	Income Statement	Change in Financial Position
Instantaneous picture of resources (assets) and obligations (liabilities)	Revenues less expenses equal earnings	Liquidity/Cash Flow position

Ratio Analysis

Since relative magnitudes are generally more revealing than absolute levels, ratios of financial aggregates have long been used to assess financial positions.[14] Ratios may be grouped into several categories. Liquidity ratios measure the firm's ability to meet its short-run obligations. Financial ratios measure the firm's long-run strengths and weaknesses. Finally, profitability and efficiency ratios reflect productivity.

Liquidity Ratios

The *current ratio*, an index of the short-run picture, is current assets (cash, short-term investments, accounts receivable, and inventories) divided by current liabilities (accounts payable, notes due in one year, and current portion of long-term debt). According to conventional wisdom, the current ratio should be two or greater. As with all ratios, however, the optimal value varies from firm to firm, industry to industry, and over time. Stable incomes and reliable sources of short-term credit lessen the need for liquid assets and therefore reduce the optimal current ratio level. Indeed, a high current ratio may indicate that resources are being tied up unnecessarily. A ratio below two is generally less worrisome than a major decline in the ratio.

The quick or acid-test ratio is defined as liquid assets (current assets less inventories) divided by current liabilities, including interim debt. Therefore inventories, which may be relatively difficult to liquidate, are part of the current ratio's numerator but excluded from the quick ratio. Most analysts recommend a quick ratio of one or more although the appropriate level varies from industry to industry, over time, and with special characteristics of the firm.

The inventory turnover ratio equals:

$$\frac{\text{Cost of good sold}}{\text{Average yearly inventory}}$$

The ideal inventory level differs with the industry and in some cases with the season and business cycle. A high turnover suggests brisk sales and well-managed inventories. A very high ratio might indicate inadequate inventories, however. A low turnover, in contrast, reflects idle resources tied up in excess inventories and/or a large obsolete inventory component.

Unless substantial losses or a major adjustment (i.e., a large merger) have clouded the picture, most established firms' short-run financial pictures will be satisfactory. Small, less-experienced firms, however, frequently encounter short-run financial difficulty either because of poor capitalizations or poor profit/cash-flow rates.

Cash to current liab.

Financial Ratios

Debt/equity and times-interest-earned ratios assess the prospects for a firm's continued success and stability. Debt/equity ratios (liabilities/net worth) vary considerably from industry to industry, firm to firm, and over time. A public utility with highly predictable earnings, a bank with very liquid assets, or a construction company that undertakes large projects may have quite a hefty ratio, such as 2:1 or even 20:1. Firms with volatile earnings (automobile manufacturers, for example) may have a much lower target ratio such as 1:10.

Borrowing is designed to increase profits relative to net worth (i.e., return on equity). Thus, heavy borrowers need to be relatively confident that their return will exceed their borrowing costs. Accordingly, a firm with a stable return is better positioned to borrow than one with a similar average but less stable profit rate. Burdensome debt obligations may in the short run force a firm with favorable long-run prospects to liquidate needed assets, and in an extreme case, to file for bankruptcy. Thus, leverage (high debt/equity) is both potentially profitable and risky. The more secure the company, the greater the percentage of debt that may be safely accepted.

A firm's appropriate debt/equity ratio varies with its earning stability. A comparison of debt/equity ratios over time and within the industry may help assess the current level's adequacy. A rapid rise in the ratio suggests that recent profit growth may not be sustainable.

Leases complicate accounting statement analysis.[15] Purchasing assets with borrowed funds increases the debt/equity ratio while leasing the same assets does not increase debt per se. The long-term obligations are, however, very similar whether the assets are leased or purchased. Thus, debt/equity ratios may not accurately reflect the financial commitment of companies that lease a large fraction of their operating assets. Firms are now required to show their capitalized long-term lease obligations on their balance sheets. Leases that call for payments of less than 80% of the asset's value need not be capitalized.

The absence of an allowance for unfunded pension liabilities can also distort a corporation's reported financial picture.[16] Rising values on pension fund portfolios are expected to pay a substantial part of the promised benefits. When the portfolio does not produce the expected gains, pension funds may be inadequate to cover pension obligations. Moreover, many pension funds are underfunded by the corporation. Pension reform legislation now requires that many benefits be paid even if the employee leaves early (vested benefits) or the firm leaves the industry. These unfunded pension liabilities have a high claim in any bankruptcy proceeding. Over the next several decades, firms must set up reserves to cover such liabilities.

Times-interest-earned (profit before tax and interest payments divided by current interest payments) also reflects a firm's debt risk. Unlike the debt/equity ratio, however, times-interest-earned relates the firm's interest obligation to its earning power. Obviously the higher the ratio, the greater probability that interest will be paid.

Profitability and Efficiency Ratios

Five important and related profitability/efficiency ratios are return on equity (ROE), return on investment (ROI), and return on sales (ROS), asset turnover and debt margin.

$$ROE = \frac{\text{after-tax profit}}{\text{shareholder's equity}}$$

$$ROI = \frac{\text{before-tax before-interest profit}}{\text{total assets}}$$

$$ROS = \frac{\text{after-tax profits}}{\text{total revenues}}$$

Asset Turnover = total revenues/total assets

Debt Margin = total assets/shareholder's equity

Note that ROE is the product of ROS, asset turnover and debt margin:

$$\text{ROE} = \text{ROS} \times \text{asset turnover} \times \text{debt margin}$$

$$\frac{\text{after-tax profit}}{\text{shareholder's equity}} = \frac{\text{after-tax profit}}{\text{total revenues}} \times \frac{\text{total revenues}}{\text{total assets}} \times \frac{\text{total assets}}{\text{shareholders equity}}$$

Thus one can examine the source of profitability or profit-problems by looking at these components of ROE.

Profitability and growth prospects are forward-looking concepts. Is the past profit and growth record likely to improve or get worse? An examination of past results helps assess various possible scenarios.

A Hypothetical Example

Consider a hypothetical group of firms each having a five-year per-share earnings growth of about 10% (Table 7.2). Firm A's sales and profits have grown proportionately while its assets have remained nearly constant. Firm B's debt has increased from 10% to 40% of its assets. Firm C's profit margin has increased from 10% to 16%. Firm D's assets, sales, and profits have all grown proportionately. Firm E has lengthened the useful-life assumption for most of its plant and equipment.

Clearly these firms' profits have grown for different reasons. Firm A's profit growth has resulted largely from increased capacity utilization. Expanding capacity to satisfy further demand growth would increase costs, thereby reducing profit growth. Firm B's profit rise is largely due to increased leverage. A further increase in the debt ratio would probably raise both the cost of borrowed funds and the risk to the stockholders. Thus, a stockholder-diluting sale of additional

Table 7.2   Sustainable Growth Is Usually Balanced

	1979	1984
Firm A (little asset growth)		
Assets	$10,000,000	$11,000,000
Liabilities	3,000,000	3,000,000
Sales	30,000,000	50,000,000
Profits	3,000,000	5,000,000
Profit Per Share	1.00	1.67
Firm B (increased debt)		
Assets	10,000,000	17,000,000
Liabilities	1,000,000	7,000,000
Sales	30,000,000	50,000,000
Profits	3,000,000	5,000,000
Profit Per Share	1.00	1.67
Firm C (increased margin)		
Assets	10,000,000	10,000,000
Liabilities	3,000,000	3,000,000
Sales	30,000,000	30,000,000
Profits	3,000,000	5,000,000
Profit Per Share	1.00	1.67
Firm D (balanced growth)		
Assets	10,000,000	17,000,000
Liabilities	3,000,000	5,000,000
Sales	30,000,000	51,000,000
Profits	3,000,000	5,000,000
Profit Per Share	1.00	1.67
Firm E (reduced depreciation)		
Assets	10,000,000	10,000,000
Liabilities	3,000,000	3,000,000
Sales	30,000,000	30,000,000
Depreciation	3,000,000	1,000,000
Profits	3,000,000	5,000,000
Profit Per Share	1.00	1.67

equity may be required for continued growth. Firm C has either raised prices or reduced its costs. In either case, further profit increases are probably constrained. A price rise may encourage greater competition, while further cost cutting could reduce quality or increase future costs. Firm E's brightened profit picture is due, at least in part, to more optimistic depreciation assumptions. As with increases in leverage, capacity utilization, and profit margins, imaginative accounting's profit enhancement potential is limited. The accountants may soon need to run very fast just to stand still. Firm D's next five year's growth may well be like the past. While other factors could intervene, at least the past growth rate has been balanced and therefore is potentially sustainable.

High growth rates resulting primarily from increased debt, higher capacity utilization, accounting changes, cost cutting, or price increases must eventually cease. Earnings forecasts should only project a more favorable margin, debt/equity ratio, output/asset ratio or depreciation rate if the projected change seems likely.

Other Ratios

In addition to the already-discussed liquidity, financial, profitability, and efficiency ratios, investors may find several other ratios useful. *Earnings per share (EPS)* is the firm's total earnings (less any preferred dividends) divided by the number of shares outstanding. Several different earnings numbers are often reported. Fully diluted EPS gives effect to the exercise and conversion of any outstanding warrants and convertibles. Earnings figures may include or exclude extraordinary items and the results from non-continuing operations. Several differing earnings numbers are often reported. The ratio of the per-share market price to EPS (PE) is a measure of relative stock price. The current annual dividend rate (usually four times the quarterly rate) divided by the price per share is the current yield. The total return reflects both capital gains and dividends. The dividend/payout ratio equals dividends per share divided by EPS. A very low payout may indicate a substantial need to finance internal growth, management's desire to expand, or abnormally high current earnings. A very high ratio may suggest few attractive investment opportunities.

Cash flow per share is the sum of after-tax profits and depreciation divided by the number of shares outstanding. When reported depreciation is overstated (understated profits) or depreciating assets are not replaced (funds available for other uses), the cash-flow-per-share figure reflects an important source of discretionary funds. Book value per share equals the firm's net worth (after subtracting that attributable to preferred shareholders) divided by its shares outstanding. A high book value relative to the stock's price may indicate either unrecognized potential or overvalued assets. Railroad book values, for example, often equal many times their stock's market price, but unless the assets can be sold for approximately their book values, the rails' modest profit rates justify their low stock prices. Alternatively, the per-share book value may be much lower than the per-share price of the stock, perhaps reflecting some hidden or undervalued assets (patents or real estate valued at historical costs). Since book values that diverge appreciably from stock prices suggest that securities may be misvalued, further analysis could be indicated. Table 7.3 summarizes the various ratios discussed herein.

Sources of Ratios

Ratios of one company are most effectively analyzed by comparing them with those of similar firms. Accordingly sources for industry ratios would be helpful. Robert Morris Associates collects data and computes ratios for a large group of industries. Other sources include Dun & Bradstreet and Standard and Poor's.

Table 7.3   Types of Fundamental Ratios

Liquidity Ratios

Current	$\dfrac{\text{Current Assets}}{\text{Current Liabilities}}$
Quick or Acid Test	$\dfrac{\text{Current Assets-Inventories}}{\text{Current Liabilities}}$
Inventory Turnover	$\dfrac{\text{Cost of Goods Sold}}{\text{Average Yearly Inventory}}$

Financial Ratios

Debt-Equity	$\dfrac{\text{Total Debt}}{\text{Shareholder's Equity}}$
Times Interest Earned	$\dfrac{\text{Profit Before Tax and Interest Payments}}{\text{Current Interest Payment}}$

Profitability and Efficiency Ratios

Return on Equity (ROE)	$\dfrac{\text{After-Tax Profit}}{\text{Shareholders Equity}}$
Return on Investment (ROI)	$\dfrac{\text{Before-Tax Before-Interest Profit}}{\text{Total Assets}}$
Return on Sales (ROS)	$\dfrac{\text{After-Tax Profit}}{\text{Total Revenues}}$
Asset Turnover	$\dfrac{\text{Total Revenues}}{\text{Total Assets}}$
Debt Margin (Leverage)	$\dfrac{\text{Total Assets}}{\text{Shareholders Equity}}$

Other Ratios

Earnings Per Share (EPS)	$\dfrac{\text{Profits After Taxes and Preferred Dividends}}{\text{Number of Shares}}$
Price/Earnings (PE)	$\dfrac{\text{Price Per Share}}{\text{EPS}}$
Current Yield	$\dfrac{\text{Indicated Annual Dividend}}{\text{Price Per Share}}$
Dividend Payout	$\dfrac{\text{Dividends Per Share}}{\text{EPS}}$
Cash Flow Per Share	$\dfrac{\text{After-Tax Profits plus Depreciation}}{\text{Number of Shares}}$
Book Value Per Share	$\dfrac{\text{Net Worth Attributable to Common Shareholders}}{\text{Number of Shares}}$

Individual industry ratios may be computed with appropriate data from several similar firms.

Profitability Models

While financial statement and ratio analysis provide a useful perspective on the firm's past and present circumstances, its stock price performance will be determined largely by its future performance, especially its profit rate.

A number of industrial organization models relate profitability to various underlying factors. Unlike the largely ad hoc and time-series-oriented earnings-prediction efforts of investment analysts, profitability models are fitted to cross-sectional data and possess some theoretical underpinnings. In spite of profit determinant's relevance to investments, the finance profession has largely ignored this literature. Since much of investment analysis assesses potential earnings growth, risk of failure, or probability of success, characteristics associated with profitability might well help judge a firm's long-run potential.

Profit determinants work has largely explored suggested relationships one or a few times. Studies of profit's relation to firm size, type of control, seller concentration, market share, buyer concentration, entry barriers, diversifications, multi-market contacts, risk, product image, advertising, capital intensity, research intensity, and leverage, have produced interesting findings but relatively few generalizable investment implications.[17] Two consulting groups' efforts to derive strategic planning profitability-models are potentially far more useful.

The Boston Consulting Group

Bruce Henderson of the Boston Consulting Group (BCG) asserted that business units (components of firms serving distinct markets) may usefully be grouped into four categories of cash-flow generator/absorbers (the growth-share matrix).[18] The high-industry-growth, high-relative-market-share group are called "stars"; high-share low-growth, "cash cows"; low-share low-growth, "dogs" and low-share high-growth, "question marks." The high-growth stars are expected to be net cash-absorbers while the cash cows generate excess cash flows (Figure 7.4). BCG suggests that some of the cow's revenue be used both to maintain its dominant market position through investment and R&D and to help the promising question marks gain share. Most of the dogs should be liquidated.

While the BCG message is designed to assist corporate managers, an implicit message applies to investors. Well-situated firms vis-a-vis the growth-share matrix are likely to be more profitable than less well-positioned firms. Stocks that do not reflect such potentials are probably misvalued.

The Strategic Planning Institute

Sidney Schoeffler's Strategic Planning Institute (SPI) uses a more detailed approach to business profitability than BCG. Also known as PIMS (Profit Impact of

Figure 7.4   The BCG Growth-Share Matrix

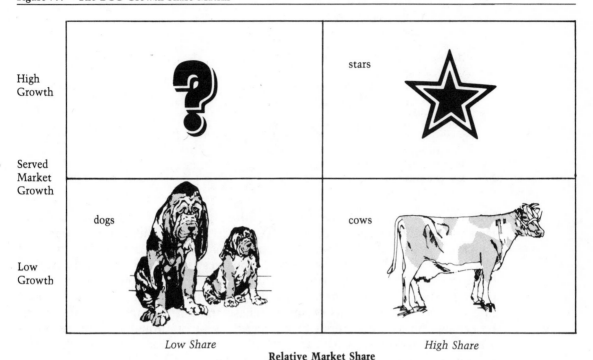

Marketing Strategies), SPI grew out of General Electric. Unlike BCG, SPI's models are based on a statistical analysis of real economic data. SPI has about 200 participating companies (a substantial percentage of whom are among *Fortune's* 500) supplying funding and detailed product-line information on about three thousand business units. This data base, which was specifically assembled for structure/strategy/performance analysis, has been used to build a number of models of product-line performance.[19] By far the best known and most widely utilized of these is SPI's Par ROI model which incorporates factors explaining approximately 70% of the ROI (Return on Investment or profit as a percentage of assets employed) variation across SPI businesses.[20] Estimated from the SPI four-year cross-sectional data base, the Par equation is designed to capture the steady-state determinants of ROI. The equation's variables were selected for their consistency with economic theory and the beliefs of knowledgeable businesspeople, statistical significance, and controllability by management. Table 7.4 lists eleven key profitability factors in the Par equation.

Competitive-position factors (market share, relative market share and relative product quality) measure a business's strengths and weaknesses within its served market. Market share reflects scale economies while relative market share

Table 7.4   The Strategic Planning Institute's Key Determinants of Profitability

	Effect on ROI
Competitive-Position Factors	
Market share	+
Relative share	+
Relative product quality	+
Market-Attractiveness Factors	
Growth in served market	+
Fixed capital intensity	−
Marketing intensity	−
Purchase amount by immediate customers	−
Joint Competitive-Position and Market-Attractiveness Factors	
Investment/Sales	−
Investment/Value added	−
Capacity utilization	+
Value added/employee	+

(this business's share relative to its top three competitors) examines share-effects from a different perspective. A 10 to 20% market share is much more impressive if no one else has as much (Exxon) than if it puts the business in third place (Chrysler). The relative quality of a business's products has a large impact on customer loyalty, repeat sales, relative price, and vulnerability to price competition. Market-attractiveness variables (growth in served market, fixed-capital intensity, marketing intensity and purchase-amount-by-immediate-customers) reflect environmental factors which affect the ease or difficulty of competing in a particular market. Operating successfully is easier in an expanding than in a declining market, as everybody can share in the growth rather than fight for the leftovers. Growth has only a modest ROI-impact because the net book value of plant and equipment tends to be underdepreciated and closer to replacement values in rapid-growth situations. On the other hand, a technology requiring a high percentage of fixed (as opposed to working) capital limits flexibility. Similarly, selling in a high-marketing-intensity market is costly. In addition to the accounting aspects of the relationship (marketing is a large cost component), marketing-intensive industries frequently experience fierce competition. Combining a high marketing level with a a relatively low selling price is an especially damaging strategy. Moreover, customers who typically place large orders (high-purchase-amount-by-immediate-customers) usually possess greater buying power and price sensitivity, thereby tending to increase the difficulty of maintaining a high margin.

The joint competitive-position and market-attractiveness factors (investment/sales, investment/value added, capacity utilization, and value added/employee) reflect both the business's within-market competitive position and the served-market environment. For example, investment intensity (a weighted average of investment/sales, and investment/value added) is affected both by how much output the business generates from its investment (its own efficiency) and by the technical nature of industry production. Similarly, capacity utilization and value added/employee are affected by both the business's own efficiency and by its industry's technical and cyclical nature. Clearly, high levels of capacity utilization and value added to investment (capital-productivity) and value added per employee (worker-productivity) contribute to business-unit success. At high operating levels, fixed costs are spread over a large output, usually reducing unit costs. Productivity and profitability go together. Businesses with heavy investment per employee tend to have high levels of value added per employee. But those that are unable to raise value added in proportion to increased investment suffer both low productivity and low profitability.

ROIs that depart from the model values tend to move back toward their Pars, indicating that Par behaves as an equilibrium.[21] SPI has also constructed other strategic planning models including those for cash flow, market share, and start-up businesses.[22] SPI members use the Par ROI equation to establish benchmarks, evaluate performance, set strategy and estimate acquisition-candidates' potentials.

Only SPI members can directly estimate profit potentials from its proprietary models and data base. Moreover, much of the needed data are not public and indeed are not even assembled by non-SPI firms. Accordingly, the model is difficult to apply directly to investment decision making. Many aspects of the model are in the public domain, however.

Estimating the relative levels of key factors (see Table 9.8) helps one evaluate long-run profit potentials. Thus a low-profit firm with high investment intensity, low market share, low capacity utilization, high marketing intensity, and low product quality may be unable to improve its profitability without strengthening its strategic position. Alternatively, an equally unprofitable firm that is appreciably stronger in most of these dimensions may more easily raise its profits.

The BCG approach emphasizes growth and market share while that of SPI utilizes a much broader array of profit determinants. Both assume that laws of the marketplace help one understand profitability relations. Clearly any superior insights into the profit prospects of investment candidates gained through these models should be helpful.[23] As yet, no empirical work tests the validity of such an approach.

RELATION OF A FIRM'S FUNDAMENTAL POSITION
TO ITS MARKET PRICE

Stock prices usually reflect their firm's industry environment, competitive position, management quality, and financial strength. Thus, a firm with a strong balance sheet, market position, profit potential, and management team operating in an industry with bright growth prospects may be fully priced. A weaker company, in contrast, is underpriced when its prospects are viewed too negatively. Accordingly, stock prices should always be evaluated in relative terms. While stronger firms deserve higher PE's than weaker firms, a strong firm with a very high PE may be fully priced while a somewhat less strong firm with a low PE may not be.

Fundamental Analysis versus Market Efficiency

If markets are relatively efficient (semi-strong form), the fundamental strengths and weaknesses of firms are already accurately reflected in their market prices and fundamental analysis is largely a waste of time. On the other hand, if the market sometimes misvalues securities vis-à-vis the available public information, fundamental analysis may be worthwhile. While the degree of market efficiency is a controversial topic, whatever level is achieved occurs because some market participants analyze fundamentals. Indeed, many investors (both large and small) devote considerable amounts of time and money undertaking and/or buying such research. If markets are efficient, those who bear the cost of making them so (i.e., those who do or pay for the fundamental analysis) are wasting their resources. The market for fundamental information is inefficient if too much is being spent on it for the benefits received. On the other hand, if such analysis does tend to pay for itself by identifying misvalued securities, the security markets are exhibiting a degree of inefficiency. Thus, either the securities market or the market for its analysis is inefficient (or possibly both are inefficient). The two markets cannot both be efficient simultaneously.

SUMMARY AND CONCLUSIONS

This chapter explored traditional approaches to economic, industry, and firm analysis. Industries exhibit very different performances, but selecting those with the best prospects is quite difficult. Past performance offers very little guide, while evaluating the industry's developmental stage may offer some modest help. Firm analysis involves assessing a company's relative strengths and weaknesses within its industry or industries. Ideally, a firm should be large enough to compete effectively but not so large as to be constrained by the threat of antitrust prosecution. Management quality, another important firm characteristic, is especially difficult to judge. Financial statement analysis utilizes a variety of different types of ratios. Liquidity ratios reflect short-run strengths and weaknesses. Financial ratios relate to a firm's longer-run prospects. Profitability and efficiency ratios reflect current operating effectiveness with an eye toward the future. Various other ratios such as earnings per share, PE, cash flow per share, payout and book value may provide additional insights. The profitability models, particularly those of BCG and SPI, may have some investment analysis potential.

The preceding discussion might be summed up as follows: Investors should acquire stocks of firms whose industry, financial, competitive, and managerial strengths are not fully appreciated by the market. While difficult to dispute, such advice is not very operational. Clearly, investors need more practical approaches.

While assessing industry and firm strengths and weaknesses is one way to search for attractive investments, such an approach is only useful if the analysis uncovers overlooked values. An efficient market has, by definition, no misvalued securities. On the other hand, an efficient market for investment analysis implies that on balance those paying for research receive full value for their costs. The security market and the market for fundamental analysis cannot both be efficient.

REVIEW QUESTIONS

1. Discuss the three principal types of accounting statements.
2. List and analyze the various classes of ratios. In general how should ratios be analyzed?
3. When examining the cause of past growth, which factors are likely to be temporary and which capable of producing sustainable growth?
4. Discuss the impact of a firm's competitive position on its investment attractiveness. Consider the saturation effect and potential antitrust problems.
5. Discuss the role of management quality in investment analysis.
6. Compare the three types of profitability models discussed in this chapter: Academic, BCG and SPI.

REVIEW PROBLEMS

1. Obtain the latest annual reports for a utility, manufacturer and bank and then compute the various ratios discussed in the text.
2. Select an industry with a number of companies having differing levels of financial strengths. Now choose a firm within that industry that is thought to be strong and another that is thought to be weak. Compute relevant ratios for each and compare. Write a report.
3. Make a list of twenty industries which are frequently mentioned in investment periodicals. Now classify each according to its life cycle stage.
4. Select three industries and read about them in the financial press. Now rank their members according to market share and competitive strength. Write a report.
5. Rank the firms in the industries selected above according to the quality of their managements. Write a report. Note this is a nearly impossible assignment even for an expert, but give it a try.
6. Obtain the year-end issues of *Forbes* and *Business Week* and read what they say in their industry analyses. Rank the industries according to *Forbes* and according to *Business Week* and compare the rankings.
7. Assemble a list of twenty large firms. Compute the stock price to per/share book value for each and plot it relative to their ROE. Do you see a pattern? If so, try to explain it.

8. Apply the equation ROE = ROS × asset turnover × total assets to the hypothetical firms of Table 7.2.
9. Select ten companies and analyze them in light of the BCG and PIMS strategic planning criteria. Follow their performance over twelve months. Write a report.

NOTES

1. P. Brown and R. Ball, "Some Preliminary Findings on the Association Between the Earnings of a Firm, Its Industry and the Economy," *Empirical Research in Accounting, Selected Studies, 1967*, Supplement to Vol. 5; *Journal of Accounting Research*, pp. 55–77.

2. B. King, "Market and Industry Factors in Stock Behavior," *Journal of Business*, 1960, pp. 139–190; S. Meyers, "A Re-Examination of Market and Industry Factors in Stock Price Behavior," *Journal of Finance*, June 1973, pp. 695–705.

3. *Wall Street Journal*, "Deere Net Fell 97% in Quarter, 71% in First Half," *Wall Street Journal*, May 26, 1982, p. 4; N. Peagan and H. Lancester, *Wall Street Journal*, June 13, 1982, p. 1, 16.

4. H. Latane and D. Tuttle, "Framework for Forming Probability Beliefs," *Financial Analysts Journal*, January/February 1968, pp. 51–61.

5. E. Brigham and S. Pappas, "Rates of Return on Common Stock," *Journal of Business*, July 1969, pp. 302–316; F. Reilly and E. Drzycimski, "Alternative Industry Performance and Risk," *Journal of Financial and Quantitative Analysis*, June 1974, pp. 423–446.

6. H. Cheney, "The Value of Industry Forecasting as an Aid to Portfolio Management," *Appalachian Financial Review*, June 1970, pp. 331–339; King, "Market and Industry Factors in Stock Price Behavior," *Journal of Business*, June 1966, pp. 139–190; J. Gaumnitz, "The Influence of Industry Factors in Stock Price Movements," Paper presented at Southern Finance Association Meeting, October 1970. Subsequently released as University of Kansas, School of Business Working Paper, June 1971; M. Livingston, "Industry Movements of Common Stocks," *Journal of Finance*, June 1977, pp. 861–874.

7. M. Tysseland, "Further Tests of the Validity of the Industry Approach to Investment Analysis," *Journal of Financial and Quantitative Analysis*, November 1971, pp. 835–847.

8. Reilly and Drzycimski, *op. cit*; M. Blume, "On The Assessment of Risk," *Journal of Finance*, March 1971, pp. 1–10; Levy, "On the Short-Term Stationarity of Beta Coefficients," *Financial Analysts Journal*, January/February 1971, pp. 55–62.

9. B. Gale and B. Branch, "Concentration vs. Market Share: Which Determines Performance and Why Does it Matter?" *The Antitrust Bulletin*, Spring 1982, pp. 83–103.

10. F. Scherer, *Industrial Market Structure and Economic Performance*, Rand McNally, Chicago, 1970, p. 77.

11. G. Bylinski, "Happily Married in Computers," *Fortune*, April 1973.

12. J. Cohen, F. Zinbarg, and Z. Zeikel, *Investment Analysis and Portfolio Management*, Irwin, Homewood, IL, 1973, pp. 324–366.

13. B. Branch, "Corporate Objectives and Market Performance," *Financial Management*, Summer 1973, pp. 24–29; S. Levin and S. Levin, "Ownership and Control of Large Industrial Firms: Some New Evidence," *Review of Business and Economic Research*, Fall 1982, pp. 36–49.

14. K. Chen and T. Shimerda, "An Empirical Analysis of Useful Ratios," *Financial Management*, Spring 1981, pp. 51–60.

15. R. Gritta, "The Impact of Lease Capitalization," *Financial Analysts Journal*, March/April 1974, pp. 47–52.

16. M. Feldstein and R. Morck, "Pension Funds and the Value of Equities," *Financial Analysts Journal*, September/October 1983, pp. 29–40.

17. H. Stekler, *Profitability and Size of Firm*, University of California Institute of Business and

Economic Research, 1963; B. Branch, "Firms Objectives and Market Performance," *Financial Management*, Summer 1973, pp. 24–30; J. Bain, "Relation of Profit Rate to Industry Concentration: American Manufacturing, 1936–1940," *Quarterly Journal of Economics*, 65, August 1951, pp. 293–324; R. Caves, B. Gale, and M. Porter, "Interfirm Profitability Differences: Comment," *Quarterly Journal of Economics*, November 1977, pp. 667–675; L. Guth, R. Schwartz and D. Whitcomb, "The Use of Buyer Concentration Ratios in Tests of Oligopoly Models," *Review of Economics* and *Statistics*, November 1976, pp. 488–572; M. Harris, "Entry and Long Term Trends in Industry Performance," *Antitrust Bulletin*, Summer 1976, pp. 295–312; S. Rhoades, "The Effect of Diversification in Industry Profit Performance in 241 Manufacturing Industries," *Review of Economics and Statistics*, May 1973, pp. 146–155; R. Caves, "The Economics of Reciprocity: Theory and Evidence on Bilateral Trading Arrangements," in W. Sellekaerts, ed., *International Trade and Finance*, Macmillan, London, 1974, pp. 17–54; D. Winn, "On the Relations Between Rates of Return, Risk and Market Structure," *Quarterly Journal of Economics*, February 1977, pp. 157–163; M. Spence, "Product Selection, Fixed Cost, and Monopolistic Competition," *Review of Economic Studies*, June 1976, pp. 218–220; H. Bloch, "Advertising and Profitability: A Reappraisal," *Journal of Political Economy*, March/April 1974, pp. 269–286; S. Schoeffler, R. Buzzell, and D. Heany, "Impact of Strategic Planning on Profit Performance," *Harvard Business Review*, 52, March–April 1974, 137–145; B. Branch, "Research and Development and Profits: A Distributed Lag Analysis," *Journal of Political Economy*, September/October 1974, pp. 481–482; G. Hurdle, "Leverage, Risk, Market Structure and Profitability," *Review of Economics and Statistics*, November 1974, pp. 481–482.

18. B. Henderson, "The Product Portfolio" (1970); "Cash Traps" (1972) and "The Experience Curve Reviewed: The Growth-Share Matrix or the Product Portfolio," Boston Consulting Group, 1973; G. Day, "Diagnosing, the Product Portfolio," *Journal of Marketing*, April 1977, pp. 29–39; B. Hedley "Strategy and the Business Portfolio," *Long-Range Planning*, February 1977, pp. 9–15; M. Coate, An Emperical Analysis of the Boston Consulting Group's Portfolio Model, FTC Working Paper #47, August 1982.

19. Strategic Planning Institute, *The PIMS Research Data Bases*, Strategic Planning Institute, 1977; H. Christensen, *Product, Market and Company Influence Upon the Profitability of Business Unit Research and Development Expenditures*, Doctoral Thesis, Columbia University, 1977; B. Gale and B. Branch, "Scale Economies of Business Unit Data: The Evidence from a Cross-Sectional Analysis," Strategic Planning Institute Staff Paper, 1979; B. Gale, "Selected Findings from the PIMS Project: Market Strategy Impact on Profitability," *American Marketing Association Combined Proceedings*, 1974.

20. B. Gale, D. Heany and D. Swire, "The Par ROI Report: Explanation and Commentary on Report," Strategic Planning Institute Staff Paper, Cambridge, MA, January 1977.

21. B. Branch, "The Laws of the Marketplace and ROI Dynamics," *Financial Management*, Summer 1980, pp. 58–65.

22. B. Branch and B. Gale, "Cash Flow Analysis: More Important Than Ever," *Harvard Business Review*, July–August 1981, pp. 131–136; V. Kijewski, "How to Formulate and Implement Your Market Share Strategy," presentation to SPI Council meeting, Held in Boston in January 1979; R. Biggadykle, "Entry Strategy and Performance," Doctoral Thesis, Harvard Business School, summer, published by Strategic Planning Institute, Cambridge, Massachusetts, August 1979.

23. M. Porter, "Industry Structure and Competitive Strategy: Keys to Profitability," *Financial Analysts Journal*, July/August 1980, pp. 30–42.

8   Misleading Accounting: The Danger and the Potential

While reported earnings per share (EPS) receive a considerable amount of investor attention, the actual numbers are prepared by company accountants and checked and attested to by auditors whose exercise of discretion can substantially affect the reported results. Moreover, the ill-defined boundaries of many accounting procedures lead to both controversy and confusion. Most users expect financial reports (balance sheets, income statements, and changes in financial position statements) to reveal an accurate picture. An uncritical acceptance of the reported data has two potential drawbacks, however. First, the legitimate application of differing accounting techniques to similar facts may properly produce very different reports. For example, Leonard Spacek illustrated how generally accepted accounting procedures could easily be used to report EPS of from $.80 to $1.79.[1] Accordingly, investors should know whether the reported figures are near the high or low end of the possible range.[2] Second, firms sometimes misuse accounting discretion to generate misleading earnings reports. Those who rely upon untrustworthy data may pay too much for a company whose books have been cooked. Overstating earnings one year usually reduces what can legitimately be reported in future years.

While most accounting statements probably represent an honest effort to reveal rather than conceal, the all-too-frequent exceptions warrant careful attention. Some problems result from a purposeful effort to misuse accounting discretion (Equity Funding, Saxon Industries).[3] Even conscientiously prepared accounting statements may be misleading, however. Thus an insightful reading of the full set of financial statements (including the footnotes) and other public data may reveal far more than a cursory glance at the key figures such as sales growth and EPS. Such a detailed analysis may either expand upon the initial perception (no surprises) or reveal a very different picture. Market acceptance of misleading financial statements may allow more knowledgeable investors to avoid or short overvalued securities (where overoptimistic accounting numbers are trusted) and buy undervalued securities (where asset values are hidden).

This chapter explores the nature of the accounting problem and how accounting discretion can affect the reported data. Both optimistic and pessimistic accounting assumptions and statements are examined and illustrated with a series of real-world examples. Finally, methods of spotting misleading accounting are discussed.

ACCOUNTING DISCRETION

Generally accepted accounting principles (GAAP) and the pronouncements of the Financial Accounting Standards Board (FASB) are designed to limit the extent of discretion and thereby enhance the consistency of accounting statements. In spite of the best efforts of the FASB and others, however, appreciable uncertainty and differences of opinion remain. Even if most accountants do a fair job under difficult circumstances, companies that report misleading results still expose their shareholders to substantial shocks.

Abraham Briloff, a pioneer in the analysis of accounting abuse, has in a series of *Barron's* articles (later compiled into several books) reported numerous examples of GAAP being perverted to produce misleading statements.[4] Since Briloff's original disclosures, accounting abuses have received additional attention, but problems persist.

The common practice of keeping more than one set of accounting records illustrates the extensive nature of accounting discretion. A company may properly maintain two sets of books—one for the IRS and one for stockholders. Some companies also keep a third set of books for their own internal use. The IRS books generally utilize every permissible deduction, writeoff, and reserve to minimize taxable profits. A more favorable view may appear in the shareholder books. The internal books may be the most realistic.

The Valuation Problem

Valuing assets and liabilities is one of the principal accounting problems. Values must be assigned to inventories, securities, plant, equipment, acquired assets, receivables, and a host of other items. Liabilities such as accrued pension benefits, long-term lease obligations, and pending damage claims also need to be valued. While valuing such money-dominated assets and liabilities as cash, receivables, and payables is rather straightforward, most valuations involve substantial subjectivity. Assets are generally valued at their acquisition cost less accumulated depreciation, or at their market value, whichever is lower. Since few usable market prices exist for plant and equipment, such assets are almost always valued at historical cost less accumulated depreciation. Even when the secondary market is relatively active (e.g., transportation equipment), historical cost less accumulated depreciation is still generally employed. With rapid inflation, however, replacement costs often exceed historical cost plant and equipment valuations. While accounting's conservative bias is supposed to reduce the likelihood of unpleasant surprises, excessive conservatism can be as misleading as excessive optimism.

Exceptions to General Accounting Rules

Accounting practice's many exceptions increase both the complexity of the process and the diversity of possible reported results. For example, the general rule that assets should be valued at cost or market, whichever is lower, does not apply to the loan and security portfolios of banks, thrift institutions, insurance companies, and other types of financial institutions (except for portfolio components slated for sale or for which payment is substantially overdue). Two justifications are offered for permitting financial firms to ignore the valuation impact of interest-rate changes. First, many such firms have offsetting liabilities whose values are reduced by rises in interest rates. That is, as interest rates rise, an institution's fixed-interest asset values will decline, but so will the market values of its fixed-rate liabilities. Second, investors and depositors or policyholders will be at least partially protected from adverse interest fluctuations as long as the institution's cash flow remains adequate. Why, so the argument goes, unnecessarily concern people with a restated balance sheet when the income picture is sound? Moreover, interest rates may eventually move in the opposite direction. Regardless of the validity of these arguments, investors should not ignore either the adverse effect of rising or the favorable effect of falling interest rates on financial institutions' balance sheets. Noting the net interest fluctuation impact reveals the firm's current worth much more clearly than do its unadjusted book values.

Other exceptions allow asset values to be increased to market. While a sale and repurchase accomplishes the revaluation by brute force, a new historical cost may be established with a partial sale. Alternatively, a swap for dissimilar assets may facilitate a revaluation. Such transactions having a legitimate business purpose may be quite proper. If a desire to increase the book valuation motivates the transaction, however, one wonders why management needs to go to such lengths. Investors are perfectly capable of looking beyond inaccurate book values.

Depreciation

Many assets offer useful service over a number of accounting periods. Expensing their costs either when the items were purchased or when they were taken out of service would be misleading. Allocating and charging off a portion of each asset's cost (depreciation) to each relevant accounting period much more closely matches revenues to expenses. If the depreciation charge estimated the decline in an asset's value due to wear, tear, obsolescence, or other factors, asset book values would approximate market values. Depreciation accounting's attempt to spread asset costs over their useful lives is, however, only tangentially related to the actual declines in asset values.

Depletion and amortization also involve charging off an asset's cost over its useful life. As a general rule, manufactured assets are depreciated; mineral resources are depleted; and intangible assets such as patents, copyrights, and goodwill are amortized. The periodic depreciation, depletion, and amortization amounts are deducted from revenues in profit determination and from the asset side of the balance sheet to determine net worth. The greater the charges, the lower the reported income, its corresponding tax liability, and the stated value of assets and net worth. Obviously, the rate at which assets are written off affects both financial statement values and after-tax cash flows.

Allowed Depreciation Methods

With straight line, a constant sum is deducted annually over the asset's estimated life. Thus, a 10-year asset with no salvage value that cost $100,000 would be depreciated at $10,000 a year. Accelerated depreciation increases (relative to straight line) chargeoffs in the early years of the asset's life, thereby postponing tax payments. For a rapidly growing firm with new depreciable assets more than replacing those whose depreciated value is approaching zero, the tax postponement is very nearly permanent. That is, taxes postponed to the current year are more than offset by taxes postponed into the following year and so on. Even when the postponement is temporary, the effect is like an interest-free term loan from the government.

In addition to choosing from among the permitted depreciation methods, some discretion may be exercised in determining an asset's depreciable life. Thus, a firm can affect its reported profits by choosing the depreciation method and by setting the depreciable life.

Accounting Abuse with Depreciation: The Leasco Example

The Leasco case illustrates the misleading results of an inadequate depreciation provision: In 1961 Leasco began offering computer rentals at lower rates than the manufacturer—commonly 82% of the manufacturer's rate. While Leasco might be more efficient than a manufacturer, highly successful companies such as IBM should be difficult to beat at their own game. Few would expect an 18% savings through greater rental efficiencies. Subsequent events revealed that the nonmanufacturer's lower rental rates largely resulted from an understated depreciation allowance.

Regardless of the method chosen, the total depreciation charge must eventually equal the acquisition cost less any salvage value. The principal question: "How should the asset's cost be allocated over its useful life?" breaks down into two questions: (1) "What is the useful life?" and (2) "At what rate should depreciation be charged at various stages of that useful life?" The useful-life estimate is central to the Leasco case.

Forecasting a computer's technological life is much more difficult than estimating its physical life. Since technological advances have quickly reduced the value of existing computers, new computers' annual rents should equal a substantial percentage of their purchase prices. A computer's rental value will decline with its rate of technological obsolescence. Depreciation should accurately reflect the computer's expected rate of obsolescence.

Leasco justified lower depreciation and rental rates by assuming that its computers' useful lives would exceed the manufacturer's estimates. Unwarranted optimism eventually resulted in large writeoffs, however. For all its accounting gimmickry, Leasco lost $7 million on its computer rentals during the seven years from 1962 to 1969.[5] When its 1970 loss of $30.8 million was reported, the firm's stock fell dramatically.

While Leasco's shareholders may not have been particularly well-served by the firm's early history, one need not shed too many tears for its founder. Saul Steinberg first burst upon Wall Street as a brash young man in his early 20s. Leasco's initial profit and growth reports inflated the stock's price, allowing Steinberg to acquire several attractive properties. While his effort to take over New York's Chemical Bank failed (largely because of vigorous establishment opposition) and the losses from the computer rental operation eventually came home to roost, Steinberg had by then acquired Reliance, a large and profitable insurance company. Leasco and Reliance were merged. Leasco was later spun off and still later acquired a substantial block of Reliance. Steinberg and his relatives owned a large share of both firms. More recently, Steinberg and his associates bought out the other shareholders and took both firms private. Still more recently, he has been extracting "greenmail" by threatening to take over firms (e.g. Quaker State and Disney) and then selling his position back to the company for a premium. Steinberg is now a very rich man due in no small part to the shareholders who made the mistake of believing his accounting numbers.

Leasco provides but one of many examples of firms whose optimistic depreciation expectations produced unrealistic reported income. Once the investment community is made aware (by a Briloff article in *Barron's*, for example) of the profit overstatement, the stock's price is almost certain to fall. Even if no one discovers the misstatements, the company's accountants will eventually run out of gimmicks, earnings will not keep pace with expectations and the stock's price will decline. Obviously depreciation accounting is one area investors should closely watch.

Kaplan and Roll examined the stock performance of 71 firms that switched back to straight-line reporting to shareholders (while continuing to use accelerated depreciation for IRS).[6] Such switches increased EPS but had no effect on cash flows and no long-term stock market impacts.

Inventory Valuation

Valuing inventories poses another difficult accounting problem. Unless one-of-a-kind type items remain in inventories for an extended period, historical cost valuations are generally adequate. When identical units are frequently added to and subtracted from the warehouse, inventories and cost of goods sold can more conveniently be valued at some cost-per-unit times the relevant number of units. Two principal techniques are used: LIFO and FIFO.

With LIFO (last in, first out), units removed from the inventories are valued at the most recent unutilized purchase price. Thus just-purchased units will be charged out (cost-of-goods-sold) at the most recent purchase price until the number of units sold exceeds the units purchased at that price. Once the most recently purchased units have been accounted for, the next most recent unutilized purchase price will then be applied and so forth.

With FIFO (first in, first out), the oldest unutilized cost figure is applied to items removed from inventories. Thus, inventories are generally valued at relatively recent costs while cost-of-goods-sold figures tend to be out of date.

Neither LIFO nor FIFO attempts to match individual physical units with their purchase prices. Thus, a firm may ship the oldest units first, but use LIFO to value them at the most recent invoice cost. Both LIFO and FIFO normally provide a reasonably consistent inventory/cost-of-goods-sold picture. With rising prices, FIFO will tend to yield a lower cost-of-goods-sold value, thereby inflating profits and ending inventory values. Compared to FIFO, LIFO generally deflates profits, taxes, and ending inventory values.

With relatively stable prices, the choice between LIFO and FIFO will not greatly affect reported earnings. With rapid price changes, the LIFO-FIFO choice does have a larger effect, but the earnings impact may still be modest if inventories are only a small part of total assets. A shift from one method to another can substantially affect reported earnings, however. Thus, until the FASB changed the rules, a poorly performing firm could switch from LIFO to FIFO in order to show a substantial one-time earnings increase. Such inventory-profits were illusory as more funds are required to replenish inventory at the higher per-unit cost. On the other hand, rapid inflation rates have encouraged some firms to shift from FIFO to LIFO and thereby reduce their inventory profits and the resulting taxes.

Chrysler's 1970 LIFO-FIFO Shift

Chrysler's 1970 results illustrate the effects of shifting from LIFO to FIFO. In early 1971, Chrysler reported a $34 million loss with a tax refund of $80 million. Using a 50% tax rate, a $34 million loss would produce a refund of $17 million while an $80 million refund would come from a $160 million dollar loss. Briloff explains this result as follows[5]:

> Start with the pre-tax loss of $34 million
> Since the "Taxes on Income" note indicates that foreign
> taxes cost Chrysler $44.5 million (the foreigners fared
> better than our IRS) assume that the foreign income was
> twice that amount, hence about   89 million
>   For a subtotal of $123 million
> Then, in another footnote, this one entitled "Invento-
> ries-Accounting Changes" we have what might be the
> rest of the jigsaw: For the period January 1, 1957 through
> December 31, 1961, the last in, first out (LIFO) method
> of inventory valuation had been used for approximately
> 60% of the consolidated inventory.
> Effective January 1, 1970, the FIFO (first in, first out)
> method of inventory was adopted for inventories previ-

ously valued using the LIFO method. Inventory amounts
December 31, 1969, and 1970 are stated higher by approximately $110 and $150 million, respectively, than
they would have been had the LIFO method been continued. The effect on 1970 income from this statement
loss vis-à-vis tax-statement loss by the difference be- $40 million
tween the $110 and $150 million, hence $163 million
   Total

But, there is yet a somewhat incomprehensible concluding paragraph in that "Inventories Accounting Change"
footnote. It reads: "For United States income tax purposes the adjustment to inventory amounts will be taken
into taxable income ratability over 20 years commencing
to January 1, 1971." Part of this was readily comprehen-
sible to me. Since Chrysler went off LIFO, the $150 mil-
lion of inventory values, heretofore suppressed, and now
surfaced, requires an additional tax of about $75 million
to be paid (again, at the 50% rate).

Clearly, the shifts from LIFO to FIFO produced a substantial accounting
gain, thereby offsetting a large portion of Chrysler's 1970 operating loss. Since
this was a one-time procedure, the unadjusted operating loss reflected ongoing
operations much more realistically.

Sunder studied the market-impact of 110 firms switching to LIFO and 22
switches to FIFO.[8] The LIFO switches showed above-market risk-adjusted returns prior to the switch and random thereafter, probably because profitable firms
tended to make the switch. On the other hand, firms switching to FIFO typically
did poorly subsequent to the switch because they were generally unprofitable.

Merger Accounting

Financial statements of merged firms may be consolidated by either pooling-of-
interest or purchase accounting. Both methods are supposed to produce consistent
financial statements that allow meaningful comparisons to be made between
pre- and post-merger operations.

With pooling-of-interest, the balance sheet values of the acquired firm's
assets and liabilities are added to the acquiring company's balance sheet at their
pre-merger book values regardless of the acquiring firm's acquisition cost. In
purchase accounting, the acquisition cost (cash or market value of the securities
used in the exchange) is distributed among the acquired firm's assets and added
to the acquiring firm's balance sheet.

The acquiring firm can report illusory gains by entering the acquired assets
on its books at unrealistically low values and then selling them at much higher
market values. Reporting profits from acquired-asset sales is perfectly appropriate

when the sold assets are valued at their fair share of the acquisition costs. Gains can be overstated by undervaluing the assets to be sold, however. Such overstatements may occur with pooling-of-interest accounting if the firm's acquisition cost substantially exceeded its book value. With purchase accounting, the acquiring firm may place unrealistically low values on assets to be sold while valuing retained assets more highly. Thus, "manufacturing" profits with pooling-of-interest accounting is easier, but purchase accounting may also be abused.

Merger Accounting Gimmicks

Briloff devoted most of three chapters of *Unaccountable Accounting* to the same basic merger accounting theme.[9] An acquired firm's assets are entered on the books at low values and then disposed of at the fair market value with the difference claimed as income. In a more recent book (*The Truth about Corporate Accounting*), Briloff criticized the allocation of acquisition costs under both types of merger accounting.[10] When, for example, General Electric acquired Utah International for approximately $2 billion, only UI's $600 million book value was entered on the GE balance sheet thereby greatly reducing depreciation and inventory costs. As Briloff put it, "$1.4 billion . . . of the cost evaporated—not even leaving the smile like that of the Cheshire cat."[11]

In the United Technologies-AMBAC merger (1978), a book value of $122 million was acquired for $220 million. Of the $98 million difference, $87.5 million was allocated to goodwill to be written off over a 25-year period. Two years earlier (1976) United Technologies had acquired Otis Elevator and in the process added $27 million in goodwill to the books. In 1979, UT acquired Mostek for $314 million of which $214 was goodwill. By year-end 1979, 32.3% of UT's book value was goodwill. While a firm's going-concern value often reflects earning potential above the sum of the assets acquired, justifying such large amounts is difficult. Moreover, UT's long-term approach to goodwill writeoff seems unwarranted.

Hong, Kaplan, and Mandelker, who studied the market response to 122 pooling and 37 purchase-accounting mergers, found no systematic reaction.[12] Investors do not seem to be fooled by "dirty pooling."

Income Anticipation and Expense Deferral

Income from an installment sale creates yet another accounting problem. The profit might logically be claimed when the purchase contract is signed, upon delivery of the product, when a given percentage of the purchase price is received, when a given percentage of the product's production cost has been incurred, upon full payment of the purchase price, or upon completion of the product. Alternatively, the profit may be prorated on the basis of the payment schedule or work fulfillment. Clearly, reported profits can depend substantially on when the profit is recognized.

Similarly, expenses may be recognized in two ways: the cost may be charged off in the year incurred (expensed) or allocated over a period of years (capitalized). Capitalization is appropriate when the benefits are expected to continue for a number of years. Otherwise the cost should be expensed. Capitalizing costs that might more appropriately be expensed tends to overstate current earnings.

Income Anticipation Gimmicks

Briloff discussed an income-anticipation abuse involving Minnie Pearl (an affiliate of National General) Franchises:

> Essentially, I am indicting the company's (and their auditor's) failure to consider the substance of the franchising agreements and instead swallowed the form. Thus, as it turned out, these officers, et al., participated importantly in forming a corporation, with only a minor capital contribution and with only limited capital resources. These corporations then entered into franchising agreements with Performance Systems whereby (and this presumes the typical franchising arrangement):
>
> 1. The newly formed franchise is obligated to pay an initial franchise fee—mostly payable in notes (with or without interest).
> 2. For this fee the franchisee receives the right to use the franchiser's name, patents, etc., for an indefinite period (frequently, however, with a right on the part of the franchiser to cancel under certain circumstances); the franchise was also entitled to assistance in site selection, lease negotiation, equipping the premises, advertising, and in selecting personnel.
> 3. The franchisee was also obligated to pay a royalty based on sales; and was frequently required to purchase inventory and supplies from the franchiser.
>
> Where then was there an abuse of logic and reality, to say nothing of fairness, in the application of GAAP? Briefly, despite the limited capitalization of the franchises, the franchiser (Minnie Pearl, for example) would pick up as income at the time of the initial franchise agreement the entire amount of the fee—even though, as we have seen, so much of it is in the form of paper generated by the undercapitalized franchisee—with little or no provision for collection and cancellation losses.
>
> All that the principals in the franchiser operations had to do was to form a corporation with a minimal capital, use some ink and paper to sign up with themselves in behalf of the franchiser, and Presto! Merlin reports income of the franchiser.[13]

Briloff also explored the anticipation of income by National Student Marketing, R. Hoe, Telex, and Memorex. In the case of National Student Marketing and R. Hoe, "fudgeness" in reporting income on the percentage basis caused the overstatement. For Telex and Memorex, inventory was, in effect, valued at retail.[14] Since these abuses came to light, FASB reforms have severely restricted the opportunity to anticipate income through franchise operations.

Land companies are criticized (Boise Cascade, AMREP, and GAC) for claiming as income the entire profit from a land sale when only a small payment is received (as little as 2 1/2% of the purchase price).[15] Another land company, Commonwealth United, offset poor operating results with the profits from an incestuous transaction. On December 31, 1968, Commonwealth purchased and resold 4,000 acres of Hawaiian property for $1,656,800 and $5,450,000 respectively. The purchasing syndicate was composed of three groups: Commonwealth's underwriters (Kleiner and Bell), the controlling stockholder of the underwriter (Shapiro) and a counsel for Commonwealth and the underwriter (Freling). The transaction involved a cash payment of $541,000 with no recourse for Commonwealth beyond reclaiming the property. This one transaction's reported profit represented 20¢ of 1968's 98¢ EPS. Also, on December 31, 1968, the underwriters purchased an office building from Commonwealth, producing another substantial portion of the company's 1968 profit. Thus, Commonwealth and its underwriter spent most of the last day of 1968 "improving" their profit report.[16]

Bernard Cornfeld of Investors Overseas Services (IOS) executed a particularly ingenious income-anticipation scheme. A portion of some Canadian Arctic oil and gas land was sold and the per-acre price applied to the entire parcel. Ordinarily, such a revaluation would be justified by an arm's-length sale of 25% or more. IOS sold less than 10% to King Resources. How independent King and IOS were was unclear, although Arthur Andersen audited both sets of books. This sale allowed IOS to claim a $102 million unrealized appreciation on the Fund of Funds it managed. Then IOS paid itself a management fee of 10% of the profit. When Robert Vesco acquired IOS from Cornfeld, he revalued the Canadian land, wiping out the profit.[17] Vesco later took $224 million dollars of IOS money with him to Costa Rica, then the Bahamas, and was last reported operating out of Cuba. Cornfeld managed to stay just clear of the law on this side of the Atlantic, but did serve time in a Swiss jail. Because of the efforts of the Canadian liquidators, however, Fund of Fund shareholders may ultimately receive liquidation payments approximately equal to their initial investments.[18] Moreover, much of the projected value is derived from the Arctic oil and gas properties that Cornfeld went to such lengths to revalue: wonders never cease!

Other Misleading Accounting Examples

Briloff, with his *Barron's* connection, is clearly the best-known authority on misleading accounting. Others have also investigated accounting gimmicks, however. For example, R. Golden, a technology specialist at Edwards and Hanly, estimated that Western Union's bookkeeping maneuvers produced about 80%

of the firm's 1972 EPS. These devices included capitalizing interest, pension and severance pay, while flowing through the net benefit of tax credits. Purchasing its own bonds below par and claiming the gain as ordinary income was especially misleading (under FASB reforms the gain is now reported as extraordinary income). Golden claimed that Western Union's $1.40 annual dividend had been covered by operating income in only one year from 1968–1972.[19] Similar motives may explain a number of proposals to exchange common for preferred or bonds; bonds for common or preferred; straight bonds for convertibles; and so forth. The firm may achieve an extraordinary gain by retiring below-par bonds early, often to offset an extraordinary writeoff or writedown.

Without claiming an attempt to mislead, Bowler points out that revised accounting methods for life insurance underwriters permit widely varying reports.

> Under statutory regulations, a company may select from a variety of reserve valuation methods, each with its own assumptions as to interest and mortality rates. The choice of methods is significant, especially to new business. For example, Company A writes a certain policy reserves of which are based on the net level premium basis (the most stringent) with interest assumed at 3%. It sets aside a reserve of $22.50.

> Company B issues a policy identical except that reserves are computed on the commissioners method, also known as modified preliminary term. It sets aside no reserves during the first year. Did Company B earn $22.50 more than Company A on this piece of business? Both methods are actuarially sound.

> And, does Company A have a liability Company B does not? As Best's points out, if a typical life insurer were to change its reserve basis from net level premium 3 1/2% to modified preliminary term 3 1/2%, its surplus would double. A change from net level 3% would triple surplus.

> The shortcomings, for shareholder purposes, of an accounting system with arbitrary variables such as these is clear. About all that can be said in favor of statutory reserve methods is that they enjoy the sanction of regulatory authorities. Under GAAP, on the other hand, policy reserve assumptions are not subject to official approval. They are made by companies in light of their own experience and judgment.[20]

Misleading Optimism

Clearly, such discretion presents some opportunities for abuse. Here are some of the areas where misleadingly optimistic accounting has occurred in the past.

- Failing to adjust book values of interest-sensitive assets to changing interest rates

- Overestimating assets' useful lives, thereby understating their depreciation
- Switching to FIFO for inventory accounting
- Undervaluing merger-acquired assets which are later sold
- Claiming income from franchise sales prior to receipt of cash flow
- Claiming income from non-arms-length sales where the seller has little recourse if the transaction is later reversed
- Claiming income from installment sales prior to the receipt of revenue
- Choosing allowed method for insurance reserve that produces the greatest current profit

UNDERVALUED ASSETS

Accounting statements may be as misleadingly conservative as the previous examples were misleadingly optimistic. Since accounting procedures are supposed to lean modestly toward conservatism, a variety of different types of assets are often substantially undervalued: developed real estate, land and mineral resources carried at historical costs, such intangible assets as tax-loss-carryforwards, patents, trademarks, copyrights, leaseholdings, government-granted privileges (such as broadcast rights and acreage allotments), and pending damage claims.

Real estate is almost always valued at historical cost, which in inflationary times is usually well below current market values. A number of different types of companies, including railroads, real estate developers, agricultural combines, paper companies, and REITs have major property holdings whose liquidation values often exceed their stock's market values. For example, one share of Tejon Ranch (AMEX) represents slightly over one-fifth of an acre of a parcel of land located halfway between Los Angeles and Bakersfield, California. Most of the real estate is farmed but part is in oil production and another part in residential development. The 1981–84 stock price range of $40–$108 is equivalent to a per-acre valuation of around $200–$500, which compares quite favorably with the 1975 average sale price of $618 for California farmland.[21] The stock's 1984 book value of $12.50 per share, in contrast, only reflected a nominal carrying value for the property. Tejon Ranch may or may not be an attractive investment but it was (in 1984) worth far more than its book value.[22]

Chicago Milwaukee Corporation, the holding company of the Chicago Milwaukee St. Paul and Pacific Railroad is (in 1984) bankrupt, but its large tracts of timberland give it an estimated $200–$300 per share breakup value compared with a 1981–84 per-share price range of $30–$192.[23] Moreover, the company's large tax-loss carryforward provides an attractive tax shelter. As with Tejon, however, its investment value may or may not approximate its liquidation value. Another group, the REITs (Real Estate Investment Trusts), are, according to some analysts, often worth far more than their stock prices (Table 8.1).

Many oil companies own reserves that may be worth considerably more than either their book or stock market values. A series of large mergers brought

Table 8.1   One View of REIT Values

STEEP DISCOUNTS

REITs' Stock Prices Belie Asset Values

	Valuation Date	Current Value	Market Price To Cur. Value
BankAmer Rlty	7/81	$38.50	— 38.3%
California REIT	10/81	14.02	— 42.0%
Federal Realty	12/80	35.65	— 39.0%
First Union Re.	12/81	25.11	— 38.7%
Intl. Inc. Prop.	6/81	11.04	— 18.5%
JMB Realty	8/81	32.26	— 38.0%
New Plan Rl. Tr.	7/81	24.28	— 44.4%
Pacific Rlt. Tr.	5/81	41.71	— 30.5%
Property Capital	7/81	29.00	— 9.0%
Rampac	6/81	a38.84	— 42.1%
Santa Anita	12/80	20.34	— 30.5%
University REIT	6/81	12.24	— 32.6%
Wells Fargo M&E	6/81	a31.04	— 30.7%

a-Entity has not revalued mortgages, which are sizeable part of assets. Share values are fully diluted. Market values are for properties, and independent appraisals concur except for JMB, New Plan and Pacific Rlt. *Source:* Audit Investment Realty Stock Review.

Source: "REITs at a Discount," *Barron's*, March 1, 1982. Reprinted by permission of *Barron's*, © Dow Jones & Company, Inc., 1982. All Rights Reserved.

particular attention to the oils. The New York Stock Exchange floor was frequently mentioned as the only place left where oil was still available at $5 a barrel (of proven reserves) compared with approximately $30 (above ground) on the open market.[24] Even allowing for the extraction costs, this differential is large. In smaller transactions, proven reserves often sold for $9–$15 per barrel. And yet on the balance sheet, proven reserves may not even be valued at $5 a barrel. Table 8.2 illustrates one media view of undervalued oil properties. Oil reserve values are, however, quite sensitive to the market price of crude. Thus, the softer oil market of 1982–84 saw a substantial decline in oil company liquidation-values.[25]

Tax-loss carryforwards are at best reported in a footnote to the financial statements. Yet such carryforwards' income tax shelter ability may be worth a substantial fraction of their dollar amount. Whether or not the carryforwards can be realized depends on the firm's future earnings potential and/or the possibility of its takeover by a firm that can utilize its tax loss. Table 8.3 exemplifies a magazine list of high-tax-loss companies.

When Can Liquidation Values Be Realized?

Firms with potentially undervalued assets such as those mentioned above have been relatively easy to find (1984). Three relevant questions relate to the ease

Table 8.2   The Price of Black Gold

The price of black gold

Has the stock market fully recognized the value of oil in the ground? Maybe not. Look at the extraordinary gap between these 34 companies' book values and the appraised values of their reserves. Then look at their stock prices.

Company	Reserves (oil & gas equivalents)		Value of reserves per barrel		Value of reserves per share		Recent stock price	52-week price range	Latest 12-months EPS	Price/ earnings ratio
	million bbls[1]	bbls per share	as reported[1]	as appraised[1]	as reported[1]	as appraised[1]				
Amerada Hess	1,258	17	$0.97	$5.60	$16.08	$ 64.65	37½	37⅝–18½	$ 7.00	5.4
Atlantic Richfield	4,884	21	0.66	5.12	13.95	109.20	59⅛	59⅛–35	6.17	9.6
BP Canada[2]	264	12	0.70	2.94	8.64	36.55	44½	57 –36[3]	4.65	9.6
Belco Petroleum	257	22	1.49	4.91	32.99	109.30	53¼	53½–29	7.28	7.3
Cities Service	1,067	13	1.02	4.25	13.00	58.20	45⅜	47¾–23⅞	5.64	8.0
Conoco	3,300	31	0.81	5.34	24.65	114.95	62⅝	62¾–39½	9.44	6.6
Dome Petroleum[2]	676	14	1.99	3.09	27.30	58.55	76⅛	95 –41½	4.56	16.7
Exxon	10,980	25	1.03	3.47	25.99	108.70[4]	75¼	75⅜–52	11.74	6.4
Getty Oil	2,463	30	1.15	4.20	34.59	103.55[4]	94½	97¾–60	10.03	9.4
Gulf Canada[2]	933	4	0.91	3.85	3.73	13.20	28⅛	36½–26½	1.55	18.1
Gulf Oil	3,092	16	1.72	5.74	27.20	79.65	45	54½–30¾	8.41	5.4
Hudson's Bay O&G[2]	883	12	0.41	4.20	4.75	45.90	32⅛	39½–25¼	1.83	17.6
Imperial Oil[2]	1,174	7	1.33	3.24	9.96	34.00[4]	43¼	59⅛–35⅛	4.36	9.9
Kerr-McGee	282	11	1.64	5.52	17.84	55.95[4]	86	87⅜–52	6.93	12.4
Marathon Oil	1,788	30	0.87	5.37	25.57	124.65[4]	64¾	73¼–40¼	6.29	10.3
Mobil	5,042	24	1.07	4.88	25.34	101.40	75¼	89½–43¼	12.59	6.0
Murphy Oil	347	9	2.17	5.61	20.17	52.20	49	49½–22½	3.49	14.0
Occidental Petroleum	960	13	0.66	1.54	8.63	20.70[4]	30¾	31⅞–19	10.49	2.9
PanCanadian Petro[2]	515	16	1.24	4.55	20.41	75.05	88⅛	92 –60¼[3]	6.62	13.3
Pennzoil	300	6	3.54	8.48	20.81	50.30	50⅜	54¼–29⅞	5.72	8.8
Phillips Petroleum	2,493	16	1.15	5.99	18.77	96.65	52½	61⅛–37⅝	6.49	8.1
Royal Dutch	5,499	41	1.53	4.41	62.75	184.84[5]	94	94 –66½	32.69	2.9
Shell Canada[2]	1,137	16	0.76	3.63	11.77	41.15	30½	44½–27⅞[3]	3.14	9.7
Shell Oil	3,477	12	2.28	6.99	25.70	78.85	48⅛	48¼–23	4.55	10.6
Shell Transport	3,666	13	1.53	4.41	20.30	59.76[5]	40⅜	41¾–27	10.25	3.9
Southland Royalty	341	7	1.37	8.02	10.12	58.45	61⅜	65 –20⅛	1.45	42.3
Standard Oil of Calif	2,941	17	1.11	5.04	19.12	91.50[4]	86¾	87¾–52½	12.99	6.7
Standard Oil, Indiana	3,681	13	1.56	6.26	19.70	105.05	71¾	73 –35¼	6.36	11.3
Standard Oil of Ohio	5,000	21	0.43	4.78	8.93	203.75[4]	65	65 –33⅞	7.04	9.2
Sun Company	1,430	12	1.25	4.45	14.80	127.85[4]	48⅞	48⅞–28¼	7.50	6.5
Superior Oil	938	37	1.80	4.58	66.48	200.45	233½	233½–99	11.39	20.5
Texaco Canada[2]	889	7	0.35	4.61	2.57	34.00	23⅛	31⅛–21¾	2.69	8.6
Texaco	4,710	17	1.11	4.92	19.35	86.15	37¼	41⅝–27	8.20	4.6
Union Oil of Calif	1,984	11	0.91	2.12	10.37	49.70[4]	43⅝	45 –19⅞	3.49	12.5

[1] Based on figures in *Oil Industry Comparative Appraisals* and *Petroleum Outlook*, John S. Herold Inc.; reserve figures used in appraisals may differ from current reserve figures. [2] Canadian dollars. [3] 1980 price range. [4] Appraisal excludes effects of windfall-profits tax on U.S. production. [5] Includes ownership in Shell Oil and Shell Canada, but excludes minority interests in those companies.

Source: "Like Buying Gold at $35 an Ounce," *Forbes*, October 27, 1980. Reprinted by permission of *Forbes* Magazine, October 27, 1980, © Forbes Inc., 1980.

or difficulty of realizing such values. First, how can asset values be estimated? Second, how does the market price compare with the hidden values? Third, if the market price does not accurately reflect the underlying asset values, will it eventually?

Determining the market value of the firm's undervalued assets is often rather easy. With the oil companies, for example, interest in the Dupont takeover of Conoco and U.S. Steel purchase of Marathon led to the publication of extensive breakup-value estimates for many of the other potential takeover targets in oil (Table 8.2) and elsewhere (Table 8.1 and 8.3). Such estimates may serve as a starting point. In other cases, the job is much more difficult. Relevant articles may appear in the financial press or inferences may be drawn from published financial reports. Moreover, current value disclosure now required of large firms may help identify companies with substantially undervalued assets.[26] Thus far, however, such disclosures seem to have been largely ignored.[27] The more difficult the valuation job, the less likely is the market to reflect such values. Thus, the most attractive opportunities may be the most difficult to uncover.

Knowing that a company's breakup value appreciably exceeds its market price does not necessarily imply that the stock is undervalued. Often the market's low valuation reflects poor earnings prospects coupled with little likelihood of early liquidation. Unless easily killed, a firm worth more dead than alive will be priced as a going concern rather than a liquidation prospect. An entrenched management with a strong ownership position often stands in the way of any outsiders who might otherwise take over and liquidate the company. Thus small stockholders may have no choice but to wait and hope for management to decide to liquidate. If the managers like their jobs, the wait may be long. On the other hand, investors who specialize in takeover and liquidation plays such as Carl Icahn, Boone Pickens, Victor Posner, and Saul Steinberg, may eventually help out.[28] Unless the investor has sufficient resources to acquire an influential position, however, he or she must wait for someone else to act.

Predicting when a liquidation might occur is hazardous, though the ease of acquiring control is one relevant factor. If the liquidation value is appreciably above the market price, if the stock's floating supply (that not locked up by those opposed to a liquidation) is a substantial percentage of the total, if the acquisition cost is not too large for those who would be inclined to take it over, and if the firm is in a relatively visible industry, takeover and liquidation is reasonably likely. Otherwise, liquidation may be a more distant prospect. If the profit potential is great enough, however, someone is eventually likely to act. Thus, a strategy of assembling a diversified portfolio of undervalued asset plays may produce enough winners to make it worthwhile. Both the Evergreen Fund and Mutual Savings Corporation have generated substantial returns with such a strategy.[29]

MISLEADING ACCOUNTING AND INDIVIDUAL INVESTORS

Work by Briloff and others have had a major impact on the accounting profession. Many reforms have taken place while many others are underway. Further changes will neither take place overnight nor eliminate the possibility of confusing and/

Table 8.3   Tax Umbrellas

Tax umbrellas

Here's a list of companies with the earnings leverage of large tax-loss carryforwards. Each lost a minimum of $25 million in at least one of the last seven years. Of course while tax-loss carryforwards can be a real shot in the arm, they're only valuable if the company has income to offset against the tax-loss carryforward.

Company[1]/principal business	Tax-loss carryforward total (mil)	Tax-loss carryforward per share	Revenues latest fiscal year (mil)	Latest 12-month earnings total (mil)	Latest 12-month earnings per share	Recent price	Price/ earnings ratio	Book value per share
(f) Allied Supermarkets[2]/grocery stores	$ 41.2	$ 7.90	$ 534.8	$ 3.2	$ 0.61	2⅛	3.5	d
American Airlines/airline	106.0	3.69	3,821.0	d125.2	d4.78	14⅞	d	$23.75
American Motors/auto	72.0	1.38	2,552.6	d197.5	d6.00	4⅞	d	9.25[3]
RL Burns/coal, oil and gas	36.3	2.27	104.9	8.2	0.54	7⅛	13.2	0.50
(f) CI Mortgage Group/real estate investment tr	33.6	6.98	11.6	2.9	0.61	7¾	12.7	9.42
Cenco/health care services	15.9	1.58	143.9	6.4	0.61	10⅝	17.4	4.85
Chicago Milwaukee/diversified holding co	173.0	70.55	111.1	2.1	0.87	39⅝	45.5	d
Chrysler/auto	2,000.0	29.86	9,225.3	d1,709.7	d26.00	6¾	d	nil[4]
(p) Commonwealth Oil Refining[2]/oil refining	20.8	1.39	1,313.2	d1.7	d0.22	2½	d	7.00[3]
Eastern Air Lines/airline	75.0[4]	3.03	3,450.0	d42.1	d1.97	9⅜	d	16.10[3]
Fedders/climate control systems	70.0	6.31	137.9	d29.0	d2.79	7⅛	d	d
First Pennsylvania/banking	150.0[4]	9.50	755.7	d164.1	d10.47	4½	d	11.98
(p) Food Fair[2,5]/grocery stores	121.0	16.44	1,124.1	17.6	2.38	4⅛	1.7	d
Genesco/apparel	29.1	2.31	834.7	4.2	0.08	7	NM	d
Great Atlantic & Pacific Tea/grocery stores	116.0	3.10	6,684.2	d49.9	d1.74	5⅜	d	10.85[3]
(f) Grolier/publishing	41.8	3.94	312.7	9.3	0.84	2⅝	3.1	d
Intl Harvester/agricultural equip	165.8	5.21	6,311.8	d271.5	d8.86	18⅞	d	53.30
(o) Itel[2]/leasing	275.0	23.02	223.8	d63.4[4]	d5.30[4]	½	d	d
Jonathan Logan/apparel	4.2	0.81	438.7	6.6	1.28	9½	7.4	25.65[3]
Leucadia National/finance	10.0	3.29	25.6	d2.8	d0.83	6⅜	d	8.20
LTV/integrated steel	200.0	4.77	8,010.0	127.9	3.95	22⅞	5.8	21.00[3]
(o) MCI Communications/telecommunications	2.6	0.08	144.3	14.8	0.12	13⅝	NM	0.40[3]
McLouth Steel/integrated steel	48.7	8.93	614.0	d55.0	d10.22	7⅞	d	22.65[3]
Memorex/computer equipment	16.0	2.21	768.7	d29.0	d4.42	13½	d	19.25[3]
National Tea/grocery stores	12.0	1.20	1,219.3	8.7	0.87	5¼	6.0	8.45[3]
The Outlet Co/broadcasting	1.0[4]	0.39	313.1	d33.3	d13.53	33⅝	d	d
Pan American/airline	130.0[4]	1.83	3,550.4	80.3	1.13	4⅞	4.3	8.30[3]
Penn Central Corp/multicompany	600.0	25.91	2,013.7	93.6	2.72	45⅝	16.8	50.70
Pier 1 Imports/retail	43.0	8.27	117.2	d2.8	d0.57	3⅛	d	2.05
Republic Airlines/airline	46.9	2.24	916.7	d24.7	d1.19	6⅞	d	5.25[3]
Sambo's/restaurants	22.0	1.71	490.1	d11.6	d0.90	5¼	d	1.75[3]
F&M Schaeffer[6]/brewing	38.0	20.42	183.5	0.6	0.14	7	50.0	d
(m) Seatrain Lines[2]/ocean transport	35.7	2.47	1,257.5	d219.6	d15.16	½	d	d
Singer Co/sewing machines; electronics	55.0	3.32	2,786.6	38.1	1.92	16⅛	8.4	13.30[3]
Teleprompter[7]/cable TV	11.0	0.65	203.6	23.2	1.36	34⅛	25.1	6.00[3]
Todd Shipyards/shipbuilding	9.6	2.25	507.4	14.3	3.08	26	8.4	28.08
UNC Resources/uranium mines	12.8	1.22	267.3	d32.0	d2.99	13⅛	d	14.37
United Merchants & Mfrs/textiles and apparel	158.0	26.63	622.0	d28.0	d4.72	5¼	d	9.63
Western Air Lines/airline	15.5	1.19	995.7	d29.6	d2.46	10⅛	d	12.60[3]
Wheeling-Pittsburgh Steel/integrated steel	4.0	1.03	1,054.1	14.7	2.85	29⅛	10.2	87.50[3]
(o) White Motor[2]/manufactures trucks	10.4	1.11	1,211.0	d56.6	d6.17	3⅝	d	NA
Wyly/computer services	20.0	1.72	117.8	19.5	1.54	11⅞	7.7	3.25

[1]All companies listed on the New York Stock Exchange except those labeled (m) Midwest Stock Exchange, (o) over-the-counter market, (p) Pacific Stock Exchange, (f) Philadelphia Stock Exchange.   [2]Company filed for reorganization under Chapter 11.   [3]Estimate from *The Value Line Investment Survey*.   [4]Estimate.   [5]Shareholders approved reorganization into a holding company: Pantry Pride.   [6]Stroh Brewery made acquisition offer @ $7.40/share.   [7]Westinghouse made acquisition offer @ $38/share.   d: deficit.   neg: negative.   nil: negligible.   NA: not available.   NM: not meaningful.

Source: S. Kichen and J. Greenberg, "From the Ashes," *Forbes*, April 13, 1981. Reprinted by permission of *Forbes* Magazine, April 13, 1981. © Forbes Inc., 1981.

or misleading financial statements. As the rules get tighter, those who would use them to mislead become more sophisticated. Moreover, the increasingly complex accounting problem for large multinational conglomerates in a period of rapidly fluctuating inflation, interest, and exchange rates is bound to magnify the ambiguities. Thus, investors may well be rewarded for reading financial statements carefully and trying to detect accounting abuses before the market does. Waiting for Briloff or someone else to expose an industry's misleading accounting risks losses that could have been avoided by sidestepping such investments. According to Kaplan and Roll, a stock's price may rise upon an inflated earnings announcement, but will usually fall once careful analysis has revealed the overstatement.[30] Both Emery and Kaplan and Roll concluded that the market usually sees through accounting manipulation eventually.[31]

Detecting Accounting Gimmicks

Even talented analysts may be unable to discover a purposeful deception from published data alone. Equity Funding's fraudulent insurance policies and Saxon Industry's bogus inventories probably could not have been exposed without insider help.[32] Even where no outright fraud was intended, detecting the misleading techniques from public documents may still be very difficult. Accounting statements are summaries containing only those aspects of financial operations that are deemed materially important. Facts the firm and its auditors consider unimportant may not appear in the statements. Finally, many investors do not have the expertise to uncover the abuses even if the necessary information is available in published records. This chapter is, however, designed to increase the reader's awareness of and ability to spot potential abuses.

To detect potentially misleading accounting procedures, investors should carefully examine published financial statements as an interdependent whole. The various pieces should form a consistent framework. The footnotes, an integral part of the financial statement, are often added at the auditor's request to present a fairer picture. The statements should also be carefully checked for internal consistency. For example, taxes should, in the absence of special circumstances, equal slightly less than half (46%) of profits before taxes. A lower tax rate has several possible explanations. The industry may receive special tax treatment; the firm may utilize tax shelters such as purchasing tax-free and local government bonds, or the firm may be reporting different results to IRS and the stockholders. Different reports to IRS and the stockholders is not necessarily improper, but does raise the possibility of optimistic reporting to stockholders. The SEC requires firms to explain greater than 5% departures from the statutory rate.

In addition to searching for inconsistencies, the investor/analyst should be familiar with the various areas where misleading accounting has been practiced: understated depreciation, inventory penetration, disposal of merger-acquired assets, anticipation of installment-sale income, and repurchase of outstanding securities. Many of the examples cited in the preceding pages are not, however, permitted by current accounting practices. Since the newly discovered gimmicks may be the most dangerous, one should not limit the analysis to areas of past abuses.[33] In summary, the following steps should help one to detect misleading accounting:

- Examine financial statements as an interdependent whole
- Carefully read all footnotes
- Check for internal consistency: taxes, depreciation, etc.
- Be familiar with past areas of abuse:
    understated depreciation
    disposal of merger-acquired assets
    anticipation of installment-sale income
    repurchase of outstanding securities
- Realize that the largest risks may come from new techniques.

SUMMARY AND CONCLUSIONS

Accounting involves substantial discretion, which may at times lead to misleading financial statements with or without the preparer's conscious efforts. Valuation involves a number of arbitrary choices in depreciation methods, inventory reporting, merger accounting, etc. The timing of income and expense recognition and the purchase of bonds below book value further complicate the picture. Such income-inflation devices as using unrealistic depreciation estimates, switching inventory methods, anticipating income, manufacturing profits through merger accounting, and reacquiring low-coupon bonds were discussed and illustrated with examples. Then we considered the profit potential of misleadingly pessimistic accounting statements. Real estate, mineral resources, and tax-loss carryforwards are especially likely to carry unrealistically low balance-sheet values. The liquidation value/stock price differential may or may not be relevant, depending on the prospects for liquidation. Finally, ways of spotting misleading accounting were considered. Statements should be examined as a whole with particular attention to footnotes, internal consistency, and areas of past abuse.

REVIEW QUESTIONS

1. Why are accounting gimmicks relevant to the stockholder?
2. Compare the various methods of depreciating assets.
3. Discuss how the use of LIFO and FIFO affect reported earnings and taxes.
4. Compare pooling of interest with purchase accounting.
5. Describe the potential abuses available to firms that must allocate income and expenses from installment sales.
6. In what way may bond refinancings lead to misleading earnings reports?
7. Discuss the difficulties of discovering accounting gimmicks.
8. Explain how one should go about checking financial statements for misleading reporting.

REVIEW PROBLEMS

1. Obtain a detailed financial statement of a savings and loan association. Using market interest rates on GNMA mortgage passthroughs and government bond quotes as a guide, estimate the value of its loan and securities portfolio. Compare these estimated values with its book values.

2. Obtain the financial statements of a firm that uses accelerated depreciation and another that uses straight line. Estimate what depreciation would be if each switched to the other's method. Use this estimate to show the impact on each firm's reported profits for the most recent year.

3. Find *Barron's* most recent Briloff article on the misleading accounting of a company or industry. Now track the performance of its securities for three months before and three months after the article appeared. Write a report.

4. Search *Barron's* and *Forbes* for a relatively recent listing of companies with liquidation values exceeding their stock's market values. Track their subsequent performance relative to the market. How many have been liquidated? How many outperformed the market? How many have been acquired? How many remain "undervalued?" Write a report.

5. Select an industry likely to contain many companies with assets whose market values substantially exceed the reported values. Estimate the liquidation values of each company. Construct a hypothetical portfolio of the most undervalued firms. Track its performance relative to the market for the succeeding six months.

NOTES

1. L. Spacek, "Business Sources" p. 27, cited in J. Lorie and M. Hamilton, *The Stock Market*, Irwin, Homewood, IL, 1973, p 146.

2. J. Siegel, "The 'Quality of Earnings' Concept—A Survey," *Financial Analysts Journal*, March/April 1982, pp 60–68; F. Black, "The Magic in Earnings: Economic Earnings versus Accounting Earnings," *Financial Analysts Journal*, November/December 1980, pp 19–25; A. Bernstein, "Reading Between the Lines," *Forbes*, May 10, 1982, pp 78.

3. R. Stern and P. Bornstein, "Now You See 'em, Now You Don't," *Forbes*, July 19, 1982, pp 34–36; J. Guyon, "Saxon Industries, 3 Ex-Aides Cited by SEC for Inflating Inventories, Falsifying Data," *Wall Street Journal*, September 10, 1982, p. 4; R. Hudson, "SEC Charges Fudging of Corporate Figures is a Growing Practice," *Wall Street Journal*, June 2, 1983, pp. 1, 19.

4. A. Briloff, *Unaccountable Accounting*, Harper & Row, New York, 1972.

5. Briloff, 1972, p 134.

6. R. Kaplan and R. Roll, "Investor Evaluation of Accounting Information: Some Empirical Evidence," *The Journal of Business*, April 1972, pp 225–257.

7. Briloff, p 37.

8. S. Sunder, "Relationship Between Accounting Changes and Stock Prices: Problems of Measurement and Some Empirical Evidence," *Empirical Research in Accounting: Selected Studies*, 1973, pp 1–45.

9. Briloff, 1972, pp 59–177 and 223–251.

10. Briloff, *The Truth About Corporate Accounting*, Harper & Row, New York, 1981, pp 90–110.

11. Ibid, p 93.

12. H. Hong, R. Kaplan, and G. Mandelker, "Pooling vs. Purchase: The Effects of Accounting for Mergers on Stock Prices," *The Accounting Review*, January 1978, pp 31–47.

13. Briloff, 1972, pp 113–114.

14. Ibid, pp 115–128.

15. Ibid, pp 163–171.

16. Ibid, pp 171–180.

17. Ibid, pp 183–192.

18. J. Dizard, "Fund of Funds: Its Long-Suffering Shareholders Are Finally Cashing In," *Barron's* February 1, 1982, p 13, 24, 25.

19. S. Jacobs, "Heard on the Street," *Wall Street Journal*, January 24, 1973, p. 39.

20. W. Bowler, "Credibility GAAP, Life Underwriters' Earnings Can't Be Taken At Face Value," *Barron's*, April 29, 1974, p 9; A. Briloff, "GAAP and the Life Insurance Companies," *Financial Analysts Journal*, March/April 1974, pp 30–38; W. Dyer, "Life Insurance Accounting Under Fire," *Financial Analysts Journal*, September/October 1974, pp 42–51.

21. G. Gilligan, *A Price Guide for Buying and Selling Rural Acreage*, McGraw-Hill, New York, 1976, pp 38.

22. D. Santry, "A $160 Per Acre Play in California Land," *Business Week*, March 19, 1979, p 144.

23. G. Putka and J. Normal, "Riding the Recovery of the Milwaukee Road," *Business Week*, August 10, 1981, p 78.

24. M. Kolbushlag, "The Luxury of Time," *Forbes*, September 14, 1982, pp 42–43.

25. G. Anders, "Breakup Values of Some Energy Firms are Cut by Herold, Depressing Shares of Small Oils," *Wall Street Journal*, April 9, 1982, pp 35.

26. W. Norby, "Application of Inflation-Adjusted Accounting Data," *Financial Analysts Journal*, March/April 1983, pp. 33–40; J. Ketz, "Are Constant Dollar Disclosures Informative?," *Financial Analysts Journal*, March/April 1983, pp. 52–55.

27. W. Bever, P. Griffin and W. Landsman, "How Well Does Replacement Cost Income Explain Stock Return?," *Financial Analysts Journal*, March/April 1983, pp. 26–32; S. Bar-Yosef and B. Lev, "Historical Cost Earnings versus Inflation Adjusted Earnings in the Dividend Decision," *Financial Analysts Journal*, March/April 1983, pp. 41–51; S. Lee, "Yawning GAAP: Why Interest in Inflation Accounting is Flagging," *Barron's*, August 15, 1983, pp. 13.

28. R. Stern and L. Saunders, "In Defense of Sharks," *Forbes*, March 15, 1982, pp 31–32.

29. B. Weberman, "Lieber's Love: Owning Takeover Candidates," *Forbes*, September 14, 1981, pp 234–235; R. Phalon, "Getting a Dollar for 50 Cents," *Forbes*, March 29, 1982, pp 146–148.

30. Kaplan and Roll, *op. cit.*

31. J. Emery, "Efficient Capital Markets and the Information Content of Accounting Numbers," *Journal of Financial and Quantiative Analysis*, March 1974, pp 139–140; Kaplan and Roll, *op. cit.*

32. *Business Week*, "Can Accountants Uncover Management Fraud?," *Business Week*, July 10, 1978, pp 92–95.

33. C. Power, "The Gimmicks of '82," *Forbes*, March 14, 1983, pp. 96–98; W. Konrad, "Reading Between the Pictures," *Forbes*, January 30, 1984, p. 126.

9 Operational Approaches to Fundamental Analysis

Investment texts traditionally devote several chapters to assessing a company's strengths and weaknesses through economic, industry and firm analysis. Identifying misvalued securities is, however, really quite distinct from analyzing a firm's prospects. Indeed practical investing requires approaches to investment selection that are both tangible and relevant. Accordingly this chapter surveys operational approaches contained in both the academic and the investor-periodical literature. We consider a variety of narrow fundamental approaches. *Forbes* magazine, *Value Line* and several other periodicals publish lists of interesting stocks. Many analysts recommend stocks with low PEs; others prefer companies with rapid growth records. Still others concentrate on small firms, R&D intensive firms, or potential takeover candidates. Avoiding firms with appreciable bankruptcy risks and buying out-of-favor stocks are yet other suggested techniques. Some services offer specialized investment advice and some analysts prefer stockholder- as opposed to management-oriented firms. The chapter concludes with an exploration of the investment implications of PE models and a discussion of several integrated methods of investment selection.

Forbes Lists

Forbes regularly assembles lists of stocks having something unusual in common. The accompanying discussion generally implies that an appreciable number are undervalued or otherwise attractive. For example, *Forbes* has since 1952 annually listed firms selling for a small fraction of their underlying assets' potential values. The criteria for "loaded-lagger" membership varies over time but always includes firms that are underpriced relative to their tangible assets. While some loaded-laggers will outperform the market, others stay on the list for years. Determining which stocks are truly undervalued is up to the investor. *Forbes'* 1980 list of "loaded laggers" and their subsequent relatively favorable performance is reproduced as Table 9.1.

While loaded laggers are compiled annually, most *Forbes* issues contain at least one list. For example: Stocks with low PEs and high growth rates, former institutional favorites, companies with dividend reinvestment plans, companies that are expected to emerge from bankruptcy with big profit potentials, potential

Table 9.1   Loaded Laggards of 1980, Revisited

Loaded laggards of 1980, revisited

If you invested $1,000 in each of the 25 stocks in the loaded laggards table FORBES printed in July 1980, your portfolio would now be worth over $39,000. That's a 56% return in about 18 months.

Company/principal business	Price June 1980	Recent price	% change
Adams Drug/retail	3⅜	4⅜	30%
American Motors/automotive	5⅜	2¾	−49
Bobbie Brooks[1]/apparel	3⅛	1⅞	−40
Ceco/construction equipment	13¾	16⅝	21
Cluett, Peabody/apparel	8⅝	15¼	77
Cunningham Drug Stores[2]/retail	8⅞	18	103
Fabri-Centers of America/textiles	5	13⅜	168
First Wisconsin/bank holding	23¼	27¾	19
Hart Schaffner & Marx/apparel	12⅜	18½	49
Helene Curtis Industries/cosmetics	6¾	13	93
House of Fabrics/textiles	4⅜	11¾	169
Jewelcor/retail	3⅝	3⅞	7
Magic Chef/home appliances	6½	8¼	27
McNeil Corp/industrial equipment	13¾	13⅝	−1
Munsingwear/apparel	14	14½	4
Outboard Marine/recreation	10⅜	19⅝	89
Oxford Industries/apparel	9⅝	31⅛	223
Pamida[3]/retail	3¼	6	85
Phillips-Van Heusen/apparel	11⅝	15¼	31
Questor/auto, recreation products	5½	9	64
Salant/apparel	5¾	9½	65
Sheller-Globe/auto parts	5⅝	12⅜	120
Springs Mills/textiles	15	24¼	62
Triangle Industries/metal fabricating	8⅝	11⅞	38
Wurlitzer/musical instruments	7⅝	4⅜	−43

[1]Firm filed Chapter 11. [2]Acquired by CD Holding at $18 a share. [3]Company sold assets and changed name to PMD Investment; offered $6 a share for all shares.

Source: S. Kichen and P. Bornstein, "The Lovely Uglies," *Forbes,* March 15, 1982. Reprinted by permission of *Forbes* Magazine, March 15, 1982. © Forbes Inc., 1982.

growth companies, stocks disliked by the experts, cash-rich and cash-poor companies, high-yield utilities, stocks that *Forbes* analysts expect to show substantial earnings increases, and emerging growth companies in a difficult market environment.[1]

Most *Forbes*-listed stocks are probably priced appropriately. Indeed some lists may contain a below-average number of undervalued situations. Stocks which appear undervalued by one criteria (such as tangible assets) may be accurately priced relative to a more important criteria (such as growth/survival prospects).

If identifying undervalued stocks were easy, we could all be rich. Nonetheless *Forbes* and *Forbes*-like lists may very well provide investors with a useful starting point. *Value Line,* for example, compiles weekly lists of the stocks that they cover for each of the following characteristics:

> Timely Stocks I (ranked #1 for next 12-month performance by *Value Line*)
> Timely Stocks II (ranked #2 for next 12-month performance by *Value Line*)
> Conservative Stocks I (ranked #1 for safety by *Value Line*)
> Conservative Stocks II (ranked #2 for safety by *Value Line*)
> High Yielding Stocks (estimated year-ahead dividends)
> High 3–5 Year Appreciation Potential
> Biggest Free Cash Flow Generators
> Best Performing Stocks (last 13 weeks)
> Worst Performing Stocks (last 13 weeks)
> Widest Discount from Book Value
> Lowest PE
> Highest PE
> Highest Annual Total Returns (3–5 years)
> Highest Estimated 3–5 Year Dividend Yield
> Highest Percentage Earned on Capital
> Untimely Stocks (ranked #5 for next 12-month performance by *Value Line*)
> Highest Yielding Non-Utility Stocks
> High Growth Stocks
> Stocks Trading at a Discount from their Liquidation Values

Low-PE versus Growth Stocks

Investment analysts have long debated the relative merits of low-PE and growth stocks. A stock's PE ratio reflects the market's view of the company's potential. A firm whose profits are expected to grow rapidly will command a high price relative to its current earnings. One with less bright prospects will generally command a lower PE. Virtually everyone recognizes that PEs should differ with the respective firms' prospects. The debate centers over how well the market prices securities (on the average) relative to their potentials. According to such well-known fundamental analysts as Graham and Templeton, the market frequently goes to extremes by overpricing stocks with exciting stories and driving those with problems well below the levels that their outlooks warrant. T. Rowe Price and other growth-stock advocates, in contrast, contended that firms with rapid growth potentials are attractive investments even at relatively high prices.[2] A high current PE may not seem overpriced relative to future earnings, and low PEs may reflect poor potentials. The two views have alternated in popularity.[3] While each viewpoint has some merit, the key question is not "can a high PE be justified?" but "are the PE's on many so-called growth stocks justified?" High

PEs can decline dramatically. For example, the Dow's composite PE rose from 12.1 on December 31, 1957, to 24.2 on September 29, 1961, only to fall to 16.2 nine months later. Since that time, the multiple has generally stayed under 20 and has often been below 10. Thus in retrospect the high-growth expectations for the soaring sixties were unrealistic.

Growth-stock advocates recommend companies with outstanding records even at high multiples. Earnings that grow at 20% will double in approximately four years. Should the multiple remain constant, the stock's price will also double over the same four-year period. The low-multiple school does not question the growth-exponents' arithmetic, but their implicit assumptions. As some have put it, very high multiples often discount not the future but the hereafter. Rapid current growth rates may simply be an anomaly. Malkiel noted in 1963 that if IBM were to grow 20% per year from 1960 to 1989, its total revenues would exceed the 1962 gross national product. Thus in a study of high-growth, high-multiple stocks, he assumed that growth rates would eventually decline to about the national average.[4] While IBM is a sizable company, many of the other traditional high-multiple stocks such as Xerox, 3M, Kodak, Disney, Avon, and Polaroid are also large. Even medium-size firms would grow to a large fraction of the economy if an abnormally high growth rate continued for several decades.

Noting that stock prices rise dramatically when both earnings and multiples increase, the low-PE advocates claim high PEs are less likely to rise appreciably than are low PEs. If a multiple may more easily increase from 5 to 10 than from 10 to 20, low-PE stocks may have a better chance of achieving truly outstanding performances. For example: a company selling initially at five times current earnings that grows at 20% per year for 10 years and doubles its multiple will sell for over 12 times its earlier price. The low-multiple advocates further contend that high-multiple stocks are particularly vulnerable to disappointing news.

The early 1970s saw the rise and fall of the "one-decision stock" concept. According to a then-popular view, certain high-quality stocks should, like Manhattan real estate, be bought, but not sold. Rapid past growth led many to expect above-average performance for the foreseeable future. Institutional investors (mutual funds, pension funds, insurance companies, and banks) scrambled to put away additional shares of 50 or so one-decision companies. The "foreseeable future" lasted about a year. The one-decision (or top-tier) stocks eventually fell dramatically toward the end of the 1974 stock market crash. Avon dropped from a 1973 high of 140 to 19; Disney from 121 to 19; and Polaroid from 143 to 14. Somewhat less dramatically, Xerox fell from 170 to 54 and IBM from 365 to 150. By comparison, the Dow Jones Industrial Average declined from 1051 to 576, about a 47% drop. Clearly, the one-decision stocks fully experienced the ravages of the 1974 decline. Indeed, nine years after 1973, the vast majority of the "nifty fifty" had failed to regain their "one-decision highs" (Table 9.2). While most of the companies have done well, their stocks have not. Revealing as Table 9.2 may be, such results need to be buttressed with academic research.

Table 9.2 ***Forbes'* Nifty Fifty in 1982**

Company	P/E ratio 1972	P/E ratio recent	Stock price range since 1972	Stock price recent	Stock price change since 1972	Earnings per share latest 12 months	Earnings per share change since 1972	Return on equity	9-year real return
Amer Hosp Supply	50	12	55⅜–18¾	39¼	–19.9%	$3.08	211.1%	14.5%	–58.5%
AMP	51	15	62½–20⅜	48⅜	13.5	3.75	316.7	24.8	–37.5
Automatic Data Proc	76	15	31¾– 5¼	23¼	1.8	1.55	434.5	17.4	–45.1
Avery Intl	64	10	51½–12¼	22¾	–47.1	2.95	227.8	15.1	–64.6
Avon Products	65	8	139¾–18⅝	29⅞	–78.2	3.66	69.4	27.1	–84.4
Bandag	59	9	43 –10⅛	24	–31.4	2.60	306.3	18.4	–61.1
CR Bard	52	15	42 – 9⅝	30⅝	–18.3	2.04	164.9	13.9	–57.2
Baxter Travenol Labs	78	17	34½–12⅛	33¾	21.1	2.15	451.3	16.2	–41.3
Black & Decker	50	11	42⅜–14¼	14¾	–59.0	1.34	88.7	16.6	–75.9
Burroughs	48	9	126⅜–27⅛	31	–71.5	3.58	52.3	3.8	–82.8
Clorox	41	6	53 – 5½	11	–76.3	1.80	68.2	14.8	–82.1
Coca-Cola	47	8	75 –22¼	31⅜	–57.7	3.58	125.2	21.1	–69.4
Colonial Penn Group	65	14	70 –12⅝	16⅝	–73.9	1.23	–5.4	14.9	–84.8
Damon Corp	53	30	70⅜– 3⅝	7¼	–88.1	d0.13	NM	4.3	–75.8
Digital Equipment	59	12	113¼–15⅛	86½	182.8	7.49	1,398.0	17.2	27.9
Walt Disney	81	14	110¼–15½	48½	–54.1	3.45	167.4	13.3	–75.9
Dr Pepper	62	9	30 – 6½	12⅛	–54.0	1.43	232.6	25.5	–70.4
Eastman Kodak	48	9	151¾–41⅛	71¾	–51.6	7.89	132.7	20.2	–70.3
Jack Eckerd	52	10	31⅞– 6¾	21⅛	–23.9	2.22	335.3	18.1	–51.6
Electronic Data Sys	49	16	32¾– 5⅜	22⅞	–15.3	1.47	177.4	24.7	–40.9
Emery Air Freight	62	8	37½–11⅜	11⅝	–61.0	1.46	175.5	30.6	–72.8
Fluor	48	9	71 – 3⅝	25½	246.7	2.83	1,786.7	26.3	119.0
Hewlett-Packard	61	16	53⅞–11½	40¼	86.1	2.55	628.6	19.2	–13.7
Intl Flavors/Fragrances	75	13	49⅜–16⅝	19⅛	–66.0	1.42	140.7	21.1	–74.7
Johnson & Johnson	61	17	44⅜–20¾	36½	–16.1	2.17	201.4	18.7	–55.3
K mart	54	8	51⅛–15⅛	15⅝	–68.0	1.88	88.0	11.5	–82.5
Eli Lilly	46	11	92½–32⅝	54	–32.2	4.76	157.3	20.3	–58.9
Longs Drug Stores	49	9	42¾–15¼	25¾	–34.4	2.79	236.1	17.4	–60.6
Marion Labs	46	25	57¾–11⅛	24¾	–44.7	0.95	0.0	12.5	–65.2
Marriott	56	11	47 – 5¾	34⅜	6.6	3.21	483.6	22.7	–47.7
Masco	46	11	42¼– 9½	35¾	26.3	3.39	413.6	20.7	–32.2
McDonald's	85	9	77⅜–21¼	59½	–22.0	6.54	595.7	21.1	–59.0
Merck & Co	45	15	103 –46⅝	81	–9.1	5.36	169.3	23.6	–46.2
MGIC Investment*	83	13	97⅞– 6⅛	50	–47.8	4.02	211.6	17.8	–72.1
Minn Mng & Mfg	40	11	91⅝–43	54¾	–36.1	5.74	164.5	21.7	–61.6
Natl Semiconductor	49	19	51½– 4⅛	19⅛	153.0	1.01	381.0	18.1	14.6
NCH	55	7	52¾–12¾	15⅛	–65.2	2.08	136.4	17.8	–81.1
Natomas	61	5	45¾– 3⅞	21	132.3	4.23	2,921.4	28.0	–64.3
Perkin-Elmer	47	15	36⅜– 7⅝	26⅜	37.9	1.76	351.3	18.7	–27.6
Polaroid	90	11	149½–14⅛	19¾	–84.3	1.87	43.8	9.0	–91.1
Ponderosa System	69	8	86¼– 3⅝	12⅛	–85.3	1.45	3.6	4.0	–91.8
Rite Aid	64	10	42½– 1⅞	27¾	–23.7	2.78	308.8	20.4	–57.9
Schering-Plough	50	8	87⅝–24⅞	28¼	–58.8	3.31	129.9	20.8	–76.0
Schlumberger	49	12	87⅛– 6⅜	50⅛	320.6	4.00	1,500.0	35.4	133.7
Simplicity Pattern	53	19	58⅞– 6⅛	9¼	–82.8	0.50	–53.3	8.3	–87.6
Sony	54	13	26⅛– 3½	16½	5.7	1.23	296.8	24.7	–45.6
Standard Brands Paint	52	9	56¾–18⅝	24¼	–55.1	2.79	173.5	16.3	–34.3
Texas Instruments	46	15	150¾–58⅝	78⅞	–13.3	5.38	147.9	19.9	–53.8
Wal-Mart Stores	52	18	43⅞– 1⅞	39¼	355.1	2.14	1,088.9	26.2	138.2
Xerox	48	5	171⅞–37⅜	40¾	–72.7	7.08	124.1	18.1	–84.3

*Baldwin-United merger offer at $52 a share. d: deficit. NM: not meaningful.

Source: Wilshire Associates

Source: M. Barnfather, "What Price Quality," *Forbes,* March 1, 1982. Reprinted by permission of *Forbes* Magazine, March 1, 1982. © Forbes Inc., 1982.

Relative PE Ratios

Several filter tests point to the selection value of low PE ratios. Breen concluded that ". . . low price-earnings multiples, measured either relative to the whole population, or to industry classification, when combined with a control on average earnings past-growth give portfolio performance which in most years exceeds that of randomly selected securities."[5] Latane and Tuttle, using seasonally adjusted data, found that 25 low-PE stocks had a six-month return (ignoring commissions) of 6.6% over the 1962–65 period compared to 3.5% for 25 high-PE stocks. For unadjusted data, the low-PE stocks returned 15.6% compared to 4% for the high-PE group.[6] Similar results were found by a number of other researchers.[7] Levy and Kripotos' study failed to support the low-PE advocates' hypothesis, however.[8]

Levy also analyzed low-PE stocks' resistance to market declines, concluding: "Low-price-earning stocks are resistant to short term declines; but that the relative advantage dissipates significantly as the downtrend is prolonged and disappears during reversals of 6 months duration."[9]

Reasons for Conflicting Results

Several factors may explain the differences in PE-subsequent performance results. First, some researchers employed more than one filter: Breen used earnings growth and Jones examined quarterly earnings reports. Thus their results may not be primarily due to the PE ratio. Second, low-PE ratio tests have usually used the Compustat data tapes which overrepresent successful firms having low beginning PEs. Only firms that grow to Compustat-size are included. Omitting a disproportionate share of unsuccessful low-PE stocks biases the results. Third, since low-PE stocks tend to be riskier than high-PE stocks, other things being equal, their apparently higher returns may simply reflect a reward for risk taking. Fourth, PE analysis relies heavily on the method of comparison. The results of those analysts who first get a "feel" for the data by experimenting with several different comparisons may fit the tested data better than reality.

The PE-performance controversy died down in the mid-1970s, only to revive with the publication of two Basu articles.[10] To overcome some of the objections to the earlier work, portfolios were formed of different PE levels and corresponding-risk-level control groups. Performance was measured from a point well after the initial earnings announcements. An extensive period and large number of stocks were covered. The results were uniformly favorable: The lowest PE portfolio outperformed the highest by 7%. While the issue remained controversial, Basu's results seemed to suggest that a low-PE selection strategy might be useful.

Combining PE Ratios with Other Factors

Bidwell and Riddle found PE ratios and a measure of abnormal quarterly earnings useful screens both separately and together.[11] Similarly Goodman and Peavy reported that company PE ratios relative to their industries' ratios were significantly related to excess returns with firms having low relative PEs outperforming those with higher ratios.[12] Most of the relevant work, however, has examined the relative roles of PEs and firm size.

Firm Size

While much of the evidence suggests that low-PE stocks tend to be underpriced, a more basic relationship may be at work. Specifically, a disproportionate number of low-PE firms may be relatively small companies that tend to outperform the market. Indeed Reinganum found that portfolios selected both on PE and firm size tended to generate abnormal returns (above the risk-adjusted market level). Moreover the PE-effect largely disappeared when size was controlled.[13] Banz found abnormal returns for small firms going back at least five years.[14] He also reported that most of the difference in returns occurred at relatively small firm sizes, while average and large firms' mean returns differed little. In a study covering the 1931–79 period, Lustig and Leinbach found significantly positive abnormal returns for small capitalization firms but not for larger firms.[15] Each author hypothesized that the small-firm effect was due to a misspecification of the Capital Asset Pricing Model (CAPM) used to adjust returns for risk. Lustig and Leinbach, for example, contend that the positive abnormal returns may simply be a reward for the extra effort of analyzing small firms. Roll argued, however, that the apparent abnormal returns of small-firm portfolios may be due to underestimating their risks.[16] Reinganum then tested Roll's hypothesis, finding that underestimates of small-firm betas could account for part but by no means all of the computed excess returns.[17] James and Edmister found that while trading activity (a measure of marketability) was related to firm size, it was not the underlying cause of the small-firm effect.[18]

The abnormal returns of small firms could be due either to superior performance relative to their fundamentals (current profitability, apparent growth potential, current leverage, per-share book value, etc.) or to underpricing relative to those fundamentals. The scale economies evidence argues against small firms consistently managing their assets more effectively than large firms.[19] On the other hand, institutional investors' preference for large firms (where they can make meaningful investments without undue price effects) and analysts' tendency to concentrate on larger firms (and thus draw attention to such stocks) may well cause such issues to be overpriced relative to the rest of the market. Indeed Arbel and Strebel find that stocks analysts ignore (whether large or small) tend to outperform the more closely followed issues.[20] Accordingly, a number of mutual funds such as the Acorn fund have sought to exploit this small-firm/neglected-firm effort by assembling portfolios of such companies.

The P/R&D Ratio

Such long-term stock market favorites as IBM, Xerox and Polaroid epitomize the growth potential of technologically derived new products. The popularity of small new high-technology companies such as Apple and Genentech illustrate the market's search for future Xeroxes. Since most new technologies require extensive research, Burgen of Dean Witter suggests using the ratio of stock prices to per-share R&D spending as a growth-potential index.[21] Firms have been required to disclose such expenditures since 1974. Burgen claims that relative R&D spending is an excellent first screen when combined with other fundamental factors.[22] Careful statistical analysis is needed to confirm (or disprove) the hypothesized relationship, however.

This author's studies of seven manufacturing industries (chemicals, electrical equipment, paper, mechanical equipment, nonferrous metals, petroleum refining, and drugs) indicate a significant causal relationship from R&D to subsequent profit and sales growth.[23] Scherer; Leonard; and Severn and Laurence reached similar conclusions.[24] While consistent with the hypothesis that R&D-intensive firms are attractive investments, the studies only tested half the relationship. Further research is needed to determine if the market price fully reflects the value of R&D activity. Indeed Doyle and Navratil reported that the market pays a premium for high R&D intensity.[25]

The P/Sales Ratio

Ken Fisher, a San Francisco money manager, contends that per-share price to per-share sales provides a more useful guide to misvalued securities than does the PE.[26] A low PE, according to Fisher, implies poor future profit expectations by the market. When, in contrast, the P/Sales is low, the market expects existing revenues to provide low profits. Since, however, P/Sales are relatively stable, a low P/Sales firm that can improve its profit margin will generate quite substantial per-share earnings. The trick, according to Fisher, is to identify firms with high sales relative to their stock prices that are likely to survive and eventually return to profitability. He argues that firms with high P/Sales may well be overpriced. Such firms typically have very high margins that may be difficult to maintain. Fisher cites a number of stock-story examples to illustrate his approach. Unfortunately, however, no one has yet subjected the P/Sales ratio screen to systematic analysis of past data.

Takeover Candidates

Buying a stock just before it becomes an acquisition target is one of the few ways of making a quick stock market killing. Acquiring firms almost always offer a substantial premium over the target firm's preannouncement price. Moreover, takeover candidates are sometimes bid up in a competition between two or more would-be suitors (National Airlines competition between Texas International and Pan Am and the Dupont/Seagrams/Mobil contest for Conoco).

Acquisitions have had a major impact on U.S. industrial structure. As the railroads linked the nation's local markets in the last half of the nineteenth century and the U.S. economy took on a national character, the resulting increase in competition led to the first great merger wave. From the Sherman Antitrust Act's passage (1890) through the turn of the century, merger activity continued at a breakneck pace. U.S. Steel, General Electric, American Can, American Tobacco, DuPont, Pittsburgh Plate Glass, International Paper, United Fruit, Allis Chalmers, Eastman Kodak and a host of others were assembled during this period. The amalgamations' promoters profitted handsomely. J.P. Morgan, for example, received $62.5 million (1901 dollars) for putting U.S. Steel together. The newly created giants' stocks were usually priced to reflect their just-acquired monopoly power. The severe recession of 1904 and antimerger ruling in *Northern Securities*[27] caused a sharp decline in merger activity. An adverse antitrust climate, weak stock market, and slow economy all tend to inhibit merger activity.[28]

A second major merger wave began during the 1920s and ended with the onset of the Great Depression. During this time the great public utility holding companies were assembled; vertical integration efforts increased and many industries saw the growth of a large "number two" firm (Bethlehem Steel, Continental Can and Allied Chemical).

A third merger wave began after the Second World War and reached a peak in the late 1960s. Since the antitrust laws blocked most significant vertical and horizontal mergers, firms such as LTV, Litton Industries, IT&T, and Gulf and Western Industries emerged through conglomerate acquisitions. The acquiring company's stock was used in virtually all of the takeovers, often at inflated prices. The depressed stock market of the early 1970s abruptly halted this game. Few rode higher or fell further than the conglomerates (LTV from 169 1/2 to 7 1/2 and Litton Industries from 94 1/2 to 2 3/4, for example).

Then in the mid-1970s a new merger wave slowly began. Unlike previous merger activity, most recent acquirers have used cash. The post-1973 depressed stock market both discouraged exchanges for the acquiring-company's stock and made cash acquisitions a cheap way of obtaining needed assets.

While the lawyers and investment bankers usually do well, most of the merger profits have been made by those who bought their stock early. Indeed the acquiring firm's shareholders almost always earn abnormal returns around the time of the takeover.[29] Unless one is an insider, identifying takeover candidates before the acquirers make their move is a difficult task. A *Business Week* article does offer some guidelines, however,[30] as does a subsequent *New York Times* article.[31] Similarly, Stavrou, an Evans and Company takeover-candidate specialist, compiled his own list.[32] Table 9.3 compares the *Business Week* and Stavrou lists.

The two sets of takeover criteria both emphasize the importance of substantial asset values, shareholders with reasons to sell, and recent large stock purchases. *Business Week* also lists prior takeover attempts and an industry with current takeover activity. Stavrou, in contrast, looks for companies with high profit potentials that are currently mismanaged.

Taking a slightly different approach, Wansley, Roenfeldt, and Cooley iden-

Table 9.3   Takeover Guidelines

Business Week	Stavrou
Low price relative to book value, cash or current assets	High liquidation value
Large shareholder ready to sell	Large shareholder ready to sell
Large recent stock purchase	A catalyst such as a large recent stock purchase
Previous takeover efforts	High market share
Industry with takeovers underway	Problems correctable by effective management

tified merger candidates solely from balance sheet/income statement information.[33] They found that acquisition candidates tended to be smaller, have lower ratios of PE, debt to assets, market value of equity to total asset value, and higher growth rates than nonmerging firms. Moreover a trading strategy of purchasing potential acquisition candidates based on these criteria generated substantial excess returns.

Acquiring companies themselves seem to be paying increasing attention to acquisitions' estimated discounted cash flows.[34] In essence the would-be acquirer treats the potential acquisition as a capital budgeting problem and assesses the prospective returns. Thus those with attractive discounted cash flows relative to their cost may be likely acquisitions.

Traders who use similar criteria may bid up many potential takeover candidates, thereby discouraging their acquisition and reducing the profit potential if the takeover proceeds. Still, an otherwise-attractive stock may be even more appealing if its takeover is likely.

Avoiding Bankruptcy Candidates

Just as selecting companies that are subsequently acquired may yield attractive returns, avoiding or perhaps even shorting companies that are likely to go bankrupt may be a profitable strategy. In 1968, Altman developed an early-warning system for identifying firms with a high bankruptcy probability.[35] Subsequent work indicates that bankruptcies are relatively predictable.[36] The Altman formula seems about as accurate at forecasting failures as most of the alternatives.[37] Whether one can profit from accurate bankruptcy predictions depends on the stock's pre- and post-bankruptcy performance. Aharony, Jones, and Swary found significantly negative risk-adjusted holding-period returns up to four years prior to a bankruptcy-filing.[38] Similarly Clark and Weinsten reported that shareholders experienced large losses during the month of a bankruptcy filing with much of the losses concentrated during the three days surrounding the announcement.[39] Taking advantage of such performance depends on having lead-time relative to the market. Using one form of risk adjustment, Altman and Brenner found predictable subsequent negative performance associated with deteriorating financial data, but the relationship disappeared when a second risk-adjustment procedure was used.[40] Thus bankruptcy-prediction models' trading signals may or may not be helpful. Those who want to try them may find a simplified form of the Altman model useful.[41] One calculates a Z-score value of credit worthiness and financial viability from the following financial data:

$$\text{Altman } Z\text{-Score} = 1.2A + 1.4B + 3.3C + 1D + .6E$$

where:

  A = working capital/assets
  B = retained earnings/assets
  C = pretax earnings/assets
  D = sales/assets
  E = market value of equities/liabilities

A firm scoring less than 1.81 is classified as troubled. A further refinement of the Altman formula has been developed by a consulting firm called Zeta Services (Morningside, New Jersey). While this proprietary model's output is sold primarily to institutional subscribers, its results are sometimes written up in places such as *Business Week* (Table 9.4). *Value Line's* Relative Financial Strength System provides similar output to its subscribers.

Contrary Opinion: Investing in Troubled Firms

Far from avoiding troubled firms, some investors seek them out. Indeed the so-called theory of contrary opinion advises investors to concentrate on out-of-favor (and therefore presumably undervalued) issues. The market will eventually return to its neglected former favorites, or so the argument goes. Contrarians may contrast their concept with what they disparagingly refer to as the "greater-fool theory." That is, those who follow fads often bid prices up to unrealistic levels hoping that still "greater fools" will pay even more.

Like many stock market concepts, contrary opinion investing is easier to discuss in the abstract than to practice. Concentrating on currently unprofitable companies is one possible approach. In 1980 *Forbes* put together a list of relatively large money losing companies. Two years later they assembled a second list along with a report on the first list's subsequent performance (Table 9.5).

The results are rather grim. Of the 90 firms, eight filed for bankruptcy and fifteen more remained unprofitable two years later. Overall the list declined 8%, which was comparable to the S&P 500's performance over the same period. Dividends were substantially higher for the S&P than the list of unprofitable firms, however. Nevertheless *Forbes* prepared a second list and argued that if the unprofitable firms can hold their own in a weak economy, just think how well they might do in an up market.[42]

Investing in low-priced stocks is another contrary opinion approach.

Table 9.4   Zeta Financial Ratings

	12 mos. ending	Vulnerability by Zeta rating*
Manufacturing		
Diversified Industries (metals, smelting)	10/81	−5.82
Elcor (building materials)	12/81	−3.45
Alpha Portland Industries (cement)	9/81	−3.40
General Refractories (furnace linings)	12/81	−2.25
NVF (steel)	12/81	−1.42
International Harvester (farm equipment)	1/82	−0.76
Allied Products (fasteners, metal stamping)	12/81	−0.75
Condec (valves, robots)	1/82	−0.57
Wheeling-Pittsburgh (steel)	12/81	−0.26
Autos		
American Motors	12/81	−3.69
Chrysler	12/81	−3.55
Airlines		
Braniff International	9/81	−4.32
Continental	12/81	−3.10
Western	12/81	−3.05
Republic	12/81	−2.86
World	9/81	−2.59
Eastern	12/81	−2.49
PSA	9/81	−2.15
Pan American	12/81	−1.74
Trucking & air freight		
Carolina Freight	9/81	−0.97
Transcon	12/81	−0.34
Tiger International	12/81	−0.03
Retailing		
Pantry Pride	10/81	−6.99
Borman's	10/81	−3.91
Allied Supermarkets	9/81	−3.35
A&P	8/81	−3.25
Genesco	10/81	−2.69
Pueblo International	10/81	−2.35
KDT Industries	10/81	−2.31
Foodarama Supermarkets	1/82	−2.22
Cook United	10/81	−2.21
Food processing & lodging		
Rath Packing	12/81	−11.09
General Host	12/81	−2.07
Ramada Inns	9/81	−1.93
United Brands	12/81	−1.48
American Bakeries	9/81	−1.48
Valmac Industries	12/81	−1.32

Data: Zeta Services Inc.

*Scores were derived through a proprietary computer analysis called "Zeta," which gauges the financial condition of a company by consolidating the effect of seven important financial ratios that measure profitability, liquidity, and leverage. The largest negative numbers suggest the highest degree of vulnerability to financial pressures.

Source: "How One Formula Rates Companies Vulnerability," *Business Week*, May 17, 1982. Reprinted by permission of McGraw-Hill, Inc.

Table 9.5   Forbes Followup

Ashes and diamonds

Here's what happened to the stock prices of FORBES' first "Red isn't dead" list of 90 moneylosing companies September 1980.

Company	% change in price	Company	% change in price	Company	% change in price
American Airlines	92%	Fotomat	−33%	Roblin Industries	−78%
American Biltrite	5	Gateway Transportation[2]	37	Ronson	−24
American Motors	−40	Gino's[2]	71	Salem Carpet Mills	−25
Arctic Enterprises[1]	−50	Goldblatt Brothers[1]	−89	Sambo's Restaurants[1]	−67
Bibb	45	Great A&P	−10	F&M Schaefer[2]	56
Bobbie Brooks[1]	−66	Hayes-Albion	−35	Seatrain Lines[1]	−96
Braniff Intl[1]	−90	Edward Hines Lumber	6	Sheller-Globe	104
Cagle's	−48	Instrument Systems[4]	−85	Soundesign[2]	172
Champion Home Bldrs	120	Intl Foodservice[2]	−64	Spector Industries[2,5]	−80
Chrysler	−28	Intl Harvester	−89	Standard Products	15
City Stores	−27	Itel[1]	−65	Superscope	−62
Coachmen Inds	35	Keystone Consolidated	4	Susquehanna	−7
Combustion Equipment[1]	−100	KLM	1	Talley Inds	−23
Commonwealth Oil	−92	Laclede Steel	−17	Texfi	−45
Continental Air Lines	−52	M Lowenstein	167	Trans World Corp	8
Culbro	166	Manhattan Industries	89	Tyson	10
Dayton Malleable	−34	CH Masland	−13	UAL	−18
Ehrenreich Photo-Opt[2]	24	Massey-Ferguson	−74	UNC Resources	−66
Elixir Industries[3]	142	McLean Trucking[2]	55	Uniroyal	67
Envirotech[2]	1	McLouth Steel	−79	US Steel	−19
Facet Enterprises	5	Memorex[2]	−10	Valmac Industries	−14
Fedders	−18	Monfort of Colorado	44	Victoria Station	−16
Filmways	−32	National Kinney	−29	Vornado	−34
Firestone	54	Orange-co	0	Ward Foods[2]	22
First Pennsylvania	−39	Ozark Airlines	71	Westmoreland Coal	−24
Fischer & Porter	−37	Pan Am World Airways	−38	White Motor	−95
Fleetwood Enterprises	91	Penn-Dixie Industries	−79	Wilson Freight[2]	−100
Food Fair (Pantry Pride)	65	Raybestos-Manhattan	−47	Winnebago Inds	117
Foodarama	0	Republic Airlines	−49	World Airways	−48
Ford Motor	−19	Robintech	−61	WTC	−7

[1]Company filed for bankruptcy within period 9/80 to present. [2]Company merged or acquired within period 9/80 to present. [3]Company went private. [4]Reverse 1/10 split in 1981. [5]Spector division of TeleCom filed Chapter 11 in 1981.

Source: S. Kichen, "Reds II," *Forbes*, July 19, 1982. Reprinted by permission of *Forbes* Magazine, July 19, 1982. © Forbes Inc., 1982.

According to Edmister and Green, such issues tend to offer superior risk-adjusted returns.[43] An even more daring contrary approach concentrates on one of the most out-of-favor groups: the bankrupts. Thus one *Barron's* author argued "Equity Funding, Penn Central, Interstate Stores and Daylin all have sought the shelter of bankruptcy. But like corporate Lazaruses, each has risen from the dead."[44] While bankrupt companies usually decline severely around the time of their filing, a few eventually come back handsomely. Many are total or near-total losses, however. Table 9.6 shows what happened to companies that filed for bankruptcy in the three years prior to 1981.

Still other contrary approaches include buying shares in a contrary-opinion mutual fund (Contrafund, for example, rose by 300% from its 1976 founding until 1982, compared with 150% for the S&P 500); seeking out liquidation-candidates; and concentrating on the depressed issues favored by insiders.[45] Greenblatt, Pzena, and Newberg find that stocks selling below their liquidation values generally provide above-average risk-adjusted returns.[46]

Table 9.6   Bankrupts' Performances

Company	Bankruptcy filing date	Stock price near filing	recent	% change
Allied Artists	4/4/79	1 3/4	1/4	−86%
Allied Supermarkets	11/6/78	5/8	1 1/16	70
Capehart	2/16/79	3/8	0	−100
City Stores	7/30/79	2 1/4	3 1/2	56
Commonwealth Oil Refining	7/23/79	10 1/4	5/8	−94
EC Ernst	12/4/78	4	1 1/4	−69
Inforex[1]	10/24/79	1 7/8	1/4	−87
Interlee (FDI)[2]	12/4/78	7 1/2	3/4	−90
Lafayette Radio Electronics[1]	1/4/80	7/8	1 1/16	21
Mansfield Tire & Rubber	10/2/79	3/4	0	−100
National Shoes	12/12/80	1 3/4	2 1/2	43
Pantry Pride (Food Fair)[2]	10/3/78	2 7/8	4 1/8	43
Penn-Dixie Industries	4/7/80	2 3/8	1 1/2	−37
Piedmont Industries	2/22/79	1 1/4	1/4	−80
Richton Int	3/18/80	1 1/4	1 1/2	20
Sam Solomon	8/21/80	3 3/4	1 1/4	−67
Tenna	12/5/79	1 3/8	0	−100
Triton Gr (Chase Man M&R Tr)[2]	2/22/79	7/8	7/16	−50
The Upson Co	6/25/80	1 1/8	1/2	−56
West Chemical Products	1/22/79	4 3/8	6 1/2	49
White Motor	9/4/80	5 3/8	1/4	−95
Wilson Freight	7/23/80	2	1/4	−88

[1]Acquired. [2]Former name.

Source: S. Kichen and A. Field, "Of Risks and Rat Holes," *Forbes*, March 1, 1982. Reprinted by permission of *Forbes* Magazine, March 1, 1982. © Forbes Inc., 1982.

Specialized Advisory Services

A variety of investment services sell very specialized advice.[47] O'Glove and Olstein (*Quality of Earnings Report*) carefully analyze published financial statements to forewarn their clients of bad news. Crary (Bear Stearns and Co.) advises clients on the likely outcomes of relevant court cases. Charles E. Simion and Company (1725 K Street, NW, Washington, DC 20006) monitor SEC filings of specific companies. Finally, Vogel and Monroe (Moore & Schley, Cameron & Co.) and several others identify potentially misvalued securities with their own stock-valuation formulas. Indeed many specialized and a host of generalized advisory services offer investment advice and forecasts. While some advisory services may be worth their cost, identifying them may be about as difficult as selecting the misvalued securities themselves.

Managerial Objectives

From Adam Smith's time (circa 1776) until the 1920s, most economists believed that firms were largely motivated by their owners' interests. With the rise of large publicly owned corporations, however, the managerial and ownership functions became increasingly separated. In 1929, 88 of the 200 largest nonfinancial firms were "management-controlled": no discernible group owned 20% or more of the stock and no smaller block showed any evidence of control.[48] By 1963, 169 of the top 200 were management-controlled, while only five were controlled by a majority-ownership group.[49] The absence of identifiable ownership groups would seem to increase manager's discretion. Thus, one wonders whether managers have any reasons to sacrifice stockholder interests, and if so, how far they can go before jeopardizing their own positions?

Baumol contends that since managerial salaries and prestige are more closely related to sales than profits, managers might sacrifice income for growth.[50] Empire-building motives may reinforce this tendency. A high preference for security can also conflict with the profit-maximizing goal. On the other hand, by doing less well than they might, managers widen the gap between their firm's actual and potential market values, increasing the risk of takeover bids, proxy fights, and bankruptcy, all of which jeopardize their jobs. Since, however, outsiders often have difficulty assessing managerial performance, stockholder interests may be sacrificed appreciably before management's position is threatened.

Even if the managers' personal investments in their firms influence their behavior, the potential for conflicting or independent interest exists. Particularly blatant types of abuse include: corporate officials overpaying themselves, trading on inside information, disposing of corporate assets at bargain prices to friends or relatives, and favoring certain suppliers.

A proposal to give 50 high-level Security Pacific Corporation officials $18 million worth of stock over a 10-year period with no established distribution-guidelines is a probable example of managers overpaying themselves.[51] Other likely abuses of power included Penn Central, Equity Funding, and Texas Gulf Sulphur officials trading on inside information. In another example, two Armour traffic officials in the 1930s directed Armour shipments to rails using specialized gears manufactured by a firm in which they owned stock. The gear manufacturer's marked share grew from 1% to 35% before the FTC stepped in.[52]

Emphasizing growth at the expense of profits may be less blatant but more damaging to stockholders. Thus excessive sales promotion, setting low margins, and especially acquiring firms at inflated prices can harm current stockholders. Organizational slack is another potential problem. When not under competitive pressure, firms may allow costs to increase and overall efficiency to decline. Moreover, managers may use the corporation to promote social and political goals having little or no relation to its business. Some social and political activity may improve the firm's public image or legal climate, but other actions may reflect the manager's own particular social goals and priorities.

While these abuses' impacts may not be measured directly, the performance of management-oriented firms can be compared with stockholder-oriented firms. In a study of management-controlled versus owner-controlled firms, Monsen, Chiu, and Cooley concluded:

> The net income to net worth ratio was 75 percent higher for owner-controlled firms than management-controlled ones over the twelve year period. This result indicates that the owner-controlled firms provide a much better return on the original investment, and suggests a better managerial capital structure and more efficient allocation of owners' resources.[53]

Similarly Masson found that "firms with executives whose financial rewards more closely paralleled stockholders' interests performed better in the stock market over the post-war period."[54] In a paper that incorporated a survey of the past 50 years of merger work and some original research of his own, Hogarty stated:

> No one who has undertaken a major empirical study of mergers has concluded that mergers are profitable, i.e., profitable in the sense of being "more profitable" than alternative forms of investment. A host of researchers, working at different points in time and utilizing different analytic techniques and data, have but one major difference: whether mergers have a neutral or negative impact on profitability.[55]

More recent studies have found that merger activity resulted in increased risk and little or no gain to acquiring-firm stockholders (while the target-firms' shareholders profit handsomely).[56] Thus, corporate officials may either be consistently misjudging merger opportunities, or merger activity has often been motivated by managerial interests.

Palmer examined the interaction of monopoly power and owner control, finding that "among firms with a high degree of monopoly power, management-controlled firms do report significantly lower profit rates than owner-controlled firms."[57] On the other hand Kamerschen found no significant difference in profitability between manager- and owner-controlled firms among Larner's sample of the 200 largest nonfinancial corporations.[58]

The evidence to date on this subject may be summarized as follows: Since managers often substitute their own interests for those of the stockholders, firms managed in stockholders' interests generally tend in some sense to outperform management-oriented firms.

Only the Masson study and more recent work by Levin and Levin[59] suggest a direct link between stock market performance and manager orientation. The other cited articles indicated a relationship between a firm's internal performance and management interest that the stock price may have already discounted. Thus manager orientation by itself may not be a particularly valuable selection criterion. A knowledge of management orientation may, however, be useful when the market price is slow to reflect the superior performance produced by a stockholder-oriented management. Accurately predicting when a firm's managers are about to become more stockholder oriented may be especially worthwhile. Management's new orientation should eventually increase earnings. Thus purchasing the stock before these results become obvious could be particularly profitable. Moreover, avoiding management-oriented companies may help sidestep some losers.

To apply these recommendations one must first identify management's goals. Management statements, such as the president's letter in the annual report, provide one clue. If growth is emphasized and profits are played down, the implications are obvious. Similarly, corporate officials can be asked to discuss goals at the annual meeting or elsewhere. Previous merger activity and management's compensation packages and portfolio composition may provide additional insight. Periodic efforts to reduce costs demonstrate that excessive organizational slack is not tolerated. A low payout ratio coupled with below-average growth suggests that management may be particularly concerned with its own interests. Management-oriented officials will vigorously oppose takeover bids or try to negotiate guarantees of their own positions. Stockholder-oriented managers will, in contrast, seek the best terms for the shareholders confident that their past performance will protect their jobs.

Encouraging a shift toward a stockholder orientation is clearly in the shareholders' interests. Accordingly, shareholders might well prefer the dissidents in a proxy fight, as a large pro-dissident vote is likely to make existing management more stockholder oriented. Asking pointed questions of management-oriented managers either by letter or at annual meetings may also signal potential stockholder-dissatisfaction.[60] Finally, a thwarted takeover bid or a new compensation scheme that ties salaries more closely to profits or stock performance may favorably affect managerial goals.

Narrow fundamental approaches as discussed here may be summarized as follows:

- *Forbes* and *Forbes*-like lists provide an interesting start in the search for undervalued securities.
- Low-PE stocks may outperform the market
- Small-capitalization stocks may outperform the market
- Stocks neglected by investment analysts may outperform the market
- R&D intense firms may be identified by observing their price/R&D spending ratio
- Low price/sales stocks may be undervalued
- Takeover candidates usually do well but anticipating the targets is difficult

- Altman's formula may help one avoid firms with a high risk of bankruptcy
- "Contrarians" advocate buying out-of-favor stocks
- Specialized advisory services offer specific types of investment advice
- Stockholder-oriented firms may outperform those with a managerial-orientation.

PE RATIO MODELS

Profit-prediction efforts presume that the market price will eventually reflect profitability changes. Attempts to establish equilibrium PE ratios for particular stocks are more direct. An effective PE ratio model could be used to predict actual PEs' movements toward their model values. If PEs migrate toward their estimated equilibrium values more quickly than those equilibrium values change, knowledge of the equilibrium estimates could help identify misvalued securities. Accordingly, a number of researchers have estimated equations of the "normal" or "predicted" PE ratio. A "normal" PE less than the actual ratio suggests the stock is overpriced. Whitbeck and Kisor's use of this technique is illustrative.[61]

Theoretical $PE = 8.2 + 1.5\,A + 6.7\,B - .2\,C$

> where
> A = growth rate
> B = payout ratio
> C = standard deviation around the trend line price   (1)

Relevant data were then used to calculate a theoretical PE for each sample company. For four different dates, the authors found that stocks with a market/theoretical PE ratio of .85 outperformed the Standard and Poor's 500 stock index. Stocks that had a ratio of 1.15 or more underperformed that same index. The Whitbeck-Kisor model was applied with Bank of New York forecasts and thus its success depended largely on the accuracy of their analysts.[62] The Bower model, which utilized historical data rather than forecasts, was, in contrast, unable to identify misvalued securities.[63] Clearly, expectational-variables play an important role in explaining PE ratios.[64]

Very little has been published on theoretical PE ratio models since the early 1970s. The computed model parameters fit one period but generally failed to hold up over subsequent periods. Thus the underlying equilibrium values for the PE ratios may change too rapidly for a dependable tendency to move toward the estimated values to emerge.

INTEGRATED APPROACHES TO FUNDAMENTAL ANALYSIS

In addition to the narrow (largely one variable) selection criteria and the PE ratio model methodologies, several integrated fundamental approaches have been devised, notably those of Graham and Templeton.

The Benjamin Graham Approach

Benjamin Graham, coauthor of the dominant investment text[65] of the 1930s, 40s and 50s, and a frequently quoted authority, advocated investment in financially strong companies with low prices relative to their underlying values. In the last years before his death in 1976, he and Dr. James B. Rea listed a set of ten simple criteria for identifying undervalued stocks.[66] These criteria can be grouped into three categories: low price, strong finances, and growing earnings. Specifically Graham and Rea suggested selecting securities with:

1. An earnings to price yield of at least twice the AAA bond yield. Thus if AAA bonds yield 10%, EPS should equal at least 20% of the stock's price (PE of 5 or less)
2. A PE ratio no higher than 40% of its five-year high
3. A dividend yield of at least two-thirds of the AAA bond yield
4. A stock price below two-thirds of tangible per share book value
5. A stock price less than two-thirds of net quick liquidation value (current assets less total debt)
6. Total debt less than tangible book value
7. Current ratio of 2 or more
8. Total debt no greater than twice the net liquidation value
9. Compound ten-year annual earnings growth of at least 7%
10. Two or fewer annual earnings declines of 5% or more in the preceeding ten years.

Very few stocks ever meet all of these criteria. Those qualifying in seven or more are said to have a high "reward-to-risk" ratio. Graham and Rea particularly stress criteria 1, 3, 5, and 6 (a low stock price relative to earnings, dividends and book value and low debt relative to book value.) They contend that individual high reward-to-risk stocks may not necessarily perform well, but a diversified group of 30 or so such securities should produce handsome returns. Rea's own work covering the 1925–75 period supports his conclusion, as does research by Robert Fargo, a financial consultant based in San Francisco.[67] Moreover several Graham-oriented money managers have produced impressive performances.[68] Two studies meeting the more exacting standards of academicians are also supportive. Oppenheimer found that Ben Graham stocks generally did particularly well each January,[69] while Oppenheimer and Schlarbaum reported that over the 1956–75 period Ben Graham-type stocks returned 3 to 3 1/2% more than the market portfolio.[70]

Graham and Rea also suggested that one should sell a stock whenever:

a) it appreciated by 50% or more
b) it had been held for more than two years
c) its dividend is eliminated
d) its earnings drop sufficiently to make it overpriced by 50% or more relative to criterion 1 (too high a PE ratio).

On the other hand, a stock that would still be bought on the basis of the original criteria should be held. Little or no research (other than that implicit in Rea's own work) supports the value of these selling rules, however.

Templeton's Approach

If results are any indication of an approach's value, that followed by John Marks Templeton deserves careful scrutiny. "According to every major mutual fund rating service . . . Templeton's Templeton Growth Fund has been the outstanding performer over the last 20 years,"[71] said a 1977 *Forbes* article. Unlike Graham and Rea, Templeton has not reduced his approach to a series of simple rules. Still, its major elements may be established from the published record:[72]

1) Templeton advocates a world view to investing. U.S. stocks are only one component. At any one time stocks are cheaper in some countries than others.
2) Like Graham and a host of others, Templeton prefers a low price relative to current earnings, asset values, and dividend yields.
3) Unlike Graham, he believes that extensive diversification with risky stocks can produce an acceptable portfolio risk.
4) He suggests selling when the market is particularly optimistic and buying when it is particularly pessimistic (who does not?).
5) He tries to assess emerging socio-economic trends and their likely investment impact. In 1977 he saw a growing economic role for government, with an especially adverse impact on the visible and therefore more vulnerable large firms. Similarly, he saw continued high inflation rates and thus advocated investments where the returns are most likely to move up with the price level.

Like Graham, Templeton seeks out-of-favor conservatively priced stocks. In addition he tries to assess the future (Will the country offer a favorable investment climate? Is the company well situated for forthcoming economic trends?) On the other hand Templeton is less concerned with individual risks than is Graham. Thus a low current ratio or high debt ratio would not necessarily bother him.

SUMMARY AND CONCLUSIONS

A wide array of fundamental approaches has been suggested. *Forbes* lists offer a useful starting point. Low-PE stocks may tend to be undervalued, but small firms ignored by the investment analysts seem to be a better bet to outperform the market on a risk-adjusted basis. High R&D intensity may be a modest plus, while an unrecognized takeover candidate could handsomely reward a timely purchase. Bankruptcy candidates and other depressed issues may be misvalued (contrary opinion), although relevant evidence is scarce. In certain circumstances, specialized advisory services and knowledge of manager orientation may help investors. PE ratio models' investment values seem limited. Of the fundamental approaches considered, the integrated methods of Graham and Templeton seem to show the greatest promise. The available admittedly limited evidence does point to their usefulness. Perhaps combining the small firm, stock holder orientation, and SPI profit-potential components with the basic Graham-Templeton framework would prove even more promising.

REVIEW QUESTIONS

1. How should one use the *Forbes* list approach to investment selection?
2. Summarize past empirical work relating the PE ratio to subsequent returns.
3. Discuss the evidence on the small-firm and neglected-firm effects.
4. Discuss the use of R&D in investment selection.
5. List and analyze the various criteria for identifying takeover candidates.
6. Discuss the principal components of the Altman bankruptcy warning formula.
7. List several specialized investment advisory services' functions.
8. What is meant by the separation of ownership and control? What is its relevance to the investor?
9. In what ways may manager and stockholder goals differ?
10. Review the empirical evidence relating to manager- versus owner-controlled firms.
11. What are the investment implications of manager versus owner control?
12. Discuss the two basic types of PE ratio models and compare the relevant evidence on their values.
13. Compare the Graham and Templeton approaches.

REVIEW PROBLEMS

1. Choose a *Forbes* list at random and follow the stocks' performances for six months. Write a report.
2. Choose five low-PE and five high-PE stocks touted for their growth prospects; follow their performance for six months. Write a report.
3. Identify a list of stocks with rumored takeovers, and a second list with takeover efforts under way. Follow their performance for six weeks after the rumor of announcement. Write a report.
4. Using the takeover criteria lists of *Business Week* and Stavrou, identify ten potential takeover candidates. Follow their stocks over one year. How many were actually taken over? How would an investor in these stocks have done? How would buyers of the others have done? Write a report.
5. Using the Altman bankruptcy model, identify five companies with

substantial bankruptcy risks. Follow them over twelve months. How many filed for bankruptcy? What was the experience of investors in the group? Write a report.

6. Refer to Figure 9.1. Look up the stock price of each listed company on May 17, 1982. How many of these companies have now gone bankrupt? What are the current prices of the stocks of those that survived? What has been the return on a portfolio of these stocks?

7. Refer to Table 9.5. Repeat the project of question 6, only use July 19, 1982, as the starting date.

8. Refer to Table 9.6. Repeat the project of question 6, only use March 1, 1982, as the starting date.

9. Using the Whitbek-Kisor relative PE ratio formula (adjust the intercept to current S&P level), identify five stocks whose PEs are too high and five that are too low. Follow their subsequent performance for twelve months. Write a report.

10. Identify ten stocks that approximately meet the Graham criteria. Follow their subsequent performance for twelve months. Write a report.

NOTES

1. S. Kichen, "Loaded Laggers," *Forbes*, July 21, 1980, pp. 76–77; S. Kichen, "A Dash of 20-10-10," *Forbes*, July 20, 1981, p. 110; *Forbes* "The Nifty Fifty Revisited," *Forbes*, December 15, 1977, pp. 72–73; *Forbes* "Compound Your Holdings," *Forbes*, April 1, 1977, pp. 22–23; R. Flaherty and S. Gilbarg, "Bargains in Bankruptcy," *Forbes*, February 4, 1980, pp. 101–102; G. Smith, "Many are Called and a Few are Chosen," *Forbes*, November 12, 1979, pp. 203–216; *Forbes* "How to Play Against the Experts and Win," *Forbes*, November 26, 1979, pp. 122–127; B. Weberman, "Rich is Better," *Forbes*, December 10, 1979, pp. 92–96; *Forbes* "Risks that Come with 12%," *Forbes*, November 26, 1979; *Forbes* "Act III," *Forbes*, April 28, 1980, pp. 110–111; S. Kichen, "The Stock Market's Flea Market," *Forbes*, October 26, 1981, pp. 210–217.

2. J. Michaels, "Thomas Rowe Price, 1898–1983," *Forbes*, November 21, 1983, pp. 51–52; A. Mandelman, "Multiple Rewards, The Case for Buying High P/E Stocks," *Barron's*, March 5, 1984, pp. 28–29.

3. D. Dreman, "Watch Those Multiples: Low Price-Earnings Ratios Yield the Best Investment Results," *Barron's*, February 28, 1977, p. 11; C. Ella, "After a Long Hiatus, Some Analysts Again Stress Growth Stocks," *Wall Street Journal*, June 3, 1977, p. 29; C. Ella, "Large Growth Stocks Are Returning to Favor with Many Investors," *Wall Street Journal*, January 25, 1979, p. 1; *Forbes*, "What Price Growth?," *Forbes*, October 13, 1980, p. 84; J. Boland, "Growth is Back," *Barron's*, November 8, 1982, pp. 13, 32; B. Edwards, "Price-Earnings Ratios: What They are, How They are Measured, and How to Use Them," *American Association of Individual Investors*, February 1984, pp. 31–33.

4. B. Malkiel, "Equity Yields: Growth, and the Structure of Share Prices," *American Economic Review*, December 1963, pp. 120–127.

5. W. Breen, "Low Price Earnings Ratios and Industry Relations," *Financial Analysts Journal*, July/August 1968 pp. 120–127.

6. H. Latane and D. Tuttle, "E/P Ratios, Changes in Earnings in Forecasting Future Prices," *Financial Analysts Journal*, January/February 1969, pp. 117–120.

7. C. Jones, "Earnings Trends and Investment Selection," *Financial Analysts Journal*, March/

April 1973, p. 82; S. Nicholson, "Price-Earnings Ratios," *Financial Analysts Journal*, July/August 1960, pp. 43–45; P. Miller and T. Beach, "Recent Studies of P/E Ratios—A Reply," *Financial Analysts Journal*, May/June 1967, pp. 109–110; J. McWilliams, "Price Earnings and PE Ratios," *Financial Analysts Journal*, May/June 1966, pp. 137–142; D. Arnold, "Small is Beautiful," *Barron's*, March 21, 1983, pp. 14, 30–32.

8. R. Levy and S. Kripotos, "Earnings Growth, P/E's, and Relative Price Strength," *Financial Analysts Journal*, November/December 1969, pp. 60, 62, 64–65.

9. R. Levy, "A Note on the Safety of Low P/E Stocks," *Financial Analysts Journal*, January/February 1973, p. 57.

10. S. Basu, "The Information Content of Price-Earnings Ratios," *Financial Management*, Vol. 4, No. 2, Summer 1975, pp. 53–64; "Investment Performance of Common Stocks in Relation to Their Price Earnings Ratios: A Test of the Efficient Market Hypothesis," *Journal of Finance*, June 1977, pp. 663–682.

11. C. Bidwell and J. Riddel, "Market Inefficiencies Opportunities for Profits," *Journal of Accounting, Auditing, and Finance*, Spring 1981, pp. 192–214.

12. D. Goldman and J. Peavy, "Industry Relative Price-Earnings Ratios as Indicators at Investment Returns," *Financial Analysts Journal*, July/August 1983, pp. 60–66.

13. M. Reinganum, "Misspecification of Capital Asset Pricing," *Journal of Financial Economics*, March 1981, pp. 19–46; M. Reinganum, "Abnormal Returns in Small Firm Portfolios," *Financial Analysts Journal*, March/April 1981, pp. 52–57; M. Reinganum; "Portfolio Strategies Based on Market Capitalization," *Journal of Portfolio Management*, Winter 1983, pp. 29–36.

14. R. Banz, "The Relationship Between Return and Market Value of Common Stocks," *Journal of Financial Economics*, March 1981, pp. 3–18.

15. I. Lustig and P. Leinbach, "The Small Firm Effect," *Financial Analyst Journal*, May/June 1983, pp. 46–49.

16. R. Roll, "A Possible Explanation of the Small Firm Effect," *Journal of Finance*, September 1981, pp. 879–888.

17. M. Reinganum, "A Direct Test of Roll's Conjecture on the Firm Size Effect," *Journal of Finance*, March 1982, pp. 27–36.

18. C. James and K. Edmister, "The Relation Between Common Stock Returns, Trading Activity and Market Value," *Journal of Finance*, September 1983, pp. 1075–1086.

19. B. Gale and B. Branch, "Concentration vs. Market Share: Which Determines Performance and Why Does it Matter," *The Antitrust Bulletin*, Spring 1982, pp. 83–105.

20. A. Arbel and P. Strebel, "The Neglected and Small Firm Effect," *Financial Review*, November 1982, pp. 201–218; Discussed in G. Putka, "Choosing Stocks that Few Analysts Followed Proved Good Strategy in the 1970s, Study Shows," *Wall Street Journal*, June 3, 1982, p. 49; A. Arbel and P. Strebel, "Pay Attention to Neglected Firms!," *Journal of Portfolio Management*, Winter 1983, pp. 37–42; A. Arbel and P. Strebel, "Giraffes, Institutions and Neglected Institutions," *Financial Analysts Journal*, May/June 1983, pp. 57–63; M. Hulbert, "Newsletter Stock Picks: The Fewer the Better?," *American Association of Individual Investors*, January 1984, pp. 16–19.

21. *Business Week*, "Using R&D as a Guide to Corporate Profits," *Business Week*, May 29, 1978, p. 75.

22. C. Ella, "Ratio of Stock Price to Firm's R&D Spending on Pre-Share Basis Found to be a Useful Gauge," *Wall Street Journal*, June 19, 1980, p. 47.

23. B. Branch, "Research and Development Activity: A Distributed Lag Analysis, *Journal of Political Economy*, September–October 1974, pp. 999–1011; and B. Branch, "Research and Development and Its Relation to Sales Growth," *Journal of Economics and Business*, Winter 1973, pp. 107–111.

24. F. Scherer, "Corporate Investment Output, Profit and Growth," *Journal of Political Economy*, June 1965, pp. 190–197; W. Leonard, "Research and Development in Industrial Growth,"

Journal of Political Economy, March–April 1971, pp. 232–256; A. Severn and M. Laurence, "Direct Investment Research Intensity and Profitability," *Journal of Financial and Quantative Analysis*, March 1974, pp. 181–193.

25. J. Doyle and F. Navratil, "The Effects of Expectations on Industrial R&D Activity: Evidence Based on the Efficient Market Hypothesis," *Nebraska Journal of Economics and Business*, Autumn 1981, pp. 17–32.

26. L. Minard, "The Case Against Price/Earnings Ratios," *Forbes*, January 13, 1984, pp. 172–176; S. Kichen, "A New Way to Spot Bargains," *Forbes*, March 12, 1984, pp. 202–208; K. Fisher, "Price-Sales Ratios: A New Tool for Measuring Stock Popularity," *American Association of Individual Investors Journal*, June 1984, pp. 13–17.

27. U.S. vs. Northern Securities Company 120 Fed. 721 (April 1903), 193 U.S. 197 (March 1904).

28. R. Metz, "Merger Mainia Slows with the Economy as Buyers Seek a Toehold and Then Wait," *Wall Street Journal*, May 7, 1982, p. 21.

29. M. Bradley, "Interfirm Tender Offers and the Market for Corporate Control," *Journal of Business*, October 1980, pp. 345–376; P. Elgers and J. Clark, "Merger Types and Shareholder Returns: Additional Evidence," *Financial Management*, Summer 1980, pp. 66–72.

30. *Business Week*, "The Profit Potential in Spotting Takeovers," *Business Week*, October 24, 1977, p. 100.

31. V. Vartan, "A Way to Spot a Takeover Target," *New York Times*, November 15, 1981, p. 14F.

32. C. Stavrou, "Choosing Candidates," *Barron's*, April 5, 1982, pp. 15–28.

33. J. Wansley, R. Roenfeldt and P. Cooley, "Abnormal Returns from Merger Profiles," *Journal of Quantitative and Financial Analysis*, June 1983, pp. 149–162.

34. *Business Week*, "The Cash-Flow Takeover Formula," *Business Week*, December 18, 1978, pp. 86–87; R. Greene and P. Bornstein, "A Better Yardstick," *Forbes*, September 27, 1982, pp. 66–69.

35. E. Altman, "Financial Ratios, Discriminant Analysis and the Prediction of Corporate Bankruptcy," *Journal of Finance*, September 1968, pp. 589–609.

36. I. Dambolena and S. Khoury, "Ratio Stability and Corporate Failure," *Journal of Finance*, September 1980, pp. 1017–1026.

37. R. Collins, "An Empirical Comparison of Bankruptcy Prediction Models," *Financial Management*, Summer 1980, pp. 52–57; E. Altman and J. Spivack, "Predicting Bankruptcy: The Value Line Relative Financial Strength System vs. The Zeta Bankruptcy Classification Approach," *Financial Analysts Journal*, November/December 1983, pp. 60–67.

38. J. Aharony, C. Jones and I. Swary, "An Analysis of Risk and Return Characteristics of Corporate Bankruptcy Using Capital Market Data," *Journal of Finance*, September 1980, pp. 1001–1016.

39. T. Clark and M. Weinstein, "The Behavior of the Common Stock of Bankrupt Firms," *Journal of Finance*, May 1983, pp. 489–504.

40. E. Altman and M. Brenner, "Information Effects and Stock Market Response to Signs of Firm Deterioration," *Journal of Financial and Quantitative Analysis*, March 1981, pp. 35–52.

41. R. Metz, "Avoiding the Stock of Risky Companies," *New York Times*, November 18, 1976.

42. S. Kichen, "Reds II," *Forbes*, July 19, 1982, pp. 102–103.

43. R. Edmister and J. Green, "Performance of Super-Low-Priced Stocks," *Journal of Portfolio Management*, Fall 1980, pp. 36–41.

44. S. Kulp, "Life After Bankruptcy," *Barron's*, February 8, 1982, p. 8.

45. F. Bleakley, "Making Money the Contrarian Way," *New York Times*, July 4, 1982, p. F13; G. Marcial, "Bargains that are Better Dead than Alive," *Business Week*, July 12, 1982, p. 68; J. Boland, "Bad News Bulls: Insiders are Buying Depressed Issues," *Barron's*, June 28, 1982, pp. 11–12.

46. J. Greenblatt, Pzena and Newberg, "How the Small Investor Can Beat the Market," *Journal of Portfolio Management*, Summer 1981, pp. 48–52.

47. D. Moffitt, "How Professional Nay-Sayers Attempt to Find Hidden Flaws in the Highfliers on Wall Street," *Wall Street Journal*, July 11, 1977, p. 28; J. Solomon, "Lawyer-Turned-Analyst Aids Investors by Calling Decisions in Corporate Suits," *Wall Street Journal*, September 30, 1980, p. 6; D. Santry, "A System for Spotting Undervalued Stocks," *Business Week*, January 23, 1978, p. 97; *Business Week*, "Morgan Stanley's Way to Spot Winners," *Business Week*, September 20, 1982, p. 101; S. Kichen, "Round Two," *Forbes*, December 1982, pp. 226–227; S. Kichen, "Shure Thing," *Forbes*, March 14, 1983, pp. 190–192.

48. A. Berle and G. Means, *The Modern Corporation and Private Property*, Macmillan, New York, 1932.

49. R. Larner, "Ownership and Control in the 200 Largest Nonfinancial Corporations, 1929 and 1963," *American Economic Review*, September 1966, pp. 777–787; R. Larner, *Management Control & the Large Corporation*, Dunellen, New York, 1970.

50. W. Baumol, *Business Behavior, Value and Growth*, Harcourt Brace & World, New York, 1967.

51. R. Metz, "Incentive Plan Under Question," *New York Times*, March 7, 1973, p. 56.

52. In re Waugh Equipment Company et. al., 15 F.T.C. 232, 242–243 (1931).

53. R. Monsen, J. Chiu, and D. Cooley, "The Effect of Separation of Ownership and Control on the Performance of the Large Firm," *Quarterly Journal of Economics*, August 1968, p. 442.

54. R. Masson, "Executive Motivations, Earning and Consequent Equity Performance," *Journal of Political Economy*, November/December 1971, p. 1278.

55. T. Hogarty, "Profits from Merger, the Evidence of Fifty Years," Conglomerate Mergers and Acquisitions: Opinion and Analysis, *St. John's Law Review*, Spring 1970, p. 389.

56. R. Harris, "The Impact of Corporate Merger on Acquiring Firms," *Journal of Financial Research*, Fall 1980, pp. 283–296; Bradley, *op. cit.*; Elgers and Clark, *op. cit.*; P. Halpern, "Corporate Acquisitions: A Theory of Special Cases? A Review of Event Studies Applied to Acquisitions," *Journal of Finance*, May 1983, pp. 297–318; T. Langetieg, R. Haugen and D. Wichern, "Merger and Stockholder Risk," *Journal of Financial and Quantitative Analysis*, September 1980, pp. 689–718; P. Malatesta, "The Wealth Effect of Merger Activity and the Objective Functions of Merging Firms," *Journal of Financial Economics*, April 1983, pp. 155–182.

57. J. Palmer, "The Profit-Performance Effects of the Separation of Ownership from Control in Large U.S. Industrial Corporations," *Bell Journal of Economics and Management Science*, Spring 1973, p. 293.

58. Larner, op. cit.; D. R. Kamerschen, "The Influence of Ownership and Control on Profit Rates," *American Economic Review*, June 1968, pp. 432–447.

59. S. Levin and S. Levin, "Ownership and Control of Large Industrial Firms: Some New Evidence," *Review of Business and Economic Research*, Fall 1982, pp. 37–49.

60. *New York Times*, "What to Ask at an Annual Meeting," *New York Times*, March 21, 1982, p. F21.

61. S. Whitbeck and M. Kisor, Jr., "A Tool in Investment Decision Making," *Financial Analysts Journal*, May/June 1963, p. 58.

62. J. Williamson, *Investments, New Analytic Techniques*, Prager, New York, 1972.

63. R. Bower and D. Bower, "Risk and the Valuation of Common Stock," *Journal of Political Economy*, May/June 1969, p. 349.

64. B. Malkiel and J. Cragg, "Expectation and the Structure of Share Prices," *American Economic Review*, September 1970, pp. 601–617; S. Hymans, *The Economic Outlook for 1980*, Research Seminar in Quantitative Economics, 1980; L. Clark, "Econometrics Gains Many New Followers, But the Accuracy of Forecasts is Unproven," *Wall Street Journal*, August 2, 1977, p. 42; W. Leontief, et. al., *Studies in the Structure of the American Economy*, Oxford University

Press, New York, 1953; R. Dorfman, P. Samuelson and R. Solow, *Linear Programming and Economic Analysis*, McGraw-Hill, New York, 1955.

65. B. Graham and D. Dodd, with C. Tatham, *Security Analysis*, McGraw-Hill, New York, 1951.

66. P. Blustein, "Ben Graham's Last Will and Testament," *Forbes*, August 1, 1977, pp. 43–45.

67. *Ibid.*

68. N. Galluccio, "There is Only One Prophet and His Name is Benjamin," *Forbes*, October 15, 1979, pp. 188; *Forbes*, "Manning and Napier—Ben Graham with a Twist," *Forbes*, April 3, 1978, pp. 52–53; R. Brammer, "Son of Graham and Dodd," *Barron's*, May 9, 1983, pp. 15, 26, 30.

69. H. Oppenheimer, "Excess January Profits: Theory and Further Empirical Evidence," Paper presented to the October 1979 Financial Management Association Meetings.

70. H. Oppenheimer and G. Schlarbaum, "Investing with Ben Graham: An *Ex Ante* Test of the Efficient Market Hypothesis," *Journal of Financial and Quantitative Analysis*, September 1981, pp. 341–360.

71. R. Flaherty, "John Marks Templeton: Serving God and Hunting Bargains," *Forbes*, May 15, 1977, pp. 72–79.

72. L. Millard, "John Templeton: Why Common Stocks are a Girl's Best Friend," *Forbes*, November 27, 1978, pp. 45–52.

10 Investment Information Sources

Effective investment analysis requires a knowledge of relevant information sources and the ability to assess their quality. Since no one knows more about a particular company than the company itself, its own reports deserve careful scrutiny. Up-to-date trading information may be found in the stock market quotations. A number of stock indexes are designed to reflect market trends. Generalized business and investment periodicals contain a substantial amount of ad hoc information. Several advisory services systematically cover groups of companies. Finally, computer-based information sources facilitate serious statistical analysis.

COMPANY REPORTS

Company-issued reports often include particularly relevant investment information (Table 10.1). Annual and quarterly reports contain the basic financial statements, a letter from the chief executive officer, the auditors' report, and a variety of additional descriptive information. The annual report also contains a section called the management's discussion and analysis, which usually offers some worthwhile commentary.[1] More detailed financial data are included in the 10K and 10Q forms that must be submitted to the SEC and listing exchange (if listed). The 10K is the counterpart to the annual report, while the 10Q is the quarterly equivalent. Shareholders of record automatically receive annual and quarterly reports as they are issued. Serious investors should, however, also obtain copies of the more detailed 10Ks and 10Qs. The firm must honor shareholder requests for its 10Ks and will usually send 10Qs as well. Copies can also be bought from firms advertising in the *Wall Street Journal* and elsewhere. Moreover, many brokerage firms have access to a large number of such reports, which they will copy for their customers. The SEC is yet another source of 10Ks and 10Qs.

The prospectus is an important company-prepared report. Unlike 10Ks and 10Qs, which are issued periodically, prospectuses are required whenever the firm publicly sells or repurchases a nontrivial amount of its securities, proposes a significant acquisition or divestiture, begins a dividend reinvestment plan, or takes any other major financial move requiring shareholder approval or notification. Because the preparers are legally obligated to reveal all relevant and material information regarding the proposal, most prospectuses are quite detailed.

226

Table 10.1   Company Reports

Report	Contents
Annual Report	Financial statements, president's letter, auditors' report, management analysis
10K	More detailed annual information
Quarterly Report	Unaudited quarterly financial statements, president's letter
10Q	More detailed quarterly information
Prospectus	All relevant facts relating to the proposed action
Proxy Statement	All relevant information relating to any item requiring a shareholder vote
Press Releases	Descriptive material on news events
13D	Extent and nature of individual large shareholdings

Including something that is not required is safer for the preparer than excluding information that a court might later determine should have been revealed.

Proxy materials also contain interesting company information. Public companies must hold annual shareholder meetings. Special meetings may also be called from time to time. Such meetings provide the vehicle for electing directors, approving auditors, and acting on a number of other matters requiring stockholder approval, such as increasing the authorized number of shares or changing the firm's legal form. Accordingly, a proxy (ballot) accompanied by relevant information on the issues (proxy statement) must be distributed to the shareholders. Proxy statements typically contain the names and holdings of the firm's principal shareholders (over 5% of outstanding shares), biographical information and stockholdings in the company of nominees to the board of directors, information on committees of the board, executive and director compensation, as well as information relating to any issue to be voted on by the shareholders. As with a prospectus, proxy statement preparers are liable for any damages resulting from incomplete disclosure.

Both prospectuses and proxy statements must be sent to shareholders. Similarly, a purchaser of an initial offering must be given a prospectus. Brokerage houses generally receive copies of both types of documents for their street-name holdings. Most companies will send copies of their prospectuses and proxy statements to anyone who requests them.

Press releases often report additional bits of company information. Unlike the official reports described above, no stringent standards or set forms apply to press releases. Companies issue press releases to disclose newsworthy information relevant to their operations. Until such information is made public, knowledgeable insiders are legally barred from trading the stock. Some press releases are automatically sent to shareholders. Those that are not are usually available upon request. Parts of company press releases generally find their way into some newspapers (such as the *Wall Street Journal*) and appear on the Dow Jones teletype. The fuller story may, however, be obtained only from the complete release.

The 13D

Owners of 5% or more of a public company's stock are required to file a 13D report with the SEC, listing exchange, and company itself. The document must reveal their holdings' extent, purpose (investment, takeover, etc.), source of their funds, and any relevant agreements (such as those with other investors). The 13D must be amended whenever a material change dates the prior filing. Since large shareholders' holdings and intentions often affect share values, 13D filings are another useful information source. For example, that a particular shareholder owns 12% of the stock, intends to purchase more, and seeks an acquirer for the company, substantially increases the possibility of a takeover.

The SEC will supply copies of 13Ds upon a written request and stated willingness to pay the copying charge. The company involved may or may not send 13D filings to those who ask. Most brokerage houses have access to 13Ds and will make copies for their customers upon request. Finally, the person making the filing will usually send a copy if asked. Such individuals normally desire good relations with other shareholders.

TRADING INFORMATION

The stock market quotations found in most daily newspapers report relevant price and volume data plus certain other items. First consider the *Wall Street Journal* stock quotations illustrated in Figure 10.1 (top). Starting at the left, two columns contain the stock's most recent 12-month high and low price, followed by an abbreviation of the company's name, its past 12-month dividend rate, the percentage yield, and price earnings (PE) ratio. Most securities without an entry in the PE column incurred recent losses. Warrants and preferred stocks also do not report a PE. The day's sales volume in units of 100 shares, and the daily high, low, and closing prices appear next. The last column reports the net change in price from the previous close.

Barron's, a major investment periodical, provides a more complete stock quotation (Figure 10.1, bottom). The yearly high and low, name of the company, dividend rate and yield, and PE ratio and sales columns are the same as in the *Wall Street Journal*. *Barron's* reports weekly sales, high, low, last, and net change figures. *Barron's* also includes additional dividend and earnings information. The first entry of the earnings columns contains the one, two, three, or all four quarter figures for the most recent period followed by the previous year's comparable number. The dividend columns begin with the amount of the latest quarterly declaration followed by the day of record and payment dates. Dividends are sent on the payment date to the owners as of the day of record.

Figure 10.1 Stock Quotations *Wall Street Journal*, June 18, 1984

52 Weeks High	Low	Stock	Div.	Yld %	P-E Ratio	Sales 100s	High	Low	Close	Net Chg.
				– A–A–A –						
20⅜	13¼	AAR	.44	2.2	21	49	20¼	20¼	20¼	+ ⅛
53¾	31½	ACF	1.40	2.6	144	132	53½	53⅜	53⅜	.....
18⅞	13⅛	AMF	.50	3.0	..	8897	17¼	16	16⅞	+1
41¼	26⅝	AMR Cp		..	5	5761	31	30	30⅛	– ¼
20⅜	17⅝	AMR pf	2.18	11.	..	6	19½	19⅜	19⅜	– ¼
41½	29⅝	AMR pf	2.13	6.5	..	37	33¼	32½	32½	– ½
26⅛	23	ANR pf	2.67	12.	..	3	23⅛	23⅛	23⅛	.....
23⅞	19½	ANR pf	2.12	10.	..	6	20⅝	20⅝	20⅝	.....
16¼	8⅜	APL		..	4	19	10⅝	10⅝	10⅝	.....
55¼	40¼	ARA	2.10	4.8	9	84	43¾	43	43¾	.....
73	50¼	ASA	3a	5.2	..	1156	60¼	57¾	58¼	–2¾
31¾	17	AVX s	.32	1.6	15	32	19⅞	19¼	19½	– ⅜
53⅜	38¼	AbtLab	1.20	2.8	14	1434	43⅜	42⅝	42⅝	– ⅜
30¼	23¾	AccoWd	.60	2.2	17	124	27	26¾	26⅞	– ⅛
27½	16½	AcmeC	.40	2.4	..	84	16¾	16⅝	16¾	.....
12⅝	8⅜	AcmeE	.32b	3.6	25	7	8⅞	8⅞	8⅞	– ⅛
24⅞	11	AdmDg	.04	.3	7	10	12	11⅝	11⅝	– ⅜
18¾	15⅛	AdaEx	2.11e	14.	..	77	15⅜	15⅛	15⅜	+ ⅛
19¾	12½	AdmMI	.28	1.7	8	22	17¼	16¾	16¾	– ¼

Source: *Wall Street Journal*, June 18, 1984. Reprinted by permission of *Wall Street Journal*, © Dow Jones & Company, Inc., 1984. All Rights Reserved.

***Barron's*, June 18, 1984**

NYSE COMPOSITE

52-Weeks High	Low	Name and Dividend	Sales 100s	Yield Pct.	P-E Ratio	Week's High	Week's Low	Last	Net Chg.		EARNINGS Interim or Fiscal Year	EARNINGS Year ago	DIVIDENDS Latest divs.	DIVIDENDS Record date	DIVIDENDS Payment date
								—A—A—A—							
20⅜	13¼	AAR .44	268	2.2	21	20¼	19¾	20¼	+ ½		Feb9m.72	.46	q.11	5-1	6-4
53¾	31½	ACF 1.40	2773	2.6	144	u53¾	53⅛	53⅜	+ ⅜		Mar3m.31	D.28	q.35	3-2	3-15
22	15½	AMCA n 1	24	6.5	...	16⅝	15½	15½	– ⅞		Mar3m.05	.11	q.25	6-1	6-29
18⅞	13⅛	AMF .50	20716	3.0	...	17¼	15½	16⅞	+ 1¼		Mar3mD.08	D.13	q.12½	5-11	6-8
51¾	49⅝	AMF pf2.96e	193	5.8	...	u51¾	51	51⅜	– ⅛	✚	....	....	1.21	6-21	7-15
41¼	26⅝	AMR Cp	26214	...	5	31¾	29⅜	30⅛	– 2⅛		Mar3m1.13	D.88	Y	...	2-15-80
20⅜	17⅝	AMR pf 2.18	x635	11.3	...	19¾	19¼	19⅜	+ ⅛		....	....	q.546⅞	6-15	7-1
41½	29⅝	AMR pf 2.13	898	6.5	...	33½	31½	32½	– 2		....	....	q.53⅛	7-15	8-1
26⅛	23	ANR pf 2.67	119	11.5	...	23¼	23⅛	23⅛	– ½		....	....	q.66⅞	5-22	6-1
23⅞	19½	ANR pf 2.12	6	10.3	...	20⅝	20⅝	20⅝	.....		....	....	q.53	5-22	6-1
16¼	8⅜	APL	63	...	4	11⅛	10⅝	10⅝	– ⅝		Mar9mD.73	.17	Y	...	4-1-80
55¼	40¼	ARA 2.10	806	4.8	9	45½	42¾	43¾	– 2		Mar26w2.71	2.42	q.52½	6-1	6-15
73	50¼	ASA 3a	2481	5.2	...	62⅝	57¾	58¼	– 4⅜		83Nov4.50	3.71	q.75	5-11	5-24
31¾	17	AVX s .32	445	1.6	15	20¾	19¼	19½	– 1¼		Mar3m.42	.07	q.08	5-9	6-1
53⅜	38¼	AbtLab 1.20	5967	2.8	14	43¾	42⅝	42⅝	– 1	✚	Mar3m.73	.62	q.30	7-13	8-15
30¼	23¾	AccoWd .60	480	2.2	17	27¼	26½	26⅞	– ⅛		84Mar1.60	1.25	q.15	6-29	7-10
27½	16½	AcmeC .40	1070	2.4	...	17½	d16½	16¾	– ¾		Mar6mD.24	D2.10	q.10	5-4	5-18
12⅝	8⅜	AcmeE .32b	22	3.6	25	9	8⅞	8⅞	– ¼		Mar39w.42	L.11	q.08	5-7	6-4
24⅞	11	AdmDg .04	x57	.3	7	12⅜	11⅝	11⅝	– ½		Mar3m.14	.14	q.01	6-15	6-30
18¾	15⅛	AdaEx 2.11e	294	13.7	...	15½	15⅛	15⅜	– ⅛	✚	83Dec.80	.91	.12	7-9	7-23

Source: *Barron's*, June 18, 1984. Reprinted by permission of *Barron's*, © Dow Jones & Company, Inc., 1984. All Rights Reserved.

While New York Stock Exchange-listed securities appear in Figure 10.1, the AMEX quotation form is identical. The *Wall Street Journal* stock quotations for OTC, regional, and foreign exchanges are less complete, however (Figure 10.2).

Figure 10.2 OTC, Regional and Foreign Stock Quotations, September 10, 1984

National Market

365-day High	Low	Stock	Sales (hds)	High	Low	Last	Net Chg.
		--A A--					
19½	14	Aaron Rents	205	17	16½	16¾	...
18⅛	8½	Acadmyln .20	1572	11⅛	10⅞	11 +	⅛
13¼	3¼	Accelratn .05b	189	11¼	10¾	10¾ –	¼
26¾	14⅛	AccurayCp .20	324	19½	19	19⅜ –	¼
14¼	2¾	Adac Labs	493	4⅝	4⅜	4½ –	⅛
28⅛	7½	Adage Inc	33	12½	12	12	...
9½	1 13-16	Advnc Circuit	155	8⅛	7⅞	7⅞ –	⅛
24	21	AEL IndusA s	4	22	22	22 +	⅞
19⅞	11½	AffilBnksh .80	12	15½	15½	15½ –	¼
22½	12¾	A F G Indust	371	17¼	16¼	17¼ +	½
27¼	15¼	AgencyRAC 5i	205	21¼	20¾	20¾ –	½
30½	9⅜	AGS Computr	67	12¾	12	12¼ –	½
14	⅜	A I A Indust	895	¾	⅝	⅝ –	⅛
14⅜	5⅞	Aircal Inc	32	7⅝	7⅜	7⅝ –	⅛
13¼	9	AirMidwst Inc	38	13¼	12¾	12¾ –	¼
18¼	8	AirWiscSv 10i	100	9¾	9¼	9⅝ +	⅛
20¼	15¾	AlaskPcB .25f	9	19¾	19¾	19¾ –	¼
29¾	24½	AlexBld s1.20	26	28¾	28½	28½	...
17	10½	Alfin Fragrnc	183	14	13½	14 +	¾
35	13½	Algorex Corp	237	14¾	13½	14 –	½
19	13½	Allegh Bev .40	9	16⅜	16⅛	16⅜	...

National List

Park Commun	6	27	28	...
Parkway Co	z11	21	21½	...
Parlex Corp	z90	12½	14	...
Par Pharmact	197	16	16½ –	1
PasqlFdA .06f	2	9½	12	...
PasqlFdB .05f	z50	10	11	...
Patlex Corp	55	4¼	4¾ –	¼
Patriot Bc pf	3	28	29½	...
Paul Revr 1.44	5	11¼	11¾	...
Pawling SvBk	62	15	15¼ +	⅜
PaxtonFrk .44	31	18	18¾ +	½
Payco Amer	4	21	22½	...
P C A Intl .48	x5	8¾	9 +	⅛

Supplemental List

22⅜	13⅜	Mack Trucks
21½	18¾	Mad GsEl 2.20
19½	9⅜	Magnetic Cont
10⅞	8⅛	Major Realty
11¾	7½	Malrite Comm
33	10	MngtSci Amer
25½	17¼	Manitowoc .80
40¾	29⅛	ManufcNatl 2
15	11⅜	Marcus .28d
9¾	6¼	Margaux Cntr
10¼	7	Marquest .05d
39	29	MdNatlCp 1.60
22¾	17¾	Masco Indust

Regional Exchange

Pacific Exchange

Sales	Stock	High	Low	Close	Chg.
600	AlaskGld	2⅝	2½	2⅝ +	⅛
100	AFn pfE	8¾	8¾	8¾	.....
100	AFn pfF	12⅜	12⅜	12⅜ +	⅛
100	AFinl pfH	29¼	29¼	29¼	.....
100	AFinl pfG	7⅜	7⅜	7⅜ +	¼
900	AFin Ent	17¾	17¾	17¾	.....
300	AmPace s	7⅛	6⅞	7⅛ +	⅛
1300	Amfac pf	13⅞	13½	13⅞ +	⅛
1800	Bastn	3¾	3¾	3¾	.....
1100	BigSky	13-32	13-32	13-32 –	1-32

Foreign Securities

Unless noted, all issues are American Depositary Receipts, or ADRs, representing ownership of securities physically deposited abroad. Quotes are in U.S. dollars. n-Not ADR. Explanatory notes on Over the Counter page.

Stock & Div	Sales 100s	Bid	Asked	Net Chg.
AUSTRALIA				
Broken Hill .55d	361	8¼	8⅜ –	⅛
GREAT BRITAIN				
BeechmGp .23b	1062	4½	4⅝	...
Burmah Oil .15d	50	2 13-32	2 15-32 –	1-32
RankOrgan .05b	93	3¼	3 5-16	...
HOLLAND				
Philps Gloeil	2794	15¼	15⅜ –	⅛
JAPAN				
Canon Inc .11d	2	25⅝	25⅞ –	⅛
Fuji Photo .06f	316	13⅜	13⅝ –	⅛

Source: *Wall Street Journal,* September 11, 1984. Reprinted by permission of *Wall Street Journal,*
© Dow Jones & Company, Inc., 1984. All Rights Reserved.

Figure 10.3 Explanatory Notes for *Wall Street Journal* Stock Quotations

EXPLANATORY NOTES

(For New York and American Exchange listed issues)

Sales figures are unofficial.

The 52-Week High and Low columns show the highest and the lowest price of the stock in consolidated trading during the preceding 52 weeks plus the current week, but not the current trading day.

u–Indicates a new 52-week high. d–Indicates a new 52-week low.

g–Dividend or earnings in Canadian money. Stock trades in U.S. dollars. No yield or PE shown unless stated in U.S. money. n–New issue in the past 52 weeks. The high-low range begins with the start of trading and does not cover the entire 52 week period. s–Split or stock dividend of 25 per cent or more in the past 52 weeks. The high-low range is adjusted from the old stock. Dividend begins with the date of split or stock dividend. v–Trading halted on primary market.

Unless otherwise noted, rates of dividends in the foregoing table are annual disbursements based on the last quarterly or semi-annual declaration. Special or extra dividends or payments not designated as regular are identified in the following footnotes.

a–Also extra or extras. b–Annual rate plus stock dividend. c–Liquidating dividend. e–Declared or paid in preceding 12 months. i–Declared or paid after stock dividend or split up. j-Paid this year, dividend omitted, deferred or no action taken at last dividend meeting. k–Declared or paid this year, an accumulative issue with dividends in arrears. r–Declared or paid in preceding 12 months plus stock dividend. t–Paid in stock in preceding 12 months, estimated cash value on ex-dividend or ex-distribution date.

x–Ex-dividend or ex-rights. y–Ex-dividend and sales in full. z–Sales in full.

pf–Preferred. rt–Rights. un–Units. wd–When distributed. wi–When issued. wt–Warrants. ww–With warrants. xw–Without warrants.

vj–In bankruptcy or receivership or being reorganized under the Bankruptcy Act, or securities assumed by such companies.

Reprinted by permission of *Wall Street Journal,* © Dow Jones & Company, Inc., 1984. All Rights Reserved.

Explanatory Notes

Quotations often include letters whose meanings are generally explained at the end of the quotation (Figure 10.3). In addition, the symbols *cv, wt,* and *pfd* stand for convertible, warrant, and preferred, respectively.

Electronic Quotations

While most stock market investors are content to follow their securities in the newspapers, others use electronic quotations for more frequent and up-to-date reports.[2] Thus Trans-Lux Corp. (110 Richards Ave., Norwalk, Conn., 06854) offers a tickertape service (each day's complete trading record for the NYSE and/or AMEX) and a service that reports sales of up to 100 stocks or futures contracts in real time (no delay in reporting). Both Quotron (1 Battery Place Plaza, New York, NY, 10004) and Bunker Ramo Information Systems (35 Nutmeg Drive, Trumbull, Conn., 06609) provide real-time access to the stock market ticker tape plus the ability to obtain last, bid and ask quotes on specified stocks and options much like a stock exchange quotation machine. All of these services involve payments for installation and monthly service, as well as additional fees to the relevant exchanges.

A less expensive system is now available to those within 50 miles of most large cities. Telenet America Inc. (Wythe St., Alexandria, Va., 22314) offers a Pocket Quote machine about the size of a hand-held calculator that will display the high, low, and last prices for any NYSE or AMEX stock on a 15-minute delay basis. The machine will also flash whenever news appears on any of up to 20 preselected stocks.

Taking electronic quotations a step further, several services will watch for major price moves on a selection of stocks and flag the movers (Spectrum Communications & Electronics Inc., Roscokrantz, Ehrenkrantz, Lyon & Ross, Hicksville, NY; Window on Wall Street, Bristol Financial Systems, Wilton, Conn.). Such services require access to a personal computer and software, and incur a monthly fee.

Standard and Poor's Stock Guide

The monthly *Standard and Poor's Stock Guide* reports considerably more data than the newspaper stock quotations. A very large number of common and preferred stocks and warrants are included. Figure 10.4 contains typical pages from the *Stock Guide*. A security is covered in a single line across two pages. Consider AAR Corp. Coverage begins with the company's ticker tape symbol followed by its name and the markets on which it is traded. For example, AAR is listed on the NYSE and the MW (Midwest Exchange). Standard and Poor's rates many of the securities from A+ to C based on the stability and consistency of their past eight years of earnings growth. An "NR" indicates that no ranking has been made (usually because of insufficient data). The security's par value

Figure 10.4 Standard and Poor's Stock Guide

HOW TO USE THE STOCK GUIDE

It is necessary to read carefully the following instructions and those on Pages 1 and 6 to correctly interpret abbreviations and data in the Guide.

Column	Explanation
INDEX	The index numbers are a visual guide to the columnar data. Stocks with options are indicated by ●; stocks in the S&P "500" are flagged with ¶.
Ticker Symbol	Ticker symbols on listed issues are those of the exchange first listed in "Market" column. OTC stocks carry NASDAQ Trading System symbols. Supplementary symbols as would appear on the ticker tape after symbol, such as "Pr" for preferred stocks, etc. are indented.
STOCKS NAME OF ISSUE (Call Price of Pfd. Stocks) Market	Names shown in this column are not necessarily the exact corporate title of the company. Also, because of space limitations, the occasional use of abbreviations has been necessary. Where the name of the company is not followed by the designation of any particular issue of its stock, it is the common or capital stock that is referred to. The Call Price of preferred stocks is shown in parentheses after the name of the issue: the footnoted data indicates year in which call price declines. Abbreviations of various provisions, etc. are shown on Page 5. Unit of Trading for stocks on the New York Stock Exchange and American Stock Exchange is indicated as follows: 10—10 shares; 25—25 shares; 50—50 shares; all others 100 shares. The markets for each issue are indicated by standard abbreviations, as shown on Page 5. The primary exchange is the first market shown.
Com Rank & Pfd Rating	Standard & Poor's Rankings and Ratings are explained on pages 6 and 7, arrows denote changes in the last 3 months.
Par Value	Present par value of the stock named. In determining transfer taxes, No Par issues are figured the same as $100 par.
Inst. Cos / * Hold Shs. (1,000)	The number of financial institutions—banks, investment, insurance, college endowments and "13F" money managers—that hold this stock and the number of shares (000 omitted) held. See explanation on Page 1.
PRINCIPAL BUSINESS	This is the principal business of the company. Where a company is engaged in several lines of business every effort has been made to list that line from which it obtains the greatest proportion of its revenue. In addition, an indication of the company's rank in the industry is given where possible.
PRICE RANGE: Historical (High, Low)	High and Low price ranges are for the calendar years indicated.
PRICE RANGE: Last Year (High, Low); Current Year (High, Low)	Price ranges are not exclusive for the exchange on which the stock is currently traded, but are based on the best available data covering the period of the column head. Price ranges of over-the-counter stocks are based on the best available high and low bid prices during the period, and should be viewed as reasonable approximations.
Month Sales in 100s	Trading volume is for the month indicated in hundreds of shrs. NYSE & ASE companies based on composite tape, all others are for primary exchange shown.
Last Month OTC—Bid Prices (High, Low, Last)	Last sales on principal exchanges are closing quotations for the preceding month. In the case of Canadian issues, prices are quoted in Canadian dollars providing the first exchange listed is a Canadian exchange. In the case of NASDAQ & OTC stocks, the latest available bid price is shown under the "Last" column.
% Div. Yield	Yields are derived by dividing total indicated dividend rate by price of stock. Such rate is based on latest dividend paid including (†), or excluding (e) extras as indicated by footnote. Additional symbols used: (s) including stock; and (‡) including extras and stock.
P-E Ratio	P-E Ratio (Price-Earnings Ratio)—See explanation on Page 1.

ALSO SEE INSIDE REAR COVER

128 Kim-Lac

Standard & Poor's Corporation

¶S&P 500 ●Options

Index	Ticker Symbol	Name of Issue (Call Price of Pfd. Stocks)	Market	Com. Rank. & Pfd. Rating	Par Val.	Inst. Hold Cos	Inst. Hold Shs. (000)	Principal Business	1971-82 High	1971-82 Low	1983 High	1983 Low	1984 High	1984 Low	Apr. Sales in 100s	April, 1984 Last Sale Or Bid High	Low	Last	%Div. Yield	P-E Ratio
¶1	KMB	Kimberly-Clark	NY,B,C,M,P,Ph	A+	5	285	13685	Consumer paper pr: newsprint	80¾	18⅝	99	65¾	92⅞	82¾	5350	91½	82¾	83⅛	5.3	10
2	KIN	Kinark Corp	AS,P	B–	10¢	5	179	Chem pkg/dstr:mfg:hotels	4¼	½	6⅞	3⅝	5⅞	4⅝	449	5	4⅝	4¾	...	11
3	KNCD	Kincaid Furniture	OTC	NR	1⅓	15	602	Mfrs bedroom,din'g furniture	....	....	16¼	12	12¾	9	534	9¾	9¼	9¾B	...	9
4	KNDR	Kinder-Care Learn'g	OTC	B+	50¢	63	5261	Operates day care centers	18⅜	¼	27¼	14¼	21⅛	14¾	13516	18¾	17	17⅝B	0.5	21
5	KRC	King Radio	AS,Ph	↓B	30¢	7	478	Aircraft electronic systems	32⅝	3¾	23¾	14¾	25	19¼	155	24	21⅝	21⅞	0.9	d
6	KEX	Kirby Exploration[54]	AS	B–	10¢	22	2555	Transp'n sv,insur,oil & gas	45¾	⅞	10¼	5¼	7⅜	5⅜	4241	6⅞	5⅝	5⅞	...	d
7	KIT	Kit Mfg	AS	C	No	4	81	Mobile hms:recr'l vehicles	23⅜	1	11	3¾	5⅝	3¾	121	5⅜	4½	4½	...	d
8	KLAC	KLA Instruments	OTC	NR	.001¢	46	4023	Electro-optical test sys	10⅛	3⅝	26½	9⁹⁄₁₆	26¾	18⅛	5645	24¼	18⅛	23½B	...	49
9	KVU	Kleer-Vu Indus	AS	B–	10¢	2	38	Plastic transparent items	2¾	⅛	6⅛	1⅞	4¼	3	961	4¼	3¼	4⅛	1.0	19
10	KLM	KLM Royal Dutch Air	NY,B,M,P,Ph	NR	j100	29	1454	Worldwide air transport	82⅞	12⅝	63¾	47	74	55¼	1983	64½	55½	55⅞	...	10
11	KLOFY	Kloof Gold Mining[57]	OTC	NR	R1	16	1349	South Africa gold mining	56	3¼	55	37	57⅜	40½	2194	53½	49½	51⅜B	4.6	11
12	KLOS	Kloss Video	OTC	NR	20¢	3	44	Mfr projection TV systems	12¾	4	14¾	5¾	8¼	6¼	343	8	7	7B	...	12
¶13●[1]	KM	K mart	NY,B,C,M,P,Ph	A–	1	512	89055	Discount: variety stores	51⅛	15⅛	39¼	21¾	33⅞	26¾	108627	30⅝	26¾	29	4.3	8
14	KMSI	KMS Indus	OTC	NR	1¢	11	649	Scientific research:optical	19	⅛	3⅝	1¾	2⅛	1½	5859	1¾	1½	1⅝B	...	78
15	KMWS	KMW Systems	OTC	NR	10¢	8	224	Mfrs electronic sys & equip	....	....	13¼	10	14¾	10¼	224	11	10½	10½B	...	21
16	KNAP	Knape & Vogt Mfg	OTC	B+	2	8	355	Mfr specialty hardware	44½	7	30¾	17¼	30	24¼	235	28	25¾	26¼B	†5.0	8
17	KNE	KN Energy	NY,M	A	5	49	3138	Natural gas,alfalfa,PL const	36⅝	10	56	23	34⅝	23¾	6740	34⅝	28¾	33⅝	4.4	14
¶18	KRN	Knight-Ridder News	NY,M	A	2½¢	142	26135	Newspapers:business info svs	25¾	3⅝	30⁷⁄₁₆	22⅛	27¾	21¼	15518	26⅛	22⅛	25¼	2.5	13
19	KNO	Knogo Corp	AS,Ph	B–	1¢	8	456	Electronic detector systems	27	³⁄₁₆	24¼	12⅛	18⅛	8⅞	1525	12⅛	8⅞	9⅞	...	18
20	KNL	Knoll Int'l Cl'A'	AS	NR	10¢	23	2837	Mfrs office furniture	....	....	17¼	12⅞	16½	10	3406	12½	10	11¼	...	12
21	KGR	Koger Co	AS	NR	10¢	31	2200	Own & operate office bldgs	19¼	13½	28½	17⅞	25⅛	22⅝	1661	25⅛	22¾	25⅛	8.8	...
22	KOG	Koger Properties	NY,M	B	10¢	28	2306	Dev & construct office bldgs	33½	4	28¾	14½	25¾	21¾	914	23⅞	21⅞	23⅝	8.6	30
23	KOLF	Kolff Medical, Inc	OTC	NR	1¢	3	112	Produces artificial hearts	....	....	12½	3⅞	5⅝	3⅝	1759	4⅝	3⅝	4⅛B	...	d
24	KOL	Kollmorgen Corp	NY,M	A–	2½	59	3174	Motor/drive:circuitry:instr	36	1¼	36¾	20¾	34	25⅝	1868	29¼	27⅝	28⅝	1.1	25
25	KOP	Koppers Co	NY,B,M,P,Ph	B+	1¼	110	13986	Forest, chemicals, road pr	35¼	7¹⁄₁₆	21⅞	15¾	23⅝	17½	16369	22½	20¼	22	3.6	19
26	Pr	4% cm Pfd (107¾)	NY([10])	A–	100	...	....	engineered metal pr:eng	62½	27¼	36	32	34	32	13	34	32¼	33¼B	12.0	...
27	Pr B	$10.00 cm Cv Pref([41]107:SF100)	[2]NY	BBB+	No	26	256	& construction	106	69	100½	85	103½	98	688	102	99¼	100½B	10.0	...
28	KOSS	Koss Corp	OTC	B	1¢	3	48	Stereophonic headphones	10⅞	1⅛	7	3	4	2	797	3⅜	2	2½B	...	d
29	KTOS	KRATOS Inc.	OTC	B–	No	5	388	Spectrometers/instrumentat'n	23¾	⅛	17¼	3¾	5½	3⅛	3420	4¾	3⅛	3¼B	...	d
30	KRMC	K.R.M. Petroleum	OTC	B–	10¢	...	....	Oil/gas prod'n,explor,devel	17⅛	1	4¾	2½	3¼	2½	130	3¼	2¾	2¾B	...	...
¶31	KR	Kroger Co	NY,B,C,M,Ph	↓A	1	193	16699	2nd lgst fd supermkt chain	47¼	7⅛	42⅞	33¾	37⅜	29½	13396	33½	29½	33½	6.0	12
32	KROY	Kroy Inc	OTC	B+	50¢	29	1207	Graphic communications pr	30¾	¼	27¾	14½	28¼	14¼	2470	17¾	14¼	15¼B	0.4	11
33	KRUE	Krueger (W.A.)	OTC	A–	31½¢	24	2711	Magazine and book printer	10⅛	⅝	18½	9⅝	18⅛	14½	2638	16½	14½	16½B	3.2	10
34	KTL	K-tel Int'l	AS,To	B–	10¢	4	402	Merchandises music prod,etc	27⅝	1⅛	12¼	6	7⅝	4¼	138	4⅞	4¼	4½	...	d
35	KTII	K-Tron Int'l	OTC	NR	1¢	1	10	Digital weight feed eq scales	20¾	4½	13½	5½	7½	3¾	675	5	3¾	3¾B	...	d
36	KUB	Kubota, Ltd ADR	NY,B,M,Ph	NR	[70]....	1	60	Agricul mchy,pipe,Japan	35	5½	28	24	31	26¼	9	30¾	28¼	27B	2.0	29
37	KUH	Kuhlman Corp	NY,M	B	1	4	90	Transformers:metal/plastic	19⅜	4¼	19¼	12⅛	19½	15½	806	19½	17	19⅝	†5.4	9
38	KLIC	Kulicke & Soffa Ind	OTC	B	No	63	3268	Equip to mfr semiconduct'rs	18¾	⅛	34¾	12¼	27¼	19½	7856	23⅞	20⅛	23⅞B	0.3	56
39	KVPH	K-V Pharmaceutical	OTC	B–	50¢	6	437	Mfr drugs for major firms	9	½	14½	6⅝	12¼	7½	1161	12¼	10¼	10¼B	...	d
40	KYLE	Kyle Technology	OTC	NR	No	...	....	Pacemaker term:connect'rs	10¾	3⅞	7	2⅝	4⅝	2¾	260	3¾	3⅛	3¼B	...	d
41	KYO	Kyocera Corp [72]ADR	NY,M	NR	[72]....	23	421	Ceramic products,elec/other	27¼	⅝	54¼	22½	62¾	51⅛	2666	60⅞	51⅛	51¾	0.6	39
42	KZ	Kysor Ind'l	NY,M	B	1	23	781	Truck eq:refrig:locks:truck'g	15	2¹⁄₁₆	22⅝	6⅝	19¾	13¾	1112	16¾	13⅞	16¾	2.4	18
43	LHC	L & N Housing	NY,M	NR	50¢	9	550	Real estate investment trust	31	19¼	31⅝	22⅞	26⅞	22⅞	378	25⅝	24⅞	24⅞	10.8	9
44	LB	LaBarge Inc	AS	B–	25¢	4	83	Tubular,electronic,furniture	8⅝	1½	6¾	2⅝	4⅞	3½	653	3⅞	3½	3⅞	1.5	23
45	LBT	Labatt(John)	To,Mo	A	No	47	1486	Beer & food products	18⅛	6⁵⁄₁₆	24½	18	25¼	17½	1300	20	17½	17⅞	5.0	6
46	LCNAF	Lacana Mining	OTC,To	NR	No	19	1888	Gold/silver prod'n:oil & gas	11⅜	2⅛	9⅞	5⅞	10⅝	8⅛	1564	10⅝	9¾	10½B	1.4	9

Uniform Footnote Explanations—See Page 1. Other: [1]CBOE:Cycle 3. [2]M. [51]△$0.62,'82. [52]Fiscal May'80 & prior. [53]12 Mo Aug,'81:Fiscal May'81 earned$0.34. [54]Vote on name chge to Kirby Exploration Co. [55]◎$0.29,'83. [56]Option,portion payable in stk. [57]ADR shrs. [58]□$0.07,'81. [59]Stk dstr of Midlands Energy Co. [60]Estimate 100% nontaxable'83. [61]Estimate 75% nontaxable'83. [62]Fiscal Mar 82 & prior. [63]□$1.84,'82. [64]□$0.36,△$0.21,'83. [65]To 12-15-84,scale to 100 in'90. [66]Estimate 100% nontaxable. [67]◎$2.76,'83. [68]□$0.23,'82. [69]°$0.22,'80. [70]ADR's equal 20 com shrs,par 50 Yen. [71]□$0.11,'80. [72]ADR's equal to 2 com par 50 yen. [73]Approx. [74]◎$0.90,'83. [75]Incl $0.07 cap gains'84. [76]8 Mo Dec'81. [77]△$0.04,'82. [78]◎$2.26,'83.

HOW TO USE THE STOCK GUIDE

It is necessary to read carefully the following instructions and those on Pages 1 and 6 to correctly interpret abbreviations and data in the Guide.

INDEX	Cash Divs. Ea. Yr. Since	DIVIDENDS Latest Payment Per $	Date	Ex. Div.	Total $ This Year	ind. rate	$ Last Year	FINANCIAL POSITION Mil. $ Cash & Equiv.	Curr. Assets	Curr. Liabs.	Balance Sheet Date	CAPITALIZATION Long Term Debt Mil. $	Shs. 000 Pfd.	Com.	Yrs. End	ANNUAL EARNINGS $ Per Share $ Latest Five Years	Last 12 Mos.	INTERIM EARNINGS OR REMARKS Period	$ Per Share $ Comparison	INDEX
Details of stock dividends and stock splits, effected during the past five years, are reported by symbol ◆ and footnotes which carry numerals corresponding to those in "Index" column. Adjustments have been made for all stock dividends.	One or more cash dividends have been paid each calendar year to date without interruption, beginning with year listed.	Latest dividend payment. If at a regular established rate, it is so noted by M—Monthly, Q—Quarterly, S—Semi-Annually, or A—Annually.	Date of disbursement of the latest payment. If an extra or stock dividend also is being paid, it is so indicated by footnote.	The date shown is that on which the stock sells "ex-dividend", that is the date on which it sells without the right to receive the latest declared dividend.	Payments made or declared payable thus far in the current calendar year, including both regular and extras, if any.	S&P projection of dividend payments for next 12 months, used to compute % Div. Yield.	Total dividend payments, including extras if any, made in the preceding calendar year. For preferred dividend accumulations to latest payment due date, see "Financial Position" or "Remarks" column.	Cash & Equivalent, Current Assets, and Current Liabilities are given in millions of dollars (000 000) omitted as 17.0—$17 000 000 1.75—$1 750 000 0.18—$175 000 etc. Where current balance sheet items are not of analytical significance, special calculations pertinent to the industry in which the company operates are presented, as tangible "Book Value per Share" for Banks; "Net Asset Value per Share" for Investment Trusts; and tangible "Equity per Share" (stockholders) for Insurance & Finance Companies. Intangibles such as goodwill, debt discount or pfd liquidating value have been deducted.				Long Term Debt is in millions of dollars, as 25.0—$25,000,000; 2.58—$2,580,000; 0.20—$200,000. It includes funded debt, long term bank loans, deferred compensations, etc. Preferred and common stocks are in shares to the nearest thousands (000 omitted), as 150—150,000; 30—30,000; 2—1,500 (due to Rounding). Outstanding shares exclude treasury stock. Figure shown under preferred shares column on company name line represents the combined number of preferred shares outstanding.				EARNINGS are in general on a "Primary" basis as reported by company, including discontinued operations but excluding extraordinary items. More detailed information on method of reporting and usage of standard footnotes can be found on Page 1. Earnings for fiscal years ending March 31 or earlier are shown under the column of the preceding calendar year. S&P Earnings Estimates are the final product of careful analysis by industry specialists of available relevant information. They are unofficial, however, and responsibility for their accuracy cannot be assumed. An arrow denotes changes in current estimate. Last 12 Mos. indicates 12 months earnings through period shown in interim earnings column, when available, or annual, if not.		Interim earnings are shown, when available, for the longest accounting interval since the last fiscal year-end. Also published in this column from time to time are references to SF provisions & divd arrears of pfds. See also Financial Position column for such notations.		The index numbers are a visual guide to the columnar data.

◆ Stock Splits & Divs By Page Reference Index.

ALSO SEE INSIDE FRONT COVER

Common and Preferred Stocks

Kim-Lac 129

Splits ◆ Index	Cash Divs. Ea. Yr. Since	Dividends Latest Payment Per$	Date	Ex. Div.	Total $ So Far 1984	Ind. Rate	Paid 1983	Financial Position Mil-$ Cash& Equiv.	Curr. Assets	Curr. Liab.	Balance Sheet Date	Capitalization Lg Trm Debt Mil-$	Shs. 000 Pfd.	Com.	Earnings $ Per Shr. Years End	1979	1980	1981	1982	1983	Last 12 Mos.	Interim Earnings Period	$ Per Shr. 1983	1984	Index
1◆	1935	Q1.10	7-2-84	6-4	3.25	4.40	4.15	34.0	826.	625.	12-31-83	p475.	...	p22796	Dc	△6.74	7.85	9.12	△8.21	8.39	8.41	3 Mo Mar	2.33	2.35	1
2	....	0.06¼	10-12-55	11-9	....	Nil	....	n/a	7.70	2.69	3-31-84	8.98	...	3510	Dc	0.32	0.02	0.12	△d0.13	0.36	0.42	3 Mo Mar	0.03	0.09	2
3	....	None Since Public			....	Nil	....	0.17	14.9	5.18	1-28-84	7.14	...	3162	Ja	....	0.17	0.57	0.83	1.05	1.05				3
4◆	1977	Q0.02¼	5-4-84	4-13	0.04½	0.09	0.08¼	103.	113.	13.0	11-25-83	218	...	17923	Au	0.22	0.33	□0.18	0.50	0.69	0.82	6 Mo Feb	0.37	0.50	4
5◆	1973	Q0.05	4-13-84	3-20	0.10	0.20	0.50	1.47	49.7	17.7	12-31-83	7.19	...	2712	Dc	3.60	2.59	2.79	0.27	■d0.98	d0.85	3 Mo Mar	0.02	0.15	5
6◆	....	None Paid			....	Nil	....	25.3	64.0	37.4	12-31-83	89.2	...	23994	Dc	0.53	0.81	△0.53	d0.44	d0.73	d0.73				6
7	....	None Paid			....	Nil	....	0.49	7.29	5.13	1-31-84	0.18	...	1465	Oc	d0.51	d1.03	▲0.37	0.03	d0.51	d0.59	3 Mo Jan	d0.22	d0.30	7
8◆	....	None Since Public			....	Nil	....	13.9	29.6	9.94	12-31-83	....	...	9975	Je	•0.03	•0.10	0.13	0.16	0.30	0.48	9 Mo Mar	0.19	0.37	8
9◆	1982	0.04	12-15-83	12-2	....	0.04	0.04	1.73	13.5	3.87	9-30-83	p10.8	...	p6079	Dc	0.02	0.23	0.25	0.26	P0.22	0.22				9
10	....	t 3.489	8-27-79	8-7	....	Nil	....	241.	626.	577.	6-30-83	*618	p2000	p7887	Mr	1.82	1.19	3.01	4.15	....	5.88	9 Mo Dec△	7.86	9.59	10
11	1970	0.856	2-24-84	12-23	0.856	2.37	2.474	236.	247.	207.	j6-30-83	....	...	±30240	Je	2.10	5.39	6.19	3.49	4.83	4.83	No interim reporting			11
12	....	None Since Public			....	Nil	....	0.16	10.3	4.40	12-31-83	0.64	...	1707	Dc	d1.07	•0.26	•0.92	0.39	0.58	0.58				12
13	1913	Q0.31	6-11-84	5-14	0.58	1.24	1.06	1028	4789	2521	1-25-84	2534	...	125911	Ja	2.84	2.07	1.75	∫2.06	∫3.80	3.80				13
14	....	None Paid			....	Nil	....	3.39	4.94	1.59	12-31-83	....	7	13569	Dc	•0.01	•0.02	□d0.11	□•0.02	•0.02	0.02				14
15	....	None Since Public			....	Nil	....	2.52	4.89	0.88	12-31-83	....	...	1401	Je	0.04	0.06	0.13	0.25	0.40	0.51	9 Mo Mar	0.27	0.38	15
16	1934	†0.40	6-1-84	5-14	†0.70	1.30	†1.20	2.08	20.5	3.45	12-31-83	....	...	1286	Je	2.95	3.00	■2.16	1.34	2.18	3.29	9 Mo Mar	1.55	2.66	16
17◆	1937	Q0.37	3-31-84	2-29	0.37	1.48	h1.48	0.88	118.	134.	12-31-83	124.	299	8786	Dc	2.23	2.44	2.78	2.85	2.37	2.37				17
18◆	1941	Q0.16	4-13-84	4-2	0.32	0.64	0.55½	43.6	276.	206.	12-31-83	77.2	...	64155	Dc	1.34	1.43	1.55	1.57	1.80	1.91	12 Mo Mar	1.64	1.91	18
19◆	....	None Paid			....	Nil	....	Equity per shr $6.35			11-30-83	3.99	...	5012	Fb	0.73	d0.38	d0.46	0.32	....	0.56	9 Mo Nov△	0.20	0.44	19
20	....	None Since Public			....	Nil	....	32.6	85.4	28.1	10-2-83	38.8	...	*11000	Dc	0.32	0.45	0.78	•0.81	P0.82	0.90	3 Mo Mar	0.07	0.15	20
21	1981	Q0.55	4-17-84	3-27	1.07½	2.20	1.85	Equity per shr $2.31			12-31-83	104.	...	7552	Dc	p0.02	p0.06	0.13	0.04	0.17	0.17				21
22	1975	Q0.50	4-17-84	3-27	1.00	2.00	1.50	Equity per shr $1.80			12-31-83	122.	...	6208	Mr	p0.40	0.55	0.49	0.68	....	0.78	9 Mo Dec△	0.62	0.72	22
23	....				....	Nil	....	20.7	21.8	0.54	12-31-83	....	...	6821	Dc	d0.01	Nil	d0.03	d0.21	d0.18	d0.14	3 Mo Mar	d0.09	d0.05	23
24◆	1943	Q0.08	6-1-84	5-15	0.16	0.32	0.32	8.38	99.9	42.9	9-30-83	*67.5	...	p9655	Dc	△1.08	1.23	1.30	1.06	P0.91	1.15	3 Mo Mar	0.11	0.35	24
25	1939	Q0.20	3-15-84	2-10	0.20	0.80	0.80	118.	527.	245.	12-31-83	249.	844	28603	Dc	3.27	1.98	1.58	□0.17	△□0.96	1.13	3 Mo Mar	d0.54	d0.37	25
26	1946	Q1.00	4-1-84	2-10	2.00	4.00	4.00					....	150	...	Dc	b4.98	b2.58	b2.04	b0.04	b1.80	....				26
27	1981	Q2.50	3-15-84	2-10	2.50	10.00	10.00	Cv at $28.75,3.478 shrs				....	694	...	Dc	....	b2.58	b2.04	b0.04	b1.80	....	SF 37,500 fr Dec'90,100			27
28◆	1979	0.04	8-25-83	8-8	....	Nil	0.12	0.32	19.6	12.1	12-31-83	4.73	...	3476	Je	0.27	•0.45	0.64	0.43	d0.01	d0.25	9 Mo Mar	0.10	d0.14	28
29◆	....	None Since Public			....	Nil	....	3.27	77.1	27.7	9-30-83	69.0	...	2824	Dc	1.17	1.33	1.10	d1.76	P■d8.09	d8.09				29
30	....	None Since Public			....	Nil	....	0.23	1.41	1.17	3-31-84	1.12	...	2255	Dc	0.39	0.60	0.57	0.16	0.03	Nil	3 Mo Mar	0.01	d0.02	30
31◆	1902	Q0.50	6-1-84	4-23	1.00	2.00	1.91	115.	1637	1298	12-31-83	900.	...	44745	Dc	3.13	□3.69	□4.56	p4.15	2.77	2.73	3 Mo Mar	0.46	0.42	31
32◆	1973	S0.03	1-3-84	12-12	0.03	0.06	0.06	0.21	34.6	14.8	12-31-83	7.66	...	5797	Mr	□0.64	0.97	1.02	0.77	....	1.33	9 Mo Dec△	0.51	1.07	32
33◆	1957	Q0.13	5-29-84	5-3	0.26	0.52	0.39	10.4	57.5	21.5	12-31-83	24.9	...	7325	Dc	0.95	1.01	1.08	□1.17	1.51	1.70	3 Mo Mar	0.22	0.41	33
34	1976	0.20	4-8-83	3-21	....	Nil	0.20	10.4	67.0	81.9	12-31-83	5.39	...	3437	Je	•0.96	•1.29	1.54	0.38	d1.19	d2.94	6 Mo Dec△	0.55	d1.20	34
35	....	None Since Public			....	Nil	....	2.61	14.1	4.24	9-30-83	3.61	...	3678	Dc	0.27	△0.58	△□0.33	△0.14	Pd0.20	d0.20				35
36	1949	0.28		4-9	0.28	0.55	0.534	294.	1416	1035	1-15-84	p518.	...	[79]p67167	Ap	1.44	1.22	1.09	0.90	0.85	0.92	9 Mo Jan	0.62	0.69	36
37	1946	Q0.22½	4-10-84	3-5	†0.57½	1.05	0.80	1.35	40.7	18.3	12-31-83	10.3	...	2039	Dc	1.56	□[71]0.13	1.80	1.31	1.93	2.23	3 Mo Mar	0.31	0.61	37
38◆	1978	Q0.02	7-9-84	6-11	0.06	0.08	0.08	35.9	82.9	17.9	12-31-83	36.4	...	7341	Sp	1.10	1.13	0.34	0.47	0.23	0.43	3 Mo Dec△	0.10	0.30	38
39◆	....	0.01¼	12-18-80	12-5	....	Nil	....	0.39	9.24	2.60	12-31-83	6.61	...	3143	Mr	0.09	0.13	d0.28	0.22	....	d0.22	9 Mo Dec△	0.19	d0.25	39
40	....	None Since Public			....	Nil	....	n/a	3.86	0.41	2-29-84	0.66	...	2573	Au	0.09	0.17	0.36	0.26	d0.09	d0.07	6 Mo Feb	d0.05	d0.03	40
41◆	1960	[73]0.191	6-30-84	3-26	[73]0.191	0.32	0.212	14.8	641.	150.	3-31-83	3.03	...	[72]69015	Mr	0.98	1.09	0.89	1.27	....	1.33	3 Mo Jun△	0.29	0.35	41
42	1982	Q0.10	7-26-84	7-5	0.25	0.40	0.20	4.08	51.3	21.3	12-31-83	19.4	...	2978	Dc	▲2.86	■1.19	▲1.04	d0.08	[74]0.92	0.92				42
43	1981	[75]0.70	5-4-84	1-24	[75]1.41	2.68	2.59	Equity per shr $23.35			12-31-83	....	...	2200	Dc	....	....	[76]2.19	3.18	2.60	2.88	3 Mo Mar	0.62	▲0.90	43
44	1974	S0.03	5-4-84	4-12	0.03	0.06	0.06	1.78	70.1	33.3	12-31-83	32.2	...	6776	Dc	0.16	0.33	▲0.41	[77]d0.01	0.13	0.17	3 Mo Mar	0.01	0.05	44
45◆	1945	gQ0.22½	4-15-84	3-23	g0.45	0.90	g0.81¾	84.2	487.	234.	j4-30-83	*300.	...	27532	Ap	0.92	□1.50	□1.73	□2.13	[78]□2.65	2.92	9 Mo Jan	□2.07	2.34	45
46	1981	g0.15	6-1-84	5-8	g0.15	0.15	g0.10	9.06	16.6	7.96	j12-31-82	11.2	...	10915	Dc	0.54	1.31	0.82	0.26	▲P1.14	j1.14				46

◆ **Stock Splits & Divs By Line Reference Index** [1]To split 2-for-1,ex May 25. [4]5-for-4,'80,'82:4-for-3,'83. [5]3-for-2,'79. [6]10-for-1,'81. [8]2-for-1 twice,'83. [9]10%,'82:2-for-1 & 3-for-2,'83:5-for-4,'82,'84. [17]10%,'80,'82:No adj for'83 spinoff. [18]2-for-1,'83. [19]2-for-1,'80. [24]2-for-1,'80:3-for-2,'81. [28]3-for-2,'80,'81. [29]2-for-1,'79:3-for-2,'80. [31]2-for-1,'79. [32]3-for-2&2-for-1,'79:2-for-1,'80,'81. [33]To split 2-for-1,ex May 30. [38]3-for-2,'79:2-for-1,'80,'83. [39]2-for-1,'81,'83. [41]6-for-5,'79,'80:10%,'82:3-for-2,'84. [45]2-for-1,'83.

Source: *Standard & Poor's Stock Guide.* Reprinted with permission.

follows the ranking. The number of institutions and their holdings takes up the next two columns. Then the firm's business is briefly described. Past price ranges, monthly sales volume, and recent prices appear next, followed by the dividend yield and PE ratio.

The first column of the opposite page contains the initial year of unbroken dividends. Relevant information on the current dividend situation appears next. If the most recent payment was quarterly, a "Q" will precede the amount. Then the payment date and ex-dividend date (dividends are paid to holders on the day-of-record, which is one day prior to the ex-dividend date) are reported, followed by the total per-share amount paid in the current year, the total indicated rate, and the amount paid in the previous year. Next, financial position data are provided, including: cash and equivalents, current assets, and current liabilities from the most recent balance sheet. Long-term debt amounts and the number of preferred and common shares then appear. Cash, assets, and debt are all in millions of dollars, while share numbers are reported in thousands. Finally, annual EPS data are reported for several years with the final column containing the most recent interim earnings.

Additional information is included on warrants and preferred stock. Item 20 in the *Stock Guide* concerns warrants for Acton Corporation. Under the name of the stock appears Wrrt(Purch 1.05 Com at 18.95). Thus the security may be used to purchase 1.05 shares of the common at 18.95 per share. Continuing across, we see under interim earnings that the warrant expires on 6/16/86.

S&P Stock Guide packs a substantial amount of relevant investor information into a very small space. Retail brokerage houses will often supply this handy reference to their customers upon request.

STOCK MARKET INDEXES

Most investors are interested in both their own stocks' price action and the market's overall moves. A number of different indexes reflect these movements. While all market indexes are based on the average prices of a sample of securities, the samples and averaging processes differ.

The Dow Jones Industrial Average

The simplest and best known of the stock indexes is the Dow Jones Industrial Average (DJIA). The Dow is an unweighted average of thirty major industrial firms. Composition changes are relatively rare.[3] The thirty stocks' prices are summed and then divided by a number called the divisor, which is adjusted to maintain comparability whenever a DJIA firm is split. Small stock dividends do not lead to a change in the divisor, however. Moreover, the declining impact of the more rapid growth of firms that tend to split biases the average downward. Nonetheless, the Dow remains the most widely followed market index. When people speak of the "Market" they usually have the DJIA in mind. While Dow

Jones Inc. also computes averages for utilities, transportation companies, and a composite sample, their industrial average receives most of the attention.

Other Stock Market Averages

Most other stock market averages are weighted to reflect the relative value of their components. Thus, the S&P composite average contains the share prices of 500 major corporations weighted according to the relative values of their outstanding shares. S&P also computes indexes of 400 industrials, 40 utilities, 40 finance and 20 transportation firms.[4]

The NYSE composite index is a value-weighted average of all stocks listed on the Big Board. Similarly, the AMEX index is a value-weighted average of AMEX stocks and the NASDAQ index is a value-weighted index of OTC stocks. Finally, the Wilshire 5000 weights stocks in all three markets. Aside from the Dow, the only other unweighted index of consequence is the *Value Line* index.

Relations Between the Indexes

Since stocks are generally affected by similar forces and since most of the indexes tend to have a common component, the indexes should move together. Table 10.2 reports correlations between some of the major averages. While the various indexes do tend to move together, they also reflect somewhat different market segments. In particular, the DJIA is representative of the larger, more established blue-chip stocks, while the NYSE and S&P 500 are broader based. The AMEX and NASDAQ indexes reflect the pricing of more speculative issues.

BUSINESS AND INVESTMENT PERIODICALS

A large number of periodicals cater to the investor/business person. Most such publications offer both factual news and opinions investors may use to stay abreast of current developments. Since the periodicals' opinions are as subject to error as those of the investment advisory services, investors should consider but not rely upon their advice.

First and foremost with current business news is the *Wall Street Journal* (WSJ), published five days a week. Most serious investors keep up with the relevant business news in the *WSJ* or the financial sections of major newspapers (the *New York Times*, for example). Both the *WSJ* and *Barron's* are published by Dow Jones, Inc., a long-time leader of the financial press. *Barron's* appears weekly and is more investor-oriented than the *WSJ*.

While *Business Week* (published weekly by McGraw-Hill) appeals principally to business people, it contains some useful investment information. For example, McGraw-Hill annually surveys and forecasts business fixed investment (new spending on long-term plant and equipment). The periodical also contains an analysis of the investment climate in its end-of-the-year issue.

Table 10.2   Stock Index Correlations

	DIJA	S&P 400	S&P 500	NYSE Composite	AMEX Value Index	NASDAQ Industrials
S&P 400	.895					
S&P 500	.916	.894				
NYSE Composite	.923	.897	.920			
AMEX Value Index	.716	.695	.727	.752		
NASDAQ Industrials	.678	.660	.682	.704	.675	
NASDAQ Composite	.794	.772	.800	.829	.788	.785

Correlation Coefficients Between Daily Percentage of Price Changes for Alternative Market Indicator Series January 4, 1972–December 31, 1979 (2,019 Observations).

Source: *Investments* by Frank K. Reilly. Copyright © 1982 CBS College Publishing. Reprinted by permission of Holt, Rinehart and Winston, CBS College Publishing.

Forbes (published twice monthly) is largely investor, as opposed to business, oriented. In addition to its lists, *Forbes* contains articles on specific companies and other relevant investment subjects. Investor-oriented magazines with a smaller readership than *Forbes* include *Financial World, Finance,* and the *Magazine of Wall Street.* More general business and money management periodicals include *Money, Fortune,* and *Fact.*

The *Financial Analysts Journal* and *Journal of Portfolio Management* publish serious work on investment theory and concepts. The typical article, while not easy reading, is at least intelligible to nonacademicians. The same could not be said for articles in the more academic finance/economics journals such as the *American Economic Review* or the *Journal of Finance.*

SYSTEMATIC COVERAGE OF COMPANIES

While the financial press covers companies unsystematically, several publications periodically report on a list of firms and thus serve as handy references. *Moody's Industrial Manual* (published annually) contains a great deal of financial information on a large number of firms' past histories. More up-to-date information on a smaller group of firms is available quarterly in *Value Line, Standard and Poor's* reports, and directly from some brokerage firms. The American Motors Corporation reports of *Moody's,* the *S&P's* reports, and *Value Line,* are illustrated below. The *Moody's* report is reproduced in Figure 10.5.

Moody's coverage is quite extensive. First the capital structure is discussed, including a list of securities followed by a brief history of the firm; a list of subsidiaries and discussions of the business and products of the firm and the firm's plants and properties; a list of managers and directors; the name of the auditor; dates of directors and annual meetings; number of stockholders and employees, the address of the general office and a report on wholesale auto sales. This is followed by income statements for the past seven years and a less extensive set of income data for twelve prior years. A balance sheet for the most recent seven years is also included. Extensive notes accompany these financial statements. Next comes a set of financial and operating information such as per-share data and financial and operation rates. A brief description of the firm's debt and equity securities appears at the end.

Coverage will vary from firm to firm, although the example cited is typical for a company the size of American Motors. Similar *Moody's* manuals are published for other types of firms. Most significant publicly held companies are included.

Although the coverage is quite extensive, *Moody's* information is largely descriptive and dated. Standard and Poor's publishes a set of manuals very similar to Moody's. They also market a more investor-oriented set of corporation reports. Figure 10.6 contains an example of such a report.

The S&P's report begins with a summary and discussion of the current outlook followed by a chart of the company's stock price action. Sales and earnings are considered next. A brief analysis of recent developments is then presented. Income and balance sheet data go back ten years. Finally, the firm's dividends, finances, and capitalization are examined.

Compared with *Moody's*, the material is briefer, more analytical, up-to-date, and investor oriented. Most listed companies and the major OTC-traded companies are covered by S&P's reports. S&P also publishes a reference book called the *Stock Market Encyclopedia*, which contains brief reports on the 500 stocks making up the S&P index.

With 90,000 subscribers, *Value Line* is several times the size of the next largest similar periodical (McGraw-Hill's *Outlook*). Figure 10.7 illustrates a *Value Line* report. *Value Line* coverage includes a chart of book value, cash flow, and price per share. Insider and institutional trading decisions are reported in boxes at the top. Some income and balance sheet data are reported along with a projection for the next fiscal year and three to five years hence. *Value Line* tables include rates of return and earnings, capital structure, and quarterly sales, earnings, and dividends for recent years. Projections are given for the next 12 months. Three boxes contain (1) a description of business, (2) an analysis of the firm's position and prospects, and (3) ratings of the firm's performance, safety, and its beta ratio.

Value Line's computer-based stock selection-timeliness ratings are its most famous statistics. Its 1,700 stocks are grouped as follows: 100 (I); 300 (II); 900 (III); 300 (IV); and 100 (V). Group one selections (ignoring commissions) have appreciated by 1,565% over the 1965–1983 period, compared with only 80% for the NYSE composite (Figure 10.8).[5] Even the well-known efficient market exponent Fisher Black acknowledges *Value Line's* past success.[6] More recently

Figure 10.5 Moody's Industrial Manual

MOODY'S INDUSTRIAL MANUAL

987

FINANCIAL & OPERATING DATA (Cont'd)

	1982	1981	1980	1979	1978	1977	1976
% net current assets to net worth	49.26	46.41	43.79	38.87	41.39	43.16	46.34
% property depreciated	50.25	47.18	45.61	43.59	42.88	43.30	45.32
% ann. dep. depl. & amor. to gr. prop.	6.66	6.47	6.39	6.09	5.66	5.47	5.32
Capitalization	%	%	%	%	%	%	%
% long term debt	24.75	25.43	27.52	27.95	29.31	27.46	27.52
% common stock and surplus	75.25	74.57	72.48	72.05	70.69	72.54	72.48
Sales ÷ inventory	6.72	6.81	6.97	6.18	5.68	5.56	5.71
Sales ÷ receivables	5.07	4.61	4.72	4.62	4.87	5.28	5.30
% sales to net property	266.47	275.38	259.95	244.53	229.23	225.94	236.17
% sales to total assets	115.23	119.05	118.42	112.74	110.06	110.00	106.29
% net income to total assets	4.40	6.43	5.45	5.96	6.17	6.27	6.78
% net income to net worth	8.58	12.89	11.09	12.51	12.43	11.93	12.33
Analysis of Operations	%	%	%	%	%	%	%
Total net sales	100.00	100.00	100.00	100.00	100.00	100.00	100.00
Cost of sales	57.21	58.72	60.36	59.87	59.25	59.77	59.06
Selling, general and other exp.	27.36	24.17	23.12	23.38	23.19	22.77	23.32
	%	%	%	%	%	%	%
Deprec., depl. and amortiz.	5.01	4.52	4.52	4.41	4.32	4.27	4.19
Research and develop. exp.	5.24	4.50	4.11	3.90	3.89	3.94	3.91
Balance	5.18	8.09	7.89	8.44	9.35	9.25	9.51
Dividends and interest						1.38	1.71
Other income	2.14	2.16	1.55	1.70	1.31	0.30	0.54
Total	7.32	10.25	9.44	10.14	10.66	10.93	11.76
Interest expense	2.00	1.86	1.82	1.97	1.81	1.79	1.58
Net income before income taxes, etc.	5.32	8.39	7.62	8.17	8.85	9.14	10.18
Income taxes and surtax	1.48	3.07	3.01	2.88	3.24	3.44	3.80
Net income	3.84	5.38	4.61	5.29	5.61	5.70	6.38

[1] As reported by company.

LONG TERM DEBT

1. American Cyanamid Co. sinking fund debenture 7⅞s, due 2001:

Rating—Aa3

AUTH.—$100,000,000; outstanding, Dec. 31, 1982, $80,000,000.

DATED—Apr. 15, 1971. DUE—Apr. 15, 2001.

INTEREST—A&O15 in NYC or by mail to holders registered on 15th day prior to interest date.

TRUSTEE—Citibank, N.A., NYC.

DENOMINATION—Fully registered, $1,000 and authorized multiples thereof.

CALLABLE—As a whole or in part, on at least 30 days' notice, to each Apr. 14, incl., as follows:

1984	.......103.32	1985	.......103.06	1986	.......102.81
1987	.......102.55	1988	.......102.30	1989	.......102.04
1990	.......101.79	1991	.......101.53	1992	.......101.28
1993	.......101.02	1994	.......100.77	1995	.......100.51
1996	.......100.26	2001	.......100.00		

Also callable for sinking fund (which see) at 100.

INTEREST—M&S 15 in NYC or by mail to holders registered F28 & A31.

TRUSTEE—Morgan Guaranty Trust Co. of N.Y., NYC.

DENOMINATION—Fully registered, $1,000 and integral multiples thereof. Transferable and exchangeable without service charge.

CALLABLE—As a whole or in part at any time on at least 30 days' notice to each Mar. 14, as follows:

1983	.......105.99	1984	.......105.67	1985	.......105.36
1986	.......105.04	1987	.......104.73	1988	.......104.41
1989	.......104.10	1990	.......103.78	1991	.......103.47
1992	.......103.15	1993	.......102.84	1994	.......102.52
1995	.......102.21	1996	.......101.89	1997	.......101.58
1998	.......101.26	1999	.......100.95	2000	.......100.63
2001	.......100.32				

thereafter at 100.

Not callable, however, prior to Mar. 15, 1986 thru refunding at interest cost less than 8.42% per annum. Also callable for sinking fund (which see) at 100.

SINKING FUND—Annually, on Mar. 15,

CAPITAL STOCK

American Cyanamid Co. common; par $5:

AUTHORIZED—60,000,000 shares; outstanding Dec. 31, 1982, 48,369,931 shares; in treasury, 535,407 shares; reserved for options, 2,504,134 shares; par $5.

Par changed from $20 to no par Mar. 27, 1929 share for share; and to $10 in Apr., 1932, share for share; $10 shares split 2-for-1 July 16, 1952 and July 12, 1957, by 100% stock dividend, from $10 to $5 Apr. 18, 1966, by 2-for-1 split.

Dividend Record (In $)

($100 par shares)

1907-22	.......Nil	1923	.......2.00	1924-25	.....6.00
1926	.......1.50				

($20 par shares)

1926	.......0.90	1927	.......1.40	1928	.......1.60
1929	.......0.80				

(No par shares)

1929-30	.....0.80	1931-32	.....Nil

(\$10 par shares)

1932-33	Nil	1934	0.25	1935	0.55
1936	1.00	[1]1937	1.60	1938	0.45
[2]1939	1.60	[2]1940	2.10	[4]1941	1.85
[4]1942-43	1.35	1944	1.35	1945	1.25
1946	1.50	1947	1.00	1948	1.50
1949	2.00	1950	4.62½	1951	4.00
1952	2.00				

(\$10 par shares after 2-for-1 split)

1952	1.00	1953-54	2.00	1955	2.50
1956	2.75	[3]1957	1.50		

(\$10 par shares after 100% stk. div.)

1957	0.85	1958-61	1.60	1962	1.70
1963	1.80	1964	2.00	1965	2.15
1966	0.62½				

(\$5 par shares)

1966	0.39¼	1967-72	1.25	1973	1.32½
1974	1.45	1975-78	1.50	1979-80	1.60
1981	1.67½	1982	1.75	[5]1983	0.43¾

[1]Of which $1 was in cash or convertible preferred, first series.
[2]Of which $1 in 1939 and $1.50 in 1940 was in convertible preferred, second series (1939) and third series (1940) (cash in lieu of fractional shares).
[3]Also 100% in stock.
[4]Includes amount paid in 5% preference stock: 1941, $1.25; 1942 and 1943, $0.75.
[5]To Mar. 25.

SINKING FUND—Annually, each Apr. 15, 1981-2000, to retire debs., cash or debs. equal to $4,000,000. Payments calculated to retire 80% of issue prior to maturity.

EXEMPTED TRANSACTIONS—Limitations described below under "Security" and "Sale and Leaseback" will not apply to a particular transaction if sum of (a) debt secured by liens the creation of which would otherwise require that Co. secure debs. plus (b) attributable debt in respect of prohibited sale and leaseback transactions plus (c) all debt and liquidation preference of all pfd. stock of restricted subsidiaries which would otherwise be prohibited, does not exceed 5% of consolidated net worth of Co. and consolidated subsidiaries.

SECURITY—Not secured. If Co. shall secure debt for money borrowed by creating a lien on any principal property, debs. shall be equally and ratably secured except for (a) liens on a Corp.'s property at time it becomes a restricted subsidiary, (b) liens on property existing at time acquired, (c) certain purchase money, exploration, drilling development and similar liens, (d) liens on debt of restricted subsidiary to Co. or another restricted subsidiary, (e) any extension, renewal or replacement thereof.

SALE & LEASEBACK—Co. or subsidiary may not sell and leaseback property unless (a) Co. could mtge. such property to secure debt in an amount equal to attributable debt with respect to sale and leaseback transaction without securing debs. or (b) Co., within 20 days, applies to retirement of senior funded debt an amount equal to greater of (i) net proceeds of sale or (ii) fair market value of principal property.

INDENTURE MODIFICATION—Indenture may be modified, except as provided, with consent of 66⅔% of debs. outstg.

PURPOSE—Proceeds to repay short-term debt.

LISTED—On New York Stock Exchange.

OFFERED—($100,000,000) at 99 (proceeds to Co., 98.125) on Apr. 21, 1971 thru White, Weld & Co. and associates.

2. American Cyanamid Co. sinking fund debenture 8⅝s, due 2006:

Rating—Aa3

AUTH—$100,000,000; outstg. Dec. 31, 1982, $99,652,000.

DATED—Mar. 15, 1976. DUE—Mar. 15, 2006.

1987-2005, cash (or debs.) to retire $4,000,000 principal amount of debs.; plus similar optional payments. Sinking fund designed to retire 76% of issue prior to maturity.

EXEMPTED TRANSACTIONS—SECURITY—Same as s.f. deb. 7⅞s, due 2001.

SALE & LEASEBACK—Co. or subsidiary may not sell and leaseback property unless (a) Co. could mtge. such property to secure debt in an amount equal to attributable debt with respect to sale and leaseback transaction without securing debs. or (b) Co., within 120 days, applies to retirement of senior funded debt an amount equal to greater of (i) net proceeds of sale or (ii) fair market value of principal property.

RIGHTS ON DEFAULT—Trustee, or 25% of debs. outstg., may declare principal due and payable (30 days' grace for payment of interest or sinking fund installments).

INDENTURE MODIFICATION—Indenture may be modified, except as provided, with consent of 66⅔% of debs. outstg.

PURPOSE—Proceeds for Co.'s capital expenditure program.

LISTED—On New York Stock Exchange.

OFFERED—($100,000,000) at 99.50 (proceeds to Co., 98.625) on Mar. 10, 1976 thru White, Weld & Co., Inc. and Salomon Brothers and associates.

3. Promissory Notes: Outstanding, Dec. 31, 1982, $193,500,000 comprised of:

(1) $43,500,000 3⅜% note due Jan. 1, 1987; prepayable at company's option at 104 to Jan. 1, 1957 and at gradually reduced rates thereafter, with required payments at rate of 6% of loans outstanding at end of 1976 or Jan. 1, 1977 and annually thereafter.

(2) $150,000,000 8¾ note, due 1988-98.

Notes contain certain restrictions, including limitations on payment of dividends. At Dec. 31, 1982, $140,400,000 of earned surplus was available for dividends.

Proceeds for working capital and general corporate proposals including capital expenditures.

4. 5.5% to 8¼% pollution control rev. bds. due through 2009:

Outstg. Dec. 31, 1982, $109,617,000. For details see Moodys' Municipal & Gov't Manual Pollution Control & Industrial Revenue Bds. section.

5. Sundry Obligations: Outstanding Dec. 31, 1982, $23,341,000.

Dividends payable quarterly Jan. 1, etc. to stock of record about Dec. 1, etc.

DIVIDEND REINVESTMENT PLAN—Company offers its holders of common stock the opportunity to buy additional shares of common stock through its Automatic Dividend Reinvestment Plan sponsored by Citibank, N.A. New York. Participating shareowners may invest monthly from $10.00 to $1,000, in addition to their dividend, at their option.

DIVIDEND RESTRICTIONS—See long term debt above.

VOTING RIGHTS—Has sole voting rights.

PREEMPTIVE RIGHTS—None except (a) for common to be issued for cash and (b) securities convertible into common and to be issued for cash other than 40,000 shares of preferred under prescribed limitations to be sold to employees.

TRANSFER, REGISTRAR AND DIVIDEND DISBURSING AGENT—Chase Manhattan Bank, N.A. New York.

LISTED—On NYSE. (Symbol: ACY); also listed on Amsterdam, Basle, Frankfurt, Geneva, Lausanne, and Zurich Stock Exchanges. Unlisted trading on Boston, Pacific and Cincinnati Stock Exchanges.

988

MOODY'S INDUSTRIAL MANUAL

AMERICAN MOTORS CORPORATION

CAPITAL STRUCTURE

LONG TERM DEBT

Issue	Rating	[1]Amount Outstanding	Interest Dates A & O 1	Times Charges Earned 1982	[4]Price Range 1982	[4]Price Range 1981	Call Price
1. 6% conv. subord. debentures, 1988		$19,699,000			83 - 49	66 - 49	[3]101.67
2. Other debt		512,674,000					
3. American Motors Overseas Corp. 6% conv. bonds, 1992		4,222,000					

CAPITAL STOCK

Issue	Par Value	Amount Outstanding	Divs. per Sh. 1982	Divs. per Sh. 1981	[2]Earned per Sh. 1982	Earned per Sh. 1981	[4]Price Range 1982	[4]Price Range 1981	Call Price
1. Class A $2.80 cum. red. preferred	$0.01	3,482,143 shs.			d$2.85	d$2.44	7¼ - 2½	4⅞ - 2⅜	
2. Common	$1.66⅔	[1]56,988,754 shs.							

[1]Excluding current portion. [2]As reported by Co. based on average shares. [3]Subject to change, see text. [4]Calendar years.

HISTORY

Incorporated in Maryland, July 29, 1916, under the name Nash Motors Company, as successor to Thomas B. Jeffery Company. Name changed to Nash-Kelvinator Corp. Jan. 4, 1937, when Kelvinator Corp. was merged and present name adopted Apr. 30, 1954 on merger of Hudson Motor Car Co.

As of January 4, 1937, acquired the business of the Kelvinator Corporation, an important manufacturer of electric refrigeration devices and household equipment, under a merger plan by which stockholders in the Kelvinator Corporation received 1⅜ shares of stock in Nash-Kelvinator Corporation for each share held. (This entailed the issuance of 1,645,600 shares of stock, or 37½% of the stock to be outstanding after completion of the merger.)

In 1945 company sold its 55% interest (acquired in 1937) in Electromaster, Inc., a manufacturer of electric ranges and water heaters.

In 1945 company purchased Kelvinator, Ltd. (England) from Kelvinator of Canada, Ltd.

In 1948 company sold 50% interest (acquired in 1936) in Appliance Manufacturing Co., manufacturers of washing machines.

On Jan. 26, 1952, acquired stove and range business of Kalamazoo Stove & Furnace Co.

In Sept., 1952, acquired controlling interest in Altorfer Bros. Co., manufacturers of laundry equipment (liquidated in May 1959).

On Apr. 30, 1954, merged Hudson Motor Car Co. Under the plan, holders of Hudson stock received 2 American Motors shares for each 3 Hudson shares; company stock was exchanged share-for-share. Unexchanged Hudson shares received $9.8125 per share cash settlement.

On Nov. 10, 1955, company sold 65% of its stock holdings in Ranco Inc. and balance was sold in 1956 for a total profit of $10,662,372.

parts for the cars are purchased from Renault. Under a licensing agreement associated with this right to manufacture, royalties are paid to Renault based on the domestically-manufactured Renault vehicles and certain service parts sold to the Company's dealers.

Pursuant to its agreements with the Company, Renault has a right of first refusal to a pro rata share of future issuances of Common Stock or Class A Cumulative Preferred Stock. As a result, simultaneously with the issuance of additional shares of Common Stock by the Company in Apr. 1983, Renault exercised its contractual right to maintain its level of ownership at approximately 46.4%, and purchased 11,484,554 shares for $63.3 million.

Total investment in the Company by Renault has been as follows:

1979—$15.0 million of Common Stock, $45.0 million 9% convertible note

1980—$122.5 million of Common Stock, $45.0 million 9% convertible note, above converted into Common Stock

1981—$45.0 million of Class A Cumulative Preferred Stock and a Warrant

1982—$40.0 million 10% Convertible Subordinated Debenture, $50.0 million 16.62% Subordinated Debenture, $52.5 million of Class A Cumulative Preferred Stock and Warrants

1983—$50.0 million 13.53% Subordinated Debenture

$62.3 million of Common Stock

In addition, Renault from time to time provides other financing to the Company in various forms, including supplier credits.

Effective as of Dec. 31, 1980, pursuant to an agreement between the Company and Renault, Renault Credit International S.A., a subsidiary of Renault, acquired a 50% interest in American Motors Financial Corporation, to establish a full service financial company to support AMC, Jeep and Renault sales in the

Strategic Plan

The Co. has embarked on a strategic plan dependent on a continuing and aggressive product development program. During the 1970's, the Co. performed erratically, both in the marketplace and financially. In the opinion of management, the principal cause was the inability of the Co. to maintain a competitive product line. Individual models appeared sporadically and, although some of these vehicles were initially well received, subsequent new models were not available to consolidate the gains made. The Company believes that, in the 1980's, it must pursue a more consistent product development program that results in a regular and timely introduction of new products. These products will draw upon the particular expertise of Renault and the Company and are expected to broaden the Company's representation in selected major market segments. In line with the Company's overall plan, it is continuing to develop front-wheel-drive passenger cars through its affiliation with Renault and new four-wheel-drive vehicles. The Company is also taking measures to strengthen its dealer network as part of its strategic plan.

On Sept. 22, 1982, the Co. met its goal of introducing the Renault Alliance, the first of its new generation of Renault passenger cars built in the United States. At the beginning of the 1984 model year, the Co. plans to introduce two new models based on the Renault Alliance platform. As with the Renault Alliance, these new models are to be built in the United States and have been modified by the Co. and Renault to meet American consumer preferences and applicable governmental requirements. During the remainder of the 1980's, the Co. expects to introduce other lines of front-wheel-drive passenger cars which will be built in the United States utilizing Renault

In June, 1967, company sold Redisco, Inc., financing subsidiary, to Chrysler Credit Corp., subsidiary of Chrysler Corp., for about $29,000,000 after setting aside $1,000,000 in escrow to provide for possible losses on certain accounts.

In July 1968, sold Kelvinator Div. (including 72% interest in Kelvinator of Canada, majority interest in Kelvinator Ltd. England and 10% interest in Kelvinator of Australia) to White Consolidated Industries, Inc. (see general index) for approx. $22,000,000 in notes and cash, retention of liquid assets of $23,000,000.

On Feb. 4, 1970 company's shareholders approved acquisition of Kaiser Jeep Corp., wholly-owned subsidiary of Kaiser Industries Corp., for $10,000,000 cash, 5,500,000 Co. capital shs. about $9,500,000 in negotiable 5-year Co. notes and about $500,000 in other assets.

In Sept. 1970, also acquired Holmes Foundry, Ltd. of Sarnia, Ont. and Windsor Plastics, Inc. (sold in 1982) of Evansville, Ind.

In Apr. 1971, formed AM General Corp. to assume the assets and government contracts of former general products division.

On Oct. 1, 1972 commenced leasing cars to public through subsidiary, American Motors Leasing Corp.

In Nov. 1972 acquired Mercury Plastics Co., Mount Clemens, Mich., manufacturer of injection molded plastic products for 611,111 common shares with 611,111 additional shares which were issued based upon an earnings formula of Mercury.

In May 1974, acquired Wheel Horse Products, Inc., South Bend, Ind., a manufacturer of lawn and garden tractors.

In Dec. 1979 sold its Richmond, Inc., engine-production plant to Klockner-Humboldt-Deutz AG, a West German manufacturer of diesel-truck and industrial engines.

Relationship with Renault:

Regie Nationale des Usines Renault ("Renault") owned 37,918,764 shares (46.4%) as of Apr. 1983 of the Company's outstanding Common Stock, and could, after exercising all rights under agreements described below, own more than 50% of outstanding shares.

The Co. is the exclusive importer and distributor of Renault passenger cars in the U.S. and Canada. The Company's wholesale sales of Renault passenger cars were 51,481 in 1982, 37,239 in 1981 and 37,792 in 1980. In 1982 Renault began distributing the Company's Jeep four-wheel-drive vehicles in France and is expected to distribute such vehicles in certain other countries. Wholesale sales of Jeep vehicles to Renault were 2,156 in 1982.

The Company began manufacture of Renault-designed Alliance passenger cars in 1982 at its facilities in the U.S. Certain component U.S, and Canada.

The principal business of AMFC is to finance the acquisition by franchised AMC/Jeep/Renault dealers of new vehicles sold by American Motors or its subsidiaries and to purchase from dealers installment obligations arising from retail sales of new products purchased from American Motors or its subsidiaries. AMFC also makes capital loans to dealers to whom wholesale financing is provided.

SUBSIDIARIES

AM General Corp.
   Amland Corp.
American Motors Sales Corp.
American Motors Realty Corp.
American Motors Leasing Corp.
American Motors Financial Corp. (50%)
Evart Products Co.
Coleman Products Co.
American Motors Pan American Corp.
Graphic Center, Inc.
Jeep Corp.
Jeep International Corp.
American Motors International Sales Corp.
American Motors International Trading Corp.
Mercury Plastics Co.
Wheel Horse Products, Inc.
Wheel-Horse Sales, Inc.
American Motors (Canada) Inc.
American Motors Overseas Corp.

Proposed Joint Venture: In May 1983, Co. announced that it has agreed to set up a joint venture with Beijing Automotive Works to construct four-wheel-drive vehicles at an existing plant in Beijing. Co. said the joint venture, which will be called Beijing Jeep Corp. Ltd., is to begin producing a version of Co.'s CJ7 Jeep by the end of 1983. Once production begins, volume is expected to double the plant's current output of 20,000 units a year. Co. said initial production will be intended for domestic use in China, but an eventual goal is to build enough for export.

BUSINESS & PRODUCTS

American Motors Corporation and its consolidated subsidiaries are engaged in the manufacture and sale of automotive vehicles. The Company entered the four-wheel-drive and tactical vehicle business through the acquisition of Jeep Corporation in 1970. Under agreements entered into with Regie Nationale des Usines Renault in 1979, the Company also imports and sells Renault passenger cars in the United States and Canada and began manufacturing Renault-designed passenger cars in the 1983 model year. The Company also is undertaking the development of new Jeep vehicle products to be introduced during the 1984 model year.

design and technology. In order to offer a range of competitive models, the Co. will continue to offer AMC Eagle and SX/4 four-wheel-drive automobiles and will supplement its domestically manufactured passenger car lines by importing selected Renault models. The Co. has decided to phase out its rear-wheel-drive passenger cars. The Co. expects that its new lines of front-wheel-drive passenger cars built in the United States, its four-wheel-drive automobiles and imported Renault passenger cars will provide a broader product line that it currently offers.

The Company's product plans also include the introduction of a new generation of Jeep vehicles, which are designed to achieve substantial fuel economy while retaining all essential Jeep vehicle characteristics. The Company plans to introduce the new Jeep vehicles with various engine-drivetrain combinations and in various models and body styles at the beginning of the 1984 model year. They will be followed by the introduction of Jeep pickup trucks derived from the Jeep series. In addition, the Co. expects to improve and continue to offer essentially all its existing Jeep series.

Business Segments

The Company's business consists principally of two segments: General Automotive and Special Government Vehicles. The General Automotive segment involves the manufacture, assembly and sale of passenger cars, four-wheel-drive automobiles and utility and recreational vehicles, and their related parts and accessories in the United States, Canada and other foreign countries, and the importation and sale of Renault passenger cars in the United States and Canada. The Special Government Vehicles segment primarily involves the assembly and sale of specialized vehicles, including tactical trucks and postal service vehicles, principally to agencies of the United States and foreign governments.

In order to concentrate its resources on its general automotive operations, the Company is seeking in 1983 to sell its Special Government Vehicles segment at a price significantly in excess of its investment.

Sales by Business Segment ($000 omitted):

	Yr. end 12/31/82	Yr. end 12/31/81	Yr. end 12/31/80
General autom. ...	$2,392,957	$2,313,332	$2,178,629
Spec. gov't vehicles	485,459	275,591	373,958
Total	$2,878,416	$2,588,923	$2,552,587

Net Earnings (Loss) by Business Segment

	Yr. end 12/31/82	Yr. end 12/31/81	Yr. end 12/31/80
General auto. ...	(193,881)	(149,748)	(210,841)
Spec. gov't vehicles	40,407	13,185	10,066
Total	(153,474)	(136,563)	(200,775)

General Automotive Segment:

Under the Renault brand name, the Company manufactures and sells the Renault Alliance pursuant to agreements between the Company and Renault. The Renault Alliance is the first of a family of Renault-designed, fuel-efficient, front-wheel-drive passenger cars to be manufactured by the Company in the United States. The Company manufactures and sells, under the AMC brand name, rear-wheel drive passenger cars, the Concord and Spirit; as of the end of April, 1983 production of the Concord and Spirit was discontinued. The Company also manufactures and sells, under the AMC brand name, four-wheel-drive automobiles, the Eagle and the SX/4. Under the Jeep brand name, the Company manufactures and sells four-wheel-drive utility and recreational vehicles consisting of the Jeep pickup truck and the Jeep CJ, Cherokee and Wagoneer, which are sports utility vehicles.

In addition, the Company presently imports and sells the LeCar, the 18i and the Fuego, which are Renault-manufactured passenger cars.

Automobiles, their parts and related accessories, are distributed by the Company and are marketed primarily by retail dealers under separate franchise agreements with the Company. The principal market area is the United States where, as of December 31, 1982, the Company had 1,786 franchised Renault, AMC and Jeep dealers compared with 1,971 as of December 31, 1981, 2,154 as of December 31, 1980 and 2,317 as of December 31, 1979. Most of these dealers are franchised to represent more than one of the Renault, AMC and Jeep brand names and many of these dealers hold franchises from other manufacturers. The strength of its dealer network is an important element of the Company's general automotive business and the Company has endeavored to maintain and enhance it through training, marketing and service programs.

The Company provides financing to certain dealers and customers through an affiliate, American Motors Financial Corporation ("AMFC"). AMFC also finances fleet sales by the Company and makes capital loans to dealers. In May 1981, AMFC entered into an agreement with Chrysler Financial Corporation ("CFC") whereby CFC provides administrative services related to automotive financing to AMFC through CFC's network of offices in the United States and Canada. This arrangement with CFC enables AMFC to provide financial services to support vehicle sales on a nationwide basis. AMFC's wholesale and

components, including forgings, stampings, engines, axles, bodies, differentials, injection molded plastic parts and interior trim. The Company purchases directly from Renault major components, including engines, transaxles and gear boxes, for the Renault Alliance, as well as service parts for the Renault passenger cars which the Company sells. The Company purchases raw and semi-finished materials, many components (including several major components) and numerous parts for its automotive products from approximately 1,200 suppliers (including other automobile manufacturers), of which approximately 1,020 are the Company's sole supplier (although in most cases other suppliers are available). Many of these suppliers employ special tools owned by the Company.

Special Government Vehicle Segment:

The special government vehicle segment, operated as AM General Corporation, supplies motor vehicles principally to military and civilian agencies of the United States and foreign governments.

During 1982, 1981 and 1980, AM General's sales to the U.S. Government amounted to approximately $234 million, $121 million and $259 million, respectively, representing 47%, 44% and 67%, respectively, of the total sales of AM General for such years.

AM General is primarily an assembler, and substantially all major components are purchased on a purchase order basis from single source suppliers.

AM General's business has been obtained from competitive and negotiated bids on U.S. Government contracts for tactical vehicles and postal service vehicles, and from direct sales of tactical vehicles to foreign governments. Tactical vehicles accounted for 81% of sales revenue in 1982, 95% in 1981, and 93% in 1980.

AM General's total backlog amounted to $1,001 million at December 31, 1982 compared with $1,021 million and $142 million at December 31, 1981 and 1980, respectively. Total backlog includes amounts relating to all funded and unfunded base contract vehicles and to funded vehicles as to which the U.S. Government has exercised its options. It is the practice of the U.S. Congress to appropriate funds annually under multi-year contracts and of the total backlog of $1,001 million at year-end 1982, $354 million represents base contract vehicles not yet funded. Included in the year-end 1982 backlog are two major multi-year con-

tract by up to 100% of base contract quantities and at year-end 1982 the Government had exercised its option relating to the 5-ton trucks for 3,140 vehicles, or 28% of the base contract quantity. The total backlog at year-end 1982 will result in approximately $581 million in sales in 1983.

AM General was awarded a contract in March 1983 from the U.S. Army for production of the 1/4 ton High Mobility Multi-Purpose Wheeled Vehicle. The contract calls for 55,000 vehicles to be delivered over a five-year period and the base contract price is approximately $1,200 million. The U.S. Army also has the option to increase vehicle quantities by up to 100%. The first deliveries of vehicles under this contract are not expected to occur until 1984, and therefore the award of the contract to AM General is not expected to contribute to the Company's 1983 revenues.

The Company has examined its business segments and long-term operating and financial resources and has concluded that it is in its best interest to concentrate its management effort and capital resources on its general automotive business. Accordingly, the Company is seeking to sell AM General Corporation, provided that an acceptable price can be obtained from an acceptable buyer.

Canadian Business:

The Company distributes passenger cars, 4-wheel-drive automobiles and Jeep 4-wheel-drive utility and recreational vehicles and service parts in Canada and manufactures certain passenger car models and 4-wheel-drive automobiles at its Brampton, Ontario, Canada plant for sale in Canada and in the United States. For 1982, 1981 and 1980 sales in Canada totaled 29,502, 26,108 and 35,228 units respectively, representing 6%, 7% and 8% respectively of the Company's total dollar sales.

International Business:

The Company distributes passenger cars, 4-wheel-drive automobiles and Jeep 4-wheel-drive utility and recreational vehicles and service parts throughout the world. International operations consist primarily of sales of domestically manufactured vehicles as knock-down units to independent licensees and distributors or to local companies in which the Company has a minority interest.

In 1982, 1981 and 1980, sales outside the U.S. and Canada represented 7%, 13% and 11%, respectively, of the Company's total dollar sales. Principal international assembly facilities for the Company's automotive vehicles retail financing notes receivable totaled approximately $110 million as of December 31, 1982.

The Company maintains facilities for the manufacture of certain major automotive tracts with the U.S. Government for 5-ton and 14-ton trucks which are valued at $728 million and $112 million, respectively. Both contracts allow the Government the option to increase quantities ratably over the life of the base contracts with the U.S. Government are located in Mexico, Egypt, Venezuela and Indonesia. The Co. also exports vehicles for use by foreign governments. In 1982 and 1981, the Co.'s exports totaled $416.4 million and $481.6 million, respectively.

PROPERTIES

Properties utilized by the Company at Dec. 31, 1982 are summarized as follows (in 000's):

| | Square Feet of Floor Space | | | | | |
| | United States and Canada | | | By Segment | | |
	Owned	Leased	Total	Automotive	Special Government Vehicles	Corporate
Manufacturing and assembly facilities	15,951	2,134	18,085	15,383	2,702	.....
Parts depots and warehouses	1,128	1,331	2,459	2,459	.....	.....
Research and engineering facilities	1,237	24	1,261	24	.....	1,237
Administration and sales office	.....	141	141	.....	.....	141
Total	18,316	3,630	21,946	17,866	2,702	1,378

The principal manufacturing and assembly plants of the automotive segment are located in Kenosha, Wisc.; Toledo, Ohio; and Brampton, Ont., Can., with component supply plants in Mich., Wisc. and Ont., Can. Administrative, research and engineering facilities are located in Southfield and Detroit, Mich. and Burlington, Wisc. The manufacturing and assembly plants of the Special Government Vehicles segment are located in Indiana.

In addition to the aforementioned properties, the Company's subsidiaries lease and sublease properties at various other locations for various purposes, including administration, warehousing, sales, service parts and accessories distribution and for other uses relating to the respective operations of the subsidiaries. Said leases are not material individually or in the aggregate.

MANAGEMENT

Officers

W.P. Tippett, Chmn. & Chief Exec. Off.
J.J. Dedeurwaerder, Pres. & Chief Oper. Off.
L.H. Hyde, Exec. Vice Pres. Pres. AM General Corp.
R.A. Calmes, Vice Pres.—Personnel & Ind. Rel.
J.E. Cappy, Vice-Pres.—Marketing Group.
T.O. Clare, Vice-Pres.—Int. Oper.
D.E. Dawkins, Vice-Pres.—Product Group
A.K. Ebersole, Vice-Pres.—Diversified Operations & Supply Group
S.W. Guittard, Vice-Pres. & Assoc. Gen. Counsel
F.A. Hainline, Jr., Vice Pres. & Genl. Counsel. Sec.

K.A. Lawton, Treas.
J.M. Lepeu, Vice-Pres.—Finance
R.C. Lunn, Vice-Pres.—Prod. Eng.
G.A. Maddox, Vice-Pres.—Mfg. Oper.
J.L. Sloan, Vice-Pres.—Pub. Rel.
M.W. Stucky, Vice-Pres.—Govt. Aff.
R.A. Teague, Vice Pres.—Styling
J.P. Tierney, Vice Pres.—Finance Staff & Contr.
P. Ventre, Vice-Pres.—Quality and Product Integrity.

Directors

(Showing Principal Corporate Affiliations)

W. Paul Tippett, Chairman and Chief Executive Officer, American Motors Corp.
Roy D. Chapin, Jr. Consultant to American Motors Corp.
Edward L. Cushman, Clarence Hilberry University Professor, Wayne State University, Detroit.
Jose J. Dedeurwaerder, President and Chief Operating Officer, American Motors Corp.
Stephen A. Girard, Chairman of the Board and Chief Executive Officer, Kaiser Steel Corp.
Bernard Hanon, Chief Executive Officer, Regie Nationale des Usines Renault.
Michel Leclere-Bessonnet, Vice-Pres. for North American Operations, Regie Nationale des Usines Renault, Paris, France.
Patricia Shontz Longe, Ph.D., Economist; Professor of Business Administration, University of Michigan, Ann Arbor. Senior Partner, Imeco-Longe Company, Mgt. Cons., Detroit.

Paul Percie du Sert, Vice-Pres., Treasurer & Deputy Chief Fin. Off. Regie Nationale des Usines Renault, Paris, France.
Felix G. Rohatyn, Senior partner of Lazard Freres & Co., N.Y.
Andrew G.C. Sage II, Managing Director of Lehman Brothers Kuhn Loeb Inc., N.Y.
Jackson W. Tarver, Vice Chairman, Cox Enterprises, Inc.
Pierre Tiberghien, Exec. Vice-Pres., Regie Nationale des Usines Renault, Paris, France, in charge of Automobile Division.
Kenneth J. Whalen, Executive Vice President, American Telephone and Telegraph Co.

Auditors: Touche Ross & Co.

Shareholder Relations: G.F. Thompson, Director Corp. Communications. **Tel:** (313)827-1830.

Director Meetings: Third Friday of each month.

Annual Meeting: Last Wednesday in April.

No. of Stockholders: May 10, 1983, 106,721.

No. of Employees: Dec. 31, 1982, 24,300.

General Office: American Center, 27777 Franklin Rd., Southfield, MI 48034. **Tel.:** (313)827-1000.

MOODY'S INDUSTRIAL MANUAL

990

STATISTICS

WHOLESALE AUTOMOTIVE UNIT SALES

	Yr. end. 12/31/82	Yr. end. 12/31/81	[1]Three mos. end. 12/31/80	[1]Yr. end. 9/30/80	Yr. end. 9/30/79	Yr. end. 9/30/78	Yr. end. 9/30/77
Domestic:							
Automobiles	159,891	157,313	39,661	185,546	159,805	172,702	187,285
Jeep vehicles	65,210	59,629	18,516	71,873	167,098	145,426	115,567
Total domestic	225,101	216,942	58,177	257,419	326,903	318,128	302,852
Overseas and Canada:							
Automobiles	35,900	49,428	13,198	56,304	47,752	41,835	40,080
Jeep vehicles	25,519	44,999	6,619	39,463	40,544	35,241	37,918
Total overseas and Canada	61,419	94,427	19,817	95,767	88,296	77,076	77,998
Total automotive sales [1]	286,520	311,369	77,994	353,186	415,199	395,204	380,850

[1]See General Note (a) below.

INCOME ACCOUNTS

CONSOLIDATED INCOME ACCOUNT
(Taken from reports filed with Securities and Exchange Commission)
(in thousands of dollars)

	Yr. end. 12/31/82	Yr. end. 12/31/81	[1]Three mos. end. 12/31/80	[1]Yr. end. 9/30/80	Yr. end. 9/30/79	Yr. end. 9/30/78	Yr. end. 9/30/77
Revenues							
Net sales	2,878,416	2,588,923	657,946	2,683,973	3,117,049	2,585,428	2,236,896
Other income	59,392	32,582	6,147	20,169	25,550	21,866	16,565
	2,937,808	2,621,505	664,093	2,704,142	3,142,599	2,607,294	2,253,461
Costs and Expenses							
[2]Cost of prod. sold, other than items below	2,584,843	2,307,508	586,133	2,454,043	2,648,518	2,198,542	1,921,358
[3]Selling, advertising & admin. exp.	341,883	320,563	75,431	300,204	278,691	241,313	211,944
Amort. of tools & dies	34,001	31,795	8,376	28,674	41,814	39,709	40,254
Depr. & amort. of plant & equip.	20,664	18,642	4,549	17,441	16,593	23,766	20,892
Cost of pensions	56,588	47,964	10,447	41,427	41,178	41,456	35,431
Interest	53,303	33,906	7,400	22,125	20,596	22,318	17,346
	3,091,282	2,760,378	692,336	2,863,914	3,047,390	2,567,104	2,247,225
Earnings before taxes on income & extraord. credits	d153,474	d138,873	d28,243	d159,772	95,209	40,190	6,236
Taxes on Income:							
United States	.....	cr2,400	100	cr16,189	14,800	12,600	1,870
Canadian and other	.....	90	700	cr3,746	12,265	3,500	1,300
Write-off of deferred income tax charges	.....	.....	.....	15,835	.....	.....	.....
	.....	cr2,310	800	cr4,100	27,065	16,100	3,170
Earnings before extraord. credits	d153,474	d136,563	d29,043	d155,672	68,144	24,090	3,066
[3]Extraordinary credits	.....	.....	.....	.....	15,800	12,600	5,200
Net earnings	d153,474	d136,563	d29,043	d155,672	83,944	36,690	8,266
Retained earnings beginning of year	d84,148	[4]d152,600	97,893	258,349	176,683	139,993	131,727
Amort. of pref. stk. disc.	d722	cr185	.....	.....	.....	.....	.....
Common dividends	.....	.....	.....	4,784	2,278	.....	.....

Retained earnings end of year, and SUPPLEMENTARY P. & L. DATA:

Retained earnings end of year	d238,344	d84,148	68,850	97,893	258,349	176,683	139,993
Maintenance & repairs	51,197	53,130	12,430	50,048	49,335	41,394	38,678
Advertising	87,128	72,677	18,493	73,408	65,453	56,979	45,636
Res. & devel.	99,300	80,300	17,600	66,700	59,800	48,400	43,289

[1] Effective Dec. 31, 1980, the Company changed from a fiscal year ending Sept. 30 to a calendar year for financial reporting purposes.

[2] Includes related portions of items shown under "Supplementary P.&L. Data" below statement.

[3] 1979: Credits due to reduction of income taxes resulting from utilization of prior years foreign tax credits, foreign net operating losses and timing differences.
1978: Credits due to reduction of income taxes resulting from utilization of net operating loss and foreign tax credit carry forward.
1977: Credits due to reduction of income taxes resulting from utilization of prior years accounting deductions.

[4] In 1981, the Company adopted FASB 43. The cumulative effect at Dec. 31, 1980 was a decrease in retained earnings of $16,250.

Consolidated Statement of Changes in Financial Position ($000):

	Yr. end Dec. 31 1982	Yr. end Dec. 31 1981	Yr. end Dec. 31 1980
Sources of Working Capital:			
Earnings (loss) bef. extraord. credits	(153,474)	(136,563)	(200,775)
Depr. & amort. of plant, equip. tools & dies	54,665	50,437	47,704
Oth. non-cash charges	7,880	25,419	17,924
Sale of Cap. Stk. to Renault	.....	.....	121,988
Iss. of debt to Renault	133,907	9,192	.....
Pro. from other l.t. debt	175,524	161,852	52,042
Pro. from sale of plant and liquidation of subsidiaries	14,047	976	.....
Pro. from sale of pref. stk. & warrant to Renault	52,500	45,000	.....
Repay. of adv. by unconsol. subsid.	9,699	25,171	.....
Iss. of Com. Stk. upon conver. of l.t. debt, ex. of options & acquisitions	166	8	45,881
Other sources	7,797	2,430	2,150
Total	302,711	183,922	86,914
Applications of Working Capital:			
Cash div.	.....	.....	2,392
Net add. to prop., plant & equip.	334,652	186,197	97,400
Conv. of l.t. debt	151	8	45,807
Curr. matur. & repay. of l.t. debt & other liab.	37,204	6,276	8,065
Inv. in and advances to uncons. subs.	10,095	12,933	16,395
Applic. of def. inc. taxes	11,400	4,286	23,197
Other	.....	.....	8,221
Total	393,502	209,700	201,477
Net incr. (decr.) in work. cap.	(90,791)	(25,778)	(114,563)

Record of Earnings, years ended Sept. 30 (in thousands of dollars):

Year	Net Sales	Inc. Bef. Taxes	Income Taxes	Income Bef. Extraord. Credits	Extraord. Credits	Net Income	Common Dividends	Com. Shs. Outstand.	Earn. Per Com. Sh.
1963	1,132,356	74,557	36,750	37,807	.....	37,807	18,783	18,789,403	2.01
1964	1,009,471	41,827	15,600	26,227	.....	26,227	21,853	19,006,495	1.38
1965	990,619	7,356	2,150	5,206	.....	5,206	16,682	19,065,464	0.27
1966	870,449	d30,918	cr15,200	d15,718	.....	d15,718	.....	19,065,464	d0.82
1967	778,009	d70,297	229	d70,526	.....	d70,526	.....	19,066,464	d3.70
1968	761,069	27,004	15,242	11,762	.....	11,762	.....	19,067,764	0.25
1969	737,449	6,978	2,050	4,928	.....	4,928	.....	19,078,554	0.26
1970	1,089,787	d56,241	.....	d56,241	.....	d56,241	.....	25,351,118	d2.22
1971	1,232,558	11,177	5,600	5,527	4,650	10,177	.....	25,395,617	0.40
1972	1,403,803	31,557	15,100	16,457	13,700	30,157	.....	25,397,150	1.18
1973	1,739,025	75,626	31,100	44,526	41,450	85,976	.....	27,100,220	3.18
1974	2,000,200	41,946	14,400	27,546	.....	27,546	5,678	29,346,952	0.94
1975	2,282,199	d35,500	cr8,000	d27,500	.....	d27,500	.....	29,685,346	d0.93
1976	2,315,470	d34,440	11,900	d46,340	.....	d46,340	.....	29,795,651	d1.56
1977	2,236,896	6,236	3,170	3,066	5,200	8,266	.....	30,101,034	0.27

MOODY'S INDUSTRIAL MANUAL

BALANCE SHEETS

COMPARATIVE CONSOLIDATED BALANCE SHEET, AS OF
(Taken from reports filed with Securities and Exchange Commission)
(in thousands of dollars)

	12/31/82	12/31/81	[7]12/31/80	[7]9/30/80	[4]9/30/79	9/30/78	[4]9/30/77
ASSETS							
Cash and short-term invest.	29,769	34,306	71,793	64,716	100,147	75,058	60,189
[2]Accounts receiv. (net)	202,696	168,814	144,296	188,355	257,949	239,873	216,939
Recoverable taxes on inc.		755	16,446	25,887			
[3]Inventories	546,881	393,665	403,263	371,738	388,596	340,155	328,532
Prepaid expenses	64,001	5,237	5,102	9,183	6,107	10,649	12,363
Deferred income tax charges					39,032	2,900	
Total current assets	843,347	602,777	640,900	659,879	791,831	668,635	618,023
Investments in & adv. to uncons. subs.	49,352	63,822	86,446	85,643	85,808	78,342	78,185
Other assets	33,722	28,353	26,950	27,243	14,251	13,967	8,003
[1]Property, plant and equipment	992,506	704,944	558,479	541,489	501,385	493,723	493,463
[1]Less accumulated depreciation	320,256	308,683	295,373	292,078	283,580	272,113	252,197
Net property account	672,250	396,261	263,106	249,411	217,805	221,610	241,266
Goodwill arising from acq.	8,648	9,507	11,555	11,643	11,991	11,517	11,866
Total assets	1,607,319	1,100,720	1,028,957	1,033,819	1,121,686	994,071	957,343
LIABILITIES							
Short-term debt	19,000	14,950	50,514	109,953	6,600	69,425	57,550
Short-term debt-affil. co.	10,000			16,500			
Current portion l. t. debt	112,777	44,709	3,918	3,908	3,213	4,404	25,973
Accounts payable trade	235,599	155,721	182,822	213,677	260,057	218,986	212,866
Accounts payable affil. co.	56,147	11,986	8,705				
Accounts payable other			50,407	70,901	113,962	77,996	88,143
Accrued liabilities	121,429	58,615	136,763	149,549	146,052	137,163	126,594
Taxes on income	214,600	152,210	1,157	712	17,730	4,038	1,032
Total current liabilities	769,552	438,191	434,286	565,200	547,614	512,012	512,158
Long term debt	395,794	272,803	108,844	76,865	64,240	87,027	90,727
Long term debt affil. company	140,801			45,000			
Other liabilities	76,039	63,562	51,580	50,187	44,271	36,040	32,536
Deferred income taxes	70,504	32,316			24,753	1,112	1,081
Class A cum. $2.80 redeem. preferred							
[5]Common stock	95,001	94,961	94,960	53,402	50,622	50,313	50,168
[6]Additional paid-in capital	297,972	283,035	270,437	145,272	131,837	130,884	130,680
Retained earnings	d238,344	d84,148	68,850	97,893	258,349	176,683	139,993
Total stockholders' equity	154,629	293,848	434,247	296,567	440,808	357,880	320,841
Total liabilities and stockholders equity	1,607,319	1,100,720	1,028,957	1,033,819	1,121,686	994,071	957,343
Net current assets	73,795	164,586	206,614	94,679	244,217	156,623	105,865
PROPERTY ACCOUNT—ANALYSIS							
Additions at cost	335,457	187,486	26,870	85,550	55,437	42,495	46,914
Retirements or sales	13,516	8,767	795	18,010	5,766	7,688	20,151
Amort. tools, dies, etc.	34,001	32,258	8,473	29,004	42,155	40,067	40,254
Other additions		4		1,568		5,520	91
Other reductions	378	612			146		725
ACCUM. DEPRECIATION—ANALYSIS							
Additions charged to income	20,265	18,158	4,451	17,089	16,230	23,387	20,500
Retirement	8,692	4,852	539	9,383	4,908	6,426	4,265
Other additions		4		792	145	2,955	1

Other reductions ....

	Book Values	Accum. Depr.
[1]Dec. 31, 1982:		
Land	9,130	
Buildings & improve.	165,404	92,351
Mach. & equip. ...	817,972	227,905

Total 992,506
[2]After reserves, 1982, $3,515,000; 1981, $3,200,000; 1980, $2,400,000; 1979, $1,100,000; 1978-77, $600,000.
[3]Lower of cost (first-in, first-out) or market as follows:

	12/31/82
Raw ma. & W.I.P.	229,731,000
Vehicles	186,445,000
Service parts	99,876,000
Supplies	30,829,000

Total 546,881,000
[4]Reclassified.
[5]Par value $1.66⅔. After deduction of treasury shares: 1975-82, 203,233.
[6]Principal "additional paid in capital" changes follow:

12/31/82: After crediting $15,000,000 for sale of Warrants, $126,000 for stock issued on conversion of long term debt and exercise of stock options and deducting $189,000 of issuance expense on common stock.

12/31/81: After crediting $12,598,000 for sale of warrant and deducting $265,000 of issuance expense for common stock.

12/31/80: After crediting $88,654,000 for sale of stock and $36,511,000 for stock issued on conversion of long-term debt.

9/30/80: After crediting $12,500,000 for sale of stock and $935,000 for stock issued on conversion of long-term debt and exercise of stock options.

617

1979: After crediting $953,000 for stock issued in acquisition, exercise of stock options, and on conversion of long-term debt.
1978: After crediting $204,000 for stock issued in acquisition and exercise of stock options.
1977: After crediting $693,000 for stock issued in acquisition and on conversion of long term debt.
[7]Effective Dec. 31, 1980, the Company changed from a fiscal year ending Sept. 30 to a calendar year for financial reporting purposes.

General Notes

(a) PRINCIPLES OF CONSOLIDATION: The consolidated financial statements include the accounts of the Company and its U.S. and Canadian subsidiaries (except those engaged in leasing, financing, retail selling and realty activities). Intercompany accounts and transactions have been eliminated. The investments in unconsolidated subsidiaries and 20% or more owned affiliates, over which the Company exercises significant influence and control, are stated at equity in net assets of such companies.

(b) INVENTORY VALUATION: Inventories are stated at the lower of cost (first-in, first-out method) or market. Market represents the lower of replacement cost or net realizable amount.

(c) DEPRECIATION AND AMORTIZATION: Property, plant and equipment is stated at cost and depreciated over the estimated useful lives of the assets. Depreciation includes the amortization of assets recorded under capital leases. The declining balance method is used for approximately 68% of the total depreciable assets and the straight-line meth-

od for the remainder. Deferred tool and die costs are amortized over periods of time representing the estimated productive use of such assets.

(d) GOODWILL ARISING FROM ACQUISITIONS: The unallocated excess of cost of investments in consolidated subsidiaries over equities in net assets acquired is being amortized over periods not exceeding forty years.

(e) AMORTIZATION OF DEBT EXPENSE: Debt discount and related issuance expenses are amortized over the life of the related debt.

(f) WARRANTY: Estimated costs related to all product warranties are provided for at time of sale.

(g) PENSION PLAN COSTS: Total pension costs include current service costs and the amortization of prior service costs over periods ranging up to forty years. The general policy is to fund accrued pension costs in the following year in accordance with ERISA requirements.

(h) INTEREST COSTS: Interest costs incurred of $21,400,000 in 1982, $7,400,000 in 1981 and $2,000,000 in 1980 have been capitalized as part of the cost of acquisition or construction of major assets.

(i) SALE OF TAX BENEFITS: The net proceeds from the sale of tax benefits are included in other income when such benefits are sold.

FINANCIAL & OPERATING DATA
Statistical Record:

	12/31/82	Yr. end 12/31/81	[5]3 mos. end. Dec. 31, 1980	[5]1980	Twelve months ended Sept. 30 1979	1978	1977
Earned per share—common:							
Earn. per shares:							
Before extraord. credits	d2.85	d$2.44	d$0.51	d$4.86	$2.24	$0.80	$0.10
After extraord. credits	d2.85	d$2.44	d$0.51	d$4.86	$2.76	$1.22	$0.27
[3]On average shares:							
Before extraord. credits	d2.85	d$2.44	d$0.81	d$4.88	$2.24	$0.80	$0.10
After extraord. credits	d2.85	d$2.44	d$0.81	d$4.88	$2.76	$1.21	$0.27
[4]On shs. fully diluted:							
Before extraord. credits	[6]	[6]	[6]	[6]	$2.07	$0.75	$0.10
After extraord credits	[6]	[6]	[6]	[6]	$2.53	$1.16	$0.27
[2]Dividends per share	Nil	Nil	Nil	$0.15	$0.075	Nil	Nil
[1]Price range stock	7¼-2½	47/8-2⅞	9½-3¾	9¼-4⅝	9¼-3¾	7⅛-3⅝	5¼-3⅝
Times charges Earned:							
Before income tax & extraord. credits					5.62	2.80	1.36
After income tax before extraord. cr.					4.31	2.08	1.18
[1]Price Range—deb. 6s, 1988	83-49	66-49	93½-57½	93½-57½	93-79½	82-61	68-59⅝
—Wts.							⅛-⅛

FINANCIAL & OPERATING DATA (Cont'd):

	12/31/82	Yr. end 12/31/81	[5]3 mos. end. Dec. 31, 1980	[5]1980	Twelve months ended Sept. 30		
					1979	1978	1977
Net tangible assets per share	$2.56	$4.99	$7.42	$8.89	$14.12	$11.47	$10.26
Net tang. asset, $1,000 long tm. debt	$1,369	$2,042	$4,833	$3,338	$7,675	$4,980	$4,406
Net current assets for $1,000 lg. tm. debt	$848	$603	$1,898	$777	$3,802	$1,800	$1,167
Number of shares:							
Year end	57,001,016	56,976,854	56,975,819	32,041,609	30,373,396	30,187,983	30,101,034
Average	56,988,754	56,975,941	35,742,090	31,909,728	30,276,713	30,186,901	30,101,034
Aver. & com. stk. equiv.	[6]	[6]	[6]	[6]	30,417,413	30,303,976	30,284,424
Shares fully diluted	[6]	[6]	[6]	[6]	33,967,946	34,023,097	34,003,545

[1]Calendar years. [2]Fiscal years. [3]Based on average capital stock and dilutive capital stock equivalents outstanding. [4]As reported, based on shares on a fully diluted basis, including shares issuable upon conversion of convertible debentures and bonds. [5]Effective Dec. 31, 1980, the Company changed from a fiscal year ending Sept. 30 to a calendar year for financial reporting purposes. [6]Dilution not applicable for loss years.

Financial & Operating Ratios

	12/31/82	Yr. end 12/31/81	[5]3 mos. end. Dec. 31, 1980	[5]1980	1979	1978	1977
Current assets÷current liabilities	1.09	1.38	1.48	1.17	1.45	1.30	1.21
% cash & securities to current assets	3.53	5.69	11.20	9.81	12.65	11.23	9.74
% inventory to current assets	64.85	60.33	62.92	56.33	49.08	50.87	53.16
% net curr. assets to net worth	47.72	56.01	47.58	31.92	55.40	43.76	33.00
% property depreciated	32.27	43.79	52.89	53.94	56.56	55.11	51.10
Capitalization:							
% long term debt	[3]79.70	[3]45.55	20.04	29.12	12.72	19.56	22.04
% common stock & surplus	20.30	49.06	79.96	70.88	87.28	80.44	77.96
[2]% ann. depr. to gross property	2.04	2.64	3.26	3.22	3.31	4.81	4.23
Sales÷inventory	5.26	6.58	[1]6.53	7.22	8.02	7.60	6.81
Sales÷receivables	14.20	15.34	[1]18.24	14.25	12.08	10.78	10.31
% sales to net property	428.18	653.29	[1]1,000.28	1,076.12	1,431.12	1,166.66	927.14
% sales to total assets	179.08	235.20	[1]255.78	259.62	277.88	260.08	233.65
% net income to total assets	.....	.....	.....	.....	7.48	3.69	0.86
% net income to net worth	.....	.....	.....	.....	23.46	11.44	2.65

[1]Sales for three months annualized. [2]Annual depreciation, amortization, etc., exclude amortization of tools and dies. [3]Including preferred stock as long-term debt.

Analysis of Operations

	%	%	%	%	%	%	%
Net sales	100.00	100.00	100.00	100.00	100.00	100.00	100.00
Cost of goods sold	89.80	89.13	89.09	91.43	84.97	85.04	85.90
Selling, adver. & adm. expense	11.88	12.38	11.46	11.19	8.94	9.33	9.48
Depreciation & amortization	1.90	1.95	1.96	1.72	1.87	2.46	2.73
Cost of pensions	1.96	1.85	1.59	1.54	1.32	1.60	1.58
Balance	d5.54	d5.31	d4.10	d5.88	2.90	1.57	0.31
Other income	2.06	1.26	.93	.75	0.82	0.85	0.74
Total income	d3.48	d4.05	d3.17	d5.13	3.72	2.42	1.05
Interest on loans	1.85	1.31	1.12	0.82	0.66	0.86	0.77
Inc. bef. inc. taxes & extraord. credits	d5.33	d5.36	d4.29	d5.95	3.05	1.56	0.28
Provisions for inc. taxes	.....	cr0.09	.12	cr.15	0.87	0.62	0.14
Extraordinary credits	.....	.....	.....	.....	0.51	0.48	0.23
Net income	d5.33	d5.27	d4.41	d5.80	2.69	1.42	0.37

LONG TERM DEBT

1. American Motors Corp. convertible subordinated debenture 6s, due 1988:
AUTHORIZED—$35,000,000; outstanding Dec. 31, 1982, $19,699,000 (net of unamortized discount of $1,509,000 and current maturities of $2,100,000).
DATED—May 1, 1969. DUE—Oct. 1, 1988.
INTEREST—A&O 1 by mail to holders registered 15th day prior to interest date.

2. Other Debt: Outstanding, Dec. 31, 1982, (excluding current portion) $512,674,000 consisting of:
(1) $17,807,000 9% bonds, net of unamortized discount of $193,000 due 1989. Bonds are payable $2,000,000 in 1984 to 1985, $3,000,000 in 1986 to 1988 and a final repayment of $5,000,000 on Jan. 15, 1989.
(2) $9,274,000 miscellaneous notes and mortgages, including capitalized leases of $5,175,000.

in 1990 and at $28.00 per share thereafter (plus cumulative dividends). Beginning in 1991, the outstanding Preferred Stock will be subject to annual mandatory redemption at $28.00 per share (plus cumulative dividends), in an amount each year equal to 10% of the total number of shares then outstanding.
The difference between the estimated fair value of Preferred Stock at date of issue and the mandatory redemption value is being recorded through periodic accretions, using the

TRUSTEE—United States Trust Co., New York.

DENOMINATION—Fully registered, $1,000 and authorized multiples thereof. Transferable or exchangeable without service charge.

CALLABLE—As a whole or in part on at least 40 days' notice at any time to each Sept. 30 as follows:

1983 .... 101.67	1984 .... 101.33	1985 .... 101.00
1986 .... 100.67	1987 .... 100.33	1988 .... 100.00

Also callable for sinking fund (which see).

SINKING FUND—Annually, to retire debs. at par, each Oct. 1, 1982-1987, cash (or debs.) amounts of $300,000 or any integral multiple thereof up to but not exceeding $2,100,000, on any sinking fund date such optional right being non-cumulative. Company will receive credit against sinking fund payments for debs. retired under optional provision and not previously credited.

Additional prepayments may be made, subject to certain provisions of agreements after Oct. 1, 1981 at prices ranging from 102.00% of principal amount in 1982 to 100% in 1987.

CONVERTIBLE—Into common at $8.16 per share (adjusted through Apr. 1983); no adjustment for interest or dividends; conversion privilege protected against dilution. No fractional shares will be issued; cash paid in lieu thereof.

SECURITY—Not secured; subordinated to all senior debt.

DIVIDEND RESTRICTIONS—Company may not pay cash dividends or acquire capital stock if aggregate amount expended would exceed 70% of consolidated net income earned subsequent to Sept. 30, 1968. See also under capital stock below.

CREATION OF ADDITIONAL DEBT—Company may not create funded debt, unless immediately thereafter, and giving effect to existence of such debt, the consolidated net tangible assets (as defined) will be not less than 200% of total funded debt, subject to certain qualifications.

RIGHTS ON DEFAULT—Trustee or majority of debs. outstanding may declare principal due and payable (15 days' grace for payment of interest).

INDENTURE MODIFICATION—Indenture may be modified except as provided, with consent of 66⅔% of debentures.

LISTED—On New York Stock Exchange.

OFFERED—($35,000,000) with warrants to purchase 875,000 common shares from time to time. Debentures and warrants were originally placed privately in units of $1,000 debs. and warrants to purchase 25 common shares; and sold by holders thereof from time to time. (Warrants expired Oct. 2, 1978).

(3) $24,363,000 two mortgage loan agreements. One agreement provides $15,863,000 and requires repayment over fifteen years commencing in 1981. The other agreement provides $8,500,000 and requires repayment over five years commencing in 1996.

(4) $250,000,000 revolving credit agreement.

Company has an unsecured revolving credit agreement with a group of banks providing for $330,000,000 through Dec. 31, 1985.

(5) $51,173,000 unsecured vehicle and component financing agreement, repayable in French francs in four semiannual installments of principal and interest through 1984.

(6) $45,057,000 unsecured tooling and equipment financing agreements totaling $87,951,000 repayable in ten semiannual installments of principal and interest.

(7) $40,000,000 10% subordinate debenture, to Renault, due March 15, 2000 convertible into Common Stock $10.01 per share (adjtd. through April 1983).

(8) $50,000,000 16.62% subordinate debenture, due March 15, 2000.

(9) $20,000,000 unsecured line of credit from Renault matures 13 months after notice of termination.

(10) $5,000,000 unsecured bank credit line matures April 1984.

3. Subsidiary Debt: Outstanding Dec. 31, 1982, $4,222,000 American Motors Overseas Corp. N.V. 6% convertible bonds, due 1992. Unconditionally and irrevocably guaranteed by American Motors Corp. Convertible into American Motors Corp. common stock at $6.56 per share (adjusted through Apr. 1983).

Subsequent Financing:

(1) In January 1983, Company sold to Renault a $50,000,000 13.5% Subordinated Debenture, due January 31, 2003.

(2) In February 1983, Company obtained a new agreement with banks providing unsecured financing of products purchased from Renault in 1983 totaling $197,000,000.

CAPITAL STOCK

1. American Motors Corp. Class A $2.80 cumulative preferred; par $0.01:

Auth., 4,500,000 shs.: outstg., Dec. 31, 1982, 3,482,143 shs., all held by Renault. The Preferred Stock (non-voting, non-participating, $28.00 involuntary liquidation preference) was sold with Warrants to purchase 13,928,572 shares of common stock at $6.31 per sh. (adj. thru Apr. 1983). The Warrants are exercisable by the tendering of Preferred Stock or the payment of cash.

The shares of Preferred Stock are redeemable, at the option of the Company, at prices per share ranging from $30.52 in 1982 to $28.28 interest method with the related charge to retained earnings.

If, at any time, the Company is in arrears as to preferred dividends or mandatory redemptions of Preferred Stock, dividends to holders of common stock are restricted. If the Company is in arrears for six quarterly dividend payments, or is in arrears as to a mandatory redemption payment, the holders of the Preferred Stock shall be entitled, only while such arrearage exists, to elect two additional members to the then existing Board of Directors. For this purpose, there shall be disregarded, until Dec. 31, 1984, dividends payable through June 30, 1983 not paid due to certain debt and share restrictions.

2. American Motors Corp. common; par $1.66⅔:

AUTHORIZED—150,000,000 shares; outstanding, Dec. 31, 1982, 57,001,016 shares; in treasury, 203,233 shares; reserved for options, 1,177,129 shares; reserved for conversion of 6% debentures, 2,514,347 shs.; reserved for conversion of 10% debentures, 3,333,333 shares; reserved for conversion of bonds, 605,738 shares; reserved for exercise of warrants, 13,928,572 shares; par $1.66⅔.

Note: See Relationship With Renault above.

Par changed from no par to $5, Dec. 23, 1936, share for share; from $5 to $1.66⅔, Feb. 10, 1960 by 3-for-1 split.

Dividend Record (in $)

(Calendar Years)

(No par shares—Nash Motors Co.)

1916-17 .... Nil	1918 .... 21.00	①1919-22 .... 16.00
1923 .... 6.00	1924 .... 10.00	1925 .... 16.00
②1926 .... 10.00		

(No par shs. afer stk. div.—Nash Motors Co.)

1926 .... 3.00	1927 .... 5.00	1928-29 .... 6.00
1930 .... 5.00	1931 .... 3.50	1932 .... 1.50
1933-34 .... 0.75	1935-36 .... 1.00	

(No par shares—Kelvinator Corp.)

1925 .... Nil	③1926 .... 1.50	1927 .... 0.50
1928-33 .... Nil	1934 .... 0.50	1935-36 .... 0.70
1937 .... 0.97		

($5 par shares—merged company)

1937 .... 1.00	1938 .... 0.12½	1939-40 .... Nil
1941 .... 0.37½	1942-46 .... 0.50	1947 .... 1.10
1948 .... 1.40	1949 .... 2.15	1950 .... 2.85
1951-53 .... 2.00	1954 .... 0.37½	1955-58 .... Nil
③1959 .... 2.40		

($1.66⅔ par shares—after 3-for-1 split)

1960 .... 1.05	③1961 .... 1.10	1962-64 .... 1.00
1965 .... 0.62½	1966-73 .... Nil	1974 .... 0.20
1975-78 .... Nil	1979 .... 0.07½	1980 .... 0.15
1981-82 .... Nil		

①Plus stock dividend of 3 shares preferred and 4 shares common for each share held, paid 1922. ②Plus 900% stock, Feb. 19, 1926.

Source: *Moody's Industrial Manual.* Reprinted with permission.

Figure 10.6 S&P Corporation Report

American Motors 150

NYSE Symbol AMO

Price	Range	P-E Ratio	Dividend	Yield	S&P Ranking
Jun. 5'84	1984				
4¼	8⅛–4	NM	None	None	C

Summary

American Motors began to build the Renault Alliance at its Kenosha, Wisconsin, plant in mid-1982. In order to provide funds for additional Renault-designed models and for a completely new series of Jeep vehicles during 1983 and 1984, the company in April, 1983 sold more than 21 million common shares to the public and Renault. In March, 1984 an additional 24.8 million shares were sold to the public and Renault, which continues to own about 46% of American Motor's common stock. Proceeds ultimately are to be used to develop new automobile and Jeep vehicle models.

Current Outlook

A modest profit of perhaps $0.10 a share or more is anticipated for 1984, in contrast to a 1983 loss of $3.61 from continuing operations.

No common dividends (omitted in June, 1980) are expected in 1984.

Increased industrywide demand for motor vehicles, a rising market share for the company's new Jeep vehicle models, and further cost-cutting measures will be helpful.

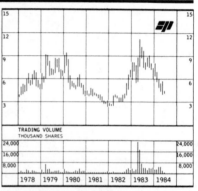

Net Sales (Million $)

Quarter:	1984	1983	1982	1981
Mar.	1,083	637	600	598
Jun.		762	667	722
Sep.		776	754	648
Dec.		1,097	857	621
		3,272	2,878	2,589

Sales for 1984's first quarter rose 70%, year to year, on a 46% gain in vehicle shipments. Helped also by a richer product mix, earnings from continuing operations were $1,679,000 (a loss of $0.01 a share after preferred dividend requirements), in contrast to a deficit of $86,465,000 ($1.57), excluding special credits of $0.04 and $0.36 a share, respectively.

Capital Share Earnings ($)

Quarter:	1984	1983	1982	1981
Mar.	d0.01	d1.57	d0.93	d0.92
Jun.	Ed0.05	d1.07	d1.24	d0.35
Sep.	E Nil	d1.24	d0.58	d0.32
Dec.	E0.16	0.06	d0.10	d0.85
	E0.10	d3.61	2.85	2.44

Important Developments

Apr. '84—The company increased its original sales forecast for its new 1984-model Jeep Cherokee and Wagoneer vehicles by 75%, from 40,000 to 70,000, for the 1984-model year.

Jan. '84—Beijing Jeep Corp., Ltd. began operations, with initial productions plans calling for about 20,000 four-wheel-drive vehicles and trucks in 1984 which will be marketed in China. Beijing Automotive Works contributed fixed assets and capital, and American Motors contributed capital and technology for a total equivalent of U.S. $51 million. AMO's equity is 31.3%, which can be increased to 49%.

Next earnings report due in late July.

Per Share Data ($)

Yr. End Dec. 31[1]	1983	1982	1981	1980	1979	1978	1977	1976	1975	1974
Book Value	0.99	1.77	4.73	7.42	14.12	11.47	10.26	10.05	11.67	12.70
Earnings[2]	d3.61	d2.85	d2.44	d6.00	[3]2.24	[3]0.80	0.10	d1.56	d0.92	[3]0.94
Dividends[5]	Nil	Nil	Nil	0.07½	0.07½	Nil	Nil	Nil	Nil	0.20
Payout Ratio	Nil	Nil	Nil	NM	Nil	Nil	Nil	Nil	Nil	21%
Prices[4]—High	11¼	7¼	4⅞	9½	9¼	7⅛	5¼	7¾	7¼	13⅜
Low	5½	2½	2⅜	3¾	4⅝	3⅝	3⅝	3⅝	3⅜	3¼
P/E Ratio—	NM	NM	NM	NM	4-2	9-5	53-36	NM	NM	14-3

Data as orig. reptd. 1. Prior to 1980 fiscal yr. ended Sep. 30. Co. earned 0.37 a sh. and decl. divd. of 0.07½ in 3 mos. ended Dec. 31, 1979. 2. Bef. results of disc. opers. of + 1.51 in 1983, bef. spec. item(s) of + 0.52 in 1979, + 0.41 in 1978, + 0.17 in 1977. 3. Ful. dil.: 2.07 in 1979, 0.75 in 1978, 0.86 in 1974. 4. Cal. yr. 5. Divds. declared. d-Deficit. NM-Not Meaningful. E-Estimated.

June 12, 1984
Copyright © 1984 Standard & Poor's Corp. All Rights Reserved

Standard & Poor's Corp.
25 Broadway, NY, NY 10004

150

American Motors Corporation

Income Data (Million $)

Year Ended Dec. 31[1]	Revs.	Oper. Inc.	% Oper. Inc. of Revs.	Cap. Exp.	Depr.	Int. Exp.	Net Bef. Taxes	Eff. Tax Rate	[3]Net Inc.	% Net Inc. of Revs.
[5]1983	3,272	d129	NM	261	87.0	99.4	[2]d258	NM	d258	NM
1982	2,878	d105	NM	335	54.7	74.7	[2]d154	NM	d154	NM
1981	2,589	d87	NM	187	50.4	41.3	[2]d139	NM	d137	NM
1980	2,553	d154	NM	97	47.7	27.0	[2]d208	NM	d198	NM
1979	3,117	149	4.8%	55	58.4	20.6	[2] 95	28.4%	68	2.2%
1978	2,585	104	4.0%	43	63.5	22.3	[2] 40	40.1%	24	0.9%
1977	2,237	68	3.0%	47	61.1	17.3	[2] 6	50.8%	3	0.1%
1976	2,315	35	1.5%	53	63.2	17.7	[2] d34	NM	d46	NM
1975	2,282	18	0.8%	90	54.5	15.9	[2] d36	NM	d28	NM
1974	2,000	66	3.3%	95	39.7	6.8	[2] 42	34.3%	28	1.4%

Balance Sheet Data (Million $)

Dec. 31[1]	Cash	Current Assets	Current Liab.	Ratio	Total Assets	Ret. on Assets	Long Term Debt	Com-mon Equity	Total Cap.	% LT Debt of Cap.	Ret. on Equity
1983	94	795	789	1.0	1,724	NM	631	81	836	75.4%	NM
1982	30	843	770	1.1	1,607	NM	537	117	762	70.4%	NM
1981	34	603	438	1.4	1,101	NM	273	281	599	45.5%	NM
1980	72	641	434	1.5	1,029	NM	109	434	544	20.0%	NM
1979	100	794	558	1.4	1,123	6.4%	65	441	529	12.2%	17.0%
1978	75	669	517	1.3	994	2.5%	87	358	446	19.5%	7.1%
1977	60	618	520	1.2	957	0.3%	86	321	408	21.1%	1.0%
1976	91	597	538	1.1	992	NM	112	311	424	26.3%	NM
1975	85	612	483	1.3	1,010	NM	128	357	499	25.7%	NM
1974	76	513	356	1.4	863	3.4%	79	383	476	16.6%	7.3%

Data as orig. reptd. **1.** Prior to 1980 fiscal yr. ended Sep. 30. **2.** Incl. equity in earns. of nonconsol. subs. **3.** Bef. spec. item(s). **4.** Net of curr. yr. retirement and disposals. **5.** Excl. disc. opers. d-Deficit. NM-Not Meaningful.

Business Summary

The company in 1983 had a 2.5% share of the domestic automobile market (including imports) and a 9.9% share of the domestic four-wheel-drive utility and recreational vehicle market. In June, 1982 it began manufacturing the Renault Alliance and subsequently the Renault Encore, both Renault-designed, front-wheel-drive passenger cars. It also manufactures the AMC Eagle, a four-wheel-drive automobile, and imports and sells the Renault Sportwagon and the Renault Fuego. Under the Jeep brand name, the company makes four-wheel-drive utility and recreational vehicles consisting of the Jeep CJ, the Jeep pickup truck, the Grand Wagoneer, and the new Jeep Cherokee and Wagoneer (a new generation of Jeep vehicles introduced in September, 1983). The company plans to introduce specialty models of Renault-designed cars in the 1985 and 1986 model years and compact and intermediate models thereafter; some will be built by the company and others will be imported from Renault. New Jeep vehicles are planned for the 1984–88 period, including a compact pickup truck in both two-wheel and four-wheel-drive versions.

Wholesale sales in 1983 totaled 383,462 vehicles (265,999 cars and 93,169 Jeeps in the U.S. and Canada and 4,020 cars and 20,274 Jeeps internationally).

Dividend Data

The most recent dividend on the common was $0.07½ paid May 5, 1980.

Finances

In March, 1984, the company sold 12,000,000 common shares through underwriters to the public at $5.375 a share for net proceeds of about $58.3 million, and also sold to Renault 12,832,000 common shares at the same price. Proceeds were to be used ultimately for the company's product development program.

Capitalization

Long Term Debt: $483,918,000.

$2.80 Class A Cum. Pref. Stk.: 3,482,143 shs. ($0.01 par); 100% owned by Renault.

Common Stock: 110,075,258 shs. ($1.66⅔ par). Regie Nationale des Usines Renault (France) owns 46.1%.
Institutions hold 4.3%.
Shareholders of record: 102,000.

Warrants: To purchase 15,444,348 com. shs. at $6.31 a sh.; 100% owned by Renault.

Office—27777 Franklin Rd., Southfield, Mich. 48034. **Tel**—(313) 827-1000. **Chrmn & CEO**—P. Tippett. **Pres**—J. J. Dedeurwaerder. **VP-Secy**—S. W. Guittard. **Treas**—K. A. Lawton. **Investor Contact**—G. F. Thompson. **Dirs**—R. D. Chapin, Jr., E. L. Cushman, J. J. Dedeurwaerder, S. A. Girard, B. Hanon, M. Leclere-Bessonnet, P. S. Longe, P. Percie du Sert, F. G. Rohatyn, A. G. C. Sage II, J. W. Tarver, P. Tiberghien, P. Tippett, K. J. Whalen. **Transfer Agent & Registrar**—Chase Manhattan Bank, NYC. **Incorporated** in Maryland in 1916.

Information has been obtained from sources believed to be reliable, but its accuracy and completeness are not guaranteed.   D. Baker

Source: Reprinted by permission of Standard & Poor's Corporation.

Figure 10.7 Value Line

AMERICAN MOTORS NYSE-AMO RECENT PRICE **4.4** P/E RATIO **14.7** (Trailing: NMF / Median: NMF) RELATIVE P/E RATIO **1.56** DIV'D YLD **Nil** | Value Line **103**

TIMELINESS **4** Below Average (Relative Price Performance Next 12 Mos.)
SAFETY **5** Lowest (Scale: 1 Highest to 5 Lowest)
BETA 1.05 (1.00 = Market)

June 29, 1984

1987-89 PROJECTIONS

	Price	Gain	Ann'l Total Return
High	12	(+175%)	29%
Low	6	(+ 35%)	9%

Insider Decisions 1983

	F	M	A	M	J	J	A	S	O	N	D	J	F	M	A
to Buy	0	0	1	9	2	1	0	1	0	0	0	0	1	0	4
to Sell	0	0	0	2	0	0	0	0	0	0	0	0	0	0	0

Institutional Decisions

	1Q'83	2Q'83	3Q'83	4Q'83	1Q'84
to Buy	8	12	9	8	9
to Sell	4	9	9	13	9
Hldg's(000)	5009	4872	4686	4559	3943

High: 14.0 11.6 9.0 10.8 9.8 13.4 7.3 7.8 5.1 7.1 9.3 9.5 4.9 7.3 11.3 8.1
Low: 8.0   5.5   5.9 6.6   6.8 3.3   3.4 3.6 3.6 3.6 4.6 3.8 2.4 2.5 5.5   4.0

(continued from Capital Structure)
$40 mill. 10% ('00) each conv. into 99.90 shs. at $10.01 (Interest not earned).

	1968	1969	1970	1971	1972	1973	1974	1975	1976	1977	1978	1979	1980	1981	1982	1983	1984	1985	87-89E
Sales per sh	39.91	38.65	42.99	48.53	55.27	64.17	68.16	76.88	77.71	74.31	85.64	102.62	83.77	45.44	50.50	40.31	46.30	47.00	50.00
"Cash Flow" per sh	.75	.80	d1.72	.76	1.21	2.15	1.48	d.27	d.77	.80	1.59	2.79	d4.31	d2.07	d2.33	d3.04	.60	.75	2.00
Earnings per sh	.17	.26	d2.22	.22	.64	1.65	.94	d.92	d1.56	.10	.80	2.24	d4.88	d2.44	d2.85	d3.61	.30	.50	1.50
Div'ds Decl'd per sh	--	--	--	--	--	.20	.20	--	--	--	--	.08	.15	--	--	--	Nil	Nil	Nil
Cap'l Spending per sh	1.00	2.47	1.62	1.07	1.21	2.51	3.24	3.00	1.76	1.55	1.37	1.80	2.63	3.27	5.87	3.17	3.00	3.00	2.50
Book Value per sh	9.99	10.69	8.02	8.43	9.61	12.68	13.05	12.03	10.45	10.66	11.86	14.51	9.26	5.16	2.71	1.63	2.70	3.30	7.75
Common Shs Outst'g	19.07	19.08	25.35	25.40	25.40	27.10	29.35	29.69	29.80	30.10	30.19	30.37	32.04	56.98	57.00	82.24	95.00	100.00	120.00
Avg Ann'l P/E Ratio	74.1	43.8	--	30.9	12.8	5.0	9.1	--	--	41.7	6.0	3.0	--	--	--	--	--	--	6.0
Relative P/E Ratio	4.46	2.66	--	1.98	.88	.49	1.27	--	--	5.46	.82	.43	--	--	--	--	--	--	.50
Avg Ann'l Div'd Yield	2.3%	--	--	--	--	--	2.3%	--	--	--	--	--	2.3%	--	--	--	--	--	Nil

Bold figures are Value Line estimates

Sales ($mill)	2000.2	2282.2	2315.5	2236.9	2585.4	3117.0	2684.0	2588.9	2878.4	3314.9							4400	4700	6000
Market Share	4.8%	4.8%	3.0%	2.0%	2.0%	1.8%	2.8%	1.8%	2.2%	3.0%							2.5%	2.5%	2.5%
Operating Margin	2.1%	NMF	NMF	1.3%	2.5%	3.4%	NMF	NMF	NMF	NMF							2.5%	3.5%	5.0%
Net Profit ($mill)	27.6	d27.5	d46.3	3.1	24.1	68.1	d155.7	d136.6	d153.5	d258.3							35.0	60.0	180
Income Tax Rate	34.3%	NMF	40.1%	50.8%	40.1%	28.4%	NMF	NMF	NMF	NMF							40.0%	40.0%	40.0%
Net Profit Margin	1.4%	NMF	NMF	.1%	.9%	2.2%	NMF	NMF	NMF	NMF							.8%	1.3%	3.3%
Working Cap'l ($mill)	157.1	128.9	59.7	98.4	151.9	235.8	94.7	121.9	73.8	6.5							100	150	400
Long-Term Debt ($mill)	78.9	128.3	111.7	86.3	78.9	56.5	164.6	272.8	536.6	630.6							600	600	800
Net Worth ($mill)	383.0	357.1	311.4	320.8	357.9	440.8	296.6	326.2	225.1	205.7							600	325	1000
% Earned Total Cap'l	6.6%	NMF	NMF	1.7%	6.2%	14.1%	NMF	NMF	NMF	NMF							9.5%	7.5%	12.5%

5.0X "Cash Flow" p sh
1.0 × Book Value
5.0X "Cash Flow" p sh
Relative Price Strength

Target Price Range 1987 1988 1989

CAPITAL STRUCTURE as of 12/31/83
Total Debt $833.1 mill. Due in 5 Yrs $668.6 mill.
LT Debt $630.6 mill. LT Interest $70.0 mill.
Incl. $17.3 mill. 6% sub. debs. ('88) callable $102.67, ea. conv. into 122.5 shs. at $8.16
(Continued on Chart)
Leases, Uncapitalized Annual rentals $9.9 mill.
Pension Liability $270 mill. in '83 vs. $267 mill. in '82

Pfd Stock $71.4 mill.   Pfd Div'd $9.7 mill.
3,482,143 shs. $2.80 cum. (arrearages $6.47 per share as of 3/31/84) (9% of Cap'l)
Common Stock 82,241,287 shs. (16% of Cap'l)

© Value Line, Inc.

7.2%	NMF	1.0%	6.7%	15.5%	NMF	NMF	NMF	15.5%	15.0%	% Earned Net Worth	18.0%
5.7%	NMF	1.0%	6.7%	14.9%	NMF	NMF	NMF	10.0%	18.0%	% Retained to Comm Eq	18.5%
21%	NMF	1.0%	3%	NMF	--	--	--	Nil	Nil	% All Div'ds to Net Prof	5%

BUSINESS: American Motors Corp. is the fourth ranking U.S. auto manufacturer. Its output was 3.0% of the U.S. industry total in calendar 1983. Makes Alliance, Encore cars, Eagle four-wheel drive autos, and Jeep (Cherokee & Wagoneer) utility and recreational vehicles. AM General subsidiary, sold in tactical trucks, postal vehicles and buses, sold in '83. Foreign sales: 6% of total. Payroll costs: about 13% of sales. '83 depreciation rate: 4.1%. Est'd plant age: 6 yrs. Employs 27,915; has 102,000 stockholders. Insiders own less than 1% of stock; Renault, 46%. Chairman: W.P. Tippet, Jr. President: J.J. Dedeurwaeder, Jr. Incorporated: Maryland. Address: 27777 Franklin Rd., Southfield, MI 48034.

AMC's U.S. auto sales are not as weak as the reported figures suggest. Unit auto volume was down about 6% in the first five months of the year, in contrast to the industry's 25% advance. But AMC's year-ago figures include sales of models since discontinued. This year's offerings consist largely of models developed in partnership with Renault, the *Alliance* and the *Encore*. But even on an apples-to-apples basis, AMC's auto sales are still down a bit. The reason, we think, is the greater popularity of larger cars. AMC's offerings are in the smaller size classes. A cutrate financing promotion might help a bit, as might some convertible models to be offered next fall. But we think the company might have market share problems until it can offer larger cars. That will probably not occur until 1987 when a new plant in Ontario is slated to come on stream. **But Jeep sales are strong.** Fuel-efficient versions of this 4-wheel drive utility vehicle have made a hit in the showrooms. Foreign sales have recovered as well.

Yet significant profits remain elusive. AMC's plants are running near full capacity, we believe. And Jeep's unit revenues and gross margins, we think, are considerably higher than those for the typical passenger car. Such circumstances would lead us to expect good profits for AMC. But it appears that the margins on its autos are very thin, as is typically true of small cars. In addition, the company's debt load, which it incurred to develop new auto and Jeep models, creates a heavy interest burden.

Prospects to 1987-89 are a little better but not all that well defined. The new Canadian plant will give AMC a broader product line. And worldwide prospects for Jeep look good. But it seems unlikely that the company will be able to develop sufficient volume to achieve share profits high enough to give the stock an appreciation potential large enough to offset the risks inherent in the company's small size and heavy debt load. Some investors may wish to speculate on a Renault takeover, but that seems unlikely, we think, since Renault has effective control. We suggest subscribers look elsewhere.

M.S./H.S.K.

CASH POSITION

	5-Year Av'g	12/31/83
Current Assets to Current Liabilities:	121%	101%
Cash & Equiv's to Current Liab'ties:	11%	12%
Working Capital to Sales:	4%	.2%

Company's Financial Strength	C
Stock's Price Stability	25
Price Growth Persistence	20
Earnings Predictability	10

Warrants (88.4 mill. fully diluted shs.) (13.9 mill. at $7 to 12/31/90)

CURRENT POSITION ($MILL.)	1981	1982	12/31/83
Cash Assets	34.3	29.8	94.5
Receivables	168.8	202.7	169.7
Inventory (FIFO)	393.7	546.9	478.3
Other	6.0	64.0	52.9
Current Assets	602.8	843.4	795.4
Accts Payable	226.3	413.2	363.1
Debt Due	59.7	141.8	202.5
Other	152.2	214.6	223.3
Current Liab.	438.2	769.6	788.9

ANNUAL RATES of change (per sh)	Past 10 Yrs	Past 5 Yrs	Est'd '81-'83 to '87-'89
Sales	-2.0%	-10.5%	2.0%
"Cash Flow"	--	--	NMF
Earnings	--	--	NMF
Dividends	--	--	NMF
Book Value	-11.0%	-22.0%	16.0%

QUARTERLY SALES ($ mill.)	Mar. 31	June 30	Sept. 30	Dec. 31	(A)Cal-endar
1981	598.4	721.8	647.5	621.2	2588.9
1982	600.2	667.2	754.3	856.7	2878.4
1983	647.9(F)	781.1	777.0	1108.9	3314.9
1984	1082.8	1100	1100	1117.2	4400
1985	1200	1200	1200	1200	4700

EARNINGS PER SHARE	Mar. 31	June 30	Sept. 30	Dec. 31	(B)Cal-endar
1981	d.92	d.35	d.32	d.85	d2.44
1982	d.93	d1.24	d.58	d.10	d2.85
1983	d1.18(F)	d1.06	d1.43	.06	d3.61
1984	.03	.10	.10	.27	.30
1985	.10	.20	.20	.50	

QUARTERLY DIVIDENDS PAID	Mar. 31	June 30	Sept. 30	Dec. 31	(C)Full Year
1980	.075	.075	--	--	.15
1981	--	--	--	--	--
1982	--	--	--	--	--
1983	--	--	--	--	--
1984	--	--	--		

(A) Fiscal year ends Sept. 30 through '80; Dec. 31st thereafter. Excl. AM General after '82. Incl. Kaiser Jeep from 70. (B) Based on avg. shs. outst'g. Excl. tax credits from loss carryforwards. Excl. non-rec. gains in '83; $1.50/sh. Next egs. rep't due late July. (C) Fully diluted 3-5 yrs. hence. (D) Incl. Dividend omitted June 20, 1980. intangibles. In '83: $1.2 mill., 15¢/sh. (E) Fully diluted 3-5 yrs. hence. (F) First quarter restated for discon. ops.

Factual material is obtained from sources believed to be reliable but cannot be guaranteed.

Source: *Value Line*, June 29, 1984. Reprinted by permission of the Publisher. Copyright, Value Line, Inc.

Figure 10.8 *Value Line*

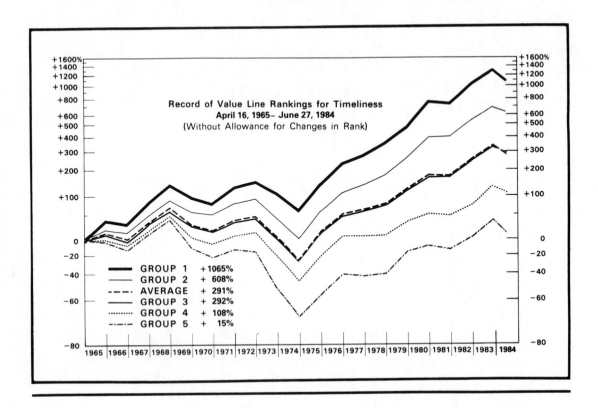

Source: *Value Line Investment Service.* Reprinted by permission of the Publisher. Copyright, Value Line, Inc.

Holloway found that while *Value Line* could not be relied upon to make after-commission trading profits, a buy and hold strategy for their selections did produce above-market risk-adjusted returns.[7]

The *Value Line* coverage is clearly quite investor oriented. While their reports contain a great deal of analysis and prediction, many interesting firms are not covered. On the other hand *Value Line* does have separate services for options, convertibles, and new issues.

The Unlisted Market Guide

Taking up where the larger publications leave off, Scot Emerich has introduced the *Unlisted Market Guide.*[8] It covers several hundred OTC companies with a format quite similar to that of S&P. To be covered in the *Guide* a firm must pay a $750 annual fee. Subscribers are charged $195 per year. Thus the *Guide* may have divided loyalties.

Brokerage House Reports

Most full-service brokerage houses either write or buy research reports that they make available to their customers. The bigger brokerage houses cover many more companies than the smaller ones (Table 10.2). Large companies are much more likely to be included. The reports may or may not be updated periodically and often are issued as part of an industry survey. In a study of one large national brokerage firm's recommendation, Stanley, Lewellen, and Scharbaum reported that over a seven-year period " . . . the firm's investment recommendations were generally timely, and conveyed information that would have permitted its customers to earn moderately above-average portfolio returns."[9]

Table 10.2 Number of Securities Covered by Brokerage Firms

BROKER	COMPANIES COVERED	BROKER	COMPANIES COVERED
Merrill Lynch	1,117	Bache Halsey	339
Salomon Brothers	879	Donaldson, Lufkin	329
Goldman Sachs	625	Lehman Brothers	325
Oppenheimer & Co.	525	Alex Brown & Sons	321
Paine Webber	522	Morgan Stanley	300
Moseley Hallgarten	510	First Manhattan	283
First Boston	480	Newberger & Barman	254
Smith Barney	430	Fohnstock & Co.	245
L.F. Rothschild	415	Cyrus J. Lawrence	225
Drexel Burnham	400	Wertheim & Co.	217
Kidder, Peabody	377	P. Eberstadt & Co.	216
Shearson Loeb Rhoades	341	Brown Bros. Harriman	212
		Wheat, First Secutities	197

Source: 1980 Directory of Securities Research

Advisory Services

A host of investment services publish newsletters dealing with both stock market timing and selection. Among the better known names in the field are Joseph Granville (whose panic sell-messages phoned across the country led to a 24 point drop in the Dow on January 7, 1981), Martin Zweig (Editor of the *Zweig Forecaster*, and frequent panelist on the Public Television Program *Wall Street Week*), and James Dines (the original "gold bug"). Much of this advice is of a very mediocre quality. Some advisory services just might be better than others, however. If past results are any indicator, *Hulbert's Financial Digest*, which tracks and evaluates advisory services recommendations, should help investors sort out the wheat from the shaft.[10] Each advisor is assumed to begin with $10,000 invested as they recommend. Table 10.3 contains Hulbert's 1983 evaluations. Investors may subscribe directly to *Hulberts* ($135 per year, 409 First Street, S.E., Washington, D.C., 20003, 800-227-1617).

Industry Periodicals

In addition to the general business/investment periodicals such as *Forbes* and the *Wall Street Journal* and the investment services such as *Moody's* and *Value Line,* some publications cover particular industries. For example, *Brewer's Digest* (monthly, Siebel Publishing Company, Chicago, Illinois 60646) reports on the beer industry. Such trade publications may contain articles relevant to potential investors, but the industry's managers are the primary readers. Some other trade periodicals, however, specialize in the stocks of particular industries. For example, *Audit's Realty Stock Review* (Audit Investment Research, 230 Park Avenue, New York, New York 10017) covers REITs and other real estate companies.

COMPUTER-BASED INFORMATION SOURCES AND SOFTWARE

The computer has in the past twenty years become an omnipresent reminder of our changing technology. Its use in investment analysis is, if anything, greater than its role in other areas. Virtually all serious empirical research utilizes the computer to manipulate data in statistically meaningful ways.

Researchers utilize a number of computer-based data sources. The best known financial data bank is the COMPUSTAT service sold by a subsidiary of Standard and Poor's (Investors Management Services, Box 23a, Denver, Co., 80201). The primary tape contains security information listed annually for the past 20 years for each of about 2,400 companies. A second tape contains quarterly data, while specialized tapes exist for various groups of companies such as OTC companies (1,000), Canadian firms (500), public utilities (175) and banks (120). Most companies with substantial investor interest are included.

The ISL (Investors Data Corporation, 122 E. 42nd St., New York, NY, 10017) and CRISPE (Center for Research in Securities Prices, University of Chicago, Graduate School of Business, Chicago, Ill., 60637) tapes are also distributed through S&P. The ISL tapes contain daily high, low, close, and volume figures for NYSE and AMEX stocks. The CRISPE tapes contain monthly price and dividend data for the NYSE for 1926 forward as well as daily NYSE stock price data from 1960 to the present. The *Value Line* data base (*Value Line* Inc., 711 Third Avenue, New York, N.Y., 10017) contains annual and quarterly data for 1,600 companies beginning in 1963 (annual data goes back to 1954), plus estimated earnings and dividends for the next year. Finally, the Media General databank (Data General Financial Services, Box 26991, Richmond, Va., 23261) includes current price, volume and financial data on 2,000 major corporations. These data bases appear to be generally but not uniformly accurate.[11]

Table 10.3   How Investment Advisers Performed in 1983

Newsletter	Gain as of 12/30/83	Clarity Rating (a)	No. of Stocks in Portfolio (b)
*Addison Report			
Conservative Stocks	+28.9%	C	17
Speculative Stocks	+89.6%	C	14
Cabot Market Letter	+7.3%	A	10
Calif. Technology Stock Letter	+5.7%	A	16
The Charted Course	+5.7%	A	32
The Chartist			
Actual Cash Account	+19.3%	A	10
Traders' Stocks	+30.5%	C	19
Dessauer's Journal	+21.1%	B	37
*The Dines Letter			
Supervised Long-Term Lists			
Good-Grade Stocks For Moderate Gains	+43.5%	A	7
Speculative Stocks	+8.6%	A	6
Income Portfolio	+13.2%	A	4
Growth Stocks	+7.0%	A	6
Prec. Metals; Deflation Hedge	+9.1%	A	1
Short-Term Trading	+90.1%	A	6
Dow Theory Forecasts			
Income Stocks List	+20.5%	C	13
Investment Stocks List	+15.6%	C	18
Growth Stocks List	+11.7%	C	19
Speculative Stock List	+11.7%	C	22
Dow Theory Letters	−6.8%	D	3
Dunn & Hargitt Mkt. Guide	+4.4%	C	20
Granville Market Letter	−25.2%	C	38
Green's Commodity Mkt. Comments	+13.6%	A	1
Growth Fund Guide			
Aggressive Growth Funds	+22.3%	C	12
Growth Funds	+24.2%	C	8
Quality Growth Funds	+19.0%	C	5
Special Situation Funds	+30.3%	C	5
*Growth Stock Outlook	+33.2%	A	20
Harry Brown's Special Reports	+8.1%	A	1
Heim Investment Letter			
Conservative Portfolio	+2.6%	A	2
Aggressive Portfolio	+2.6%	A	2
High Technology Investments			
Long-term Portfolio	+2.3%	A	5
Trading Portfolio	−19.2%	A	2
Holt Investment Advisory	−8.6%	B	36
Howard Ruff's Financial Survival Report	−16.3%	A	9
Indicator Digest	+11.8%	C	14
Int'l. Harry Schultz Letter	+1.6%	C	17
Kinsman's Low-Risk Advisory	+8.1%	A	11

Table 10.3   Continued

Newsletter	Gain as of 12/30/83	Clarity Rating (a)	No. of Stocks in Portfolio (b)
*Market Logic	+28.0%	B	37
Myer's Finance & Energy	−0.9%	D	1
New Issue Investor	+6.6%	C	14
New Issues	+11.6%	C	34
Nicholson Report			
Stocks for the Longer-Term Investor	−12.9%	C	24
Stocks for Aggressive Traders	−9.0%	C	5
The Option Advisor			
Conservative Portfolio	−97.2%	A	1
Moderate-Risk Portfolio	−92.9%	A	1
Aggressive Portfolio	−93.4%	A	1
Outlook			
Foundation Stocks	+12.3%	C	5
Growth Stocks	+10.5%	C	6
Speculative Stocks	+21.4%	C	9
Income Stocks	+28.0%	C	3
Peter Dag Investment Letter	+6.0%	A	3
Professional Investor			
NYSE Scan	+14.1%	C	47
AMEX Scan	+48.2%	C	51
OTC Scan	+29.3%	C	50
Investment Grade Stk Scan	−18.5%	C	12
Professional Tape Reader	−9.8%	B	31
Professional Timing Service	+22.4%	C	11
Prudent Speculator	+72.9%	A	63
RHM Survey of Wrts., Opts., and Low-Priced Stocks	+8.6%	C	25
Smart Money	−59.1%	C	10
Speculator	+8.8%	C	11
Successful Options Investing	−18.9%	C	21
Switch Fund Advisory	+16.4%	A	6
Systems & Forecasts	−6.9%	B	14
Telephone Switch Newsletter			
Equity-Cash Switch Plan	+19.0%	C	5
Gold-Equities Switch Plan	−7.8%	C	4
Tony Henfrey's Gold Letter	+6.9%	C	0
United Business & Investment Reports			
Growth Stocks	+1.7%	C	30
Cyclical Stocks	+7.0%	C	24
Income Stocks	+14.7%	C	10
*Value Line Investment Survey	+34.8%	C	100
*Value Line OTC Spec. Sit. Survey	+24.1%	C	26
Zweig Forecast	+1.5%	A	16
Zweig Performance Ratings Report	+17.5%	C	27
THE "RISKLESS' RATE OF RETURN: You could have earned this by investing only in Treasury Bills:	+8.6%		

Table 10.3 Continued

Newsletter	Gain as of 12/30/83	Clarity Rating (a)	No. of Stocks in Portfolio (b)
STOCK AVERAGES:			
By way of comparison, the major market averages have performed as follows (dividends not included):			
DJIA	+20.3%		
NYSE Composite	+17.5%		
AMEX Market Value Index	+31.0%		
Standard & Poor's 500	+17.3%		
NASDAQ OTC Composite	+19.9%		
Wilshire 500 Equity Index	+18.8%		

*TOP-PERFORMING LETTERS

Notes: If a newsletter has more than one model portfolio, their returns have been averaged. For example, the portfolios in the Addison Report had an average gain of 57.9%.
(a) Some letters precisely specify all elements necessary to construct a model portfolio, thus rating an A. But many indicate allocations unsystematically and in general terms. Where such vagueness is acute—C or D—measuring the portfolio is necessarily more difficult.
(b) T-Bills don't count, so a portfolio entirely in T-Bills or the equivalent rates a "O."

Source: S. Duffy, "Who Was Hot and Who Was Cold," *Barron's*, January 16, 1984. Reprinted by permission of Barron's, © Dow Jones & Company, Inc., 1984. All Rights Reserved.

Programs utilizing these data bases as input can screen the data banks for certain characteristics and/or perform numerous manipulations of the available data. Some of these programs are marketed primarly to institutions. Others are available free to people connected with an academic institution. The growth of personal computers will undoubtedly make computer analyses much more accessible to many individual investors. Indeed a number of investor-oriented programs, most of which are for technical analysis (Table 10.4) and a variety of data-sources are available to those with personal computers (Table 10.5). Before purchasing a software package and data service, one might wish to refer to one of the publications which reviews computer investment programs: *Financial and Investment Software Review* (Quarterly, $45 per year, Box 6, Riverdale, NY, 10471); *Wall Street Computer Review* (Monthly, $139 per year, Dealer's Digest Inc., 150 Broadway New York, NY, 10038) and *Computerized Investing* (bimonthly $44 per year, American Association of Individual Investors, 612 N. Michigan Avenue, Chicago, Ill. 60611).

The ultimate in computerized investing allows one to trade securities directly in the marketplace. A pilot program of Instinet (122 E. 42nd Street, New York, NY, 10017) enables, one to dial into the network and first obtain a quote and then execute a trade for any security traded on the Pacific Stock Exchange.

Investment Implications of the Computer

Since the computer and computer-based data sources play a large and growing role in investment analysis, investors should be aware of their availability. Those simply wishing to apply the results of such research may find the computer useful, but not essential. Mutual funds and other institutions in the best positions to utilize computers have not produced particularly impressive performances with or without them.

INVESTOR ASSOCIATIONS

Three associations are designed to assist small investors. The National Association of Investment Clubs (Box 220, Royal Oak, Michigan, 48068) helps groups of small investors establish investment clubs and provides a vehicle for investment clubs to communicate with each other. The association now has 5,000 clubs representing 90,000 members. For $25 per club plus $6 per member one can obtain the association's assistance in establishing a club.

The American Association of Individual Investors (612 North Michigan Avenue, Chicago, Illinois, 60611) offers a wide variety of services for its $44 annual membership: 1) A journal of investment theory and practice that appears ten times a year; 2) An investor's guide to no-load mutual funds; 3) Local chapter membership where available in a number of metropolitan areas; 4) A series of home computer programs for investors; 5) A tax-planning guide; 6) Access to a number of seminars, a variety of home study material, and a bi-monthly periodical on computerized investing (optional for extra cost).

The American Association of Microcomputer Investors (Box 1384, Princeton, NJ 08542; 609/737-3972) is the newest of these small investor organizations. Its $49 annual enrollment fee entitles one to the *AAMI Journal*, which offers articles on investment software and data bases; the AAMI *Investment Software Directory*; free computer programs from the public domain and AAMI staff; discounts on other investment software; and a number of study guides for investors.

At the other end of the spectrum the Investment Company Institute (1775 K Street, Washington, D.C., 20006; 202/293-7700) services mutual funds and other institutional investors. The Institute publishes a periodical called the *Mutual Funds Forum*.

BUSINESS NEWS PROGRAMS

Television's only nationwide business news program during the 1970s was *Wall Street Week* (WSW). Hosted by Louis Rukeyser and a rotating series of panelists (including Martin Zweig), the program has continued to draw a substantial audience. The Public Broadcasting System (PBS) program combines a format of moderator commentary, panelist discussion, viewer questions, and guest interviews.

The growth of cable systems and the "narrowcasting" approach to programming has, however, led to the introduction of a rash of new business programs in the early 1980s.[13] For example Friday nights' *WSW* is now accompanied on PBS by the *Nightly Business Report*, which appears daily (five days a week).

Table 10.4   Computing the Expense of Computer Investing

Program	Maker	Cost	Features
Advisor	Kate's Komputers, Sausalito, Calif.	$600	Provides instant analysis of portfolio value and tracks options approaching parity, gains or losses and stop points.
Analyst	Kate's Komputers	$600	A stock, bond, currency and option charting system with usual features like a split screen. Files are large enough to encompass 20 years of price data.
CompuTrac	Technical Analysis Group, New Orleans	$1,800, plus $200 annual fee	Advanced technical analysis programs including such mathematical exotica as regression analysis, momentum charting and demand aggregates. It combines price, volume and open interest figures into one indicator.
Intra-day Analysis	Technical Analysis	$1,500	Calculates up-to-the-minute quotes and emits an "audible alarm" when any of up to 20 commodity contracts exceeds a stop point.
Investpak	McGraw Hill, N.Y.	$200	Computes, among other things, transaction costs, stock and portfolio valuations and upside breakeven points for a strip straddle on several options.
Market Analyzer	Dow Jones & Co., Princeton, N.J.	$350	Is an assortment of basic and intermediate technical analysis procedures like oscillators of moving averages and cumulative volume indicators.
Market Microscope	Dow Jones & Co., N.Y.	$700	Simultaneously analyzes up to 20 of 68 financial variables on 3,200 stocks, and can rank securities based on estimated earnings.
Micro/Scan	ISYS Corp., Cambridge, Mass.	$3,600	Price includes monthly updates of prices and corporate financial data for a fundamental analysis of 1,400 stocks; 26 variables can be selected and companies ranked by stock market price multiple, discount to book value and other combinations.
Stockpak	Standard & Poors Corp., N.Y.	$50, plus $200 annual update fee	A beginner's fundamental analysis kit, containing 30 financial categories on 900 companies; runs on only Radio Shack personal computers.
DATA SERVICES			
The Source	Readers Digest Assn., McLean, Va.	$100 subscription fee, plus $7.75 per-hour user fee	Price, volume, sales, earnings and 51 other financial benchmarks for 3,100 companies can be grouped and ranked for screening.
News/Retrieval	Dow Jones & Co.	$50 basic fee plus $75 annual charge & 10 cents & up per minute user fee.	Market Prices, news and earnings estimates on 2,400 companies. Wall Street Week transcripts and 10-K extracts.
CompuService Information Service	H&R Block, Columbus, Ohio	$30 one-time fee, plus user fee of $5 per hour, plus 3 cents and up per item.	Oldest data base, with prices, volume and dividend data on 40,000 stocks, bonds and options issued since 1974. It also includes Standard & Poor's and Value Line corporate files.

Source: L. Marion, "Investing by Computer: More Programs for Individuals Hit Market," *Barron's*, October 9, 1982. Reprinted by permission of *Barron's*, © Dow Jones & Company, Inc., 1984. All Rights Reserved.

Table 10.5   The Leading 'Libraries' that a Personal Computer User Can Consult

Service	Hookup cost, charges*	Number of subscribers	Main services offered	Startup date
Dow Jones News/Retrieval	$50, 10¢–$1.20/minute	60,000	Business and economic news, stock quotes, investment information	Nov. 1977
CompuServe Information Service	$20–$40 (depending on software package purchased), $5–$22.50/hour	36,000	Financial information, banking, games, shopping, weather, encyclopedia, newspapers, bulletin boards	July 1979
The Source	$100, $5.75–$29.75/hour	26,000	News and research tools, consumer tips, market quotes, travel, shopping, games, bulletin boards	June 1979
NewsNet	No hookup fee, $18–$24/hour, extra to read newsletters not already subscribed to, up to $96/hour	300	More than 80 newsletters covering many subjects	Apr. 1982
Dialog Information Services Inc.'s Knowledge Index	$35, $24/hour	NA	Descriptive indexes of articles, books, and reports; newspapers	Dec. 1982
DRI-VisiCorp	$250 for VisiLink software package; $10–$125 per data base	NA	58 updated data bases: economic forecasts, foreign exchange, individual industries	Jan. 1983
BRS/After Dark	$50, $6–$15/hour	NA	Abstracted indexes of articles, from science to education	Jan. 1983

*Hookup costs include differing amounts of free time and sometimes are waived in certain promotions. Charges vary according to time of day, data base used, and transmission speed
Data: BW
NA= not available

Source: "How to Pick Your Stocks by Computer," *Business Week*, September 12, 1983. Reprinted by permission of McGraw-Hill, Inc.

This half-hour program is devoted to business, and particularly stock market, news. It ends with a segment by one of its ten regular commentators. *Insider Business Today*, a third PBS offering, is a weekly interview program.

The Cable News Network (CNN) originates three business news programs. *Moneyline*, with a heavy concentration of economic and market information, appears daily. *Moneyweek* is a weekly compilation of some of the *Moneyline* stories. *Inside Business* provides an in-depth look at corporate leaders.

The Financial News Network offers twelve hours of programs daily. Its *FNN Final* provides an hour of in-depth business and financial news. *Moneytalk* is a call-in show for viewer questions.

Other business-oriented programs include the *Wall Street Journal Report*, produced weekly by Dow Jones and broadcast by Independent Network News;

Biz Net News Today, produced daily by the U.S. Chamber of Commerce and broadcast by the Modern Satellite Network; *Business Times,* the Entertainment and Sports Network's daily briefing for top executives, and *Moneyworks,* an interview program produced by Mintzer.

SOURCES OF INVESTMENT IDEAS

The preceeding discussion of the financial press and other investment information sources has left out many publications and data sources while only briefly touching others. Readers might follow up this discussion by examining some of the relevant periodicals in the library. With these sources, where should an investor go for investment ideas? The financial press is constantly suggesting interesting investment situations. Brokers also recommend investments as part of their "service." Friends, neighbors, relations, and local business people sometimes have ideas worth considering. *Forbes, Value Line* and some other periodicals frequently list stocks with particular characteristics in common (very low PE ratios, large cash positions, etc.), which may serve as useful beginning points. One interested in a particular industry can begin with the *Value Line* sample.

Examining the entire list of NYSE, AMEX or the national OTC securities may sometimes be useful. For example, one may believe that many warrants, convertible bonds, or high-yield bonds are underpriced. A quick check through the most recent *Wall Street Journal* will reveal those listed on each exchange. Warrants have a "wt" after their name; convertibles have a "cv" after theirs; and high-yield bonds have high numbers in the yield column.

SUMMARY AND CONCLUSIONS

An individual following a particular stock should refer to company-prepared documents such as 10Ks, 10Qs, prospectuses, proxy materials, press releases, and annual and quarterly reports. 13D filings report large ownership positions. Stock quotations and indexes contain price and other information on individual securities and the market. Business news is discussed in publications such as the *Wall Street Journal* and *Business Week,* while *Barron's* and *Forbes* offer more investor-oriented coverage. Investors seeking information about specific firms may wish to consult *Moody's Industrial Manuals,* the *Standard & Poor's Reports, Value Line,* or brokerage-house reports. Tapes containing a number of years of financial information for many firms are very nearly essential for serious statistical analysis. A variety of investment-related computer software is available to those with personal computers.

REVIEW QUESTIONS

1. Discuss the information available in corporate reports.
2. Compare a *Barron's* and *Wall Street Journal* quotation. What additional information is in the *Standard & Poor's Stock Guide?*

3. Discuss the various stock market indexes.
4. Compare the coverage in *Moody's Manuals*, the *Standard & Poor's Reports* and *Value Line*.
5. Discuss the computer's role in investments.

REVIEW PROBLEMS

1. Select a company and obtain each of its various reports (see Table 10.1 for a list). Read and analyze each report. Analyze the company on the basis of these reports.
2. Compare the coverage in your local newspaper with the *Wall Street Journal* quotations of Tables 10.1 and 10.2.
3. Compute the daily percentage change in each of the following market indexes for ten days: S&P 500, *Value Line*, Dow Jones Industrials, NYSE, AMEX and Wilshire 5000. Repeat for monthly changes over past year. Compare the performances.
4. For the same company as was selected in question 1 obtain current reports in *Value Line*, *Moody's*, *S&P* and from a brokerage house. Read and analyze each report. Write your own report on the company. Compare it with the one you write from company-only data.
5. Read through several recent issues of *Forbes* and identify a list of ten companies which the magazine has featured favorably. Now consult *Value Line*, *Moody's* and S&P on each. Finally obtain company reports on each. Evaluate each company on the basis of each set of reports.
6. Write for literature from the various vendors of investment related computer software and data sources. Write a report.
7. Sketch the type of features that would be desirable to have in a computer investing software package.

NOTES

1. C. Power, "Light in Dark Corners," *Forbes*, August 1, 1983, p. 133.

2. D. Dunn, "Devices that Let You Track Stocks Like a Floor Trader," *Business Week*, July 25, 1983, pp. 83–84; R. Rusting, "Computers Help Investors Follow Stocks that may be Affected by Insider Trading," *Wall Street Journal*, June 11, 1984, p. 27.

3. M. Farrell, ed., *The Dow Jones Investor's Handbook*, Dow-Jones Books, Princeton, NJ, 1980; H.L. Butler, Jr. and J.D. Allen, "The Dow-Jones Industrial Average Re-Reexamined," *Financial Analysts Journal*, November/December 1979, pp. 23–30; R.D. Milne, "The Dow-Jones Industrial Average Re-examined," *Financial Analysts Journal*, November/December 1966, pp. 83–88; E. Carter and K. Cohen, "Bias in the DJIA Caused by Stock Splits," *Financial Analysts Journal*, 1966, pp. 90–94; L. Schellbach, "When Did the DJIA Top 1200?," *Financial Analysts Journal*, 1967, pp. 71–73.

4. *S&P 500 Stock Index Adds Financial Transportation Groups*, Standard and Poor's Corporation, New York, 1976; *Trade and Securities Statistics*, Standard & Poor's Corp., New York, 1981.

5. A. Bernhard, *How to Use the Value Line Investment Survey*, Arnold Bernhard & Co., New York, 1982; *Value Line*, "The Value Line Ranking System at Midyear," *The Value Line Investment Survey*, July 24, 1983, pp. 443–445.

6. F. Black, "Yes Virginia, There is Hope: A Test of the Value Line Ranking System," *Financial Analysts Journal*, September 1973, p. 10.

7. C. Holloway, "A Note on Testing an Aggressive Investment Strategy Using *Value Line* Ranks," *Journal of Finance*, June 1981, pp. 711–720.

8. C. Jakobson, "Diamonds to Dogs, a New Service Covers Them All," *Barron's*, February 6, 1984, pp. 16–18.

9. R. Stanley, W. Lewellen, and G. Sharbaum, "Further Evidence on the Value of Professional Investment Research," *Journal of Financial Research*, Spring 1981, pp. 1–10.

10. P. Brimlow, "Box Score on Advisers," *Barron's*, April 20, 1981, pp. 9, 23, 25, 29; M. Hulbert, "Gambling on Advisors' Performance," *American Association of Individual Investors Journal*, October 1983, pp. 22–28; M. Hulbert, "The Financial Digest," *American Association of Individual Investors Journal*, April 1984, pp. 21–22.

11. B. Rosenberg and M. Houglet, "Error Rates in CRSP and Compustat Data Bases and Their Implications," *Journal of Finance*, September 1974, pp. 1, 303, 310; R. Bennin, "Error Rates on CRISP and Compustat: A Second Look," *Journal of Finance*, December 1980, pp. 1,267–1,271; R. McElreath and C. Wiggins, "Using the COMPUSTAT Topics in Financial Research Problems and Solutions," *Financial Analysts Journal*, January/February 1984, pp. 71–76.

12. R. Stern, "What's in it for Your Broker?" *Forbes*, September 26, 1983, p. 96.

13. D. Kelley, "Sons of Wall Street Week," *Barron's* September 5, 1983, pp. 14, 32, 33.

Section IV:
Investment Timing

Selecting attractive investments is only one part of an effective investment program. Investors also want to take advantage of the market's ups and downs. This section explores market timing in three separate chapters. The following case illustrates some of the issues to be examined.

STARTING A NEWSLETTER

You and a friend in the brokerage industry have decided to start an investment newsletter. Your friend plans to quit her job and you will be passing up a job offer in banking to pursue this option. Your friend will be in charge of marketing while your primary job will be to write the articles. Since startup costs (principally advertising) are expected to be quite heavy, you must find some backers. Another friend has assembled a list of potential investors but they are sure to want some evidence of your potential. You have agreed to put together a sample of what your newsletter will contain. Accordingly you must write a sample letter. The proposed sample is to contain three sections. First you will analyze the current and anticipated state of the economy and its likely impact on stock prices. Second you will assess the market's tone and emotional state. Finally you will recommend some specific stocks that you expect to make short-term moves. Since your letter will be in your potential backers' hands for several weeks before they decide what to do, they will have an opportunity to compare your forecast with the market's actual performance.

The three sections of your proposed newsletter correspond to the three chapters of this section. Chapter 11 deals with relations between the stock market and the economy. Business-cycle stock market relations are explored first. Various ways of forecasting economic activity are examined with much attention focused on relations between monetary policy and stock market movements. The remainder of Chapter 11 discusses relations between the stock market and the inflation rate. Noneconomic factors that may be used to forecast stock market activity are explored in Chapter 12. Specifically, timing the market with percentage changes from previous highs, market PEs, market PEs relative to interest rates, recession patterns, election-year cycles, official pronouncements, discount rate changes, company share repurchase, and various technical market indicators are all discussed. Finally Chapter 13 examines various methods of timing individual security trades. Chart reading is briefly considered along with anxious-trader effects, adjustment lags, and speculative bubbles.

11 The Stock Market and the Economy

While not necessarily the key to short-term trading profits, understanding stock market/economy relationships may help investors avoid some unprofitable moves. Is a falling stock price an encouragement to buy? Perhaps or perhaps not. It depends, for example, on whether a changed economic outlook has greatly altered profit expectations. A solid understanding of stock market/economy relationships, coupled with an ability to forecast the economy's future, may indeed facilitate profitable trading. Accordingly, this chapter is designed to help investors understand such relationships. First, various ways of forecasting economic activity are considered, including econometric models, leading indicators, and investor-constructed forecasts. To help investors understand how to formulate a forecast, fiscal and monetary policies' economic impacts are examined. Then we explore the empirical relations between stock performance and economic policy, giving particular emphasis to monetary policy. The remainder of the chapter discusses the theoretical arguments and empirical evidence relating to inflation's impact on returns.

FORECASTING ECONOMIC PERFORMANCE

Chapter 7 discussed theoretical relations between the stock market and the economy. We saw how the business cycle affected firms' profits, dividends, and stock prices. In general, an expanding economy causes sales to rise, inventory levels to decline, working hours to expand, income to increase, and thus corporate profits and dividends to rise. This generally causes stock prices to rise as well. A weak economy, in contrast, generally affects the stock market adversely. Now we shall consider how one might forecast economic activity and thus seek to anticipate stock market moves.

Econometric Forecasts

A number of professional econometricians forecast economic activity by applying the latest economic information and expectations to their own models. One may (at a substantial cost) subscribe directly to such services, or follow the reports on them in the financial press (the *Wall Street Journal*, *Business Week*, etc.).

Economic forecasts have several noteworthy limitations, however. First, the periodic predictions do not reflect interim developments. Second, stock prices themselves may already incorporate the relevant information. Third, the forecaster's past records are far from perfect, although they may be improving.[1] Table 11.1 illustrates their relatively unsuccessful 1983 performance.

Leading Indicators

"Leading indicators" are also designed to forecast economic activity. The NBER and Commerce Department have identified 12 monthly data series that tend to lead the business cycle: stock prices, average work week, average unemployment claims, net business formations, new consumer goods and material orders, contracts for plant and equipment, new building permits, change in book value of inventories on hand and on order, change in sensitive materials' prices, index of slow deliveries from suppliers, change in money supply (M2), and change in business and consumer credit. The list is revised from time to time, however.[2]

A study by Heathcotte and Apilado suggested that trading decisions based on the eleven non-stock indicators could outperform a buy and hold strategy.[3] Simonson, however, criticized the work as lacking a firm theoretical basis and relying on hindsight-based filter rules.[4] More recent research by Wertheim and Company and Geoffrey Moore found leading indicators quite accurate at forecasting economic turns but offering about the same amount of lead time as the stock market itself.[5] That is, by the time the leading indicators forecast an economic turn, the stock market is already anticipating the move.

The *Business Week* Leading Index (BWLI), which appears in its "Financial Figures of the Week" section, provides an alternative index.[6] Geoffrey Moore, who originated the original NBER/Commerce Department index, has assembled a new weekly index that appears to outperform his earlier creation. Based on seven data series (initial unemployment claims, bond yields, money growth, stock prices, real estate loans, business failures, and materials prices), the index appears to give rather accurate advance warning of economic downturns, but less timely notice of upturns.

Homemade Forecasts

While leading indicators' and econometric forecasts' stock-timing values appear to be limited, early accurate homemade economic predictions might facilitate more profitable performance. Like the weather, almost everyone has an opinion on the economy. Such opinions should be based on an accurate understanding of how the economy operates. Malabre argues that understanding economics sufficiently to formulate a forecast is not especially difficult.[7] Investors who prefer not to forecast GNP, unemployment, and inflation precisely may be more inclined to estimate the direction and perhaps the general magnitude of the changes in each. That is, few individuals would feel comfortable forecasting an increase in GNP of 7.8% but many might be capable of correctly predicting more growth

Table 11.1   1983 Economic Results vs. Forecaster Predictions

REAL GNP	INFLATION	UNEMPLOYMENT
Actual +3.4%	Actual +3.3%	Actual 9.5%
Morris Cohen +4.0%	Citicorp +5.6%	Evans Economics 10.6%
Eggert Enterprises +3.8%	Conference Board +5.6%	Wharton Econometrics 10.3%
Citicorp +3.4%	BankAmerica +5.2%	Chase Econometrics 10.1%
Peter L. Bernstein +2.8%	Data Resources +5.2%	Data Resources 10.1%
Wharton Econometrics +2.8%	Evans Economics +5.2%	Man. Hanover 10.1%
Conference Board +2.6%	Man. Hanover +5.2%	Peter L. Bernstein 10.0%
BankAmerica +2.5%	Chase Econometrics +5.1%	Conference Board 10.0%
Chase Econometrics +2.4%	Eggert Enterprises +5.1%	BankAmerica 9.9%
Data Resources +2.2%	Wharton Econometrics +5.0%	Citicorp 9.7%
Man. Hanover +2.2%	Morris Cohen +4.9%	**Morris Cohen 9.5%**
Evans Economics +1.4%	Peter L. Bernstein +4.7%	Eggert Enterprises 9.2%

Source: Eggert Economic Enterprises, from P. Kilborn, "Why Prognosticators Strayed," *The New York Times*, December 16, 1983. © 1983 by The New York Times Company. Reprinted by permission.

than last year's 4%. Indeed just knowing whether to expect a recession, continued rapid growth, or a pause should help in investment timing as much as most professional forecasts.

Serious efforts to predict economic activity should take account of the government's economic policy. Government spending and taxing policy (fiscal policy), and any activity affecting interest rates and the money supply (monetary policy) all have important economic impacts.

Fiscal Policy

Government spending affects the economy in several ways. First, when the economy has some slack, increased government expenditures call forth additional production. Thus a public works project will employ people to produce the structure and the required inputs (cement, steel, etc.). They will spend most of their income on consumer goods and services, thereby creating demands that put others to work and so on. While this "multiplier" process increases employment and production, at each stage a portion of the extra income is saved, taxed, or spent on imported goods. These so-called leakages reduce the multiplier's power. Moreover, the additional spending forces the government to increase its borrowing or taxes, thereby crowding out other borrowers and/or reducing other disposable incomes. Thus less goes to each succeeding round. In fact, leakages are so pervasive that the GNP typically increases only by about twice the amount of the government spending increase.

A tax decrease's effect is similar to a government spending increase. Lower tax rates and reduced withholdings increase after-tax income, causing spending to rise. This spending increase in turn leads to additional production, jobs, and income, which cause further increases. Thus both a government spending increase and a tax decrease stimulates the economy while a government spending decrease and a tax increase restrains the economy. A change in spending, however, has a greater economic impact than an equivalent-size tax change, since the full amount of the spending change affects GNP, while a portion of the tax change affects savings. When, in contrast, the economy is already operating near its capacity, stimulative economic policy has little or no output or employment impact, but does tend to increase prices.

Monetary Policy: The Fed's Tools

The Federal Reserve System's (Fed) economic impact stems from its power to influence credit conditions. The M1 money supply, which consists of all cash and coin in circulation outside banks, plus all depository accounts on which check-like instruments may be drawn, is largely determined by the Fed. Federally chartered banks and state banks with Fed memberships are required to maintain reserves with the Fed equal to a percentage of their deposits. The Monetary Control Act of 1980 envisions subjecting all depository institutions (banks, S&Ls, credit unions, etc.) to the Fed's reserve requirements over a three- to seven-year period.

The Fed can influence the money supply by raising or lowering the reserve requirement. If the reserve requirement is decreased, banks need less reserves to support their existing deposits and thus may increase their loans. An increase has the reverse effect. Banks grant loans by making deposits to the borrowers' account. Checks written against these deposits flow largely into other bank accounts. Loan-induced increases in cash holdings are generally small relative to the increase in banking system deposits. The increased deposits create additional lending power which, when utilized, generate still more lending power via the so-called money multiplier. The reserves freed by the reduced reserve requirement will eventually be utilized by increased lending, however.

Rather than changing reserve requirements, the Fed generally prefers to influence the banking system through open-market operations. A large portion of the Fed's reserves are represented by United States government debt, whose coupon income substantially exceeds the Fed's own expenses. The Fed's portfolio management dramatically affects the banking system. The Fed pays for bonds with drafts (checks) that increase the recipient banks' reserves. These increased reserves allow a multiple increase in deposits and loans. Similarly, a Fed sale of government securities reduces reserves, thereby forcing deposits and loans to contract. The Fed buys and sells Treasury securities daily and thereby pumps in or takes out a targeted amount of reserves. The change in reserves then affects the aggregate money supply.

The Fed also loans reserves (discount loans) to member banks. Stressing that discounting is a privilege, not a right, the Fed only makes such loans on a short-term basis (as a safety valve). By adjusting the rate and willingness to grant loans, the Fed makes discounting more or less attractive. Compared with changing reserve requirements and open market operations, however, discounting is a relatively minor tool used principally to signal changes in other Fed policy. In addition to the "discount window," depository institutions having a temporary shortage may borrow reserves from others with a temporary excess in the so-called Federal Funds market. Table 11.2 lists the Fed's principal policy tools.

Table 11.2   The Fed's Principal Policy Tools

Reserve Requirement	Increasing (Decreasing) the ratio reduces (raises) the amount of money that can be supported by a given reserve base.
Open Market Operations	Fed purchases (sales) of government securities increase (decrease) the reserves available to support the money supply.
Discount Loans	Increasing (Decreasing) the discount rate and decreasing (increasing) its willingness to grant discount loans tightens (eases) monetary policy

Monetary Policy's Economic Impact

How does an increase in deposits and loans affect the economy? Money in the form of transactions balances (e.g., checking deposits) and near money in the form of short-term highly liquid securities (e.g. T-bills) are useful commodities. An increase in the supply of money and near money encourages many people to spend more. These additional expenditures tend to create more income and jobs and stimulate additional spending. A reduction in deposits and loans, in contrast, tends to reduce spending and income. As with fiscal policy, stimulatory monetary policy tends to increase real (noninflationary) output when the economy has slack resources and to increase prices when bottlenecks appear.

Monetary and Fiscal Policy: Some Qualifications

The economy may be stimulated by increased government spending, lower taxes, and an increase in the money supply; it can be restrained by the reverse processes.

Several factors complicate this seemingly simple relationship, however.

First, changes in tax rates and government spending (fiscal policy) or in the reserve requirement, discount rate, and open-market policy (monetary policy) take time to work through the economy. Thus the direction of government monetary and fiscal policy can help forecast economic behavior.

Second, monetary and fiscal policies' sensitivities to political pressures differ. Monetary policy is formulated by the Federal Reserve Board's governors and its Open-Market Committee, whose members are appointed by the President for long, staggered terms. Furthermore, the Fed is not dependent on Congressional appropriations because its own interest income is more than adequate to cover its expense. Thus the Fed can pursue a relatively independent monetary policy. Fiscal policy, on the other hand, is formulated jointly by Congress and the administration, both of which are influenced by diverse interest groups. As a result, short-term pressures increase the difficulty of implementing long-run fiscal policies.

Third, the stock market also monitors economic policy. Thus investors need a superior understanding of economic policy/economy/stock market relationships if they are to have an advantage. Since such economic forecasts should be based on an assessment of likely future economic policy, one needs to understand the policymakers' goals.

Goals of Monetary and Fiscal Policy

Monetary and fiscal policymakers' primary economic goals are full employment and price stability. Inflation is a general rise in the price level. A 12% inflation rate implies that $1.12 is required to buy the same diverse market basket of goods and services as could be acquired for $1 last year. The unemployment rate is defined as the percentage out of work of those who are employed or actively seeking employment. Extensive government statistics are compiled on both employment and inflation. Additional concerns include: economic growth, increased productivity, balance of payments equilibrium, a strong dollar (internationally), environmental protection, energy independence, economic freedom, equal economic opportunity, consumer protection, and product safety. Policies designed to achieve some of these goals frequently conflict with other goals, however.

Virtually everyone agrees that price stability and full employment are desirable. Unemployment-reducing policies may, however, accelerate inflation because of what might be termed the "capacity effect." Stimulating the economy depletes the reservoir of unemployed workers, resources, and excess capacity. Eventually those bidding for an inadequate supply of inputs will force prices to rise. Some stimulation may be administered to a slack economy before bottlenecks accelerate the inflation rate, however.

Figure 11.1 Unemployment and Economic Cycles

Percent
Unemployment

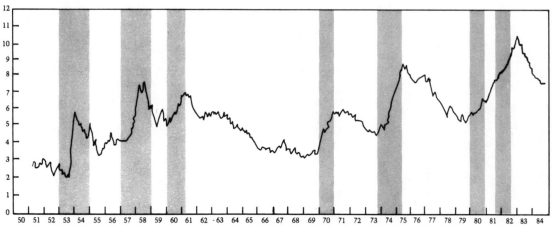

Periods of business recessions as defined by National Bureau of Economic Research

Source: National Bureau of Economic Research.

Some unemployment is inevitable. People change jobs (frictional unemployment), work at seasonal jobs (seasonal unemployment), or are unemployed because of location, background, or training (structural unemployment). Increasing numbers are employed in unreported underground economy jobs.[8] These various classes of unemployed and unreported-employeds create an almost irreducible floor for reported unemployment. The height of this floor, however, changes as the economy evolves (Figure 11.1).

Similarly the inflation rates' recent history (Figure 11.2) and performance relative to unemployment (Figure 11.3) may provide clues to its future behavior. Figure 11.3 illustrates the inflation/unemployment tradeoff. In the early 1960s, unemployment was relatively high and the inflation rate relatively low. Stimulative economic policy (first the Kennedy tax cut and then the Vietnam war) tended to reduce unemployment and increase the inflation rate. Once inflation got out of hand, the rate spiraled upward and unemployment also rose. In the late 1970s and early 1980s we had very high unemployment coupled with a high inflation rate. More restrictive economic policy led to still higher unemployment but some fall in the inflation rate. By late 1984 the unemployment rate was declining and inflation seemed to be rising somewhat.

Figure 11.2 Change in the Consumer Price Index: 12-Month Change in the CPI-U

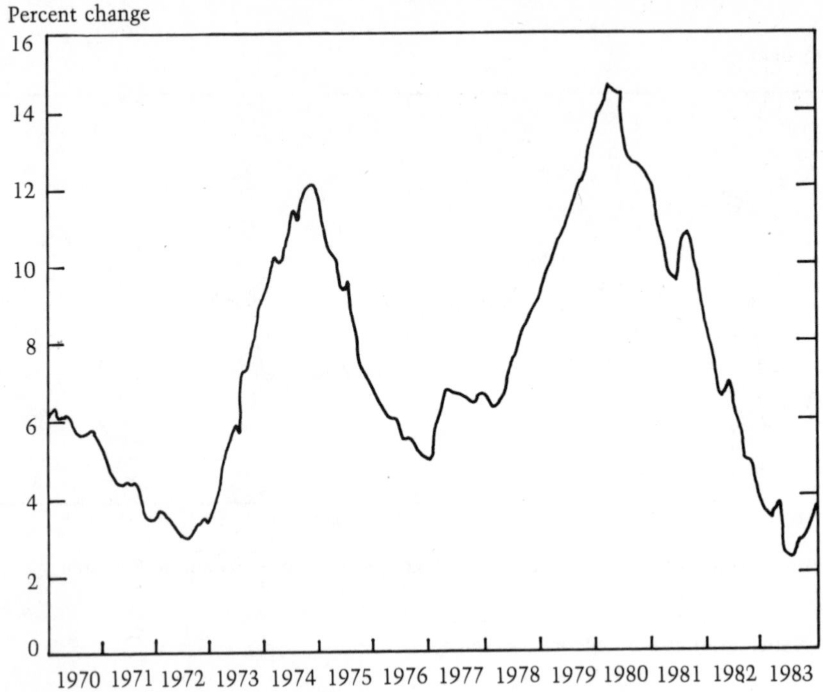

Percent change

Source: Department of Labor.

Predicting a Shift in Economic Policy

Whether economic policy is more likely to be expansionary or contractionary depends largely on unemployment's and inflation's relative importance to policymakers. While the tradeoffs are quite complex, some guidelines may be helpful.

Most economists once thought that 4% unemployment represented full employment. Those occasions when unemployment dipped below 4% (1966–69) were followed by accelerating inflation. Since 1975, however, unemployment above 4% has not relieved inflationary pressures. Thus most policymakers now believe reported unemployment of 5% or even 6% is acceptable (full employment).[9] Unemployment above 7 or 8% is still a major concern, however. Stimulatory monetary and fiscal policy becomes more likely with every tenth of a percentage point rise toward 8%. Once begun, stimulation usually continues until inflation becomes a more pressing problem or unemployment is reduced to the 5 to 6% range.

Figure 11.3 Inflation and Unemployment Rate

Inflation (Percent)[1]

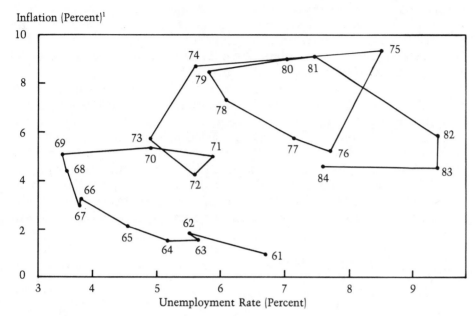

[1]Percent change in GNP implicit price deflator.

Source: Department of Commerce and Department of Labor.

In the 1950s and 1960s, a 3% inflation rate was generally considered a problem. The double-digit inflation of the 1970s and early 1980s made policymakers long for such creeping inflation. Indeed, a 5 to 7% inflation rate may be marginally acceptable. The desire to reduce inflation further has not been abandoned, but may be unrealistic in the post-1974 environment. That is, after 10–14% inflation, both the public and the policymakers seem reasonably willing to settle for restraining inflation to half that rate. A given inflation rate's acceptability depends greatly on recent experience, however: if inflation can be kept in the high single digits for a time, policymakers may seek a rate in the mid-to-low single digits.

When the inflation rate is considered too high and unemployment is between 6 and 8%, economic policy is especially difficult to forecast. Other things being equal, higher inflation and lower unemployment increase the likelihood of contractionary economic policy. Restrictive economic policy is quite likely with a problem inflation rate and unemployment below 7%. On the other hand, with 7.5% unemployment and a marginally unacceptable inflation rate, stimulation is likely. Economic policy forecasts should be based on up-to-date knowledge of what levels are acceptable, however. For example, in 1984, most economic policymakers would have been quite pleased with unemployment and inflation below 6%. Twenty years earlier, however, the goals were around 4% for unemployment and 2% for inflation. No doubt the acceptable (or tolerable) unemployment and inflation levels will continue to vary.

The fiscal and monetary authorities tend to be more concerned, other things being equal, with a rising than a constant inflation rate. On the other hand, a falling inflation rate may increase the likelihood of stimulative actions. Similarly, the longer inflation has persisted at an unacceptably high level, the greater the probability of restraint.

The overall unemployment rate's composition also provides clues to likely future monetary and fiscal policy. Unemployment rates are reported for various subgroups. The so-called central unemployment rate for males between the ages of 25 and 54 is particularly relevant. The central rate is usually well below

Figure 11.4 Selected Unemployment Rates

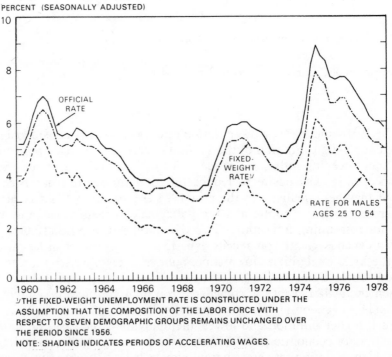

Sources: Department of Labor and Council of Economic Advisors.

the global rate (Figure 11.4). For a given overall rate, the lower the central rate, the less likely is economic policy to be stimulating. When the central rate is low, further stimulation tends to be especially inflationary. Furthermore, the central group's political pressures are generally more effective than those of other labor force components.

While the Administration, Congress, and the Fed usually attempt to coordinate monetary and fiscal policy, differences can occur. Since stimulus is politically more acceptable than restraint, the Fed must sometimes make the initial restrictive move. Like the Supreme Court, however, the Fed does "follow the election returns." Indeed, the Fed's chairman must often answer pointed questions before Congressional committees and is ever mindful that the legislation under which it operates can be changed. Moreover the President can fill Fed vacancies with people who he or she expects to pursue policies similar to the Administration's.

The unemployment/inflation tradeoff also has important political ramifications. All administrations seek low unemployment and stable prices. The more liberal (conservative) the administration, however, the greater its desire to reduce unemployment (inflation). Thus the Truman and Kennedy-Johnson administrations sought low unemployment and tolerated increased inflation while the Eisenhower, Nixon and Ford administrations generally sought to reduce inflation at the cost of higher unemployment rates. The Carter administration had the worst of both worlds but became increasingly concerned with inflation as time went by. The Reagan administration's overriding concern with inflation abated only when unemployment reached double digits and inflation declined dramatically. Table 11.3 summarizes the factors affecting shifts in economic policy.

Table 11.3   Factors Affecting the Likelihood of a Shift in Monetary and Fiscal Policy

A Shift toward Greater Stimulation is more likely if:	A Shift toward Greater Restrictiveness is more likely if:
Unemployment is far above its goal	Unemployment is near its goal
Inflation rate is near its goal	Inflation rate is far above its goal
Unemployment is increasing	Unemployment is decreasing
Inflation is decreasing	Inflation is increasing
Administration is liberal	Administration is conservative
Presidential election is approaching	Presidential election is far off

The Disproportionate Impact of Monetary Policy
Stock market analysts pay particular attention to monetary (as opposed to fiscal) policy for several reasons: first, monetary policy has differential industry effects. Second, monetary policy is usually easier (although not necessarily easy) to track

Figure 11.5   Monetary Coverage by the Press

M1 Surges $3.1 Billion, but Bonds Rise On Report That Borrowings From Fed Fell

By EDWARD P. FOLDESSY
Staff Reporter of THE WALL STREET JOURNAL

NEW YORK—The nation's money supply surged $3.1 billion, the Federal Reserve Board reported, leaving the growth of the weekly measure close to the upper limit of the Fed's target range.

But bond prices edged higher, as dealers were encouraged by other Fed figures indicating the banking network was relatively flush with funds. These figures showed that borrowings from the Fed by banks and savings institutions declined to an average of $512 million from the previous week's estimated $1 billion.

Credit Markets

Borrowings from the Fed are watched closely for clues to the central bank's credit policy. Still, many analysts cautioned against placing too much weight on the latest figure, saying the drop in borrowings might be only temporary. Some warned that the Fed may be forced to further tighten its credit hold, pushing interest rates higher, in order to slow the money supply's rapid growth and keep inflation in check.

'A Danger Signal'

The $3.1 billion surge in the basic money supply, known as M1, in the week ended June 4 "throws up a danger signal," said David M. Jones, an economist at Aubrey G. Lanston & Co. If money growth should exceed the central bank's target, "it will force the Fed to consider a future tightening move," he added.

Philip Braverman, chief economist at Briggs, Schaedle & Co., believes the Fed may already be in the process of a "passive" credit-tightening move, allowing market forces to push up the important interest rate on federal funds. "Money and credit growth has been excessive" and could easily "justify a Fed firming move," he said.

Nevertheless, prices of some Treasury bonds rose more than ½ point yesterday, or more than $5 for each $1,000 face amount of securities. The bellwether 30-year, 13¼% bond closed at 100 6/32, up from 99⅝ Wednesday. That lowered the yield to 13.22% from 13.30%. As recently as May 30, the bonds traded at 94 22/32 to yield 14%.

Interest Rates

Helping buoy credit markets recently have been signs that the economic expan-

sion is beginning to slow from its rapid first-quarter clip. Some analysts argue that a cooling of business activity will allow the Fed to avoid a tougher credit policy, at least temporarily.

Maury N. Harris, a vice president and economist at Paine Webber Group Inc., predicts interest rates will be little changed at least through summer. "Much of the rise in rates since the beginning of the year has been due to the surprisingly strong economic performance," he said. "As the economy moderates, the upward pressure on interest rates will abate," he said.

The gross national product, adjusted for inflation, is growing at a 3%-to-4% annual rate this quarter, Mr. Harris estimated. That would be down from the first quarter's 8.8% pace and would "dictate an unchanged credit policy," he said. The slowdown is sufficient to "prevent further interest-rate increases," he contends.

Federal Funds Rate

Kathleen Cooper, senior financial economist for Security Pacific National Bank, Los Angeles, disagrees. She contends interest rates will continue to rise this year, reflecting what she expects to be continued "high credit demand." The interest rate on federal funds, which are reserves banks lend each other, will increase to about 11¾% by the end of the year, she predicted. The funds rate strongly influences other interest rates. It hovered between 10⅞% and 11% much of yesterday, after averaging 10.85% in the week ended Wednesday.

"The Fed is focusing much more on the economy and credit growth than on the money supply" in setting policy, Miss Cooper said. Although the economic expansion has slowed from the torrid pace of the first quarter, it hasn't slowed enough to allow the Fed to relax its credit grip, she said.

"The best that we can hope for is that the Fed will stand pat," Miss Cooper said. She added that she expects "some pickup" in the economy this month and in the third quarter, pressuring the Fed to "tighten another notch" this summer.

Figures released by the Fed yesterday afternoon showed that the basic money measure, M1, averaged a seasonally adjusted $545.2 billion in the latest week, up from a revised $542.1 billion the previous week. The prior week's figure originally was estimated at $541.9 billion.

That left M1 only $1.4 billion below the upper end of the Fed's target range, which calls for 4% to 8% growth this year. The measure is the total of private checking deposits plus cash held by the public. Because it represents funds readily available for spending, M1 is considered by many analysts to be an important determinant of the economy and inflation.

Even with the latest weekly jump, monthly figures showed that M1 was within the Fed's target band in May. The Fed estimated that M1 averaged $541.1 billion last month, up from $535.3 billion in April.

Other figures showed that M2, a broader money-measure, rose $17.2 billion in May, while an even broader measure, M3, increased $24.2 billion.

Broader Money-Supply Measures

The Fed said M2 averaged $2.259 trillion in May, compared with $2.242 trillion a month earlier. M3 increased to an average of $2.815 trillion from $2.791 trillion. So far this year, M2 has grown at an annual rate of 7.1%, while M3 has expanded at a 9.7% clip. The central bank is seeking 6%-to-9% growth in each of the two measures this year.

Demand for credit also has been growing briskly. The Fed reported that the total debt of the nation's non-financial sector grew at a 13.4% annual rate in April, the latest period for which figures are available. The central bank's guideline calls for growth of 8% to 11% this year in the credit yardstick. According to the Fed, such debt outstanding averaged $5.431 trillion in April, up from a revised $5.371 trillion in March.

The Fed also reported that commercial and industrial loans on the books of the 10 leading New York City banks soared $1.11 billion in the week ended June 6. That contrasted with a $295 million decline the previous week and brought the total of such loans outstanding to $63.32 billion.

Commercial Paper Outstanding

Commercial paper, or corporate IOUs, outstanding in the U.S. fell $1.21 billion in the June 6 week to $213.51 billion. A week earlier such paper diminished by $650 million. The decline in the latest week, however, was due to a record drop in the amount of paper issued by banking concerns.

Paper issued by banking institutions and financial companies tumbled $3.34 billion in the latest week, while paper sold by non-financial companies jumped $2.13 billion.

Separately, the Fed disclosed that loans it made to troubled Continental Illinois National Bank & Trust Co. had been reclassified as "extended credit." The Continental loans have averaged $2 billion a day in recent weeks. They previously had been carried by the Fed as "adjustment borrowings," a designation assigned to loans that usually are granted banks that simply misjudged their reserve needs for a specific accounting period.

In the credit markets yesterday, most short-term interest rates were little changed. The Treasury's latest 26-week bill closed at 10.37% bid, down slightly from 10.40% Wednesday. The bid on the companion 13-week issue was unchanged at 9.88%.

On the corporate front, a $100 million offering of 15% first-mortgage bonds by Arizona Public Service Co. sold briskly, according to underwriters led by First Boston Corp. The issue, priced at 99.5 to yield 15.1% to maturity in 1994, is rated Baa-2 by Moody's Investors Service Inc. and triple-B-plus by Standard & Poor's Corp.

Also offered yesterday was a $250 million issue of extendible notes by Citicorp. The notes, carrying an initial rate of 13.6%, were priced at par. Holders have the right to redeem the securities in two years. At the same time, the bank holding company has the right to extend the maturity date to 1999. The issue is rated double-A-1 by Moody's and double-A by S&P.

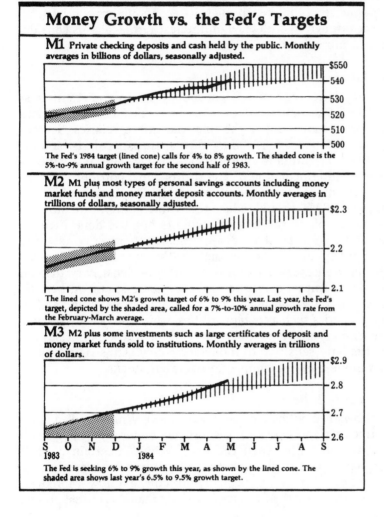

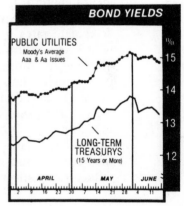

and perhaps easier to predict. The Fed's weekly monetary data releases are intensively analyzed by the financial press.[10] Moreover monetary policy can shift emphasis more quickly than can fiscal policy. Thus Fed action may have to shoulder the entire macroeconomic adjustment burden when political pressures inhibit discretionary fiscal policy. Third, an influential group of economists (monetarists largely associated with the University of Chicago) assert that money drives the economy while fiscal policy plays a more modest role. Fourth, monetary policy not only affects the stock market through its economic impact, but also has a more direct effect through its influence on interest rates.[11] Let us consider each of these matters in more detail.

Differential Industry Effects

Monetary policy works by rationing credit. Tight money not only raises interest rates (at least in the short run) but restricts loans to weaker credit risks and influences the allocation of funds among the financial intermediaries. Savings and loan associations and mutual savings banks (thrifts) are particularly hard hit when tight money causes depositors to move toward higher-yield investments such as money funds ("disintermediation"). The thrifts' large portfolios of low-yield long-term mortgages makes them quite vulnerable. Over time, a shift to adjustable rate mortgages (ARMs) should reduce this vulnerability. The move to deregulate rates has helped offset the loss of accounts but has done little to reduce the resulting profit squeeze. This disintermediation process not only depresses the thrifts' earnings, but also reduces the availability of mortgage money from which much of their business is derived. The thrifts' sensitivity to high interest rates and the adverse impact of disintermediation increases the real estate, construction, building materials, and major appliance industries' vulnerability to tight money. Other industries such as public utilities, which are heavily levered, and auto and farm machinery manufacturers, the bulk of whose purchases are financed, are also particularly sensitive to monetary policy. Thus tight money differentially affects various types of companies and their stocks.[12]

Monetary Policy is Easier to Follow

The financial press follows Fed policy closely (Figure 11.5). While the Fed itself has some difficulty tracking and controlling short-run monetary aggregates,[13] monetary policy is easier to follow than the lengthy and uncertain path of authorizations, appropriation and implementation of government expenditures. Tax legislation, fiscal policy's other side, is equally difficult to follow. Moreover, monetary policy's greater volatility leads to more signals than does fiscal policy.

Monetarists versus Fiscalists

Since Keynes published his *General Theory* in 1936, the monetarists have debated with those who emphasize the importance of fiscal policy (fiscalists).[14] While the fiscalists dominated the 1940s and 1950s, by the early 1960s the debate was again in full swing. The dispute continues although the issues may be narrowing. During much of the post-1936 period the fiscalists were far more influential in and out of government. Since the late sixties, however, both groups have had substantial influence. Most economists now agree that both monetary and fiscal policy affect the economy but disagree on their relative importance. Unless monetary and fiscal policy are working at cross purposes, both economic schools expect the same direction (if not the magnitude) of impact. Moreover, monetary and fiscal policies' conflicts usually arise because monetary policy is leading and fiscal policy will soon follow. Therefore investors, who are principally concerned with direction rather than magnitude, need not assess the relative merits of the monetarists' and fiscalists' arguments.

Monetary Policy's Direct Effect on the Stock Market

Monetary policy indirectly influences the stock market through its effect on the economy and corporate profits. It also has a direct effect in three related ways: first, since stock prices reflect the present value of expected future income streams, interest rates influence the rate at which stocks' expected incomes are discounted. Second, investors find bonds relatively more attractive as yields-to-maturity increase, thereby shifting some investors from stocks to bonds. Finally, higher interest rates mean higher borrowing costs for margin investors who will demand a higher expected return to justify the higher cost of financing their margin purchases. Thus higher interest rates should depress stock prices because they imply a higher discount rate, more attractive returns for bonds, and higher costs for margin debt. Lower interest rates have the opposite effect. Figure 11.6 illustrates the linkages between monetary policy and stock prices.

Figure 11.6 Links Between Monetary Policy and the Stock Market

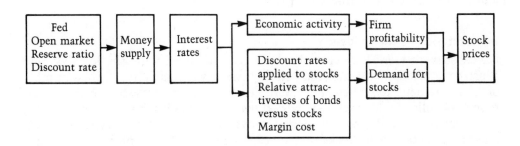

Empirical Research on Money/Stock Market Relationships

While everyone agrees that monetary policy affects the stock market, the relationship's dependability and time frame are highly controversial. Beryl Sprinkel (then with the Harris Trust and Savings Bank of Chicago, more recently Assistant Secretary of the Treasury) wrote two books on the money-stock price relationship.[15] Sprinkel argued that monetary policy shifts tended to lead stock price changes and thus generate useful timing signals. Sprinkel's empirical analysis only employed visual, impressionistic, and relatively simplistic evidence, however. In a more sophisticated (i.e., econometric) test, Homa and Jaffee estimated a constant-lag relationship between the money supply and a stock price index.[16] Using it to signal a switch between stocks and Treasury bills produced a higher after-commission return (8.6%) than a buy-and-hold strategy (7.6%). Several other researchers reached similar conclusions.[17] Malkiel and Quandt, in contrast, reported that when a revised and extended money supply data series was employed, a buy-and-hold strategy outperformed a switching strategy based on monetary signals. Moreover a model using economic variables related to corporate profits and sales (e.g., interest rates) outperformed predictions based solely on the money supply.[18]

Two subsequent studies sought to resolve the conflicts raised by the earlier work. First Rozeff, who identified various methodological flaws in the studies favorable to the money supply-leads-stock-price-movements hypothesis, concluded: "Stock prices do not lag behind growth rates of the money supply, nor would we expect them to do so in an efficient market."[19] In perhaps the most extensive study of the issue, Rogalski and Vinso noted several shortcomings in all the prior literature (including Rozeff):[20] Specifically, failing to remove serial correlation and not accounting for release lags and frequent revisions of monetary statistics. Their conclusions were, however, virtually identical to those of Rozeff: "[I]nformation concerning the actual rate of growth of the money supply is incorporated into stock returns as purported by various monetary portfolio theorists . . . [T]he stock market is efficient with respect to monetary information."[21] In still more recent studies Davidson and Froyen and Mitchell and Stansell reached similar conclusions.[22]

Interpretation of the Evidence

No subsequent work has seriously challenged the Rozeff and the Rogalski and Vinso conclusions that a monetary timing strategy is ineffective. Still, a number of issues remain unsettled. For example, since many investors believe that monetary policy yields useful signals, knowledge of their trading-patterns might help explain some day-to-day market movements.[23] Second, monetary signals may still help one trade stocks that are especially sensitive to interest rate/money supply moves. Third, most of the tests have only considered monetary signals in isolation. Possibly money supply data incorporated into a well-specified economic model (containing interest, unemployment, and inflation rates, for example) would yield more positive results. Finally, virtually all prior work has tested relations between actual (as opposed to anticipated)[24] money supply changes and stock market performance. Clearly stock prices and money supply changes are related but the lags seem to be short or nonexistent. Sorenson tested the timing value of predicted money supply changes, however. Utilizing Barro's[25] money growth-rate equation he found stock prices related to anticipated but not unanticipated changes in the money supply. He concluded that "[t]he potential ability of some analysts to form superior expectations of future money, and act on those expectations, may be the force which drives what has long been accepted as a direct relationship between money and stock prices."[26] Figlewski and Urich found that a simple average of twenty security dealer's forecasts of weekly money supply changes accurately predicted the direction of T-bill price changes.[27]

An Integrated Approach

Trading decisions based on actual monetary policy changes seem unlikely to outperform a buy and hold strategy. Accurately predicting monetary policy changes, supplementing the analysis with knowledge of other economic influences, and concentrating on interest-sensitive securities might prove more effective. Forecasted fiscal policy changes and other factors having a short-run economic impact might also be considered. In particular, consumer spending and business fixed plant, equipment, and construction spending often have substantial and sometimes unexpected economic effects. The Survey Research Center of the University of Michigan periodically surveys and reports on consumer sentiments.[28] Similarly, McGraw-Hill surveys and reports business capital expenditure plans (in a November issue of *Business Week*, a McGraw-Hill publication—Table 11.4), as does the Commerce Department (in the December *Survey of Consumer Sentiments*). The Conference Board compiles quarterly capital appropriation statistics (reported in *Manufacturing Industrial Statistics*). These forecasts are widely reported in the press.

Differing economic conditions' impacts on particular firms and industries might also be considered. Construction-related and other interest-sensitive companies are especially vulnerable to tight money. Moreover postponable expenditures (e.g., autos and consumer durables) are typically depressed by recessions, while other industries (e.g., utilities and beer) suffer only slightly. Few industries are truly recession proof, their own claims notwithstanding, but vulnerability to the economic climate does vary.[29] Recession-sensitive (e.g. smokestack) companies may be poor performers just before a downturn, while they generally rally just before an upturn.

While these suggestions seem logical, little or no relevant empirical research has yet tackled the issues. Success in using an understanding of economy/stock market relations will depend upon investors' astuteness vis-a-vis the

Table 11.4   McGraw-Hill Report

Spending plans shrink in major economic sectors

Plans for 1982 capital spending

	November '81 survey	March '82 survey
	Percent change from 1981	
All business	**9.6**	**6.9**
Mining	24.8	−3.1
Railroads	23.4	3.1
Rubber	21.2	11.5
Food & beverages	20.6	2.7
Nonferrous metals	18.2	−4.6
Petroleum	16.8	8.2
Communications & other	12.2	7.8
Electrical machinery	10.4	6.2
Autos, trucks & parts	10.2	2.6
Gas utilities	8.7	−3.5
Textiles	2.5	−0.9

Source: "Capital Spending Takes a Dive," *Business Week*, March 22, 1982. Reprinted by permission of McGraw-Hill, Inc.

market consensus. If the market-consensus analysis is effective, few investors are likely to do better. If market analysts frequently err avoidably, however, those with superior analytical abilities should profit. Clearly further research is needed.

THE INFLATION-STOCK MARKET RELATION

The stock market is influenced by both the business cycle and the inflation rate. While investors might seek to maximize their expected risk-adjusted return regardless of inflation, they should consider various investment types' differential inflation protection. For example, potential investors' propensities to spend (particularly on durables) may be affected by their expected real (noninflationary) returns. Second, since different investments may offer varying degrees of long-term inflation protection, some assets' appeals may depend on the expected long-term inflation rate. Third, investors who are able to anticipate changes in the inflation rate may be able to shift profitably between more and less inflation-resistant investments.[30]

The Wall Street View of Stocks as an Inflation Hedge

Until the 1970s, most analysts thought stocks offered substantial inflation protection. Stockbrokers and mutual fund salespeople argued that equity returns would tend to keep up with inflation better than would fixed-return securities.

Early thought often confused two rather different inflation-hedge concepts. According to one view, an inflation hedge's market value should rise with the general price level. Thus a perfect inflation hedge's real return should be independent of price changes. A perfect inflation hedge yielding 4% with stable prices would return 4% + x% for an inflation rate of x%. While few ever claimed that stocks offered complete protection, many believed that if consumer prices changed by x%, average stock would yield a% + bx% where b was some positive number less than unity. In a second form of the inflation-hedge concept, average long-run stock returns are expected to exceed the rise in the general price level. Thus capital would tend to be preserved in spite of inflation. This latter form is less strong, as it permits the market to be affected adversely (if temporarily) by high and/or rising inflation rates. In spite of media coverage of the 1970s experience with rapid inflation and poor stock market performance (Table 11.5), the view persists that stocks somehow still protect investors from inflation.[30]

Theoretical Underpinnings of the Stock Market Inflation-Hedge Hypothesis

To provide effective short- or long-run inflation-protection, companies must recapture higher costs through higher prices.[31] Stocks represent ownership of real assets whose replacement values and abilities to generate income may well rise with the price level. Thus if firms are able to raise their prices sufficiently, the real (inflation-adjusted) value of dividends and share prices may keep pace with price-level increases. A number of considerations limit their ability to raise prices by enough to preserve investment values, however.

For example, three aspects of our tax system penalize investment income at high inflation rates.[32] First, IRS requires that firms report as profits sums that reflect the difference between the historical cost and the replacement value of inventory, plant, and equipment. Inflation increases these differences and the profit tax on them. Thus, the real after-tax component of reported profits tends to fall as prices increase. Second, until indexing, inflation tended to push investors into higher marginal tax brackets, further increasing the penalty. Third, individuals must pay taxes on sums (dividends and capital gains) that often contain a substantial inflation component. Thus even if the before-tax return rose point for point with the inflation rate, the after-tax return would not. For example: a one-third tax rate applied to a 3% nominal return and zero-inflation (a 3% real return before taxes) provides a 2% after-tax real return. A 6% nominal return with a 3% inflation rate produces a real after-tax return of only 1%. A 9% nominal return and 6% inflation rate would yield a real after-tax return of 0%. For nominal returns above 9%, a 3% before-tax real return results in negative real after-tax returns. Borrowing makes the relationship considerably more complex, however. Randall has shown that high tax-bracket investors can usually enhance their yields by borrowing to finance capital-gains oriented investments.[33] Margin

Table 11.5   Media Publicity for Stock Return Record

There's no return like a real return

Adjust the numbers to reflect price increases, and many stocks have been lousy investments since 1972. Column five gives the bad news.

Company	Price 12/31/72	Price 12/31/81	Inflation-adjusted price 12/31/81	Inflation-adjusted total return value	9-year real return
Abbott Laboratories	$ 8.75	$27.00	$12.24	$15.06	72.1%
Aetna Life & Casualty	24.38	44.00	19.95	30.74	26.1
Alum Co of Amer	17.71	25.63	11.62	16.63	−6.1
Amax	21.92	47.25	21.43	31.52	43.8
Amerada Hess	18.88	24.13	10.94	13.56	−28.2
American Brands	21.06	36.75	16.67	31.92	51.6
Amer Electric Power	30.00	16.25	7.37	18.58	−38.1
American Express	64.88	44.13	20.01	27.16	−58.1
Amer Home Products	40.67	36.50	16.55	23.55	−42.1
AT&T	52.75	58.75	26.64	52.97	0.4
Anheuser-Busch Cos	55.25	41.13	18.65	23.98	−56.6
Atlantic Richfield	19.44	46.88	21.26	28.97	49.0
Baker International	8.47	38.00	17.23	19.20	126.7
Baxter Travenol Labs	27.88	33.50	15.19	16.40	−41.2
Boeing	5.56	22.50	10.20	14.39	158.8
Bristol-Myers	34.50	53.13	24.09	32.18	−6.7
Burlington North Inds	24.75	53.63	24.32	33.33	34.7
Caterpillar Tractor	44.33	55.50	25.17	33.69	−24.0
Cities Service	15.53	46.00	20.86	32.81	111.3
Coca-Cola	74.25	34.75	15.76	30.71	−58.6
Commonwealth Ed	35.88	19.88	9.01	21.94	−38.9
Conn General Ins	37.06	50.00	22.67	29.03	−21.7
Consolidated Ed	25.00	32.50	14.74	34.44	37.8
Cooper Industries	9.25	51.50	23.36	30.32	227.8
Deere & Co	22.88	35.50	16.10	23.57	3.0
Digital Equipment	30.58	86.50	39.23	39.22	28.3
Dow Chemical	25.38	26.25	11.90	16.46	−35.1
Dresser Industries	11.69	33.25	15.08	18.56	58.8
EI Du Pont	59.17	37.25	16.89	26.73	−54.8
Eastman Kodak	148.38	71.13	32.26	44.23	−70.2
Emerson Electric	45.63	45.38	20.58	26.95	−40.9
Exxon	21.88	31.25	14.17	25.95	18.6
Fluor	7.35	30.00	13.60	16.15	119.7
Ford Motor	63.70	16.75	7.60	14.44	−77.3
Gannett	25.67	36.13	16.38	21.06	−18.0
General Electric	72.88	57.38	26.02	38.18	−47.6
General Motors	81.13	38.50	17.46	35.51	−56.2
General Tel & Elec	30.13	32.00	14.51	29.31	−2.7
Georgia-Pacific	20.98	20.13	9.13	12.21	−41.8
Getty Oil	23.50	64.63	29.31	35.15	49.6
WR Grace	$26.50	$45.75	$20.75	$36.11	36.3%
Gulf Oil	27.00	35.38	16.04	30.41	12.6
Halliburton	23.38	52.13	23.64	27.27	16.6
Hewlett-Packard	21.63	39.63	17.97	18.72	−13.5
Hughes Tool	7.10	40.13	18.20	20.38	187.0
IBM	80.40	56.88	25.79	36.43	−54.7
International Paper	41.88	39.13	17.74	26.47	−36.8
IT&T	60.25	29.75	13.49	25.01	−58.5
Johnson & Johnson	43.50	37.13	16.84	19.70	−54.7
K mart	48.88	15.75	7.14	8.59	−82.4

Company	Price 12/31/72	Price 12/31/81	Inflation-adjusted price 12/31/81	Inflation-adjusted total return value	9-year real return
Kerr-McGee	32.94	37.38	16.95	20.25	−38.5
Eli Lilly	79.63	56.00	25.40	32.83	−58.8
Litton Industries	10.56	56.38	25.57	26.32	149.2
McDonald's	76.25	65.38	29.65	31.32	−58.9
Merck & Co	89.13	84.75	38.43	48.06	−46.1
Minn Mining & Mfg	85.63	54.50	24.72	32.94	−61.5
Mobil	18.50	24.13	10.94	19.22	3.9
Monsanto	49.63	70.13	31.80	49.46	−0.3
NL Industries	8.44	39.75	18.03	29.60	250.7
Occidental Pet	11.75	24.00	10.88	17.16	46.0
Pacific Gas & Elec	32.63	21.00	9.52	22.50	−31.0
JC Penney	90.38	28.63	12.98	18.68	−79.3
Pennzoil	17.83	48.00	21.77	34.52	93.6
PepsiCo	29.04	36.38	16.50	22.17	−23.7
Pfizer	42.88	53.25	24.15	31.93	−25.5
Philip Morris	29.56	48.75	22.11	28.16	−4.7
Phillips Petroleum	22.19	40.50	18.37	25.15	13.3
Procter & Gamble	111.50	80.38	36.45	48.81	−56.2
Raytheon	8.41	37.38	16.95	21.32	153.5
RJ Reynolds Inds	25.81	47.13	21.37	35.53	37.7
Rockwell Intl	16.19	32.75	14.85	26.72	65.0
Santa Fe Industries	11.08	21.13	9.58	15.66	41.3
Sears, Roebuck	58.00	16.13	7.31	11.06	−80.9
Shell Oil	13.72	44.00	19.95	30.17	119.9
SmithKline	14.60	67.63	30.67	55.88	282.7
Southern Calif Ed	27.75	28.75	13.04	30.17	8.7
Southern Co	20.13	12.00	5.44	14.26	−29.2
Standard Oil Calif	19.91	42.88	19.44	32.61	63.8
Standard Oil Ind	21.88	52.00	23.58	35.11	60.5
Standard Oil Ohio	11.55	41.50	18.82	23.49	103.4
Sun Co	17.75	45.50	20.63	30.41	71.3
Superior Oil	13.86	36.88	16.72	17.85	28.8
Tandy	2.88	33.75	15.31	15.33	432.3
Teledyne	7.84	138.50	62.81	62.80	701.1
Tenneco	29.00	33.50	15.19	27.17	−6.3
Texaco	37.50	33.00	14.97	29.11	−22.4
Texas Instruments	90.94	80.50	36.51	42.09	−53.7
Texas Oil & Gas	7.30	35.00	15.87	15.26	109.0
Texas Utilities	34.00	19.63	8.90	17.11	−49.7
Time Inc	15.81	38.25	17.35	24.93	57.7
Travelers	38.88	43.88	19.90	30.43	−21.7
Union Carbide	50.00	51.38	23.30	37.87	−24.3
Union Oil Calif	9.97	37.63	17.06	23.80	138.7
Union Pacific	17.25	52.00	23.58	32.18	86.6
United States Steel	20.33	29.88	13.55	22.24	9.4
United Technologies	22.25	41.75	18.93	29.77	33.8
Warner Comm	10.41	54.88	24.89	31.20	199.7
Westinghouse Elec	43.00	25.50	11.56	19.05	−55.7
Weyerhaeuser	28.19	29.00	13.15	16.91	−40.0
Xerox	149.25	40.50	18.37	23.44	−84.3

Source: Reprinted by permission of *Forbes* Magazine, February 15, 1983, © Forbes Inc., 1983.

restrictions and the scarcity of investments with reliable capital gains yields limit investors' abilities to exploit this ploy, however.

In addition to the inflation-imposed tax penalty, other considerations increase the difficulty of offsetting inflation's adverse effect. One might suspect that cost and price increases of x% would (neglecting tax-effects) approximately maintain the firm's financial position. In fact, however, higher prices and costs generally require a contemporaneous and disproportionate increase in capital to finance inventories, accounts receivable, and new plant and equipment.[34] Any increased revenues derived from higher prices come in more slowly. Moreover if higher inflation rates are associated with higher interest rates, both the amount and cost of financing tends to increase with inflation.[35]

Thus to offset the effect of taxes on nominal profits and to finance the increased capital requirements at higher interest rates, prices must be raised proportionally more than the direct cost increase. To offset the increased retained-earnings requirement (needed to support the additional borrowings) and the investor's inflation-imposed tax burden, prices must rise still more.

Many firms are, however, unable to raise prices sufficiently to recapture their increased production costs, to say nothing of increasing them sufficiently to offset tax and financing effects. The more rapid the inflation, the greater the likelihood of governmental action such as fiscal and monetary restraint, jawboning, and/or price controls or guidelines designed to reduce demand-side pressures, as well as supply-side efforts to increase efficiency and competition through regulatory reform. To the extent that these various policies succeed, even if only in the short-run, profits may also be reduced. Moreover, competition from substitutes whose costs may be more stable may limit firms' abilities to raise their prices. Finally, international competition tends to hold some prices down depending on the interplay of such factors as domestic versus international inflation rates; changes in exchange rates; tariffs and import quotas; and the foreign competition's pricing responses. Similar considerations influence the ability of domestic exporters to pass on their higher costs internationally. Thus both governmental pressure and foreign competition constrain many firm's opportunities to raise prices sufficiently to offset inflation's negative effect. Table 11.6 summarizes the various adverse stock market impacts of inflation.

Finally, two highly-regarded economists, Modigliani and Cohen, argue that investors make two basic errors in pricing securities in the presence of inflation.[36] First, investors are said to capitalize equity earnings incorrectly by comparing equities' current cash earnings with the nominal, rather than real, bond returns. Bond returns are fixed until maturity while profits and dividends tend to rise over time. Second, they contend that investors have failed to take proper account of inflation's impact on the real value of corporate debt. According to Modigliani and Cohen, these two alleged mispricing effects reduced the S&P 500 stock index by 50% in 1977. Writing in 1982, however, Cagen asserted that the market seemed to be as underpriced as it was alleged to be in 1977.[37]

In summary, stocks may for a variety of reasons perform less well during

Table 11.6   Inflation's Adverse Stock Market Impact

Tax Impact	Cost Impact	Price Impact
Corporate taxes are applied to historical cost plant, equipment and inventories	Greater capital needs for new plant, equipment accounts receivable and inventories	Resistance to price increases Government pressure to restrain prices
Investors are pushed into higher tax brackets*	Higher interest costs incurred on borrowings	Competition from substitutes
Individual taxes are applied to nominal dividend and interest income	Revenues come in more slowly	International competition

*Indexing, if retained, should help ameliorate this effect.

rapid-inflation periods. Taxes tend to reduce real after-tax profits because they are applied to noninflation-adjusted before-tax profits and may reduce the real investment return because they are applied to the nominal returns paid to investors. Some of the inflation-caused higher costs may not be quickly recaptured, even if prices are raised proportionally with costs. Cost increases may not always be passed on because of government pressure, competition from substitutes, and/or international competition. Finally, in an inflationary environment, the stock market itself may not price securities correctly.

While the above-stated considerations increase the difficulty of fully offsetting inflationary impacts, stocks need to provide a positive expected real return in order for firms to attract capital. The capital markets are supposed to assure sufficient capital availability for consumer-identified expansion candidates. Since investors have little incentive to invest at a loss, firms must be able to offer positive expected returns. If new investments yield positive real returns, the shares of firms owning equivalent existing capacity should be bid up to their replacement values. This process may not take place quickly, completely, or for all industries, but should on balance operate to provide adequate expansion and modernization capital. The less capital the system supplies, the more valuable is the existing capital in those industries where consumer demand is outstripping supply. Eventually this process should insure that an appreciable fraction of real returns are at an acceptable level.

Taken together, these various considerations suggest that the stock market's short-run inflation-adjustment process may be painful for investors. In the longer run, however, a functioning capitalist system must offer positive expected real after-tax returns, even in an inflationary environment.

Empirical Studies of Inflation/Stock Market Relations

In the first serious research on the stock market's inflation impact, Alchian and Kessel reported that net monetary debtor corporations experienced an increase in their equity value greater than that of net monetary creditors.[38] Net monetary debtors' assets whose nominal values are independent of price changes (such as money, time deposits, and bonds) are exceeded by their corresponding liabilities (such as loans, bonds outstanding, and accounts payable). Subsequently, Reilly, Johnson, and Smith found that the average real return on several well-known stock indexes was negative or below the indexes' long-term average return in each of five rapid-inflation periods.[39] Since two of the periods began during expansions and ended during recessions, two began during peacetime and ended during war, and one straddled the 1966 credit-crunch, non-inflationary factors may have contributed to the poor performance. In a third study, Keran found that inflationary expectations depressed stock prices (as measured by Standard & Poor's 500), which is inconsistent with an inflation-hedge theory.[40]

Cagan on the other hand, found that U.S. stock prices increased by 3% more annually than wholesale prices over 1871–1971.[41] Moreover, British and French stock prices outperformed the annual inflation rate (before adding dividends) by 1.3% and .1% respectively over similar periods. The degree of outperformance varied inversely with the three country's inflation rates, however. Moreover a typical group of German stocks purchased in 1914 would have lost three-fourths of their value by the end of the hyperinflation in 1924. Similarly, Branch reported that the stocks of those countries with the highest inflation rates tended to rise faster than those of countries with lower rates.[42]

In an update, Reilly, Smith, and Johnson reported that the stock market's inflation protection depended on the inflation rate's direction.[43] Thus stocks may perform better with a constant or declining rate than a rising rate. Similarly, Jaffee and Mandelker, and Nelson concluded that once the market adjusted to anticipated inflation, it generally provided an acceptable expected real return.[44] Unanticipated inflation rate-rises typically had a negative effect, however.

Unlike other researchers, Bodie defined common stocks' hedge value in terms of their ability to reduce the real return variability of a portfolio of one-year T-bills.[45] According to Bodie, only a short position in stocks would have reduced inflation risk. Unlike Albian and Kessel, Hong found no inflation-induced transfer from creditor- to debtor-companies but he did find a differential tax-induced transfer from business to government.[46]

A more recent study by Fama challenged all previous work in the area. Specifically Fama claimed that:

> The negative stock return-inflation relations are induced by negative relations between inflation and real activity which in turn are explained by a combination of money demand and the quantity theory of money.[47]

Both Fama's theoretical model and empirical tests seem to support his contention that the observed simple stock market/inflation relation results from the proxy effects of an underspecified model. Similarly Geske and Roll have developed and tested a model that explains the negative relation between stock returns and inflation as due to rational investors realizing the adverse impact of inflation on future economic policy.[48] Empirical studies by both Solnik and Gultekin support the Geske/Roll findings.[49]

Finally Hendershot used a theoretical model to test four separate inflation-related hypotheses designed to explain the post-1960s stock price decline: (1) Tax-law impacts on real share values; (2) Modigliani-Cohn inflation-induced valuation errors; (3) Increased uncertainty leading to a higher risk premium; and (4) Biases in the tax laws, valuation errors, and risk-premium impacts on real after-tax debt yields.[50] The first three explanations were not by themselves consistent with Hendershot's model and the observed historical behavior. An increase in the risk premium, coupled with the tax bias did, however, seem to fit the observed decline in real after-tax debt yields and real share values.

Assessment of the Evidence

Overall, the empirical work suggests that stocks tend to provide long-term inflation protection and possibly some short-term protection from anticipated inflation. Knowing that stock price rises may eventually offset inflation is, however, small comfort to investors who must sell before the market rebounds. If, as much of the research suggests, unexpected inflation rate rises depress stock prices, the real value of investments fall both with the rise in the price level and with the decline in the position's nominal value. Some investors may be able to ride out such market declines but others will not. Perhaps non-stock investments provide more dependable inflation protection.

THE INFLATION-PROTECTION OF OTHER INVESTMENTS

Stock-related securities such as common stock mutual funds, convertible bonds, preferreds and options probably behave much like stocks vis-a-vis inflation. Debt securities, commodities, real estate, and collectibles, in contrast, may offer different levels of inflation protection.

Both Jaffee and Mandelker, and Levi and Makin found that the returns on fixed income securities tended to compensate for anticipated but not for unanticipated inflation.[51] This conclusion, while similar to that reached in several stock market inflation studies, has a very different implication. Unlike stocks, debt securities mature. An inflation rate rise that depresses security prices locks in stock investors, while bond principal may be reinvested at maturity. For example: purchasers of bonds yielding 10% in an 8% inflation environment might see inflation rise to 12% and equivalent debt yields increase to 14% shortly thereafter. With short maturities, such an unanticipated inflation rate rise will only cause a modest return loss. Even a longer-maturity bond's principal will eventually become available for reinvestment.

That debt securities, particularly short-term debt securities, seem to provide a degree of current inflation protection leads us to wonder about their long-run performance. For the 1926–74 period, Ibbotson and Sinquefield found an average inflation-adjusted return of 6.1%, 1.4%, 1.0%, and 0.0% for common stocks, long-term corporates, long-term governments, and Treasury bills respectively.[52] Thus the securities that offer the greatest short-run protection (T-bills) yield the least long-term and vice versa.

Bodie and Rosanski reported that for 1950–76, commodity futures prices tended to move inversely with stock prices and to do best during periods of rapid inflation.[53] The commodity markets are rather far afield for most security-market investors, however.

Real estate might well provide substantial inflation protection. Since replacement costs of developed property vary with labor and material costs (correlated with consumer prices), real estate construction costs should rise with consumer prices. These increased construction costs should eventually affect real estate values, although demand considerations may have a greater short-term effect. Fama and Schwartz, in fact, find that real estate offers a complete hedge against both expected and unexpected inflation.[54] Since real estate has its own set of drawbacks (e.g., illiquidity), its inflation-protection history is not in itself sufficient justification for investing in real estate.

The same underlying factors that cause consumer prices to rise may increase collectible prices. That is, higher money incomes chasing a fixed quantity of collectibles should bid prices up more rapidly the higher the inflation rate. Collectors' items have generally done well in the recent inflationary environment.[55] Whether this performance is because of or in spite of the high inflation rate requires further study.

While stocks in the aggregate offer little or no inflation protection, Bernard and Frecka find that certain stock portfolios have provided significant inflation hedges.[56] Selecting stocks on the basis of their 1969–74 performance, they were able to form portfolios that effectively hedged against the 1974–79 inflation.

SUMMARY AND CONCLUSIONS

The economy's effect on the stock market interests investors who want to understand and/or forecast the market's behavior. Both monetary and fiscal policy have a substantial economic impact. Economic policy attempts to maintain price stability and full employment. Stimulation is designed to reduce unemployment, while restraint is applied when inflation is the primary concern. Which is the overriding goal varies with a variety of considerations, including their relative severities and the policymakers' judgments. Understanding the government's likely reactions should help one forecast economic activity and perhaps stock market performance. Relations between monetary policy and the stock market receive particular attention. Monetary policy affects the stock market both indirectly through its economic effect and directly via its interest-rate effect. While some earlier work seemed to find monetary signals helpful, the most careful and comprehensive recent studies found no usable lag between changes in monetary policy and changes in stock prices. Trading on predicted monetary policy changes may well be profitable, however.

Inflation/stock market relations were also considered. According to pre-1970 Wall Street wisdom, companies could offset inflation's impact by raising their own prices. Tax effects, government anti-inflation pressure and international competition, however, often make implementing the necessary price rises difficult. Still, to allocate capital properly, the market must offer the prospect of a positive real after-tax return. Some empirical research suggests that in the short run, unanticipated rises in inflation have affected the stock market adversely. In the longer run, however, average market returns may exceed the inflation rate. Debt securities, particularly short-term debt securities, seemed to provide more effective protection from the adverse inflation impacts, but their long-term return only marginally exceeded the inflation rate. Both commodities and real estate offer intriguing inflation protection, but present security market investors with a variety of other problems.

REVIEW QUESTIONS

1. Trace the relationship between the economy and the stock market.
2. Discuss the uses and limitations of econometric and leading-indicator forecasts of economic activity. How might they be used in stock market analysis?
3. Explain how fiscal policy operates through taxes and government spending.
4. Discuss the Fed's three principal tools and how they are used to affect the economy.
5. Discuss how one can predict changes in fiscal and monetary policy.
6. Why do stock analysts give so much attention to monetary policy?
7. Why might one think stock prices adjust for inflation? What factors may retard this adjustment?
8. Summarize the findings of past work linking inflation and stock price performance.
9. How do bonds, real estate, and commodities behave relative to inflation?

REVIEW PROBLEMS

1. Obtain a number of economic forecasts for the most recently completed year and compare them with that year's actual result. Write a report.
2. Update Figures 11.1, 11.2 and 11.3 and comment on the implications of the newer data vis-a-vis politically acceptable levels of unemployment and inflation.
3. Analyze the current state of the economy. Forecast GNP, unemployment and inflation for next year. Write a report explaining your forecast. Read it a year later.

4. Assess the current state and forecast the future direction of monetary and fiscal policy. Review fiscal and monetary policy six months later. Explain why your forecast erred. If it didn't, repeat the process for the next succeeding six months.

5. Assemble a list of five interest-sensitive stocks. Plot their performance relative to a series of interest rates. Write a report.

6. Update Table 11.5 with current stock prices and returns. Compare the returns with those of T-bills over the same period.

7. Assemble a list of fifteen stocks and group them into three categories: those best able to pass costs along, those least able to pass cost along and those with an average ability to pass costs along. Plot their monthly returns and the monthly inflation rates over three years. Write a report.

NOTES

1. J. Schall, "To Divine is to Err: Econometricians Prosper Despite Bum Forecasts," *Barron's,* March 23, 1982, pp. 15, 30, 35; L. McGinley, "Forecasters Overhaul 'Models' of Economy in Wake of 1982 Errors," *Wall Street Journal,* February 17, 1983, pp. 1, 20; F. Black, "The Trouble with Econometric Models," *Financial Analysts Journal,* March/April 1982, pp. 29–37.

2. A. Malabre, "Economists Start Revising Some Indexes," *Wall Street Journal,* December 10, 1981, p. 33; *Business Week,* "Why Economic Indicators are Often Wrong," *Business Week,* October 17, 1983, pp. 168–169.

3. B. Heathcotte and V. Apilado, "The Predictive Content of Some Leading Economic Indicators for Future Stock Prices," *Journal of Financial and Quantitative Analysis,* March 1974, pp. 247–258.

4. D. Simonson, "Comment: The Predictive Content of Some Leading Economic Indicators for Future Stock Prices," *Journal of Financial and Quantitative Analysis,* March 1974, pp. 259–261.

5. W. McConnell, *Investment Manager's Review,* Wertheim & Company, Inc., March 23, 1981, p. 10; G. Moore, *Business Cycles Inflation and Forecasting,* National Bureau of Economic Research Studies in Business Cycles No. 240, Ballinger Publishing, Cambridge, Massachusetts, 1980.

6. *Business Week,* "A New Economic Index that Provides Early Forecasts," *Business Week,* November 14, 1983, pp. 154–155.

7. A. Malabre, "How to Become Your own Economist: Facts that Count are Easy to Get and Understand," *Wall Street Journal,* March 21, 1977, p. 36.

8. P. MacAvoy, "The Underground—No Recession There," *New York Times,* July 4, 1982, p. F3; S. Maital, "Only the Shadow Knows the Underground Economy's Real Size," *Barron's,* November 4, 1983, pp. 16, 44, 46, 48.

9. R. Hershey Jr., "When Is Unemployment 'Natural'?," *New York Times,* October 25, 1982, p. 416; J. Lubdin, "As Joblessness Rises, Economists Wonder Why There's Little Outcry," *Wall Street Journal,* May 27, 1982, p. 31; K. Abraham, "Structural/Frictional vs. Deficient Demand Unemployment: Some New Evidence," *American Economic Review,* September 1983, pp. 708–724.

10. L. Asinof, et. al., "Fed Watching Grows in the Markets Spurring Frenzied Anxious Trading," *Wall Street Journal,* November 8, 1982, pp. 31, 47; G. Marcial and B. Riemer, "The Friday Follies of Wall Street's Fed Watchers," *Business Week,* August 29, 1983, p. 20; *Business Week,* "Where Wall Street's M1 Junkies Get Their Weekly Fix," *Business Week* October 3, 1983, pp. 114–116; T. Petzinger Jr., "More Concerns Hire Fed Watchers to Interpret Central Back's Policies," *Wall Street Journal,* October 21, 1983, p. 31.

11. F. Wright, "The Link Between Money and Stock Prices," *Financial Analysts Journal*, May/June 1976, pp. 35–45.

12. M. Jochuk and W. Petty, "The Interest Sensitivity of Common Stock Prices," *Journal of Portfolio Management*, Winter 1980, pp. 19–25.

13. S. Edgar, "Product Control is a Problem at the Fed," *Financial Analysts Journal*, January/February 1974, pp. 82–91; B. Moore, "The Difficulty of Controlling the Money Stock," *Journal of Portfolio Management*, Summer 1981, pp. 7–14.

14. J. M. Keynes, *The General Theory of Employment Interest and Money*, Macmillan, London, 1936.

15. B. Sprinkel, *Money and Markets: A Monetarist's View*, Irwin, Homewood, Ill., 1971; *Money and Stock Prices*, Irwin, Homewood, Ill., 1964.

16. K. Homa and D. Jaffe, "The Supply of Money and Common Stock Prices," *Journal of Finance*, December 1971, pp. 1045–1066.

17. M. Hamberger, and L. Kochin, "Money and Stock Prices: The Channels of Influence," *Journal of Finance*, May 1972, pp. 231, 249; M. Keran, "Expectations Money and the Stock Market," *Federal Reserve Bank of St. Louis*, January 1971, pp. 16–31; F. Reilly and J. Lewis, "Monetary Variables and Stock Prices," Working Paper #38, University of Kansas, Lawrence, March 1971; Rudolph, "The Money Supply and Common Stock Prices," *Financial Analysts Journal*, March/April 1972, pp. 19–25; M. Gupta, "Money Supply and Stock Prices: A Probabilistic Approach," *Journal of Financial and Quantitative Analysis*, January 1974, pp. 57–68.

18. B. Malkiel and R. Quandt, "Selected Economic Indicators and Forecasts of Stock Prices," Finance Resource Center, research memorandum #9, Princeton University, Princeton, NJ, 1971; J. Pesando, "The Supply of Money and Common Stock Prices: Further Observations on the Econometric Evidence," *Journal of Finance*, June 1974, pp. 909–922; B. Malkiel and R. Quandt, "The Supply of Money and Common Stock Prices: Comment," *Journal of Finance*, September 1972, pp. 921–926; R. Cooper, "Efficient Capital Markets and the Quantity Theory of Money," *Journal of Finance*, June 1974, pp. 887–908.

19. M. Rozeff, "Money and Stock Prices' Market Efficiency and the Lag in Effect of Monetary Policy," *Journal of Financial Economics*, September 1974, p. 301.

20. R. Rogalski and J. Vinson, "Stock Returns, Money Supply and the Direction of Causality," *Journal of Finance*, September 1977, pp. 1017–1030.

21. *Ibid.*, pp. 1027–1028.

22. L. Davidson and R. Froyen, "Monetary Policy and Stock Returns: Are Stock Market's Efficient?," *Federal Reserve Bank of St. Louis Review*, March 1982, pp. 3–12. C. Mitchell and S. Stansell, "Stock Yields, Bond Yields, and the Money Supply: A Study of the Causal Relationships," *Review of Business and Economic Research*, Winter 1982, pp. 46–54.

23. T. Ulrich and P. Wachtel, "Market Response to the Weekly Money Supply Announcements in the 1970s," *Journal of Finance*, December 1981, pp. 1063–1072; B. Cornell, "The Money Supply Announcements Puzzle: Review and Interpretation," *American Economic Review*, September 1983, pp. 644–657; T. Herman, "MI Mania Inks Fed, But Monetary Data Still Rattle Markets," *Wall Street Journal*, January 24, 1984, pp. 1, 19.

24. P. Phaff, "Evaluation of Some Money Stock Forecasting Models," *Journal of Finance*, December 1977, pp. 1639–1646.

25. R. Barro, "Rational Expectations and the Role of Monetary Policy," *Journal of Monetary Economics*, January 1976, pp. 1–32; "Unanticipated Money Growth and Unemployment in the United States," *American Economic Review*, March 1977, pp. 101–115; "Unanticipated Money, Output, and the Price Level in the United States," *Journal of Political Economy*, August 1977, pp. 549–580.

26. E. Sorensen, "Rational Expectations and the Impact of Money upon Stock Prices," *Journal of Financial and Quantitative Analysis*, December 1982, pp. 649–662.

27. S. Figlewski and T. Urich, "Optimal Aggregation of Money Supply Forecasts: Accuracy, Profitability and Market Efficiency," *Journal of Finance*, June 1983, pp. 695–710.

28. G. Katona, *Psychological Economics*, Elsevier, New York, 1975.

29. J. Curley, "Games, Other Luxuries Sell Well As Slump Slows Sales of Durables," *Wall Street Journal*, May 6, 1982, pp. 31; T. O'Donnell and S. Kichen, "Strong-Arming the Recession," *Forbes*, July 5, 1982, pp. 99–106.

30. B. Malkiel, "Common Stocks—The Best Inflation Hedge for the 1980's," *Forbes*, February 18, 1980.

31. J. Gipson, "Growth on the Demand Curve: The New Kind of Growth," *Journal of Portfolio Management*, Winter 1980, pp. 46–48.

32. M. Feldstein, "Inflation and the Stock Market," *American Economic Review*, December 1980, pp. 839–847; G. Benson, "The Synergistic Impact of Taxes and Inflation on Investment Return," *Financial Analysts Journal*, March/April 1973, pp. 74–75; U. Yaar, D. Palmon and M. Marcus, "Stock Prices Under Inflation with Taxation of Nominal Gains," *Financial Review*, Winter 1980, pp. 38–54; J. McCain, "The Interaction Between Federal Income Taxes and Inflation," *Nebraska Journal of Economics and Business* Spring 1982, pp. 27–38.

33. M. Randall, "Investment Planning in an Inflationary Environment," *Financial Analysts Journal*, January/February 1981, pp. 68–70.

34. P. McCauley, "The Quick Asset Effect: Missing Key to the Relation Between Inflation and the Investment Value of the Firm," *Financial Analysts Journal*, September/October 1980, pp. 57–66; B. Gale and B. Branch, "Cash Flow Analysis: More Important Than Ever," *Harvard Business Review*, July–August 1981, pp. 131–136.

35. J. Linter, "Inflation and Security Returns," *Journal of Finance*, May 1975, pp. 259–280.

36. F. Modigliani and R. Cohen, "Inflation, Rational Valuation and the Market," *Financial Analysts Journal*, March/April 1979, pp. 24–44.

37. P. Cagan, *Stock Prices Reflect the Adjustment of Earnings for Inflation*, NYU Monograph Series in Finance and Economics, 1982.

38. Alchian and R. Kessel, "Redistribution of Wealth through Inflation," *Science*, September 4, 1959, p. 538.

39. F. Reilly, G. Johnson, and R. Smith, "Inflation, Inflation Hedge, and Common Stocks," *Financial Analysts Journal*, January/February 1970, pp. 104–110.

40. M. Keran, "Expectations, Money and the Stock Market," *Federal Reserve Bank of St. Louis*, January 1971, pp. 16–31.

41. A. Malabre, "The Outlook," *Wall Street Journal*, December 17, 1974, p. 1; P. Cagan, "Common Stock Values and Inflation: The Historical Record of Many Countries," *National Bureau Report Supplement*, March 1974, pp. 1–10.

42. B. Branch, "Common Stock Performance and Inflation: An International Comparison," *Journal of Business*, January 1974, pp. 48–52.

43. F. Reilly, R. Smith and G. Johnson, "A Correction and Update Regarding Individual Common Stocks as Inflation Hedges," *Journal of Financial and Quantitative Analysis*, December 1975, pp. 871–880.

44. J. Jaffee and A. Mandelker, "The 'Fisher Effect' for Risky Assets: An Empirical Investigation," *Journal of Finance*, May 1976, pp. 447–458; C. Nelson, "Inflation and Rates of Return on Common Stocks," *Journal of Finance*, May 1976, pp. 471–482; J. Ang, J. Chua and A. Desai, "Evidence that the Stock Market Adjusts Fully for Expected Inflation," *The Journal of Financial Research*, Fall 1979, pp. 97–109; S. Moosa, "Inflation and Common Stock Prices," *Journal of Financial Research*, Fall 1980, pp. 115–128; C. Chu and D. Whitford, "Stock Market Returns and Inflationary Expectations: Additional Evidence for 1975–1979," *Journal of Financial Research*, Fall 1982, pp. 261–271.

45. Z. Bodie, "Common Stocks as a Hedge Against Inflation," *Journal of Finance*, May 1976, pp. 459–470.

46. H. Hong, "Inflation and Market Value of the Firm: Theory and Tests," *Journal of Finance*, September 1977, pp. 1031–1048.

47. E. Fama, "Stock Returns, Real Activity, Inflation and Money," *American Economic Review*, September 1981, pp. 545–565.

48. R. Geske and R. Roll, "The Fiscal and Monetary Linkage Between Stock Returns and Inflation," *Journal of Finance*, March 1983, pp. 1–34.

49. B. Solnik, "The Relation Between Stock Prices and Inflationary Expectations: The International Evidence," *Journal of Finance*, March 1983, pp. 35–48; N. Gultekin, "Stock Market Returns and Inflation: Evidence From Other Countries," *Journal of Finance*, March 1983, pp. 49–66; N. Gultekin, "Stock Market Returns and Inflation Forecasts," June 1983, pp. 663–673.

50. P. Hendershott, "The Decline in Aggregate Share Values Taxation: Valuation Errors, Risk, and Profitability," *American Economic Review*, December 1981, pp. 909–922; R. Pindyck, "Risk, Inflation and the Stock Market," *American Economic Review*, June 1984, pp. 335–351.

51. J. Jaffe and G. Mandelker, "Inflation and the Holding Period Returns on Bonds," *Journal of Financial and Quantitative Analysis*, December 1979, pp. 959–979; M. Levi and J. Makin, "Fisher, Phillips, Friedman and the Measured Impact of Inflation and Interest," *Journal of Finance*, March 1979, pp. 35–52.

52. R. Ibbotson and R. Sinquefield, "Stocks, Bonds, Bills and Inflation: Year-by-Year Historical Returns, (1926–1974)," *Journal of Business*, January 1976, pp. 11–47.

53. Z. Bodie and V. Roasanki, "Risk and Return in Commodities Futures," *Financial Analysts Journal*, May/June 1980, pp. 27–40; Z. Bodie, "Commodity Futures as a Hedge Against Inflation," *Journal of Portfolio Management*, Spring 1983, pp. 12–17.

54. E. Fama and W. Schwertz, "Asset Returns and Inflation," *Journal of Financial Economics*, November 1977.

55. T. O'Donnell, "Stocks or Collectables," *Forbes*, September 15, 1980, pp. 70–71; J. Ang, J. Chua, and W. Reinhart, "Monetary Appreciation and Inflation-Hedging Characteristics of Comic Books," *Financial Review*, May 1983, pp. 196–205.

56. V. Bernard and J. Frecka, "Evidences of the Existence of Common Stock Inflation Hedges," *Journal of Financial Research*, Winter 1983, pp. 301–312.

12 Stock Market Timing and Forecasting

The stock market seems to respond both to economic (business cycle, money supply, inflation, interest rates, etc.) and non-economic forces. Indeed stock prices often appear to swing between extremes of optimism and pessimism. This chapter explores whether such moods can be identified and used to trade profitably. We first consider the stock market's tendency to overreact and then discuss efforts to recognize such overreactions while they are underway. Declines from previous highs, market PE ratios and their relation to interest and inflation rates, behavior during recessions, the election-year cycle, official pronouncements, margin rate changes, company stock repurchases, Dow Theory, and investment advisors are all examined in a search for reliable market-timing devices. Then various technical indicators (data series or combinations of data series which are purported to forecast market turns) are discussed in some detail. Specifically short interest, odd-lot trading, premiums and discounts on closed-end investment companies, specialist short selling, mutual fund cash positions, secondary distributions, the *Barron's* confidence index, floor trader activity, and the Treasury bill rate are all explored in the context of several relevant empirical studies. We then examine additional market indicators: the short-term trading index, urgent selling index, January indicator, advisors' sentiments indicator, and advance/declines. Finally Monday-Friday price patterns are discussed.

DOES THE STOCK MARKET OVERREACT?

When asked to predict stock market performance, J. P. Morgan once replied: "It will continue to fluctuate." Anyone who has followed stocks understands the irony of this statement. While the market's direction may be difficult to predict, its continued volatility is not. Stock prices often change dramatically. Specific stock groups frequently go through fads. At one time, a stock may rise on a rumor that the firm was entering the nursing home (or gambling, motor homes, genetic engineering, etc.) industry while later that same industry is anathema to the market. News sometimes has almost no impact while at other times the market is just looking for an excuse to move. To attribute such gyrations to a careful analysis of new information (market efficiency) seems questionable at best.

298

While most investors would probably agree that the market has an emotional side, some supporting evidence is called for. In this regard Malkiel examined the implications of early 1960s growth-stock pricing.[1] From the December 1961 peak to the June 1962 trough the Standard and Poor's 425 Industrial Average declined 28.5%, while an index of high-quality growth stocks (constructed by Malkiel) fell by 52.2%. Assuming an eventual decline to the economy's growth rate, Malkiel determined the required current-rate growth needed to justify the market price. Over the December 1961–June 1962 period the average required years of abnormal growth for Malkiel's growth-stock sample fell from 6 to 2 1/2 as their average multiple declined from 62.9 to 24.9. Changes in these companies' earning-prospects seemed unlikely to have caused such drastic reevaluations.

In a more sophisticated study of a similar phenomona, Shiller found that if real stock prices and dividends are stationary stochastic processes, stock price volatility is inconsistent with market efficiency.[2] Specifically, changes in real dividends are far too modest to account for the historical pattern of real stock price changes in an efficient market. A number of popular authors also believe that the market has become especially volatile as the role of institutions has grown.[3]

Are Overreactions Identifiable While They Are Happening?

Baylis and Bhirud followed up on Malkiel's work by suggesting the number of years of above-average growth needed to justify current multiples (which they called the "gamma" factor) be used as an investment tool.[4] Noting that the gamma factor for the institutions' growth-stock favorites increased markedly over the 1967-73 period, they wondered if the market was overreacting. At about the same time Silen and Safir expressed a similar opinion in *Barron's* as did Loomis in *Fortune*.[5] Soon thereafter these so-called top-tier stocks followed the rest of the market into a deep depression.[6] Thus whether by superior insight or luck, a number of analysts correctly identified this particular emotional peak. More recently Joseph Granville flashed a sell signal to his subscribers when the Dow hit a four-year high of 1004.69 on January 6, 1981. The Dow fell 23.80 points the next day on record volume. While it did reach a high of 1024.05 in late April of 1981, the subsequent trend was clearly down (reaching a low of 776.92 on August 12, 1982). Granville had also called an earlier market bottom when he turned bullish on April 21, 1980, with the Dow at 759.13. The Dow climbed 30.72 the following day beginning the advance which led to the four-year high of January 6, 1981. Indeed Baesel, Shows, and Thorp found that Granville's six market timing signals over the December 1978-January 1981 period were significantly better (statistically) than chance.[7] These impressive Granville forecasts contrast sharply, however, with his relatively poor prior and subsequent timing record and record in selecting individual stocks.[8] Moreover, the publicity of Granville's successes gave him considerable market influence. Thus rather

Table 12.1   News Events and Stock Market Reactions (Dow-Jones Industrial Average)

		Close Trading Day Before	Same Day Close	Close Trading Day After	3 Trading Days Later	21 Calendar Days Later
Korean war*	6-24-50	224.35	213.94	212.07	206.72	197.63
Eisenhower heart attack	9-24-55	487.45	445.56	465.93	468.68	416.13
Egypt seizes Suez Canal*	7-26-56	514.13	515.85	512.30	517.81	517.19
Hungarian revolt*	10-23-56	485.27	485.05	482.67	486.06	486.69
Sputnik I	10-4-57	465.82	461.70	452.42	451.40	435.15
U-2 shot down*	5-1-60	601.70	599.61	607.73	608.32	623.66
Berlin Wall erected*	8-12-61	722.61	718.93	716.18	721.84	718.72
Cuban missile crisis*	10-22-62	573.29	568.60	558.06	570.86	624.41
John Kennedy assassinated	11-22-63	732.65	711.49	743.52	750.52	760.17
Dominican Republic invasion*	4-28-65	918.16	918.86	918.71	922.11	932.12
Israel-Arab war*	6-5-67	863.31	847.77	862.71	873.20	872.11
U.S.S. Pueblo seized*	1-23-68	871.71	864.77	862.23	865.06	831.77
Soviets invaded Czechoslovakia*	8-20-68	887.66	888.67	888.30	896.13	919.38
Cambodian invasion*	4-30-70	737.39	736.07	733.63	709.74	665.25
U.S. mines North Vietnam harbors*	5-9-72	937.84	925.12	931.07	941.83	971.18

*International political (war-related) events.

Source: D. Dorfman, "Heard on the Street," *Wall Street Journal*, May 18, 1972. Reprinted by permission of *Wall Street Journal*, © Dow Jones & Company, Inc., 1972. All Rights Reserved.

than predicting, Granville may have caused the January 1981 selloff.[9] Since some analysts will always be predicting an up market and others predicting a fall, some will be correct just by chance.

More Evidence on Overreactions

A *Wall Street Journal* study of reactions to fifteen dramatic news events also suggests a tendency for the market to overreact. Most of these events made headlines but had no lasting market impact (Table 12.1).

Table 12.2, which reports the annual performance of S&P's 500 average, further illustrates the market's volatility.

Annual price changes varied from a +45% in 1954 to a −27.1% in 1974. Only four of thirty-four annual moves are within 3% of the overall average (8.5%). Clearly stock prices fluctuate greatly from year to year. For example, the 14% decline in 1957 was followed by a 38% gain and 1974's 27% decline was succeeded by a 29% rise. Fluctuations such as these reflect the market's tendency to react vigorously to short-term factors. In fact Table 12.2, which relates only to year-end price changes, understates the extent of the market's fluctuations. Table 12.3 presents within-year high and low price data.

The long-term upward trend tends to mask considerable within-year movement. For example, the index recorded a low of 34.58 in January 1955 and a high of 46.41 in November of the same year. In 1975 the index varied from 62.28 to

Table 12.2   Annual Performance of Standard & Poor's 500

Annual Changes Year-End	Standard & Poor's 500 Stocks	Annual Changes Year-End	Standard & Poor's 500 Stocks
12/31/50	+15.0%	12/31/67	+20.1
12/31/51	+16.3	12/31/68	+7.7
12/31/52	+11.8	12/31/69	−11.4
12/31/53	−6.6	12/31/70	+0.1
12/31/54	+45.0	12/31/71	+10.8
12/31/55	+26.4	12/31/72	+18.2
12/31/56	+2.6	12/31/73	−21.1
12/31/57	−14.3	12/31/74	−27.1
12/31/58	+38.1	12/31/75	+29.0
12/31/59	+8.5	12/31/76	+19.2
12/31/60	−3.0	12/31/77	−13.0
12/31/61	+23.1	12/31/78	+1.1
12/31/62	−11.8	12/31/79	+12.3
12/31/63	+18.9	12/31/80	+25.9
12/31/64	+13.0	12/31/81	−9.7
12/31/65	+9.1	12/31/82	+14.7
12/31/66	−13.1	12/31/83	+17.3

79.80. Looking at each year's mean index value suggests an upward trend. Noting the differences between highs and lows of the same and succeeding years reveals substantial short-term variability, however. Moreover, most individual stocks and portfolios experience considerably greater year-to-year return variability.

Taken together, the preceding review of stock market performance illustrates the market's pervasive time series variability. An unemotional market reacting only to relevant newly public information should be less volatile. The observed volatility does not in and of itself *prove* that the market overreacts but does at least *suggest* that a mood-based market timing strategy would be effective. This leads into the next topic: How can market extremes be identified; or can they?

BUY CHEAP AND SELL DEAR: WHEN ARE STOCKS CHEAP?

Buying and selling at the appropriate times is at least as important as identifying misvalued securities. Most mutual funds' relatively unspectacular performance illustrates the difficulty of anticipating major market moves. Treynor and Mazuy, for example, found that none of the 57 mutual funds studied was able to anticipate market moves successfully.[10] Still, the rewards from accurate timing encourage us to search for any shred of useful evidence.

We can begin by lowering our sights a bit. No one should expect to identify the market's tops and/or bottoms consistently. Some investors may be able to develop a feel for when stocks are too high or too low, but even this may be expecting too much. After the 1929 crash, stocks continued to sink lower and lower as what seemed like bargain prices were later shown to be expensive (Table 12.4). A similar, if somewhat shorter-run, phenomenon occurred during the market decline of 1973–1974.

Table 12.3   Standard & Poor's 500 Stock Composite Index (1941–1943 = 10)—Annual Data

	DAILY CLOSING PRICES			EARNS. PER SHARE	DIVS. PER SHARE	BOOK VALUE* PER SHARE	PE RATIO	DIVIDEND YIELD		
Year	High	Low	Last	$	$	$	Last	High	Low	Last
1983	172.65	138.34	164.93	14.07	7.09	130.00	11.7	5.1	4.1	4.3
1982	143.10	103.75	140.64	12.65	6.87	123.00	11.1	6.2	4.8	4.9
1981	138.10	112.80	122.60	15.24	6.63	117.20	8.1	5.8	4.7	5.4
1980	140.30	98.22	135.80	14.86	6.16	108.30	9.2	6.3	4.5	4.7
1979	111.30	96.13	107.90	14.86	5.65	18.71	7.3	5.9	5.2	5.6
1978	107.00	86.90	96.11	12.33	5.07	89.72	7.8	5.7	9.9	5.1
1977	107.00	90.71	95.10	10.89	4.69	82.21	8.7	5.2	3.9	5.1
1976	107.80	90.90	107.50	9.91	4.05	72.26	10.8	4.2	3.6	3.9
1975	95.61	70.04	90.19	7.96	3.08	70.84	11.3	5.3	3.9	4.1
1974	99.80	62.28	69.94	9.25	3.66	67.81	7.6	5.8	3.5	5.3
1973	120.24	92.16	97.55	8.16	3.38	62.84	12.0	3.7	2.6	3.4
1972	119.12	101.67	118.05	6.42	3.15	58.34	18.5	2.6	3.1	2.7
1971	104.77	90.16	102.09	5.70	3.07	55.28	17.9	2.9	3.4	3.0
1970	93.46	69.29	92.15	5.13	3.14	52.65	18.0	3.4	4.5	3.4
1969	106.16	89.20	92.06	5.78	3.16	51.70	15.9	3.0	3.5	3.4
1968	108.37	87.72	103.86	5.76	3.07	50.21	18.0	2.8	3.5	3.4
1967	97.59	80.38	96.47	5.33	2.92	47.78	18.1	3.0	3.6	3.0
1966	94.06	73.20	80.33	5.55	2.87	45.51	14.5	3.1	3.9	3.6
1965	92.63	81.60	92.43	5.19	2.72	43.50	17.8	2.9	3.3	2.9
1964	86.28	75.43	84.75	4.55	2.50	40.23	18.6	2.9	3.3	2.9
1963	75.02	62.69	75.02	4.02	2.28	38.17	18.7	3.0	3.6	3.0
1962	71.13	52.32	63.10	3.67	2.13	36.37	17.2	3.0	4.1	3.4
1961	72.64	57.57	71.55	3.19	2.02	34.87	22.4	2.8	3.5	2.8
1960	60.39	52.30	58.11	3.27	1.95	33.74	17.8	3.2	3.7	3.4
1959	60.71	53.58	59.89	3.39	1.84	32.26	17.7	3.0	3.4	3.1
1958	55.21	40.33	55.21	2.89	1.75	30.65	19.1	3.2	4.3	3.2
1957	49.13	38.98	39.99	3.37	1.79	29.44	11.9	3.6	4.6	4.5
1956	49.74	43.11	46.67	3.41	1.74	26.53	13.7	3.5	4.0	3.7
1955	46.41	34.58	45.48	3.62	1.64	25.09	12.6	3.5	4.7	3.6
1954	35.98	24.80	35.98	2.77	1.54	22.01	13.0	4.3	6.2	4.3
1953	26.66	22.71	24.81	2.51	1.45	20.76	9.9	5.4	6.4	5.8
1952	26.59	23.09	26.57	2.40	1.41	20.15	11.1	5.3	6.1	5.3
1951	23.85	20.69	23.77	2.44	1.41	18.66	9.7	5.9	6.8	5.9
1950	20.43	16.65	20.41	2.84	1.47	16.77	7.2	7.2	8.8	7.2
1949	16.79	13.55	16.76	2.32	1.14	15.17	7.2	6.8	8.4	6.8
1948	17.06	13.84	15.20	2.29	0.93	14.53	6.6	5.5	6.7	6.1
1947	16.20	13.71	15.30	1.61	0.84	12.49	9.5	5.2	6.1	5.5

*S&P 400

Source: Reprinted by permission of Standard & Poor's Corporation.

Table 12.4   1929 Crash and Recovery

	CLOSING PRICES				
	Sept. 3, 1929	Nov. 13, 1929	July 8, 1931	July 8, 1932	July 8, 1933
Dow Jones Industrials	381.17	198.69	143.83	41.22	105.15
Dow Jones Railroads	189.11	128.07	81.21	13.23	55.67
AT&T	302 1/2	207	177 3/8	72 1/8	132
Anaconda	130 7/8	70 1/2	25 3/4	4	21 1/4
Bethlehem Steel	136 3/4	79 1/4	48 1/8	8 3/8	47 5/8
DuPont	215	90	86	22 3/8	80 3/4
Erie Railroad	90 3/4	42 3/4	22 7/8	3	20 1/8
General Motors	71 3/4	36 1/8	37 3/8	7 3/4	32 1/2
IBM	241 3/4	112 1/2	147	54 1/2	139
ITT	147 1/8	53 1/2	32 3/8	3 7/8	19 1/2
Montgomery Ward	134 3/8	49 7/8	19 1/2	4 3/8	27 3/4
Radio Corp. (RCA)	98 1/8	28 3/4	17	3 5/8	12
Sears	171	81 3/8	55 1/8	10 1/4	44 1/8
U.S. Steel	257 5/8	151 1/2	96 1/8	21 1/2	65 1/4
Warner Brothers	60 1/2	30 1/4	7 1/4	5/8	6 3/4
Westinghouse	285 7/8	105	67	15 7/8	54 5/8
Zenith	45 1/2	10 1/8	2 3/4	1/2	2 1/4

Source: G. Gilmar, "A Day to Remember: When the Worst Bear Market Ever Came to No End,"
Barron's, July 5, 1982. Reprinted by permission of *Barron's*, © Dow Jones & Company, Inc., 1982.
All Rights Reserved.

Table 12.5   Yearly Highs and Lows of Dow Jones Averages

	INDUSTRIALS		TRANSPORTATION		UTILITIES	
	High	Low	High	Low	High	Low
1984 (prelim)	1286.64	1086.57	612.63	444.03	134.83	122.25
1983	1284.65	1027.04	590.04	434.24	140.08	119.51
1982	1070.55	776.92	455.69	292.12	122.83	103.22
1981	1029.05	824.01	447.38	335.48	117.81	101.28
1980	1000.17	759.13	381.08	233.69	117.34	96.05
1979	897.61	796.67	271.77	205.78	109.78	98.24
1978	907.74	742.12	261.49	199.31	110.98	96.35
1977	899.75	800.85	264.64	199.60	118.67	104.97
1976	1014.79	858.71	237.03	175.69	108.67	84.52
1975	881.81	633.04	174.57	146.47	87.07	72.02
1974	891.66	577.60	202.45	125.93	95.09	57.95
1973	1051.70	788.31	228.10	151.97	120.72	84.42
1972	1036.27	889.15	275.71	212.24	124.14	105.05
1971	950.82	797.97	248.33	169.70	128.39	108.03
1970*	842.00	631.16	183.31	116.69	121.84	95.86
1969	968.85	769.93	279.88	169.03	139.95	106.31
1968	985.21	825.13	279.48	214.58	141.30	119.79
1967	943.08	786.41	274.49	205.16	140.43	120.97
1966	995.15	744.32	271.72	184.34	152.39	118.96

Table 12.5   Continued

	INDUSTRIALS		TRANSPORTATION		UTILITIES	
	High	Low	High	Low	High	Low
1965	969.28	840.59	249.55	187.29	163.32	149.84
1964	891.71	766.08	224.91	178.81	155.71	137.30
1963	767.21	646.79	179.46	142.03	144.37	129.19
1962	726.01	535.76	149.83	114.86	130.85	103.11
1961	734.91	610.25	152.92	131.06	135.90	99.75
1960	685.47	566.05	160.43	123.37	100.07	85.02
1959	679.36	574.46	173.56	146.65	94.70	85.05
1958	583.65	436.89	157.91	99.89	91.00	68.94
1957	520.77	419.79	157.67	95.67	74.61	62.10
1956	521.05	462.35	181.23	150.44	71.17	63.03
1955	488.40	388.20	167.83	137.84	66.68	61.39
1954	404.39	279.87	146.23	94.84	62.47	52.22
1953	293.79	255.49	122.21	90.56	53.88	47.87
1952	292.00	256.35	112.53	82.03	52.64	47.53
1951	276.37	238.99	90.08	72.39	47.22	41.47
1950	235.47	196.81	77.89	51.24	44.26	37.40
1949	200.52	161.60	54.29	41.03	41.31	33.36
1948	193.16	165.39	64.95	48.13	36.04	31.65
1947	186.85	163.21	53.42	41.16	37.55	32.28
1946	212.50	163.12	68.31	44.69	43.74	33.20
1945	195.82	151.35	64.89	47.03	39.15	26.15
1944	152.53	134.22	48.40	33.45	26.37	21.74
1943	145.82	119.26	38.30	27.59	22.30	14.69
1942	119.71	92.92	29.28	23.31	14.94	10.58
1941	133.59	106.34	30.88	24.25	20.65	13.51
1940	152.80	111.84	32.67	22.14	26.45	18.03
1939	155.92	121.44	35.90	24.14	27.10	20.71
1938**	158.41	98.95	33.98	19.00	25.19	15.14
1937	194.40	113.64	64.46	28.91	37.54	19.65
1936	184.90	143.11	59.89	40.66	36.08	28.63
1935	148.44	96.71	41.84	27.31	29.78	14.46
1934	110.74	85.51	52.97	33.19	31.03	16.83
1933	108.67	50.16	56.53	23.43	37.73	19.33
1932	88.78	41.22	41.30	13.23	36.11	16.53
1931	194.36	73.79	111.58	31.42	73.40	30.55
1930	294.07	157.51	157.94	91.65	108.62	55.14
1929	381.17	198.69	189.11	128.07	144.61	64.72
1928***	300.00	191.33	152.70	132.60	—	—
1927	202.40	152.73	144.82	119.29	—	—
1926	166.64	135.20	123.33	102.41	—	—
1925	159.39	115.00	112.93	92.98	—	—

  * Jan. 2, 1970 Transportation Average replaced Railroad Average.
 ** From June 2, 1938, the Utility Average was based on 15 stocks instead of 20 as formerly.
*** On March 7, 1928, the list of rails was increased to 20 from 12.

Declining market trends do eventually reverse, however. One would like to buy when the market has completed most of its downward movement but has not yet risen much above its low. If the precise bottom is not usually identifiable, perhaps buying can at least be concentrated in depressed periods. Such a strategy requires some idea of when stocks are near their cyclical lows.

Declines from a Previous High

Investment analysts continually compare average stock prices with their prior levels in hopes of finding evidence that will help them forecast the future. A basic source are the Dow's annual highs and lows since 1925, shown in Table 12.5. Table 12.6 reports the major declines since 1919. Purchases near these bottoms were generally superior to purchases at most other times. The problem, however, is to identify when the market is near a low.

Table 12.6   Major Market Declines

	DJIA High	DJIA Low	Down (%)
1984	1286.64	1086.57	16%
1981–82	1024.05	776.92	24
1976–78	1014.79	742.12	27
1973–74	1051.71	577.60	45
1971	950.82	797.97	16
1968–70	985.21	631.16	36
1966	995.15	744.32	25
1961–62	734.91	535.76	27
1960	685.47	566.05	17
1957	520.77	419.79	19
1948–49	193.16	161.60	16
1946	212.50	163.12	23
1939–42	155.92	92.92	40
1937–38	194.40	98.95	49
1929–32	381.17	41.22	89
1919–21	119.62	63.90	46

The post-1960 experience is revealing. In the 1961–62 crash, the Dow fell from 734 to 535, while the 1966 decline was from 955 to 744. In 1968–70 the Dow declined from 985 to a 1970 low of 631. In 1971 the market fell from a high of 950 to a low of 797. The Dow declined from a peak of 1051 in 1973 to a low of 577 in December 1974. The 1976–78 drop was from 1015 to 742. In 1981–82 the Dow declined from 1024 to 776. The Dow also dropped from 1287 to 1087 in 1984. In percentage terms the declines were 27%, 25%, 36%, 16%, 45%, 27%, 24%, and 16%. One who bought when the market was off 15% would have been near the low twice and far from it six times. Those who bought when the market had declined 25% would have missed the 1969–70, 1981–82, and 1984 bottoms. One waiting for a 35% drop might buy stocks only once a decade. Apparently past trading patterns provide very little help with timing.

The Market PE Ratio as a Signal

The market average PE ratio, which measures relative prices, might be used to identify tops and bottoms. For example, the Dow PE ratio's rise from 12.1 in 1957 in 24.2 (a level seen only once during the post World War II period) in 1961 was clearly overdone. In retrospect, the subsequent fall to 16.2 might have been expected. In 1966 the ratio rose to 18.1, only to fall to 13.5 in the same year. The ratio fell from 16.9 to 11.7 in 1969–70, and in 1971 it fell from 17.3 to 16.2. In 1973–74 the ratio fell from 16.5 to 6.1. It rose somewhat from that low but ended the decade at 8. It has stayed within the 6 to 9 range during the 1980–81 period but exploded in 1982–83, reflecting large losses by some of the component firms (Table 12.7).

Table 12.7   Dow Jones Industrial Average, Earnings, P/E and Dividends Quarterly

		DOW JONES INDUSTRIAL AVERAGE				
	Quarter Ended	Clos. Avg.	Qtrly Earns	12-Mth. Earns	P/E Ratio	Qtrly Divs.
1984	June 29	1132.40	35.02	102.07	11.1	14.98
	Mar. 30	1164.89	30.12	87.38	13.3	13.94
	Sept. 28	1206.71				14.72
1983	Dec. 30	1258.64	13.89	72.45	17.4	14.77
	Sept. 30	1233.13	23.04	56.12	30.0	13.98
	June 30	1221.96	20.33	11.59	105.4	13.70
	Mar. 31	1130.03	15.19	9.52	118.7	13.88
			72.45			56.33
1982	Dec. 31	1046.54	d2.44	9.14	114.4	13.03
	Sept. 30	896.25	d21.49	35.15	25.5	13.44
	June 30	811.93	18.26	79.90	11.2	13.75
	Mar. 31	822.77	14.82	97.13	8.5	13.92
			9.15			54.14
1981	Dec. 31	875.00	23.56	113.71	6.9	13.73
	Sept. 30	849.98	23.26	123.32	6.9	13.73
	June 30	976.88	35.49	128.91	7.6	14.19
	Mar. 31	1003.87	31.40	123.60	8.1	13.86
			113.71			56.22
1980	Dec. 31	963.99	33.17	121.86	7.9	14.40
	Sept. 30	932.42	28.85	111.58	8.4	13.53
	June 30	867.92	30.18	116.40	7.5	13.20
	Mar. 31	785.75	29.66	120.77	6.5	13.23
			121.86			54.36
1979	Dec. 31	838.74	22.89	124.46	6.7	13.87
	Sept. 28	878.67	33.67	136.26	6.4	12.51
	June 29	841.98	34.55	128.99	6.5	12.49
	Mar. 30	862.18	33.35	124.10	6.9	12.11
			124.46			50.98
1978	Dec. 29	805.01	34.69	112.79	7.1	14.34
	Sept. 29	865.82	26.40	101.59	8.5	11.41
	June 30	818.95	29.66	91.37	9.0	11.62

Table 12.7   Continued

	Quarter Ended	Clos. Avg.	Qtrly Earns	12-Mth. Earns	P/E Ratio	Qtrly Divs.
		DOW JONES INDUSTRIAL AVERAGE				
	Mar. 31	757.36	22.04	89.23	8.5	11.15
			112.79			48.52
1977	Dec. 30	831.17	23.49	89.10	9.3	13.24
	Sept. 30	847.11	16.18	89.86	9.4	10.73
	June 30	916.30	27.52	97.18	9.4	11.41
	Mar. 31	919.13	21.91	95.51	9.6	10.46
			89.10			45.84
1976	Dec. 31	1004.65	24.25	96.72	10.4	12.13
	Sept. 30	990.19	23.50	95.81	10.3	9.85
	June 30	1002.78	25.85	90.68	11.1	10.19
	Mar. 31	999.45	23.12	81.87	12.2	9.23
			96.72			41.40
1975	Dec. 31	852.41	23.34	75.66	11.3	9.63
	Sept. 30	793.88	18.37	75.47	10.5	9.05
	June 30	878.99	17.04	83.83	10.5	8.97
	Mar. 31	768.15	16.91	93.47	8.2	9.81
			75.66			37.46
1974	Dec. 31	616.24	23.15	99.04	6.2	10.45
	Sept. 30	607.87	26.73	99.73	6.1	9.43
	June 28	802.41	26.68	93.26	8.6	8.87
	Mar. 29	846.68	22.48	89.46	9.5	8.97
			99.04			37.72
1973	Dec. 31	850.86	23.84	86.17	9.9	10.62
	Sept. 28	947.10	20.26	82.09	11.5	8.36
	June 29	891.71	22.88	77.56	11.5	8.27
	Mar. 30	951.01	19.19	71.98	13.2	8.08
			86.17			35.33
1972	Dec. 29	1020.02	19.76	67.11	15.2	8.99
	Sept. 29	953.27	15.73	62.15	15.3	7.76
	June 30	929.03	17.30	58.87	15.8	7.87
	Mar. 30	940.70	14.32	56.76	16.6	7.65
			67.11			32.27
1971	Dec. 31	890.20	14.80	55.09	16.2	7.85
	Sept. 30	887.19	12.45	53.43	16.6	7.51
	June 30	891.14	15.19	53.45	16.7	7.80
	Mar. 31	904.37	12.65	52.36	17.3	7.70
			55.09			30.86

This fluctuating market PE experience illustrates the unreliability of a multiple-based timing strategy. Holmes' composite PE average of 14 of all NYSE stocks (1871–1971) provides a very rough guide at best.[11] Perhaps from a historical perspective a Dow of 10 or less is below average. From 1954 to '73 the Dow did not go lower than 9. In 1949 and 1951 the ratio was around 7, and has since 1974 often been even lower. The low multiple value of 6 to 7 during 1974 and again in 1976-81 was largely due to concern over high interest rates and

rapid inflation. The ratio was above 13 in the 1930s, and until 1947 it was usually above 10. The 1934 multiple of almost 90 and over 110 in late 1982 reflected
abnormally low aggregated earnings. That is, large losses by a few firms (Chrysler, International Harvester, U.S. Steel, etc.) offset most of the other firm's earning. Thus little or no pattern is revealed. Determining when the market PE is
in unsustainably high territory is equally difficult. As the multiple rises close
to or above 18, a reversal seems increasingly likely. The market has turned down
on many occasions when the Dow's multiple was well below 18, however.

Clearly the market multiple has been an undependable basis for timing
decisions. Since what seems like a very high (or low) multiple in one economic
climate may be quite justified in another, perhaps multiple analysis could usefully be combined with some knowledge of the prevailing conditions and
expectations.

The Gray Approach: PE Ratios Relative to Interest Rates

Since market interest rates form the basis for discounting expected income
streams, Gray contends that such rates and stock multiples should be related.[12]
Noting that a stock's return is equal to its dividend yield plus its appreciation
rate, and that the dividend yield equals its earning/price ratio (1/PE) times its
payout ratio, Gray wrote:

$$i = \frac{D}{E} \frac{(E)}{(P)} + G$$

where: i = return on stock
   D = dividend per share
   E = earnings per share
   P = price per share
   G = long-term growth rate in price per share (assumed to
      average 5%)

Note: D/E = payout ratio (assumed to average 55%)
   E/P = earnings-price ratio

Gray found that the higher the AA utility bond yield, the lower the spread
between i (the "Common Stock Sustainable Return") and bond yields. This spread
is regressed on the yield and the deviation from the values predicted by the
regression plotted over time (Figure 12.1).

Gray suggests using a spread greater than .2% below or above its predicted
value (the shaded areas of Figure 12.1) as a buy or sell signal. During the test-
periods the predictions were generally correct directionally. The reliability of
Gray's and similar devices should be assessed cautiously, however. While many
trading rules generate abnormal returns over the test period, some trading strategies will "work" once, just by chance, particularly if the data are "mined". A
rule derived from one period's analysis and tested successfully over a second
period is much more likely to reflect a continuing relationship.

Gray did not test his approach on a second period nor did he take account

Figure 12.1 Gray's Stock Price Movement Results

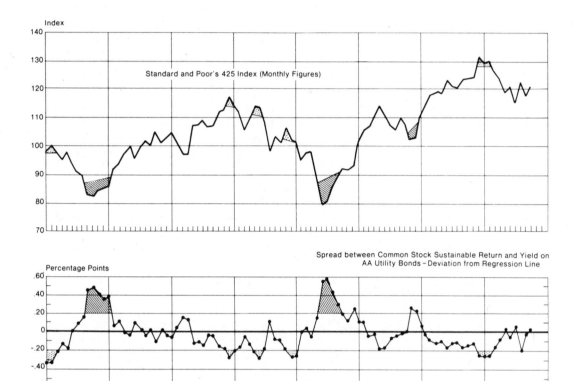

Source: W. Gray, "The Application of Discontinued Rates in Forecast; Returns for Stocks and Bonds," *Financial Journal*, May–June 1974. Reprinted with permission.

of commissions and other trading costs. A predictor that seems correct directionally may not be sufficiently reliable or predict moves of great enough magnitudes to overcome the extra trading costs. Moreover rules should only be tested with information when it would have been available. Since Gray's study and most of the other work discussed herein fail to take any of these precautions, their results are only suggestive.

PE Ratios Relative to Inflation Rates
Miller, the chief investment officer of Donaldson, Lufkin and Jenrette advocates a trading strategy based on the relation of stock prices to inflation rates.[13]

Figure 12.2 PEs and Inflation

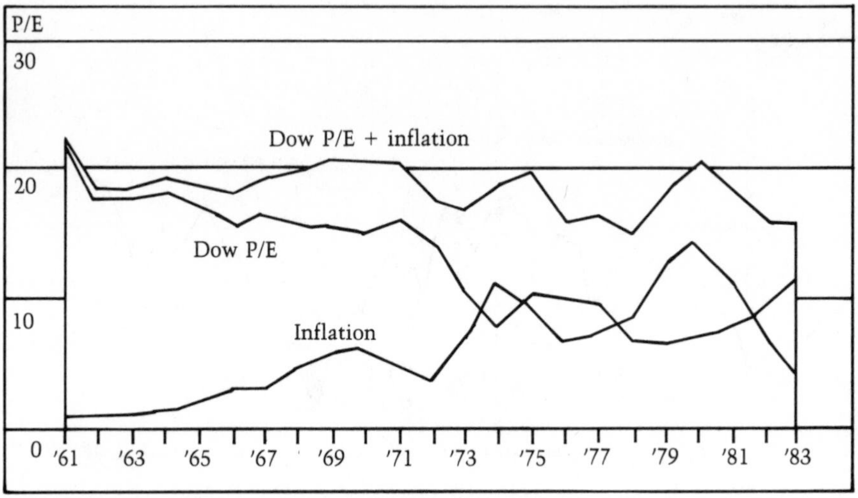

Source: S. Kichen, "The Rule of 20," *Forbes*, July 20, 1983. Reprinted by permission of *Forbes* Magazine, © Forbes Inc., 1983.

Specifically he asserts that the Dow Jones Industrial average's PE ratio added to the inflation rate tends to move up or down toward 20. That is, since inflation tends to reduce the real return on stocks, PEs tend to decline with rises in the inflation rate and vice versa. Figure 12.2 seems to support Miller's view. As the sum rises toward 20 it becomes more likely to decline. Note, however, that the actual average of the sum is 18.5 not 20. Moreover, like Gray, Miller has not carefully tested his approach.

Market Behavior During Recession

Stock market performance during recessions and the subsequent recoveries may follow a predictable pattern. Cullity examined seven postwar economic contractions (1949, 1954, 1958, 1961, 1963, 1967, and 1970) five of which were official recessions as defined by the National Bureau of Economic Research (NBER).[14] The 1963 and 1967 contractions are unofficial mild pauses. Two important conclusions emerged from Cullity's study. First, a pattern of rising markets during recessions is revealed (Figure 12.3). Second, stock price advances are more vigorous after more severe contractions. Somewhat more recently Malabre contended that the market usually turns up when the economy is still deep in a recession and goes nowhere in the subsequent recovery.[15] Piccini, who studied 13 twentieth century business cycles, found ". . .investors can often sell stocks without penalty as much as eight months before an expansion peaks and begin repurchasing six months after a recession has begun."[16] While buying

Figure 12.3 Recovery Patterns of New York Stock Exchange Composite Index

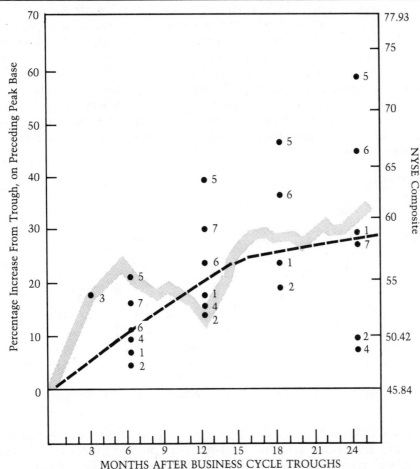

Arabic numerals identify recovery periods arranged according to the severity of the preceding recessions, beginning with the mildest. The periods start with business cycle troughs as follows: 1, January 1963; 2, June 1967; 3, November 1970; 4, February 1961; 5, August 1954; 6, October 1949; 7, April 1958.

■■■Median of previous recoveries that followed mild or moderate recessions. The unbroken line indicates present expansion.

Source: J. Cullity, "Stock Price Recoveries Following Recessions: A Second Look," *Financial Analysts Journal*, January–February 1974. Reprinted with permission.

after the economic recovery begins does not require a forecast, selling before an economic peak assumes an ability to predict economic cycles. Thus Piccini's findings are only modestly helpful to those who cannot forecast the economy's direction.

The Election-Year Cycle

Administrations frequently stimulate the economy in presidential election years and then put on the breaks following the voting. As a result, notes C. Rolo, "[s]ince 1948, the economy has peaked seven months, on average, after Presidential Election Day and sunk to its low 11 months later."[17] Indeed "[o]ver the 1961–78 period, stocks returned an average 21.7 percent in the year beginning two years prior to a presidential election, 15 percent in the year of the election, 3.6 percent in the year immediately following and −15.2 percent in the second following year."[18] Thus if this pattern persists, one should expect market lows one and a half to two years after a presidential election and highs about six months after (Figure 12.4).

Figure 12.4 The Election-Year Cycle

Post-election sags, pre-election fling

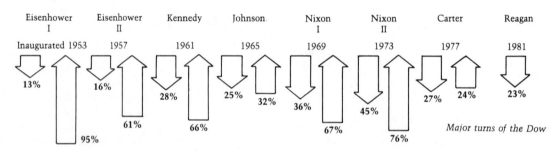

Source: C. Rolo, "Anticipates Major Ups and Downs Moves," *Money* Magazine, June 1982. Reprinted with permission.

Riley and Laksetich, who studied a variety of Wall Street election-year stock cycle folklore, found that positive short-run performance generally followed a Republican's election and negative followed that of a Democrat.[19] They also reported that the market generally rose after the election outcome was known but fell after an incumbent lost. They even found that ". . .rules triggered by a Republican victory and/or the anticipation of such victory, consistently earned positive returns."[20]

Official Comments, Margin Rate Changes and Company Stock Repurchases

Government officials (President, Secretary of Treasury, Chairman of the Council of Economic Advisors, Fed Chairman, etc.) sometimes comment publicly on the level of the stock market. Such pronouncements may either reflect inside information about future economic policy or be designed to bolster the stock market for political purposes. As with everyone else's advice, investors should listen to but not rely upon government officials' opinions.

Changes in the margin rate are also sometimes used as timing signals. According to this view, as expressed by Burke, the Fed usually lowers the margin rate near the bottom:

> In recent decades, each reduction in margin requirements has been associated with a rise in stock market credit, and ultimately with a rise in stock prices, although sometimes with a considerable lag. Margin requirements were cut in January 1958, July 1960, July 1962, May 1970, and December 1971, and in each case the end result was a sharp reversal of the previous downward movement of credit and stock prices. Of course, other more important factors were present in each case, including a general easing of credit conditions. Thus margin policy may have some forecasting powers.[21]

Another bit of evidence on the market's state relates to firm repurchases of their own stock. Before about 1960, many repurchases were to facilitate acquisitions, stock dividends, and conversions. More recent purchases, however, are viewed primarily as ". . .a good investment of excess cash."[22] Companies often repurchase their stock at bargain prices, although they do not always pick the bottom.[23]

Dow Theory
Dow Theory as originated by Charles Dow is one of the earliest approaches to market timing. Charles Dow was the founder and first editor of the *Wall Street Journal*. He hypothesized that the market moves in trends that are revealed by the relations between two indexes of market performance. Specifically he asserted that a continuing trend may be identified by looking first for a new high in an index defined as primary (such as the Dow Jones Industrial Average) and then seeking confirmation from a second (such as the Dow Jones Transportation Average). Thus if the Industrials reach a new high followed quickly by a new high for the Transports, the up trend is said to be intact. In a study of the 1971–80 period, Glickstein and Wubbles found the technique to have produced useful timing signals.[24]

Table 12.8 summarizes the preceding discussion of market timing approaches.

Market Forecasters
Rather than trying to identify the tops and bottoms themselves, many investors rely on those who make their living forecasting the market. Depending on professional investment managers and stock market analysts has a number of drawbacks (unimpressive past records, substantial fees, and the problem of deciding which to use). Similar difficulties arise for market-timing experts. Nonetheless such services are a significant part of the investment scene.

Stock market forecasters utilize a variety of techniques. One well-known market forecaster with a reasonably successful recent record is Francis Kelly,

Table 12.8   Market Timing Approaches

Declines from a previous high	Market's previous declines exhibit no consistent pattern
Market PE ratio	Movements in the market PE are an undependable basis for investment-timing
Gray Approach	Market PEs relative to interest rates may offer useful timing-signals
Rule of 20	The market PE plus the inflation rate may tend toward 18.5
Behavior during recessions	Market tends to turn up early in a recession
Election-Year Cycle	Market tends to peak shortly after a presidential election
Official Pronouncements	Administration officials may occasionally make statements that are useful to investors
Margin Rate Changes	Announcements of margin rate changes may help one time the market
Company Stock Repurchases	Large stock repurchases by many firms may signal that a market bottom is near
Dow Theory	An uptrend is confirmed when a high in the primary index (i.e. DJIA) is soon followed by a high in the secondary index (i.e. DJTA)

chairman of Dean Witter's investment policy committee. Kelly, a fundamentalist, bases his forecasts on share prices relative to future prospects. He is also a contrarian who is happiest when no one agrees with him.

Martin Zweig, one of the best known forecasters and frequent panelist on "Wall Street Week" (Public Television's weekly stock market program), publishes a newsletter with over 8,000 subscribers. Zweig is best described as an eclectic-technician. He relies heavily on his assessment of Fed policy and various technical market indicators. His advice is often very short term. Those who follow Zweig do a lot of trading but have, according to Connelly, tended to make money.[25] Furthermore Zweig topped Hulbert's advisor ratings in both 1981 and 1982.[26] He did not do nearly as well in 1983, however (see Table 10.3).

Paul Desmond, president of *Lowery's Reports*, continues a technical advisory service that began in 1938. The "Lowery method" attempts to detect supply (selling power) and demand (buying power) through changes in price and trading volume.

Robert Farrell, vice president and manager of market analysis of Merrill Lynch, considers himself a "market psychologist." He tries to track the behavior of institutional investors and advocates trading against their emotional reactions.

With 10,000 subscribers for his *Professional Tape Reader*, Stan Weinstein has one of the widest followings. His recommendations are based largely on his readings of 47 technical indicators.

The following list of market forecasters (assembled from a *Money* article by Peter Kadis),[27] may be helpful, although the present author does not recommend any of them. Most have trial subscriptions.

Table 12.9   Market Timing Letters Recommended by *Money* Magazine

Letter	Author	Frequency	Cost Per Year	Address
Zweig Forecaster	Martin Zweig	Every 3 weeks	$195	747 Third Avenue New York, New York 10017
Professional Tape Reader	Stan Weinstein	Twice a month	$250	Box 2407 Hollywood, Fla 33022
Lowery's New York Stock Exchange Market Trend Analysis	Paul Desmond	Weekly	$200	Royal Palm Way Palm Beach, Fla 33480
Granville Market Letter	Joseph Granville	Weekly	$250	Drawer 0 Holly Hill, Fla 32017
Market Logic	Normal Fosback	Twice a month	$ 95	3471 N. Federal Highway Fort Lauderdale, Fla 33306

Investors who wish to know what such market forecasters are saying may subscribe directly or read articles reporting analysts' opinions in the popular press. Others may prefer to assess the data the the forecasters use.

TECHNICAL MARKET INDICATORS

Thus far we have examined market forecasts based on relative declines in the Dow, market multiples, market multiples relative to interest and inflation rates, historical relationships during recessions, election-year cycles, official pronouncements, discount rate changes, share repurchases, Dow Theory, and market analysts' opinions. "Technical market indicators" are also used to predict market moves. Many analysts claim to see timing signals in the behavior of certain data series or combinations of data series such as short-interest, odd-lot behavior, specialist short-selling, and a host of other factors.

Short-Interest

At one time short-sellers (those who sell borrowed stock which they hope later to replace at a profit) were thought to be sophisticated traders able to anticipate market turns. Thus an increase in short-interest (uncovered short-sales) was said to forecast a market decline and vice versa. Others, in contrast, argue that short-interest reflects potential demand from covering short-traders. According to this view, a rise in short-interest forecasts a market rally. Several studies, however, found that short-interest was largely unrelated to market rises and falls.[28] While some technicians claim that the short-interest ratio (number of shares sold short/volume) is a useful indicator, Kerrigan showed that its apparent value is principally due to fluctuations in the denominator (volume).[29]

Odd-Lot Activity

According to some analysts, small (odd-lot) traders tend to buy at tops and sell at bottoms. Thus when odd-lotters are buying on balance, the market may be poised for a fall, and when small investors are largely selling, the market may be ready to turn up. Raihall and Jepson attempted to refine the indicator by taking account of the relative prices of odd-lot trades and noting that buy/sell ratios for odd-lotters should be related to past values of the ratios rather than unity.[30] Even with these refinements their results were inconclusive. Gup did find a significant relationship for the 1955–70 period, however.[31]

Odd-Lot/Short Ratio

According to a related hypothesis, odd-lot short-sellers are particularly unsophisticated investors. Thus when odd-lot short-sales are high, the market may be near bottom and vice versa. Figure 12.5, which compares the ratio of odd-lot short-sales to total odd-lot sales with the Dow, does suggest some relationship. For example the high level reached in 1974 preceded a subsequent market bottom, while the low of 1975 was followed by market rises. The relatively flat performance since 1976 reveals few signals, however.

Zweig devised a somewhat more sophisticated odd-lot index. He reasoned that when optimism runs rampant, investors eventually exhaust their buying power and stocks are likely to fall. At other times, very pessimistic investors have sold most of their stock so that a modest demand increase can push prices up. The problem then is to measure this investor sentiment.

> Traditionally, odd-lot short selling activity has been measured by the Odd-Lot Short Ratio, which is calculated by dividing odd-lot short sales over some time period by total odd-lot sales. One difficulty, however, with the ratio is that both numerator and denominator show degrees of pessimism. An alternative might be to use odd-lot purchases in the denominator. This ratio would better record the differences in expectations between bullish investors (odd-lot purchasers) and bearish speculators (odd-lot short sellers).

> Again, this ratio is not entirely satisfactory because of cyclical swings in the balance between O.L. purchases and O.L. sales. For example, in most periods, purchases by odd-lotters exceed sales, but in the past three years the reverse has prevailed for all save a single day. In order to adjust for such cyclical tendencies in O.L. behavior, we have calculated relative O.L. purchases and sales in the denominator. The resulting fraction is called the Total Odd-Lot Short Ratio (TOLSR). Furthermore, in order to smooth out daily aberrations, the TOLSR is computed on the basis of a 10-day moving average.[32]

Zweig's analysis of TOLSR performance for 1947–73 seemed to suggest some value for the index.

Figure 12.5 Odd Lot Short Sale Ratio

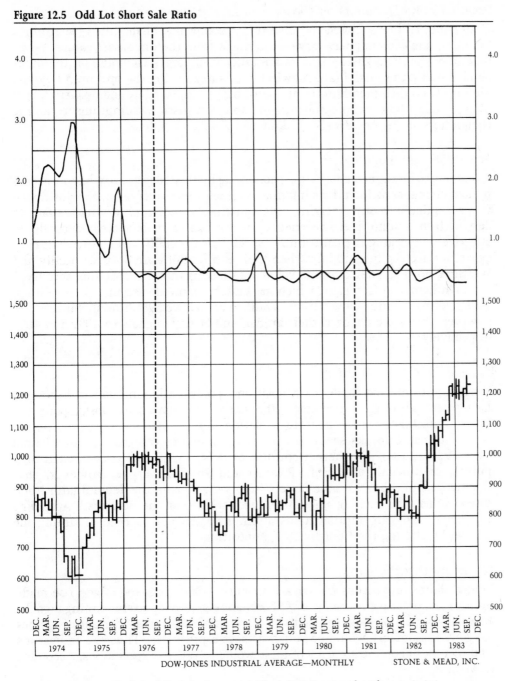

DOW-JONES INDUSTRIAL AVERAGE—MONTHLY   STONE & MEAD, INC.

Source: *Long-Term Technical Trends*, Stone and Mead, Inc. Reprinted with permission.

Premiums and Discounts on Closed-End Investment Companies

Unlike mutual funds, closed-end investment companies' share prices (determined by supply and demand) may vary substantially from their net asset values. When premiums are high, Zweig expects a market rise. Large discounts, on the other hand, are said to signal a fall. A switching strategy using the optimum buy/sell filter based on their premiums or discounts outperformed a buy and hold strategy.[33] Missing data, lack of risk adjustment, and optimistic assumptions regarding transactions costs, however, cast doubt on Zweig's results.

Specialists' Short-Selling

According to Kent, specialists are especially sophisticated investors, having access to nonpublic trading intentions information (their limit order book) and positioned to react quickly to any emerging developments.[34] Since their profits are largely derived from trading their assigned stocks, much of their success depends on effectively managing their inventory. Specialists generally sell short when they expect a price decline and buy when their expectations are positive. Reilly and Whitford, however, failed to find value in following their short-selling activity.[35]

Wirtheim and Company, which has closely followed specialist short-sellings, once said that a ratio below 47% was bullish and above 59% bearish. Since 1976, however, they have changed their bullish and bearish signals to 40% and 46% respectively.[36]

Mutual Fund Cash Position

When equity mutual funds' cash positions (potential buying power) become a large percentage of their total assets, the market may have some upside potential. Figure 12.6 illustrates the historical relationship.

The market peaks seem to be closely related to troughs in mutual fund cash (1976, 81, 83). The market bottoms of 1974, 78, 80 and 82 occured at high points for mutual fund cash. Ranson and Shipman argue, however, that fluctuations in the ratio came largely from variations in the denominator (total assets) rather than differing amounts of funds waiting on the sidelines.[37] According to Cheney and Veit, mutual funds attempt but do not succeed in timing the market by altering their portfolios' compositions.[38]

Secondary Distributions

Merjos claims that secondary stock distributions (offerings too large to be made through the ordinary exchange or OTC channels) provide useful timing signals. A dearth of such offerings indicates that potential sellers consider current prices too low. Presumably would-be sellers expect a price rise. Thus the indicator's value depends upon the accuracy of these would-be seller's expectations. According to Merjos:

Secondary volume seems to have a definite relationship with major tops

Figure 12.6 Mutual Fund Cash Position

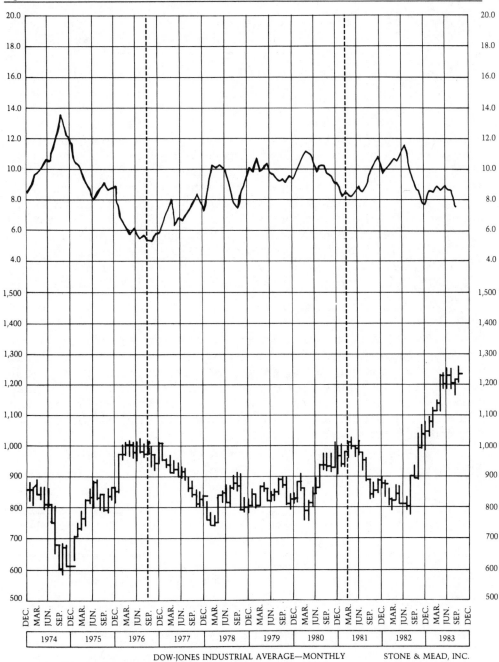

DOW-JONES INDUSTRIAL AVERAGE—MONTHLY   STONE & MEAD, INC.

Source: *Long-Term Technical Trends*, Stone and Mead, Inc. Reprinted with permission.

and bottoms. It fell to very low levels in 1960, 1962, 1966 and 1970—years when the market did in fact make major lows. The 10-week volume in those years dropped to lows ranging from 4 to 13, or to about one a week. Conversely, volume was particularly high in 1961, 1965, 1968, 1971 and 1972—years when intermediate or major tops were made. The 10-week totals rose to highs, ranging from 64 to 161, or the equivalent of more than 6 to 16 a week.[39]

The Barron's Confidence Index

The *Barron's* confidence index is the ratio of ten high-grade corporate bond rates relative to the more speculative Dow Jones bond index rates. The ratio appears in *Barron's* "Market Laboratory" section, a source of many of the underlying data used to compute market indicators.[40] This index's users believe that "smart money" will move toward quality bonds when the outlook is unfavorable and toward speculative bonds when the outlook is favorable. According to Ring, the index predicted peaks reasonably well but was less accurate in predicting troughs.[41]

As with most of the indicators discussed thus far, the evidence is suggestive but not conclusive. Even in forecasting tops, the results are not especially encouraging. A lead varying from one to fourteen months is quite undependable.

Floor Traders

Floor traders who, like specialists, have seats on the exchange and buy and sell for their own accounts should be rather sophisticated investors. Since small gains on large-volume trades are unlikely to be offset by commissions, they are well-positioned to profit from short-term moves. Accordingly, short-selling by floor traders might forecast a fall and vice versa. Zweig, however, asserts that floor traders are subject to the same emotional pressures that lead odd-lotters to sell at bottoms and buy at peaks.[42]

Table 12.10 summarizes the preceding discussion of technical market indicators.

Table 12.10 Technical Market Indicators

Total Odd-Lot Short Ratio	When odd-lot short-sales are abnormally high (low), the market is said to be near a bottom (top).
Specialist Short Selling	High (Low) specialist short selling is thought to forecast a market decline (rise)
Mutual Fund Cash Position	Mutual fund cash is an indication of potential future demand for stocks
Secondary Distributions	A dearth (flood) of secondary offerings indicates that potential sellers believe prices are too low (high)
Barron's Confidence Index	Ratio of high grade to average grade bond yields reflects confidence of "smart" investors
Floor Traders	Floor trader activity may be a useful contrary-indicator

Treasury Bill Rate

The borrowing and lending market may also affect the rates used to discount stocks' expected income streams. One index of such conditions is the interest rate on 90-day Treasury Bills.

Branch Study

Past work suggested that subsequent market movements were related to odd-lot short-selling, specialist and floor trader activity, premiums and discounts on closed-end investment companies, mutual fund cash positions, secondary stock sales, interest rates, and *Barron's* confidence index. Most early research examined each indicator separately, using past market behavior to set arbitrary buy and sell signals, which were then tested in an ad hoc fashion. The signal was judged successful if the market eventually moved in the forecasted direction. A more definitive test would examine the indicators simultaneously and constrain the investigator from using hindsight to call an eventual market move a success. Multiple regression analysis permits such a test. Accordingly, this author examined the predictive power of the market indicators mentioned in the beginning of this paragraph for the 1960–1974 time period.[43] Separate tests were performed on data for the 1960–67 and 1968–74 periods. While most of the variables tested did have the expected signs, many of the coefficients were insignificant. Dropping the insignificant variables revealed four consistently significant indicators: confidence index, mutual fund cash position, specialists' short-selling, and the 90-day Treasury Bill rate. These variables had the expected signs and the relationships persisted over both periods.

Daigler-Fielitz and Landingham Studies

More recently Daigler and Fielitz and Landingham tested a number of daily market indicators (indicators on which daily data are available).[44] Using multiple discriminant analysis, Daigler and Fielitz were able to develop three trading rules that showed profit potential on a before-commission basis, but failed to cover trading costs. Landingham results were similar. While more sophisticated statistically than my own study, the Daigler-Fielitz and Landingham studies' concentration on daily indicators and daily price movements restricts their analysis' generalizability. Most market indicators are designed to call market turns rather than short-term moves.

Assessment of the Studies

Clearly a careful long-period study of market indicators is needed to resolve the current controversy. My study failed to test actual trading rules or take account of commissions, while both the Daigler-Fielitz and the Landingham studies only analyzed relatively short-term moves. Nonetheless, all three studies seemed to find some predictive value in technical market indicators. Even forecast methods that fail to produce above-commission excess returns can help time trades that will be made anyway.

While the just-discussed work suggests that technical indicators may well have some value, the relationships may or may not persist. If, for example, the market pays careful attention to these relations, knowledge of them would become valueless. On the other hand, many indicators have long been touted without losing their followers.

MORE MARKET INDICATORS

Subsequent to the publication of my article, market indicator articles appeared in the financial press (*Barron's, Wall Street Journal*, etc.) with some frequency.[45] Discussing a few of the more interesting indicators is instructive.

Short-Term Trading Index

According to Turov, the short-term trading index has a relatively accurate forecasting record. The index, which attempts to measure the degree to which volume is concentrated in declining and advancing stocks, is defined as follows: "The number of advancing stocks is divided by the number of declining ones: that equals A. The volume of advancing stock is divided by the volume of declining ones: that equals B. The short-term trading index is A divided by B."[46] The indicator is available on most stock quotation machines.

A little manipulation reveals that the index is the average volume of declining stocks relative to the average volume of advancing stocks. The lower the ratio, the greater is the volume in advancing stocks. According to Turov, the ratio is generally between .70 and 1.30. He contends that a low ratio (high volume in advancing stocks) is a sell signal and a high ratio is a buy signal. Turov suggests .90 in a bear market and .80 in a bull market as a sell signal. The figures for buying are respectively 1.45 and 1.30 in a bear and bull market. Turov's article in December 1974 correctly called a major market bottom.

Eight years later Zweig studied and in the process refined the indicator. Using a ten-day smoothed value and testing over the 1964–82 period, Zweig found the (impressive) results reported in Table 12.11. A study such as this one should, however, be subjected to the professional review that publication in an academic journal implies.

Urgent Selling

Introduced by James Alphier, a market analyst and portfolio manager, the urgent selling indicator is based on the market's performance over the past fifteen trading days.[47] A period of "urgent selling" occurs when any broad market average closed lower four times more often than it closed higher, including at least twelve down days. According to Alphier, after a period of urgent selling, two out of three times the next 20% move will be up. Over the 1885–1978 period, 62 instances

Table 12.11 Zweig's Tests of the Short Term Trading Index

TRIN vs. S&P 500, 10-Day Smoothed
1964 to 1982

TRIN Range	S & P Performance		Probability of Up Market
	Period	% Change	
Above 1.5	1 Month Later	+4.97%	63%
0.7 to 1.5	1 Month Later	+0.22%	54%
Under 0.1	1 Month Later	+0.17%	73%
Above 1.5	3 Months Later	+6.55%	78%
0.7 to 1.5	3 Months Later	+0.67%	55%
Under 0.7	3 Months Later	+0.35%	73%
Above 1.5	6 Months Later	+20.07%	96%
0.7 to 1.5	6 Months Later	+1.49%	55%
Under 0.7	6 Months Later	−1.62%	30%
Above 1.5	1 Year Later	+29.99%	96%
0.7 to 1.5	1 Year Later	+3.13%	62%
Under 0.7	1 Year Later	−8.58%	17%

TRIN 10-Day Simple Average 1.5 or Greater
1964 to 1982

Date	3 Months Later		1 Year Later	
	Dow	ZUPI	Dow	ZUPI
09/07/66	+4.0%	+6.3%	+16.9%	+43.6%
10/06/66*	+4.1%	+10.9%	+19.6%	+47.9%
05/04/70	+1.5%	−11.3%	+31.2%	+29.2%
09/30/74	−0.8%	−3.6%	+38.2%	+32.1%
11/19/74*	+21.1%	+27.1%	+39.6%	+39.0%
03/24/80	+14.6%	+20.0%	+31.2%	+47.2%
Avg./Pd.:	+8.0%	+8.4%	+28.2%	+37.8%
$10,000 =	$14,667	$14,993	$28,733	$39,091
Annualized				
Return	+35.9%	+38.3%	+28.2%	+37.8%
Months:	15	15	51	51

*Repeat signal in 1966 includes the one-month return on the first signal (measure is for 4, 7 & 13 months). Repeat signal in 1974 includes two-month returns on the first signal (measure is for 5, 8 & 14 months). ZUPI = Zweig Unweighted Price Index

Source: M. Zweig, "Handy Trader's Tool," *Barron's*, May 24, 1982. Reprinted by permission of *Barron's*, © Dow Jones & Company, Inc., 1982. All Rights Reserved.

of urgent selling occurred. The next 20% move was up for 41 of these and down for only 21.

While interesting, this indicator does have its shortcomings. First, signals only occur about once every year and a half. Thus long periods can pass without a signal. Second, since the signal is judged successful if the market eventually moves up 20% before it moves down by that amount, one might wait a long time for such a "success." Third, the indicator has not been reexamined on more recent data and thus may only have worked over the test-period.

The January Indicator

The January indicator is a rather simplistic tool that receives a good bit of attention at the first of each year: A market that rises in January is expected to rise during the year and vice versa.[48] While conceding its apparently high success rate (24 of 29 correct up market calls over the 1934–76 period), Madrick pointed out a number of flaws.[49] Since the market generally rises in both January and for the year, its success may easily be overstated. Several other months seem to do about as well. Moreover, one who followed a straightforward buy and hold strategy would have a higher-valued portfolio (even ignoring transaction costs) over the 1952–1976 period than one who had used the January-indicator as a trading signal.

The Advisors' Sentiments Indicator

One of the most intriguing of the new wave of market indicators is that based on the investment analysts themselves. A contrary opinion approach would expect the market to peak when advisors' sentiment was most bullish and reach a bottom when sentiment was most bearish. Utilizing an index compiled by Cohen of Investor's Intelligence Inc., Boland found that over the 1978 to August 1980 period, the Dow tended to reach a peak just after investment advisors were most bullish and a bottom just after they become most bearish.[50] Figure 12.7 illustrates the 1963–81 behavior of the advisors' sentiment index relative to the market. The two series do seem to move together.

Figure 12.7 Sentiment Index of the Leading Investment Services

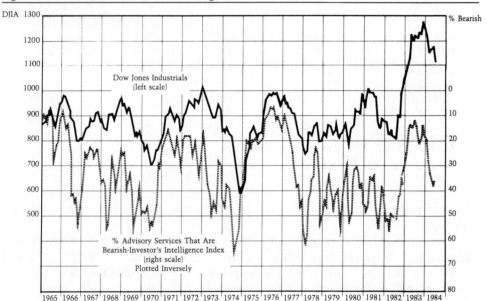

Source: *Investment Strategy Highlights*, Goldman, Sachs & Co., June 1984. Reprinted with permission.

Daily Indicators

Most indicators are designed to predict intermediate or long-term market trends. Day-to-day moves are not nearly as interesting to most people because of the high trading costs relative to the typically modest day-to-day moves. Nonetheless, those who trade at little cost (specialists, floor traders, those receiving institutional discounts, etc.), or who will trade anyway, might as well take advantage of any predictable daily price moves. The Advance/Decline and Monday-Friday price patterns represent two approaches to forecasting such short-term moves.

Advance/Decline Patterns ✳

The market's strength may be gauged by the ratio of the number of stocks advancing to the number declining. Philippatos and Nowroki found a tendency for past ratios to persist.[51] That is, if a particular day has many declines relative to the historical average, the next day's declines were likely to lie somewhere between the last day's results and the average. Similar findings for the London and Amsterdam stock exchanges were cited in their study.

Monday-Friday Price Patterns

Unusual price behavior has also been found for Mondays and Fridays. Cross reported that the Standard & Poor's composite average rose on 62.2% of the Fridays and on only 39% of the Mondays during the 1953–70 period.[52] These differences were statistically significant. The market was consistently more likely to be up on Friday than on Monday for each of the eighteen years of the sample. After a decline on Friday, the chances of a rise on Monday were only 24%. If Friday had shown an increase, the chances of an increase on Monday were about 50%. The government's practice of sometimes withholding unpleasant economic news until the market's Friday close may account for the phenomona.

Cross's original study ended with 1970. Subsequent work has refined and extended the analysis. For example, French, who studied the 1953–77 S&P 500,

Table 12.12 Additional Market Indicators

Short-Term Trading Index	High (Low) relative volume of advancing stocks is a sell (buy) signal
Urgent Selling	When at least twelve of the last fifteen days have been down, the market is said to be approaching a bottom
January Indicator	January performance is said to forecast the year but the evidence is unimpressive
Advisors' Sentiments	Investment advisory sentiment is said to be a contrary-indicator
Advance/Decline Patterns	Past advance/decline patterns tend to persist
Monday-Friday Price Pattern	Market tends to rise on Fridays and fall on Mondays

found positive returns for Tuesday, Wednesday, Thursday, and Friday and negative returns for Monday, during each of five five-year subperiods.[53] Similarly Gibbons and Hess found Monday mean Treasury Bill and stock returns low or even negative.[54]

These day-of-the-week price effects suggest that if no overriding considerations intervene, investors might as well sell on Fridays and wait until late in the day on Mondays to buy. Mondays after a Friday decline may offer somewhat more attractive buying opportunities. Table 12.12 summarizes the discussion of these additional market indicators.

SUMMARY AND CONCLUSIONS

The evidence discussed herein reveals an emotional side to the market. Many efforts to identify market tops and bottoms have been offered but none contain a magic formula. Percentage declines from previous peaks appear to be approximately random. The market PE ratio is almost useless in isolation but when PE ratios are low (high) relative to their past relationship to interest and inflation rates, a market rise (fall) may be likely. Stocks generally rise early in a recession and go sideways during most of the recovery period. The election-year cycle provides an interesting approach to market timing. Official pronouncements, discount rate changes, stock repurchases and Dow Theory may occasionally be helpful. A large number of analysts sell newsletters that attempt to forecast market trends (and make money for them). Some have reasonably accurate records.

Most of the remainder of this chapter dealt with technical market indicators (short-interest, odd-lot, premiums and discounts on closed-end investment companies, specialists' short-selling, mutual fund cash positions, secondary distributions, *Barron's* confidence index, floor trader activity, and the Treasury bill rate). My own study found four of these reasonably reliable in a multiple regression context: Specialist short-selling, mutual fund cash position, *Barron's* confidence index, and the Treasury bill rate. Studies by Daigler and Fielitz and by Landingham, however, failed to establish after-commission trading profits from daily market-indicator signals. Of the indicators not considered in the Branch study, the advisors' sentiments index appeared most promising. In conclusion, the market's emotional volatility seems to be very difficult but perhaps not impossible to predict. Clearly this area needs much more study.

REVIEW QUESTIONS

1. Does the stock market overreact? Explain why or why not.
2. Describe and discuss the relevance of the market's major contractions since 1960.
3. Discuss the usefulness of market average PE ratios in forecasting the market's direction.

4. What is the Grey approach? How should it be tested further?
5. How does the market generally perform during recessions?
6. Discuss the election-year cycle.
7. Assess the forecasting-value of official pronouncements, discount rate changes, and corporate stock repurchases.
8. What common disadvantages do investment managers, stock analysts, and market forecasters have?
9. Discuss the relevance of short interest and odd-lot behavior in market timing.
10. Identify the hypothesized relationships for the following indicators: Premiums and discounts on closed-end investment companies, specialist short-selling, mutual fund cash, secondary distributions, *Barron's* confidence index, and floor trader activity.
11. Summarize and compare the Branch, Daigler-Fielitz, and Landingham studies.
12. Identify the hypothesized relationships for the following indicators: short-term trading, urgent selling, January, advisor's sentiments, advance/decline, and Monday-Friday.

REVIEW PROBLEMS

1. Identify five stocks that traditionally have high PEs and are touted for their growth prospects. Track these stocks' performances over the most recent major up and down moves in the market. Compare their performances with that of market averages.
2. Identify five major news events occuring over the past year or two. Track the market's reaction for thirty days after each event. Write a report.
3. Track the performances of a list of major stocks over the most recent market slide and recovery. (See Table 12.4 for an example.) Describe the result.
4. Plot market PE ratios (e.g. S&P 500) and AAA bond rates monthly for the past five years. Do you see any useful trading rules? Recommend a trading strategy. Now go back another five years and apply it. Would you have made money? Discuss your results in a report.
5. Plot the stock market's performance relative to the unemployment rate, inflation rate, and prime rate for the last two business cycles. Do you see any exploitable patterns? Formulate a trading strategy and test it over two other business cycles. Would it have made money? Describe your experience in a report.
6. Plot market performance around the time of the most recent presidential election. Is any pattern apparent? Formulate a trading rule and apply it to a prior presidential election period. Would you have made money? Describe your results in a report.

7. Obtain trial subscriptions to five market forecasters and compare each forecast with subsequent performance. Identify the one with the best and the worst records for the period you studied. Get a friend to obtain a second trial subscription to these two forecasters and again compare their performance with the market. Write a report.

8. Select five market indicators that can be computed from the data in *Barron's* market laboratory section. Compute the indicators weekly for twelve weeks and compare their signals with actual market performance. Choose the two with the best and the two with the worst records and follow them for another twelve weeks. Write a report.

9. Track the Monday-Friday pattern for the past year on both the NYSE and the AMEX. Write a report.

NOTES

1. B. Malkiel, "Equity Yields, Growth, and the Structure of Share Prices," *American Economic Review*, December 1965, pp. 1004–1031.

2. K. Shiller, "The Use of Volatility Measures in Assessing Market Efficiency," *Journal of Finance*, May 1981, pp. 291–303.

3. T. Carrington and D. Hertzberg, "Stock Prices Become More Volatile as Role of Institutions Grows," *Wall Street Journal*, November 30, 1982, pp. 1, 21; *Business Week*, "Behind the Market's Wild Ride," *Business Week*, October 25, 1982, pp. 98–103.

4. R. Baylis and S. Bhirud, "Growth Stock Analysis: A New Approach," *Financial Analysts Journal*, July/August 1973, pp. 63–72.

5. *Barron's*, "New Investment Era? The Long-Run Market, say Smilen and Safir, It's Ended," *Barron's*, July 30, 1973, pp. 3, 10, 14; C. Loomis, "How the Terrible Two-Tier Market Came to Wall Street," *Fortune*, July 1973, pp. 82–89.

6. F. Reilly and E. Drzycimski, "An Analysis of the Effects of a Multi-Tiered Stock Market," *Journal of Financial and Quantitative Analysis*, November 1981, pp. 559–576.

7. J. Baesel, G. Shows and E. Thorpe, "Can Joe Granville Time the Market?," *The Journal of Portfolio Management*, Spring 1982, pp. 5–9.

8. G. Putka, "Joe Granville's Followers Defecting As He Sticks With Bearish Outlook," *Wall Street Journal*, November 12, 1982, pp. 29–49.

9. C. Elia, "How a Market Guru Called the Big Drop—Or Else Set it Off," *Wall Street Journal*, January 8, 1981, pp. 1, 17.

10. J. Treynor and K. Mazuy, "Can Mutual Funds Outguess the Market?," *Harvard Business Review*, July–August 1966, pp. 131–136; F. Fabozzi and J. Francis, "Mutual Funds Systematic Risk for Bull and Bear Markets," *Journal of Finance*, December 1979, pp. 1243–1250; E. Theodore and J. Cheney, "Are Mutual Funds Market Timers?," *Journal of Portfolio Management*, Winter 1982, pp. 35–42.

11. J. Holmes, "100 Years of Common Stock Investing," *Financial Analysts Journal*, November/December 1974, pp. 38–44.

12. W. Gray, "The Application of Discount Rates in Forecasting; Returns for Stocks and Bonds," *Financial Analysts Journal*, May/June 1974, pp. 53–61; W. Gray, "Developing a Long-Term Outlook for the U.S. Economy and Stock Market," *Financial Analysts Journal*, July–August 1979, pp. 29–39.

13. S. Kichen, "The Rule of 20," *Forbes*, June 20, 1983, p. 31.

14. J. Cullity, "Stock Price Recoveries Following Recessions: A Second Look," *Financial Analysts Journal*, January/February 1974, pp. 45–58.

15. A. Malabre, "Following the Script: Gain in Share Prices in Midst of Recession Adheres to Pattern," *Wall Street Journal*, April 18, 1975, p. 1; A. Malabre, "Shifting Stocks: Today's Zigzag Market is Typical of Periods of Business Expansion," *Wall Street Journal*, September 29, 1975, p. 1; A. Malabre, "Just as the Economy May be Recovering, Share Prices Wobble," *Wall Street Journal*, February 3, 1981, pp. 1, 22.

16. R. Piccini, "Stock Market Behavior Around Business Cycle Peaks," *Financial Analysts Journal*, July/August 1980, pp. 55–57.

17. C. Rolo, "Anticipating Major Ups and Downs," *Money*, June 1982, pp. 44–50.

18. F. Allvine and D. O'Neill, "Stock Market Returns and the Presidential Election Cycle," *Financial Analysts Journal*, September/October 1980, pp. 47–56; V. Vartan, "Stocks in An Election Year," *New York Times*, December 29, 1983, pp. D1, D5.

19. W. Riley and W. Laksetich, "The Market Prefers Republicans: Myth or Reality," *Journal of Financial and Quantitative Analysis*, September 1980, pp. 541–560.

20. Ibid., p. 557.

21. W. Burke, "How Now, Dow Jones?" *Business and Financial Letter*, Federal Reserve Bank of San Francisco, January 11, 1974, pp. 1–2; M. Zweig, "Fed Indicator," *Barron's*, January 20, 1975, p. 11.

22. H. Baker, P. Gallagher and K. Morgan, "Management's View of Stock Repurchase Programs," *Journal of Financial Research*, Fall 1981, pp. 233–248.

23. A. Merjos, "Corporations Have Been Canny Buyers of Their Own Stock," *Barron's*, May 28, 1973, pp. 9, 15; A. Merjos, "Good on the Rebound: Company Stock Buy-Backs Work Only in Rising Markets," *Barron's*, March 15, 1982, pp. 28–30.

24. D. Glickstein and R. Wubbels, "Dow Theory is Alive and Well!," *Journal of Portfolio Management*, Spring 1983, pp. 28–35.

25. J. Connelly, "Seven Forecasters With Foresight," *Money*, June 1982, pp. 54–58.

26. P. Brimelow, "Rating the Advisers," *Barron's*, January 10, 1983, pp. 11, 12, 48; *Business Week*, "The Hottest Gurus on the Street," *Business Week*, February 14, 1983, pp. 116–117.

27. P. Kadis, "First-Class Market-Timing Letters," *Money*, June 1982, pp. 63.

28. T. Mayor, "Short Trading Activity and the Price of Equities: Some Simulation and Regression Results," *Journal of Finance and Quantitative Analysis*, September 1968, pp. 283–298; R. Smith, "Short Interest and Stock Market Prices," *Financial Analysts Journal*, November/December 1968, pp. 151–154; J. McDonald and D. Baron, "Risk and Return on Short-Position on Common Stocks," *Journal of Finance*, March 1973, pp. 97–107.

29. R. Cole, "Tracking the Short Interest Reports," *New York Times*, March 28, 1982, p. 14F; C. Comer, "Bullish Indicator, The Short Interest is Signaling Higher Share Prices," *Barron's*, November 21, 1983, p. 26; R. Russell, "Bearish is Bullish, Analyzing the Stunning Series of Short Interest Ratios," *Barron's*, December 26, 1983, p. 34; T. Kerrigan, "Behavior of the Short Interest Ratio," *Financial Analysts Journal*, November/December 1974, pp. 45–49.

30. D. Raihall and J. Jepson, "The Application of Odd Lot Buy Singles to Dividend Stocks," *Mississippi Valley Journal of Business and Economics*, Winter 1972–73, pp. 19–30.

31. B. Gup, "A Note on Stock Market Indicators and Pricing," *Journal of Financial and Quantitative Analysis*, September 1973, pp. 673–682.

32. M. Zweig, "Stalking the Bear: A New Odd Lot Indicator Has Just Turned Bullish," *Barron's*, July 3, 1973, p. 11.

33. M. Zweig, "An Investor Expectation-Stock Rise Prediction Model Using Closed-End Premiums," *Journal of Finance*, March 1973, pp. 67–78.

34. W. Kent, *The Smart Money*, Doubleday, Garden City, NY, 1972.

35. F. Reilly and D. Whitford, "A Test of the Specialists' Short Sale Ratio," *Journal of Portfolio Management*, Winter 1982, pp. 12–19.

36. *Investment Manager's Review*, Wirtheim Co. Inc., March 23, 1981, p. 19.

37. D. Ransom and W. Shipman, "Institutional Buying Power and the Stock Market," *Financial Analysts Journal*, September/October 1981, pp. 62–69.

38. J. Cheney and T. Veit, "Evidence of Shifts in Portfolio Asset Composition as a Market Timing Tool," *Financial Review*, February 1983, pp. 56–78.

39. A. Merjos, "Few Big Sellers: The Dearth of Secondary Distributions is Bullish," *Barron's*, October 15, 1973, p. 5.

40. M. Zweig, *Understanding Technical Forecasting: How to Use Barron's Market Laboratory Pages*, Dow Jones Inc., 1978.

41. J. Ring, "Confidence Index, It Works Better at Tops than at Bottoms," *Barron's*, March 25, 1974, p. 11.

42. M. Zweig, "Uncanny Floor Traders," *Barron's*, April 22, 1974, p. 11.

43. B. Branch, "The Predictive Power of Market Indicators," *Journal of Financial and Quantitative Analysis*," June 1976, pp. 269–286.

44. R. Daigler and B. Fielitz, "A Multiple Discriminant Analysis of Technical Indicators on the New York Stock Exchange," *Journal of Financial Research*, Fall 1981, pp. 169–182; M. Landingham, "The Day Trader: Some Additional Evidence," *Journal of Financial and Quantitative Analysis*, June 1980, pp. 341–356.

45. C. Stabler, "The Switchers: More Investors Shuttle Their Cash to Catch Sharp Market Trends," *Wall Street Journal*, June 7, 1978, p. 1; R. Forsyth, "Barometer for Bonds: Market Vane Calls the Turn on Capital Markets," *Barron's*, September 13, 1982, pp. 30, 32; P. Roth, "Weighting Options: Put-Call Ratios Can be Useful in Calling Turns," *Barron's*, October 11, 1982, pp. 34, 36; R. Klempin, The Coppock Curve: A Famous Indicator Flashes a Long-Term Buy Signal," *Barron's*, November 22, 1982, pp. 20–21.

46. D. Turov, "Buy Signal? A New Technical Indicator is Flashing One," *Barron's*, December 9, 1974, p. 11.

47. J. Alphier, "Urgent Selling," *Barron's*, February 26, 1979, pp. 11–22.

48. J. Allan, "The Winds of January on Wall Street," *New York Times*, January 18, 1976, p. 20; *Business Week*, "Five Days in January Foretell an Upbeat Year," *Business Week*, January 23, 1984, p. 111; L. Pittel, "Stocks for January," *Forbes*, January 16, 1984, p. 125.

49. J. Madrick, "Shooting Holes in the January Indicator," *Business Week*, January 31, 1977, p. 71.

50. J. Boland, "Stock Market Seers? Investment Advisors are Usually Wrong at Turning Points," *Barron's*, September 1, 1980, pp. 11–14.

51. G. Phillippatos and D. Nawroki, "The Information Inaccuracy of Stock Market Forecasts: Some New Evidence of Dependence on the New York Stock Exchange," *Journal of Financial and Quantitative Analysis*, June 1973, pp. 443–458.

52. F. Cross, "The Behavior of Stock Prices on Fridays and Mondays," *Financial Analysts Journal*, November/December 1973, pp. 67–69; A. Merrill, *The Behavior of Prices on Wall Street*, Analysis Press, Chautauqua, NY, 1966; B. Branch, "Explaining Nonrandom Behavior of Stock Prices," *Financial Analysts Journal*, March/April 1974, p. 10.

53. K. French, "Stock Returns and the Weekend Effect," *Journal of Financial Economics*, March 1980, pp. 55–70.

54. M. Gibbons and P. Hess, "Day of the Week Effects and Asset Returns," *Journal of Business*, October 1981, pp. 579–596.

13 Timing Individual Security Trades

Investment timing involves both anticipating market trends and formulating reliable expectations for price changes relative to those trends. This chapter explores this latter topic (generalizable factors that may affect individual security prices). We first consider the theoretical arguments and empirical evidence on technical analysis. Then a variety of specialized price dependencies (tendencies for prices to behave in a particular fashion) are discussed, including the impact of block trades, secondary distributions, intraday dependencies, tax-loss trading, earnings and dividend-change announcements, *Wall Street Journal* announcements, broker sell recommendations, bond-rating changes, pollution disclosures, corporate crime disclosures, *Wall Street Week* recommendations, trading suspensions, option expirations, option listings, insider-trading reports, splits, reverse splits, stock dividends, tender offers, mergers, liquidations, stock repurchases, rights offerings, forced conversion, and voluntary spinoffs. Finally we examine the timing issues related to cross-correlations, volume effects, brokerage share prices, dividend reinvestment plans, dollar averaging, and a trading strategy called "cut your profits and let your losses run."

TECHNICAL ANALYSIS

Since chart reading is still widely practiced, no treatment of investment timing would be complete without some discussion of the technical approach. Chart-readers contend that price/volume patterns reveal future demand and supply relations by reflecting evolving market psychology. Technical analysts seek to identify favorable buying and selling opportunities from repeating price patterns. Consider, for example, the "head and shoulders" formation, a classic pattern of chartists (Figure 13.1). Lerro and Swayne explain this pattern as follows:

> This pattern is referred to as a "head and shoulders.". . . it has a remarkable resemblance to the human form.
> A closer inspection of the configuration reveals the following stages of development:
> *Left Shoulder.* The shoulder builds up as a result of a strong rally, accompanied by significant volume. Thereafter, a profit taking reaction occurs

Figure 13.1 Head and Shoulders Formation

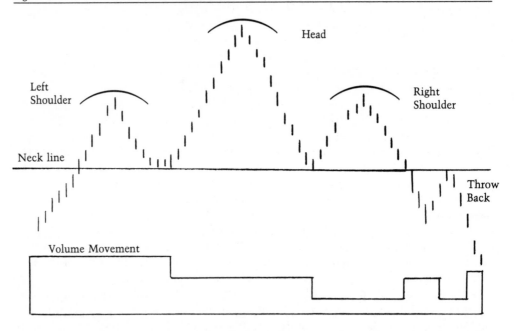

Source: Lerro, Anthony J. and Swayne, Jr., Charles B., *Selection of Securities: Technical Analysis of Stock Market Prices.* Copyright 1974 General Learning Corporation. Reprinted by permission of Silver Burdett Company.

which forms the right leg. Volume is noticeably reduced on the downward slope.

Head. Rising prices and increased volume initiate the left leg of the head pattern followed by a contraction, on reduced volume, which extends to the neckline. Observe that the head extends well above the left shoulder.

Right Shoulder. Another price rally produces the left leg of this shoulder and finally the rally breaks up and the prices slide downward. Volume action is quite different than in the left shoulder and head formation. More often than not, volume is decidedly smaller than under the left shoulder and head. The right shoulder tends to be equal in height with the left shoulder; it is always well below the head.

The unwary trader who unfortunately bought late, usually has an opportunity to redeem himself when a brief minor rally pulls price back to the neckline. There is no guarantee that such an event will always occur, but, as a rule, a continued downtrend is normally followed by a slight recovery. Once the throw back is completed, prices tend to break down into a strong retreat. High volume is apparent in this latter phase representing an obvious reversal pattern.[1]

According to the chartists, this pattern forecasts a major decline. The inverted head and shoulders formation is said to give a buy signal. Numerous books discuss many such configurations, with more published every year.

Chart-Reading and Market Efficiency

The weak form of the efficient-market hypothesis implies that past market behavior contains no useful investment-timing information. That is, investors' efforts to find hidden values should, according to efficient-markets adherents, cause stock prices to reflect all relevant public information (including any information implicit in past price patterns) accurately and quickly. Thus, Samuelson showed that a stock price will follow a random walk if its "... present price is set at the expected discounted value of its future dividends; where the future dividends are supposed to be random variables generated according to any general (but known) stochastic process."[2] Indeed if many traders recognized repeating patterns, their rapid reaction would cause an almost immediate change to the predicted level. Eventually some investors' efforts to react to partial patterns would eliminate most repeating patterns.

Technical analysts, in contrast, assert that their system, while not infallible, does provide useful signals. Why else, they ask, do so many investors continue to pay for and follow their advice? Why indeed? Why do otherwise-intelligent people go to astrologers and fortune tellers?

The efficient-market proponents respond that some successes may be due to combining other information with charts and giving credit to the charts alone, while other technicians may simply have been lucky. Just as enough monkeys and enough typewriters will produce a "King Lear," enough analysts and enough market turns will reveal some very high "success" rates. The relevant question is: "Do such successes repeat themselves?" Hearing from the winners (who are likely to be vocal), but not from losers (who are unlikely to advertise their failures), gives a distorted view. A *Business Week* story featured a technical analyst who correctly called a declining market the day after the market hit its peak January 1, 1973. This analyst continued to forecast a decline at least up to August 31, 1974, when the market itself was still declining.[3] The *Wall Street Journal* featured another successful analyst a few years later.[4] We have already seen how Joe Granville called several market turns.[5] Indeed at any stage of the market cycle some analysts are likely to have a sufficiently impressive record to justify an article touting their "wisdom." While such track records are impressive, one cannot help wondering how many other technical analysts made disastrous forecasts during similar periods. Granville himself, after correctly calling a couple of turns, totally missed the very strong market upturn that began in August of 1982.[6]

Evidence such as that cited in Chapter 6 suggests that past price behavior contain little or no generally useful information.[7] Any generalized time series dependencies exhibited by past price behavior appear to be too weak to offset transaction costs. A closer look suggests that the issues may not be quite so simple, however.

SPECIALIZED DEPENDENCIES

Smidt argues that certain types of specialized time-series return dependencies should be expected.[8] First, large orders of anxious traders may cause short-run price reactions that when dissipated, produce a price reversal. Second, lags in reaction to new information may lead to short-run price trends. Third, excessive speculation may cause speculative bubbles with subsequent reversals.

Anxious-Trader Effects

Block trades, secondary offerings, intraday-dependencies and tax-loss trading may lead to temporary supply-demand imbalances with resulting anxious-trader price effects.

Block Trades and Secondary Offerings

Grier and Albien examined a filter rule of buy-on-block-trades, expecting a reversal.[9] For the first decile of block trades ranked by size of open-to-block-price decline, profits from buying at the block price and selling at the close only slightly exceeded commissions. Specialists and floor traders, who incur much lower trading costs, could (and probably do) profit substantially, however. A subsequent study by Dann, Mayers, and Raab found that block trades with large (greater than 4.56%) open-to-block-price-declines have by the close generally risen by more than enough to cover transactions costs.[10] Five minutes after the block trade, however, the price-recovery had usually progressed too far to afford after-commission profits, and within fifteen minutes most prices had fully recovered. As a practical matter, only specialists and floor traders are positioned to react within these time frames. One advisory service (Xerox's Auto Ex division) does report trading interest of 230 major institutions and 120 brokerage houses.[11] While designed to facilitate institutional block trades, the system can be used to forecast such trades (for $1,000 a month).

Scholes reported an average price decline of .5% on large secondary distributions on the day of the sale and 2.2% at the end of fourteen days.[12] He also found that secondary distributions of corporate insiders, investment companies, and mutual funds were followed by appreciably greater price changes than when the sellers were banks, insurance companies, estates, trusts, or individuals. Scholes reasoned that the former were more likely to have sold on fundamental grounds while the latter may have simply needed liquidity. These secondary distribution results do not exhibit any anxious-trader effects per se, but perhaps daily close price data are too crude to reveal them.

General Intraday Dependencies: Specialists and Limit Orders

While persuasively arguing that stock prices closely resemble a random walk for daily movements, Granger and Morgenstern did find temporary intraday barriers to price movements and nonrandom overnight price changes.[13] They ascribed these patterns to the interaction of specialists and limit orders. Specialists are charged with keeping an orderly market (avoid excessive volatility) in their assigned stocks with a combination of limit orders and their own buying and selling. Since limit orders tend to collect at even values (whole numbers and halves as opposed to quarters, quarters as opposed to eighths, etc.), they may act as temporary barriers to price movements. Once the market has executed a stack of whole-number limit orders, only a few orders may restrict further movement. Thus, continued buying activity may lead to a rather rapid price increase until a new barrier is encountered. For example, buying pressure may move a price from 18 5/8 to 18 7/8, and once 19 is penetrated, continued buying could quickly propel the price to 19 7/8, with 20 becoming the next barrier.

Granger and Morgenstern also found similar-magnitude overnight and overday price fluctuations, even though the former involve much lower volume.[14] Accumulated overnight orders and the specialist's own account are used to set the opening price. Since price swings trigger limit orders on which specialists are paid a fee, the authors concluded that a fluctuating overnight price is often profitable for the specialists. Lacking the necessary data on specialists' dealings, however, Granger and Morgenstern were unable to prove their suspicions.

Niederhoffer and Osborne also found unmistakable evidence of nonrandom behavior in transaction-sign reversals.[15] After a positive price change, the next nonzero price change has a 3 to 1 chance of being a decline. Similarly, a negative price change is much more likely to be followed by an increase. This nonrandom transaction price behavior is caused by the interaction of market orders with the bid-asked spread. Market orders to buy are immediately executed at the current asked. A subsequent order to sell will produce a reversal, while a buy will leave the price at the asked. Indeed, this intraday price behavior indicates that the last trade price (the quote the broker usually gives) is not the best index of the market price. For example a last trade in XYZ at 23 5/8 could be associated with any of the following:

  a) Bid 23 5/8   Ask 23 7/8
  b) Bid 23 3/8   Ask 23 5/8
  c) Bid 23 1/2 ˙Ask 23 3/4

In rare instances the market may even have moved away from the last reported price:

  d) Bid 23 7/8   Ask 24 1/2
  e) Bid 23 1/8   Ask 23 3/8

Thus interested traders should always request reports on the current bid and asked prices rather than rely only on the previous trade's price. Complete knowledge of the current quote is particularly relevant to those who want to place limit orders. Traders should also usually ask for a size (number of shares sought at the bid and available at the ask).

Tax-Loss Trading

Yet another area of possible anxious-trader impacts involves year-end selling to establish a tax loss. While their methodologies differ somewhat, separate studies by McEnally, Dyl, Branch, Branch and Ryan, Roll and Givoly, and Ovadia all suggest that tax-loss trading has dramatically affected some year-end stock prices.[16] Branch and Ryan, who studied the first-of-the-year returns over the 1965-78 period, found average four-week price moves relative to the market of 6.67% and 14.75% (which were statistically different from zero) for NYSE and AMEX year-end lows respectively. Similarly McEnally found that stocks which fell by the greatest percentage over the preceding twelve months were most likely to rise after the first of the year. Such findings suggest (assuming the observed relations persist) that one should sell tax-loss candidates well before year end and that the year end is an attractive time to purchase stocks that are under tax-loss selling pressure. More recent work by Branch and Chang, however, indicate that tax-loss trading did not have a similar price pattern in the 1979–82 period.[17] They did find that stocks which declined most in December were most likely to rise in January. Both Roll and Givoly and Ovadia find that most of the turn-of-the-year effect occurs at the small-firm level.

Assessment: Anxious-Trader Effects

The anxious-trader effects evidence seems relatively persuasive. Block and tax-loss trading have in the past both tended to depress prices temporarily, generally followed by a reversal. Secondary offerings are also associated with modest price declines. Intraday price-dependencies related to specialist trading and limit order activity also reveal some anxious-trader effects. With the possible exceptions of the tax-loss results, however, the dependencies appear to be too small to permit after-transactions-cost trading profits. On the other hand, those who intend to trade anyway might as well take advantage of whatever forecasting value these relationships may offer. Table 13.1 summarizes our discussion of anxious-trader effects.

Adjustment-Lags

Adjustment-lags are a second category of specialized dependencies. Specifically, prices may take time to react to such factors as earnings announcements, dividend changes, ex-dividend dates, *Wall Street Journal* announcements, broker sell-recommendations, bond rating changes, pollution disclosures, corporate crime disclosures, *Wall Street Week* recommendations, trading suspensions, option expirations, option listings, insider-trading reports, splits, stock dividends, tenders,

Table 13.1 Anxious-Trader Effects

Block Traders	Prices tend to decline with block trade and regain most of the loss by day's end
Large Secondary Distributions	Modest decline on day of and following a secondary distribution
Intraday Dependencies	Result from incoming market orders causing prices to bounce between bid and ask
Overnight Price Changes	Volatility may result from specialist seeking to trigger limit orders
Tax-Loss Trading	Issues under year-end tax selling pressure may rise at first of the year

mergers, liquidations, share repurchases, rights offerings, forced conversions, and voluntary spin-offs. Moreover, cross-correlations and volume effects may also be used to identify adjustments in process.

Earnings Announcements, Dividend Changes and Ex-dividend Dates

While prices may not adjust instantly to earnings and dividend announcements, the lags appear to be quite short. Ashley reported that the reaction to dividends or earnings news was essentially complete within two or three days.[18] Jones, in contrast, found that favorable earnings announcements were not fully discounted by the market until professional analysts had digested and interpreted the results.[19] Several studies have reported a relatively slow market reaction to unexpected earnings changes.[20] Richards and Martin found that the reaction to changes in earnings forecasts continued for as much as five months after the revision.[21]

Several different studies found that reactions to dividend increases are often substantial and usually completed by the day of the announcement or soon thereafter.[22] Ex-dividend price reactions were also predictable to an extent. Dividends are paid to stockholders of record on a prespecified date. Dividends on purchases made the day after the ex-dividend date go to the prior owner. Campbell and Beranek reported that the price tends to fall by 90% of the dividend on the ex-dividend date, although the relationship was far from exact.[23] On the other hand Kalay and Subrahmanyam report that call option prices tend to fall on the ex-dividend day for the underlying stock.[24] The predictability of ex-dividend price reactions has led several authors to suggest trading strategies. Since 85% of intra-corporate dividends are untaxed, Joehnk, Bowlin and Petty advocate buying preferreds just before the day-of-record and selling quickly thereafter.[25]

Wall Street Journal Announcements and Broker Sell-Recommendations

Morse examined price and volume effects for *Wall Street Journal* announcements of earnings and dividend announcements, large product sales, earnings forecasts, acquisitions, stock splits, and labor strikes for 50 companies over the eleven trading days surrounding the announcement. He found a significant price effect the day before the announcement appeared in the *Journal* (but probably the same day as it was reported on the Dow Jones News ticker) as well as on the day the story appeared.[26] In most cases the excess returns were in the expected direction. Volume was also usually high at the time of the announcement. Bidwell and Kolb found that broker sell-recommendations had a negative short-run impact on security returns.[27] Such abnormal returns could, however, only be exploited profitably by those who incur low transactions costs and have prior warnings of the recommendations. On the other hand, stocks depressed by the sell-recommendations tended to generate subsequent above-normal returns.

Bond Rating Changes, Pollution Disclosures, Corporate Crime Disclosures, "Wall Street Week" Recommendations, and Trading Suspensions

Griffin and Sanvicente, who examined the stock-price reaction to bond rating changes, reported an appreciable downgrade effect, but an insignificant effect for upgrades.[28] Since only monthly data were examined, the study did not reveal whether the reaction proceeded too quickly to be exploited by traders.

Jaggi and Freedman found a significant investor reaction to firms' disclosing the extent of their pollution-control spending intentions, particularly in the disclosure month.[29] Firms that made such disclosures generally experienced superior investor reaction compared with nondisclosing firms in the same industries. Since only monthly data were examined, the timing of the reactions was not explored closely enough to determine if trading profits were possible. Strachen, Smith, and Beedles found a significant market reaction to disclosures of allegations of illegal corporate behavior, virtually all of which occurs at the time of the announcement.[30]

In a particularly ingenious study Fosback explored the market reaction of 200 stocks recommended by guests of the public television program *Wall Street Week (WSW)* from December 1980 to April 1982.[31] On the average, the stocks rose .4% two weeks before the show; .8% the week before; 2.1% the day after and then fell 3.2% over the next month and a half. Fosback concluded that most WSW guests are unable to select winners, but that the market does pay attention to the program.

Schwartz's study of market behavior during and following trading suspensions implied a relatively efficient pricing process.[32] The specialists' "indications" of reopening ranges almost always contained the actual reopening price and post-suspension price movements seemed approximately random.

Option Expirations and Option Listings

Two additional events with possible associated price-dependencies involve options. Specifically Officer and Trennepohl found a modest but statistically significant tendency for the underlying stock's price to be depressed two days prior to option expirations.[33] The price effects were, however, too small to yield trading profits after taking account of the impacts of taxes, transactions costs, and search-costs.

Branch and Finnerty found that initial call option listings were associated with stock price increases, but the magnitude was generally too small to be exploited profitably after allowing for transactions costs.[34] Whiteside, Dukes, and Dunne, in contrast, found little or no impact of option listing on either the price or volume of the underling shares' trades.[35]

Insider Trading

Insider information appears often to facilitate a relatively accurate stock evaluation. While noninsiders must generally wait until that information is publicly released, traders can observe insiders' decisions and act accordingly. Zweig surveyed five academic studies of insider-trading signals; all reached similar conclusions: signals based on significant insider trading allowed one to outperform the market by a substantial margin.[36] Thus, insider trading appears to be one market signal whose value is well supported by careful academic analysis. According to Nunn, Madden, and Gambola, CEOs' and directors' inside trades are a better predictor of subsequent performance than those of vice presidents and beneficial owners.[37] Apparently the CEOs and directors have better access to information. Trivoli finds even more favorable results from joint use of financial ratios and insider-trading data.[38]

Since insiders must report their trades to the SEC, one could consult the SEC records to determine their actions on a particular stock. Insider trading activity is sometimes discussed in the financial press, at least on an ad hoc basis,[39] and some investment services report SEC insider-trading data to subscribers. Among such services are the following.

> Securities and Exchange Commission Monthly Report on Insider Trades (Washington, DC, $70 a year)
> *Consensus of Insiders*, Perry Wysong, (Box 10247, Fort Lauderdale, FL, 33334; weekly, $247 a year)
> *Insider Indicator*, J. Michael Reid, (2230 NE Brazee St., Portland, OR, 97212; semimonthly, $145 a year)
> *The Insiders*, Norman Fosback, (3471 N. Federal Hwy., Fort Lauderdale, FL, 33306; semimonthly, $49 a year)
> *The Insiders' Chronicle*, William Mehlman, (Box 9662, Arlington, VA, 22209, 50 issues a year, $325 a year)
> *The Insiders Edge Highlights Report*, Richard Horowitz (122 Spanish Village, Suite 644, Dallas, TX, 75248; monthly $79 a year)

Stock Splits, Reverse Splits, and Stock Dividends

Investors are believed to prefer per-share prices of $20 to $60. Very low-priced stocks are considered too speculative, and high-priced stocks are costly to purchase in round lots. Accordingly, stock distributions are used to reduce the per-share prices of high-priced stocks, while reverse stock splits may be employed for very low-priced issues.[40] Copeland found, however, that post-split shares usually incur proportionately higher commission-charges and bid-ask spreads.[41] Thus splits generally increase trading costs, as well as incurring the additional costs of officers' time, printing stock certificates, handling fractional shares, revising the stockholder ledger, communicating with shareholders, transfer taxes, and listing fees.

Since the price of a stock usually rises prior to a split or stock dividend, one might trade on prior knowledge or accurate forecasts of splits.[42] The former strategy is illegal while the latter's success-rate is untested. We do know, however, that unless the dividend is later increased, subsequent performance is not usually favorable.[43] On the other hand, Woolridge and Chambers found significant negative price performance associated with reverse splits around the time of the proposal, approval, and ex-split dates.[44]

Three further stock-distribution studies reveal additional relationships. First, Nicholes and Brown, who examined earnings and split announcement effects over time, found no indication that the market was becoming more efficient.[45] Second, Nicholes reported that for small stock distributions, a positive impact in the announcement month was followed by a negative adjustment over the succeeding three months.[46] Finally Woolridge found that investors interpret stock dividends as signals from management on the firm's future.[47] The larger the dividend, the greater is the market reaction.

Tender Offers, Mergers and Liquidations

Tender offers, mergers, and liquidations may present still other attractive trading opportunities. Holders usually profit when a stock is tendered for and/or merged into another company, as the offering price almost always exceeds the previous level.[48] A variety of different types of people may benefit from such transactions. Those who put the deals together are always well rewarded, as are the target firms' advisors. Even the acquired firms' managements are usually well compensated when they are forced to leave. Those who know of planned mergers before the announcement may (illegally) trade on that knowledge. Large investors like Carl Icahn may buy a sizable position in a company and then try to either force takeover from the inside or get the company to pay a premium to repurchase his shares. The company's own assets are often used as collateral to finance the full takeover. Yet another ploy is to acquire a large position in an undervalued company and then have the company buy out most or all of the small public shareholders. Taking a company "private" in this way not only buys out most shareholders at depressed prices but also eliminates much of the stockholder-relations cost. Finally, a company whose assets are worth more than the market price of its shares may be bought as a liquidation prospect.

While these various maneuvers may yield handsome returns, traders need either inside information of planned takeovers (and a willingness to break the law) or the resources to influence the relevant firms. Small investors can only try to anticipate forthcoming acquisitions and be in the right place at the right time when such moves are announced. Once a takeover looks like a success, tendering is almost always advisable, as small holdings of other companies' subsidiaries usually have little speculative appeal.

Share Repurchases, Rights Offerings, Forced Conversions, and Voluntary Spinoffs

While earnings retention and minor debt decisions continually alter capital structures, some actions have more substantial impacts. Any change that appreciably alters the number of shares outstanding and/or the firm's debt ratio can dramatically affect the shareholders' expected income streams and risks. Capital structure changes that affect the relative amounts of dividend and interest payments also have important tax implications. Thus, the market may well react to such events as share repurchases, which decrease outstanding shares, and rights offerings and forced conversions, both of which increase outstanding shares.

Masulis found the following market reactions to capital structure changes: 1) Changes affecting expected taxes and/or the relative values of stocks versus bonds were associated with significant security price moves in the predicted directions; 2) different classes of security-holders were often affected differentially by the shift; and 3) shareholders were generally adversely affected by a decrease in leverage.[49]

Studies by Vermaelen and Dann indicate both that firms use share repurchases to signal their belief that their stocks are undervalued and that the common shareholders usually benefit from such repurchases.[50] Bondholders, on the other hand, do not seem to be either helped or hurt by the repurchases. Market reaction occurs within one day of the announcement, however. Share repurchases also have the advantage of transfering funds to shareholders in the form of capital gains, as opposed to dividends.[51]

On the other hand, Bradley and Wakeman find that stock repurchases designed to remove potential takeover threats tend to lower the values of the affected firm's stock.[52] Similarly Dann and DeAngelo find that standstill agreements (agreements between management and large shareholders that limit these shareholders' options by, for example, agreeing not increase their ownership position or seek to gain control of the firm for a specific period) also tend to harm nonparticipating shareholders.[53] Dodd and Warner find that proxy contests generally enhance stock prices temporarily.[54] The stock's price usually falls once the day of record for voting passes, however.

Share repurchases decrease shares outstanding and tend to increase per-share prices, while rights offerings have the opposite effect. White and Lusztig reported that investors generally have reacted negatively to a rights offering on the announcement day, and the market has not regained any of the lost ground by the fifth day after the announcement.[55]

Like rights offerings, forced conversions of convertible debentures and convertible preferreds increase shares outstanding and reduce leverage, thereby tending to lower both per-share earnings and risk. Calling convertibles will only force conversion if the stock price has appreciated sufficiently for the conversion value to exceed the call price by a substantial amount. Not surprisingly, Alexander and Stover find that forced conversions are generally preceded by a strongly positive abnormal return.[56] More surprisingly, however, such forced conversion announcements are also associated with subsequent negative abnormal returns for a period of up to twelve months.

A spin-off occurs when a parent company distributes shares in a heretofore subsidiary company to its shareholders. While no new assets result from the distribution, value may be created if separating the parent from the former subsidiary enhances their freedom or the market's perception of their combined values. Miles and Rosenfeld studied 55 such spin-offs, finding that most such events were associated with abnormal returns prior to the announcement, but random ones thereafter.[57]

Cross Correlation and Volume Effects

Investment analysts have often asserted that particular stock groups tend to lead other groups (i.e. trunk airlines move before the feeder airlines; interest-sensitive stocks tend to lead the market; high-risk stocks are hit first and hardest in an economic downturn; low-PE stocks hold up best in a down market; etc.). An efficient market should not exhibit such leads and lags, however. While academics have not yet tested specific lead-lag hypotheses, work by Hawawini and others bear on the generalized lead-lag phenomenon.[58] Apparently some securities do tend to lead while others lag. Whether such leads and lags can be profitably exploited remains to be seen, however.

Morse's price/volume relationships study provides a final bit of information on adjustment lags.[59] He hypothesized that investors with information not yet fully impounded into the market price have an incentive to trade on one side of the market until the price has fully adjusted. His results confirm that expectation. Price trends are frequently accompanied by abnormally high volume.

Assessment: Adjustment-Lags

The market appears to adjust quickly to a variety of different types of announcements. Reactions generally occur within a day or so of the following types of announcements: earnings reports, dividend changes, bond rating changes, *Wall Street Journal* reports, *Wall Street Week* mentions, allegations of corporate crimes, option listings, stock dividends, share repurchases, and rights offerings. Reactions tend to precede the announcement or event for splits, tender offers, mergers, option expirations, and voluntary spin-offs. Thus, trading on such relationships would normally require prior knowledge or accurate forecasts. On the other hand, revisions of earnings forecasts, insider trading signals, forced conversions, and possibly ex-dividend date reactions may produce usable price relations (i.e. those that take place over a long enough period to be exploited by non-members of the listing exchange). Table 13.2 summarizes our discussion of adjustment lags.

Table 13.2   Adjustment Lags

Earnings Announcements	Quick market reaction to earnings news
Dividend Announcements	Quick market reaction to dividend news
Ex-dividend date	Stock price tends to fall by somewhat less than the amount of the payment on ex-dividend date
Wall Street Journal Announcements	Significant price effects the day before and day of significant stories in the *Wall Street Journal*
Broker Sell-Recommendations	Sell-recommendations tend to depress price, generally followed by a reversal
Bond Rating Changes	Appreciable price reaction to downgrades but not for upgrades
Pollution Disclosures	Disclosing firms tended to do better than nondisclosers in subsequent market trading
Alleged Corporate Crime	Quick market reaction to news of alleged illegal activity
Wall Street Week Recommendations	Recommended stocks tended to rise the Monday after the show and decline over the next six weeks
Trading Suspensions	Specialists' reopening-range indications almost always contain the actual reopening price
Option Expirations	Tendency for underlying stock's price to be depressed two days before expirations
Option Listings	Stock prices may increase modestly at initial call listings
Insider trading	Reports of insider trades appear to provide profitable trading signals
Stock Splits and Dividends	Stock prices usually rise prior to, but not after, a split announcement
Reverse Splits	Stock prices generally decline after reverse splits
Tender Offers	Holders usually profit from tender offers, but anticipating such offers is difficult
Share Repurchases	Share repurchases often indicate that management believes the stock is undervalued but those designed to remove takeover threats tend to depress prices
Rights Offerings	Shareholders generally react negatively to announcements of rights offerings
Forced Conversions	Strong positive performances generally precede forced conversion announcements with negative performances after the announcements
Voluntary Spin-offs	Positive performances prior to announcements followed by random performances
Cross Correlations	Some securities tend to lead while others tend to lag the market
Price-Volume Effects	Price trends are frequently accompanied by abnormally high volume

Speculative Bubbles

Some contend that the market often gets carried away, only to reverse itself when faced with reality. Indeed Malkiel goes so far as to argue that investors should seek out stocks where a subsequent positive overreaction is likely:

> I have stressed the importance of psychological elements in stock price determination. Individual and institutional investors are not computers that calculate warranted price-earnings multiples and print out buy and sell decisions. They are emotional human beings driven by greed, gambling, instinct, hope, and fear in their stock market decisions. This is why successful investing demands both intellectual and psychological acuteness.
>
> Stocks that produce "good vibes" in the minds of investors can sell at premium multiples for long periods, even if the growth rate is only average. Those not so blessed may sell at low multiples for long periods even if their growth rate is above average. To be sure, if a growth rate appears to be established, the stock is almost certain to attract some type of following. The market is not irrational. But stocks are like people—What stimulates one may leave another cold, and the multiple improvement may be smaller and slower to be realized if the story never catches on.
>
> So my advice is to ask yourself whether the story about our stock is one that is likely to catch the fancy of the crowd. Is it a story on which investors can build castles in the air—but castles in the air that really rest on a firm foundation?[60]

Stocks with a story certainly do attract Wall Street's attention.[61] While general tests for speculative bubbles would be virtually impossible, market reactions to new issues and new listings do provide possible examples of the phenomena.

The New-Issue Market

New-issue (first public sale of stock in a heretofore privately held company) prices often rise dramatically in the immediate post-sale period. While such trends might be exploited by buying at issue and selling quickly thereafter, most attractive new issues' supplies are rationed. Thus often only the underwriting brokers' best customers may be able to buy at the issue price.

A number of studies covering various periods reached the same conclusion: new issues generally produced abnormal short-run returns followed by below-market returns for somewhat longer holding periods. For example, Reilly examined 53 new issues over the 1963–65 period. One week after the initial sale the average new-issue gained 9.9%, but only 8.7% by the fourth week. The Dow in comparison gained 3% and 5% over these periods.[62] Even more impressively, Ibbotson found a risk-adjusted excess return of 11.4% in the month of issue.[63] Logue pointed out that, in the absence of vigorous competition, the underwriters would have an incentive to underprice.[64] Similarly Baron showed that investment bankers who are better informed than their clients have an incentive to underprice new issues.[65] Since the underpricing will be passed along to the issuer, the sale will be made easier and buyers happier at little cost to the underwriters. Thus, if future new-issue performance is like the past, one should generally realize gains soon after the initial purchase.

Neuberger and Hammon, Logue and Lindvall, and Newberger and La Chapelle all found that issues handled by nonprestigious underwriters tended to show greater appreciation than those of more prestigious firms.[66] In addition, Neuberger and Hammon found that secondary offerings of already issued securities tended to appreciate less than new issues.[67] Nelson argued, however, that the underpricing tendency occurred during periods when the public was enamored with new issues.[68] New issues are typically quite risky. For example, an SEC study of the 960 firms going public between 1952 and 1962 found that by 1963, 37% had failed while only 34% were showing profit.[69] Perhaps underwriters initially price securities closer to their risk-adjusted intrinsic values than does the market.

Much of the new-issues work was conducted in the early 1970s on data from the new-issue boom of the late 1960s. With the relatively depressed market that followed, both new issues and new-issue studies went into decline. By late 1980, however, the new-issue market, particularly that for energy and high technology companies, had taken off again.[70] Much of the action was in the Denver OTC market where a familiar pattern emerged: strong immediate post-offering returns followed by weaker subsequent performance.[71] The most publicized example of these new issues was Genentech, which went public at 35 only to rise to 89 in the immediate after-market. Prior year's profit amounted to 2¢ per share. At its high, this company with an unproven genetic engineering technology had a market value of two-thirds of a billion dollars. Investors were again paying a high price for hope and a promise. By Spring 1982, Genentech's price was below its original-issue level and had touched as low as 25. Similarly, the Denver Penny market, which had been the center of much of the new-issue hysteria, had declined dramatically.

Two somewhat more recent studies add to our knowledge of new-issue performance. Downs and Heinkel reported that new issues whose entrepreneurs' confidence is reflected in their large ownership positions tended to do well, but that dividend policy was unrelated to subsequent performance.[72] Then Hess and Frost, who studied new issues of seasoned securities, found no significant price effects from the offerings.[73]

New Listings

The pattern for newly listed stocks appears similar to that of new issues. Several studies indicate that when an OTC stock gains a listing, or when an AMEX stock is listed on the NYSE, the price tends to rise and then to fall back to the previous level.[74] Goulet contends that since the firm and its insiders may utilize the post-listing period to sell stock, both the number of shares outstanding and the number publicly held tend to increase, thereby depressing the price.[75] Thus the short-term price runup associated with a new listing or listing on a more prestigious exchange may offer an attractive selling opportunity.

Assessment: Speculative Bubbles

The evidence on new-issue and new-listing price reactions does tend to support the speculative bubble hypothesis. Both new issues' and newly listed issues' price rises tend to be followed by a reversal. While the percentage moves of new issues seem large enough to yield abnormal after-commission returns, the difficulty of buying at issue may substantially reduce the profit potential. Moreover, new-listing price effects are generally too small to cover transactions costs. Table 13.3 summarizes our discussion of speculative bubbles.

Table 13.3   Speculative Bubbles

Story Stocks	Market often gets carried away with stocks having an attractive story
New Issues	New issues generally appreciate in the immediate after-market followed by a subsequent decline
New Listings	Prices tend to rise prior to listing and subsequently decline to previous level

Overall Assessment: Special Situations Dependencies

At least some evidence can be found for all three of Smidt's hypothesized special situation price dependencies. The vast majority of the documented dependencies, however, either occur too quickly for most non-exchange members to profit or the magnitudes of the average price effects are too small to be exploited by those who must pay commissions (even at a modest discount). On the other hand, a few of the dependencies seem sufficiently large and long lasting to yield abnormal returns. Specifically tax-loss candidates, insider trading, and new issues all may offer exploitable price trends. Morover those who have already decided to trade may be able to take advantage of other more modest price-effects. Note, however, that the reported results reflect historical average relationships. Even if such relations continue, a large portfolio managed over a relatively long period may be necessary to generate results close to the average.

OTHER MARKET TIMING ISSUES

Certain timing topics do not fit into any of Smidt's categories. Accordingly, market moves and brokerage shares, dividend reinvestment plans, dollar averaging, and "cut your profits and let your losses run" are now discussed outside the Smidt context.

Market Moves and Brokerage Share Performance

While brokerage houses were long organized as partnerships or closely held corporations, most have now gone public, revealing interesting stock trading patterns. Stock market volume seems to vary directly with the market averages. Brokerage profits, which are highly dependent on stock market volume, are particularly strong when the market is rising and weak when it is falling.[76] As a result brokerage stock prices tend to fluctuate disproportionately with the market. Thus those who think they can call market turns may find brokerage house stocks useful trading vehicles.

Dividend Reinvestment Plans

Deciding whether or not to participate in a dividend reinvestment plan raises another timing issue. Since Allegheny Power started the practice in 1968, many nonfinancial firms have begun allowing their stockholders to reinvest their dividends directly into the company's stock. Prior to that time a number of financial corporations had such plans.

In October 1973, at least 264 nonfinancial firms offered reinvestment programs.[77] By year-end 1980, the number had risen to over 1,102.[78] Typically the corporation sends the dividends of participating stockholders to the bank's trust department, which maintains an account for each shareholder. The managing bank purchases stock on the open market, crediting each participant with his or her shares less brokerage fees and administrative costs. Many plans also permit additional stock purchases. Large round-lot purchases by the plan tend to reduce brokerage fees.

In 1969 American Telephone & Telegraph became the first company to sell newly issued stock through a reinvestment plan. Then in 1975 AT&T started the practice of offering 5% discounts on the exchanged stock. By 1980, at least 110 companies gave discounts on their dividend reinvestments. Public utilities offered many of these plans, qualifying them as tax-free distributions.

Dividend reinvestment plans have a number of advantages. From the firm's standpoint, the plans: 1) add to stockholder goodwill; 2) increase demand for the firm's stock; 3) save some dividend-related expenses; and 4) encourage small stockholders to increase ownership. In addition, plans involving new share purchases: 1) reduce the firm's debt/equity ratio; 2) provide a regular source of equity capital; and 3) permit new equity to be sold without incurring underwriting fees or other flotation costs. In addition, the plans have several direct benefits to stockholders: 1) brokerage costs are reduced; 2) dollar averaging is encouraged; 3) dividend payments are immediately reinvested; 4) some plans offer a discount; 5) public utility plans generally offer tax-free dividend reinvestment; and 6) the program provides a form of forced savings. The plans also have a number of disadvantages: 1) stockholder diversification may be adversely affected; 2) the liquidity of stockholders is reduced; 3) new-share issues may cause some dilution; and 4) individual participation may be reduced.

Pettway and Malone found that firms with such plans tended to have higher payout ratios and lower PE ratios, earnings growth, and debt/equity ratios, and thus were generally less risky than firms not offering plans.[79] Pettway also found that the stocks of firms introducing reinvestment plans usually rose in the short term, suggesting that an attractive time to sell is shortly after a firm first offers the option.[80]

Thus reinvestment plan participation reduces flexibility, but largely avoids commissions and may both allow investors to acquire stock at a discount and reduce their tax liability. For most investors, however, the amounts involved are small and participation does reduce the opportunity to invest dividend payments elsewhere.

Cut Your Profits and Let Your Losses Run

The timing strategies discussed thus far have all been subjected to at least a cursory look at some evidence. Numerous trading strategies are, in contrast, offered without a shred of supporting evidence. An example of such gratuitous advice is that recommended by one Jeremy Grantham, a founder of Batterymarch Financial Management. In a convolution of the well-known Wall Street principle that one should sell losers and stay with winners, Grantham advises investors to ride their losers until they become winners. The British-born Harvard MBA seems to believe that whatever goes up is likely eventually to come down and vice versa.[81] That is, high-priced, highly profitable firms are likely to attract competitors who erode their profits, while poorly performing firms tend to become more profitable as their competition drifts away. No supporting evidence is offered. According to Grantham, investors should sell their strong performers and use the proceeds to double up on the poorly performing holdings. The proposal is an intriguing twist on the theory of contrary opinion. Like so many proposed trading strategies, however, this one has not been rigorously (or even casually) tested by any competent academician. One has to accept or reject such advice totally on faith.

Dollar Averaging

Investors who have little confidence in their ability to forecast market and/or individual security movements may prefer to invest a fixed dollar amount per period (dollar averaging) and thereby buy more shares when prices are low than when they are high. In a purported refinement, Emory recommends that after a portfolio has shown a profit for a time, the owner should sell some components to realize a tax loss.[82] When the portfolio begins to show losses, the reserve accumulated from past selling should be used to add to the portfolio. In this way one hopes to buy when the market is depressed and sell when it is high.

Similarly Lichell suggests a systematic investment plan involving stocks and savings accounts.[83] One puts aside a set amount each month with the percentage going into stocks determined by the previous price performance. When the market price is below the investor's average price, the percentage committed to stocks is increased and vice versa. This approach is designed to produce a maximum gain in a fluctuating market that does eventually rise. Sloane discusses dollar cost averaging applied to selling. Those with mutual fund redemption plans are advised to sell a fixed number of shares per period rather than constant dollar value, thereby selling more shares at higher prices.[84]

Tomlinson notes, however, that periodic fixed-amount purchases perform poorly if the bulk of the transactions take place at prices that are higher than end-period levels. This would in fact have happened to investors over a number of different ten-year periods.[85] Similarly, Baldwin points out that no arbitrary timing system can substitute for careful analysis.[86]

SUMMARY AND CONCLUSIONS

We began this survey of individual security timing-devices by examining technical analysis and found that the chart-reader's magic appears to be worthless. On the other hand, some specialized dependencies may well be profitably employed in trading decisions. Following Smidt, we explored special dependencies associated with anxious-trader effects, lags in reaction to new information, and speculative bubbles. Anxious-trader effects were observed in the market's reaction to block trades, tax-loss selling, secondary offerings, and intraday interactions of the bid/ask spread with the specialist's quotes. In the realm of adjustment lags, very quick reactions were found for announcements of: earnings, dividend changes, bond rating changes, *Wall Street Journal* stories, option listings, share repurchases, and rights offerings. Moreover the market tended to anticipate splits, tender offers, mergers, and voluntary spin-offs. On the other hand, insider-trading signals, forced conversion, and ex-dividend date reactions may produce exploitable patterns. Finally, the price effects of new issues and new listings seemed to reflect a speculative bubble phenomena. Overall tax-loss candidates, insider trading and new issues seem to have offered the most exploitable price trends. The usefulness of most of the other observed dependencies is largely limited to selecting the best times to make a particular trade.

The tendency of brokerage shares to magnify market moves makes them interesting trading vehicles, at least for those with forecasting ability. Since many companies offer dividend reinvestment plans, their investors need to know the pros and cons of participation. "Cut your profits and let your losses run" was included as an example of totally unsubstantiated investment timing advice. Dollar averaging provides an alternative to trying to time individual purchases.

REVIEW QUESTIONS

1. Compare the positions of chartists and those who subscribe to the random walk hypothesis.

2. Discuss the three types of situations Smidt believes are likely to lead to specialized time series dependencies in stock prices. What evidence relates to these hypothesized dependencies?
3. How do specialists and limit orders affect intraday and overnight stock prices?
4. Why should traders always ask for a price quote which includes both the bid and ask as well as the last price?
5. How do new issues and newly listed stock prices typically perform?
6. How might one use tax-loss trading, merger, tender offer, and liquidation relationships in stock market timing?
7. How do brokerage stock prices fluctuate with the stock market?
8. Discuss and analyze the impact of stock splits, stock dividends, and reinvestment plan.
9. Discuss dollar-average buying and selling.

REVIEW PROBLEMS

1. Determine the large block trades for a recent week from *Barron's* market laboratory section. Collect data on the stocks' highs and lows for the week before, during, and after the trade. Compute the average price variability for each week. Do the same for a matched set of companies. Write a report.
2. Call the nearest stock exchange and ask to have a specialist call you after trading hours so that you can interview him or her for a class project. Ask the specialist how he or she sets the bid and ask and thus the spread. Ask about limit orders and limit order book. Keep a record of all that is said. Write a report.
3. Assemble a list of stocks that reach lows near year-end and have fallen a great deal from their earlier levels. Track their performance after year-end. Write a report.
4. Assemble a list of ten stocks for a year. Track their performances around each earnings announcement, dividend announcement, and ex-dividend date. Write a report.
5. Assemble a list of ten stock split and reverse split announcements in the *Wall Street Journal*. Now track their performances for three months before and three months after the split announcements. Write a report.
6. Assemble a list of ten tender offers. Plot performances from two weeks before the announcements to the time the tender offers are complete or withdrawn. Write a report.
7. Assemble a list of ten rights offerings. Plot the performances of the underlying stocks for a period of two weeks before the announcements until the offers are complete. Write a report.
8. Assemble a list of five stocks that fit Malkiel's "Castles in the Air"

criteria. Plot their performances for six months. Write a report.

9. Assemble a list of ten stocks that were new issues six months ago. Plot their performances from then until now. Write a report.

10. Assemble a list of five stocks that have recently been listed on the NYSE. Track their performances for six weeks before and six weeks after their listings. Write a report.

11. Assemble a list of five large brokerage stocks. Plot their performances relative to the NYSE average over a two year period (by months). Formulate a trading rule and test it over the preceding two years. Write a report.

NOTES

1. A. Lerro and C. Swayne, *Selection of Securities Technical Analysis of Stock Market Prices*, General Learning Press, Morristown, NJ, 1970, pp. 30–31.

2. P. Samuelson, "Proof that Properly Discounted Present Values of Assets Vibrate Randomly," *Bell Journal of Economics and Management Science*, Autumn 1973, pp. 369–374.

3. *Business Week* "The Technical Analysts Who Called it Right," *Business Week*, August 31, 1974, pp. 54–55.

4. Laing, "The Technician: Don Hahn Calls Turns of Market with Help of Graphs, Psychology," *Wall Street Journal*, December 23, 1977, p. 1.

5. *Business Week*, "Why Granville Can't Be Ignored," *Business Week*, October 12, 1981, p. 134.

6. J. Baesel, G. Shows and E. Thorpe, "Can Joe Granville Time the Market?," *The Journal of Portfolio Management*, Spring 1982, pp. 5–9; G. Putka, "Joe Granville's Following Defecting As He Sticks with Bearish Outlook," *Wall Street Journal*, November 12, 1982, pp. 29, 49.

7. W. Granger and O. Morgenstern, *Predictability of Stock Market Prices*, Heath, Lexington, MA, 1970; E. Fama, "Random Walks in Stock Market Prices," *Financial Analysts Journal*, September/October 1965, pp. 55–59; R. Levy, "Random Walks: Reality or Myth," *Financial Analysts Journal*, November/December 1967; E. Fama and M. Blume, "Filter Rules and Stock Market Trading," *Journal of Business*, January 1966, pp. 226–241; M. Jensen and G. Benington, "Random Walks and Technical Theories: Some Additional Evidence," *Journal of Finance*, May 1970, pp. 469–482.

8. S. Smidt, "A New Look at the Random Walk Hypothesis," *Journal of Financial and Quantitative Analysis*, September 1968, pp. 235–262.

9. P. Grier and P. Albien, "Nonrandom Price Changes in Association With Trading in Large Blocks," *Journal of Business*, July 1973, pp. 425–433.

10. L. Dann, D. Mayers and R. Raab, "Trading Rules, Large Blocks and the Speed of Adjustment," *Journal of Financial Economics*, January 1977, pp. 3–22.

11. S. Kichen, "Predicting the Big Blocks," *Forbes*, February 2, 1981, p. 103.

12. M. Scholes, "The Market for Securities: Substitution versus Price Pressure and the Effects of Information on Share Prices," *Journal of Business*, April 1979, pp. 170–211.

13. Granger and Morgenstern, *op. cit.*

14. Granger and Morgenstern, *op. cit.*, especially pp. 151–176.

15. V. Niederhoffer and M. Osborne, "Market-Making and Reversal on the Stock Exchange," *Journal of American Statistical Association*, December 1966, pp. 897–917.

16. R. McEnally, "Stock Price Changes Induced by Tax Switching," *Review of Business and Economic Research*, Fall 1976, pp. 47–54; E. Dyl, "Capital Gains Taxation and Year-End Stock Market Behavior," *Journal of Finance*, March 1977, pp. 165–175; B. Branch, "A Tax Loss

Trading Rule," *Journal of Business*, April 1977, pp. 198–207; B. Branch and C. Ryan, "Tax Loss Trading: An Inefficiency Too Large To Ignore," *The Financial Review*, Winter 1980, pp. 20–29; R. Roll, "Vas ist Das?" *Journal of Portfolio Management*, Winter 1983, pp. 18–28; D. Givoly and A. Ovadia, "Year-End Tax-Induced Sales and Stock Market Seasonality," *Journal of Finance*, March 1983, pp. 171–816.

17. B. Branch and K. Chang, "Tax-Loss Trading, is the Game Over or Have the Rules Changed?," Unpublished working paper presented at 1983 Financial Management Association meeting.

18. J. Ashley, "Share Prices and Changes in Earnings and Dividends: Some Empirical Results," *Journal of Political Economy*, vol. 70, 1962, pp. 82–85.

19. C. Jones, "Economic Trends and Investment Selection," *Financial Analysts Journal*, March/April 1973, pp. 79–83.

20. H. Latane and L. Jones, "Standardized Unexpected Earnings - A Progress Report," *Journal of Finance*, December 1977, pp. 1457–1467; D. Joy, R. Litzenberger and R. McEnally, "The Adjustment of Stock Prices to Announcement of Unanticipated Change in Quarterly Earnings," *Journal of Accounting Research*, Autumn, 1977, pp. 207–224; R. Rendleman, C. Jones and H. Latane, "Emperical Anomolies Based on Unexpected Earnings and the Importance of Risk Adjustments," *Journal of Financial Economics*, November 1982, pp. 219–288.

21. M. Richards and J. Martin, "Revisions in Earnings Forecasting How Much Response?," *Journal of Portfolio Management*, Summer 1979, pp. 47–52.

22. C. Kwan, "Efficient Market Tests of the Information Content of Dividend Announcements: Critique and Extension," *Journal of Financial and Quantitative Analysis*, June 1981, pp. 193–206; J. Aharony and I. Swary, "Quarterly Dividend and Earnings Announcements and Stockholders Returns: An Empirical Analysis," *Journal of Finance*, March 1980, pp. 1–12; R. Pettit, "Dividend Announcements, Security Performance and Capital Market Efficiency," *Journal of Finance*, December 1972, p. 1006; R. Watts, "The Information Content of Dividends," *Journal of Business*, April 1973, pp. 191–211; A. Divecha and D. Morse, "Market Responses to Dividend Increases and Changes in Payout Ratios," *Journal of Financial and Quantitative Analysis*, June 1983, pp. 163–174; G. Benesh, A. Keown and J. Pinkerton, "An Examination to Market Reaction to Substantial Shifts in Dividend Policy," *Journal of Financial Research*, Summer 1984, pp. 131–142.

23. J. Campbell and W. Bernek, "Stock Price Behavior on Ex-Dividend Date," *Journal of Finance*, December 1955, pp. 425–429; A. Kalay, "The Ex-Divided Day Behavior of Stock Prices: A Reexamination of the Clientel Effect," *Journal of Finance*, September 1982, pp. 1059–1070.

24. A. Kalay and M. Subrahmanyam, "The Ex-Dividend Day Behavior of Option Prices," *Journal of Business*, January 1984, pp. 113–128.

25. M. Joehnk, O. Bowlin and J. Petty, "Preferred Dividend Rolls: A Viable Strategy for Corporate Money Managing?," *Financial Management*, Summer 1980, pp. 78–87; J. Finnerty, "The Behavior of Electric Utility Common Stock Prices Near the Ex-Dividend Date," *Financial Management*, Winter 1981, pp. 59–68.

26. D. Morse, " *Wall Street Journal* Announcements and the Securities Markets," *Financial Analysts Journal*, March/April 1982, pp. 69–76.

27. C. Bidwell and R. Kolb, "The Impact and Value of Broker Sell Recommendations," *Financial Review*, Fall 1980, pp. 58–68.

28. P. Griffin and A. Sanvicente, "Common Stock Returns and Rating Changes: A Methodological Comparison," *Journal of Finance*, March 1982, pp. 103–120.

29. B. Jaggi and M. Freedman, "An Analysis of the Information Content of Pollution Disclosures," *Financial Review*, September 1982, pp. 142–152.

30. J. Strachan, D. Smith and W. Beedles, "The Price Reaction to (Alleged) Corporate Crime," *Financial Review*, May 1983, pp. 121–132.

31. J. Scholl, "Before and After: What Happens to Stocks Recommended on 'Wall Street Week,'" *Barron's*, October 25, 1982, pp. 32–33.

32. A. Schwartz, "The Adjustment of Individual Stock Prices During Periods of Unusual Disequilibria," *Financial Review*, November 1982, pp. 228–239.

33. D. Officer and G. Trennepohl, "Price Behavior of Corporate Equities Near Options Expiration Dates," *Financial Management*, Summer 1981, pp. 75–80.

34. B. Branch and J. Finnerty, "The Impact of Option Listing on the Price and Volume of the Underlying Stock," *Financial Review*, Spring 1982, pp. 1–15.

35. M. Whiteside, W. Dukes and P. Dunne, "Short Term Impact of Option Trading on Underling Securities," *Journal of Financial Research*, Winter 1983, pp. 313–322.

36. M. Zweig, "Canny Insiders," *Barron's*, January 21, 1976, p. 5.

37. K. Nunn, G. Madden and M. Gombola, "Are Some Insiders More 'Inside' Than Others?," *Journal of Portfolio Management*, Spring 1983, pp. 18–22.

38. G. Trivoli, "How to Profit from Insider Trading Information," *Journal of Portfolio Management*, Summer 1980, pp. 51–56.

39. J. Boland, "Canny Insiders: It Usually Pays to Follow their Lead," *Barron's*, January 26, 1981, pp. 9, 20, 21, 24; J. Boland, "Insider Favorites: They Range from Burroughs to Weatherfron Instructional," *Barron's*, February 8, 1982, pp. 15, 29; J. Boland, "Ahead of the Crowd," *Barron's*, December 27, 1982 pp. 14, 18.

40. W. Baker and P. Gallager, "Management's View of Stock Splits," *Financial Management*, Summer 1980, pp. 73–77; L. Ingrassia, "Recent Increase in Share Prices Has Led to Flurry of Stock Splits, Stock Dividends," *Wall Street Journal*, January 27, 1983, p. 56; D. Harris, "The Inside Track on Stocks," *Money*, December 1983, pp. 131–140.

41. T. Copeland, "Liquidity Changes Following Splits," *Journal of Finance*, March 1979, pp. 115–142.

42. E. Fama, L. Fisher, M. Jensen, R. Roll, "The Adjustment of Stock Prices to New Information," *International Economic Review*, February 1969, pp. 1–21; F. Reilly and E. Drzycimski, "Short-Run Profits from Stock Splits," *Financial Management*, Summer 1981, pp. 64–74.

43. J. Miller and B. Fielitz, "Stock Split and Stock Dividend Decisions," *Financial Management*, Winter 1973, pp. 35–46; T. Lueck, "Stock Splits - Not Always a Bonanza," *New York Times*, July 3, 1983, p. 15F.

44. J. Woolridge and D. Chambers, "Reverse Splits and Shareholder Wealth," *Financial Management*, Autumn 1983, pp. 5–15.

45. W. Nichols and S. Brown, "Assimilating Earnings and Split Information," *Journal of Financial Economics*, September 1981, pp. 309–316.

46. W. Nichols, "Security Price Reaction to Occasional Small Stock Dividends," *Financial Review*, Winter 1981, pp. 54–62.

47. J. Woolridge, "Stock Dividends As Signals," *Journal of Financial Research*, Spring 1983, pp. 1–12.

48. G. Madden, "Potential Corporate Takeover and Market Efficiency," *Journal of Finance*, December 1981, pp. 1181–1196; R. Masulis, "Stock Repurchase by Tender Offer: An Analysis of the Cause of Common Stock Price Changes," *Journal of Finance*, May 1980, 305–318; S. Andreder, "Up the Down Staircase: Takeover Candidates Continue to Buck the Market Trend," *Barron's*, July 12, 1982, pp. 25–27; P. Asquith and E. Kim, "The Impact of Merger Bids on the Participating Firm's Security Holders," *Journal of Finance*, December 1982, pp. 1209–1228; J. Wansley, W. Lane and H. Yang, "Abnormal Returns to Acquired Firms by Type of Acquisition and Method of Payment," *Financial Management*, Autumn 1983, pp. 16–22; P. Asquith, "Merger Bids, Uncertainty, and Stockholder Returns," *Journal of Financial Economics*, April 1983, pp. 51–80.

49. R. Masulis, "The Effects of Capital Structure Change on Security Prices," *Journal of Financial Economics*, June 1980, pp. 139–178.

50. T. Vermaelen, "Common Stock Repurchases and Market Signaling: An Empirical Study," *Journal of Financial Economics*, June 1981, pp. 139–184; L. Dann, "Common Stock Repur-

chasing: An Analysis of Returns to Bondholding and Stockholders," *Journal of Financial Economics*, June 1981, pp. 113–138.

51. W. Baldwin, "A Modest Proposal," *Forbes*, August 2, 1982, pp. 31–33.

52. M. Bradley and L. Wakeman, "The Wealth Effects of Targeted Share Repurchases," *Journal of Financial Economics*, April 1983, pp. 301–328.

53. L. Dann and H. DeAngelo, "Standstill Agreements, Privately Negotiated Stock Repurchases and the Market for Corporate Control," *Journal of Financial Economics*, April 1983, pp. 275–300.

54. P. Dodd and J. Warner, "On Corporate Governance: A Study of Proxy Contests," *Journal of Financial Economics*, April 1983, pp. 401–438.

55. R. White and P. Lusztig, "The Price Effects of Rights Offerings," *Journal of Financial and Quantitative Analysis*, March 1980, pp. 23–40.

56. G. Alexander and R. Stover, "The Effect of Forced Conversions Common Stock Prices," *Financial Management*, Spring 1980, pp. 39–45.

57. J. Miles and J. Rosenfeld, "The Effect of Voluntary Spin-off Announcements on Shareholder Wealth," *Journal of Finance*, December 1983, pp. 1519–1528; D. Heath and J. Zaira, "Voluntary Corporate Divestiture and Value," *Financial Management*, Spring 1984, pp. 10–16; G. Alexander, G. Benson and J. Kampmeyer "Investigating the Valuation Effects of Announcements of Voluntary Corporate Selloffs," *Journal of Finance*, June 1984, pp. 503–517.

58. G. Hawawini and A. Vora, "Evidence of International Systematic Risk in the Price Movements of NYSE and AMEX Common Stocks," *Journal of Financial and Quantitative Analysis*, June 1980, pp. 331–340; G. Hawawini, "The Intertemporal Cross Price Behavior of Common Stocks: Evidence and Implications," *Journal of Financial Research*, Summer 1980, pp. 153–167.

59. D. Morse, "Asymmetrical Information in Securities Markets and Trading Volume," *Journal of Financial and Quantitative Analysis*, December 1980, pp. 1129–1148.

60. B. Malkiel, *A Random Walk Down Wall Street*, WW Norton, New York, 1973, p. 243.

61. F. Bleakley, "Story' Stocks Come Back into Vogue," *New York Times*, April 17, 1983, p. 10F; *Business Week*, "Are High-Tech Stocks Flying Too High?," *Business Week*, March 21, 1983, pp. 126–127; E. Spragins, "Remember Transitron?," *Forbes*, June 6, 1983, p. 200.

62. F. Reilly, "Further Evidence on Short-Run Results for New Issues Investors," *Journal of Financial and Quantitative Analysis*, January 1973, pp. 83–90.

63. R. Ibbotson, "Price Performance of Common Stock New Issues," *Journal of Financial Economics*, September 1975, pp. 235–272.

64. D. Logue, "On the Pricing of Unseasoned Equity Issues, 1965–1969," *Journal of Financial and Quantitative Analysis*, January 1973, pp. 91–104.

65. D. Baron, "A Model of the Demand for Investment Banking Advising and Distribution Services for New Issues," *Journal of Finance*, September 1982, pp. 955–996.

66. B. Neuberger and C. Hammond, "A Study of Underwriters' Experience with Unseasoned New Issues," *Journal of Financial and Quantitative Analysis*, March 1974, pp. 165–177; D. Logue and J. Lindvall, "The Behavior of Investment Bankers: An Econometric Investigation," *Journal of Finance*, March 1974, pp. 203–215; B. Newberger and C. La Chapelle, "Unseasoned New Issue Price Performance on Three Tiers: 1975-1980," *Financial Management*, Autumn 1983, pp. 23–28.

67. *Ibid.*

68. E. Nelson, "Comment: 'A Study of Underwriters' Experience with Unseasoned New Issues'," *Journal of Financial and Quantitative Analysis*, March 1974, pp. 179–180.

69. U.S. Securities and Exchange Commission, 1963 *Special Study of Securities Markets*, 1963, p. 551.

70. N. Galluccio, "Isn't This Where We Came In?," *Forbes*, September 29, 1980, pp. 160–162; R. Dustin and G. Getschow, "New Issues Stock Boom Nears Danger Point Some Regulators

Warn," *Wall Street Journal*, November 211, 1980, pp. 1, 20; S. Kichen, "New Issues Pick up Steam," *Forbes*, March 30, 1981, p. 138.

71. R. Angell and J. Hunt, "Is the Denver Market Efficient?," *Journal of Portfolio Management*, Spring 1982, pp. 10–16.

72. D. Downes and R. Heinkel, "Signaling and the Valuation of Unseasoned New Issues," *Journal of Finance*, March 1982, pp. 1–10.

73. A. Hess and P. Frost, "Tests for Price Effects of New Issues of Seasoned Securities," *Journal of Finance*, March 1982, pp. 11–26.

74. R. Furst, "Does Listing Increase the Market Price of Common Shares?," *Journal of Business*, April 1970, pp. 174–180; J. Van Horne, "New Listings and Their Price Behavior," *Journal of Finance*, September 1970, pp. 783–794; F. Fabozzi, "Does Listing on the AMEX Increase the Value of Equity," *Financial Management*, Spring 1981, pp. 43–50; S. Kichen and J. Schriber, "The Big Board is a Roller Coaster," *Forbes*, August 31, 1982, pp. 162–165; J. McConnell and G. Sawyer, "A Trading Strategy for New Listings on the NYSE," *Financial Analyst Journal*, January/February 1984, pp. 34–38.

75. W. Goulet, "Price Changes, Managerial Actions and Insider Trading at the Time of Listing," *Financial Management*, Spring 1974, pp. 30–36; *Business Week*, "Now the Best Investment May be Your Broker," *Business Week*, June 20, 1983, pp. 166–167.

76. R. Stovall, "Strictly for Swingers: Brokerage Shares Lead the Market-Violently-Up or Down," *Barron's*, June 12, 1978; P. Meyer, "Riding the Brokerage Stocks," *Forbes*, August 6, 1982, pp. 31–32.

77. R. Pettway and R. Malone, "Automatic Dividend Reinvestment Plans and Non-Financial Corporations," *Financial Management*, Winter 1973, pp. 11–18.

78. *Forbes*, "Off the Street," September 15, 1980, pp. 148–151.

79. Pettway and Malone, *op. cit.*

80. R. Pettway, "Automatic Dividend Reinvestment Plans, Valuation, and Dividend Policy," unpublished working paper.

81. *Forbes*, "The Man who Loves Dogs," December 11, 1978, pp. 87–90.

82. E. Emory, *When to Sell Stocks*, Dow Jones-Irwin, Homewood, IL 1973.

83. R. Lichell, *Superpower Investing*, Farnsworth, Lynnbrook, NY, 1974.

84. L. Sloane, "Cost Averaging In Reverse," *New York Times*, May 7, 1983, p. 30.

85. L. Tomlinson, "Overrated Technique: Dollar Cost Averaging Has Failed to Pay Off," *Barron's*, October 20, 1975, pp. 5–11.

86. W. Baldwin, "All Coins Have Two Sides," *Forbes*, May 23, 1983, pp. 188–189; W. Baldwin, "The Dollar-Cost Sure Thing," *Forbes*, August 15, 1983, pp. 114–115.

Section V:
Mutual Funds, Bonds and Options

The first four sections of this book deal largely with stock market investing. While common stocks are important, the universe of investable assets is much broader. Indeed mutual funds, bonds, and options, investment types related to but distinct from common stocks, have grown in relative importance in the last several years. The following case illustrates many of the issues that you will encounter in this section.

Passing the CFA Exam

You have been working as a broker in a middle-size brokerage firm for two years. While your client list has grown and the firm seems happy with your work, you want to move up. One component of your advancement strategy is to become Chartered Financial Analyst (CFA). Accordingly you signed up for their course and exam. Your work as a stockbroker has made you quite familiar with stocks, so you expect no trouble with that part of the exam. You know, however, that mutual funds, bonds, and options will also be covered on the exam. Moreover your own clients have been asking you more and more questions about these investment types. You feel that now is the time to diversify securities market knowledge.

The chapters of this section provide an extensive background on these non-stock investment types. Chapter 14 discusses mutual funds and other types of pooled portfolios. The types, organizational structures, performance, and advantages of such investments are considered. Chapters 15 and 16 cover fixed income securities. Chapter 15 examines the characteristics and types of both short- and long-term debt securities. Various factors that affect yields are considered in Chapter 16, specifically default risk, term structure, duration, the coupon effect, and a variety of specialized characteristics yield effects. Chapter 17 explores the nature of and various ways of trading pure option securities, including puts, calls, warrants, and rights. Chapter 18 takes up convertibles and other types of combination securities, as well as hedging and arbitraging, trades which often involve combination securities.

14 Mutual Funds and Similar Types of Investments

Mutual funds and similar types of pooled portfolios are designed for investors who want some of their wealth managed by "professionals." While average risk-adjusted mutual fund performance approximates that of the market, their convenience, diversification, recordkeeping, security-safekeeping, and portfolio management appeal to many investors.

We begin this chapter by discussing the various types of pooled-portfolio arrangements. Next the funds' organizational structures, sales fees, asset compositions and investment priorities (income, growth, liquidity, capital-preservation, tax-preference) are explored, followed by a listing of some mutual fund information sources. We then examine fund performance, giving particular attention to the difficulty funds have in outperforming the market. Finally fund selection criteria are explored.

DIFFERING WAYS OF ORGANIZING FUNDS

Mutual funds and similar investments assemble and maintain pooled portfolios for individual investors. Each share (or unit) of such an investment represents a fraction of its portfolio. A share's pro rata ownership of the portfolio is called its net asset value (NAV). For example: a $100,000,000 portfolio divided among 10,000,000 shares would have a per-share NAV of $10. If the portfolio's value rose to $110,000,000, NAV would increase to $11, assuming no change in shares outstanding.

Load versus No-Load Funds

Mutual funds may be bought directly from the company (no-load) or through a stockbroker or mutual fund salesperson (load). Load fund purchases incur a sales fee ranging from 8.5% on small acquisitions (under $10,000) to 1% on very large purchases (over $1 million). The standard $850 fee on a $10,000 load fund purchase compares unfavorably with the 2% to 3% average commission on direct stock acquisitions. Front-end loading of long-term purchase agreements is particularly costly to buyers. Under the Securities Amendments Act of 1970, purchasers have 45 days to cancel for a full refund; the front-end load cannot exceed 50% of the initial year's payment, and cancellation within a year reduces the load to 15%.

Even so, separate yearly purchases are less expensive. For example: in a ten-year plan to invest $1,000 annually, the first year's commission would be $500 and reduced to $150 if the plan were cancelled within a year. A simple $1,000 purchase would, in contrast, only incur an $85 commission.

Direct sales of no-load funds do not involve an agent or sales fee. Load and no-load average portfolio-performances have been comparable.[1] Selling expenses borne by the no-load fundholders are, in contrast, relatively small. While mutual fund agents know their product, most investors can find suitable no-load funds themselves with a bit of research. Avoiding a fee of $85 per thousand invested provides a very good reason for most investors to prefer no-load funds. The sales disadvantage of their extra cost has led many funds to convert to no-load status.

Prospectuses for no-load funds may be obtained by responding to advertisements in the financial press or writing to the funds listed in such guides as Weisenberger (available in most libraries). Several directories are devoted exclusively to no-load funds. Published annually, they list various types of funds, along with their services, minimum investment amounts, addresses and telephone numbers. One such guide is available for $1 from the No-Load Mutual Fund Association, Valley Forge Colony Building, Valley Forge, PA. 19481. The *Handbook for No-Load Fund Investors*, $24, from P.O. Box 283, Hastings-on-Hudson, N.Y. 10706 is more comprehensive. *The Individual Investor's Guide to No-load Mutual Funds* is available to all members of the American Association of Individual Investors (Membership fee of $44 per year, 612 N. Michigan Avenue, Chicago, Ill. 60611).

Closed-End Investment Companies

Mutual funds' numbers of outstanding shares increase or decrease with sales and/or redemptions. Normally the number of closed-end investment company shares outstanding remains constant, with supply and demand determining share prices. The shares may sell for a premium or, more commonly, at a discount from their NAV. Boudreau suggests that the divergence of per-share prices from their NAVs reflects differences in expected future performance.[2] Malkiel's in-depth empirical study ascribed part of the discount to unrealized appreciation, capital gains distributions policy, and letter and foreign stock investments.[3] Most of the discounts, however, seemed to result from the lack of broker incentives (their fee on a load fund is much higher than for a closed-end fund). Leonard and Noble, in contrast, argue that the discounts and premiums are related to uncertain future risk levels and the difficulty of forcing a liquidation.[4]

Richards, Fraser, and Groth found that over the 1970–76 period, deep-discount funds generally outperformed the market.[5] Large shareholders sometimes take over closed-end funds and convert them to open-end.[6] Thus a 10,000,000 share closed-end fund with a per-share NAV and market price of $10.00 and $7.50, respectively, might offer a tempting target. While a takeover effort would probably drive the price up, perhaps 3,000,000 shares could be purchased over time at an average cost of $8.50. If the remaining stock is widely dispersed, 30% of the outstanding shares should be sufficient for control. The new controlling group could quickly convert to an open-end fund. By offering to buy back shares at their NAV, the fund would immediately make each holder's shares worth the $10 NAV (assuming no price change while the takeover was underway). Relatively large resources are required to force such a reorganization, but small fundholders will also profit.

Investment Company Quotations

Figure 14.1, a closed-end fund quotation, was taken from the *New York Times*. Similar quotations appear in the *Wall Street Journal, Barron's* and elsewhere. Funds are grouped into two categories: diversified common stock funds and specialized equity and convertible funds. The NAV, stock price, premium and discount are reported.

Figure 14.1   Closed-End Quotation

Closed End Bond Funds

TUESDAY, JAN. 24, 1984

Unaudited net asset values of closed-end investment bond fund shares, recorded by the companies as of Friday. Also shown is the closing listed market price or a dealer-to-dealer asked price of each fund's shares, with the percentage of difference.

	N.A. Value	Stk Price	% Diff		N.A. Value	Stk Price	% Diff
AmCap	19.28	18⅞	- 2.1	ItcpSe	18.11	18⅛	+ 0.08
Bunk H	17.45	17⅝	+ 1.0	HanJI(a)	18.78	17⅞	- 4.8
CircleIn	12.32	13¾	+11.6	HanJS	14.06	13	7.5
CNAI	10.72	10¼	- 4.4	LincPI	23.53	20⅝	-12.4
CurrInc	10.05	9½	- 5.5	Mas Inc	10.94	11⅝	+ 6.3
DrexB	17.27	17⅞	+ 3.5	Mon St	17.34	17½	- 1.2
Exclsr	16.51	15⅝	- 5.4	MutOm	12.86	12⅝	- 1.8
FtDear	12.28	11⅝	- 5.3	PacAS	13.94	12⅜	-11.2
HatSe	15.49	15¾	+ 1.7	SPaul	10.27	10	- 2.6
INAIn	16.72	16½	- 1.3	StaMSe	10.72	10	- 6.7
IndSqlSc	15.80	17¼	+9.2	TranInc	19.34	18¾	- 3.1
				Uslife	9.65	9⅝	-0.3

*Thursday's Price.
(a) Ex Dividend.**Prices Monthly.
n.a. Not Available.

Publicly Traded Funds

February 3, 1984
Following is a weekly listing of unaudited net asset values of publicly traded investment fund shares, reported by the companies as of Friday's close. Also shown is the closing listed market price or a dealer-to-dealer asked price of each fund's shares, with the percentage of difference.

	N.A. Value	Stk Price	% Diff		N.A. Value	Stk Price	% Diff
Diversified Common Stock Funds				BancrftCv	a25.16	24	- 4.6
AdmExp	17.18	16⅜-	4.7	Castle	30.79	32½+	5.6
BakerFen	40	34½-	13.8	CentSec	14.02	12¾-	9.1
EqStrat	b12.11	11½-	5.0	Claremonta	34.81	29⅜-	15.6
GenAInv	16.52	18⅛+	9.7	CLAS	.69		....
Lehman	14.71	15½+	5.4	CLAS Pfd	39.10	1⅞	....
NiagaraSha	17.65	18⅝+	5.5	Cyprus	55.0	3⅞+	559.1
OceasSec	4.46	7¼+	12.2	Engex	23.72	19	-19.89
Source	32.14	31¼-	2.8	Japan	14.41	14	- 2.8
Tri-Conti	24.51	24⅜-	.6	Mexico	b3.38	3¾+	10.9
US&For	23.34	22⅜-	4.1	Nautilus	33.09	36½+	10.3
Specialized Equity and Convertible Funds				NewAnFd	38.91	35¼-	9.4
AmCapCv	30.73	32 +	4.1	Pete&Res	28.71	28⅜-	.3
ASA	b60.33	61¾+	2.4				

a-Ex-dividend. b-As of Thursday's close. z-Not available.

The closed-end quotations may be compared with the *New York Times* mutual fund quotation in Figure 14.2. Similar quotes appear in the *Wall Street Journal* and most major newspapers. The offer price reflects the load if any. No-load funds sell at their NAVs. Many fund groups such as the American Express Funds or the Dreyfus Group are managed by the same company but appeal to different investors' needs and goals.

Figure 14.2 Mutual Fund Quotation

Mutual Funds

	N.A.V.	Buy	Chg.
DMC			
Decat	14.49	15.84+	.11
Delaw	17.09	18.68+	.03
Delch	6.96	7.61-	.06
Tx Fre	6.52	6.83-	.05
Delta	10.99	12.01-	.05
DIT CG	9.91	NL +	.16
DIT AG	15.10	NL +	.05
DIT CI	9.01	NL -	.09
Dir Cap	.82	NL	
DG Div	21.69	NL +	.24
DodCx Bl	24.39	NL +	.23
DodCx St	22.75	NL +	.27
Drex Bur	16.34	16.93+	.13
Dreyfus Grp:			
A Bnd	12.00	NL -	.11
CalTx	12.67	NL -	.13
Dreyf	11.36	12.42+	.09
Interm	12.00	NL -	.08
Levge	15.40	16.83+	.14
GthOp	9.59	NL +	.03
NY Tx	12.72	NL -	.10
Spl Inc	7.04	NL	
Tax Ex	10.52	NL -	.08
Thrd C	6.49	NL +	.03
Eagl Gth	6.63	7.25+	.03
Eaton Vance:			
EHBal	7.17	7.73+	.07
EHStk	10.91	11.76+	.17
Grwth	6.18	6.75+	.06
HiYld	4.42	4.83-	.02
IncBos	8.23	8.99-	.02
Invest	7.24	7.91+	.04
SpEqt	17.46	18.82+	.09
TaxM	12.93	14.13+	.12
VS Spl	12.77	13.96+	.08
Eberstadt Group:			
Chem	9.05	9.89+	.10
EngRs	11.65	12.73	
Survey	12.76	13.95+	.09
EnguTil	19.15	NL +	.18
Evrgrn r	36.14	NL +	.16
EvrgrTtl	13.67	NL +	.04
FPA Par	12.78	13.97+	.09
FPA Per	14.12	15.43+	.06
Frm BG	12.79	NL +	.15
Federated Funds:			
Am Ldr	11.00	11.76+	.12
Exch	21.82	NL +	.28
FdlIntr	9.08	NL -	.06
GNMA	9.58	NL -	
Hi Icm	10.99	11.75-	.07
Inco	9.47	NL -	.16
Short	10.07	NL -	
Stock	14.25	NL +	.20
Tx Fre	8.37	8.76-	.06
US Gvt	7.72	8.08-	.14
Fidelity Invest:			
Bond	6.12	NL -	.03
Congrs	49.57	NL +	.55
Conffd	9.29	NL +	.01
Dstny	12.24..	-	.01
Discv	17.10	NL +	.02
Eq Inc	21.48	21.92+	.10
Exch	41.25	NL +	.55
Fredm	11.22	NL +	.10
Magel	29.71	30.63+	.18
Mun Bd	6.39	NL	
Fidel	13.77	NL +	.12
Gvt Sec	8.67	NL -	.08
Hilnco	8.15	NL -	.03
Hi Yld	10.63	NL -	
Lt Mun	7.86	NL -	
MassTx	9.31	9.40-	.01
Merc	11.16	11.51+	.07
Purifn	11.33	NL +	.03
SelEn	9.86	10.06+	.03
SelFin	16.01	16.34+	.01
SelHlt	16.04	16.37+	.07
SelMtl	14.00	14.29+	.07
SelTch	20.45	20.87+	.36
SelUtil	14.40	14.69+	.10
SpecSit	9.94	10.25+	.02
Thrift	9.03	NL -	
Trend	34.48	NL +	.11
FiduCap	16.18	NL +	.03
Financial Prog:			
Bond	6.09	NL -	.12
Dyna	6.69	NL +	.05
FnclTx	13.40	NL -	.01
Indust	3.86	NL +	.05

	N.A.V.	Buy	Chg.
IRI Stck	13.10	13.72+	.14
IDS Mutual:			
IDS Bd	4.41	4.57-	.02
IDS Dis	6.63	6.98+	.02
IDS Ex	4.68	4.93	
IDS Grt	14.86	15.64+	.18
IDS HiY	3.73	3.93-	.02
IDS ND	8.13	8.56+	.05
IDS Prog	6.45	6.79+	.04
Inv Mtl	10.38	10.93+	.02
IDS Tx	3.25	3.42-	.02
Inv Stk	15.05	15.84+	.13
Inv Sel	7.32	7.71-	.03
Inv Var	7.28	7.66+	.07
ISI Group:			
Grwth	6.14	6.71-	.01
Incom	3.42	3.74-	.04
Trst Sh	10.24	11.19-	.05
Industry	6.80	NL +	.07
Inf Invst	14.25	15.57-	.04
InvP Eqty	8.63	NL +	.13
InvP HiY	8.33	NL -	.04
ITB Group:			
InvBos	8.93	9.63+	.04
Hilnco	13.16	14.19-	.02
MasTF	13.97	14.67+	.01
Inv Resh	4.87	5.32+	.03
Istel	13.53	NL -	
IvyGth	12.16	NL +	.04
Ivyinst	95.51	NL +	.38
JP Grth	12.78	13.89+	.14
JP Inco	7.23	7.86-	.08
Janus	11.38	NL +	.05
John Hancock:			
Bond	12.90	14.02-	.09
Grwth	11.52	12.52+	.16
US Gvt	7.94	8.63-	.08
Tax Ex	8.90	9.67	
Kaufmn	.10	NL	
Kemper Funds:			
CalTx	11.46	12.00-	.05
Incom	7.78	8.28-	.03
Grow	12.26	13.40+	.17
Hi Yld	9.64	10.34-	.03
IntlFd	13.86	15.15-	.09
Mun B	7.57	7.92-	.06
Optn	11.39	12.45+	.11
Summ	22.07	24.12+	.31
Tech	11.30	12.35+	.15
Tot Rt	12.22	13.36+	.11
US Gvt	8.29	8.64-	.05
Keystone Mass:			
Cus B1 r	14.12	NL -	.10
Cus B2 r	16.96	NL -	.06
Cus B4 r	7.51	NL -	.01
Cus K1 r	8.22	NL	
Cus K2 r	5.95	NL +	.06
Cus S1 r	18.43	NL +	.22
Cus S3 r	8.27	NL +	.08
Cus S4 r	5.69	NL +	.04
Intl r	4.72	NL +	.04
TxFr r	7.34	NL -	.01
Mass	11.68...		
LeggMas	18.29	NL +	.06
LehCap	19.12	NL +	.11
LehInvst	16.73	NL +	.24
Levrge	6.58	NL +	.09
Lexington Grp:			
CpLdr fr	10.69	11.51+	.04
Goldfd	4.15	NL +	.01
GNMA	7.02	NL -	.08
Grow	7.33	NL +	.02
Resh	14.36	NL +	.10
Lindnr	18.30	NL +	.03
Loomis Sayles:			
Capit	16.30	NL +	.33
Mut	15.10	NL +	.05
Lord Abbett:			
Affiltd	8.49	9.15+	.10
Bnd db	9.62	10.51+	.02
Dev Gt	7.30	7.98-	
Incom	2.79	3.01-	.01
ValAp	7.82	8.55+	.05
Lowry	8.86	9.68+	.02
Lutheran Bro:			
Fund	13.21	13.91+	.13
Incom	7.85	8.26-	.09
Muni	6.53	6.87-	.05
Mass Financl:			
InTrB	9.71	10.47-	.14
MIT	10.62	11.45+	.15

	N.A.V.	Buy	Chg.
Neuberger Berm:			
Enrgy	17.80	NL +	.14
Guard	35.40	NL +	.33
Libty	3.74	NL -	.03
Manht	5.84	NL +	.07
Partn	14.15	NL +	.05
NY Mun	1.04	NL -	.01
NY Vent	7.26	7.93+	.04
Newt Gt	24.31	NL +	.18
Newt Inc	7.89	NL -	.01
Nichola	22.41	NL +	.05
Nichinc	3.41	NL -	.03
NE InTr	10.46	NL	
NE InGt	10.11	NL +	.08
NovaFd	11.91	NL +	.09
Nuveen	6.97	NL -	.03
Omega	9.49	NL +	.09
Oppenheimer Fd:			
AIM	17.01	18.59+	.09
Direct	17.51	19.14+	.13
EqInc	6.87	7.51-	
Oppen	7.82	8.55+	.05
Gold	8.43	9.21-	.01
Hi Yld	16.87	18.09-	.04
Prem	22.56	24.66+	.25
Rgcy	12.88	14.08+	.02
Specl	19.61	21.43+	.20
Target	15.49	16.48+	.01
Tx Fre	7.54	7.90-	.03
Time	11.99	13.10+	.14
OTC Sec	14.21	15.45+	.02
PwbAtl	8.34	9.11+	.02
PwbAm	12.17	13.30+	.01
PaxWld	10.45	NL -	
Penn Sq	8.17	NL +	.10
Penn Mu	5.58	NL	
PermPrt	11.01	NL -	
Phila	8.29	9.06+	.11
Phoenix Series:			
Balan	9.77	10.68-	.05
CvFd	15.45	16.89+	.13
Grwth	12.11	13.23+	.03
HiYld	8.68	9.33	
Stock	10.33	11.29+	.03
PC Cp	11.89...	+	.09
Pilgrim Grp:			
Mag C	6.19	6.67+	.02
Mag In	7.34	7.91-	.01
PAR	22.28	22.62-	.02
Pilg Fd	12.12	13.07+	.04
Pioneer Fund:			
Bond	8.38	9.16-	.04
Fund	18.79	20.54+	.17
II Inc	14.27	15.60+	.09
III Inc	12.25	13.39-	.02
Plitrnd	11.75	NL +	.13
PrecMtl	18.56	NL -	.04
Price Funds:			
Grwth	12.90	NL +	.23
GthInc	11.75	NL +	.09
Incom	8.07	NL -	.01
Intl	13.02	NL -	.10
N Era	15.98	NL +	.15
N Horiz	12.44	NL +	.04
ShTrBd	4.89	NL -	.01
TxFrI	8.24	NL -	.01
TxFrSi	4.91	NL	
Pro Services:			
MedT	8.46	NL +	.06
Fund	8.97	NL +	.07
Incom	8.02	NL -	.02
Prudential Bache:			
AdiPfd	24.06	NL -	.04
Equity	12.94	13.88+	.08
GvtSc	9.40	9.49-	.04
HiYld	9.36	10.04-	.01
HYMu	13.26	13.88-	.02
NDec	11.41	12.24+	.08
Option	13.42	14.39+	.18
Qualty	13.98	14.99-	.10
Rsch r	8.25	NL -	.02
TxMng	20.44	21.92+	.14
Putnam Funds:			
Conv	12.07	13.19+	.07
CalTx	12.86	13.50-	.12
Capit	6.43...	+	.09
CCsArp	46.74	47.94-	.07
CCsDsp	46.91	48.11+	.13
InfoSc	11.01	12.03+	.20
Int Eq	14.84	16.22...	
Georg	10.22	11.17+	.07

	N.A.V.	Buy	Chg.
HiYld	17.33	18.24-	.10
MMun	12.57	13.23-	.10
NYMun	13.41	14.12-	.11
Sherm D	6.73	NL -	
Sierra Gt	11.04	NL +	.11
Sigma Funds:			
Capit	11.84	12.94+	.06
Inco	6.88	7.52-	.04
Invest	7.02	7.67+	.05
Spcl n	6.38	6.97+	.05
Trust	10.12	11.06+	.04
Vent	8.62	9.42+	.02
SB Eqty	12.45	NL +	.16
SB I&Gr	8.07	8.56+	.04
SoGen In	13.23	13.85-	.03
SwinInc	4.30	NL -	.04
Sover In	17.43	18.35+	.12
State Bond Grp:			
Com St	4.78	5.22+	.06
Divers	5.68	6.21+	.05
Progrs	7.60	8.31+	.06
StFrm Gt	8.84	NL +	.07
StFrm Bl	11.87	NL +	.01
StStreet Inv:			
Exch	76.50	NL +	1.15
Grwth r	49.49	NL +	.77
Intl	66.10	66.47+	1.01
Steadman Funds:			
Am Ind	3.01	NL +	.03
Assoc	.85	NL	
Invest	1.38	NL +	.01
Ocean	6.10	NL +	.01
Stein Roe Fds:			
Bond	7.83	NL -	.06
Cap Op	20.08	NL +	.60
Discv	7.39	NL +	.06
Specl	13.29	NL +	.05
Stock	13.46	NL +	.15
TaxEx	7.43	NL -	.02
TotRet	19.71	NL +	.26
Univ	14.86	NL -	.02
StratCap	7.11	7.77+	.07
StratInv	9.51	10.39-	.14
Strat Gth	16.18	NL +	.07
Strongin	16.41	NL +	.03
StrngT	15.06	NL +	.01
Tel IncSh	12.11..-		
Templeton Group:			
Frgn	10.48	11.45+	.03
Global I	31.22	NL -	.11
Glob II	9.33	10.20-	.02
Grwth	8.82	9.64+	.08
World	11.71	12.80+	.09
Thomson McKinnon:			
Gwth	x10.17	NL +	.05
Inco	x 9.23	NL -	.08
Opor	x10.27	NL +	.08
Trns Cap	8.65	9.40+	.05
TrnsNew	7.58	NL -	.03
Tudr Fd	16.53	NL +	.08
20th Century:			
Gift r	3.92	3.93+	.02
Grwth	11.72	NL +	.26
Select	20.67	NL +	.21
Ultra r	6.40	6.43+	.09
USGv	93.05	NL -	.47
Vista r	4.22	4.24+	.03
USAA Group:			
Grwth	12.10	NL +	.09
Inco			
Sblt	13.37	NL +	.04
TXEH	11.26	NL -	
TXEIt	10.73	NL -	
TXESh	10.18	NL -	
Unified Mgmt:			
Acum	7.79	NL +	.03
Gwth	15.24	NL +	.05
Inco	11.17	NL -	
Mutl	11.43	NL +	.06
United Funds:			
Accm	6.92	7.56+	.05
Bond	4.97	5.43-	.04
IntGth	5.91	6.46-	.01
Con Inc	12.66	13.84-	.01
Hi Inc	12.31	13.45-	.02
Incom	11.76	12.85+	.13
Muni	5.93	6.18-	.04
NwCcpt	4.65	5.08...	
Retire	5.56	6.08+	.01
ScEng	9.19	10.04+	.11
Vang	5.20	5.68...	
Utd Services:			
GldShr	8.20	NL -	.05
GBT	11.79	NL +	.08
Growth	7.57	NL +	.08
Prspct	.80	NL -	.01

Source: *New York Times*, © 1984 by The New York Times Company. Reprinted by permission.

Redemption of Funds

Most mutual funds permit easy redemption at their NAV. Normally one who calls (toll free) or writes for a partial or full redemption receives a speedy reply. Most funds also have an automatic withdrawal plan. Thus one can have a constant monthly sum sent from the fund, as long as the remaining balance is sufficient. Some funds charge a redemption fee; most do not. One can normally switch funds within the same group without incurring a load fee or even very much paperwork, encouraging some investors try to profit from market swings by switching between a group's stock and money-market funds.

Variable Annuities and Unit Investment Trusts

Some insurance companies sell investments called variable annuities which, except for their regulators, differ little from mutual funds and closed-end investment companies.

Unit investment trusts are similar to, but distinct from, mutual funds and other investment companies. Units of such trusts, like mutual fund shares, represent part ownership of a common portfolio; unlike mutual funds, unit trust portfolios are unmanaged. The absence of management expenses tends to enhance the return. Once assembled, most debt security portfolios can appropriately be left unmanaged until they mature. While such trusts do trade in a secondary market, it is relatively inactive. Thus unit trusts are costly to trade prior to maturity. Since few investors would want to hold an unmanaged equity security portfolio, most unit trusts own portfolios of debt securities. Table 14.1 illustrates the various types of funds by organizational structure.

Table 14.1   Pooled Portfolio-Type Funds By Organizational Structure

Type	Characteristics
Mutual Funds	Open ended; price based on NAV
load funds	Sold through salesperson for a commission
no-load funds	Sold directly without a commission
Closed-end Investment	Corporation owning a managed portfolio; Stock traded on
Companies	an exchange or OTC, usually at a discount from NAV
Variable Annuities	Mutual fund type instrument sold by insurance companies
Unit Investment Trusts	Unmanaged; self-liquidating; largely for debt securities

DIFFERING TYPES OF MUTUAL FUND PORTFOLIOS

Most mutual fund portfolios consist of stocks and/or bonds, including money market securities and long-term debt securities (Table 14.2). Mutual funds can, however, be set up to manage almost any types of investible asset including commodities, options, coins, art, precious metals, etc.

Bond and Balanced Funds

Bond funds are available in a host of different types. Money market funds manage short-term debt security portfolios. Several categories of long-term bond funds

Table 14.2 Fund Type by Type of Investments

Type	1975 Funds	1975 Assets ($ billions)	1981 Funds	1981 Assets ($ billions)
Common Stock Funds	282	$32.4	287	$ 38.2
Balanced Funds	28	5.1	20	2.8
Bond, Income Funds	80	4.7	134	11.0
Municipal Bond Funds	0	0	46	3.1
Money Market Funds	36	3.7	160	181.9
Total	426	$45.9	647	$237.0

Source: *Mutual Fund Forum*, May 1983. Reprinted with permission.

manage portfolios of corporates, governments, or municipals. These broad categories may be further divided into subcategories such as high-risk corporates and intermediate-term governments. Balanced fund portfolios combine common stocks with bonds and preferred stock and tend to have slightly riskier portfolios with somewhat higher expected yields than comparable-maturity bond funds. The remainder of the chapter will deal with equity (common stock) mutual funds. Other types of funds will be discussed in subsequent chapters.

Common Stock Funds' Differing Goals

Common stock funds may be classified into a number of categories reflecting their managers' stated goals. Such funds differ principally in their risk orientation. Performance or "Go-Go" funds (a type largely confined to the late 1960s and early 1970s) are exceptionally risk oriented. Growth funds emphasize appreciation potential and often accept considerable risk. Income funds concentrate on high-dividend, low-risk stocks with modest growth potentials. Middle-of-the-road funds tend to place a somewhat higher premium on stability than growth funds but less than the income funds. A fund's risk orientation may be determined from its prospectus. Mead and *Standard & Poor's Stock Guide* both contain extensive fund classifications.[7] Table 14.3 shows these general characteristics.

Specialized Types of Common Stock Funds

Specialized common stock funds may invest in specific industries (Chemical Fund), types of companies (Technology Fund), or regions (Northeast Fund). Hedge funds attempt to take advantage of market downswings by shorting some stocks while establishing long positions in others. International funds participate in some foreign markets. Dual funds assign their portfolio's capital gains to half of the shareholders while accruing dividends to the other half. Share selections depend principally on one's preferences and tax status. Swap funds permit purchases with stock of other companies. Tax-managed funds are organized as corporations to take advantage of the 85% dividend tax exclusion. Unlike most

Table 14.3   General Types of Common Stock Funds

General Categories

Type	Characteristics
Performance Funds	Exceptionally risk oriented
Growth Funds	Emphasizes price appreciation
Middle-of-the-Road Funds	Seeks a balance between price-appreciation and stability
Income Funds	Assembles a low-risk high-yield portfolio

Specialized Categories

Industry Funds	Swap Funds
Special types of companies	Tax-Managed Funds
Regional Specialization	Index Funds
International Funds	Socially Responsible Funds
Dual Funds	Penny Funds

funds, the tax-managed funds retain their portfolio's dividends and in effect convert them to tax-preferred capital gains. Index funds are managed to duplicate the performance of some stock index such as the S&P 500. Socially responsible funds restrict their portfolio to companies not involved in activities they consider objectionable (polluters, war materials, South Africa, tobacco, alcohol, etc.). Penny funds concentrate on low-priced stocks.

MUTUAL FUND INFORMATION SOURCES

The most comprehensive mutual fund information source is *Investment Companies*, published by Arthur Weisenberger Services. This annual publication covers over 500 funds with a page-long description of each fund's history, objectives, special services, advisors, sales charges, and ten-year performance. Weisenberger also publishes *Management Results* every three months to update the long-term performance of over 400 funds, and *Current Performance and Dividend Record*, which updates the short-run performance monthly.

United Business Service Company publishes *United Mutual Fund Selection* twice a month. Each issue contains articles on mutual funds and the first issue of each month reports changes in NAV for the covered funds. *Forbes* examines mutual funds in one of its two August issues. Recent and ten-year returns are reported along with sales charges and expense ratios. The monthly *S&P Stock Guide* surveys about 400 funds. Each issue contains data on goals, type, size, NAV, distributions, prices, and yields. *Barron's* covers mutual fund performance quarterly. Several newsletters advise investors on when to switch between a common stock and a money market fund to catch the market turns. This category includes *Telephone Switch* (Huntington Beach, Calif.); *Switch Fund* (Gaithersburg, Md.); *Prime Investment Alert* (Portland, Maine); and *Systems and Forecasts* (Great Neck, NY). Most of these funds have a taped telephone advisory (not toll free) as well as a newsletter. Newsletters that concentrate on fund selection and performance include *No Load Fund X* (San Francisco); *Growth Fund Guide* (Rapid City, SD); *No Load Fund Investor* (Hastings, NY); *United Mutual Fund Selector* (Boston); and *The Mutual Fund Letter* (Chicago). The *Mutual Funds Forum* (Investment Company Institute, 1775 K Street NW Washington, DC 20006) publishes articles of general interest to the industry.

MUTUAL FUND PERFORMANCE

The remainder of this chapter considers fund performance relative to goals, the market, potential, and individual investor performance, as well as predicting their future performance.

Fund Performance Relative to their Goals

Funds usually perform according to their goals. That is, funds that assemble risky portfolios generally achieve somewhat above-average long-term returns. Less risk-oriented funds are usually more stable but offer lower expected returns. Ang and Chua also found a high random component in mutual fund performance, however.[8]

Mutual Fund and Other Institutional Investor Performance

According to many different studies, average risk-adjusted mutual fund performance rarely outperforms the market.[9] In a relatively favorable study of mutual fund performance, Mains reported (after correcting some earlier researchers' errors) that mutual funds did tend to outperform the market before but not after deducting expenses.[10] Shawky found that fund performance was substantially better in the 1970s than before, but that their average returns still only approximated that of the NYSE index.[11] Indeed in 1983 the average stock mutual fund gained 20.2%, compared with 22.6% for the S&P 500.[12] A variety of studies have found that many mutual funds attempt to time the market, but few do so successfully.[13]

The available information suggests that non-mutual fund institutional investors' risk-adjusted performance is no better than that of mutual funds. For example, Schlarbaum[14] found that 20 property liability insurance company portfolios' 1958–67 performance was significantly below the market's average. Bogle and Twardowski reported that among institutional investors, mutual funds did best, followed by investment counselors, and then insurance companies, with banks having the poorest relative record.[15] Long-term performance for the various types of institutional investors was relatively similar, however.

While most mutual funds do not earn abnormal risk-adjusted returns, outperforming a relatively efficient market is difficult. Still, mutual funds do have the resources to hire the best talent, collect the most useful information, and analyze it with the most sophisticated techniques. Furthermore, their large size should facilitate operational efficiency—especially when securities are bought in quantities qualifying for commission discounts. Why then, with all these advantages, do the funds so rarely outperform the market?

Why Mutual Funds Rarely Outperform the Market

Outperforming the market average is difficult for institutional investors who make up a large part of that average. Institutions hold approximately 40% of the total value of U.S. stocks, and an even larger proportion of the larger listed issues that make up most of the market indexes (Table 14.4).[16]

Table 14.4 Market Value of Stockholdings of Institutional Investors and Others (Billions of Dollars, End of Year)

	1973	1974	1975	1976	1977	1978	1979	1980
1. Private Noninsured Pension Funds	90.5	63.4	88.6	109.7	101.9	107.9	123.7	175.8
2. Open-End Investment Companies	43.3	30.3	38.7	43.0	36.2	34.1	34.8	44.5
3. Other Investment Companies	6.6	4.7	5.3	5.9	3.1	2.7	1.8	2.3
4. Life Insurance Companies	25.9	21.9	28.1	34.2	32.9	35.7	40.5	52.9
5. Property Liability Insurance Companies[1]	19.7	12.8	14.2	16.9	17.1	19.4	24.8	32.3
6. Personal Trust Funds[2]	101.3	72.0	86.9	100.8	97.1	95.1	106.1[r]	132.9
7. Mutual Saving Banks	4.2	3.7	4.4	4.4	4.8	4.8	4.7	4.2
8. State and Local Retirement Funds	20.2	16.4	24.3	30.1	30.0	33.3	37.1	44.3
9. Foundations	24.5	18.4	22.7	27.1	26.1	27.0	31.2[r]	32.9
10. Educational Endowments	9.6	6.7	8.8	10.4	9.8	10.2	10.2	10.4
11. Subtotal	345.8	250.2	322.0	382.5	359.0	370.2	414.9	532.5
12. Less: Institutional Holdings of Investment Company Shares[3]	6.7	6.5	8.6	10.0	10.5	10.3	8.5	12.6
13. Total Institutional Investors	339.1	243.7	313.4	372.5	348.5	359.9	406.4[r]	519.9
14. Foreign Investors[4]	37.0	28.4	52.6	63.9	67.7[r]	80.0[r]	92.0[r]	114.5
15. Other Domestic Investors[5]	525.3	369.6	483.5	569.2	529.6[r]	548.2[r]	679.2[r]	938.9
16. Total Stock Outstanding[6]	901.4	641.7	849.5	1,005.6	945.8	988.1	1,177.6[r]	1,573.3

r = revised
[1]Excludes holdings of insurance company stock
[2]Includes Common Trust Funds
[3]Excludes institutional holdings of money market funds
[4]Includes estimate of stock held as direct investment
[5]Computed as residual (line 15=16-14-13) Includes both individuals and institutional groups not listed above
[6]Includes both common and preferred stock. Excludes investment company shares but includes foreign issues outstanding in the U.S.
Source: *Statistical Bulletin*, August 1981, Securities and Exchange Commission.

Each type of institutional investor (investment companies, insurance companies, pension funds, college endowments, foundations, and bank trust departments) has access to similar managerial talent, sources of information, and types of analysis. Furthermore, private investment managers, individuals with large sums to invest, and non-financial corporations with large stock portfolios all have equivalent advantages. Thus mutual funds must compete with other similarly positioned institutional and non-institutional investors. Since their abilities and resources are comparable, their average performances should be similar.

Some investors may have an advantage over most institutional investors. For example, companies appear to be particularly adept at choosing attractive times to purchase their own stock.[17] Indeed corporate officials sometimes take advantage of a firm's stock-repurchase decision to sell their own holdings. Insider sales may often signal a price decline.[18] While institutions sometimes trade on inside information, insiders have better access and may more effectively conceal their activities. Users of inside information do so at the expense of the remainder of the market. Thus some non-institutional and corporate investors have advantages that allow them to forecast market performance at least as well as, and often better than, mutual funds. Moreover, many small-to-moderate-sized investors are at least as sophisticated as the large institutions.

Unsophisticated investors with small to moderate-sized portfolios make up the remainder of the market. The average large investor (institutional or otherwise) can only outperform the market at the expense of these less sophisticated investors. This is a difficult task for several reasons. Unsophisticated small investors are a relatively small part of the market, so a substantial amount of small investor underperformance is required to permit any appreciable overperformance by the remainder. Small investor performance may, however, be largely random and thus similar to the market as a whole. In addition, mutual funds themselves have a number of disadvantages (noted below) that tend to lower their returns by more than any likely advantage they may have vis-a-vis unsophisticated investors.

Mutual Fund Disadvantages

Only if a mutual fund's portfolio outperforms the market by more than their management fees, which average about .5% per year, will its owners' returns exceed the market return. Furthermore, load-fund owners incur both the load and the commissions the fund pays when it trades. Investors who acquire stock directly or through no-load funds will, in contrast, only pay commissions on the stocks purchased. Quantity discounts on large institutional trades reduce but do not eliminate the double-commission disadvantage of load funds.

Second, funds, particularly those with large portfolios, often adversely affect the market prices of the stocks that they trade. Sizeable purchases tend to be above the most recent market price, and large sales below it. About 20% of institutional trading is in blocks of 10,000 shares or more. Radcliff reported price concessions of up to 12% on such trades, and the Institutional Investor Survey suggests average concessions of 1% to 3%.[19] Similarly Krause and Stoll found a tendency for prices to fall after institutional purchases and rise after institutional sales.[20] In an extensive study of trading costs for one institutional investor (Banker's Trust Company), Condon found average price concessions of .92% on purchases and .18% on sales.[21] Loeb found that trading costs varied directly with market capitalization and inversely with block size, both of which adversely affect large investors such as mutual funds.[22] Small investors, in contrast, can generally purchase up to several round lots with little price-effect. Funds sometimes attempt to counteract this problem (as well as the control problem) by assigning portions of their portfolio to several managerial groups. Such subdividing may reduce but is unlikely to eliminate the adverse price effects of their large trades. Furthermore, managing costs may be increased by subdividing.

Third, large institutions are vulnerable to certain management abuses that reduce their returns. Some managers may churn their accounts, producing commissions for their broker-friends, but reducing their fund's return. A high turnover rate may represent window dressing dumping of "losers" before quarterly reporting, frustration with past failures, a conspiracy to milk the fund through commission payments, or a sincere belief that active trading may increase the fund's return.[23] Fund returns are often reduced by rapid turnover, however. Fund managers may also be taken in by false claims designed to support a declining stock. Pre-bankruptcy trading in Equity Funding and Penn Central Railroad provide examples of managers seeking to prop up the stock while they unload. Small investors may also be adversely affected by such activities, although the institutional investors are, because of their size, the most likely targets for the tempting fruit of supposedly inside information. On occasion managers intentionally defraud their fund's owners, as in the case of Robert Vesco and Investors Overseas Service.[24]

Fourth, institutional investors typically restrict their analysis to a small percentage of traded stocks. Institutions frequently focus on 25 to 300 companies, compared with about 5,000 listed securities and at least 20,000 traded OTC. Institutional holdings concentrate on the larger firms,[25] reducing by their attention the likelihood of finding undervalued situations. Other stocks may remain misvalued because much of the market ignores them.[26]

In summary, mutual fund performance is often no better than the market averages for the following reasons:

- Institutional investors such as mutual funds constitute a large part of the market
- Some other types of large investors (wealthy individuals, large corporations, etc.) have advantages similar to those of the institutions
- Some investors such as corporate insiders have even greater advantages than institutional investors
- Unsophisticated small investors make up only a small part of the market
- Mutual funds have a number of disadvantages relative to many other types of investors:

    Management fees, expenses and loads for load funds reduce their returns

    Large investors such as mutual funds usually adversely affect the market when they trade

Institutions are vulnerable to management abuses that reduce their returns

Institutions usually restrict their analysis to a small percentage of traded stocks

Mutual-Fund Versus Individual Performance

While institutions, including mutual funds, do not generally outperform the market, comparable evidence on individual investor performance is limited. The average small investor's risk-adjusted return could be inferior to the market's or the average mutual fund's. Investors who trade in small lots generally pay full (undiscounted) commissions, and their small portfolios are unlikely to be well-diversified.

Predicting Fund Performance

The evidence and considerations discussed above imply that funds do not, on the average, outperform the market. Recognizing this difficulty, many money managers have sought to equal market performance by assembling a portfolio of stocks (index fund) having characteristics like the S&P 500. Others have wondered if some especially well-managed funds might consistently outperform the market. To test this proposition, Williamson ranked a sample of 180 funds' risk-adjusted returns and found no significant correlation between the 1961–65 and 1966–70 rankings. The funds in the top 20% and 40% tended to persist there, but the composition of the bottom 20% and 40% was essentially random. Rudolph suggests that management turnover may help explain why past performance does not appear to provide a particularly useful prediction of future fund performance.[27] Williamson also found the availability of net new money was uncorrelated with past or future performance.[28]

Elsewhere I investigated the effect of turnover, size, and load on subsequent return.[29] Turnover appeared to increase costs and reduce returns. Large funds tended to have lower returns than small funds, perhaps because of the greater adverse price effects of their typically larger trades and more restricted sample of stocks. That load fund returns are inferior to those of no-load funds is not surprising, as the load is largely a dead-weight cost. While the selection of a small, low-turnover, no-load fund may produce returns above those of the average fund, more than 80% of the return variation was left unexplained by the Branch model. In earlier work, Friend, Blume, and Crockett found that return tended to increase with turnover and was unrelated to size.[30] Investors themselves seem to be largely uninfluenced by most of the criteria discussed above. Size, marketing effort, and prior performance do appear to affect investor choice, however.[31]

Mutual Funds and the Small Investor

If funds do not generally outperform random selection, and if accurately predicting future fund-performance is very difficult, should such funds be purchased? In other words, should one pay for professional management that does not increase the risk-adjusted expected return? Levy and Sarnat make such a case.[32] They contend that mutual funds help spread risks, provide safekeeping for securities, offer accurate recordkeeping, manage portfolios, and obtain discount commissions. Funds have generally offered relatively attractive expected returns, a large variety of expected risk-return tradeoffs, and an opportunity to spread risk more efficiently than small investors can do on their own.

Where does this leave small investors? Those who have a fund manage their investments should expect no better than average performance. Investors who believe that they can outperform the market may appropriately manage their entire portfolios. Relatively modest resources (e.g., $10,000) may be sufficient to construct a well-diversified portfolio. Investors who are not especially risk averse may properly choose to manage even very small portfolios. Risk averters of modest means with little confidence in their investment skills, and investors with limited time for investment management, may well wish to have a mutual fund manage part or all of their wealth. Investors in mutual funds will find relatively few reliable selection guidelines. Clearly investors should prefer a no-load fund with a risk level corresponding to their preferences. Also, a small, low-turnover fund with favorable past performance may do a bit better than average.

SUMMARY AND CONCLUSIONS

This chapter has considered various aspects of mutual funds and related investments. First, the types of funds were explored. Funds differ on the basis of organizational structure, load versus no-load, types of portfolios, and risk-orientations. Their performance was discussed next. Mutual funds and similar investor-types generally fail to outperform the market for a variety of reasons. Professionally managed portfolios are a large part of the total market, their expenses reduce their net returns, they affect the market when they trade, they are subject to various management abuses, and they are often restricted to relatively few companies. Then, the difficulties involved in predicting mutual fund performance were considered. Small, no-load, low-turnover funds with favorable past performance may or may not outperform the averages. Finally, reasons for buying mutual funds in spite of their poor performance were examined. They offer a convenient and relatively cost-effective way of diversifying. Investors who do not wish to manage their portfolios may well prefer to let a mutual fund handle their investment decisions.

REVIEW QUESTIONS

1. Discuss load funds, no-load funds, and front-end loading.
2. Compare mutual funds, closed-end funds, and unit investment trusts.
3. List the kinds of assets owned by the various types of mutual funds.

4. Describe the various types of risk orientations of common stock funds. Also describe other types of common-stock funds.
5. In general how do mutual funds perform relative to the market?
6. Why do most mutual funds rarely outperform the market?
7. What factors may be used to predict mutual fund performance?
8. Make a case for purchasing mutual funds in spite of their relatively poor risk-adjusted return history.

REVIEW PROBLEMS

1. Update Table 14.2 by going to the library and obtaining recent data on the number and asset-size of the various types of mutual funds. Compare the most recent numbers with those in the table.
2. Compare the coverage of mutual funds in each of sources discussed in the text. Write a report.
3. Assemble a list of five load and five no-load funds having similar objectives. Plot their annual performances for the past five years. Compare the returns to investors in the two groups. Write a report.
4. Assemble a list of five closed-end investment companies and plot their performances and premium/discounts for the past six months. Devise a trading rule. Test it over the next preceding six months. Write a report.
5. Write for five no-load mutual fund information packages and study them carefully. Then invite a mutual fund salesperson to give you his or her sales pitch. Be sure and inform the agent that this is all part of a class project. When the agent gets through ask what portion of the load goes to the seller. Write a report.

NOTES

1. G. Perritt, "Mutual Funds," *American Association of Individual Investors Journal*, June 1984, pp. 18–22; U.S. Securities and Exchange Commission, *Institutional Investor Study Report*, No. 6, 1971, p. 31.
2. K. Boudreau, "Discounts and Premiums on Closed-End Market Funds: A Study in Valuation," *Journal of Finance*, May 1973, pp. 525–528.
3. B. Malkiel, "The Valuation of Closed-End Investment-Company Shares," *Journal of Finance*, June 1977, pp. 847–859.
4. D. Leonard and N. Noble, "Estimation of Time-Varying Systematic Risk and Investment Performance: Closed-End Investment Companies," *Journal of Financial Research*, Summer 1981, pp. 109–120.
5. R. Richards, D. Fraser and J. Groth, "Winning Strategies for Closed-End Funds," *Journal of Portfolio Management*, Fall 1980, pp. 50–55.
6. *Forbes*, "Open Season on Closed-Ends?", *Forbes*, November 26, 1979, pp. 82–83; J. Bettner, "Speculators Buy 'Closed-End' Mutual Funds with Eye to Opening Them Up for Big Profits," *Wall Street Journal*, March 29, 1982, p. 40; T. Hertzfeld, *The Investor's Guide to Closed-End Funds*, McGraw-Hill, New York, 1980.
7. S. Mead, *Mutual Funds: A Guide to the Lay Investor*, General Learning Press, Braintree, MA, 1971, pp. 40–41; *Standard and Poor's Stock Guide*, published monthly by Standard and Poor's Corporation.

8. J. Ang and J. Chua, "Mutual Funds: Different Strokes for Different Folks?," *Journal of Portfolio Management*, Winter 1982, pp. 43–50.

9. J. Williamson, "Measuring and Forecasting of Mutual Fund Performance: Choosing an Investment Strategy," *Financial Analysts Journal*, November/December 1972, pp. 78–84; M. Zweig, "Darts Anyone?" *Barron's*, February 19, 1973, p. 11; W. Sharpe, "Mutual Fund Performance," *Journal of Business*, January 1966, pp. 119–138; J. Treynor and K. Mazuy, "Can Mutual Funds Outguess the Market?" *Harvard Business Review*, July–August 1966, pp. 131–136; M. Jensen, "Problems in Selections of Security Portfolios," *Journal of Finance*, May 1968, pp. 389–416; E. Chang and W. Lewellen, "Market Timing and Mutual Fund Investment Performance," *Journal of Business*, January 1984, pp. 57–72; R. Henriksson, "Market Timing and Mutual Fund Performance: An Empirical Investigation," *Journal of Business*, January 1984, pp. 73–96.

10. N. Mains, "Risk, the Pricing of Capital Assets, and the Evaluation of Investment Portfolios: Comment," *Journal of Business*, July 1977, pp. 371–384.

11. H. Shawky, "An Update on Mutual Funds: Better Grades," *Journal of Portfolio Management*, Winter 1982, pp. 29–34.

12. G. Putka, "Mutual Funds, 20.2% Gain in '83 Trailed S&P's 500 Rise, but Some Ran Far Ahead," *Wall Street Journal*, January 5, 1984, p. 7.

13. M. Ferri, D. Oberhelman and R. Roenfeldt, "Market Timing and Mutual Fund Portfolio Composition," *Journal of Financial Research*, Summer 1984, pp. 143–150; R. Merton, "On Market Timing and Investment Performance," *Journal of Business*, July 1981, pp. 363–406.

14. G. Schlarbaum, "The Investment Performance of the Common Stock Portfolio of Property-Liability Insurance Companies," *Journal of Financial and Quantitative Analysis*, January 1974, pp. 89–106.

15. J. Bogle and J. Twardowski, "Institutional Investment Performance Compared," *Financial Analysts Journal*, January/February 1980, pp. 33–41.

16. D. Farrar and L. Girton, "Institutional Investors and Concentration of Financial Power: Berle and Means Revisited," *Journal of Finance*, May 1981, pp. 369–381.

17. A. Merjos, "Taking the Long View: Corporations Have Been Canny Buyers of Their Own Stock," *Barron's*, May 24, 1973, p. 9.

18. J. Kwitney, "As Firms Repurchase Stock, Some Insiders Unload Part of Theirs," *Wall Street Journal*, June 20, 1974, p. 1; M. Zweig, "Multiple Inside Sales, They're a Useful Guide to What a Stock May Do," *Barron's*, December 17, 1973, pp. 9–21; D. Petty, "An Analysis of Corporate Insider Trading Activity," *Journal of Economics and Business*, Fall 1973, pp. 19–24; J. Jaffee, "Special Information and Insider Trading," *Journal of Business*, July 1974, pp. 410–428.

19. D. Radcliff, "Liquidity Costs and Block Trading," *Financial Analysts Journal*, July/August 1973, pp. 73–80; U.S. Securities and Exchange Commission, *Institutional Investors Study Report*, no. 6, 1971, pp. 81–94.

20. A. Kraus and H. Stoll, "Price Impacts of Block Trading on the New York Stock Exchange," *Journal of Finance*, June 1972, pp. 569–588; A. Kraus and H. Stoll, "Parallel Trading by Institutional Investors," *Journal of Financial and Quantitative Analysis*, December 1972, pp. 2109–2138; M. Scholes, "The Market for Securities: Substitute versus Price Pressures and the Effects of Information on Share Prices," *Journal of Business*, April 1972, pp. 179–211.

21. K. Condon, "Measuring Equity Transaction Costs," *Financial Analysts Journal*, September/October 1981, pp. 57–61.

22. T. Loeb, "Trading Cost: The Critical Look Between Investment Information and Results," *Financial Analysts Journal*, May/June 1983, pp. 39–45.

23. *Wall Street Journal*, "More Funds Stepping Up Portfolios Turnover in Bid to Boost Performance," *Wall Street Journal*, July 12, 1982, p. 37, S. Kon, "The Market-timing Performance of Mutual Fund Managers," *Journal of Business*, July 1983, pp. 323–348.

24. A. Briloff, *Unaccountable Accounting*, Harper & Row, New York, 1972, pp. 183–192.

25. Farrar and Girton, *op. cit.*

26. A. Arbel and P. Strebel, "The Neglected Firm and Small Firm Effect," Competative Paper winner 1982, Eastern Finance Association Meetings, *Financial Review*, November 1982, pp. 201–218.

27. B. Rudolph, "Know the Men Behind the Numbers," *Forbes*, June 6, 1983, pp. 194–196.

28. Williamson, *op. cit.*

29. B. Branch, *Fundamentals of Investing*, Wiley/Hamilton, 1976, pp. 205–206.

30. I. Friend, M. Blume and J. Crockett, *Mutual Funds and other Institutional Investors*, New York, McGraw-Hill, Inc., 1970.

31. W. Woerheide, "Investor Response to Suggested Criteria for the Selection of Mutual Funds," *Journal of Financial and Quantitative Analysis*, March 1982, pp. 129–138.

32. H. Levy and S. Sarnat, "Investment Performance in an Imperfect Securities Market and the Case for Mutual Funds," *Financial Analysts Journal*, March/April 1972, pp. 77–81.

15 Types of Fixed-Income Securities

Fixed-income securities provide the principal alternative to common stocks for both issuers and buyers. The same brokers and similar markets are used to trade them and many companies issue both types of securities. Their similarities notwithstanding, many stock investors ignore the bond markets. Such neglect was understandable when bond yields averaged 4 to 5% and the stock market's long post-World War II rally was underway, but times have changed. Far from being a mundane backwater, fixed income securities' diversity and high yields make them very competitive with common stocks. Fixed income securities' volatility, attention, number of types, ways of participating, and small investor involvement have all increased in recent years. While bonds may not belong in every portfolio, all serious investors should at least consider them.

This chapter explores the characteristics of the various types of short- and long-term debt instruments along with the mutual funds that invest in them. We first consider money market and other short-term securities: large CDs, T-bills, acceptances, commercial paper, Eurodollars, federal funds, repurchase agreements, discount loans, money funds, short-term unit trusts, and low-denomination bank-issued securities. Then various long-term securities are discussed including governments, agencies, mortgage-related securities, municipals, corporates, long-term bank CDs, income bonds, floating-rate notes, zero-coupon bonds, Eurobonds, insurance-company-assembled debt, private placements, and preferred stock.

TYPES OF DEBT SECURITIES

The federal government, state and local governments, corporations, foreign governments, and international organizations all sell fixed-income securities. Almost all debt securities promise to pay a fixed periodic coupon amount and return their face value at a prespecified time. They vary in a number of ways, including length to maturity, coupon rate, type of collateral, convertibility, tax treatment, and restrictions placed on the borrower.

Debt instruments largely compete with other similar-maturity instruments. Securities maturing in a year or less are considered short-term. High-quality short-term debt obligations trade in what is called the money market.

THE MONEY MARKET AND OTHER SHORT-TERM DEBT SECURITIES

Money market instruments are highly liquid, quite marketable, and bear very little risk. The principal money market instruments are large bank CDs, Treasury bills, commercial paper, banker's acceptances, and Eurodollar deposits. Very short-term lending and borrowing in the federal funds market, repurchase agreements, and the Fed's discount window round out this market. In addition, money market mutual funds, short-term unit investment trusts, short-term municipals, and certain securities and accounts of banks and other financial institutions also compete in the short end of the debt security market.

Large CDs

The unregulated interest rates on bank and thrift-issued CDs of $100,000 and above usually exceed the rates payable on smaller balances. About 25 New York-based CD dealers handle most secondary market trading.[1] CDs are subject to the same up-to-$100,000 government-guarantee as other bank and thrift institution issues. While the very high-denomination CDs are largely uninsured, most CDs are quite safe. Those issued by troubled banks, such as Continental Illinois in 1984, may be risky, however. Moody's now rates the quality of some CDs. Most CDs have short-term maturities.

Their relatively high minimum denomination puts large CDs beyond the range of small investors. Funds for one large CD may be assembled from several investors, however. Many banks will lend individuals the funds needed to reach the minimum. Typically the loan rate slightly exceeds the CD rate, but the holding's net yield may still be relatively attractive.

Treasury Bills and Other Short-Term Governments

Short-term United States government securities (governments) make up one of the money market's largest segments. This market consists of bills and other securities maturing within a year. T-bills are issued at a discount and mature at par (face value), while other governments are sold initially near par and pay a coupon return. Most governments are issued in $10,000 minimum denominations. Short-term governments possess excellent (OTC) marketability, frequent original offerings, very low perceived risk, and competitive yields. They are not subject to state and local taxes, which could appreciably increase their relative after-tax yield. A number of non-Treasury government agencies also issue short-term securities.[2]

While T-bills can be bought through a broker or bank for a commission of $20, $50 or more, a direct purchase from the nearest Federal Reserve Bank can be made for the cost of first-class postage. One simply writes a letter stating a desire to purchase 13-week or 26-week bills at the noncompetitive (average of competitive) bid for the next weekly auction. The letter indicates the amount desired ($10,000 minimum and $5,000 multiples thereafter) and includes a certified or official bank check for the bill's face value. A refund for the discount on the security will be sent immediately after the next auction. Investors in T-bills can either have the face value automatically reinvested or sent to them at maturity.

A Treasury bill quotation for June 20, 1984, is illustrated in Table 15.1. The first entry was to mature on June 21, 1984. One could sell the security prior to maturity at a price yielding 10.75%, while a purchaser would receive a 10.59% return. Note that the final column in the Treasury bill quote reports the return on a coupon-equivalent basis, as opposed to the discount basis used in the bid/ asked columns. A special feature, *The Mathematics of Yields*, discusses the relationship between coupon and discount yields.

Table 15.1   Treasury Bill Quotation, June 20, 1984

U.S. Treas. Bills Mat. date	Bid	Asked	Yield	Mat. date	Bid	Asked	Yield
			Discount				Discount
-1984-				10-11	10.20	10.14	10.61
				10-18	10.22	10.16	10.66
6-21	10.75	10.59	0.00	10-25	10.21	10.15	10.67
6-28	8.00	7.70	7.82	11- 1	10.34	10.28	10.83
7- 5	9.21	9.15	9.31	11- 8	10.38	10.32	10.90
7-12	9.30	9.26	9.44	11-15	10.38	10.32	10.92
7-19	9.25	9.19	9.38	11-24	10.48	10.42	11.06
7-26	9.18	9.12	9.33	11-29	10.55	10.49	11.16
8- 2	9.50	9.44	9.68	12- 6	10.61	10.55	11.25
8- 9	9.70	9.62	9.88	12-13	10.63	10.57	11.29
8-16	9.65	9.61	9.89	12-20	10.60	10.56	11.31
8-23	9.72	9.68	9.58	12-27	10.65	10.59	11.35
8-30	9.82	9.74	10.06	-1985-			
9- 6	9.98	9.94	10.29	1-24	10.57	10.51	11.27
9-13	9.92	9.84	10.21	2-21	10.73	10.67	11.50
9-20	9.91	9.89	10.28	3-21	10.76	10.70	11.58
9-27	10.04	9.98	10.40	4-18	10.95	10.89	11.87
10- 4	10.16	10.10	10.55	5-16	11.02	10.96	12.02
				6-13	11.06	11.04	12.20

Source: *Wall Street Journal*, June 21, 1984. Reprinted by permission of *Wall Street Journal*, © Dow Jones & Company, Inc., 1984. All Rights Reserved.

Commercial Paper

Commercial paper is usually issued by large corporations with solid credit ratings to finance short-term needs. The notes are only secured by the issuer's good name. Commercial paper issuers generally pay slightly less than bank rates (the prime rate), but eliminating the intermediary's compensation allows them to pay investors a slightly higher rate.[3] Commercial paper is rated, but as a practical matter only high-grade issues are very saleable. Paper is marketed in round lots of $250,000 and is seldom available in smaller than $100,000 denominations. Most commercial paper is payable to the bearer, although it may be registered.

Acceptances

An acceptance is an obligation to pay a certain amount at a prespecified time. The obligation is accepted by a bank; hence the name "acceptance." Acceptances

SPECIAL FEATURE: **THE MATHEMATICS OF YIELDS**

While the term *yield* is often used as if its meaning were unambiguous, yield can actually be taken to mean a number of different things. For example, the "current yield" reported in newspaper quotations is simply the coupon rate divided by the current price. Thus an 11% percent coupon on a bond quoted at 85 would have a current yield of:

$$\text{Current Yield} = \frac{110}{850} = 12.94\%$$

While such a computation does not consider the discount or premium from par, a more complex concept, the *yield-to-maturity*, does. To compute the yield-to-maturity, one solves for the rate that would make the present value of the income payments equal the price of the bond (see Chapter 4).

The *yield-to-earliest-call* is often computed for bonds that are likely to be called before maturity. The computation is similar to that for the yield-to-maturity, except that the earliest call date and the call price are used rather than the maturity date and face value.

Those who sell prior to maturity may compute yet another yield, the *holding period* or realized yield. This is the rate that makes the present value of the payments and sale price equal the purchase price.

Most yields, especially long-term yields, are quoted in *coupon-equivalent* terms. Short-term yields, in contrast, are often stated in what is called the *discount basis*. The two yields are computed differently and can produce rather different numbers. Coupon-equivalent yields assume that interest payments take place semiannually and are based on a 365-day year. Discount yields, in contrast, work with a 360-day year and assume that the interest is deducted at the outset. As a result, stated discount-basis yields are somewhat below the coupon-equivalent yield computed for the same security.

The formula for a one-year security's discount-basis yield is:

$$d = \frac{D}{F} \tag{1}$$

where: d = discount-basis yield
F = face value
D = discount in face value

Thus a $1,000 face value one-year bond selling for $900 would be priced at a $100 discount and offer a discount yield of 10% ($100/$1,000).

A slightly more complicated formula is required for maturities of less than one year:

$$d = \frac{D}{F}\left(\frac{360}{M}\right) \tag{2}$$

where: M = number of days to maturity

Accordingly, the yield for a Treasury bill with 250 days until maturity selling for $9,500 would be computed as follows:

$$\frac{\$500}{\$10,000} \times \frac{360}{250} = 7.20\%$$

We can compute the simple-interest yield from the discount-basis yield with the following formula:

$$i = \frac{365\,d}{360 - d\,M} \tag{3}$$

where: i = simple-interest yield

Applying formula (3) to our previous example produces:

$$i = \frac{365\,(.072)}{360 - (.072)(250)} = 7.68\%$$

Thus we see that the simple-interest yield (7.68%) appreciably exceeds the discount-basis yield (7.20%) for this security. Table 15.1A illustrates the differential in the two yields.

The simple-interest yield approximates but does not equal the coupon-equivalent yield. The two yields differ because the simple-interest formula assumes that the interest payments are received at maturity while the coupon-equivalent yield takes account of semiannual interest payments. When a security has less than six months to run, the two rates are equivalent. For longer-maturity instruments, however, the following formula is employed to compute the coupon-equivalent yield on a security that is priced on a discount-basis.

where: r = coupon-equivalent yield
P = price as a percentage of face.

Thus a six-month Treasury bill selling at $9,506.53 with 190 days to run would be handled as follows:

$$r = \frac{\dfrac{2M}{365} + 2\sqrt{\left(\dfrac{M}{365}\right)^2 - \left(\dfrac{2M}{365} - 1\right)\left(1 - \dfrac{1}{p}\right)}}{\dfrac{2M}{365} - 1}$$

$$r = \frac{\dfrac{2(190)}{365} + 2\sqrt{\left(\dfrac{190}{365}\right)^2 - \left(\dfrac{2(190)}{365} - 1\right)\left(1 - \dfrac{1}{.950635}\right)}}{\dfrac{2(190)}{365} - 1} = 9.95\%$$

Table 15.1A Comparisons at Different Rates and Maturities between Rates of Discount and the Equivalent *Simple Interest* Rates on a 365-Day-Year Basis

Rate of Discount (percent)		Equivalent Simple Interest (percent)		
		30-Day Maturity	182-Day Maturity	364-Day Maturity
4	....	4.07	4.14	4.23
6	....	6.11	6.27	6.48
8	....	8.17	8.45	8.82
10	....	10.22	10.68	11.27
12	....	12.29	12.95	13.84
14	....	14.36	15.28	16.53
16	....	16.44	17.65	19.35

usually arise in the course of foreign trade, but occasionally result from domestic trade. First Boston describes a hypothetical acceptance as follows:

> Creation and Life of an Acceptance: Consider a coffee processor in the United States who wishes to finance the importation of Colombian coffee on an acceptance basis. The American importer, after negotiating with the exporter in Colombia, arranges with his/her American commercial banker for the issuance of an irrevocable letter of credit in favor of the exporter. The letter of credit specifies the details of the shipment and states that the Colombian exporter may draw a time draft for a certain amount on the American bank. In order for the acceptance to be eligible for discount by the Federal Reserve, the period of time specified, based on the estimated number of days required to liquidate the transaction, may be a maximum of 180 days. The Colombian exporter, in conformity with the terms of the letter of credit, draws a draft with his local bank, receiving immediate payment. The Colombian bank then forwards the draft and the shipping documents conveying title to the coffee to the United States for presentation

to the bank that issued the letter of credit. This bank stamps the draft "accepted"—the American bank has accepted an obligation to pay the draft at maturity. An acceptance has been created.

The new acceptance is either returned to the Colombian bank or sold to an acceptance dealer and the proceeds credited to the account of the Colombian bank. The shipping documents are released to the American importer to process and sell the coffee. The proceeds of the coffee sales are deposited by the importer at the accepting bank in time to honor the acceptance. At maturity, the acceptance is presented for payment by its owner and the transaction is completed.[4]

Once created, the acceptance trades like other money market securities. Acceptances are available in a wide variety of denominations and maturity dates. A small number of dealers buy and sell acceptances, quoting spreads of about 1/4 of 1%. Acceptances, like most money market securities, can be purchased through a stock broker.

Eurodollar Deposits

Eurodollar deposits are dollar-denominated liabilities of banks located in Europe or anywhere else outside the United States. Most Eurodollars are held as fixed-rate time deposits of $250,000 to $5,000,000, with maturities of from one day to several years. Eurodollar yields are quite competitive with other money market rates. U.S. investor's Eurodollar deposits may occasionally be difficult to repatriate, and disputes between borrower and lender must be settled without the protections of the U.S. legal system. Issuing banks' depositors are rarely as protected by insurance and government regulation as those of U.S. banks. Since many issuers are subsidiaries of U.S. banks and others are large institutions with long histories of sound operations, the Eurodollar market's risks should not be overemphasized. Defaults have been very rare in the post-World War II period.

Federal Funds, Repurchase Agreements, and Discount Loans

Banks and other types of financial institutions also participate in several very active short-term debt markets. The federal funds market arose to facilitate overnight bank borrowing and lending of excess reserves. Subsequently other financial institutions and even some foreign banks and government security dealers entered the market.[5] This federal funds market in fact encompasses all unsecured overnight loans in immediately-available, reserve-free funds.

Repurchase agreements (repos) are sales of securities whose guaranteed repurchase at a prespecified price and date (usually one day later), establishes their return. Payment is generally in immediately-available reserve-free funds transferred between financial institutions. Many banks and other depository institutions now offer retail repos that pay unregulated interest rates on investments of below $100,000. While these arrangements had been considered quite safe, the default of Drysdale Government Securities illustrated their potential risk.[6]

Discount loans, another part of the money market, are extended by the Fed to member banks and certain other institutions to cure a short-term reserve deficiency. The Fed often signals monetary policy shifts with changes in the rate charged on such loans (discount rate).

Except for retail repos, this part of the money market is almost exclusively restricted to depository institutions such as commercial banks and savings and loan associations. Indeed most money market instruments are only available to those investors with sufficient resources to purchase at least one (high-denomination) unit.

Money Market Mutual Funds

Interest-rate ceilings on many bank savings instruments, coupled with generally higher money market rates, led to the development of money market mutual funds and short-term unit investment trusts. The money funds invest resources from many small investors in a large portfolio of money market securities. Most funds set a $1,000 minimum account size. The portfolio's net income is distributed to the fund's owners and may be paid monthly or reinvested. Small investors generally earn about one half of a percentage point below the prevailing rates. Because such funds concentrate on very liquid short-term instruments, adverse interest moves are unlikely to affect the fund's share prices significantly. Most money market instruments must be sold at the prevailing market price less commissions in discrete and relatively large units. Money market funds shares can, in contrast, be redeemed in whole or in part on very short notice without a redemption charge. Most funds permit several types of redemption: the fundholder can write or call toll-free for an immediate check-mailing or wire-transfer into the fundholder's bank account. Most funds also permit checks of $500 or more to be written on the account, thereby allowing the funds to earn interest until the check clears.

Individual money funds have somewhat different risk, return, and marketing characteristics. Some invest only in Treasury bills; other portfolios contain slightly riskier money market investments. Some funds only hold very short-term instruments while others incur the reduced liquidity of slightly longer maturities. Still others vary their average maturity on the basis of their interest rate expectations.[7] Some short-term municipal funds offer (lower) tax-free yields. Thus different types of money funds appeal to various investor types.

While most money funds of a given class (general, governments-only, or municipal) offer very similar risks and returns, they do differ somewhat.[8] Two groups, William Donoghue and the Institute for Econometrics, now rate the safety and performance of the money funds.[9] Standard & Poor's also rates funds that agree to pay a fee for the service. Most funds see little value in the rating services, however.[10]

Short-Term Unit Investment Trusts

Short-term unit investment trusts offer many of the same advantages as money funds: low risk, low-denomination investment, and money market yields. On the other hand, the money funds are managed and continuous; the unmanaged unit trusts mature. Furthermore, the unit trusts' expenses are appreciably below those of the money market funds, but trusts are less convenient than the money funds.[11] Units must be held until maturity (generally six months) or sold in a relatively inactive secondary market. Because short-term unit trusts invest in longer-term securities than most money funds, they are somewhat less liquid. Unlike the money funds, unit trust yields are established when they are purchased. If market rates move up subsequently, the trustholder must wait until maturity to reinvest at the higher rate. On the other hand, if interest rates decline, the holder will receive an above-market rate until the trust matures. Compared with money funds, their principal advantage is a lower expense ratio and thus, other things equal, a higher yield. They are, however, less convenient and more exposed to interest-fluctuation risk than most money funds.

Low-Denomination Short-Term Securities of Banks and Other Intermediaries

In the past several years, banks and other financial intermediaries have been permitted to offer an increasing number of low-denomination securities. The relevant regulations have and will no doubt continue to change, largely in the direction of reduced regulation. In 1984, banks and thrifts continued to offer the traditional passbook-type savings account which allows immediate withdrawals and pays 5-1/2%. Money market rates have, however, almost always been above 5-1/2%. Money market certificates with 31-day-or-longer maturities and a $500 minimum have no interest ceilings. Thus banks can pay whatever competition requires on such certificates. Depository institutions may also sell repurchase agreements, which are not subject to minimum-amount or maximum-yield restrictions. Technically such repos can be written for any maturity and denomination, but most are relatively short term. Repos are not government insured, however. Beginning in late 1982, banks and other deposit institutions were allowed to offer an account that competes directly with the money funds. The so-called money market accounts have a $2,500 minimum and are restricted to six withdrawals per month, only three of which may be by check. These accounts' yields are not regulated, so the depository institutions can compete for funds by paying what they like.

The response to money market accounts was quite favorable.[12] Unlike Treasury bills, bank and thrift institution certificates and accounts are subject to state and local income taxes. Thus the after-tax yield on T-bills is generally higher than the yield on equivalent depository institution certificates.

While most debt securities may be sold prior to maturity at the market price, small denomination CDs are generally nontransferable. One can redeem them before maturity at the issuing bank, but up to 90 days' interest is sacrificed. Alternatively one may borrow the needed sum using the CD as collateral. Thus before redeeming a CD early, one should compare the interest sacrifice with the net cost of such a loan.

As with all nonmunicipal debt securities, CD interest income is fully taxable at the federal level. Since small CDs are bought and sold at par, capital gains and losses are impossible. On the other hand, the risk of loss through bankruptcy is nil. The FDIC, or in the case of S&Ls, the FSLIC, guarantees the security up to $100,000, and very few deposit institutions fail. Thus small short-term CDs appeal to safety-oriented investors.

Money Market Rates

The rates on CDs, bankers' acceptances, and commercial paper tend to move together very closely. Treasury bills generally offer a slightly lower yield because of their somewhat greater security and marketability.[13] Eurodollar rates tend to exceed other money market rates slightly, reflecting their modestly greater risk. Figure 15.1 is typical of the *Wall Street Journal* money rate quotations.

Implications of the Money Market for Individual Investors

The market for short-term debt instruments has grown dramatically in recent years. High short-term and volatile long-term rates have encouraged many investors to shift toward short-term securities.[14] While some individuals may buy money market securities directly, their large denominations ($10,000 for Treasury bills, $100,000 for CDs, $250,000 for commercial paper), put the market out of reach for investors of modest means. Money funds, short-term unit trusts, and bank money certificates and money market accounts do, however, offer a viable alternative for those desiring a highly liquid low-risk instrument. Table 15.2 lists the market's various components.

LONG-TERM DEBT INSTRUMENTS

A wide variety of types of long-term debt securities are also available. Most such securities fall into three categories: government bonds (including agencies); municipals; and traditional corporate bonds. Other categories include mortgages and mortgage-related securities, bank CDs, bond funds, income bonds, floating-rate notes, zero-coupon bonds, Eurobonds, insurance company debt securities, private placements, and preferred stock.

Treasury Notes and Bonds

In addition to T-bills, the Treasury Department also issues both intermediate and long-term debt instruments. Typical bond and note quotations are reproduced in Table 15.3. The original issue rate appears first, followed by the maturity date. Notes are denoted with an "*n*" following the maturity date, while the others are bonds which were originally issued for longer than ten years. The bid and

Figure 15.1 Money Rates

Money Rates

Wednesday, June 20, 1984

The key U.S. and foreign annual interest rates below are a guide to general levels but don't always represent actual transactions.

PRIME RATE: 12½%. The base rate on corporate loans at large U.S. money center commercial banks.

FEDERAL FUNDS: 15% high, 11¾% low, 13% near closing bid, 14% offered. Reserves traded among commercial banks for overnight use in amounts of $1 million or more. Source: Prebon Money Brokers Inc., N.Y.

DISCOUNT RATE: 9%. The charge on loans to member depository institutions by the New York Federal Reserve Bank.

CALL MONEY: 12½%. The charge on loans to brokers on stock exchange collateral.

COMMERCIAL PAPER placed directly by General Motors Acceptance Corp.: 11% 30 to 59 days; 10.90% 60 to 89 days; 10.80% 90 to 119 days; 10.70% 120 to 149 days; 10.60% 150 to 270 days.

COMMERCIAL PAPER: High-grade unsecured notes sold through dealers by major corporations in multiples of $1,000: 11.10% 30 days; 11.15% 60 days; 11.15% 90 days.

CERTIFICATES OF DEPOSIT: 11.40% one month; 11.50% two months; 11¾% three months; 12.35% six months; 13.20% one year. Typical rates paid by major banks on new issues of negotiable C.D.s, usually on amounts of $1 million and more. The minimum unit is $100,-000.

BANKERS ACCEPTANCES: 11.35% 30 days; 11.35% 60 days; 11.30% 90 days; 11.30% 120 days; 11.40% 150 days; 11.40% 180 days. Negotiable, bank-backed business credit instruments typically financing an import order.

LONDON LATE EURODOLLARS: 11⅝% to 11½% one month; 11¾% to 11⅝% two months; 11⅞% to 11¾% three months; 12% to 11⅞% four months; 12 5/16% to 12 3/16% five months; 12½% to 12⅜% six months.

LONDON INTERBANK OFFERED RATES (LIBOR): 11¾% three months; 12⅜% six months; 13¼% one year. The average of interbank offered rates for dollar deposits in the London market based on quotations at five major banks.

FOREIGN PRIME RATES: Canada 12%; Germany 7.75%; Japan 5.70%; Switzerland 6%; Britain 8.50%. These rate indications aren't directly comparable; lending practices vary widely by location. Source: Morgan Guaranty Trust Co.

TREASURY BILLS: Results of the Monday, June 18, 1984, auction of short-term U.S. government bills, sold at a discount from face value in units of $10,000 to $1 million: 10.01% 13 weeks; 10.49% 26 weeks.

FEDERAL HOME LOAN MORTGAGE CORP. (Freddie Mac): Posted yields on 30-year mortgage commitments for delivery within 30 days. 14.62%, standard conventional fixed-rate mortgages; 13.02%, one-year adjustable rate mortgages.

MERRILL LYNCH READY ASSETS TRUST: 10.24%. Annualized average rate of return after expenses for the past 30 days; not a forecast of future returns.

Source: *Wall Street Journal.* Reprinted by permission of *Wall Street Journal,* © Dow Jones Company, Inc., 1984. All Rights Reserved.

asked prices appear next, followed by the change in the bid and the yield.

Governments may either be bearer (payable to bearer) or registered (payable only to the registered owner). Unlike bearer bonds, lost or stolen registered securities will be replaced by the issuer. Bearer bonds appeal to those who would like to conceal their income and/or wealth. Since mid-1983, all newly issued

Table 15.2 Short-Term Debt Securities

Type	Money Market Issuer	Minimum Denomination
Large CDs	Banks and Thrifts	$100,000
Treasury Bills	U.S. Treasury	$ 10,000
Acceptances	Foreign Companies but bank-guaranteed	varies
Commercial Paper	Secure Corporations	$250,000
Eurodollars	Foreign-Based Banks	$250,000

Intra-Institutional Market

Federal Funds	Loans between Fed Members
Repurchase Agreements	Sale and guaranteed buy-back of securities
Discount Loans	Loans from Fed to Fed Members

Small Investor Market

	Term	Minimum Denomination
Money Funds	On Demand	$ 1,000
Short-term Unit Trusts	Six months	$ 1,000
Low Denomination Bank Securities (several types)	31 days or longer	$ 500
Retail Repos	varies	varies
Money Market Accounts	Only six withdrawals per month	$ 2,500

governments must be registered. Governments are generally traded in an over-the-counter market composed of about two dozen dealers, most of whom are New York City investment or commercial bankers.[15] Governments are also traded on the NYSE. The Treasury conducts an active original-issue market for governments, and banks and others may bid for newly issued bills or bonds. Because of their very large volume and active trading, governments generally have modest spreads: on short-term issues, 1/32 to 4/32 (par of 100) is common. A spread of 1/32 on $10,000 bonds amounts to only $3.125; 4/32 is only $12.50. Longer-term, less-active issues may have somewhat higher spreads. Governments may be bought through stockbrokers, commercial banks (for a fee), or directly from the Fed.

The federal government's securities will be considered secure as long as it is willing and able to raise sufficient tax revenues to finance the debt. Because of their lower risk, governments generally yield less than highly rated corporate securities. Governments are not subject to state and local income taxes, however.

Certain United States government bonds issued prior to March, 1973 may be used at their face value to pay estate taxes. Thus a bond purchased for $750 may be worth $1,000 in estate taxes. To be used for estate-tax purposes, how-

Table 15.3 ***Wall Street Journal*** **Treasury-Issue Quotations, June 20, 1984**

Treasury Issues/*Bonds, Notes & Bills*

Wednesday, June 20, 1984

Representative mid-afternoon Over-the-Counter quotations supplied by the Federal Reserve Bank of New York City, based on transactions of $1 million or more.

Decimals in bid-and-asked and bid changes represent 32nds; 101.1 means 101 1/32. a-Plus 1/64. b-Yield to call date. d-Minus 1/64. n-Treasury notes.

Treasury Bonds and Notes

Rate	Mat.	Date	Bid	Asked	Bid Chg.	Yld.
8⅞s,	1984	Jun n	99.28	100	– .1	8.51
14⅜s,	1984	Jun n	100	100.4	....	8.12
13⅛s,	1984	Jul n	100.8	100.12	+ .1	9.12
6⅜s,	1984	Aug	99.10	99.28	....	7.49
7¼s,	1984	Aug n	99.14	99.18	....	9.99
11⅝s,	1984	Aug n	100.4	100.8	....	9.93
13¼s,	1984	Aug n	100.11	100.15	+ .1	9.60
12⅛s,	1984	Sep n	100.7	100.11	....	10.54
9¾s,	1984	Oct n	99.15	99.19	....	10.78
9⅞s,	1984	Nov n	99.11	99.15	....	11.08
14⅜s,	1984	Nov n	101.2	101.6	– .1	11.09
16s,	1984	Nov n	101.23	101.27	....	10.97
9⅜s,	1984	Dec n	98.30	99.2	....	11.27
14s,	1984	Dec n	101.8	101.12	....	11.22
9¼s,	1985	Jan n	98.19	98.23	– .1	11.49
8s,	1985	Feb n	97.22	97.26	....	11.58
9⅝s,	1985	Feb n	98.18	98.22	– .2	11.65
14⅝s,	1985	Feb n	101.21	101.25	....	11.71
9⅝s,	1985	Mar	98.11	98.15	– .1	11.74
13⅜s,	1985	Mar n	101	101.4	– .2	11.82
9½s,	1985	Apr n	98	98.4	– .2	11.86
3¼s,	1985	May	94.9	95.9	....	8.83
4¼s,	1975-85	May	94.14	95.14	....	9.67
9⅞s,	1985	May n	98.2	98.6	– .2	11.97
10⅜s,	1985	May n	98.25	98.29	– .2	11.69
14⅛s,	1985	May n	101.19	101.23	– .3	12.05
14⅜s,	1985	May n	101.26	101.30	– .3	12.04
14s,	1985	Jun n	101.23	101.27	– .3	12.03
10s,	1985	Jun n	97.31	98.3	– .3	12.04
10⅝s,	1985	Jul n	98.9	98.13	– .4	12.20
8¼s,	1985	Aug n	96.6	96.13	– .4	11.68
9⅝s,	1985	Aug n	97.6	97.10	– .3	12.20
10⅝s,	1985	Aug n	98.1	98.5	– .4	12.33
13⅛s,	1985	Aug n	100.23	100.27	– .4	12.32
10⅞s,	1985	Sep n	98.6	98.10	– .4	12.34
15⅞s,	1985	Sep n	103.28	104	– .3	12.39
10½s,	1985	Oct n	97.16	97.20	– .6	12.45
9¾s,	1985	Nov n	96.12	96.16	– .6	12.56
10½s,	1985	Nov n	97.6	97.10	– .7	12.60
11¾s,	1985	Nov n	99.1	99.5	– .7	12.43
10⅞s,	1985	Dec n	97.14	97.18	– .9	12.69
14⅛s,	1985	Dec n	101.24	101.28	– .11	12.73
10⅝s,	1986	Jan n	96.30	97.2	– .12	12.70
10⅞s,	1986	Feb n	97.2	97.6	– .14	12.77
13½s,	1986	Feb n	100.28	101	– .11	12.81
9⅞s,	1986	Feb n	95.18	95.22	– .10	12.86
14s,	1986	Mar n	101.19	101.23	– .11	12.89
11½s,	1986	Mar n	97.21	97.25	– .15	12.94
11¾s,	1986	Apr n	97.31	98.1	– .15	12.98
7⅞s,	1986	May n	91.24	91.28	– .13	12.83
9⅜s,	1986	May n	94	94.4	– .14	12.96
12⅝s,	1986	May n	99.7	99.11	– .17	13.02
13¾s,	1986	May n	101.4	101.8	– .18	12.99
14⅞s,	1986	Jun n	103.1	103.5	– .20	13.05
8s,	1986	Aug n	90.20	90.24	– .20	13.07
11⅜s,	1986	Aug n	96.25	96.29	– .19	13.07
12¼s,	1986	Sep n	98.8	98.12	– .22	13.10
6⅛s,	1986	Nov	88.28	89.28	– .16	11.04
11s,	1986	Nov n	95.23	95.27	– .20	13.07
13⅞s,	1986	Nov n	101.13	101.21	– .19	13.05
16⅛s,	1986	Nov n	105.28	106.4	– .22	13.07
10s,	1986	Dec n	93.8	93.12	– .21	13.17
9s,	1987	Feb n	90.24	90.28	– .21	13.19
10⅞s,	1987	Feb n	94.26	94.30	– .24	13.20
12¾s,	1987	Feb n	98.31	99.3	– .24	13.17
10¼s,	1987	Mar n	93.2	93.6	– .24	13.26
12s,	1987	May n	97.6	97.10	– .25	13.14
12½s,	1987	May n	98.2	98.4	– .25	13.30
14s,	1987	May n	101.17	101.25	– .25	13.24
10½s,	1987	Jun n	92.30	93.2	– .27	13.36
13¾s,	1987	Aug n	100.30	101.2	– .28	13.33
11⅛s,	1987	Sep n	94.6	94.10	– .28	13.32
7⅝s,	1987	Nov n	85.14	85.30	– .21	12.86
12⅝s,	1987	Nov n	98.2	98.6	– .26	13.31
11¼s,	1987	Dec n	94.4	94.8	– .28	13.35
12⅜s,	1988	Jan n	97.4	97.8	– .28	13.37
10⅛s,	1988	Feb n	90.16	90.20	– .27	13.46
12s,	1988	Mar n	95.21	95.25	– .27	13.46
13¼s,	1988	Apr n	99.17	99.25	– .25	13.32
8¼s,	1988	May n	84.25	85.1	– .28	13.29
9⅞s,	1988	May n	89.3	89.7	– .29	13.52
14s,	1988	Jul n	101.22	101.30	– .28	13.37
10½s,	1988	Aug n	90.19	90.23	– .28	13.49
15⅜s,	1988	Oct n	105.30	106.6	– 1	13.44
8¾s,	1988	Nov n	84.26	85.2	– .28	13.35
11¾s,	1988	Nov n	94.6	94.10	– .30	13.51
14⅝s,	1989	Jan n	103.20	103.24	– .30	13.50
11⅜s,	1989	Feb n	92.22	92.26	– .31	13.51
14⅜s,	1989	Apr n	102.28	103	– 1	13.51
9¼s,	1989	May n	85.13	85.21	– .31	13.33
11¾s,	1989	May n	93.21	93.25	– .31	13.53
14½s,	1989	Jul n	103.12	103.16	– .28	13.52
13⅞s,	1989	Aug n	100.31	101.1	– 1	13.56
11⅞s,	1989	Oct n	93.28	94	– .24	13.49
10¾s,	1989	Nov n	89.14	89.18	– .28	13.54

Source: *Wall Street Journal*, June 20, 1984. Reprinted by permission of *Wall Street Journal*,

ever, these bonds (called "flower bonds") must be part of the estate prior to the owner's death. Because of their value in estate settlement and their relatively limited supply, flower bonds' yields-to-stated-maturity are generally well below otherwise-equivalent governments.[16] Thus only those expecting to die soon will find flowers attractive.

Agency Securities

Several other government agencies also issue debt obligations. These include the Federal Intermediate Credit Banks, The Banks for Cooperatives, and the Federal

Land Banks, which supply farm credit, and the Federal Home Loan Bank System, which supplies mortgage credit. A typical daily newspaper quotation summary is shown as Table 15.4. By the end of 1980, over $160 billion in agencies were outstanding compared with only $1.6 billion thirty years earlier.

Table 15.4 *Wall Street Journal* Agency Quotations, June 20, 1984

Government, Agency and Miscellaneous Securities

Wednesday, June 20, 1984

Mid-afternoon Over-the-Counter quotations; sources on request.

Decimals in bid-and-asked and bid changes represent 32nds; 101.1 means 101 1/32. a-Plus 1/64. b-Yield to call date. d-Minus 1/64. n-Treasury notes.

FNMA Issues

Rate	Mat	Bid	Asked	Yld
8.20	7-84	99.26	99.30	9.06
9.05	7-84	99.27	99.31	9.27
11.10	8-84	99.29	100.1	10.45
7.95	9-84	99.10	99.14	10.34
9.75	9-84	99.23	99.27	10.48
10.05	9-84	99.21	99.25	10.48
11.70	10-84	100	100.4	11.02
14.90	10-84	100.29	101.1	11.06
17.20	11-84	102.1	102.5	11.24
6.90	12-84	97.31	98.3	11.15
7.55	12-84	98.7	98.11	11.24
15.05	12-84	101.16	101.20	11.35
9.90	1-85	99.1	99.5	11.49
17.00	2-85	102.28	103	11.90
7.65	3-85	97.2	97.6	11.79
14.25	3-85	101.15	101.19	11.81
13.75	4-85	101.5	101.9	11.96
11.30	5-85	99.6	99.10	12.10
15.25	5-85	102.12	102.16	12.14
8.60	6-85	96.27	96.31	12.00
9.95	6-85	98	98.2	12.12

Fed. Home Loan Bank

Rate	Mat	Bid	Asked	Yld
9.60	6-84	99.30	100.1	6.48
14.00	6-84	99.31	100.2	7.83
15.55	7-84	100.12	100.16	9.60
7.85	8-84	99.13	99.17	10.20
16.00	8-84	100.26	100.30	10.27
13.85	9-84	100.21	100.25	10.43
16.40	9-84	101.9	101.13	10.46
14.45	10-84	101	101.4	10.82
7.38	11-84	98.13	98.17	10.89
12.25	12-84	100.12	100.18	11.21
13.55	1-85	100.29	101.1	11.65
7.38	2-85	97.8	97.12	11.47
10.80	3-85	99.4	99.8	11.80
12.10	4-85	99.28	100	12.15
14.55	4-85	101.29	102.1	11.89
8.13	5-85	96.19	96.23	11.92
12.00	5-85	99.25	99.29	12.08
12.20	6-85	100	100.4	12.06
15.00	6-85	102.21	102.25	11.99
12.80	7-85	100.13	100.17	12.24
13.90	7-85	101.18	101.20	12.17

| 7.75 | 1-86 | 92.28 | 93.4 | 12.83 |

Federal Farm Credit

Rate	Mat	Bid	Asked	Yld
9.63	7-84	99.28	100	9.00
9.75	7-84	99.29	100.1	8.34
14.80	7-84	100.8	100.12	9.94
15.25	7-84	100.9	100.13	10.01
9.55	8-84	99.25	99.29	10.03
9.63	8-84	99.25	99.29	9.87
9.63	9-84	99.19	99.23	10.49
9.95	9-84	99.23	99.27	10.43
11.75	9-84	100.2	100.6	10.14
9.90	10-84	99.20	99.22	10.56
10.60	10-84	99.25	99.29	10.70
12.85	10-84	100.14	100.18	10.89
14.35	10-84	100.28	101	11.01
9.70	11-84	99.10	99.14	10.91
10.50	11-84	99.22	99.26	10.88
9.55	12-84	99.3	99.7	11.32
10.10	12-84	99.6	99.10	11.36
10.65	12-84	99.17	99.21	11.39
11.45	12-84	99.27	99.31	11.46
10.75	1-85	99.14	99.18	11.36
10.90	1-85	99.17	99.21	11.49
14.35	1-85	101.13	101.17	11.51
10.70	2-85	99.6	99.10	11.73
11.95	3-85	99.27	99.31	11.93
13.20	3-85	100.23	100.27	11.84
13.25	4-85	100.25	100.29	12.02
14.80	4-85	102	102.4	11.99
9.20	6-85	97.13	97.15	12.09
11.60	7-85	99.6	99.10	12.27
10.00	7-85	97.18	97.22	12.32
12.75	9-85	100.4	100.8	12.48
14.90	9-85	102.17	102.21	12.40
14.30	12-85	101.30	102.2	12.68
17.00	12-85	105.14	105.18	12.65
10.75	8-87	93.4	93.20	13.30

15.13	12-91	104.12	104.28	14.05
5.38	4-92	61.24	62.24	13.15
14.75	6-92	103.8	103.24	13.95
13.63	9-92	98.4	98.20	13.90
10.90	3-93	85.16	86	13.70
10.38	5-93	81.16	82	13.95
5.88	9-93	60.12	61.12	13.25
6.50	3-94	62.8	63.8	13.35
6.38	10-94	60.12	61.12	13.40
8.63	8-95	70.20	71.4	13.75
8.13	8-96	66.24	67.8	13.75
9.35	12-00	70.20	71.4	13.85
8.85	7-01	67	67.16	13.85
8.38	12-01	63.24	64.8	13.85
8.25	5-02	62.24	63.8	13.85
8.35	8-02	63.8	63.24	13.85
12.38	10-02	90.12	90.28	13.75

Federal Land Bank

Rate	Mat	Bid	Asked	Yld
8.10	7-85	95.21	95.25	12.35
7.95	10-85	94.16	94.20	12.43
8.80	10-85	95.18	95.22	12.38
7.60	4-87	86.26	86.30	13.27
7.25	7-87	84.15	84.19	13.52
7.85	1-88	84.18	84.22	13.36
8.20	1-90	79.24	80	13.39
7.95	4-91	75.26	76.2	13.40
7.95	10-96	66.22	67.6	13.47
7.35	1-97	63.2	63.10	13.48

Inter-Amer. Devel. Bk.

Rate	Mat	Bid	Asked	Yld
4.50	11-84	97.4	97.16	11.50
8.25	1-85	97.20	98	12.00
8.00	3-85	97	97.12	12.10
8.38	2-86	93	93.12	13.05
14.00	12-86	100.28	101.8	13.35

Asian Development Bank

Rate	Mat	Bid	Asked	Yld
8.63	8-86	92.4	92.20	12.70
	7-92	34.16	35	13.45
7.75	4-96	65.4	65.20	13.70
11.13	5-98	82	82.16	14.00

GNMA Issues

Rate	Mat	Bid	Asked	Yld
8.00		67.15	67.23	13.73
9.00		71.22	71.30	13.99
9.50		74.7	74.15	14.03
10.00		76.21	76.29	14.10
11.00		81.29	82.5	14.14
11.50		84.26	85.2	14.11
12.00		87.30	88.6	14.04
12.50		90.5	90.13	14.20
13.00		93.3	93.11	14.12
13.50		95.23	95.31	14.26
14.00		98.23	98.31	14.12
15.00		102.12	102.20	14.57
16.00		106.21	106.29	14.79

FIC Bank Debs.

Rate	Mat	Bid	Asked	Yld
7.95	4-86	91.29	92.5	13.01
6.95	1-87	86.23	86.29	13.18

Student Loan Marketing

Rate	Mat	Bid	Asked	Yld
11.25	10-87	94.10	94.18	13.33
10.10	1-88	90.8	90.12	13.61
11.70	7-88	94.30	95.6	13.27
12.85	9-89	97.8	97.16	13.52
10.50	2-90	89.12	89.20	13.56
10.50	4-93	83.18	83.26	13.71

Private Expt. Fndg. Corp.

Source: *Wall Street Journal*, June 20, 1984. Reprinted by permission of *Wall Street Journal*, © Dow Jones & Company, Inc., 1984. All Rights Reserved.

Like Treasury issues, those of the Federal Home Loan Bank System and those of the sponsored farm credit agencies are not subject to state and local taxes. The Federal National Mortgage Association (FNMA) and the Government National Mortgage Association (GNMA) securities are taxed at the state and local level, however. Agency securities generally bear a slightly higher interest rate than comparable-maturity Treasury issues. Why, if the guarantees are similar, are the agency yields usually higher? Marketability differences account for part of the difference. Because most agency issues' trading volumes are less than those of Treasury issues, the market is narrower and spreads wider.[17] Marketability only concerns investors who may need to sell prior to maturity, however. Holding for a substantial period spreads the buying and selling costs over several years. Along with higher trading costs, the confusingly wide choice of agency issues dampens some investors' enthusiasm. Taking time to learn about agencies, though, is a small price to pay for a significantly higher return.

Mortgages and Mortgage-Related Securities

Many agency and some types of non-agency securities are either backed by or represent ownership in a pool of mortgages. The vast majority of outstanding mortgage debt is collateralized by a first claim (first mortgage) on developed real estate such as single homes or commercial property. Most such mortgages require a minimum initial down payment of 20% to 25% (the borrower may put down more) and are amortized with level monthly payments over an extended period (20 to 30 years is typical). Since the property securing the mortgage usually appreciates, causing the ratio of collateral value to mortgage debt remaining to rise as time passes, first mortgages are usually rather low- and declining-risk investments. Even in a default and distress-sale of the property, the mortgage holder is likely to recover a high percentage of the outstanding debt.

Financial intermediaries such as banks, savings and loan associations, and insurance companies write the vast majority of mortgages. Some mortgages are guaranteed by the federal government through the Veterans Administration (VA) or the Federal Housing Administration (FHA), which adds further protection. Several federal agencies and some other groups promote mortgage lending by purchasing mortgages from the originator.

Virtually all actively traded mortgage-related securities are issued by two federal agencies, one former federal agency, and a handful of large banks. The oldest and largest of these is the FNMA, which began as a federal agency designed to channel funds to the mortgage market. The FNMA purchases mortgages from original mortgage lenders (mortgage bankers, commercial banks, S&Ls, and savings banks) with the proceeds of its own debt security sales. Its bonds, which have fixed coupons and maturities, trade in a secondary market much like other bonds. In 1968 FNMA was separated into two parts, one of which—the current FNMA—became a publicly traded profit-oriented corporation. The other part of the old FNMA became the GNMA, which continues to promote mortgage lending on a non-profit basis. GNMA guarantees the timely payment of principal and interest on securities issued by private mortgage institutions and backed by pools of government-insured-or-guaranteed mortgages. Since the pools only contain FHA and VA guaranteed mortgages, GNMA passthroughs are very secure debt instruments. These passthroughs' principal drawbacks are a relatively high minimum denomination ($25,000, but may be bought in $5,000 units thereafter) and uncertain amortization-rate. One literally owns a part of a mortgage pool. Passthrough owners receive monthly interest and amortization payments (less a small service fee to GNMA and the financial institution that administers the mortgage). Mortgages written for specific periods are sometimes prepaid. Depending on such matters as the divorce rate and mobility in the relevant geographic area, a mortgage's expected maturity can be well under or well above the twelve-year average that is usually assumed. Moreover high mortgage rates have discouraged the prepayment of old low-rate mortgages. In spite of these drawbacks, GNMA's relatively high secure yields make them quite attractive.

The Federal Home Loan Mortgage Association (Freddie Mac) also sells mortgage-related securities. While GNMA is an agency under the Housing and Urban Development Department, Freddie Mac is an adjunct of the Federal Home Loan Bank Board that regulates the savings and loan industry. Freddie Mac purchases conventional (not government-insured) mortgages, pools them, and sells participations which have much in common with GNMA passthroughs. Freddie Mac participations trade in $100,000 minimum denominations. Since substantial collateral generally underlies the mortgages and Freddie Mac guarantees them, the participations are also considered quite safe.

Encouraged by the success of FNMA, GNMA and Freddie Mac, several large banks led by Bank of America have begun packaging and marketing their own mortgage pools. These pools offer somewhat higher yields and risks than the agency securities. While not government-guaranteed, these private passthroughs are backed by the underlying mortgage collateral and most have a partial guarantee from a private insurer. For example, defaults equal to the first 5% of principal on the Bank of America passthroughs are insured by the Mortgage Guarantee Insurance Corporation (MGIC). Since defaults rarely exceed 5% of principal, such insurance offers considerable protection. Some depository institutions also sell mortgage-backed bonds. Such securities are, however, just another type of corporate bond which happens to have mortgages as collateral. Some mutual funds manage mortgage portfolios, thereby allowing small investors easy access.

Direct Mortgage Investment

Individuals can also participate directly in the mortgage market. High interest rates and rapidly rising housing prices have led more and more property owners into seller financing. Individual investors can extend collateralized loans much like those originated by financial intermediaries. All that is required is a legal document setting forth the rights and obligations of the borrower and lender. The mortgage may be a "first" or it may be junior to some other obligations. The mortgage agreement contains the borrower's pledge to pay principal and interest at a prespecified rate that amortizes the loan. If the payment is not made promptly, the lender has the right to seize and dispose of the collateral for the debt, with the proceeds first repaying the loan and collection expenses. The lender still has a claim against the borrower for any remaining deficit. Unlike "firsts," most second mortgages are written for relatively short periods (e.g., five years) and require principal repayment at maturity (the balloon). With a second mortgage, the lender generally has the right, if not repaid, to assume the borrower's position. Thus the second mortgage holder may make up back payments, and when the first mortgage is paid off, take possession of the property. Alternatively, the second mortgage holder can sell or let his or her interest lapse. Second mortgages are usually written for an appreciable fraction of the asset's remaining value (after subtracting the first mortgage), and those who use them are often overextended. Second mortgage holders are frequently asked to extend the repayment dates when the mortgagee cannot pay the balloon. Thus such instruments are often quite risky and generally trade in a relatively thin secondary market.[18]

Mortgage Investment Assessment

The advantages and disadvantages of indirect mortgage ownership are similar to those of bonds, though the various passthroughs and participations offer a less certain maturity and payout rate than do most bonds. Direct mortgage participations (especially seconds if competitive) usually bear a high interest rate reflecting the greater risk and trouble involved. Clearly, potential investors should approach direct mortgage lending cautiously.

State and Local Government Debt Obligations

The debt security markets also contain a large number of state and local government securities called "municipals." The issuing agency may be as well-known as the state of New York or the New York Port Authority, or as obscure as a small rural Alabama water district. Obviously, the adequacy of these units' tax bases varies enormously. In 1975 for example, New York City was forced to halt the direct sale of its debt obligations. First New York State and then the federal government had to step in to help avoid a default.[19] Cleveland did actually default. More recently (1983), the Washington Public Power System (WPPS) defaulted on $2.25 billion of its bonds.

Investors should carefully evaluate the financial resources of the issuing municipal unit.[20] While many of these bonds are rated by Standard & Poor's and Moody's investor services, effective municipal investing involves substantial individual monitoring. Many of the newer issues are guaranteed by one of several companies.[21] Treynor contends that the primary determinant of municipal bond quality is the unit's ability to pay as measured by its taxable property.[22]

Municipal bond interest is not subject to federal income tax or state and local tax in the state of issue. Capital gains on municipal holdings are taxable, however. Municipals' tax advantage allows issuers to offer lower before-tax returns than otherwise-similar taxable bonds. The relative after-tax return depends on an individual's tax bracket and the differential yields. Obviously, tax-free income becomes more attractive the higher one's tax bracket. Those with marginal tax rates of 25% or more will generally find their after-tax return on municipals above that of similar-risk taxable bonds. Below that rate, the taxable bonds tend to offer the higher after-tax yield. One should evaluate the situation on an individual basis, however, as relative interest rates vary over time and with maturity. At times a 20% tax rate is the dividing line, while at other times it is 30%.

Comparing after-tax returns is quite straightforward. First the investor determines his or her marginal rate. For example: a joint taxable income of $25,000 in 1984 would have been taxed $3,465 plus 25% of the excess over $24,600, or $3,625. Thus 25% was the marginal tax rate. On December 28, 1983, the New

York State Power Authority 9 7/8% bonds maturing in 2020 were offered at 100, which corresponded to a before- and after-tax yield of 9 7/8%. Southern Bell Telephone 12 7/8% bonds maturing in 2020 were also selling for 100, for a before-tax yield of 12 7/8%. The maturity dates on these two low-risk securities are almost identical. The after-tax return on taxable bonds is: before-tax return × (1 − marginal tax rate). In this case, 12.875% (1 − .25) = 9.66%.

Thus for one in the 25% tax-bracket, the after-tax return on the AT&T bond was slightly lower than the Power Authority bond. With a marginal tax rate of 22%, however, the after-tax return on AT&T would be 10.0%, which is greater than that of the municipal bond. Note also that the computation would be more complex for bonds trading at a discount, as capital gains taxes would have to be paid on both types of issues. State and local income taxes, if applicable, would further complicate the comparison. The presence of such taxes does enhance tax-free returns, however. For example, a New York City resident excapes federal, state, and city income taxes on any interest income from bonds issued by New York municipal units.

Municipal Bond Funds
While individuals can assemble their own portfolios of municipals, a rather large sum would be required to spread risks effectively. Municipal bond funds assemble and manage well-diversified portfolios that appeal to moderate-means investors seeking tax-exempt income. Many fund's portfolios are, however, weighted toward high-risk securities.[23]

Like the money funds, municipal bond funds compete with unit investment trusts. The comparisons are relatively similar. The municipal unit trusts' risk-adjusted yields are somewhat higher, but they are somewhat less convenient to own than the municipal bonds funds.[24] A number of funds invest only in the securities of a single state, which allows their residents to take full advantage of the tax-free status of the income at the federal, state, and local levels.

Corporate Debt Obligations

Corporations constitute the third principal category of bond issuers (in addition to governments and municipals). Both convertible and nonconvertible corporate instruments, like government bonds, bear interest and mature. In addition, convertibles (which will not be discussed further here) may at the owner's option be exchanged at some fixed rate for stocks of the issuing corporation. Now consider the corporate bond quotations of Table 15.5.

Corporate bond quotations read much like stock quotations. The first column contains the issuing company's name followed by the bond's coupon rate and the maturity date. For example, the APL quote indicates that the APL bond pays 10 3/4% on its face value and matures in 1997. The current yield, 14% in this case, is the coupon rate divided by the current price. Next comes the number

Table 15.5 New York Exchange Bond Quotation, June 20, 1984

CORPORATION BONDS
Volume, $$30,000,000

Bonds	Cur Yld	Vol	High	Low	Close	Net Chg.
APL 10¾97	14.	1	74¼	74¼	74¼	.....
ARA 4⅝s96	cv	6	57	57	57	+ ¾
AVX 13½00	16.	20	86⅜	86⅜	86⅜	+ ¼
AetnLf 8⅛07	13.	7	63⅜	63⅜	63⅜	− ½
AlaBn 10.65s99t	11.	10	99¼	99¼	99¼	− ⅜
AlaP 8½s01	14.	15	62⅛	61⅜	61⅜	−1⅛
AlaP 8⅞s03	14.	35	63½	63⅜	63½	− ½
AlaP 9¾s04	14.	14	68½	68½	68½	+ ¼
AlaP 8¾07	14.	8	61	61	61	−1
AlaP 8⅝87	10.	5	86¼	86¼	86¼	− ¾
AlaP 9½08	14.	5	67⅛	67⅛	67⅛	+ ⅝
AlaP 15¼10	15.	1	101⅜	101⅜	101⅜	−1⅛
AlaP 17⅜11	16.	6	109½	109½	109½	−1
AlskA 9s03	cv	10	91½	91½	91½	.....
AlskH 16¼94	15.	15	110	109	110	+5
AlskH 16¼99	15.	13	107⅝	107⅝	107⅝	−1⅞
AlskH 17¾91	16.	18	113½	111⅛	113½	+ ½
AlskH 18⅜01	17.	69	110¼	109¼	110⅛	+1
AlskH 15s92	15.	20	102⅜	102⅜	102⅜	−1⅛
AlldC zr87	..	10	67	67	67	+1
AlldC zr98s	..	8	17½	17	17	.....
AlldC zr2000s	..	3	14½	14½	14½	− ½
AlldC d6s88	8.2	6	74	73½	73½	− ½
AlldC d6s90	9.1	41	67½	65⅝	65⅝	.....
AlldSt 9½07	cv	20	111½	110½	111½	−1½
AlsCha 16s91	16.	5	100⅞	100⅞	100⅞	−1
Alcoa 7.45s96	12.	2	62	62	62	− ⅛
AluCa 9½95	12.	15	77⅞	77¾	77¾	− ⅛
AMAX 8s86	8.7	7	92⅛	92⅛	92⅛	+ ⅜
AForP 5s30	14.	17	38	35¼	35¼	−2¾
AAirl 4¼92	7.9	1	54	54	54	+ ½
AAirl 11s88	11.	9	100	100	100	.....
AAirl 5¼98	11.	6	48¼	48¼	48¼	+ ¼
ACan 3¾s88	5.2	1	71½	71½	71½	.....
AExC 10.1s90	12.	25	86	85⅝	86	+ ⅜
AExC 12⅞91	13.	25	96½	96½	96½	− ½
AExC 14¾92	14.	9	102¾	102¾	102¾	− ¾
AmGn 11s07	cv	28	123½	122½	122½	+ ¼
AmGn 11s08	cv	65	123	122½	122½	−1½
AInvt 8¾s89	11.	20	78⅝	78⅝	78⅝	+ ½
AmMed 9½01	cv	101	114	111¼	114	+2
AmMed 8¼08	cv	42	85	84⅛	85	+1
AmMed 13s01	cv	14	149¾	149	149¾	+1¾

New York Exchange Bonds

Wednesday, June 20, 1984

Total Volume $30,190,000

	Domestic Wed.	Domestic Tue.	All Issues Wed.	All Issues Tue.
Issues traded	854	879	856	884
Advances	237	387	239	388
Declines	470	319	470	323
Unchanged	147	173	147	173
New highs	2	7	2	7
New lows	46	41	46	44

SALES SINCE JANUARY 1

1984	1983	1982
$3,271,208,000	$4,128,073,000	$2,704,839,000

Dow Jones Bond Averages

−1982− High	−1982− Low	−1983− High	−1983− Low	−1984− High	−1984− Low		Wednesday −1984−		Wednesday −1983−		Wednesday −1982−	
71.52	55.67	77.84	69.35	71.75	64.81	20 Bonds	65.87	− .11	73.60	+ .44	58.60	+ .18
72.71	53.80	78.88	65.76	69.31	59.43	10 Utilities	60.92	− .04	72.46	+ .21	56.24	+ .11
71.23	57.36	77.13	71.51	74.37	69.61	10 Industrial	70.82	− .18	74.73	+ .66	60.95	+ .25

Bonds	Cur Yld	Vol	High	Low	Close	Net Chg.
CIT 15½87	15.	5	105½	105½	105½	.....
CNA 8½95	13.	2	66⅝	66⅝	66⅝	.....
Caesr 12½00	16.	2	80	80	80	−4¼
Campbl 9⅞90	11.	50	87	87	87	−1
CPc4s perp	11.	31	35	34	34⅞	− ⅛
CaroT 9⅛00	14.	17	66⅜	66⅜	66⅜	− ⅝
CartH 9¼96	13.	10	70⅞	70⅞	70⅞	+1⅞
CatTr 5½00	cv	10	90	88¼	90	− ½
Cave 11½00O	16.	20	73¾	73¾	73¾	−1⅛
Cave 11½00N	15.	2	76⅜	74½	76⅜	− ⅛
Celanse 10⅞87	12.	5	93	93	93	− ⅞
Cenco 5s96	cv	5	64	64	64	+ ½

Bonds	Cur Yld	Vol	High	Low	Close	Net Chg.
ConEd 9⅛04	14.	30	67⅜	67⅛	67⅜	− ⅛
CnNG 4½87	5.4	5	83	83	83	.....
CnNG 4⅜88	5.9	2	74⅛	74⅛	74⅛	−3⅛
CnPw 4½88	7.2	15	62½	62½	62½	− ½
CnPw 4⅝89	7.5	4	61⅜	61⅜	61⅜	+1⅜
CnPw 4⅝90	8.6	30	53⅝	53½	53½	− ⅛
CnPw 4⅝91	9.3	50	50	50	50	.....
CnPw 5⅞96	13.	7	44½	44½	44½	+1¼
CnPw 6⅝98	15.	12	46	45¼	45¼	+ ¼
CnPw 7⅝99	16.	20	47½	47⅛	47½	+ ⅛
CnPw 8⅝00	17.	5	51⅜	51⅜	51⅜	.....
CnPw 8⅛01	16.	1	49½	49½	49½	.....

Source: *Wall Street Journal*, June 20, 1984. Reprinted by permission of *Wall Street Journal*,

of bonds traded during that day. Finally, the high, low, and closing prices and the net change are reported. Corporate bonds are usually sold in $1,000 face value units, while quotations are given in parts of one hundred. Thus the APL quotation of 74 corresponds to $740 per bond. A bond trading for less than 100 is selling at a discount from its face or par value, while one selling at above 100 is trading at a premium.

Corporate bonds also trade in a very active OTC market. One wishing to buy or sell a large dollar value of bonds should check the OTC bond quotations to see which market offers the better price. Small amounts of bonds are also traded on some other exchanges, including the AMEX.

High-Risk Corporates

Bonds were once thought of as very secure low-risk investments. More recently, however, many bonds are viewed as very risky, and thus bear commensurate yields. One observer reports that 93% of low-rated issues have paid off and that such issues' substantial yield-premiums tend to offset their default risks.[25] Indeed junk-bond speculators have often done quite well.[26] Table 15.6 illustrates some mid-1982 yield differentials.

Table 15.6 Differential Bond Yields on May 19, 1982

Company		Coupon	Maturity	Price	Current Yield
Very Secure Bonds	AT&T	13-1/4	1991	96-1/4	13.7
	GE Credit	13-5/8	1991	97	14.0
Risky Bonds	Eastern Airlines	17-1/2	1998	92-7/8	18.8
	Rapid American	11	2005	57-5/8	18.9
	World Airlines	11-1/4	1994	52-7/8	22.3
Very Risky Bonds	International Harvester	9	2004	28-1/2	31.6
	Braniff (in default)	10	1986	32-1/2	30.8*

*if paid

These enormous indicated yield differentials reflect appreciable differences in risk. While ill-suited to the needs of cautious investors, many risk-oriented investors are attracted to junk bonds. Risk and potential returns can be as great as with many stocks. Indeed a risky firm's bonds sometimes offer a more attractive speculation than its stock. The troubled firm only has to avoid bankruptcy or maintain a substantial value in a reorganization for the bondholders to be rewarded. The stockholder's return, in contrast, may not be attractive unless the firm both avoids bankruptcy and becomes relatively profitable. A study by Chandy and Cherry strikes a cautious note for would-be investors in junk bonds, however.[27] The authors found that while the average realized yields on junk bonds generally exceeded that for high-grade bonds, volatility was proportionately even greater. In periods of rising interest rates, investment-grade bonds offered both less volatile yields and higher realized returns.

While always an important investment goal, diversification is crucial for junk-bonds, where defaults are not infrequent. A defaulting issue may eventually pay off, but the wait can be long and tedious. Thus having a diversified portfolio, which substantially lessens the impact of a single default, is especially advisable for junk-bond investors. Junk-bond funds, however, provide small investors with an effective diversification vehicle. In fact the growth of such funds has encouraged some firms with relatively low credit ratings to return to the market. Interest in such issues, however, may have grown to the point where the market has become overcrowded.[28]

Corporate Bond Funds

Corporate bond funds have existed for many years. With the stock market depressed and interest rates at historic highs, bond fund yields became increasingly attractive in the early 1970s. The very high interest environment of the early 1980s further enhanced their yields and attractiveness.

As with other types of securities, bond funds may be load or no-load, open-end or closed-end, and managed or unmanaged (unit trusts). As with stock funds, the no-load-type fund is generally preferred. Most closed-end funds sell at a discount from their NAV.[29] Both open-end and closed-end bond funds have similar advantages and drawbacks vis-a-vis direct bond ownership as do common stocks and their mutual funds. They offer diversification, convenience, and low-denomination purchase, but the expenses incurred in selling and operating the funds reduces yields somewhat. As with other types of funds, unmanaged funds have lower expenses, which means that more of their portfolios' yields flow through to their unit holders.

OTHER TYPES OF DEBT INSTRUMENTS

While the already-discussed debt instruments (money market, governments, municipals, traditional corporates) constitute the bulk of the debt market, a number of other debt security types bear mentioning. Long-term CDs, income bonds, floating-rate notes, and zero-coupon bonds have unusual interest provisions. In addition, Eurobonds, insurance company debt instruments, private placements, and even preferred stock have characteristics similar to other long-term debt instruments.

Long-Term Certificates of Deposit

Commercial banks and other financial intermediaries also sell a variety of longer-term debt instruments. Technically they can pay whatever rate they choose on securities with $100,000 or greater denominations or on repos of any denomination. As a practical matter, however, repos and large CDs very seldom have maturities of longer than a year. Banks and other deposit institutions are also permitted to pay unregulated rates on low-denomination CDs ($500 or greater) with maturities of 31 days or longer.

Income Bonds

Most bonds either pay the agreed-upon coupon or default. "Income bonds," in contrast, pay interest only if it is earned. Passed coupons may or may not accumulate. Bonds with large unpaid arrearage may offer attractive speculations. Specific indenture provisions indicate when earned income is sufficient to require an interest payment. Most income bonds originated in a reorganization exchange, but some were sold originally as income bonds. Even though income bonds offer issuers as much flexibility as preferred stock plus the right to deduct the interest payments, they are much rarer than preferreds. McConnell and Schlarbaum, who studied the issue, were unable to explain their relative scarcity satisfactorily.[30]

Floating-Rate Notes

In 1974, Citicorp introduced a novel type of variable-rate security. Soon thereafter several other corporations offered their own floating-rate notes. The Citicorp coupon is adjusted every six months to yield 1% over the three-month Treasury bill rate. After an initial two-year holding period, the bond became redeemable at par every six months and matured in fifteen years. The redemption feature makes such securities quite liquid, and their floating rate tends to price them close to par.

Relatively few corporate floating-rate notes have been sold in the past few years. The student loan programs in Kansas, Kentucky, and Minnesota have, however, all issued intermediate term notes with tax-free interest pegged at approximately 70% of the T-bill rate.[31] Similarly, the Student Loan Marketing Association (Sallie Mae, a government-chartered but privately owned corporation) has sold notes backed by government-guaranteed student loans whose interest rates are adjusted weekly to .75% above the 91-day T-bill rate.[32] Floating-rate issues are also relatively common in the international market, especially in Asia.[33] A few companies have also issued floating-rate preferreds.[34]

Zero-Coupon Bonds

Treasury bills and certain other securities, such as U.S. Savings Bonds, have long been sold on a discount basis with their return derived from the difference between their purchase price and maturity value. More recently, a number of long-term corporate issues have become available. Such securities' precisely identifiable maturity values appeal to IRA and Keogh accounts. The end-period value of funds invested in coupon-yielding bonds, in contrast, is affected by the rate earned on the reinvested coupon payments. Because of this potentially attractive feature, and because of their relative scarcity, zero-coupon bonds have tended to sell for somewhat lower yields than equivalent-risk coupon bonds. Nonetheless, the zero-coupon bonds lock both the buyer and the issuer into a long-term rate. If rates go up the buyer suffers, while the issuer loses if rates decline.[35] For a given change in interest rates, zero-coupon prices change proportionately more than do coupon bond prices. Coupon bond owners may at least reinvest the interest at higher rates when rates rise. Similarly, the issuer may be able to call a coupon bond and refinance more cheaply if interest rates fall. Zero-coupons, in contrast, are generally callable at par, which would almost always be far above their market value.

Zero-coupon bonds may also be created from some types of bonds by separating the coupons from the principal portion.[36] While most bonds pay interest to the bearer, some have attached coupons that may be clipped and sold to one seeking periodic income. The bond without its coupons attached is called a strip bond.

Merrill Lynch has created yet another type of zero-coupon security which it calls a Treasury Investment Growth Receipt (Tiger). A pool of U.S. government securities is purchased and used to guarantee the issue. Like other zero-coupons, Tigers pay no coupon, but mature at face value and are sold at a discount. Other brokerage firms offer similar instruments also bearing feline names (Cats, Lions, Cougars, etc.).

Eurobonds

While Eurodollars are dollar-denominated accounts held by individuals, firms, or governments domiciled outside the U.S., Eurobonds are denominated either in dollars or in some other currency, but traded internationally. U.S. and foreign bonds, in contrast, are only traded in one country. The Eurobond issuer benefits from the wider distribution and the absence of restrictions and taxes that are placed on national bonds. Eurobond buyers may obtain more attractive rates and greater diversification than from U.S. bonds alone. Moreover those bonds denominated in a foreign currency offer investors an opportunity to speculate against the dollar.[37]

Most Eurobonds are issued by multinational corporations, governments, and international organizations, and most are denominated in dollars or marks. By mid-1984, over $210 billion were outstanding. They may take on any of the forms of regular bonds: straight bonds, convertibles, floating-rate notes, zero-coupons, etc. Most are issued in bearer form. Yields are generally competitive with those in the U.S. market.

Insurance Company Debt Assemblies

Two types of insurance company-assembled debt instruments are designed for fixed-income-oriented investors. One seeking a tax-deferred yield may find single-premium (one initial payment) deferred-annuity contracts attractive.[38] The invested funds generate interest that accumulates while taxes may (depending on IRS rulings) be deferred until the retiree begins withdrawals, when most other incomes are lower. Such issues are only as secure as the issuer, however.[39] A second type of insurance company issue, the guaranteed-interest contract (GIC), promises a high interest rate over the security's life, as well as the opportunity to earn the same or a higher guaranteed rate on additions. While these plans are principally designed for pension funds, individual investors can also participate.[40] Investors with sufficient resources to assemble their own diversified bond portfolios may not need either type of issue. The instruments do appeal to those with more limited resources, however.

Private Placements

Approximately one third of all debt instruments sold are placed privately to a few large buyers (often insurance companies) and publicly announced in the financial press. Such announcements are generally referred to as "tombstones" because of the large white spaces and small amount of lettering. Even if the typical private placement's large size (tens of millions of dollars) rules out direct purchases, one may participate indirectly through one of the closed-end funds that specialize in such investments.[41] Private placements generally yield 1/2% to 1% more than equivalent-risk bonds, but lack marketability.[42] Private placements offer issuers greater flexibility, as they can be tailored for specific buyers and do not require a prospectus.[43] The underwriting cost-savings largely offsets their somewhat higher coupon, and the relatively few owners makes it easier to renegotiate terms when necessary.

Preferred Stock

Preferred stock is an equity security with many similarities to debt instruments. Preferred dividends must be declared if common dividends are paid. Moreover, most preferreds are cumulative, which means that accumulated dividends (unpaid) must be made up before the common dividend can resume. Thus many companies' preferred dividends are almost as dependable as their bond interest. A weak company's preferreds may, however, be almost as risky as its common.[44] Some preferreds are participating, which means that they may receive an extra dividend payment if a high enough dividend is paid to the common shareholders.

Preferred stockholders are residual claimants, only one step ahead of the common stockholders. Unless creditors' claims are fully satisfied, nothing will be left for either class of stockholders. Unlike corporate interest payments, preferred dividends paid to corporations are 85% tax free. That is, only 15% of dividends that one corporation receives from another is taxable. For a corporation in the 46% tax bracket, a 12% preferred yield is equivalent to an after-tax yield of 11.3%. A fully taxable yield of 20.9% would, in contrast, be needed to generate 11.3% after taxes. Thus preferreds have become very popular with corporate investors—particularly banks and insurance companies.[45] Because this tax advantage is only available to corporations, most individual investors will not find preferreds attractive.

Implications of the Long-Term Bond Market for the Investor

As with the market's short end, investors may choose from a large number of long-term debt security types. Governments and agencies offer very secure yields. Municipal coupons are tax sheltered. Corporates and municipals can be bought in a wide array of risk and return categories. Specialized types have coupons that vary with earnings or market rates. Still others pay no coupon but mature for substantially more than their issue price. The various types are summarized in Table 15.7.

SUMMARY AND CONCLUSIONS

Security market investors should at least consider the wide variety of risks, returns, marketabilities, liquidities, and tax treatments offered by the bond market. A

Table 15.7   Long-Term Debt Securities

	Issue Type	Characteristic
Primary Types	Treasury Notes and Bonds	lowest risk category
	Agency Issues	slightly higher risks and yields than Treasuries
	Mortgage-Related Securities	
	FNMA	mortgage-backed (VA and FHA)
	GNMA	passthroughs (VA and FHA)
	Freddie Mac	conventional mortgages with Freddie Mac guarantee
	Bank Issued	conventional mortgages often with a private guarantee
	Direct Mortgage	risk varies, seconds are usually quite
	seller financing	risky
	Municipals	tax-free, risk varies
	Municipal bond funds	diversified, may be open or closed-end
	Corporates	vary greatly in risks and yields
	Corporate bond fund	diversified, may be open or closed-end
	Junk bond fund	high-risk portfolio
Specialized Types	Long-Term CDs	limited variety
	Income Bonds	interest only paid if earned
	Floating-Rate Notes	coupon varies with market rates
	Zero-Coupon	sold at a discount, pays no coupon
	Eurobonds	traded internationally
	Insurance Company Debt	
	Single-Premium	taxes may be deferred until maturity
	GIC	allows additions at high yield
	Private Placements	large and flexible
	Preferred Stock	85% tax-sheltered to corporations

well-diversified portfolio containing both equity and debt securities is likely to be less risky than a well-diversified portfolio of stocks or bonds alone. Investors should have little difficulty finding issues bearing risks corresponding to their own preferences.

The money market provides relatively attractive short-term rates on high-quality securities such as T-bills, commercial paper, large bank CDs, banker's acceptances, and Eurodollar loans. Small investors can participate in this market through money market mutual funds, short-term unit investment trusts, and the money market certificates and accounts of commercial banks and thrift institutions. Larger investors can assemble their own money market portfolios.

Treasury and federal agency securities make up a large part of the long-term debt security market. Most such issues are untaxed at the state and local level. The agencies tend to offer slightly higher yields, but are somewhat less marketable than Treasury issues. A large part of the agency security market is mortgage-related. The various bonds, passthroughs, and participations of FNMA, GNMA, Freddie Mac, and the large bank pools offer high, safe monthly income combined with a somewhat uncertain maturity.

State and local issues, whose interest payments are untaxed at the federal level, form another major segment of the debt security market. Most municipals offer relatively low before-tax yields, which primarily appeal to those in high tax brackets. Municipal bond funds and municipal unit investment trusts provide small investors various ways to enter this market.

Corporate securities vary greatly in risk. Some high-risk issues offer very high yields. Corporate bond funds (including high-risk bond funds) and closed-end bond funds permit small investors to own part of a diversified debt-security portfolio.

Other types of debt securities include income bonds, floating-rate notes, zero-coupon bonds, Eurobonds, insurance company-assembled debt securities, privately placed issues, and preferred stock (an equity asset priced primarily on its stated yield). Each of these securities appeals to specialized segments of the marketplace.

Thus the debt security market offers a wide array of risk/return tradeoffs, maturities, and tax treatments. In the last few years, a variety of new instruments have improved the small investors' access to these markets. Since a number of mutual funds and short-term unit trusts facilitate investing in money market, municipal, corporate, high-risk corporate, and various other more specialized types of debt securities, access is no longer restricted by the difficulty of diversifying across a variety of high-denomination securities.

REVIEW QUESTIONS

1. Discuss each of the various classes of money market securities.
2. Discuss the short-term debt securities that are available to the small investor.
3. Describe the three principal types of bonds by issuer.
4. Discuss the relation between Treasury and agency securities.
5. Compare the various types of mortgages and mortgage-related securities.
6. What types of long-term debt securities can banks sell?
7. Explain how to compare municipal bond yields with those of other types of debt issues.
8. Discuss income bonds, floating rate notes, and zero-coupon bonds.
9. Discuss Eurobonds, insurance company debt instruments, private placements, and preferred stocks.
10. Describe the various types of mutual funds, unit trusts, and closed-end funds which participate in the short- and long-term bond markets.

REVIEW PROBLEMS

1. Using the formulas on page 376 and the quotations of Table 15.1 (or a more current quote if desired), compute the actual bid and ask prices for a sample of five T-bills. Now compute the coupon equivalent yields for the issues. Compare the two sets of yields.

2. Make a list of the various money market instruments and track their yields weekly for eight weeks. Which yields are generally highest? How do the yield-spreads vary over time? Write a report.

3. Make a list of five money market mutual funds and five short-term unit trusts. Compare their performances over four six-month cycles (you will have to identify a new list of unit trusts each time). Write a report.

4. Ask five or more local banks and other depository institutions what their current rates are on money market accounts. Compare these rates with those paid by money market mutual funds.

5. Compare the rates on ten Treasury issues with similar maturity and coupon agencies.

6. Make a list of the various mortgage-backed and mortgage-related securities. Plot their rates monthly for twelve months. Which offers the highest yields? How does the market vary over time? Write a report.

7. Choose five municipal issues of differing investment quality and plot their rates monthly over two years. Compare the plot with a similar plot for Treasurys and corporates. Write a report.

8. Assemble a list of five bond funds and five long-term unit trusts. Compare their yields. Write a report.

9. Update Table 15.6 with the most recent price quotes. How would an investor in each of these bonds have done?

10. Identify five companies in financial trouble and obtain copies of successive credit agreements. Examine the progression. Assess the relative damage to the bankers and bondholders. Write a report.

11. Assemble a portfolio of five high-risk bonds and five high-quality bonds. Track the portfolio for one year. Compare the returns. Write a report.

12. Assemble a list of five preferred stocks and track their performance relative to portfolios of the same companies' underlying common and debentures. Compare the returns. Write a report.

13. Select three corporate bonds of varying maturities and three comparable municipal bonds. Compute the marginal tax bracket at which each pair of bonds offers equivalent after-tax returns.

14. Select five T-bills and five U.S. notes with comparable maturities from Tables 15.1 and 15.3 (or current quotes if you prefer). Convert the T-bills' discount yields to coupon-equivalent returns and compare the two sets of returns.

NOTES

1. B. Summers, "Negotiable Certificates of Deposit," *Economic Review*, July/August 1980, pp. 8–19.

2. D. Howell, "Federally Sponsored Credit Agency Securities," Brick editors, *Financial Markets*, R. Dame, Richmond, Va., 1981, pp. 31–44.

3. P. Abken, "Commercial Paper," *Economic Review*, March/April 1981, pp. 11–22.

4. First Boston Corporation, *Handbook of Securities of the United States Government and Federal Agencies*, First Boston Corporation, 1972, p. 11.

5. C. Lucas, M. Jones and T. Thurston, "Federal Funds and Repurchase Agreements," *Quarterly Review*, Summer 1977, pp. 33–48.

6. T. Carrington and G. Anders, "Drysdale's Default Shows Danger of Intricate Financing Agreements," *Wall Street Journal*, May 20, 1982, p. 29; P. Phalon, "Repos and Regrets," *Forbes*, September 13, 1982, p. 32.

7. J. Blyskel, "Very Lucky or Very Good," *Forbes*, March 29, 1982, pp. 140–149.

8. G. Mahon, "Safe, Not Sorry: There are Distinctions Between Money-Market Funds," *Barron's*, October 5, 1981, pp. 4, 5, 34 and 41; *Consumer Reports*, "How to Judge Money-Market Funds," *Consumer Reports*, January 1983, pp. 30–34.

9. D. Rankin, "How They Rate the Money Funds," *New York Times*, March 7, 1982, p. 12F.

10. M. Brady, "Poor Ratings," January 25, 1982, *Barron's*, pp. 9, 30 and 31; *Business Week*, "Will Ratings Catch on For Money Funds?," *Business Week*, January 23, 1984, pp. 112–113.

11. T. Cook and J. Duffield, "Short-Term Investment Pools," *Economic Review*, September/October 1980, pp. 3–23.

12. *Wall Street Journal*, "New High-Interest Bank Accounts Luring Cash from Money Funds," *Wall Street Journal*, December 16, 1982, p. 33.

13. M. Ferri and J. Gaines, "A Study of Yield Spreads in the Money Market: 1971–1978," *Financial Management*, Autumn 1980, pp. 52–59; T. Cook, "Determinants of the Spread Between Treasury Bill and Private Sector Money-Market Rates," *Journal of Economics and Business*, Spring/Summer 1981, pp 177–187.

14. T. Herman, "Many Investors Turn to Short-Term Issues for Safety, Liquidity," *Wall Street Journal*, June 15, 1982, pp. 1, 21.

15. C. McCurdy, "The Dealer Market for U.S. Government Securities," *Quarterly Review*, Winter 1977–78, pp. 33–47.

16. D. Fraser and J. Stern, "Flower Bonds, Tax Changes and the Efficiency of the Bond Markets," *Review of Business and Economic Research*, Winter 1983, pp. 13–24.

17. L. Banks, "The Market for Agency Securities," *Federal Reserve Bank of New York*, Spring 1978, Vol. 3, No. 1, pp. 7–21; D. Puglisi, A. Vignola, "An Examination of Federal Agency Debt Pricing Practices," *Journal of Financial Research*, Summer 1983, pp. 83–92.

18. R. Guenther, "Lower Interest Rates Create Good Opportunity to Sell Mortgage Loans to Investors for Cash," *Wall Street Journal*, February 7, 1983, p. 42.

19. D. Kidwell and C. Trzcinka, "Municipal Bond Pricing and the New York City Fiscal Crisis," *Journal of Finance*, December 1982, pp. 1239–1246; D. Kidwell and C. Trzinkka, "The Impact of the New York City Fiscal Crisis on the Interest Cost of New Issue Municipal Bonds," *Journal of Financial and Quantitative Analysis*, September 1983, pp. 381–400.

20. B. Klapper and V. Pappas, "Wall Street is Forcing Cities to Disclose More when Floating Bonds," *Wall Street Journal*, June 30, 1977, p. 1; *Business Week*, "A Risky New Breed of Tax-Exempts," *Business Week*, August 16, 1982, p. 95; A. Gunn, "Defensive Tax-Exempts; Quality, Sinking Fund, 'Cushion' Issues, Minimize Hazards," *Barron's*, August 22, 1977, pp. 9–13; T. Schlindwein, "Municipal Bond Investing," *American Association of Individual Investors Journal*, November 1983, pp. 4–10.

21. B. Shakin, "Insurance of Municipal Bonds Grows More Popular," *Barron's*, November 29, 1976, pp. 11–15; R. Braswell, E. Nosar; and M. Browning, "The Effect of Private Municipal Bond Insurance as the Cost to the Issuer," *Financial Review*, November 1982, pp. 240–251.

22. J. Treynor, "On the Quality of Municipal Bonds," *Financial Analysts Journal*, May/June 1982, pp. 25–31.

23. L. Asinof, "Municipal-Bond Funds Offer Tax-Exemption, Diversification and Minimum—but some—Risk," *Wall Street Journal*, March 21, 1983, p. 42.

24. D. Moffitt, "Investors for the Long Haul Should Consider Unit Trusts Before Buying Muni-Bond Funds," *Wall Street Journal*, Octobet 17, 1977, p. 48; D. Stock, "Does Active Management of Municipal Bond Portfolios Pay?", *Journal of Portfolio Management*, Winter 1982, pp. 51–55.

25. S. White, "Not for Widows, Orphans: But Speculative Opportunities Abound in Junk Bonds," *Barron's*, March 8, 1976, p. 9.

26. L. Richert, " 'High-Yield' Bonds Offer Speculators Large Price Gains," *Wall Street Journal*, March 15, 1976, p. 21; *Business Week*, "Why Junk-Bonds are Suddenly Glittering," *Business Week*, September 5, 1983, pp. 85–86.

27. P. Chandy and R. Cherry, "The Realized Yield Behavior of Junk Bonds," *Review of Business and Economic Research*, Winter 1983, pp 40–50.

28. R. Phalon, "One Junk Dealer too Many," *Forbes*, February 14, 1983, pp. 174–155.

29. R. Richards, D. Fraser and J. Groth, "The Attractions of Closed-End Bond Funds" *Journal of Portfolio Management*, Winter 1982, pp. 56–61; E. Sanger, "Best of Both Worlds, That's the Promise of Closed-End Bond Funds," *Barron's*, October 31, 1983, pp. 28–31.

30. J. McConnell and G. Schlaubaum, "Returns and Prices of Income Bonds 1956–76 (Does Money Have an Odor?)," *Journal of Business*, January 1981, pp. 33–64.

31. R. Stern, "Will Alter to Fit," *Forbes*, March 29, 1982, pp. 89–90.

32. *Business Week*, "Sallie Mae's 'Floating Winner'," *Business Week*, February 22, 1982, p. 101.

33. E. Browning and V. Fung, "Asian Borrowers Attract New Investors with Rush of Floating-Rate Note Issues," *Wall Street Journal*, May 21, 1982, p. 34.

34. *Business Week*, "Companies Love the New Preferreds," *Business Week*, August 23, 1982, p. 92.

35. J. Bettner, "New Wave of Zero-Coupon Bonds for IRAs Could Sink Investors if Interest Rates Rise," *Wall Street Journal*, March 22, 1982, p. 50; S. Chakravarty, "Things Won't go Better with Pepsi," *Forbes*, May 24, 1982, p. 177; J. Yawitz and K. Maloney, "Evaluating the Decision to Issue Original Issue Discount Bonds: Term Structure and Tax Effects," *Financial Management*, Winter 1983, pp. 36–46; R. Smith, "Zero-Coupon Bonds' Price Swings Jolt Investors Looking for Security," *Wall Street Journal*, June 1, 1984, p. 27.

36. *Business Week*, "Strips' Tempt the Bond Trade," *Business Week*, May 3, 1982, p. 111.

37. D. Moffitt, "Little Known in U.S., 'Sumari' Bonds Offers Haven for Some Investors with a Yen for Yen," *Wall Street Journal*, March 27, 1978, p. 36; M. Winkler, "Big Eurobond Market Has Expanded Sharply But Faces Competition," *Wall Street Journal*, May 29, 1984, pp. 1, 16.

38. D. Moffitt, "High Tax-Deferred Yields on Annuity Policies Give Them Fresh Appeal to Some Investors," *Wall Street Journal*, May 2, 1977, p. 32.

39. D. Rankin, "The Diminished Allure of Annuities," *New York Times*, April 24, 1983, p. 11F.

40. *Business Week* "The Fund Officers Still Like the GICs," *Business Week*, April 26, 1976, p. 67; R. West, "When is a GIC not a GIC," *Financial Analysts Journal*, January/February 1983, pp. 24–26.

41. Federal Reserve Board Staff, "The Private Placement Market," Brick, *op. cit.*, pp. 161–165; A. Glenn, "Private Placements: They Pay Off for Borrower and Lender Alike," *Barron's*, December 12, 1977, p. 3.

42. B. Zwick, "Yields on Privately Placed Corporate Bonds," *Journal of Finance*, March 1980, pp. 23–30.

43. A. Kalotay, "Innovations In Corporate Finance: Deep Discount Private Placements," *Financial Managerial*, Spring 1982, pp. 55–59.

44. D. Smith, "A Framework for Analyzing Nonconvertible Preferred Stock Rick," *Journal of Financial Research*, Summer 1983, pp. 127–139.

45. E. Sorensen and C. Hawkins, "On the Pricing of Preferred Stock," *Journal of Financial and Quantitative Analysis*, November 1981, pp. 515–528.

16 The Determinants of Fixed-Income Security Yields

The prices of all investments (including debt securities) are affected by the general level of interest rates, which are in turn related to such factors as the supply and demand for credit, the economy's strengths and weaknesses, inflationary expectations, and energy prices. The relative discount rate applied to an individual debt security's promised income stream will vary with a number of other characteristics including its default risk, length to maturity and the timing of its promised future cash flows. This chapter explores the impacts of such factors. Default risk, a primary determinant of yields, is given considerable attention with near-default workouts, Chapter XI and X bankruptcy proceedings, and bond rating each considered. We also explore the impacts of term structure, duration, coupon effect, seasoning, marketability, call protection, sinking-fund provisions, me-first rules, usability, industrial classification, condition of collateral, and listing status. The chapter ends with a discussion of bond portfolio management and the relative performance of bonds and stocks.

DEFAULT RISK

No one wants to buy bonds in a seemingly secure company that subsequently goes bankrupt. Defaulting bonds may eventually pay part or all of their principal and accrued interest—or its owners may be left with nothing more than a tax write-off. While some investors achieve high yields from diversified portfolios of bonds in or near default, the strategy is risky, difficult, and trying. Most bond investors prefer simply to collect their principal and interest when due. Such investors should avoid unduly risky bonds while simultaneously seeking to maximize the return for their desired risk level. Distinguishing safe from unsafe bonds and determining the appropriate risk premium for bonds having particular default risks is a difficult task, however. The issuer's promises to the bondholders is one place to start.

Indenture Provisions

Bond indentures contain a number of provisions, the most important of which relate to each issue's interest and maturity obligations. The borrower agrees to a specified coupon payment until maturity, when principal is to be returned. A trustee, usually a bank, is charged with enforcing each indenture provision.

Debt obligations may be backed by specific collateral and/or by the issuer's general credit. The issuer agrees to maintain any pledged assets or acceptable substitutes in good repair. The equipment trust certificates of railroads and other transportation companies constitute a major portion of the collateralized corporate bond market. Even weak companies can issue relatively low-risk (and therefore low-yielding) equipment trust certificates because of the collateral's quality. For example, the bankrupt Penn Central continued to pay interest on its equipment trust certificates to maintain control over its rolling stock.

Most corporate bonds, called *debentures*, are not backed by any specific collateral. Many firms' credit ratings are satisfactory without collateral; other issuing firms own no usable collateral. Debenture holders normally have the same standing as the firm's other general creditors.

In addition to interest-, principal-, collateral-, and liquidation-requirements, a bond's indenture may provide for a sinking fund and/or call-privileges as well as dividend and certain other restrictions. Sinking funds require that a portion of the issue be retired periodically. To meet this provision, bonds may be bought in the open market or called, or funds may be set aside in an escrow account for the issue's eventual retirement. A call privilege permits the issuer to redeem the securities before maturity at a prespecified price. The call price normally exceeds the bond's face value by an amount that declines as maturity is approached. For example: ten years before maturity, the bond might be called at 105 with the call premium declining by .5 per year thereafter. Falling interest rates encourage issuers to call and refinance their debt at lower rates. Some bond's no-call features prohibit calls for part or all of the bond's life, however. Investors should be wary of call rights. Calling high-coupon bonds, which often trade for substantial premiums over face, would cost the bondholder the difference between the pre-call market price and the call price. Dividend restrictions are designed to preserve the firm's capital. Thus dividends might be limited to a certain percentage of profits unless the firm's net worth exceeds some specific level. A minimum current ratio may be set and "me-first" rules may restrict the future borrowing level. All of these features are designed to protect the creditors. Since the value of these provisions depends on how they are enforced, we need to consider what usually happens in a default.

Defaults and Near-Defaults

Firms rarely choose not to pay required interest and principal. They sometimes have no choice, however. Indeed the large number of financially troubled firms in the early 1980s—Braniff, Chrysler, AM International, International Harvester, Saxon Industries, Wicks, Mego, Manville, World Airways, etc.—has heightened interest in the default issue.

A firm technically defaults whenever any of its bond indenture provisions are violated—or for that matter any of the terms of its other debt agreements. Many minor defaults (e.g. the working capital ratio falls below the stipulated minimum) do not lead to a bankruptcy filing. The trustee may permit the violation or the matter may be quickly cured. Even a failure to pay stipulated interest and principal will not automatically force a bankruptcy proceeding, as a late payment may quickly rectify the default. Indeed most defaults do not lead to bankruptcy filings and most bankruptcies do not lead to liquidations. Rather defaults, and indeed many near-defaults, usually result in a formal or informal reorganization that stops short of a long and costly liquidation. Where a few large creditors (such as banks who have extended substantial loans) can be identified, the troubled borrower may seek concessions to avoid a bankruptcy. Such lenders may be asked to accept a payment stretchout, interest rate reduction, swap of debt for equity or tangible assets, reduction in loan principal, and a change or waiver of certain default provisions. Lenders often agree to such restructurings in the hopes of eventually recovering more than they would in a formal bankruptcy. Because obtaining concessions from all of the numerous bondholders would be difficult, they are rarely asked. Accordingly, the bondholders obtain the benefit of the large lenders' concessions without making any corresponding sacrifice. If the effort fails, the bondholders still retain their priority in formal bankruptcy proceedings.

Bankruptcy proceedings may begin with a petition from either a creditor or the firm itself. The firm may choose to file under Chapter XI, which allows time to propose an arrangement with a majority of its creditors (numerically and by dollar amount). Once a majority agree and the court approves, the agreement may be imposed on the rest.[1] Only unsecured creditors may be involved in such arrangements, however. Secured creditors retain their rights in Chapter XI reorganizations.

An unsuccessful Chapter XI reorganization effort usually leads to a Chapter X proceeding. Other cases may begin as Chapter X bankruptcies. Either way, the Chapter X process is slower, more costly, and may result in the firm's liquidation. When a defaulting firm is thought to be worth more dead than alive, its assets may be sold and the proceeds distributed according to the absolute priority of claims followed in bankruptcy and liquidation proceedings:

1. Expenses incurred in administering bankrupt estate (legal fees, operating expenses, debt obligations issued after bankruptcy)
2. Wages and salaries earned within six months of filing for bankruptcy— up to $600 per employee
3. Federal, state, and local taxes
4. Secured creditors up to the value of pledged collateral, with the remaining claims moved to the unsecured level
5. Unsecured creditors (may be subordinated)
6. Preferred stockholders
7. Common stockholders

Under the absolute-priority-of-claims principle, the valid claims of each priority class are fully satisfied before the next class receives anything. The marginal priority group receives proportional compensation. Thus if the firm's recoverable value exceeds the legitimate claims of categories 1, 2, 3 and 4, but does not fully cover category 5's additional claims, the unsecured creditors would receive a fraction of their claims, while the higher classes would be fully compensated. Priority classes 6 and 7 would receive nothing, unless all of the valid claims of 5 were fully satisfied or unless the bankruptcy involved fraud. Several factors limit the applicability of the absolute-priority-of-claims principle, however. First, because the firm's going-concern value is subjective, the lower priority claimants will seek to increase the sum available for their priority level by arguing for a higher overall valuation. Second, the values of any securities issued by the reorganized firm are somewhat uncertain, and thus their abilities to satisfy claims are subject to dispute. Third, the low-priority claimants may use various legal maneuvers to tie up the proceedings for an extended period unless they are given something. Accordingly, most informal workouts and reorganizations ultimately allocate lesser-priority claimants somewhat more than the absolute-priority-of-claims principle requires. Thus in practice, unsecured and subordinated creditors can generally make enough noise to obtain some share of the assets even when senior creditors' claims exceed the firm's remaining asset value after taking care of priorities 1–3. Moreover, most creditors are prevailed upon to accept lower-priority securities of the reorganized firm. Thus senior creditors may receive debentures or preferred shares, while junior creditors could be given common stock and warrants. The reduced debt burden generally permits the reorganized firm to remain solvent. New equity holders may have a long wait before receiving any common or preferred dividend payments, however.

Bond Ratings

Both municipal and corporate bond default risks are rated by Standard & Poor's, Moody's, and Fitch investor services. Ratings are based on each services' evaluation of the firm's financial position and earnings prospects.[2] Table 16.1 describes the two principal agencies' rating categories. While the agencies do not release their specific rating formulas or analysis, a number of academic studies reveal a rather predictable pattern. Ratings tend to rise with profitability, size, and earnings-coverage, decrease with earnings-volatility, leverage, and pension obligations, while varying with industry classification.[3] Occasionally ratings differ between the rating agencies, usually reflecting a close call on fundamentals. A subordinate issue will usually receive a lower rating than a more senior security of the same issuer. While the rating agencies do follow issues over time, rating changes occur relatively infrequently and often take place long after the underlying fundamentals change.[4] Accordingly, several services now offer more up-to-date analyses including a prediction of rating changes.[5] Many brokerage firms have begun paying increasing attention to bond analysis.

Table 16.1 Bond Rating Categories

Moody's	Standard & Poor's	Description
Aaa	AAA	Highest rating—has extremely strong capacity to pay principal and interest.
Aa	AA	High grade—has a strong capacity to pay principal and interest but lower protection margins than Aaa and AAA.
A	A	Upper medium grade—has many favorable investment attributes, but may be vulnerable to adverse economic conditions.
Baa	BBB	Medium grade—generally adequate capacity to pay interest and principal coupled with a significant vulnerability to adverse economic conditions.
Ba	BB	Somewhat speculative—has only moderate protection during both good and bad times.
B	B	Speculative—generally lacks characteristics of other desirable investments. Interest and principal payments over any long period of time are not safe.
Caa	CCC	Poor quality—in danger of default.
Ca	CC	Highly speculative—often in default.
C		The lowest rated class of bonds—extremely poor prospects.
	C	Income bonds on which no interest is being paid.
	D	Issues in default with principal and/or interest payments in arrears.

Adapted from: *Bond Guide* (Standard & Poor's Corporation); *Bond Record* (Moody's Investor Services). Used with permission.

Investors can use financial ratios and bankruptcy-prediction models to perform their own bond analysis. An examination of the level and trend in the current, quick, debt-equity, return on equity, times-interest-earned, and other relevant ratios compared with industry and national averages might reveal current deficiencies and/or significant long-term risks. Clearly, high debt-equity ratios and low times-interest-earned percentages are not reassuring. Unfortunately, such analysis can only provide part of the story. Bondholders should also be interested in the firm's future prospects. For example, a seemingly shaky current financial position may be offset by an upcoming product introduction. Alternatively, a firm with a solid financial position may be trapped in an industry that is slowly being eliminated by changing technology.

Bond Ratings and Performance
According to Pye, no bonds that Moody's rated in the top four classes (Aaa, Aa, A, or Baa) defaulted in the 1950s or 1960s.[6] A small number of railroad bonds

rated Ba or less did default, however. The experience of the 1920s and 1930s is rather different to be sure, but Pye argued that major firms seldom go bankrupt except during major depressions, which economists and government officials now know how to avoid. Subsequent to the Pye article, however, several large firms did go under: W.T. Grant, Franklin National Bank, Penn Central, Braniff, AM International, Penn Square Bank, Continental Airlines, and Manville (with close calls for International Harvester and the Continental Illinois bank). Government bailouts were required to save Lockheed and Chrysler. Pye also found that at least down to Baa, default-risk differences could not justify the return differentials. That is, even after subtracting default losses, one achieves a significantly higher return with Baa than with Aaa issues. In the 1920s and 1930s, on the other hand, the average yield differences accurately reflected default experience. Pye reasons that the substantial premium returns on less highly rated issues results from risk aversion. With default experience as low as it has been, highly rated issues' slight additional safety margins may not be worth the interest sacrifice.

The after-default-loss yield experience of below-Baa bonds is less clear. West notes that below-Baa bonds usually command risk premiums above what would be expected on the basis of traditional ratio analysis (leverage, profitability, etc.).[7] Since many institutional investors are not permitted to own below-Baa bonds, such securities may well offer superior risk-adjusted yields. Thus diversified portfolios of medium- to high-risk bonds might outperform similarly diversified high-quality bond portfolios. Diversification across industries would spread the default risk, and the higher indicated yield might more than offset any default losses. McConnell and Schlarbaum, however, found that at least one subcategory of high-risk bonds appears to be efficiently priced:[8] income bonds with interrupted interest payments tend to offer yields that, while high, are commensurate with their risks.

THE TERM STRUCTURE OF INTEREST RATES

Yields to maturity tend to vary systematically with length to maturity. Plotting yield versus maturity for issues with otherwise-similar characteristics (risk, coupon, call-feature, etc.) reveals rising, falling, unvarying, or complex patterns at various times.

Before discussing the various hypothesized explanations for yield-curve shapes, let us review the relationship between an expected income stream's price and its discount rate. While all bond prices move inversely with market rates, interest rate sensitivity increases with maturity. Consider a 100-year bond with a $100 coupon rate. For such a far-off maturity, the simplified formula *Price = Coupon/Discount Rate* is a very close approximation. Accordingly, when corresponding market rates are 10%, this bond will sell for $1,000 ($100/.10). Should market rates on equivalent-risk issues rise to 11%, this bond's price will fall to $909 ($100/.11). On the other hand, a 9% market rate would price the bond at $1,111 ($100/.09). Since most investors are risk averse, the possibility

Figure 16.1 Types of Yield Curves

A Rising Yield Curve: Yields are low on short-term issues and rise on long maturities, flattening out at the extremes.

A Declining Yield Curve: High short-term yields decline as maturity lengthens.

A Flat Yield Curve: Approximately equal yields on short-term and long-term issues.

A Humped Yield Curve: Intermediate-term yields are above those on short-term issues. Long-term rates decline to levels below those for short-term and then level out.

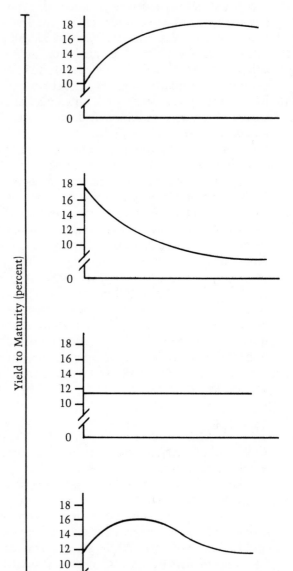

of an interest rate rise and the consequent capital loss generally causes the greater concern. Furthermore, a bond's call feature limits its upside potential.

Both short- and long-term bond prices respond to changes in market rates. The imminent return of principal limits short-term issues' interest rate sensitivity, however. For example: a one-year $100 coupon-rate issue should sell for $1,000 when interest rates are 10%. If rates rise to 20%, the issue must be priced to offer a 20% return. A one-year 10% coupon note selling at $916 would yield about 20% by providing $100 in interest and $84 in capital gains (184/916 = .20). A very long-term bond with an equivalent $100 coupon would, in contrast, need to fall to about $500 ($100/.20). We see that a doubling of interest rates would cause the very long-term bond's price to fall to nearly half its previous value, while the shorter-term issue's price would decline by much less. Thus in a sense short-term issues are less risky to investors than are longer-term securities. Borrowers, on the other hand, may prefer the security of a fixed long-term rate and thus find distant-maturity issues less risky for them. Some investors may also prefer longer-term issues as they offer an assured long-term rate. Clearly the relative risk of a particular maturity depends upon one's perspective (investment horizon, timing of cash needs, etc.)

Term Structure Hypotheses

The segmented markets, liquidity preference, and unbiased expectations hypotheses all seek to explain the yield curve's shape. The segmented markets hypotheses asserts that each market segment's supply and demand determine interest rates for that maturity-class. According to this hypothesis, the yield curve simply reflects that particular time's supply and demand for each maturity-class. Some investors are thought generally to prefer to lend short; many borrowers prefer long-term obligations. Thus rates are often lower for short maturities.

The liquidity preference hypothesis assumes that markets are not segmented per se, but that lenders generally prefer to lend short while borrowers prefer to borrow long. Thus a rising yield curve is generally needed to compensate for the greater time commitment.

The unbiased expectations hypothesis asserts that long rates reflect the market's expectation of current and future short rates. Thus the one-year rate is simply the geometric average of the current six-month rate and the expected six-month rate six months hence. If the twelve-month rate is Y%, unbiased expectations asserts that the market anticipates the six-month rate six months from now to be the rate necessary when coupled with the current six-month rate to yield a twelve-month return of Y%. For example: six- and twelve-month yields of 8% and 9% imply an expected six-month yield in six months of 9.6% $(1.04 \times ? = 1.045^2)$. According to this view, potential arbitrage activity always drives the yield curve into the shape appropriate for that set of expectations. If long rates seem too high vis-a-vis expected future short rates, some short-horizon investors will move toward longer-term issues, while some longer-horizon lenders will switch toward shorter-term borrowing. Such activity should quickly drive rates into the appropriate relationship. All three hypotheses recognize the existence of such arbitraging activity, but only unbiased expectations asserts its overriding power. Table 16.2 summarizes the three term structure hypotheses.

Table 16.2 Term Structure Hypotheses

Segmented Markets	Yields reflect supply and demand for each maturity-class
Liquidity Preference	Lenders generally prefer to lend short and borrowers prefer to borrow long, tending to produce an upward-sloping yield curve
Unbiased Expectations	Long rates reflect the market's expectation of current and future short rates

Each hypothesis explains the various yield curve shapes slightly differently and has somewhat different implications. According to liquidity preference, yield curves typically rise because, on balance, lenders prefer the short end and borrowers the long end. Segmented markets is also consistent with a tendency for yield curves to rise, as lenders may be relatively more numerous at the short end. Unbiased expectations, in contrast, asserts that yield curves only rise when interest rates themselves are expected to increase, while a constant-yield curve indicates neutral expectations. A falling yield curve reflects an expectation that rates will fall, causing borrowers (bond issuers) to rely on short-term financing until the expected fall occurs. Accordingly, borrowers anticipating a decline in interest rates tend to shift demand from the long- to the short-term market, thereby bidding up short rates relative to long rates.

Lender-expectations have a similar effect. Lenders (bond buyers) want to profit from the expected interest-rate decline by owning long-term bonds as falling rates cause their prices to rise relative to shorter-term issues. Thus investors who expect rates to fall will tend to favor the longer maturities, thereby pushing downward on long-rates and upward on short-rates. In summary, when rates are expected to fall, the actions of both lenders and borrowers will tend to twist the yield curve downward, causing short-term rates to exceed long-term rates. The very tight monetary policy in 1974 and again in 1980–81 created just such circumstances: very high short-term rates with lower long-term rates.

None of the three term-structure hypotheses has gained overwhelming acceptance or been completely ruled out. On theoretical grounds, unbiased expectation is generally favored, while liquidity preference may have a slight edge in explaining the data.[9] Most academicians believe that modern debt markets are not segmented per se, but appreciable numbers of borrowers and lenders may have "preferred habitats." From the investor's viewpoint, the relative strengths and weaknesses of the hypotheses are less important than an understanding of the empirical relationship between yield and maturity.

The Term Structure's Investment Implications

Yield curve relationships may provide bond traders with two opportunities. First, securities whose yields are some distance from curves plotted with otherwise-similar issues may well be misvalued. Thus bonds whose yields exceed their respective yield curve values may be underpriced. If their market prices adjust more quickly than the curve itself shifts, the strategy would produce an above-market return. Indeed Brennan and Schwartz find profit potential in purchasing bonds that are underpriced vis a vis their own yield-curve model.[10]

A second strategy involves what is called riding the yield curve. A steeply rising yield curve may offer an attractive trading opportunity. Suppose, for example, that one-year T-bills yield 14%, compared with 12% on six-month securities. Both the six-month bill and a twelve-month bill sold six months later would generate a six-month return. If six-month T-bills are still yielding 12% six months later, the return on the latter strategy will be quite a bit higher than 12%, and indeed above 14% as well. To yield 12% with six months to go, the 14% one-year T-bill must return approximately 15% in the first six months ($1.06 \times 1.075 = 1.14$). Such a riding-the-yield-curve strategy does risk an adverse interest rate move, however. Should six-month rates rise to 16%, the six-month return on the twelve-month bill would only be around 11% ($1.08 \times 1.055 = 1.14$). According to Osteryoung, McCarthy, and Roberts, riding the yield curve tended to increase both returns and risks, at least for the test-period (1976–78).[11]

DURATION

Term-to-maturity does not fully reflect a payment stream's timing. Bonds with coupons close to market yields sell near par. Others having coupon rates that are very low or very high compared to market rates will be priced far from par. Computed yields to maturity will have somewhat different implications for each such issue. The greater the proportion of the return coming from the coupon, the more of the return will be paid prior to maturity. Thus a higher coupon is somewhat akin to shortening the issue's maturity. On the one hand, a high coupon reduces vulnerability to adverse interest rate moves, as at least the coupon can be reinvested as received. On the other hand, coupons cannot, in a period of falling yields, be reinvested at rates as high as the bond's initial yield. Thus a high-coupon bond has less interest fluctuation risk but greater reinvestment risk than one with a lower coupon.

Duration, the weighted average time to full recovery of principal and interest payments, captures the impact of differing payback rates. The formula for duration (D) is:

$$D = \frac{\sum_{t=1}^{N} \frac{C_t (t)}{(1 + i)^t}}{\sum_{t=1}^{N} \frac{C_t}{(1 + i)^t}}$$

where:

t = payment date of coupon or principal
C_t = payment in period t
i = market yield
n = number of periods to maturity

Now consider the durations of two bonds maturing in 5 years. Bond A has a 14% coupon while bond B has a 4% coupon. Table 16.3 reports the results of computing both bonds' durations using a 14% discount rate.

Table 16.3   Duration Computation Example

1	2	3	BOND A 4	5 PV as Proportion	6
Year	Cash Flow	PV at 14%	PV of Flow	of Price	1 × 5
1	140	.877	122.78	.12278	.12278
2	140	.769	107.66	.10766	.21532
3	140	.675	94.50	.09450	.28350
4	140	.592	82.88	.08280	.33152
5	1140	.519	591.66	.59166	2.95830
Sum (Market Price of Bond)			999.48	.99948	3.91142

Duration = 3.91 years

			BOND B		
1	40	.877	35.08	.05348	.05348
2	40	.761	30.44	.04641	.09882
3	40	.675	27.00	.04116	.12348
4	40	.592	23.68	.03610	.13440
5	1040	.519	539.76	.82285	4.11425
Sum (Market Price of Bond)			655.96	1.00000	4.52443

Duration 4.52 years   .

Thus bond B's lower coupon corresponds to a duration of about a half year longer than that of bond A. For equivalent maturities, the lower the coupon the longer the duration. Since bond price movements with interest rate changes vary proportionately with duration,[12] duration reflects interest sensitivity more accurately than does time-to-maturity. Duration also provides a better measure of the wait to payoff than does time-to-maturity.

Immunization

Minimizing the reinvestment-risk on a bond-portfolio is called "immunization."[13] One way of immunizing a portfolio is to buy bonds with durations equal to their planning horizon. For example: suppose Jane R. Nearretirement plans to retire in seven years (her planning horizon), at which time she will use her retirement savings to buy a lifetime income (annuity). A portfolio of bonds having a seven-year duration minimizes her reinvestment risk. Note, however, that to maintain the desired immunization over time, she may have to sell some bonds and buy others. Only zero-coupon bonds' durations decrease as rapidly as their lengths to maturity.

Three methods may be used to immunize a portfolio. Purchasing zero-coupon bonds equal to the planning horizon is by far the easiest. Thus, for example, a large pension fund with relatively easily forecasted payment obligations could purchase a series of zero-coupon securities that matured at times and in amounts that correspond to the projected net cash outflows. Such a strategy encounters two basic difficulties, however. First, cash outflows can rarely be forecasted very precisely. Second, zero-coupon bonds may not be available in the exact maturities needed. Moreover, since the assembled zero-coupons (i.e. the Tigers) are priced to generate after-expense profits for the assemblers, their yields tend to be somewhat below otherwise-equivalent coupon issues. Accordingly, most immunization strategies involve some degree of managing (with or without some zero-coupons in the portfolio).

A second method involves assembling and managing a bond portfolio so that its average duration equals the owner's (i.e. pension fund's) planning horizon. Over time, the fund would probably receive in-payments as well as coupon- and-principal payments on its portfolio and would have to pay benefits out of the fund. Its initial portfolio components' maturities would grow shorter. Inevitably the fund would find itself faced with either a cash imbalance (depending on cash inflows versus outflows) and an average duration which differed appreciably from its initial target. The fund might use its net cash flows to purchase bonds that moved the portfolio's duration toward its target. Alternatively, some portfolio components could be replaced with others whose durations more closely matched the target. Thus bonds purchased ten years earlier that were now close to maturity might be sold, and new longer-term bonds bought with the funds.

The third and most sophisticated approach to immunization combines a portfolio of debt securities with interest rate futures positions (commodity contracts calling for the subsequent delivery of debt instruments such as short- or long-term governments) to achieve the desired duration level. Kolb and Gay have shown how such a strategy can largely eliminate the need to buy and sell bonds.[14] One simply purchases interest futures contracts in amounts and maturities corresponding to the portfolio's forthcoming coupon payments. Thus the inpayments can be immediately reinvested at known rates by taking delivery of the debt securities promised by the interest futures contracts.

In summary, the three methods of immunization are:

- Purchasing zero-coupon bonds equal to the planning horizon

- Assembling and managing a bond-portfolio with an average duration equal to the planning horizon
- Combining a portfolio of debt securities with interest rate futures positions to achieve the desired duration-level

The Coupon-Effect

The relative amounts of coupon and price-appreciation returns also have tax implications. Most bond interest income is fully taxed, while long-term capital gains on bond holdings are taxed at 40% of the investor's ordinary rate. Thus price-appreciation income is tax preferred. Note, however, that the imputed yield from price appreciation on zero-coupon bonds is taxed as if it were received periodically. Only bonds originally issued at or near par generate a capital gains tax break. Still, the market contains many deep-discount, low-coupon bonds which, if held to maturity, will produce a substantial capital gain. Moreover bonds priced well below par (and therefore below their call price) are much less likely to be called than those trading near or above par. Accordingly, investors tend to prefer deep-discount bonds to higher coupon issues.[15] The before-tax yields to maturity on low-coupon, deep-discount issues are usually somewhat below yields on otherwise-similar issues trading nearer to par. This relationship is called the "coupon-effect." Those in high tax brackets will generally find deep-discount issues attractive even when their before-tax yields are appreciably below issues whose yields are fully taxable.

OTHER FACTORS AFFECTING BOND PRICES AND YIELDS

The characteristics already discussed (general interest rate levels, default risk, maturity duration, coupon effect) constitute the principal price/yield determinants of specific bonds. Somewhat less important characteristics include: marketability, seasoning, call protection, sinking-fund provisions, me-first rules, usability, industrial classification, condition of collateral, and listing status.

The vast majority of bond trading takes place in high-volume markets with narrow spreads and deep supply and demand. Many lower-volume issues, however, trade in thin markets with spreads of 5 and even 10 points. A quote of 70 bid to 80 asked implies a 14% spread. Unless a limit order can be used to reduce the spread's impact, trading such an issue is extremely costly. Other things equal, the less marketable the issue, the higher the yield required to make the bond attractive to investors.[16]

Seasoned issues are established in the marketplace (traded at least a few weeks beyond completion of the initial sale). As with new stock issues, new issues of bonds seem to be priced a bit below equivalent seasoned issues.[17] Martin and Richards, however, contend that the apparent yield-differences can be explained by the existence of tax, call-provision, and other issuer-specific factors.[18]

Call protection varies appreciably from issue to issue. Some bonds are callable when sold, while many others may not be called for the first five or ten years of their life. Callable issues that are reasonably likely to be redeemed (high yields) should be evaluated on their yield-to-earliest-call rather than their yield-to-maturity. In marginal cases, both yield figures should be computed. While call protection tends to increase a bond's price, Van Horne finds that the market tends to overvalue call protection.[19] Thus callable issues may generally be a better buy.

The sinking fund's presence increases demand slightly and reduces the probability that refinancing will burden the issuer. Thus other things equal, a sinking fund adds modestly to a bond's value.[20] Such funds do not appear to reduce the debt-issuer's ex-post cost, however.[21]

Me-first rules protect existing bondholders from having their claims weakened by a firm that issues additional debt with a priority higher or equivalent to theirs. Brauer finds that such rules significantly enhance the market values of the protected bonds.[22]

Usable bonds are worth their par value in exercising the firm's outstanding warrants. If such bonds sell for less than par, exercising with them is cheaper than with cash. If the stock price is near or below the point where exercising is attractive, the usability feature may add to the bond's value.[23] Usability's price impact depends on the relative magnitude of the bond's straight-debt value versus its value in exercising the warrant as well as the relative supply of usable bonds and warrants outstanding.

Boardman and McEnnally, who exhaustively studied the factors that affect bond values, found that (1) industrial and transportation issues tend to command higher prices than otherwise-equivalent utility issues, (2) the status of collateral affects values especially when the issue would otherwise have a low rating, (3) listing has little or no price impact.[24] Table 16.4 summarizes the various factors affecting bond yields.

ASSEMBLING AND MANAGING A BOND PORTFOLIO

Diversified bond portfolios are managed to meet their owner's needs. A half dozen different bond issues are usually sufficient to achieve relatively effective diversification. Bonds should also be selected to produce the desired level of maturity/duration, default-risk/quality rating, coupon/price appreciation, etc. Bonds may be part of a larger portfolio that includes stocks and perhaps some other types of assets. Accordingly, a bond's role in providing liquidity, dependable income, etc., should be viewed in that larger portfolio context.

Estimated betas may be computed for bonds as well as for stocks. Such beta estimates may be used, particularly in a portfolio context, to assess the securities' sensitivities to market fluctuations. Most bonds have low but positive betas.[25] Thus far, at least, few bond traders have made much use of the concept.

Table 16.4   Factors Affecting Bond Yields

General Credit Conditions	Affects all yields to one degree or another
Default risk	Riskier issues require higher promised yields
Term structure	Yields vary with maturity reflecting expectations for future rates
Duration	Measures average wait till payback
Coupon effect	Low-coupon issues offer yields which are partially tax-sheltered
Seasoning	Newly issued bonds may sell at a slight discount to otherwise-equivalent established issues
Marketability	Actively traded issues tend to be worth more than otherwise-equivalent issues that are less actively traded
Call protection	Protection from an early call tends to enhance a bond's value
Sinking-fund provisions	Sinking funds increase demand and reduce the risk of refinancing thereby tending to enhance a bond's value
Me-First Rules	Bonds protected from the diluting effect of additional firm borrowings are generally worth more than otherwise-equivalent unprotected issues
Usability	Bonds usable at par to exercise warrants tend to be worth more than otherwise-equivalent issues
Industrial Classification	Industrial and transportation issues tend to command higher prices than otherwise-equivalent utility issues
Collateral Status	Well-maintained collateral tends to enhance bond values relatively to less well-maintained collateral
Listing	Exchange listing appears to have little or no impact on bond yields

Bond Swaps

Portfolio managers frequently liquidate one bond position to finance another's purchase. Such bond swaps may be designed to increase yield-to-maturity or current yield, to adjust duration or risk, or to establish a tax loss. Since many swaps are not executed simultaneously, traders risk making one side of the swap (say the sell), only to encounter an adverse price move before the other side is accomplished. Transactions costs may also reduce some of the swap's expected benefits. Nonetheless, a variety of circumstances make swaps attractive. For example, a low-coupon, deep-discount issue might be sold and the proceeds used to purchase a higher-coupon issue. The sale would normally generate a tax loss, and the purchased issue is likely to offer a higher yield. On the other hand, the swap would probably increase both the call- and the reinvestment-risk. In another swap an investor might sell one issue held at a loss and then purchase another very similar issue. Such a pure tax swap establishes a loss while leaving the portfolio's basic character unchanged. In yet another type of swap, a bond originally purchased as a long-term issue may have moved much closer to maturity. Swapping it for a long-term bond would restore the desired maturity level and possibly enhance yield as well (if long rates are above short rates).

Possible bond swaps are illustrated with the help of the quotes in Table 16.5. One owning the AT&T 3 7/8s of 1990 could greatly increase the current yield with a switch to the 10 3/8s of 1990 (10.5% versus 5.6%). The yield-to-maturity would also rise (10.6% versus 9.4%). A tax swap requires a switch to a different issuer. Thus one holding the AT&T 3 7/8s or 10 3/8s of 1990 could trade them in for GM Acceptance 11 5/8s of 1990. The maturities are similar and the GMA quality is only slightly below that of AT&T (AA+ versus AAA). Maturity-swaps could be made between either AT&T 1990 issues and the 8.80s of 2005 or between the GMA 11 5/8s of 1990 for the GMA 11 3/4s of 2000.

Table 16.5 Selected Bond Quotations for December 31, 1981

Issuer	Rating	Coupon	Maturity	Price	Current Yield	Yield-to-Maturity
AT&T	AAA	3 7/8	1990	69 1/2	5.6%	9.4%
AT&T	AAA	10 3/8	1990	98 7/8	10.5%	10.6%
AT&T	AAA	8.80	2005	79 5/8	11.1%	11.3%
GM Acceptance	AA+	11 5/8	1990	101 3/4	11.4%	11.3%
GM Acceptance	AA+	11 3/4	2000	97	12.1%	12.2%

Other Aspects of Bond Portfolio Management

Managing a bond portfolio effectively can involve much more than the simple types of swaps mentioned above.[26] One might, for example, speculate on a bond upgrade by buying an issue that the market views pessimistically. Margin may be used to magnify potential gains. Some bonds may have higher promised long-term yields than the current cost of margin money. Whether such apparently attractive yield spreads should be exploited depends on the likelihood that they will persist, and the high-yielding issues' default risks. If market interest rates rise, the margin borrowing rate will increase and bond prices will decline. Still more complicated maneuvers involve the use of interest futures and hedges between a company's bond and its other securities. For example, a long position in a company with a high default risk might be hedged with a short position in the firm's stock. If the firm goes bankrupt, the stock could become almost worthless while its bonds still retain some value in a reorganization or liquidation. If the company survives, the bonds will eventually pay off, while the stock may not do well unless it prospers. Finally, portfolio managers can trade on the basis of their interest-rate forecasts.[27] If interest rates are expected to fall, portfolio maturities should be lengthened; an expected rise should cause the manager to

Table 16.6   Interest Rates, Money and Capital Markets

Averages, percent per annum; weekly and monthly figures are averages of business day data unless otherwise noted.

Instrument	1981	1982	1983	1984 Jan.	Feb.	Mar.	Apr.	1984, week ending Mar. 30	Apr. 6	Apr. 13	Apr. 20	Apr. 27
MONEY MARKET RATES												
1 Federal funds[1,2]	16.38	12.26	9.09	9.56	9.59	9.91	10.29	9.97	10.41	10.13	10.37	9.98
2 Discount window borrowing[1,2,3]	13.42	11.02	8.50	8.50	8.50	8.50	8.87	8.50	8.50	8.71	9.00	9.00
Commercial paper[4,5]												
3 1-month	15.69	11.83	8.87	9.23	9.35	9.81	10.17	10.04	10.16	10.11	10.23	10.16
4 3-month	15.32	11.89	8.88	9.20	9.32	9.83	10.18	10.09	10.15	10.12	10.22	10.21
5 6-month	14.76	11.89	8.89	9.18	9.31	9.86	10.22	10.11	10.17	10.13	10.26	10.27
Finance paper, directly placed[4,5]												
6 1-month	15.30	11.64	8.80	9.20	9.34	9.76	10.08	9.95	10.16	10.08	10.04	10.00
7 3-month	14.08	11.23	8.70	9.08	9.14	9.54	9.86	9.74	9.81	9.87	9.83	9.92
8 6-month	13.73	11.20	8.69	9.02	9.06	9.38	9.76	9.60	9.66	9.72	9.80	9.86
Bankers acceptances[5,6]												
9 3-month	15.32	11.89	8.90	9.23	9.38	9.88	10.22	10.12	10.20	10.15	10.26	10.26
10 6-month	14.66	11.83	8.91	9.19	9.35	9.91	10.26	10.15	10.22	10.15	10.33	10.34
Certificates of deposit, secondary market[7]												
11 1-month	15.91	12.04	8.96	9.33	9.43	9.91	10.24	10.18	10.26	10.19	10.28	10.24
12 3-month	15.91	12.27	9.07	9.42	9.54	10.08	10.41	10.34	10.40	10.33	10.42	10.46
13 6-month	15.77	12.57	9.27	9.56	9.73	10.37	10.73	10.59	10.69	10.61	10.76	10.84
14 Eurodollar deposits, 3-month[8]	16.79	13.12	9.56	9.78	9.91	10.40	10.83	10.61	10.79	10.73	10.89	10.89
U.S. Treasury bills[5]												
Secondary market[9]												
15 3-month	14.03	10.61	8.61	8.90	9.09	9.52	9.69	9.72	9.74	9.65	9.76	9.64
16 6-month	13.80	11.07	8.73	9.02	9.18	9.66	9.84	9.85	9.91	9.79	9.86	9.79
17 1-year	13.14	11.07	8.80	9.07	9.20	9.67	9.95	9.86	9.96	9.82	9.98	10.00
Auction average[10]												
18 3-month	14.029	10.686	8.63	8.93	9.03	9.44	9.69	9.76	9.67	9.66	9.80	9.64
19 6-month	13.776	11.084	8.75	9.06	9.13	9.58	9.83	9.88	9.83	9.82	9.92	9.74
20 1-year	13.159	11.099	8.86	9.04	9.24	9.68	9.86	.....	.....	.....	9.86	.....
CAPITAL MARKET RATES												
U.S. Treasury notes and bonds[11]												
Constant maturities[12]												
21 1-year	14.78	12.27	9.57	9.90	10.04	10.59	10.90	10.79	10.91	10.76	10.94	10.98
22 2-year	14.56	12.80	10.21	10.64	10.79	11.31	11.69	11.54	11.67	11.55	11.69	11.79
23 2-1/2-year[13]	.....											
24 3-year	14.44	12.92	10.45	10.93	11.05	11.59	11.98	11.80	11.96	11.84	11.85	12.08
25 5-year	14.24	13.01	10.80	11.37	11.54	12.02	12.37	12.20	12.36	12.24	12.38	12.47
26 7-year	14.06	13.06	11.02	11.58	11.75	12.25	12.56	12.39	12.54	12.41	12.58	12.66
27 10-year	13.91	13.00	11.10	11.68	11.84	12.32	12.63	12.46	12.61	12.49	12.66	12.74
28 20-year	13.72	12.92	11.34	11.82	12.00	12.45	12.65	12.51	12.54	12.52	12.73	12.78
29 30-year	13.44	12.76	11.18	11.75	11.95	12.38	12.65	12.47	12.60	12.50	12.70	12.76

	12.87	12.23	10.84	11.29	11.44	11.90	12.17	12.00	12.13	12.05	12.21	12.27
30 Composite[14] Over 10 years (long-term)	12.87	12.23	10.84	11.29	11.44	11.90	12.17	12.00	12.13	12.05	12.21	12.27
State and local notes and bonds												
Moody's series[15]												
31 Aaa	10.43	10.88	8.80	9.00	9.04	9.41	9.54	9.40	9.50	9.60	9.50	9.55
32 Baa	11.76	12.48	10.17	10.10	9.94	10.22	10.30	10.25	10.30	10.30	10.30	10.30
33 Bond Buyer series[16]	11.33	11.66	9.51	9.63	9.64	9.94	9.96	9.93	10.04	9.97	9.89	9.94
Corporate bonds												
Seasoned issues[17]												
34 All industries	15.06	14.94	12.78	12.92	12.88	13.33	13.59	13.48	13.53	13.51	13.60	13.70
35 Aaa	14.17	13.79	12.04	12.20	12.08	12.57	12.81	12.71	12.74	12.71	12.79	12.95
36 Aa	14.75	14.41	12.42	12.71	12.70	13.22	13.48	13.33	13.42	13.36	13.48	13.62
37 A	15.29	15.43	13.10	13.13	13.11	13.54	13.77	13.70	13.74	13.73	13.75	13.84
38 Baa	16.04	16.11	13.55	13.65	13.59	13.99	14.31	14.15	14.21	14.22	14.37	14.41
39 A-rated, recently-offered utility bond[18]	16.63	15.49	12.73	12.99	13.05	13.63	13.96	13.80	13.86	13.87	14.05	14.18
MEMO: Dividend/price ratio[19]												
40 Preferred stocks	12.36	12.53	11.02	11.35	11.16	11.39	11.66	11.52	11.79	11.63	11.62	11.60
41 Common stocks	5.20	5.81	4.40	4.27	4.59	4.63	4.64	4.57	4.63	4.70	4.62	4.61

1. Weekly and monthly figures are averages of all calendar days, where the rate for a weekend or holiday is taken to be the rate prevailing on the preceding business day. The daily rate is the average of the rates on a given day weighted by the volume of transactions at these rates.

2. Weekly figures are averages for statement week ending Wednesday.

3. Rate for the Federal Reserve Bank of New York.

4. Unweighted average of offering rates quoted by at least five dealers (in the case of commercial paper), or finance companies (in the case of finance paper). Before November 1979, maturities for data shown are 30–59 days, 90–119 days, and 120–179 days for commercial paper; and 30–59 days, 90–119 days, and 150–179 days for finance paper.

5. Yields are quoted on a bank-discount basis, rather than an investment yield basis (which would give a higher figure).

6. Dealer closing offered rates for top-rated banks. Most representative rate (which may be, but need not be, the average of the rates quoted by the dealers).

7. Unweighted average of offered rates quoted by at least five dealers early in the day.

8. Calendar week average. For indication purposes only.

9. Unweighted average of closing bid rates quoted by at least five dealers.

10. Rates are recorded in the week in which bills are issued. Beginning with the Treasury bill auction held on Apr. 18, 1983, bidders were required to state the percentage yield (on a bank discount basis) that they would accept to two decimal places. Thus, average issuing rates in bill auctions will be reported using two rather than three decimal places.

11. Yields are based on closing bid prices quoted by at least five dealers.

12. Yields adjusted to constant maturities by the U.S. Treasury. That is, yields are read from a yield curve at fixed maturities. Based on only recently issued, actively traded securities.

13. Each biweekly figure is the average of five business days ending on the Monday following the date indicated. Until Mar. 31, 1983, the biweekly rate determined the maximum interest rate payable in the following two-week period on 2-½-year small saver certificates. (See table 1.16.)

14. Averages (to maturity or call) for all outstanding bonds neither due nor callable in less than 10 years, including several very low yielding "flower" bonds.

15. General obligations based on Thursday figures; Moody's Investors Service.

16. General obligations only, with 20 years to maturity, issued by 20 state and local governmental units of mixed quality. Based on yields to maturity on selected long-term bonds.

17. Daily figures from Moody's Investors Service. Based on figures for Thursday.

18. Compilation of the Federal Reserve. This series is an estimate of the yield on recently-offered, A-rated utility bonds with a 30-year maturity and 5 years of call protection. Weekly data are based on Friday quotations. The Federal Reserve previously published interest rate series on both newly-issued and recently-offered Aaa utility bonds, but discontinued these series in January 1984 owing to the lack of Aaa issues.

19. Standard and Poor's corporate series. Preferred stock ratio based on a sample of ten issues: four public utilities, four industrials, one financial, and one transportation. Common stock ratios on the 500 stocks in the price index.

Source: *Federal Reserve Bulletin*, May 1984, p. A24.

shift toward near-cash securities. Such a strategy assumes that the manager can accurately forecast interest rate changes, however.

Comparison of Yields for Various Securities

Now that the various types of debt securities have been discussed, their past returns may be usefully examined as a clue to future rates. Table 16.6, reproduced from a *Federal Reserve Bulletin*, provides such a historical overview. The reported rates are not realized returns, but yields-to-maturity for the particular time. For money market instruments, this qualification is of little importance as the price fluctuation impact on realized-yields is minor. In other words, for short-term securities, the yield-to-maturity and the realized returns for actual holding periods will normally not differ greatly. For longer-term issues, however, the possible deviation of realized returns and yields-to-maturity is substantial. One might, for example, have purchased a long-term (30-year) government bond in 1981 when its yield-to-maturity was 13.44% and then sold it in January 1984 when its yield was 11.75%. Over that holding period the return would be considerably more than the 13.44% return that would be realized if the security were held until maturity.

Comparative rates on preferred and common stocks are also included in the long-term securities data. Table 16.6's current yield on the current price data are not adjusted for capital gains or losses, however. Since preferreds are primarily income securities, the stated rates may approximate their long-term yields. For common stocks, the data are not comparable, as dividends constitute only a fraction of their average returns. While failing to allow for capital gains or losses is clearly misleading, any estimated allowance would be arbitrary. Past historical returns may bear little relation to the future, while expected returns are unobservable.

Bond Returns Versus Stock Returns

Since many investors at least consider both bonds and stocks, a comparison of their historical return relationships is worthwhile. Bonds are widely believed to offer a lower but less-risky expected return than stocks. Norgaard, for example, found that over the 1926–69 period, average stock returns almost always exceeded average after-tax bond returns.[28] Specifically, the mean return on stocks exceeded that on bonds by about 5.5%, so that even when stock returns were appreciably below their means, they were still likely to be above those of bonds. Furthermore, a balanced portfolio of bonds and stocks performed little better than the all-bond portfolio. Thus Norgaard's study implies that a well-diversified portfolio of stocks has generally offered a greater expected return with less risk than a bond or balanced bond/stock portfolio. Massey, and still later Grauer and Hakansson, obtained similar results for subsequent periods.[29] Finally, a very comprehensive study by Ibbotson, Carr, and Robinson found that stocks tended to offer higher returns than bonds in most countries over most time periods.[30]

One who has a specific time horizon may still prefer the certainty of bonds, however. Similarly, tax-exempt bonds are attractive to many investors. High-risk bonds may well offer expected returns similar to those of stocks. Thus the results of Norgaard and others question the general attractiveness of bonds, but do not rule out the use of bonds for certain people at certain times.

SUMMARY AND CONCLUSIONS

A variety of factors influence bond yields. General market forces affect both the level and term structure of rates. For a given maturity class and market environment, rates differ primarily with default risk. Informal workouts may reduce the impact of technical defaults and near-defaults, while Chapter XI proceedings are less costly than the more formal Chapter X process. Rating agencies assess bonds' default risks and their issuer's financial strengths.

Various hypotheses attempt to explain the term structure of interest rates. Segmented markets ascribes rates to supply and demand for each maturity class. Liquidity preference asserts that borrowers generally prefer the long end, while lenders prefer the short. Unbiased expectations holds that the term structure reflects a contiguous set of short-term interest rate expectations. Investors may use the term structure relationship to identify securities that are potentially mispriced. Some investors may "ride" a yield curve that is expected to remain approximately stable.

Duration, the weighted average term of the payment stream, is a more accurate measure of repayment timing than is length-to-maturity. Investors and portfolio managers may utilize duration in a strategy designed to immunize their portfolios from reinvestment risk. Specifically, they may minimize the potentially adverse impacts of being unable to reinvest coupons at attractive rates by assembling portfolios with durations equal to their planning horizons.

The coupon effect refers to the price impact of relative taxation of capital gains and coupon income. Low-coupon, deep-discount bonds are generally preferred to otherwise-equivalent issues because a higher percentage of their income is tax sheltered. In addition, prices tend to be higher for more marketable, seasoned issues with sinking funds, me-first rules, and call protection. Usable bonds may also command higher prices. Industrial classification, condition of collateral, and listing status may have some minor price impacts.

Managing a bond portfolio can involve a variety of complicated maneuvers such as immunizing, swaps, and hedges. A number of researchers have found that average stock returns generally exceeded average bond returns. This relation may or may not continue.

REVIEW QUESTIONS

1. List and discuss the principal provisions of bond indentures.

2. What is a default? How does it relate to bankruptcy and liquidation?
3. Describe the various possible outcomes of defaults and near-defaults.
4. What is meant by the absolute priority of claims principle? What is its relevancy to most bankruptcies?
5. How do Chapter X and Chapter XI bankruptcies differ?
6. Discuss bond ratings and default risks.
7. How does performance vary with bond ratings?
8. Describe the three proposed explanations for the term structure of interest rates.
9. What are the implications of the term structure for individual investors?
10. How do yields vary with duration and the coupon effect? What is immunization? How are they related?
11. Discuss the impacts of marketability, seasoning, call protection, sinking-fund provisions and usability on yields.
12. What is involved in managing a bond portfolio? What are bond swaps?
13. How have bond and stock yields compared over time?

REVIEW PROBLEMS

1. Plot the term structure of interest rates using government bonds. Repeat the process for AAA corporates, A corporates, B corporates, AAA municipals, and A municipals. Compare the structures. Write a report.
2. Assemble a list of similar-risk and similar-maturity bonds having varying coupon rates. Plot their current yields-to-maturity versus maturity. Repeat the process for three prior years. Analyze the relationships. Write a report.
3. For the above list compute each bond's duration. Plot current yields-to-maturity versus duration. Repeat the process for three prior years. Analyze the relationship. Write a report.
4. Obtain a troubled firm's bond indenture along with its most recent set of financial statements. Identify as many technical defaults as you can.
5. Obtain a reorganization plan for a firm that has recently come out of bankruptcy. Compare the payouts with those that would have been made under the absolute-priority-of-claims principle.
6. From the S&P Bond Guide select twenty bonds with similar maturities and coupons but different ratings. Plot their yields-to-maturity versus their ratings.
7. Go back to an S&P Bond Guide of five years ago and select portfolios of five bonds for each rating class. In each case try to identify bonds with approximately equivalent maturities and coupon rates. Now compute the annual returns on each portfolio up to the present.
8. Assume you have a $100,000,000 portfolio to manage for the next three years. Your incentive compensation depends upon promising as high

a return as you can while making sure that you deliver. Obviously you want to immunize the portfolio as best you can. Using current market quotes, compare the return you could promise if you purchased zero-coupon bonds (backed by governments) or bought a portfolio of governments and interest futures contracts for the coupon payments. Compute the end value and return for each approach and compare the results.

9. Assemble a list of ten usable bonds and collect data on monthly prices of the bonds, warrants and underlying stocks for the past year. Plot each of the price series over time. Compute the cost of exercising with cash and bonds for each time and compare that with the cost of an outright purchase of the stock.

10. Update Table 16.5 to the present time. Now compute the relative attractiveness of the various bond swaps discussed in the chapter.

NOTES

1. K. Klec, "All You Ever Wanted to Know About Cram Down Under the New Bankruptcy Code," *American Bankruptcy Law Journal*, Volume 53, 1979, pp. 133–172.

2. Standard and Poor, *Standard and Poor's Rating Guide*, McGraw-Hill, New York, 1979; H. Rudnitsky, "What's in a Rating?" *Forbes*, September 12, 1983, p. 41; Standard and Poor's, *Credit Overview: Corporate and International Ratings*, Standard and Poor's Corporation, New York, 1982.

3. Horrigan, "The Determination of Long-Term Credit Standing with Financial Ratios," *Empirical Research in Accounting: Selected Studies*, 1966, Supplement to *Journal of Accounting Research*, Vol. 4, pp. 44–62; Thomas F. Pogue and Robert M. Soldofsky, "What's in a Bond Rating?" *Journal of Financial and Quantitative Analysis*, June 1969, pp. 201–208; R. West, "An Alternative Approach to Predicting Corporate Bond Ratings," *Journal of Accounting Research*, Spring 1970, pp. 118–125; and G. Pinches and K. Mingo, "A Multivariate Analysis of Industrial Bond Ratings," *Journal of Finance*, March 1973, pp. 1–18; A. Bulkaou, "Industrial Bond Ratings: A New Look," *Financial Management*, Autumn 1980, pp. 44–51; R. Morris III, "Fundamental Factors Affecting Electric Utility Bond Ratings: A Qualitative Approach," *Financial Analysts Journal*, September/October 1982, pp. 59–61; L. Martin and G. Henderson, "On Bond Rating and Pension Obligations," *Journal of Finance and Quantitative Analysis*, December 1984, pp. 463–470; L. Perry, G. Henderson and T. Cronan, "Multivariate Analysis of Corporate Bond Ratings and Industry Classifications," *Journal of Financial Research*, Spring 1984, pp. 27–36.

4. M. Backer and M. Gosman, "The Use of Financial Ratios in Credit Downgrade Decisions," *Financial Management*, Spring 1980, pp. 53–56.

5. C. Curtis, "The Ratings According to Hosinger," *Forbes*, September 27, 1982, pp. 194–195; L. McAdams, "How to Anticipate Utility Bond Rating Changes," *Journal of Portfolio Management*, Fall 1980, pp. 56–60; G. Anders, "As Bankruptcies Mount, Bond Analysts Start to Win Notice for Spotting Likely Candidates," *Wall Street Journal*, May 25, 1982, p. 53.

6. G. Pye, "Gauging the Default Premium," *Financial Analysts Journal*, January/February 1974, pp. 49–52.

7. R. West, "Bond Ratings, Bond Yields and Financial Registration: Some Findings," *Journal of Law and Economics*, April 1973, pp. 159–168.

8. J. McConnell and G. Schlarbaum, "Another Foray into the Backwaters of the Market," *Journal of Portfolio Management*, Fall 1980, pp. 61–65.

9. J. Cox, J. Ingersoll and S. Ross, "A Reexamination of Traditional Hypotheses about the Term Structure of Interest Rates," *Journal of Finance*, September 1981, pp. 769–800; K. Price and J. Brick, "The Term Structure: Forecasting Implications," Brick, *op. cit.*, p. 379.

10. M. Brennan and E. Schwartz, "Bond Pricing and Market Efficiency," *Financial Analysts Journal*, September/October 1982, pp. 49–56; M. Brannard and E. Schwartz, "An Equilibrium Model of Bond Pricing and a Test of Market Efficiency," *Journal of Financial and Quantitative Analysis*, September 1982, pp. 301–330.

11. J. Osteryoung, D. McCarthy and G. Roberts, "Riding the Yield Curve with Treasury Bills," *Financial Review*, Fall 1981, pp. 57–66.

12. F. Macauley, *Some Theoretical Problems Suggested by the Movements of Interest Rates, Bond Yields and Stock Prices in the United States since 1856*, New York, National Bureau of Economic Research, 1938; G. Bierwag, G. Kaufman and A. Toevs, "Duration: Its Development and Use in Bond Portfolio Management," *Financial Analysts Journal*, July/August 1983, pp. 37–43; C. Hessel and L. Huffman, "Incorporation of Tax Consideration into the Computation of Duration," *Journal of Financial Research*, Fall 1983, pp. 213–215; L. Fisher and R. Weil, "Coping with the Risk of Interest Rate Fluctuations: Returns to Bondholders from Naive and Optimal Strategies," *Journal of Business*, October 1971, pp. 408–431; R. Weil, "Macaulay's Duration: An Appreciation," *Journal of Business*, October 1973, pp. 589–592; "Duration as a Practical Tool for Bond Management," *Journal of Portfolio Management*, Summer 1977, pp. 53–57; M. Leibowitz, "How Financial Theory Evolves into the Real World-or Not: The Case of Duration and Immunization," *Financial Review*, November 1983, pp. 271–280.

13. C. Gushee, "How to Immunize a Bond Investment," *Financial Analysts Journal*, March/April 1981, pp. 44–51; R. McEnally, "How to Neutralize Reinvestment rate Risk," *Journal of Portfolio Management*, Spring 1980, pp. 59–63; H. Fong and O. Vasicek, "The Tradeoff Between Return and Risk in Immunized Portfolios," *Financial Analysts Journal*, September/October 1983, pp. 73–78.

14. R. Kolb and G. Gay, "Immunizing Bond Portfolios with Interest Rate Futures," *Financial Management*, Summer 1982, pp. 81–89; G. Gay, R. Kolb and R. Chiang, "Interest Rate Hedging: An Empirical Test of Alternative Strategies," *Journal of Financial Research*, Fall 1983, pp. 187–197.

15. T. Cook, "Some Factors Affecting Long-Term Yields Spreads in Recent Years," *Economic Review*, September 1973, pp. 2–14; R. Roll, "After-Tax Investment Results from Long-Term vs. Short-Term Discount Coupon Bonds," *Financial Analysts Journal*, January/February 1984, pp. 47–54.

16. C. Boardman and R. McEnally, "Factors Affecting Seasoned Corporate Bond Prices," *Journal of Financial and Quantitative Analysis*, June 1981, pp. 207–226; K. Slater, "Before Selecting Municipal Bonds, Buyers Should Judge Issue's Future Marketability," *Wall Street Journal*, January 30, 1984, p. 35.

17. Andrew F. Brimmer, "Credit Conditions and Price Determination in the Corporate Bond Market," *Journal of Finance*, September 1960, pp. 353–370; and Mortimer Kaplan, "Yields on Recently Issued Corporate Bonds: A New Index," *Journal of Finance*, March 1962, pp. 81–109; John R. Lindvall, "New Issue Corporate Bonds, Seasoned Market Efficiency and Yield Spreads," *Journal of Finance*, September 1977, pp. 1057–1067.

18. J. Martin and R. Richards, "The Seasoning Process for Corporate Bonds," *Financial Management*, Summer 1981, pp. 41–48.

19. J. Van Horne, "Called Bonds: How Does the Investor Fare?" *Journal of Portfolio Management*, Summer 1980, pp. 58–61.

20. E. Dyl and M. Joehuk, "Sinking Funds and The Cost of Corporate Debt," *Journal of Finance*, September 1979, pp. 887–893.

21. A. Kalotay, "Sinking Funds and the Realized Cost of Debt," *Financial Management*, Spring 1982, pp. 43–54; W. Lloyd and C. Edmonds, "The Impact of a Sinking Fund on the Firm's Cost of Debt," *Review of Business and Economic Research*, Spring 1982, pp. 74–82.

22. G. Brauer, "Evidence of the Market Value of Me-First Rules," *Financial Management*, Spring 1983, pp. 11–18; M. Brody, "Controversial Issue: A Leveraged Buy-Out Touches Off a Bitter Dispute," *Barron's*, September 19, 1983, pp. 15, 19, 22.

23. L. Post, "Yield to Early Maturity: An Important Factor with Useable Bonds," *Financial Analysts Journal*, November/December 1973, pp. 72–73; B. Weberman, "How to Use Usables," *Forbes*, July 18, 1983, p. 163.

24. Boardman and McEnally, op. cit.

25. M. Weinstein, "The Systematic Risk of Corporate Bonds," *Journal of Financial and Quantitative Analysis*, September 1981, pp. 257–278.

26. F. Trainer, "The Uses of Treasury Bond Futures in Fixed-Income Portfolio Management," *Financial Analysts Journal*, January/February 1983, pp. 27–34; *Business Week*, "New Ways to Play the Interest Rate Markets," *Business Week*, February 8, 1982, pp. 102–106.

27. M. Lane, "Fixed-income Managers must Time the Market!" *Journal of Portfolio Management*, Summer 1979, pp. 36–40; J. Cheney, "Rating Classification and Bond Yield Volatility," *Journal of Portfolio Management*, Spring 1983, pp. 51–57; C. Billingham, "Strategies for Enhancing Bond Portfolio Returns," *Financial Analysts Journal*, May/June 1983, pp. 50–56.

28. R. Norgaard, "An Examination of the Yields of Corporate Bonds and Stocks," *Journal of Finance*, September 1974, pp. 1275–1286.

29. J. Massey, "For the Long Haul: Stocks Invariably Outperform Both Bills and Bonds," *Barron's*, January 31, 1977; R. Grauer and N. Hakansson, "Higher Returns, Lower Risk: Historical Returns on Long Run, Actively Managed Portfolios of Stocks, Bonds, Bills, 1936–1978," *Financial Analysts Journal*, March/April 1982, pp. 39–54.

30. R. Ibbotson, R. Carr and A. Robinson, "International Equity and Bond Returns," *Financial Analysts Journal*, July/August 1982, pp. 61–83.

17 Pure Option Securities

Most types of securities can only be bought, sold, or held. Option securities, in contrast, may be exchanged (with or without additional funds) for some other security or, in the case of puts, permit their owner to sell some other security for a prespecified price. Warrants, rights, calls, and puts are pure options; convertible bonds, convertible preferreds, and certain other security types are combinations. Combination securities derive value both from their convertibility and promised income. Pure options' values, in contrast, are solely related to what they can do to facilitate a particular purchase or sale. Because option securities constitute an interesting and important component of the investment scene, two chapters of this book are devoted to them.

This chapter concentrates on pure options, beginning with a discussion of puts, calls, and their markets; special terminology; leverage potential; quotations; valuation; performance in various types of markets; covered and naked writing; spread trades; tax implications; option mutual funds; institutional participation; and commissions. We next consider some of the special traits of warrants and rights, including their exercise with usable bonds and what happens in a takeover. The final sections discuss rights and how they are valued.

PURE OPTION SECURITIES: WARRANTS, RIGHTS, CALLS, AND PUTS

Warrants, rights, and calls are all options to purchase a prespecified number of units of a particular security at a prespecified price over a prespecified (and almost always limited) period. Puts, in contrast, are options to sell a prespecified number of units at a prespecified price over a prespecified period. A few warrants permit one to purchase bonds, but the vast majority of option securities facilitate the purchase or sale of common stock.

Warrants and rights are company-issued securities; calls and puts are private contracts between individual buyers and sellers. The issuing company almost always satisfies warrant- and right-exercisers by issuing additional units of its securities. Put and call exercises, in contrast, do not alter the number of shares outstanding. Call-writers (sellers) must stand ready to supply already-issued stock (either from their own portfolio or by an open market purchase). Put-writers must be prepared to purchase existing shares. Puts and calls are normally written for relatively short periods (nine months or less is typical), while warrants often have lengthy exercise periods (e.g. five years). Rights, in contrast, must generally be exercised within a few weeks of their issue. Companies distribute rights to their shareholders in order to raise equity capital. Rights are usually exercisable at an appreciable discount from the stock's pre-offering market price, and normally trade in the secondary market.

Unlike rights, newly issued warrants are typically exercisable at prices well above those of the underlying securities. Warrants generally trade in the secondary market until near their expiration and then are only exercised if doing so is profitable.

Option Terminology

Option traders have their own special vocabulary. Several key terms will first be defined and then put to use:

Striking Price (strike)—price at which the option is exercisable (sometimes called the exercise price)

Intrinsic Value—price of the underlying security less the striking price of the option or zero if the strike is above the market price

Time Value—option price less its intrinsic value

In-the-Money Option—option with a positive intrinsic value (striking price below market price for a call)

Out-of-the-Money Option—option with a zero intrinsic value (striking price above market price for a call)

Premium—option price (equal to the sum of the intrinsic and time values). Note some people use premium to refer to the time value. At the option exchanges, however, it is used as defined here.

The Speculative Appeal of Options: Leverage

Options on a large number of units of the underlying security can be bought for relatively small sums. Such an option position greatly magnifies (levers) the upside effect of price moves in that security. For example, the largest rise among NYSE issues in 1982 was Chrysler, which went from just above 3 to slightly above 18 (about a sixfold increase). Its warrants, however, rose from 1 1/8 to 10 1/8, an increase of 933%. On the other hand, an option's price can at worst fall to zero. Because of this upside leverage and downside-loss limitation, in-the-money options are typically priced appreciably above their intrinsic values. Moreover options with time remaining before expiration and striking prices that are not too far below the stock's market price may also command nontrivial prices. Far out-of-the-money options and any out-of-the-money options near their expirations are, in contrast, usually almost worthless. Consider the following examples:

In 1956 General Tire and Rubber Company stock was selling at 50, while warrants with a 70 striking price and 1959 expiration were trading at 4 1/2. By 1959, the stock price had reached 98 1/2 and the warrant 39. In percentage terms, the warrants had increased 770% compared with a 97% rise in the stock's price. Thus General Tire warrantholders earned eight times the percentage return of the shareholders. While limited to the initial purchase price, the downside risk of options is still substantial. For example: in 1960 the common of Molybdenum Corporation of America sold for 42, while warrants permitting one to purchase the stock at 30 were available at 16. When the warrants expired in 1963, the stock had fallen to 29. Thus warrantholders experienced a 100% loss at expiration regardless of their purchase price. Stock acquired at 42, in contrast, had lost 32% of its value when the stock reached 29.

In these examples, the warrants' striking prices were 70 for General Tire and 30 for Molybdenum. With the stock at 50, General Tire warrants had an intrinsic value of 0. At the later date the intrinsic value was 28 1/2 (98 1/2 − 70). With warrant prices at 4 1/2 and 39, the time values were 4 1/2 and 10 1/2 respectively. With the stock at 42 and warrants at 16, Molybdenum warrants had intrinsic and time values of 12 and 4 respectively. These statistics are summarized in Table 17.1.

Table 17.1   General Tire and Molybdenum Warrants

	General Tire	
	1956	1959 (near expiration)
Stock Price	50	98 1/2
Striking Price	70	70
Warrant Price	4 1/2	39
Intrinsic Value	0	28 1/2
Time Value	4 1/2	10 1/2
	Molybdenum	
	1960	1963 (at expiration)
Stock Price	42	29
Striking Price	30	30
Warrant Price	16	0
Intrinsic Value	12	0
Time Value	4	0

The above examples clearly illustrate the leverage of warrants. Because a given sum can purchase far more options than underlying shares, an upward stock price movement will generally lead to a greater percentage gain for warrantholders than for stockholders. If, on the other hand, the stock price is below the striking price as maturity approaches, the warrants quickly lose their value.

The following hypothetical example further illustrates the relationship between a stock's price and that of its associated option. This relationship is graphically represented by Figure 17.1. Suppose a stock selling for 100 has a call to

Figure 17.1 Option and Stock Returns Compared

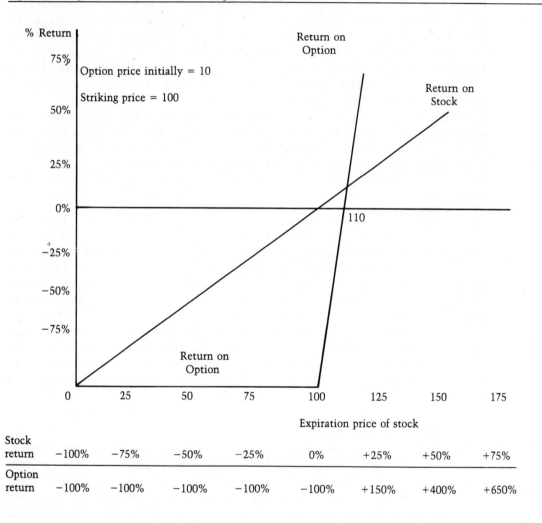

Stock return	−100%	−75%	−50%	−25%	0%	+25%	+50%	+75%
Option return	−100%	−100%	−100%	−100%	−100%	+150%	+400%	+650%

buy it at 100; the call sells for 10. (Striking price = 100; intrinsic value = 0; and time value and premium = 10). Near expiration, the call should be priced very close to its intrinsic value. For any price below 100, the call will expire worthless, and callholders will lose their total investment. At a price of 100 to 110, the call's expiration price will be less than its cost. For any stock price above 110, the callholder makes money. Thus at prices below 100 the stockholder experiences a partial loss compared with a total loss for the callholder. At any price between 100 and 110, the stockholders profit. Callholders' profits rise disproportionately with the stock price. For prices very slightly above 110, the stockholders' percentage returns are greater, but at somewhat higher prices the callholders' percentage returns greatly exceed the stockholders'. At 111, for example the callholder's return is 10%, compared with 11% for the stockholder (ignoring dividends). At 112, however, the callholders earn 20%, compared with 12% for the stockholders. A price of 120 produces a 20% gain for the stockholders while the callholders realize a 100% gain.

Note that the gain on the call rises dramatically as the price of the stock increases. For a stock price of 150, callholders earn 400%, compared with 50% for the stockholders. Commission and dividend effects have been ignored in the analysis, but their net impact would generally be modest.

Options Markets

Actively traded rights and warrants are generally listed on a stock exchange. Most put and call trading takes place on the option exchanges. Unlisted puts and calls and less actively traded warrants and rights are traded over the counter.

Before listed options appeared, option expiration dates and striking prices varied greatly, making secondary market trading very haphazard. Listed puts and calls expire every three months, with three sets of expiration dates traded at any particular time. Their standardized striking prices and expiration dates facilitate a continuous market in identical securities. The listed option market experienced spectacular growth throughout the latter half of the 1970s. By 1984, four exchanges (CBOE, AMEX, Philadelphia, and Pacific) were listing options on approximately 400 stocks. Option trading in these issues often exceeds that of the underlying shares.

Put and Call Quotations

Figure 17.2 illustrates typical listed put and call quotations. The *Wall Street Journal* system (followed by most daily newspapers) is considerably more compact than *Barron's*. The left hand column of the *WSJ* quotation contains the name of the company or an abbreviation, with the New York Stock Exchange closing price for the stock appearing below it. For example the "Bris My" abbreviation corresponds to Bristol Myers. The striking price is listed next. Apache strikes are available at 10 and 15. Then the calls' closing prices are reported, followed by similar quotes for puts. The price is quoted per share even though puts and calls trade in 100-share units. Thus one call or put represents an option on 100 shares. An *s* signifies that no option was listed, while an *r* indicates none were traded on that day. The more complete *Barron's* quotation contains the volume,

Figure 17.2 ***Barron's*** **and** ***Wall Street Journal*** **Option Quotations**

BARRON'S/MARKET WEEK

OPTIONS TRADING

June 15, 1984

Put and call options printed on these pages include only options that traded a minimum volume of fifty contracts during the week. Each put option gives the holder the right to sell at the striking price one hundred shares of the underlying stock and each call option gives the holder the right to buy at the striking price one hundred shares of the underlying stock. Options may be exercised prior to the expiration date (usually the Saturday following the third Friday of the expiration month). Open interest indicates the number of contracts outstanding at Thursday's close. All other figures are as of Friday's close. A weekly total of open interest and put and call volume appears at the conclusion of each exchange listing.

Options Trading (CBOE)

Option name Expire date Strike price	Sales	Open Int.	Week's High	Low	Price	Net Chg.	N.Y. Close
Apache Jun10..	158	329	1⅞	1⅞	2	− 1¼	12
Apache Sep15..	61	2872	5-16	3-16	3-16	− ¼	12
Apache Dec10..	62	72	3¾	3	3	− ½	12
Atl R Jul40.....	804	1577	8½	5	5	− 4	44½
Atl R Jul40 p...	700	2720	3-16	1-16	⅛	+1-16	44½
Atl R Jul45...	1547	6631	4½	1 7-16	1 7-16	−3 3-16	44½
Atl R Jul45 p..	2776	4285	1¼	3-16	1¼	+ 1	44½
Atl R Jul50...	4723	18116	1	⅛	3-16	−15-16	44½
Atl R Jul50 p..	532	3141	5½	1⅞	5¼	+ 3⅝	44½
Atl R Jul55.....	194	1860	⅛	1-16	1-16	− ⅛	44½
Atl R Oct40 p..	176	476	½	5-16	½	+3-16	44½
Atl R Oct45....	369	1253	4¼	2½	2½	− 2¾	44½
Atl R Oct45 p..	276	632	2½	⅞	2¼	+ 1¼	44½
Atl R Oct50..	1268	4832	2½	15-16	15-16	−1 7-16	44½
Atl R Oct55.....	143	1113	⅞	¼	¼	−9-16	44½
Atl R Jan45...	76	59	5	3⅝	3⅝	− 2¼	44½
Atl R Jan45 p..	110	100	2½	1⅜	2¼	+ ¾	44½
Atl R Jan50..	403	734	3⅜	1½	1 9-16	−1 11-16	44½
Atl R Jan55...	136	454	1½	¾	¾	− ⅝	44½
Avon Jul20.....	778	6766	1 1-16	9-16	13-16	− ¼	19⅞
Avon Jul20 p...	700	3187	⅞	9-16	¾	+3-16	19⅞
Avon Jul25.....	217	5465	⅛	1-16	1-16	−1-16	19⅞
Avon Oct20.....	384	2587	1 13-16	1¼	1 11-16	.....	19⅞
Avon Oct20 p..	155	1213	1½	1 3-16	1½	+3-16	19⅞
Avon Oct25.....	504	3560	7-16	¼	¼	−3-16	19⅞
Avon Oct30.....	52	1706	⅛	⅛	⅛	......	19⅞
Avon Jan20.....	187	1421	2 7-16	1¾	2 5-16	−1-16	19⅞
Avon Jan20 p..	61	333	1 15-16	1½	1 11-16	.....	19⅞
Avon Jan25.....	110	1218	¾	⅝	⅝	−3-16	19⅞
BankAm Jul15 p	935	2412	9-16	3-16	½	+ ¼	15½
BankAm Jul20.	249	7058	⅛	1-16	1-16	......	15½
BankAm Jul20 p	285	1203	4⅜	3½	4⅜	+ ⅞	15½
BankAm Oct15	197	1380	2⅜	1 5-16	1⅜	− 1⅛	15½
BankAm Oct15 p	152	789	15-16	½	⅞	+ ¼	15½
BankAm Oct20	223	5226	⅜	¼	¼	− ⅛	15½
BankAm Oct20 p	308	1914	4⅝	3⅝	4⅝	+ 1	15½
BankAm Oct25.	128	3124	⅛	1-16	1-16	−1-16	15½

THE WALL STREET JOURNAL
Monday, June 18, 1984

Option & NY Close	Strike Price	Calls—Last Jun	Sep	Dec	Puts—Last Jun	Sep	Dec
Apache	..10	2	2	3	r	r	r
12	 15	r	3-16	9-16	3¼	2 11-16	2½
BrisMy	..40	6⅜	7½	r	r	¼	½
46½	... 45	1⅜	3¼	4½	r	1⅛	1⅝
46½	... 50	1-16	15-16	2⅛	3½	4	r
Bruns	. 22½	5⅛	s	s	r	s	s
27½	. 27½	1-16	s	s	1-16	s	s
27½	... 20	7¼	r	r	r	r	r
27½	... 25	2⅛	3½	4¼	r	9-16	1⅛
27½	... 30	1-16	1 1-16	1 13-16	2 9-16	3	r
Celan	70	1-16	r	4⅜	2⅛	r	r
Chamln	. 20	1-16	1¼	r	⅜	r	1 9-16
19½	... 25	r	r	½	r	r	r
19½	... 30	r	1-16	r	r	r	r
CompSc	. 10	1¾	r	2¾	r	r	r
11¼	... 15	r	7-16	¾	3⅝	3½	3¼
Dow Ch	. 25	2⅛	3¼	3⅝	r	7-16	⅞
27¼	... 30	1-16	13-16	1½	2⅝	3½	3¾
27¼	... 35	r	3-16	7-16	8	r	r
Esmark	. 45	14¾	14¾	r	r	r	r
59⅞	... 50	9⅞	r	r	r	r	r
59⅞	... 55	s	4⅞	r	s	1-16	r
59⅞	... 60	s	1-16	3-16	s	⅜	¼
FBost	... 30	r	r	r	r	½	r
36⅜	... 35	2	3¾	r	1-16	r	r
36⅜	... 40	1-16	1½	2¾	r	r	r
36⅜	... 45	r	¼	1	r	r	r
36⅜	... 50	r	¼	s	r	r	s

Source: *Wall Street Journal* and *Barron's*. Reprinted by permission of *Wall Street Journal* and *Barron's*, © Dow Jones & Company, Inc., 1984. All Rights Reserved.

open interest (contracts outstanding), high, low, and change in the price.

Striking prices are initially set at levels that are divisible by 5 or 10 and closest to the current stock price. As a stock price moves away from the available strikes, trading becomes unattractive in the existing options. For example: a call with a strike of 30 on a stock selling for 50 will be priced too high to offer very much leverage, while a call with an 80 strike on a stock trading at 60 is so likely to expire worthless that it has very little speculative appeal. Since stock prices can move quite a bit in a few months, some strikes may differ substantially from the current quote. Accordingly, new strikes are authorized at levels close to the stock's current quote whenever its price changes appreciably. The older strike options continue to be traded but are not replaced with more distant expirations as they mature unless the underlying stock's price moves back into range.

Turov's Formula

Turov's formula shows the rate of appreciation in the underlying stock necessary to make the option attractive. The formula is primarily useful for one who has some expectations for the underlying stock's future price range. That is, a warrant's or call's relative attractiveness is related to the price the stock must reach by expiration to generate equal percentage gains on the stock or option. If the stock's price rises above this level, the option will show the greater gain. Otherwise the stock will have a larger gain or lesser loss. This value equals the striking price divided by the stock price minus the current warrant price. Thus:

$$f = e/(s - w) \tag{1}$$

where f = appreciation of stock necessary to generate equal gains in the stock and warrant
     e = striking price of warrant
     s = current price of stock
     w = current price of warrant

Turov subsequently revised his formula to take account of dividends, but noted that in practice the adjustment's impact was minor.[1]

An Example of Turov's Formula

On November 9, 1983, the Charter company's stock was trading for 9 1/8 while its warrants, exercisable at 10 (expires 9/1/88), sold for 4 1/8. Applying Turov's formula to these data reveals:

$$f = \frac{10}{9\ 1/8 - 4\ 1/8} = \frac{10}{5} = 2$$

Thus if the price of Charter doubles, investments in the stock and warrant would offer equivalent returns. In that instance, the stock would trade for 18 1/4 and the warrant's intrinsic value would rise 8 1/4, or twice its current market price. If one expects Charter to appreciate by more than that amount before its warrants expire (1988), the warrants are the more attractive investment.

THE VALUE OF AN OPTION

The valuation of options long intrigued financial theorists. Following work by Shelton, Samuelson, and Parkinson, Black and Scholes (BS) wrote the classic theoretical option pricing work.[2] They reasoned that if one could buy the underlying stock and write calls so as to maintain a fully hedged position, any change in the stock's price would be offset by an equivalent but opposite change in the short position's value. Thus if a $1 change in the stock price caused a 50¢ change in the call price, one could construct a fully hedged position by writing calls on twice as many shares as are bought. Since the investor is short two calls, a $1 increase (decrease) in the stock price would be matched by a $1 decrease (increase) in the call position's value. In fact, any move in the stock's price would be precisely offset by a change in the option position's value. The hedge may be maintained by adjusting the ratio of stocks to calls whenever necessary. Thus what is termed a riskless hedge has been created. Assuming that an investment in the combined riskless position should earn the riskless interest rate (approximately the rate on short-term governments), BS were able to develop a call-valuation formula that is a function of five variables: call values increase with time-to-maturity, interest rates, the underlying stock's price and volatility, and decrease as the striking price increases. Active option traders often use programmable calculators to compute BS prices. Such traders may follow a strategy of buying undervalued (vis-a-vis the model) options and writing overvalued ones. One who becomes deeply involved in option trading should learn more about the specifics of the BS model (see Appendix A).[3]

Empirical Studies of the Black/Scholes Model

Not surprisingly, the BS model led to a host of studies designed to test the correspondence between BS prices and model prices and/or whether apparent price disparities offered profitable trading opportunities. In a study of over 2,000 OTC calls and 3,000 straddle contracts (combination put and call on the same security), BS themselves found a significant tendency for low-variance options to be overpriced and high-variance options to be underpriced.[4] When transaction costs were considered, however, the profit potential of a buy-high variance and sell-low variance options strategy disappeared. Gali, who studied initial CBOE option pricing, found that trading against calls whose prices were out of line with the BS formula generally produced profits before, but not after, commissions.[5]

The original BS empirical study utilized OTC calls (before the CBOE began), and Gali worked with data for an early period of option trading. More recent work has produced a variety of results. For example Gultekin, Rogalski, and Tinic found near-expiration options were often mispriced.[6] Trennepohl found that BS model prices adjusted for dividends were significantly lower than observed prices.[7] Gleit and Branch reported that a strategy of buying undervalued and writing overvalued options (vis-a-vis BS model prices) might be profitable.[8] Bhattacharya, in contrast, found no systematic mispricing of options except for those very close to maturity.[9] Phillips and Smith reported that taking the bid/ask spread into account eliminated most apparent mispricings.[10] Similarly Whaley, MacBeth and Merville; Geske and Roll; and Sterk were able to explain option prices well with more sophisticated versions of the model.[11] On the other hand, a study by Manaster and Rendleman found that option prices contained information relevant to future movements in the underlying stock's prices.[12]

On balance, these results suggest that option pricing is a relatively efficient process. No doubt some mispricings do occur, but most seem to be relatively brief and only allow profitable trades for those who can buy and sell at minimum transactions costs. In any case, the key to successful option trading is effective analysis of the underlying stock's potential. One who can somehow identify misvalued stocks may be able to magnify the profit potential with options. Options are short-term wasting assets, however. Even investors who correctly analyze stock values may lose money on options unless the market price adjusts before their options expire. All too often one may be right on fundamentals but wrong on timing and lose money as a result.

Put/Call Parity

Put/call parity represents another theoretical aspect of option pricing. A put-like position can be created from a call and short-position in the stock (manufactured put). Similarly a long-position in the stock plus a put (manufactured call) has the same kind of payoff as a call. Since a put can be converted into a manufactured call and a call can be converted into a manufactured put, the two options' prices should be related. Indeed according to "the law of one price" whenever two assets offer equivalent payoff matrices, their prices must be identical (or within a range permitted by such arbitrage expenses as transactions costs).

While traders normally prefer to buy puts or calls directly, some people will choose to manufacture puts from calls or vice-versa when prices get out of line. Some brokerage firms try to profit from apparent price disparities by taking offsetting positions in the manufactured and nonmanufactured puts and calls ("conversions").[13] Such arbitrage-activity tends to drive the prices back toward their proper parity. Indeed Klemkosky and Resnick found that the relatively rare departures from put/call parity price relationships seldom persist long enough for one to profit (even for those on the exchange).[14] As with the BS formula, the precise form of the put/call parity formula is a bit too complex to discuss in this treatment, but serious option traders should be aware of its existence. The explicit relationship is presented in Appendix B.

In addition to manufacturing calls from puts and puts from calls, one can manufacture option-like positions with stock and cash. For example, a long stock position coupled with sufficient borrowing is equivalent to a call. While limited by margin restrictions, such a strategy can provide a viable alternative to an over-the-counter call when none is listed.[15]

OPTION TRADING STRATEGIES

One can buy calls outright, engage in combination option trades called spreads, write calls on stock already owned (covered writing), or write calls on stock the writer does not own (naked writing). A similar matrix of put-trades is possible.[16] Still other trades involve combining pure options with other securities such as short positions in the underlying stock or long positions in bonds or convertibles. The following pages explore some of the various types of trades.

Buying Calls

Many option traders simply purchase individual calls on underlying stock that they hope will rise sufficiently to produce a profit. The following hypothetical example illustrates the desired outcome.

Buying Calls in a Rising Market

| | XYZ August 35 | | 100 Shares XYZ | |
	Price	Cost	Price	Cost
Purchase date value	$2 1/2	$250	$35 1/4	$3,525
Sale date value				
(6 months later)	$5 1/4	$525	$39 1/2	$3,950
Profit		$275		$ 425
Return		110%		12.05%

This example demonstrates the upside leverage of options. A small stock price rise led to a much larger option price increase. The callholder earns 110%— almost 10 times as much as the stockholder. Notice that the hypothetical call's time value decreased as time advanced and as the option moved deeper into the money. In this instance the option-position's value increased by $275 while the underlying stock position (on an equivalent number of shares) rose by $425. Although hypothetical, this example is not atypical. Some actual moves over the week of May 28 to June 4, 1982, are reported below.

Actual Stock-Call Price Moves May 28–June 4, 1982

	May 28	June 4	% Change
Esmark—June 45	1	1 5/8	62.5
Esmark Common	45 1/4	46 1/4	2.2
South West Airline—			
September 35	5	7	40
Southwest Common	34	35 7/8	5.5
Whittaker—			
September 20	3 1/4	4 5/8	34.6
Whittaker Common	22 1/4	22 7/8	2.8
Armco, November 20	1/2	3/4	50
Armco Common	16 5/8	17 1/2	5.2

While these reported gains are attractive, optionholders should also expect some substantial losses. The next example illustrates the result from a long option-position in a falling market:

Buying Calls in a Falling Market

| | XYZ August 35 | | 100 Shares XYZ | |
	Price	Cost	Price	Cost
Purchase date value	$2 1/4	$225	$35	$3,500
Value three months later	$1	$100	$31 1/2	$3,150
Expiration (6 months later)	$0	$0	$31 1/2	$3,150
Loss		$225		$ 350

Both the stock's price decline and the passage of time reduced the option's price. In this example the optionholder's loss is $225 compared with a $350 loss for a 100-share stock position. In percentage terms, however, the stock declined by only 10% while the option price fell 100%.

In-the-Money versus Out-of-the-Money Options

In-the-money calls (calls whose striking prices are below their underlying stock's market prices) tend to reflect moves in the stock's prices more fully (larger dollar-for-dollar price effect) than out-of-the-money calls. In-the-money calls will retain some value at expiration as long as they stay in-the-money; an out-of-the-money option will expire worthless unless the stock's price rises sufficiently. On the other hand, in-the-money calls' higher prices reduce their leverage. Out-of-the-money calls will generally produce a larger gain than in-the-money calls when the underlying stock price increases rapidly. A slow price rise, in contrast, may be offset by a reduction in the option's time value as it approaches maturity.

Exercise versus Sale of a Call

Exercising options much before they expire is rarely attractive. Because such options generally retain substantial time value, one can usually acquire the stock at a lower cost by selling the call and buying the stock outright. The one exception is when a stock is about to go ex-dividend for a substantial payment. Rather than lose the dividend, one may choose to exercise or sell the option while its price still reflects the anticipated dividend payment.

Commissions are almost always lower for selling in-the-money options than for exercising and simultaneously selling the stock. Option exercisers incur commissions on both the stock's purchase and its sale compared to a single commission for the option-seller. Moreover the much lower dollar value of the option trade generally results in a considerably smaller commission than each stock transaction's commission. On the other hand, one wanting to hold the underlying stock would only incur a single commission by exercising, compared with two commissions on the option sale and stock purchase.

Option traders should also consider the impact of time value in exercise-or-sell decisions. As expiration approaches, options may trade at a slight discount from their intrinsic values (negative time values). For example, a soon-to-expire call with a strike of 45 on a stock trading at 46 might sell for 7/8 (1/8 below its intrinsic value). The call's $12.50 per 100-share discount below its intrinsic value represents what option market makers might require to cover their costs of buying and exercising the option and then selling the underlying stock. Few individual investors could trade that cheaply and thus are still generally better off to sell the option unless they want to own the stock. Normally, arbitrage trading will keep even very short-term option prices close to their intrinsic values.

Call Writing

Every purchased call contract has a call writer on the other side. Call writers may write calls on stock they own (covered writing) or be uncovered (naked writing). Covered call writing offers stockholders additional income and some downside protection. That is, the premium provides the call writer with income that at least partially offsets any stock-price decline. On the other hand, the writer risks having the stock called away and losing the additional profit on the rising stock price. Thus covered writing reduces both downside risk and upside potential. Suppose XYZ is now selling at 50. The writer of a call on XYZ at $50, in return for a $4 premium, has for the life of the option limited further upside potential to $54, while the stock could move down to $46 before a loss (relative to an immediate sale at 50) is incurred. Even at prices below $46, the loss on the stock-call position is below that of the pure stock-position.

Writing Calls in a Rising Market

	XYZ August 35 Price	Premium	100 Shares XYZ Price	Cost
Purchase date	$2 1/2	$250	$35 1/4	(owned)
Call exercised	$4 1/2	$450	$39 1/2	$3,950
Proceeds of sale			$35	$3,500
Loss versus selling on open market				$450
Less premium received				$250
Net (opportunity) loss before commission				$200

Note that the opportunity loss of $450 relative to what the writer would have received by selling the stock in the open market is partially offset by the initial option-sale premium of $250, producing a net loss of $200 plus commissions. In this case, the covered writer would have earned more by not writing the call. Now consider the impact of a decline in the optioned stock's price.

Writing Calls in a Declining Market

	XYZ August 35 Price	Premium	100 Shares XYZ Price	Cost
Purchase date	$2 1/4	$225	$35	(owned)
Value three months later	$1	$100	$31 1/2	
Expiration	$0	$0	$31 1/2	(owned)
Paper loss				$350
Less premium received				$225
Net paper loss				$125

Covered call writers are, however, concerned with both up and down movements in the underlying stock. A fall in the stock's price reduces the value of their stock position, which may be only partially offset by the call premium received, while a stock price rise exposes them to the risk of exercise.

Only near-expiration in-the-money options are likely to be exercised; writers may avoid such exercises by buying identical calls. If the stock price increased (decreased) between the time the call (put) was written and repurchased, the covering transaction may incur a loss. That loss could be partially offset by writing another option at a higher striking price. Once again, however, the writer would be obligated to sell the stock at the new price. The following examples illustrate this point.

As the stock drops to $31 1/2, the stockholder's $350 loss is reduced by the $225 call premium (to $125). The writer would have been better off to have sold the stock initially, but less is lost than if the option had not been written. Presumably the writer retains the stock and writes another $35 option for a lower premium after the first one expires. Now consider what happens if the stock price is relatively stable.

Writing Calls in a Stable Market

| | XYZ August 35 | | 100 Shares XYZ | |
	Price	Premium	Price	Cost
Purchase date	$2 1/4	$225	$35	(owned)
Value three months later	$2	$200	$35	
Expiration	$0	$0	$35	(owned)
Profit or loss				0
Plus premium received				$225
Net positive cash-flow increase				$225

A stable stock price is attractive for the option writer. Suppose the stock also pays a $1.50 dividend each six months. The writer would receive $2.25 in call premiums and $1.50 in dividends, for a total of $3.75 per share. This is equivalent to a six-month return of 10.7% on the stock ($3.75/$35.00). If the stock price goes up, however, the shares may be called away, while a price fall cuts into the return.

Research by French and Henderson, Yates and Kopprasch, and particularly Mueller, suggests that covered writing tends to yield attractive returns.[17] Indeed, Mueller asserts that a strategy of writing three-month covered calls with striking prices slightly below the stock price also reduces portfolio risk.

Naked Writing

Selling calls on stock that is owned (covered option writing) is considered fairly conservative. The covered writer of a stock that trades in a relatively narrow range can sell new options each time the old ones expire unexercised. Writers of options that are not exercised need not have owned the stock. This brings up the topic of naked writing. Naked writers do not own any of the underlying stock. Such writers hope that the optioned stock will not rise above the striking price while the option remains in force. Suppose one writes a $50 call on 100 shares of the stock for $4 per share. If the option expires unexercised, the naked writer has made $400 (less commissions). If the call is exercised, the naked writer is forced to buy 100 shares at the market price (at say $60) and immediately sell them to the optionholder for $50, taking a loss ($1,000 less the premium). He or she also must pay a commission on each trade. Alternatively, the naked writer could have covered the in-the-money call (buy back equivalent position) prior to its exercise and avoided one commission.

Naked writing is similar to selling short. Both the naked writer and short-seller profit from a price decline and have potentially unlimited loss exposure. Like selling short, naked writing requires a margin deposit sufficient to guarantee the stock's purchase if required. The potential profit in naked option writing is limited to the premium received. The potential loss is theoretically unlimited, since the stock could rise to any price.

The following example illustrates the dangers of naked writing. In early 1981, near-expiration calls on AMAX 50s were trading for 50¢. Since the AMAX stock was then under 40, the likelihood of exercise seemed remote. Just before they were about to expire, however, Socal offered to acquire AMAX for a price in the 70s. The market value of the AMAX 50s shot up to over 10. Many option-traders who had written AMAX 50s for 50¢ were forced to cover at $10 or more. Some option-buyers were later shown to have had prior knowledge of the Socal offer. Because of this insider trading, a court settlement may eventually bail out the writers.

A similar dramatic price run-up occurred when Gulf tried to take over Cities Service. Cities Service, which was trading at 42, increased to 53 1/8 when Gulf announced its $63 offer. June (1982) calls at 45 (which had only two days until expiration) rose from 1/8 to 9 1/2. Thus a $1,000 investment multiplied to $76,000. Again some naked writers were severely hurt.[28]

Puts

A put contract enables the holder to sell 100 shares of a specific stock for a set striking price at any time up to a specified expiration date. Put holders profit if the stock price declines sufficiently. Put writers, in contrast, profit if the stock price does not rise or rises only modestly. Theoretical put-valuation models are very similar to those for calls.[19]

Strategies Using Puts

Puts can be used in a variety of strategies. For example, a speculator may buy a put in the hopes of profiting from a projected decline in the underlying stock's price. On the other hand, a speculator who feels that a particular stock is going to rise may buy the stock and hedge the position with a put. A decline in the stock's price increases the put's value, thus largely offsetting the loss in the stock. If the stock price rises, the put is allowed to expire unexercised. Such a strategy's payoff matrix is very similar to that for a call position.

Speculators who believe that a stock will be stable or rise may buy the stock and sell a put on it. The stock's cost is in effect reduced by the put premium. If the stock rises, the trader profits both from the put premium and the stock's price appreciation. If it falls, however, both positions will show a loss.

Put Terminology

The Options Clearing Corporation considers a put writer to be covered if and only if he or she also holds a put of the same class with an equal or higher striking price. The term *in-the-money* implies that the option has a positive intrinsic value. An *out-of-the-money* option has no intrinsic value, which for a put means that the underlying stock's price is higher than the option's exercise price, e.g. the stock is selling at $50 and the put's striking price is $45.

Manufacturing a Put

A speculator who believes that a stock's price is about to fall can short the stock and hedge the position with a call. The resulting position is very similar to that of buying a "put." In general, buying a put incurs lower commissions than buying a call and shorting the stock. When only calls are listed, however, investors who want a put-like position have no choice but to manufacture it.

Put Buying versus Short-Selling

Rather than hedging with a call, some speculators may simply short the stock. The unhedged short seller, put buyer, and manufactured-put buyer all seek to profit from a price decline. Buying or manufacturing a put has several advantages vis-a-vis taking an unhedged short position. These include:

- The risk is limited to the original put investment
- Puts generally offer greater leverage
- Puts involve less psychological pressure to cover
- Puts do not require short dividend payments (but manufactured puts do)
- Put commission costs are lower (but manufactured puts' commissions are not)

On the other hand, leverage cuts both ways, and time works against the put buyer, as puts expire.

Exercise versus Selling In-the-Money Puts

As with calls selling, an in-the-money put is generally more attractive than exercising and simultaneously buying the underlying stock. On the other hand, if the putholder would like to sell the stock anyway, exercising is usually desirable.

Straddles, Strips and Straps

A straddle is a put and a call on the same stock, with identical striking prices and expiration dates. As with other option writers, straddle writers may be covered or naked. Writing straddles against a stock position is similar to writing a covered call option. Straddle writers have some downside protection and an opportunity to profit if the stock price rises or remains constant. In return for the additional premium, however, the straddle writer undertakes to buy more stock if the put side of the straddle is exercised.

Referring back to Figure 17.2, we see that with the stock at 46 1/2, Bristol Myers December 45 calls are available for 4 1/2, while the puts sell for 1 5/8. Thus a straddle would cost 6 1/8. If the stock were to fall to 38, the put side of the straddle would be worth (intrinsic value) 7, while a rise to 52 would give the call side an intrinsic value of 7. Indeed for any price below 38 7/8 or above 51 1/8, the straddle shows a profit (neglecting commission). Thus the straddle investor is looking for a large move either up or down in the stock. On the other hand, a straddle writer will make money if the stock stays near the striking price.

In the prelisted-option days of the old Put and Call Dealers Association, two other types of put-call combinations were frequently encountered: strips and straps. A strip is a combination of two puts and one call, while a strap is two calls and a put. With most puts and calls trading separately on the option exchanges, strips, straps and straddles are now only rarely encountered.

Spreads

An option spread is a simultaneous short and long position in options on the same stock. The options differ either in strike, expiration, or both. Similar types of combination trades are also possible with different-delivery commodity futures contracts. Unlike the case of strips, straps, and straddles, many option trades do involve spreads. The two basic types of option spreads are vertical and horizontal. A vertical spread involves short and long positions at different striking prices, while a horizontal spread consists of short and long positions for different expirations. Spreads can best be illustrated by considering some examples.

The following constellation of call option prices for Ford on June 15, 1984 are used in the examples below:

Ford Call Prices for June 15, 1984, with Ford Common at 36 3/8

Strike	June	September	December
30	4 7/8	5 7/8	6 1/2
35	1/16	2 1/2	3 5/8
40	1/16	7/8	1 3/4
45	r	3/16	13/16

Vertical Spreads

One who expected Ford to rise from 36 3/8 to about 40 might have bought the December 35s at 3 5/8. Alternatively, one could have bought the December 35s at 3 5/8 and simultaneously written the December 40s at 1 3/4, for a net cost (neglecting commissions) of 1 7/8 (3 5/8 − 1 3/4). A rise to 40 would produce a gain of 3 1/8 (5 − 1 7/8) compared with a profit of 1 5/8 (5 − 3 5/8) if only the long position were taken. Moreover losses are limited to 1 7/8 (compared with 3 5/8 on the long-position alone). Indeed for every price up to 41 1/4, a greater dollar gain is realized on the spread than on the simple long-position. Above 41 1/4, however, the short-position limits the gain (i.e., profits are less than those on the long-position by itself). Thus compared with only buying the December 35, this spread reduces risk and increases gains for modest price moves. For larger favorable price moves, however, the gains would be higher on the long-position alone. Indeed for prices above 41 1/4, the spread position's profits are lower with the long side alone. Note, however, that even for prices somewhat above 41 1/4, the percentage profit is higher on the spread, as the unhedged position requires a higher initial investment (1 7/8 on spread versus 3 5/8 for the December 35 call alone). Indeed, in the above example the stock would have to rise to 44 5/8 for the percentage gains to be equivalent. At that level, the call alone has has an intrinsic value of 9 5/8 (44 5/8 − 35), which represents a gain of 6 (9 5/8 − 3 5/8). This is equivalent to a gain of about 66% (6 ÷ 3 5/8), which is about the same as that on the spread (3 1/8 ÷ 1 7/8).

A vertical spread such as the one discussed above is designed to take advantage of an expected stock price rise. Writing the lower strike option covered by the purchase of a higher strike, in contrast, creates a spread that will show gains if the stock's price falls. Thus writing the September 35s while buying the September 40s would initially yield 1 5/8 (2 1/2 − 7/8). Should the stock drop below 35 at expiration, the spreader would be able to keep that sum (1 5/8), and would show a gain for prices at expiration of as much as 36 5/8. According to a study by Frankfurter, Stevenson, and Young, a strategy of writing in-the-money calls against out-of-the-money calls would have produced substantial trading profits for the examples that they examined.[20]

Horizontal Spreads

Investors who expected a modest short-run price rise for Ford could have bought the December 40s and sold the September 40s for a net cost of 7/8 (1 3/4 − 7/8). If Ford traded at or just below 40 in September, the September 40s would expire worthless. The December 40s, in contrast, would still have three months to run and be worth about 2. At these prices the trade would earn around 100%. If the stock goes to 45, however, both the September 40s (the short position) and the December 40s would rise. The difference in the two option prices may either increase or decrease slightly, thereby producing little or no gain or loss. Alternatively, the stock could fall from 36 3/8 to, say, 25, in which case both the September and December 40s will fall dramatically. If in September the Decembers were still worth 3/8, the initial spread would narrow from 7/8 to 3/8 (1/2). The loss, while not total, is still substantial. Thus the spread-trader will not make money under every scenario but losses are limited. With spreads, adverse moves in the short position tend to be offset by favorable moves in the long position and vice versa.

Assembling Spreads

Spreads may be bought and sold as a package or put on one side at a time (legged on). Option market makers normally quote a price that reflects the ask on the long side and the bid on the short side. One may use limit orders to "leg on" a somewhat better price on each side. Such a piecemeal approach does incur some risks, however. To avoid putting up margin, the long side needs to be purchased first. Once the long side is on, the short side's price could move adversely (down) before the spread is fully established. One would normally close a spread position by covering the short side first (to avoid being short without a hedge).

Regardless of how they are assembled, spreads are relatively complicated trades, only briefly explored here. Brokers can, however, supply interested investors with a set of pamphlets from the options exchanges explaining spreads and various other aspects of option trading in much greater detail.

Tax Implications

Option trading involves a number of relevant tax implications, several of which are noted below:

1. Option profits and losses are treated as capital gains or losses, provided the trader is neither a broker nor a full-time trader (i.e., one's principal income source is not from trading). Holding periods are almost always too short for pure option trades to qualify for long-term treatment, however.
2. The profit or loss on an exercised call is not realized for tax purposes until the stock is sold. Thus one can carry over profits to a following year and stretch short-term gains into long-term gains.
3. An option writer who is exercised (this problem could have been avoided by covering prior to expiration) will have to sell stock at the striking price and thereby perhaps incur a large taxable gain. The writer can avoid realizing such a gain by purchasing the stock on the open market for delivery at the striking price. For example, one might have written options at 70 on stock purchased at 40, only to see the stock's price rise to $80. Delivery of the original stock would produce a profit of $3,000 per 100 shares. If taking additional capital gains this year is unattractive, the investor might cover with newly purchased stock.

Option Mutual Funds

Thus far, option mutual funds are only a small factor in option trading and no more than a small segment of the mutual fund industry. They do offer investors an additional choice, however. Because option prices are particularly volatile, any mutual fund whose portfolio consisted principally of calls could conceivably lose its entire investment in a down market. Accordingly, most recently established funds have chosen more conservative strategies, such as writing in-the-money covered options on dividend-paying stocks.[21] A second approach keeps most of the fund's assets in low-risk investments such as Treasury bills, and uses the remainder to speculate in options.[22] The covered-option-type fund is suited for conservative investors, while the fractional-option-investment-type is more interesting to risk-oriented investors.

Institutional Participation in the Option Markets

While option funds are a very minor factor, other institutional investors such as pension funds and bank trust departments have become increasingly active. Such investors can write options against their large stock portfolios. The substantial commission discounts available to such institutions makes certain types of combination trades attractive. In particular, conversions (offsetting positions in calls and manufactured calls) can sometimes be structured to yield relatively attractive riskless returns for those who can trade at minimal costs.

Brokerage Commissions on Options

Most brokerage firms have a separate commission schedule for options based on the number of options and dollar volume of the trade. Optionholders who exercise will pay a commission on the purchased stock, and the writer will pay a selling commission on the called-away stock. Because the gross profits on option trades, particularly spreads, are often relatively thin, one should pay careful attention to the impact of commissions.

WARRANTS AND RIGHTS

As pure options, warrants and rights have much in common with calls. The same basic valuation principles and risk/return tradeoffs are present with all three types of securities. Each option type has some distinctive characteristics, however.

Special Situations and Warrants

Warrants are often sold in a package with bonds that may be used at par to exercise the warrant. When the bond's price is below par, exercise becomes more attractive with *usable bonds* (bonds exercisable at their face value as a substitute for cash) than with cash. For example, a warrant may permit the purchase of XYZ stock at 20 when the market price is 15. No one would use cash to exercise at such prices. If usable bonds are selling at 60, however, a bond costing $600 could be used with the appropriate number of warrants to purchase 50 shares of stock having a market value of $750. Both Post and Weberman suggest that usable bonds are sometimes an attractive speculation. Rush and Melicher found that the existence of usable bonds tends to increase the warrant's market price.[24]

A takeover threat increases the risk of warrant ownership. For example, Indian Head warrants permitted the holder to purchase stock at 25. Prior to its takeover by the Dutch holding company, Thyssen Bornemisza, Indian Head stock was trading at 22 and the warrants at 5. Thyssen offered 27 for the stock and 2 for the warrants (the difference between the striking price, 25, and the purchase price of the stock, 27). The Thyssen action caused the warrant price to fall to 2 1/4 even though the warrants will not expire until 1990. Warrantholders apparently believed that the takeover would leave too thin a market for Indian Head to make the warrants attractive. While the warrantholders could reject the Thyssen offer, the warrants' value was greatly reduced by the Dutch company's takeover of Indian Head.[25]

A 1971 Internal Revenue Service ruling encouraged firms to extend the life of warrants that would otherwise expire unexercised, thereby increasing the danger of warrant short selling. IRS now requires firms to report as profits the sale price of any warrant that expires unexercised. Exercised warrants, in contrast, do not incur taxes for the issuer.

Warrant-issuing companies occasionally try to ensure that their warrants are exercised by supporting their stock price above the warrant's strike price near expiration. For example: in 1976, Tesovo engaged E. F. Hutton to stabilize (put a floor under) their stock price at $14.50 so that soon-to-expire warrants with a $13.80 strike would be exercised.[26] AT&T engaged Morgan Stanley for a similar operation in 1975.

Rights

Since offering stock to new buyers would dilute the existing stockholders' interests, corporations sometimes sell stock through a rights offering. For example: a company with 10 shareholders, each having 1,000 shares (10% of the company), might want to raise additional equity capital by selling another 10,000 shares. Offering these shares to the highest bidder might well deny them to the current shareholders and thus dilute their positions. If all of the new stock was bought by outsiders, the existing shareholders would see their interest reduced by half. They had each owned 10% of 10,000, or 1,000 shares each. Now they each own 5% of 20,000 shares.

To avoid diluting existing shareholder's positions, a company that needs additional capital may issue rights that give them first refusal on the new stock. The right will specify the terms for the stock purchase (price and time frame). Shareholders wishing to maintain their interest would simply exercise their rights. Most holders of a trivial percentage of a very large company may prefer to sell their rights on the open market. Rights usually offer new stock at a discount from the current market price, thereby giving the right an intrinsic value. If the stock then rises further, the right's value will also increase. Rights trading is relatively speculative, as most rights have a very short lifespan—often only a few weeks.

Rights are Usually Issued for Fractional Shares

One right is issued for each outstanding share. Such rights typically give the holder an option on a fraction (say 1/4) of a share. Thus the holder of 100 shares of the underlying stock might receive 100 rights, which would entitle him or her to buy 25 shares. Because rights are generally issued for short-exercise periods at striking prices far in-the-money, they are generally priced very close to their intrinsic values (little or no time value).

Cum-Rights and Ex-Rights

As with dividends, rights-offering announcements specify a day-of-record for people owning the stock to receive the rights—the *cum-rights period*. After this date, the stock sells *ex-rights*. Setting the record date a few days after the ex-rights date allows time for record keeping. Generally, the shares go ex-rights in the marketplace four business days before the record date. For example:

Typical Timing of a Rights Offering

Date	Day	Event
January 15	Monday	Rights offering announced for shareholders of record on Monday, February 5
January 29	Monday	Last day to buy the shares cum-rights
January 30	Tuesday	Shares go ex-rights
February 5	Monday	Record date

The underlying stock's value depends on whether it is selling cum- or ex-rights. The stock's price will generally drop on the day it goes ex, since subsequent buyers will not receive the rights.

Valuation During the Cum-Rights Period

Assume that buying 10 XYZ shares at $40 gives one enough rights to buy one additional share at $38. Thus, one can buy 10 + 1 shares of stock for: (10 × $40) + (1 + $38) = $438. Therefore, the shares' average price is $438 divided by 11, or $39.82, and the intrinsic value of one right is $40 minus $39.82 = 18¢.

One owning 100 shares should be able to sell the rights for $18. Thus the intrinsic value of one right during cum-rights period:

$$= \frac{\text{market price of stock} - \text{subscription price}}{\text{number of shares needed to subscribe to one share} + \text{one share}}$$

Applying this formula to the above example yields:

$$\frac{\$40 - \$38}{10 + 1} = \frac{\$2.00}{11} = 18\text{¢}$$

The right's market value may, however, differ from its intrinsic value (time value).

Valuation During the Ex-Rights Period

As a stock goes ex-rights, its market value will usually decline slightly (as with the ex-dividend date). The adjusted formula becomes:

$$= \frac{\text{market value of stock} - \text{subscription price}}{\text{number of shares needed to subscribe to one share}}$$
$$= \text{intrinsic value of one right during ex-rights period}$$

If the stock dropped by 25¢ to $39.75 when it went ex-rights:

$$\frac{\$39.75 - \$38.00}{10} = \frac{\$1.75}{10} = 17.5\text{¢}$$

How Leverage Works with Rights

Suppose that the stock rises to $45 after it goes ex-rights, but before the rights expire. The new intrinsic value becomes:

$$\frac{\$45.00 - \$38.00}{10} = \frac{\$7.00}{10} = 70\text{¢}$$

Investors who bought at 20¢ ($2,000 plus commission) and sold at 70¢ would have more than tripled their money in a few weeks. Had the stock dropped below the striking price, however, a total loss would result. Out-of-money rights that are about to expire have very little value. Thus trading rights can be a rather risky short-term speculation.

The Decline of Pre-emptive Rights

At one time most corporate charters contained a pre-emptive rights clause that guaranteed shareholders the opportunity to maintain their proportional ownership. This provision has been voted out of many corporate charters, however. Companies claim that they need increased flexibility to sell shares in whatever manner seems most attractive at the time of the sale. As a result, most new stock issues do not involve rights.

SUMMARY AND CONCLUSIONS

Option securities offer many diverse investment opportunities. Pure options such as warrants, rights, puts, and calls tend to magnify the gains or losses from price changes in the associated stock. Such securities' owners obtain substantial upside potential, while their loss exposure is limited to the cost of their positions. Put and call writers, in contrast, take the opposite side of the bet. They have limited profit potential coupled with very substantial risk exposure. Actively traded options are usually listed on an exchange, while more thinly traded issues trade OTC. According to the Black/Scholes valuation formula, a call's value should increase with its underlying stock's price and volatility, time to maturity, and the interest rate. It should move inversely with its strike price. Options seem to be priced relatively efficiently vis a vis the theoretical model. Put/call parity relates the price of puts to that of corresponding calls. Options may be bought, sold, or exercised, or one may write them against owned stock (covered writing), other options (spreads), or nothing but sufficient assets to cover (naked writing). As with most investments, option securities are generally priced to reflect their potential. Thus to make money with options, one generally needs to have a better idea than the market how the underlying stock's price is likely to move.

APPENDIX A: THE BLACK/SCHOLES FORMULA

The Black/Scholes (BS) formula may be derived precisely given the following assumptions:

1. Frictionless capital markets: No transactions costs or taxes and all information simultaneously and freely available to all investors.
2. No short-sale restrictions
3. All asset prices following a continuous stationary stochastic process
4. A constant riskfree rate over time
5. No dividends
6. No early exercise

The resulting formula is:

$$C = S_o N (d_1) - \frac{S \times N (d_2)}{e^{rt}}$$

$$d_1 = \frac{\ln (S_o/S) + (r + 1/2 \, \sigma^2) \, t}{\sigma \sqrt{t}}$$

$$d_2 = \frac{\ln (S_o/S) + (r - 1/2 \, \sigma^2) \, t}{\sigma \sqrt{t}}$$

where:

C = option value
r = continuously compounded riskless interest rate
S_o = stock price
S = strike price of option
e = 2.718
t = time to expiration of option as a fraction of a year
σ = the standard deviation of the continuously compounded annual rate of return
$\ln = (S_o/S)$ = natural logarithm of S_o/S
$N(d)$ = value of the cumulative normal distribution evaluated at d

APPENDIX B: PUT-CALL PARITY

The formula relating the value of a put to that of a call may be written as:

$$(C_o - P_o) = \frac{(1 + r_f) S_o - S}{1 + r_f}$$

where:

C_o = call value
P_o = put value
r_f = riskfree rate
S_o = stock price
S = striking price

REVIEW QUESTIONS

1. Distinguish between a put and a call option.
2. What kind of option would a bearish speculator buy? Why?
3. What kind of option activity would an investor carry out to protect a profit in a stock he or she owns?
4. What is a straddle?
5. What risk does the writer of a naked put take?
6. What obligation does the writer of a covered call undertake?
7. What type of option trading activity would a bullish speculator carry out?
8. What type of option trading activity would a short-seller carry out?
9. Explain the striking price.
10. Discuss the various types of spreads.
11. Distinguish between a warrant and a right.

12. Rights do/do not lead to dilution (explain).
13. Warrants do/do not lead to dilution (explain).
14. Exercising warrants increases/decreases earnings per share (explain).

REVIEW PROBLEMS

1. Identify a list of five puts and five calls. Now compute the time value and intrinsic value for each.
2. Apply Turov's formula to three of the above call options.
3. Select five put/call combinations and compute their put/call parity values. Compare them with the actual relations. Realize that nonsimultaneous closes, commissions, and bid-ask spread would all work against parity. Explain.
4. Repeat the above process, this time using the Black/Scholes formula (you will have to estimate stock variances).
5. Identify five stocks with high dividend rates and formulate a covered writing strategy for each. Track your performance over time. Write a report.
6. Identify five long-term calls that you would feel least uncomfortable writing naked. Track their performance and assess the results. Write a report.
7. Assemble five vertical spreads and track their performances. Write a report.
8. Assemble five horizontal spreads and track their performances. Write a report.
9. Identify five companies with outstanding warrants and listed calls. Track their performances relative to the common for the life of each call. Write a report.
10. XYZ stock is selling ex-rights at $50. The rights entitle the holder to 10 shares at $48. What is their theoretical value?

NOTES

1. D. Turov, "Dividend Paying Stocks and Their Warrants," *Financial Analysts Journal*, March/April 1973, pp. 76–79; D. Turov, "Speculative Security, Warrants, Argues a Fan, Have a Lot Going for Them," *Barron's*, November 28, 1983, pp. 38, 47.

2. J. Shelton, "The Relation of the Price of a Warrant to the Price of Its Associated Stock," *Financial Analysts Journal*, May/June 1967 and July/August 1967, pp. 134–151; P. Samuelson, "Rational Theory of Warrant Prices," *Industrial Management Review*, Spring 1965, p. 20; P. Samuelson, "Mathematics of Speculation Price," *SIAM Review*, January 1973, pp. 1–42; M. Parkinson, "Empirical Warrant Stock Relationships," *Journal of Business*, October 1972, pp. 563–569; F. Black and M. Scholes, "The Pricing of Option Contracts and Corporate Liabilities," *Journal of Political Economy*, May–June 1973, pp. 637–654.

3. E. Elton and M. Gruber, *Modern Portfolio Theory and Investment Analysis*, John Wiley and Sons, New York, 1981, pp. 441–478.

4. F. Black and M. Scholes, "The Valuation of Option Contracts and a Test of Market Efficiency," *Journal of Finance*, May 1972, pp. 399–417.

5. P. Gali, "Tests of Market Efficiency of the Chicago Board Options Exchange," *Journal of Business*, April 1977, pp. 167–197.

6. N. Gultekin, R. Rogalski and S. Tinic, "Option Pricing Model Estimates: Some Empirical Results," *Financial Management*, Spring 1982, pp. 58–69.

7. G. Trennepohl, "A Comparison of Listed Option Premiums and Black/Scholes Model Prices: 1973–1979," *Journal of Financial Research*, Spring 1981, pp. 11–20.

8. A. Gleit and B. Branch, "The Black/Scholes Model and Stock Price Forecasting," *Financial Review*, Spring 1980, pp. 13–22.

9. M. Bhattacharya, "Empirical Properties of the Black/Scholes Formula under Ideal Conditions," *Journal of Financial and Quantitative Analysis*, December 1980, pp. 1081–1106.

10. S. Phillips and C. Smith, "Trading Costs for Listed Options: The Implications for Market Efficiency," *Journal of Financial Economics*, June 1980, pp. 179–201.

11. R. Whaley, "Valuation of American Call Options on Dividend-Paying Stocks: Empirical Tests," *Journal of Financial Economics*, March 1982, pp. 29–58; J. MacBeth and L. Merville, "Tests of the Black/Scholes and Cox Call Option Valuation Models," *Journal of Finance*, May 1980, pp. 285–300; W. Sterk, "Tests of Two Models for Valuing Call Options and Stocks with Dividends," *Journal of Finance*, December 1982, pp. 1229–1238; W. Sterk, "Comparative Performance of the Black-Scholes and Roll-Geske-Whaley Option Pricing Models," *Journal of Financial and Quantitative Analysis*, September 1983, pp. 345–354; R. Geske and R. Roll, "On Valuing American Call Options with the Black-Scholes European Formula," *Journal of Finance*, June 1984, pp. 443–455; W. Sterk, "Option Pricing Dividends and the In- and Out-of-the-Money Bias," *Financial Management*, Winter 1983, pp. 47–53.

12. S. Manaster and R. Rendleman, "Option Prices as Predictors of Equilibrium Stock Prices," *Journal of Finance*, September 1982, pp. 1043–1057.

13. R. Stern, "Reverse Conversions," *Forbes*, May 10, 1982, p. 61.

14. R. Klemkosky and B. Resnick, "An Ex-ante Analysis of Put-Call Parity," *Journal of Financial Economics*, December 1980, pp. 363–379.

15. M. Rubenstein and H. Leland, "Replicating Options with Positions on Stock and Cash," *Financial Analysts Journal*, July/August 1981, pp. 63–72.

16. W. Welch, *Strategies for Put and Call Option Trading*, Winthrop Publishers, Cambridge, Massachusetts, 1982; P. Ritchken and H. Salkin, "Safety First Selection Techniques for Option Spreads, *Journal of Portfolio Management*, Spring 1983, pp. 61–67.

17. D. French and G. Henderson, "Substitute Hedged Option Portfolios: Theory and Evidence," *Journal of Financial Research*, Spring 1981, pp. 21–32; J. Yates, and R. Kopprasch, "Writing Covered Call Options: Profits and Risks," *Journal of Portfolio Management*, Fall 1980, pp. 74–79; P. Mueller, "Covered Options: An Alternative Investment Strategy," *Financial Management*, Autumn 1981, pp. 64–71.

18. G. Anders, "Cities Service Call Options, Nearing Expiration, Provide Holder with Windfall After Gulf Bid," *Wall Street Journal*, June 23, 1977, p. 1.

19. W. Eckhardt Jr., "The American Put: Computational Issues and Value Comparisons," *Financial Management*, Autumn 1982, pp. 42–52.

20. G. Frankfurter, R. Stevenson and A. Young, "Option Spreading: Theory and an Illustration," *Journal of Portfolio Management*, Summer 1979, pp. 59–63.

21. A. Fredman and R. Moore, "Cutting Losses and Gains, Most Option Funds use Surprisingly Cautious Strategies," *Barron's*, October 18, 1982, pp. 44, 45 and 60; W. Baldwin, "Risk and Reward," *Forbes*, November 18, 1982, pp. 256–257.

22. *Business Week*, "Option Funds: A Popular Cushion for Investor," *Business Week*, January 16, 1978, pp. 90–91.

23. L. Post, "Yield to Early Maturity: An Important Factor with Usable Bonds," *Financial Analysts Journal*, November/December 1973, pp. 72–73; B. Weberman, "How to Use Usables," *Forbes*, July 18, 1983.

24. D. Rush and R. Melicher, "An Empirical Exmination of Factors Which Influence Warrant Prices," *Journal of Finance*, December 1974, pp. 1449–1466.

25. W. Shepherd, "New Risk in Warrants," *Business Week*, August 3, 1974, p. 42.

26. *Business Week*, "Propping Stock so Warrants Sell," *Business Week*, October 25, 1976, p. 92.

18 Convertibles and Other Combination Securities

Several types of instruments combine option features with characteristics of other securities. Convertible debentures and convertible preferreds are the two primary types, while hybrid convertibles, equity notes, commodity-backed bonds, and stock-indexed bonds are much rarer. Convertible preferreds are a type of preferred stock. Convertible debentures, hybrid convertibles, equity notes, and commodity-backed and stock-indexed bonds are all debt securities. Each type of combination security may be exchanged for a set number of common shares or, in the case of commodity-backed and stock-indexed bonds, their redemption value or coupon rate is indexed to some other price. Except for equity notes, conversion is at the security owner's option.

This chapter examines the various types of combination securities, giving particular attention to convertible debentures. Convertibles' investment appeal, specialized terminology, call risk, and conversion premiums are all addressed. Then we briefly explore convertible preferreds, hybrid convertibles, equity notes, and commodity-backed and stock-index bonds. Finally hedges and arbitrages, trades which often involve pure and combination option securities, are discussed.

COMBINATION SECURITIES' APPEAL

Combination securities derive value both from their current return (preferred dividends or interest) and potential to become common stock or some other asset. If the underlying common's price rises sufficiently, the convertible owner can either acquire stock at a below-market price or sell the combination security at a price that reflects the stock's value. If the underlying stock's price does not rise sufficiently to make conversion attractive, the owners still receive income on the securities as preferreds or debentures. The market contains very few free lunches, however. While convertibles do offer an attractive combination of upside potential and downside protection, the convertibility feature is acquired at the cost of reduced interest or dividend income.

Convertible Terminology

As with pure options, a number of specialized terms are involved with convertibles:

453

Conversion ratio—Number of shares into which the security is convertible
Conversion price—Face value of the security divided by its conversion-ratio
Conversion value—Current stock price times the conversion-ratio
Straight-debt value—Market value of an otherwise-equivalent bond lacking a conversion feature
Conversion-premium—Bond price less its conversion-value
Premium over Straight-debt value—Bond price less its straight-debt value

To understand the use of these terms consider a 12% issue with a face value of $1,000, convertible into 50 shares of CVD stock (its *conversion-ratio*) at any time over the next 20 years. For a $20-a-share stock price, the convertible's *conversion value* equals the bond's face value ($20 × 50 = $1,000). Thus the *conversion price* is $20 per share. If the stock sells for $15 a share when the bonds are issued, the bond's conversion value equals $750. Such bonds will generally trade at a price that more closely reflects their value as bonds—*straight-debt value* of their 12% coupon rate. Thus if the market rate on similar-risk long-term bonds is 14%, this bond should sell for at least $860 [12%/14% = .86]. If the underlying stock's price rose sufficiently for the conversion value to approach the convertible's straight-debt value, the bond's price would begin behaving more like that of its underlying stock. If, for example, the stock rose to $30 a share, the convertible would sell for at least its $1,500 conversion value and move up and down largely with the stock's price.

While conversion and straight-debt values tend to place a floor under the price, convertibles normally yield appreciably less than otherwise-similar nonconvertibles because of their *equity kicker*. Thus a convertible with a 10% coupon would typically command a somewhat higher price than a similar-quality 10% nonconvertible. The difference between the bond's conversion value and market value is known as the *conversion premium*. The difference between the convertible's market price and straight-debt value is called the *premium over the straight-debt value*. Assume the CVD bonds sold for $950 when the stock traded at 15, and similar nonconvertibles were selling for $875. The conversion premium would be $200 ($950 − $750) and the premium over straight-debt value would be $75 ($950 − $875). Table 18.1 contains data on some real world convertibles.

Because convertible bonds are often almost as risky as stocks, the same margin percentage is required: in 1984, 50% versus 30% for straight bonds. Convertibles' coupon payments may offset part or all of the interest cost of a margin-purchase. Buying convertibles on margin may be appealing if the (short-term) margin rate is low relative to the (longer-term) bond rate. Indeed, low conversion-value convertibles often pay relatively high yields and sometimes even return to life.[1]

Table 18.1   Selected Convertible Bond Data for February 1, 1983

Convertible issue	S & P Rating	Conversion Ratio	Stock Price	Conversion Value	Estimated Straight-Debt Value	Market Price
AVCO 5 1/2 93	BB−	18.52	27 5/8	$ 512	$500	$ 670
Central Tel 9s 98*	B	117.65	9	$1,059*	$810	$1,045*
GELCO 14s 01	BB−	22.13	42 3/8	$ 938	$950	$1,010
GTE 5s 92	BBB	22.98	40 3/4	$ 936	$560	$ 962
Life Mark 11s 02	BB+	30.30	34 7/8	$1,057	$840	$1,215
Ramada Inns 10s 00	B−	129.03	5 3/4	$ 742	$710	$ 960

*Note that the conversion value is almost always below the market price of a convertible. The anomaly revealed here may reflect quotations at different closing times for the convertible and underlying stock, or the bond may have closed at the bid while the stock closed at the asked. Arbitrage profits would of course have been possible if one could have traded at these prices.

Why Buy Convertible Bonds?

Convertible bonds offer both a fixed coupon (usually a bit below the market rate on equivalent-risk straight-debt securities) and the possibility of a capital gain. They should not be bought either as income securities (straight bonds almost always offer a higher risk-adjusted yield) or as pure stock plays (the stock itself will usually rise proportionately more in a strong market). Rather, convertibles appeal to investors who find the related stock's prospects attractive but desire the straight-debt value's income and protection.

Convertibles have two basic advantages over the underlying common. First, the security's current return is usually higher than the corresponding common's dividend yield. Second, convertibles' fixed coupons give them considerable resistance to downward moves in the common's price. Convertible prices do tend to move inversely with interest rates, however. Moreover, they normally yield less than otherwise-similar nonconvertible debentures. Finally, the conversion feature will only have value as long as the stock price has a reasonable potential of rising enough for the conversion value to exceed the straight-debt value.

According to Stevenson, deep-discount convertibles are often particularly attractive.[2] *Business Week* cited the following example:[3] In the depressed market of August 1974, the Chase Manhattan Bank's 4 7/8% bond sold for $630 (a 9% yield), which equaled its estimated straight-debt value. Moreover the market price only exceeded the conversion value by 10%. A 25% increase in the stock price would lead to a bond price increase of about 18%. A 25% fall in the stock price (assuming interest rates held steady) would, in contrast, probably have produced about a 3% reduction in the bond's price. A substantial decline in the bond's price would require both an increase in interest rates and a fall in the stock's price. Even in this instance, one could simply hold the bond to maturity and collect a 9% return.

Convertible's Call Risk

While most debt securities are callable, the call feature is especially relevant to convertible holders. Ingersoll showed that corporations should force conversion whenever the call price is safely below the bond's conversion value.[4] Since following such a policy would severely limit convertibles' upside potentials, they may only offer attractive returns (vis-a-vis nonconvertibles) if the conversion value exceeds the call price soon after the security is issued.[5] Mikkelson finds that calling to force conversion generally depresses the underlying stock's price.[6]

The Theoretical Value of Convertibles

Because they contain both debt and equity elements, convertibles' theoretical values are relatively difficult to define. Debt values will depend upon the coupon, default risk, maturity date, and other indenture provisions. The conversion feature's value is affected by the firm's risk and capital structure, dividend policy, calling policy, conversion terms, and the current stock price.

As with call valuation, a convertible's theoretical value should not offer assured arbitrage profits to either buyers or short-sellers. Values derived from the Black/Scholes contingent-claim pricing model (used to derive theoretical values for options) have been applied to convertible pricing by Ingersoll, McDaniel, Brennan, and Schwartz.[7]

Calculating the price the stock must reach to make investments in convertibles or their associated stocks equivalent is also much more complex than with warrants (Turov's formula). Both the premium over conversion and the difference between interest and expected dividend income must be considered. Liebowitz has identified three plausible definitions of equivalent return.[8]

The Conversion Premium

The conversion premium, which indicates the amount over the underlying stock value paid for the straight-debt value protection, is of considerable interest to investors. Weil, Segal, and Green assembled the following list of potential determinants of the conversion-premium.[9]

1. **Transaction costs:** Since bond commissions are generally less than those of equivalent-value stock, buying bonds and converting them may incur lower transactions costs than purchasing stock directly.
2. **Income differences:** The bond's coupon yield is usually greater than the dividend yield on equivalent stock.
3. **Antidilution clause:** The indenture gives some protection against the diluting effect of additional stock sales or distribution of assets. The specifics of these provisions may affect the premium.
4. **Price floors:** The convertibles' straight-debt value protects holders from stock price falls.

5. **Volatility of the underlying stock:** As with pure options (BS formula), a volatile stock price increases the likelihood of a large payoff.
6. **Length to maturity:** The longer the life of the conversion option, the more time the stock has to reach an attractive level.

On a priori grounds, WSG ruled out antidilution clauses, stock volatility and length to maturity, which left transaction costs, income differences, and price floors. In their empirical work, the income-differences variable had the proper sign and was statistically significant. The transaction-cost variable had an unexpected negative sign, however. The floor variable added little explanatory power and was not generally statistically significant. WSG believed that the floor variable was unimportant in their equation because it offered relatively little protection. They suggested that similar protection could be obtained with a stop-loss order. Their sample, however, only contained convertibles priced well above their straight-debt values so that the floor was likely to be almost irrelevant. Stop-loss orders liquidate one's holdings, while the convertible's floor reduces the potential loss as one waits for the stock to rise again. The floor is more nearly equivalent to a put at the floor level lasting for the bond's expected life. Such a put would probably be quite expensive.

WGS's statistical methodology was criticized by Duvel, and Murry questioned their assertion that a stop-loss order provided equivalent protection.[10] Work by both Walter and Que, and West and Largay confirmed the importance of the floor variable.[11] In a reply, WGS conceded this point while demonstrating the relatively modest effect of the floor, especially when the premium over the straight-debt value is large.[12] Thus income differences and floors both affect the conversion premium. Subsequently, Jennings found the conversion premium to be related to undiversifiable risk.[13] He also noted that income and transaction cost differences are relevant only if the future conversion value is expected to exceed the future straight-debt value. In addition, he found that bonds whose conversion premiums were below his predicted value tended to appreciate relative to bonds with overvalued conversion premiums.

Convertible Preferreds

While less popular than convertible debentures, convertible preferreds have become much more numerous in the past few years. In 1983, forty-three new issues worth over $3 billion were sold, a tenfold increase over 1982. Much of this increase results from various mergers, acquisition, and leveraged buyouts in which the acquirer issues new securities rather than purchasing with cash.

Convertible preferreds promise (but do not guarantee) a fixed dividend and can be converted into a stated number of common shares within a prespecified period. The convertibility feature may eventually expire, at which time the stock becomes a normal fixed-income preferred. As with convertible bonds, convertible preferreds behave more like the underlying stocks when the market price is close to their conversion values, and more like straight preferreds when the conversion value is well below the value as a preferred.

The number of common shares that one can obtain by converting is called the conversion ratio. Thus, a preferred convertible into four common shares would have a ratio of 4.00. This conversion ratio may change with time. For example: an issue might be convertible into four shares for the first 10 years after issue, two shares for the next 10 years and then may become a straight preferred.

A preferred's conversion value is the current price of the common stock multiplied by the conversion ratio. A preferred convertible into four shares of common stock selling at $10 would have a conversion value of $40. A market price of $50 would reflect a conversion premium of $10. The conversion premium is normally expressed as a percentage:

$$\text{conversion premium} = \frac{\text{market price of preferred less conversion value}}{\text{conversion value}} \times 100$$

The conversion premium in the above example is:

$$\frac{\$50 - \$40}{\$40} = \frac{\$10}{\$40} = 25\%$$

Knowing the conversion premium may help an investor determine whether the convertible preferred or the common is more attractive. For example, one might have a choice between a company's 12% convertible preferred selling at $50 and its common stock bearing a 6% dividend yield selling for $20. If the conversion ratio is two and the conversion value is $40, the conversion premium is 25%:

	CVP	Common
Price	$50	$20
Dividend	$3.50	$1.00
Yield	12%	9%

For the 25% premium, an investor buying the 12% convertible preferred receives a higher current yield (12% versus 6%—6% more income), a more stable dividend (a characteristic of preferreds), and the option of converting the issue into common. Of course the higher the conversion premium, the more remote will be the chance of an attractive conversion, and the lower the gain, even if conversion does become profitable. Moreover, convertible preferreds are exposed to the same kind of call- and interest rate risks as are convertible bonds.

Hybrid Convertibles

While convertible bonds and preferreds are the primary types of convertible securities, other types of combination securities also bear mentioning. Unlike traditional convertibles, hybrids are convertible into stock of different companies from those that issue them.[14] For example: in 1980, Textron sold debentures convertible into Textron-owned shares of Allied Chemical (at 66). At about the same time, Mesa Petroleum sold a security convertible into General American. Companies with substantial stock portfolios may find hybrids a useful source of funds. Hybrids are about as attractive to investors as the underlying company's straight convertibles. The bond's default risk depends on the issuing company's financial position, however. The conversion of a regular convertible is a tax-free exchange, while any profit realized when a hybrid is converted is immediately taxable.

Equity Notes

Equity notes were developed to meet the capital needs of banks.[15] Such notes are issued as debt that yield a fixed coupon until maturity, when they are automatically converted into common. For example: Manufacturers' Hanover Trust (Manny Hanny) sold $100 million in ten-year equity notes in April 1982. Such notes yield 15 1/8% and in 1992 must be converted into Manny Hanny shares at a price equal to the 30-day average price prior to maturity, with upper and lower limits of 55.55 and 40 (Manny Hanny was then selling for around 32).

Commodity-Backed and Stock-Indexed Bonds

Commodity-backed bonds are debt instruments whose values are potentially related to the price of some physical commodity. For example: in 1980 Sunshine Mining (silver) sold $57.5 million in 8 1/2% bonds whose redemption value is tied to the price of silver. For prices below $20 per ounce, the bonds mature at face; at higher prices, the bond's redemption value rises proportionately. Thus such bonds allow the owner to speculate on a silver price rise while earning a modest return. When the bonds were issued, silver sold for $14 to $15 per ounce. At year-end 1982 silver was down to $10 only to rise to around $14 a few months later. Silver traded at between $7 and $8 during most of 1984. The bond's price has moved up and down with the silver price and interest rates.

In 1981 Oppenheimer and Co. marketed a $25 million stock-index bond. The coupon rate is indexed to stock trading volume with a maximum of 22%, compared with an initial rate of 18%. High stock volume means booming business for Oppenheimer, so they can afford to pay a higher interest rate.

Both commodity-backed and stock-indexed bonds were designed to appeal to speculative investors with options that specially-positioned issuers can offer.[16] Additional types of innovative combination securities will probably be devised as time passes. Table 18.2 lists the various types of combination securities.

HEDGING AND ARBITRAGING

As markets have become more sophisticated, the diversity of security types increased, and takeover activity more widespread, hedging and arbitrage trading has risen markedly. Both brokerage firms and individual investors have gotten into the act.

Table 18.2   The Types of Combination Securities

Convertible Bonds	Debt securities which may be exchanged for common stock at a fixed ratio
Convertible Preferreds	Preferred stock which may be exchanged for common stock at a fixed ratio
Hybrid Convertibles	Debt securities of one company convertible into the common of another company
Equity Notes	Debt securities with a mandatory conversion
Commodity-Backed Bonds	Debt securities whose potential redemption-values are related to the market price of some physical commodity such as silver
Stock-Indexed Bonds	Debt securities whose yields are related to stock market volume

Hedging

Hedging involves taking opposite positions in related assets to profit (or reduce losses) from hoped-for relative price movements. For example, one might buy stocks and short corresponding warrants or vice versa. Arbitragers, in contrast, simultaneously buy and sell equivalent securities in separate markets, profiting from temporary price differences. Arbitragers will generally take advantage of any appreciable price disparities for securities traded on both the Pacific Stock Exchange and the NYSE or any other combination of exchanges. In addition to their use in debt- and equity-related securities trading, hedging and arbitraging also take place in a wide variety of other markets, including those for currencies and commodities.

Both hedging and arbitraging may be classified into risk and pure forms. A pure hedge is designed to reduce risk. For example, most silver mining companies have relatively stable extraction and processing costs combined with considerable output-price volatility. Periodically selling its planned production in the commodity futures market would substantially reduce such a firm's price-fluctuation risk. Hedge trades establish a dependable price well before the silver is ready for sale. Mining companies that hedge each projected output increment largely insulate themselves from subsequent silver spot (immediate delivery) price fluctuations. Pure hedging may be advisable whenever establishing a forward price reduces an important business risk. Such pure hedges are incidental to hedgers' main spot-market business.

Risk hedges, in contrast, are designed to yield a relatively likely profit. Rather than reduce the impact of potentially adverse price moves, risk hedgers seek to profit from potentially favorable relative price movements while minimizing their exposure to potentially adverse moves. Put and call spreads are examples of risk hedges.

Arbitraging

Pure arbitragers assume opposite positions on equivalent (or convertible to equivalent) assets when prices in separate markets diverge sufficiently. Pure arbitrage produces a quick, certain profit. Risk arbitragers, in contrast, take offsetting positions in securities that are only potentially equivalent, such as the shares of an acquisition candidate and its proposed acquirer.[17] An exchange for debt or equity securities may or may not be hedged by the arbitrager. A tender for cash does not require the arbitrager to make an offsetting trade, however. Table 18.3 summarizes the various types of hedges and arbitrages.

Table 18.3   The Types of Hedges and Arbitrages

Pure hedging	Reducing the risk of an exposed asset position by making an offsetting trade
Risk hedging	Taking offsetting positions in related assets in the hopes of profiting from relative price moves
Pure arbitraging	Simultaneously buying and selling identical assets on different markets at price differences which guarantee a profit
Risk arbitraging	Taking offsetting positions in the securities of an acquisition candidate and its proposed acquirer at prices that guarantee a profit if the takeover succeeds

A proposed merger involving an exchange of shares will generally leave the two stocks' relative prices somewhat out of line with the merger terms. For example: XYZ may offer two of its shares for each share of UVW Corporation. If pre-offer prices of XYZ and UVW were 50 and 65 and immediate post-offer prices move to 53 and 85, the UVW stock would still be underpriced relative to the XYZ offer. UVW shares can (assuming the merger agreement takes effect) be exchanged for two XYZ shares worth a total of 106, which is a premium of 26% over the current market price. One can profit from this discount by buying UVW and shorting twice as many XYZ shares. If, for example, the acquisition is completed in six weeks and commissions and financing costs amount to 5%, the arbitrager would earn a 20% profit, equivalent to 173% per annum. If the proposed merger falls through, however, the acquisition candidate's stock might decline to its pre-offer level, while the acquiring company's stock could remain largely unchanged, thereby forcing the arbitrager to incur a considerable loss to reverse the trade. Sometimes antitrust problems, shareholder opposition, or a management reassessment blocks a proposed deal. In other cases a hostile takeover attempt may be derailed by insufficient tenders or the target firm's legal maneuvers. Nonetheless, many large sophisticated investors have generated substantial profit rates through risk arbitrage, but it is not a game for the faint of heart.[18]

Most hedge and arbitrage trades are designed to produce relatively modest short-term profits (in percentage terms). Very nimble movements and minimum commissions are needed since profits often depend upon obtaining favorable overall prices in both markets. Few amateur investors have sufficient funds, time, expertise, and courage to undertake serious arbitrage plays. Even professionals have to move quickly when profitable price relationships open up. Hedging, which is somewhat less demanding than arbitraging, is more suited to amateur traders.

Real World Hedges

During July and August 1974, *Business Week's* "Wall Street" section discussed three hedge recommendations of independent investment analysts.[19] While *Business Week* did not specifically endorse any of the hedges per se, the attention paid to the proposals suggested they were worth considering. The hedges' outcomes were examined for those who closed out their positions on either December 16, 1974 or January 24, 1975 (approximately six months after the recommendations were published). The results for other nearby dates were similar.

Northwest Airlines Hedge

The Situation

Investor Jones buys 300 shares of Northwest Airlines at 21 1/4 a share. The cost of the stock after commissions is $6,472. He can hedge against a price decline of as much as 20%, and increase his profits on a rise of up to 18%, if he simultaneously sells 13 six-month call options on the Chicago Board Options Exchange at $150 apiece. Each option entitles the buyer to purchase 100 Northwest shares at $25 a share. The income from the 13 call options after commissions is $1,841.

The Outcome
Possible Result A

The stock is at 25 when the option expires. The option is not exercised, so Jones keeps the $1,841 from the option sale and the value of his stock is up by $1,125.

Possible Result B

The stock is more than 25 when the option expires and Jones is in trouble. He is, in effect, short the 1,000 shares he must buy if the option is exercised, so he loses $1,000 for every $1 the stock climbs over 25. If the stock hits 28, both the income from the option sale and the gain on his stock from 21 1/4 to 25 (the option price), less commission, are lost.

Possible Result C

The stock falls below 21 1/4. The option will not be exercised and Jones has the $1,841 from the option sale. Not until the stock falls to 15 1/8 will he actually lose money.

Had Northwest's stock price stayed between 15 1/8 and 28, the hedger would have made money. The stock, however, closed at 11 7/8 on December 16, 1974, producing an after-commissions loss of $2,989 ($6,472 − $3,483), which was only partially covered by the profit on the call short sale. Covering the calls for

1/16 would have produced a profit of $1,760 ($1,841 − $81), leaving a net loss on the transaction of $1,229 ($2,989 − $1,760). On January 24, 1975, the stock had risen to 12 7/8, which would have reduced the loss by about $300.

AT&T Hedge

American Telephone warrants are so low—1 7/8 at midweek—that it might seem sheer folly to sell them short. But AT&T shares, now below 44, have a long way to go before the warrants, exercisable at 52 until they expire next May, take on any real value. So some speculators are trying an offbeat hedge—shorting the warrants and buying October calls to protect themselves if the warrants rise. As explained by Reynolds Securities' Leroy Gross, the hedge works this way, with commissions figured in:

The speculator shorts 5,000 warrants at 1 7/8, for which he receives $8,978. He also buys 50 calls—each on 100 shares—expiring in October. They trade at 3/8, or $37.50 per call, so the hedger puts up $2,157. Gross—whose Stockbroker's Guide to Put and Call Option Strategies was recently published by the New York Institute of Finance—outlines three ways the hedger could profit by October.

The shares remain at 45 or below. The calls expire worthless, so the hedger loses $2,157. But the warrants drop to 5/8. The hedger buys warrants for $3,345 to cover the shorts he sold for $8,978, for a gain of $5,634. His net profit is $3,477.

The shares rise to 55. The warrants will trade at 4, Gross figures, so the hedger loses $11,557 covering. But the calls have jumped to 5 ($500), for a profit of $21,039. The net gain: $9,482.

The shares rise only to 50. Gross estimates that the warrants will trade at 1 1/2, for a $1,027 gain, while the calls will be 1/2 ($50), for a $70 profit—a total gain of $1,097. The danger is in Gross underestimating how much people will pay for warrants with six months to run. Suppose the warrants were to trade at 2 1/2 instead of 1 1/2: the hedger's profit would turn into a $4,000 loss.

By December 16, 1974, the calls had expired worthless while the AT&T warrant traded at 9/16. Covering the warrant short sale would have cost $2,953, producing a gain of $6,025 on the warrant part of the transaction ($8,978 − $2,953 = $6,025). The calls cost $2,157 so the net gain on the full hedge would have been $3,868 ($6,025 − $2,157). The hedger was unprotected once the October calls expired, however. On January 24, 1975, the warrants were still trading at 9/16, so the hedger's profit would not have changed by waiting an additional 5 1/2 weeks.

An IBM Tax Hedge

The IBM hedge was designed to convert capital losses into ordinary losses. In September 1973, the IRS ruled that writers must treat the profits on called-away stock as capital gains. The difference in the repurchase (zero if it expires) and selling price of an unexercised call is, however, treated as an ordinary gain or loss. To take advantage of this rule, investors were urged to write "in-the-money" calls that were very likely to be exercised. The following example was used to illustrate the point.

With IBM common trading at 209 and June 200 calls available at 25, the investor was advised to buy 100 shares of IBM common and write CBOE calls on 200 shares of stock. If the price of IBM stock was higher when the calls expired, the hedger would take an ordinary loss on the calls and realize a long-term gain on the stock. For example, if the stock was at 250 on January 31, 1975, he or she would lose $5,000 on the two calls but make $4,100 on the stock. Someone in the 50% tax bracket would have had a net after-tax gain of $1,475. In other words, the before-tax loss would be $900, but the $5,000 ordinary loss would reduce taxes by $2,500, while the $4,100 gain only would increase taxes by $1,025 for a net tax advantage of $1,475. If the stock's price declined, the tax advantage would disappear, but the hedge might still make money. A trader in the 50% bracket would show a profit if the stock stayed between 184 and 269. The hedge did, however, envision investing $20,900 in the stock, which was only offset by the $5,000 received for the calls. Moreover, commissions and foregone return on the funds committed would narrow the profitable trading range somewhat.

On December 16, 1974, IBM closed at 165 1/4 while the calls sold for 2. Selling the stock would have produced $16,450 after commissions while covering the calls would have cost $425, producing a net loss of $134 (−$4,525 on stock + $4,489 on call). On January 24, 1975, IBM had fallen to 162 7/8, while the calls were trading at 1/16, producing a net gain of $112 (−$4,763 on stock + $4,875). Since the calls were not exercised at either date, both the gain and loss would have been short term; thus the hedge failed to yield any tax-advantage.

An Evaluation

The Northwest Airlines hedge lost approximately $1,000 on a $6,500 commitment. The AT&T hedge earned almost $4,000, but incurred considerable risk once the call expired. The IBM hedge failed to produce any tax advantage and essentially broke even. Thus one of the three proposed hedges produced a substantial loss, one broke even, and the one profitable set of trades became quite risky once the call protection expired. An investor undertaking all three hedges would have earned about $3,000, or 9%, of the $27,000 initial investment. A six-month holding period return of 9% is unspectacular, considering the risks. The one profitable trade was the short sale of the AT&T warrants, which fell from 1 7/8 to 9/16.

The short sale would have required a margin deposit of one-half the dollar value of the sale. Thus short-sellers had to put up about $1 for each warrant sold, for a gain of about $1.25, or 125%. Clearly this single trade was quite profitable whether part of a hedge or not. Indeed with most hedges, one side makes money while the other side almost always loses. A hedger's net profits or losses depend on the relative sizes of the two sides' profits and losses. When they were recommended, each of the just-discussed hedges appeared likely to show profits. If only IBM (then at 209) had stayed between 185 and 269 and if only Northwest Airlines (then at 21 1/4) had stayed between 15 1/8 and 28, the hedges would have generated profits. IBM, however, fell to 165 and Northwest to 11 1/4, so both hedges lost money. Investors should never underrate the possibility of a particular security's price moving outside a prespecified range over a given period.

SUMMARY AND CONCLUSIONS

Combination securities include convertible bonds, convertible preferreds, hybrid convertibles, equity notes, commodity-backed bonds and stock-index bonds. Each combines a fixed-income security with an option (or in equity note's case, an obligation) to convert the security to common stock or some other asset. Thus such securities offer some of the upside potential of a stock, with the downside protection of a bond or preferred. Since combination securities are priced to reflect their profit and risk characteristics, buyers usually obtain the upside potential at the cost of a lower yield than otherwise-equivalent straight debt or straight preferred securities. Moreover, the call risk further limits the upside potential. Pure and combination option security positions are often combined with each other and/or with nonoption securities to produce hedges and arbitrages. Clearly investors considering some companies' common should also weigh the pros and cons of a position in their other securities.

REVIEW QUESTIONS

1. Discuss the appeal of convertibles.
2. Why is call risk particularly relevant to convertibles?
3. Discuss the various factors that affect a convertible's premium over conversion value.
4. What are hybrid convertibles and equity notes?
5. Discuss the two types of hedging and arbitraging.

REVIEW PROBLEMS

1. A convertible preferred selling at $100 may be exchanged for two shares of common, trading at $40. What is the conversion premium?
2. In the above example, what should the convertible preferred sell for if the common goes to $60?

3. Assemble a list of ten convertible bonds. Compute their conversion value, and from their rating, coupon and maturity, estimate their straight-debt value. Plot their market price versus their conversion value and versus their straight-debt value. Now plot the premium over the conversion value versus the premium over the straight-debt value.

4. Assemble a list of five convertibles and compute their conversion premiums.

5. For the above list compute the premiums over their straight-debt values.

6. Assemble a list of three recommended hedge trades and track their performances. Write a report.

NOTES

1. *Forbes*, "When Burnt Out Convertibles Come to Life," *Forbes*, February 6, 1978, p. 74; B. Weberman, "Busted Converts," *Forbes*, June 20, 1983.

2. R. Stevenson, "Deep-Discount Convertible Bonds: An Analysis," *Journal of Portfolio Management*, Summer 1982, pp. 57–64.

3. *Business Week*, "An Opportunity for the Next Bull Market," *Business Week*, August 24, 1974.

4. J. Ingersoll, "An Examination of Corporate Call Policies on Corporate Securities," *Journal of Finance*, May 1977, pp. 463–478.

5. H. Bierman, Jr. "Convertible Bonds as Investments," *Financial Analysts Journal*, March/April 1980, pp. 59–62.

6. W. Mikkelson, "Convertible Calls and Security Returns," *Journal of Financial Economics*, September 1981, pp. 237–264.

7. Ingersoll, *op. cit*; M. Brennan and E. Schwartz, "Analyzing Convertible Bonds," *Journal of Financial and Quantitative Analysis*, November 1980, pp. 907–930; W. McDaniel, "Convertible Bonds in Perfect and Imperfect Markets," *Journal of Financial Research*, Spring 1983, pp. 51–66.

8. M. Liebowitz, "Understanding Convertible Securities," *Financial Analysts Journal*, November/December 1974, pp. 57–67.

9. R. Weil, J. Segall, D. Green, "Premiums on Convertible Bonds," *Journal of Finance*, June 1968, pp. 928–930.

10. D. Duvel, "Premiums on Convertible Bonds: Comment," *Journal of Finance*, September 1970, pp. 923–927; G. Murry, "Premiums on Convertible Bonds: Comment," *Journal of Finance*, September 1970, pp. 928–930.

11. J. Walter and A. Que, "The Valuation of Convertible Bonds," *Journal of Finance*, June 1973, pp. 713–732; R. West and J. Largay, "Premiums on Convertible Bonds: Comment," *Journal of Finance*, December 1972, pp. 1156–1162.

12. R. Weil, J. Segall, and D. Green, "Premiums on Convertible Bonds," *Journal of Finance*, December 1972, pp. 1163–1170.

13. H. Jennings, "An Estimate of Convertible Bond Premiums," *Journal of Financial and Quantitative Analysis*, January 1974, pp. 33–56.

14. R. Phalon, "Wall Street's Latest—Hybrid Convertibles," *Forbes*, August 18, 1980.

15. *Business Week*, "A Cool Welcome for Equity Notes," *Business Week*, May 10, 1982, pp. 183–184.

16. D. Hertzberg, "Some Gimmicks Used to Sell Bonds Sour as Rates Fall, Inflation Slows," *Wall Street Journal*, December 18, 1982, p. 33.

17. G. Wyser-Pratte, *Risk Arbitrage II*, Monograph Series in Finance and Economics, Solomon Brothers Center for the Study of Financial Institutions, Monograph 1982—3-4.

18. G. Marcial, "Risk Abitrage: Now Open to the Public," *Business Week*, August 29, 1983, p. 65; W. Baldwin, "Does It Work for Mere Mortals, too?" *Forbes*, September 12, 1983, pp. 103–106; K. Noble, "Playing the Game of Arbitrage," *New York Times*, September 20, 1981, p. 14F; M. Laws," Risk and Reward, The Arbitrage Game Provides Plenty of Both," *Barron's*, November 30, 1981, pp. 9, 18 and 20.

19. *Business Week*, "Support Grows for Arbitrage Play," *Business Week*, July 13, 1974, p. 54; *Business Week*, "An Offbeat Hedge in AT&T," *Business Week*, July 22, 1974, p. 53; *Business Week*, "Abracadabra with Tax Losses," *Business Week*, August 10, 1974, p. 109.

Section VI:
Commodities and Real Estate

Section V dealt with mutual funds, bonds, and options; Section VI discusses commodities and real estate. While somewhat more distantly related to stocks, both of these investment types have an important place in the economy. The following case illustrates some of the issues that are explored in this section.

Making Partner

Having paid your dues by obtaining a CFA and working as a stockbroker, securities analyst, and newsletter writer, you are about to be made partner of a diversified financial services firm. While you have considerable background in most aspects of your firm's business, commodities and real estate are largely foreign to you. Merrill, Shearson, and Jenrette has long been in commodities and has recently acquired Epoch 21 and its nationwide chain of real estate brokerage offices. Because of your highly respected managerial skills, you expect to be given a supervisory role in Epoch 21. Alternatively you may be moved to the Chicago office with responsibility over the commodity operations. The decision is expected to be taken shortly after you become a partner. You will have very little time to prepare for your expected new assignment. Your bonus will, however, be tied to the performance of your division. Accordingly you want to learn what you can now. This section should get you started.

Commodities, perhaps the least understood of the major investment types, are examined in Chapter 19. Futures contracts are defined and their uses discussed. Then we identify the various types of traders and explore the methods of making trading decisions. Finally such topics as specialized commodity investments and strategic metals are examined. Chapter 20 explores real estate investing in some detail. Real estate's investment suitability is considered, along with a series of investment principles and three different approaches to valuing real estate investments. Then various types of real estate investments are considered, including duplexes, apartment buildings, commercial property, undeveloped land, and real-estate-oriented stock.

19 Commodities and Related Investments

Though a bit off the beaten path compared with more traditional investments (stocks, bonds, and real estate), commodities constitute an important investment area. The dollar value of futures contracts traded substantially exceeds that of securities. Moreover, the commodity market's dramatic price swings appeal to many speculators. Finally, futures prices reflect anticipated market conditions in many important consumer goods and services (meat, grain, sugar, silver, lumber, interest rates, etc).

The commodities market challenges even the most skillful traders. Nonetheless, investors need some understanding of the market to decide intelligently whether to participate. This relatively brief introduction is not designed to equip one to trade commodities, but should provide sufficient background to go further.[1] We begin by examining the nature, growth, and diversity of commodity futures contracts. The types of professional commodity traders are considered next, followed by a discussion of several large and disruptive individual commodity trades. We then explore various aspects of trading decisions including fundamental and technical analysis. Finally, a variety of specialized commodity types are examined, including interest rate and stock market futures, commodity options, commodity mutual funds, and such commodity-related investments as gold bullion, gold mining stocks, Krugerrands, silver coins, and strategic metals.

WHAT ARE COMMODITIES?

In spite of the commodity market's size, activity level, and economic relevance, relatively few security market investors understand clearly how and why it works. The word *commodity* refers largely to deferred-delivery contracts traded on a futures exchange. A commodity futures contract might obligate one side (the seller) to deliver a specific quantity of wheat on a prespecified date to a prespecified location or set of locations. The other side (the buyer) would promise to pay for the wheat upon delivery. Such contracts allow those who expect later to have or need wheat to establish a price and quantity when the contract is initially traded.[2] Standardizing the contract's terms (grade, quantity, delivery location, and date) facilitates active trading.

Futures may be used to hedge spot (immediate delivery) positions or to speculate on commodity price changes. Rather than make or take physical delivery,

469

most hedgers and speculators eventually close their positions with offsetting trades. Spot and futures market prices that move too far out of line do encourage some traders to make or take delivery, however. Indeed, the threat of such arbitraging activity generally drives spot and near-delivery futures prices together.

Since most commodities can be traded with margins (earnest money) of from 5% to 15% of the contract's value, even a small change in their price can produce a very substantial profit or loss. Margin percentages are generally set just high enough to limit default-risk.[3]

The Growth of Commodity Trading

Though organized futures trading is almost as old as organized securities trading, the latter's size and scope has seemed to dwarf the former. Only a small fraction of those who own stocks and bonds have ever traded commodities. Various factors have, however, contributed to commodity trading's recent growth. As investors sought alternatives to the generally depressed stock market of the 1970s and early 1980s, many commodity prices rose dramatically with inflation. Moreover, the commodity exchanges have devised a variety of intriguing new futures contracts. As a result, commodity trading has grown at a time when stockholder numbers have declined. The value of a Chicago Board of Trade (the largest commodity exchange) seat (membership) generally exceeds that for the New York Stock Exchange by a wide margin.

Commodity Trading is not Popular with Everyone

While some politicians blame commodity speculators for the high cost of food and other raw materials, most economists believe that commodity trading has little or no long-run price effect. Large speculators can temporarily drive up any commodity's price by absorbing enough of the available supply, but they almost always eventually sell exactly as much as they buy. Thus speculators rarely, if ever, affect a commodity's long-run scarcity. Indeed, some argue that speculators' efforts are more likely to be stabilizing than destablizing.[4] Those rare commodity traders who do take delivery of a substantial amount of the physical commodity often get hurt more than they hurt others (the Hunts). Efforts to "corner" a market almost never succeed in the long-run. Commodities trading does serve a number of useful functions, such as facilitating hedging, providing a mechanism for allocating supplies over time, and generating information on future price expectations.[5]

The Different Types of Commodities

Listed futures contracts exist for three basic classes of delivery vehicles: agricultural, mineral, and financial commodities. The principal foods include cattle, hogs, chickens, wheat, oats, corn, soybeans, barley, sugar, potatoes, coffee, and cocoa. The commodity exchanges also trade non-food agricultural items such as lumber, plywood, cotton, and wool. The minerals traded on futures exchanges include heating oil, copper, zinc, gold, silver, platinum, tin, and lead. Such financial futures as those for Treasury bills, long-term government bonds, CDs, GNMA passthroughs, several stock market indexes, and various currencies have grown increasingly popular in the past few years. The prices of all these items are quite volatile, reflecting their underlying supply and demand variability. While no legal or theoretical barriers prevent futures trading in rhubarb or peppermint, interest would probably be insufficient to justify such listings. Commodity exchanges do, however, frequently try to establish futures trading in new commodities.[6] For example, contracts for turkeys, shrimp, apples, and diamonds were tried and failed, while live cattle, pork bellies, lumber, plywood, heating oil, and a number of financial futures have been more successful. Many other items such as steel girders, pig iron, scrap aluminum, returnable drink bottles, uranium, milk, butter, coal, cement, cinder blocks, farmland, apartments, shopping centers, tulip bulbs, sulfur, and nails might or might not support futures trading. Predicting which futures contracts will succeed is quite difficult. Successful contracts have, however, generally possessed most of the following characteristics: (1) a relatively competitive spot-market; (2) a meaningful standardized contract; (3) storability or its equivalence (a call on production); and (4) sufficient price volatility to attract speculative and hedging interest.

Differences Between Commodities and Securities Markets

The commodities and securities markets differ in a number of important respects.

Table 19.1 Commodities versus Stocks

Commodities	Stocks
limited term	unlimited term
maximum daily price moves	no limit on daily price moves
delivery possible	never becomes spot
margins of 5% to 15%	margins of 50% or more
long-interest = short-interest	short-interest is usually only a small fraction of long-interest
no short-restrictions	short-sales must not be on a downtick
no interest charged on unpaid margin	margin debt incurs interest
no specialist system	market making by specialists
commission discounts on special types of trades	no commission discounts for discounts for special trades
positions must be opened and closed with same brokerage firm	positions may be opened and closed with different firms

Since futures terms rarely exceed 18 to 24 months, long-term commodities investment is restricted to those willing to take possession and pay storage. Futures have maximum daily trading limits that prevent prices from moving up or down by more than a set amount. The inability to trade once the price has reached its daily limit may delay timely coverage of an exposed position. Holding near-delivery futures positions risks having to make or take delivery. Margins are much lower on commodities than on securities; 15% or less is common. Security market short-selling restrictions (must not be on a downtick) do not apply to the commodities market. Short-interest in securities is usually a small fraction of long-interest, while commodity short and long positions are numerically equal. Unpaid commodity margin balances do not incur interest, as actual payment only takes place at delivery. The futures market has no specialist system. Certain types of commodity transactions receive commission discounts, but no similar discounts apply to securities transactions. Commodity and option positions must be closed with the brokerage firm that handled the initial transaction. Stocks and bonds may, in contrast, use different brokerage firms to buy and sell. Table 19.1 summarizes these differences.

Commodity Quotations

Commodity quotations (Figure 19.1) are no more difficult to read than those for stocks and bonds. Each commodity's heading (e.g. Corn (CBT)—5000 bu.; cents per bu.) contains the name of product on which the contract is written; an abbreviation of the listing-exchange; a single contract's size and pricing units. Each individual quotation lists the months in which contracts become due, followed by that day's opening, high, low, and settlement prices, along with the change from the previous day's settle. The remaining three columns contain the lifetime highs and lows plus each listing's number of outstanding contracts (open interest). Total daily volume is also included under the price quotation. As an example, consider the coffee quotations. Coffee is traded on Coffee, Cocoa, and Sugar exchange (CCSE) contracts of 37,500 lbs. Its price is quoted in cents per pound. Contracts expire five times a year: September, December, March, May, and July, with contracts running up to about fourteen months out. On June 12, 1984, the July 1984 contract opened at 146.25¢ per lb.; reached a high of 147.10, a low of 145.26, and closed at 146.63. This represented a change of .10 from the previous close. This contract has traded as high as 158.42 and as low as 106.25. As of this quote (open interest), 2,649 July 1984 contacts were outstanding.

The Different Types of Commodity Traders

Many different types of professional commodity traders play distinct roles in the market. Large firms in commodity-related industries (mining, baking, meat packing, grain, etc.) often maintain traders on the relevant exchanges to provide a future supply or market for their product. These professionals' access to and understanding of the latest crop estimates, cost comparisons, weather reports, information on possible government policy changes, and other useful data gives them a decided advantage. Other classes of professional traders include scalpers, day traders, position traders, and arbitragers. Like stock exchange floor traders and specialists, these traders usually have seats on the exchange and trade for their own accounts. Scalpers seek to buy at slightly below or sell at slightly above the previous price, hoping to close out at a modest profit. Scalpers are not expected to make a market, but their activity does help keep trading more orderly.

Figure 19.1 Typical Commodity Quotation

Futures Prices

Tuesday, June 12, 1984
Open Interest Reflects Previous Trading Day.

—GRAINS AND OILSEEDS—

	Open	High	Low	Settle	Change	Lifetime High	Lifetime Low	Open Interest
CORN (CBT) 5,000 bu.; cents per bu.								
July	347¾	348¼	344¾	346¼	− 2½	388	286¼	69,658
Sept	321	322	318¾	319¾	− 1¼	356½	295½	28,144
Dec	300	300¾	298¾	299	+ ½	330	279¾	44,163
Mar85	310	310¾	308¾	309	....	319	289¾	7,833
May	315	315½	313¾	313¾	− ¼	322	295½	1,556
July	317½	317½	316¾	316¾	....	323¼	307½	560
Sept	309½	309½	309	309	....	315	307	14
Est vol 32,800; vol Mon 34,416; open int 151,928, −3,263.								
CORN (MCE) 1,000 bu.; cents per bu.								
July	347¾	348	345	346¼	− 2½	388⅛	288½	4,582
Sept	320	321¼	319⅝	319¾	− 1¼	355	298½	1,060
Dec	299¾	300½	398⅞	299	+ ½	330	281¼	5,685
Mar85	310	310	308⅞	309	....	319	292¼	325
May	315	315	315	313¾	− ¼	321	292	52
July	317¼	317¼	317¼	316¾	....	323¼	309¾	24
Sept	....	....	....	309	....	308½	308½	2
Est vol 850; vol Mon 977; open int 11,730, −109.								
OATS (CBT) 5,000 bu.; cents per bu.								
July	182½	183	180	182¼	+ ½	226	166¼	1,808
Sept	179	179½	178	178¾	+ ¼	219	164¾	1,100
Dec	181	181½	180¾	181½	+ ¾	193¼	168½	953
Mar85	185¼	185½	185	185½	+ ½	196½	181¾	288
May	186½	186½	186½	186½	+ ½	191	186	2
Est vol 550; vol Mon 547; open int 4,151, +40.								
SOYBEANS (CBT) 5,000 bu.; cents per bu.								
July	785	794	779½	785¼	− ¾	992½	639½	40,963
Aug	786	792	777½	783	− 1	956¾	630	19,841
Sept	745	749	739	739½	− 5½	860	705½	9,571
Nov	715	717	705	705½	− 7	772¼	661	24,203
Jan85	727	729	717½	717¾	− 8¼	765½	676	5,722
Mar	738	740	730	730½	− 7½	776	692	1,825
May	750	750	740½	740½	− 7½	784	729½	639
July	751	755	745½	745½	− 7½	784	742	110
Est vol 52,700; vol Mon 69,726; open int 102,874, −2,520.								
SOYBEANS (MCE) 1,000 bu.; cents per bu.								
July	787	794½	780	785¼	− ¾	992½	645	10,628
Aug	784	792	778	783	− 1	955	646	2,600
Sept	746	749	739	739½	− 5½	853	708	607
Nov	716	717	706	705½	− 7	772¼	661	4,159
Jan85	723½	727½	719	717¾	− 8¼	766	678	745
Mar	739	739	729½	730½	− 7½	776	722	385
May	747	747	746	740½	− 7½	783	733	131
July	....	....	....	745½	− 7½	777	748	32
Est vol 6,400; vol Mon 13,006; open int 19,287, −351.								
SOYBEAN MEAL (CBT) 100 tons; $ per ton.								
July	185.50	185.50	182.40	182.70	− 1.80	267.50	180.50	20,938
Aug	187.50	188.00	185.20	185.70	− 1.70	241.00	183.30	12,360
Sept	188.50	189.00	185.50	186.00	− 1.70	243.00	184.40	6,954
Oct	181.00	181.50	177.10	177.30	− 3.20	240.00	177.10	9,294
Dec	184.00	184.00	179.50	180.10	− 3.10	227.00	179.50	14,000
Jan85	186.00	186.00	182.00	182.00	− 3.00	208.00	182.00	2,661
Mar	188.00	188.50	185.00	185.00	− 3.00	209.00	185.00	804
May	191.00	191.00	189.00	189.00	− 1.50	205.00	189.00	78
Est vol 13,500; vol Mon 23,011; open int 67,089, −336..								
SOYBEAN OIL (CBT) 60,000 lbs.; cents per lb.								
July	33.60	34.46	33.40	33.97	+ .49	39.75	20.00	20,395
Aug	33.00	33.70	32.75	33.32	+ .53	38.45	20.30	12,739
Sept	31.60	32.25	31.31	31.94	+ .43	36.15	23.45	6,890
Oct	29.55	30.15	29.31	29.80	+ .33	33.05	23.50	9,615
Dec	28.45	28.85	28.20	28.60	+ .27	30.90	23.45	8,867
Jan84	28.20	28.60	28.10	28.35	+ .27	30.25	24.05	2,166
Mar	28.00	28.50	28.00	28.00	− .26	30.25	25.25	845
May	....	....	....	28.03	+ .25	29.90	27.50	7
July	....	....	....	28.02	+ .24	30.25	29.50	0
Est vol 21,000; vol Mon 23,511; open int 61,524, +883.								
WHEAT (CBT) 5,000 bu.; cents per bu.								
July	357	358	354	354½	− ¾	427	322	20,245
Sept	363	363¼	360	360½	− 1	432	325	12,052
Dec	377½	378½	375	375½	− ½	418	337½	13,310
Mar85	387½	388¼	385¼	385½	− ¾	404	344	3,234
May	390	390	387¾	387¾	− 1¼	405	367¼	169
July	374	374	371½	371½	− 1	390	371½	83
Est vol 14,700; vol Mon 10,049; open int 49,093, +75.								

—FOOD & FIBER—

	Open	High	Low	Settle	Change	Lifetime High	Lifetime Low	Open Interest
COCOA (CSCE) —10 metric tons; $ per ton.								
July	2,410	2,414	2,383	2,406	+ 35	2,755	1,894	4,877
Sept	2,438	2,459	2,422	2,454	+ 44	-2,747	1,987	9,353
Dec	2,350	2,370	2,339	2,363	+ 42	2,680	2,040	5,872
Mar85	2,330	2,335	2,320	2,342	+ 42	2,570	2,090	3,301
May	....	....	....	2,362	+ 42	2,570	2,275	535
July	....	....	....	2,382	+ 42	2,400	2,400	129
Sept	....	....	....	2,402	+ 42	....	....	3
Est vol 3,846; vol Mon 6,413; open int 24,070, −495.								
COFFEE (CSCE) —37,500 lbs.; cents per lb.								
July	146.25	147.10	145.26	146.63	− .10	158.42	106.25	2,649
Sept	145.75	145.75	144.75	144.95	− 1.22	155.87	110.50	3,965
Dec	145.25	145.49	144.65	144.90	− 1.10	154.50	116.40	1,919
Mar85	144.00	144.25	143.65	143.65	− 1.23	153.50	123.50	1,172
May	....	....	....	142.93	+ .82	152.00	122.01	307
July	....	....	....	142.38	− .12	149.20	121.00	112
Sept	....	....	....	140.50	− .75	147.50	127.00	36
Est vol 1,325; vol Mon 1,207; open int 10,160, +96.								
SUGAR—WORLD (CSCE) —112,000 lbs.; cents per lb.								
July	5.71	5.72	5.52	5.53	− .20	14.95	5.48	25,178
Sept	5.96	5.98	5.79	5.79	− .21	14.93	5.79	4,007
Oct	6.20	6.23	6.06	6.07	− .16	15.30	6.03	44,646
Jan85	6.80	6.80	6.68	6.65	− .17	13.10	6.60	561
Mar	7.36	7.38	7.22	7.23	− .15	13.60	7.19	13,044
May	7.63	7.65	7.51	7.52	− .14	10.50	7.51	4,169
July	7.95	7.95	7.81	7.82	− .12	9.95	7.81	1,961
Sept	8.20	8.20	8.20	8.05	− .18	9.75	8.10	84
Oct	8.43	8.43	8.35	8.33	− .12	9.05	8.30	640
Est vol 12,865; vol Mon 7,442; open int 94,290, −257.								
SUGAR—DOMESTIC (CSCE) —112,000 lbs.; cents per lb.								
Sept	22.10	22.11	22.10	22.11	....	22.58	21.50	2,549
Nov	21.80	21.81	21.80	21.81	+ .01	2.19	21.65	2,096
Jan85	....	....	....	21.80	....	22.20	21.66	521
Mar	21.85	21.87	21.85	21.86	+ .01	22.30	21.70	2,240
May	21.95	21.95	21.95	21.95	....	22.40	21.75	1,118
July	....	....	....	22.03	....	22.43	21.90	627
Est vol 195; vol Mon 362; open int 9,151, −362.								

—METALS & PETROLEUM—

	Open	High	Low	Settle	Change	Lifetime High	Lifetime Low	Open Interest
COPPER (CMX) —25,000 lbs.; cents per lb.								
June	61.00	61.20	61.00	60.90	− .10	72.10	61.00	6
July	61.45	61.75	60.60	61.30	− .15	89.80	60.60	31,225
Aug	....	....	....	62.00	− .15	....	....	0
Sept	62.80	63.15	62.00	62.65	− .15	90.80	62.00	24,735
Dec	64.95	65.25	64.05	64.75	− .15	92.70	64.05	16,678
Jan85	65.60	65.80	65.25	65.45	− .15	92.00	65.25	257
Mar	67.10	67.30	66.15	66.85	− .15	93.20	66.15	7,938
May	68.45	68.65	67.50	68.25	− .15	92.50	67.50	4,487
July	70.00	70.00	69.25	69.65	− .10	88.25	69.25	2,457
Sept	71.20	71.20	70.75	71.05	− .10	82.10	70.75	1,003
Dec	73.80	73.80	72.85	73.20	− .10	84.25	72.85	1,460
Jan86	74.35	74.35	74.35	73.95	− .10	84.20	70.00	66
Mar	75.55	75.80	75.00	75.40	− .10	80.00	75.00	562
Est vol 13,000; vol Mon 17,165; open int 90,874, −1,109.								
GOLD (CMX) —100 troy oz.; $ per troy oz.								
June	374.80	375.70	372.00	374.40	+ 1.10	580.00	370.00	853

Source: *Wall Street Journal.* Reprinted by permission of *Wall Street Journal,* © Dow Jones & Company, Inc., 1984. All Rights Reserved.

Day traders, who usually close their positions by the end of each day, trade somewhat less frequently than scalpers and also hope to profit from modest price moves. Unlike scalpers and day traders, position traders seek to profit from fundamental or technical forces that may manifest themselves over several days. Finally, arbitragers try to exploit relative prices that vary from expected relationships. Table 19.2 summarizes these types.

Table 19.2 Professional Commodity Traders

Firm Representatives	Hedge needs or outputs of commodity-related firms
Scalpers	Seek to take advantage of very short-run imbalances in supply and demand
Day-trader's	Short-run traders who close their positions each day
Position-traders	May hold positions for several days based on fundamental or technical factors
Arbitragers	Seek to exploit departures from expected relative price relationships

Disadvantages of Commodity Trading for Amateurs

Compared with amateurs, professional traders have better access to relevant information, lower cost trading, and/or quicker executions.[7] Incurring a significant disadvantage relative to a large part of the market should discourage most small investors. Moreover, the number of listed commodities is much smaller than the number of actively traded stocks. Thus each commodity receives proportionately more attention, thereby increasing the difficulty of finding misvalued contracts. In addition, unlike the securities market, each futures contract has equal numbers of shorts and longs. If the price declines, the shorts gain what the longs lose and vice versa. If the professionals make money on balance, the amateurs must lose. Furthermore, both losers and winners must pay commissions. One very out-of-date study of grain trading over the 1924–32 period, sponsored by the Commodity Exchange Authority (CEA), suggested that professionals outperformed the rest of the market.[8]

Hedge-Trading Results

Since hedging is akin to purchasing insurance, one might well expect that those who facilitate hedge trading (speculators) would generally earn a risk premium. Identifying risk takers and hedgers from aggregated data is relatively difficult. Hypothesizing that most hedgers are short and most speculators are long, Dusak found overall returns of long hedgers in wheat, corn, and soybeans very close to zero, and largely uncorrelated with other investment returns for the 1952–67 period. These results suggest that at least for the three commodities tested, returns from long positions were small. The contracts did, however, appear to offer substantial diversifying value.[9]

Rockwell's earlier and considerably broader study of 25 markets over an 18-year period reached the following conclusions:[10]

1. Small traders lost slightly more on short positions than they made on long positions.
2. Large speculators profited at the expense of hedgers with the greatest profits made in large active markets.
3. Hedgers tended to do well in low-volume markets; the profits of large speculators in high-volume markets comes mainly from the small speculator.

Thus professionals may well profit at the expense of small traders and speculators do not seem to receive a risk premium for their risk taking. In other words, would-be commodity traders appear to face a very difficult market.

LARGE TRADES AND BIG TRADERS

In addition to the aforementioned difficulties, large traders can disrupt the markets, thereby hurting many small speculators. To be on the same side and helped is, of course, equally possible. Commodity markets are only infrequently dominated by any single trader or small group of traders, but large traders pose very real risks.

The Russian Wheat Deal

The best known and most massive of the disruptive large trades involved the Russians. In the early 1970s, poor weather and an unsuccessful harvest created a major Soviet grain shortage. Apparently unaware of the severity of their problem, the Nixon administration allowed the Soviets to purchase massive quantities of U.S. wheat and corn. The Russians negotiated shrewdly, separately, and secretly with several of the nation's largest grain dealers. Each dealer, thinking it was the primary Soviet agent, hedged its Russian orders with futures contracts. Their strategy allowed the Soviets to accumulate their entire needs before the price ran up very much. Thus massive Russian purchases not only wiped out our long-held grain surpluses, but once its full dimensions were known, threatened to create a severe wheat shortage. Bread prices did not reach the feared dollar-a-loaf level, but the wheat price did trade in a range not seen before or since. Those who were short wheat while this trade unfolded were substantial losers.

The Russian wheat deal is now ancient history. Rumors of a new buying spree by the Russians, Arabs, or perhaps the Chinese still sweep the exchange floors from time to time, however. Only super large traders have much impact on the grain markets. In other markets, smaller but still large traders can also have an impact. The great potato scandal of 1976 involved just such a market.

The Great Potato Default

Although most potatoes are grown in Idaho and nearby states, futures trading is largely in Maine potato delivery contracts. Since the two types of potatoes compete for the same markets, the New York Mercantile Exchange's Maine potato contract should provide an acceptable vehicle for hedging either type.[11] Most

Maine potatoes are grown by relatively small individually motivated farmers. Idaho's, in contrast, are dominated by the potato baron J.R. Simplot. In the mid-1970s, Simplot and Taggares (another large factor in the Western potato market) thought that the abundant supply of Idahos would cause the Maine potato price to fall by the time the May 1976 futures contracts became deliverable. Simplot and Taggares ultimately undertook an obligation to deliver 50 million pounds of Maine potatoes. In a competitive market, their abundant stocks of Idahos should have depressed the futures price sufficiently to allow them to close their positions profitably prior to delivery. They had not, however, counted on the short-squeeze that soon ensued. Some of the longs, knowing of the large open-interest (numbers of outstanding contracts) in near-delivery contracts, tied up most of the supply of Maine potatoes. By purchasing some potatoes for cash and stranding other stockpiles by renting the available boxcars, these longs prevented Simplot and Taggares from delivering enough potatoes to satisfy their short-positions. These longs hoped to force the shorts to bid up the price. Rather than be bullied, Simplot and Taggares chose to default. The shorts were sued for not fulfilling their contracts. The longs were charged with attempting to corner the market. The exchange and the defaulting-customers' brokers were each accused of improper surveillance. The Commodity Futures Trading Commission (CFTC) investigated and complained but was itself criticized for allowing the default to develop. The courts took years to sort this matter out. When all was said and done no one emerged a winner.[12]

The Hunts: Silver I

While Simplot and Taggares are big men in Idahos, they are small potatoes compared to the Hunts. H.L. Hunt, the father of a rather large clan, made quite a lot of money in oil and various other ventures. He supported a number of right-of-center causes, and his family had a major role in establishing the American Football League. H.L. Hunt died several years ago; his family, particularly his older sons, have carried on in the best Dallas wheeler-dealer tradition. Their substantial resources gave the Hunts an apparent advantage in commodity trading. Among their hobbies are commodities beginning with "S". The Hunts began with silver futures. Convinced that the metal was underpriced, Nelson Bunker Hunt and his brothers Herbert and Lamar purchased millions of ounces of futures contracts which bid up the price. Rumors of large unknown silver buyers propelled the price to still higher levels. Once the shorts compared the Hunt-held silver contracts with the amount of qualified physical silver available, they became very nervous. While silver was plentiful, relatively little of the metal was refined to the proper purity, inspected and deposited in the appropriate warehouses. The Hunts liquidated their positions by selling some of their contracts at the higher prices then obtaining, taking delivery on some contracts and rolling others forward by selling near-delivery futures and replacing them with more distant-delivery contracts. They made a killing in their first silver venture (but not the second time around as we shall soon see).

The Hunts: Sugar

After their silver coup the Hunt brothers seemed to stumble onto sugar. A stockbroker friend put them into a small (one million dollar) investment in Great Western United (the nation's largest beet-sugar refiner) at just about the time sugar futures were moving from under 10¢ per pound to over 60¢. Finding the company in a state of disarray, the Hunts had no choice but to buy everyone else out. They next acquired a cane sugar refining capability and negotiated agreements with cane sugar producing countries to swap silver for unrefined cane. Then (after a big court battle) Great Western United acquired a large interest in the Sunshine Mining company, a major silver producer. Later they recapitalized Great Western United, renamed it Hunt International Resources and sold its interest in Sunshine Mining for a handsome profit.

The Hunts: Soybeans

With Silver, Sugar and Sunshine Mining already tapped, what commodity is left but Soybeans? When their experts predicted a protein shortage (beans are very high in protein), they began their purchases. No unhedged trader or group of traders is permitted to hold more than three million bushels of bean contracts. The Hunts argued that each family member could buy contracts on three million bushels, however. Eventually the family owned contracts on twenty-four million bushels. Since the Hunt contracts amounted to a substantial fraction of the amount left until the next harvest (the carryout), they were positioned to create an artificial shortage. Taking a dim view of this prospect, the CFTC tried to force the Hunts to sell. Claiming that each Hunt acted individually, they refused to unload. The CFTC revealed the Hunt's trading positions, thereby increasing bean price volatility. The Hunts and CFTC each brought separate suits alleging the other attempted to manipulate prices. While different-level courts issued various opinions, the matter was left at a draw. The Hunts were told not to do it again but were assessed no penalties. Apparently the Hunts left the bean pits a bit richer than when they entered.

While the Hunts were sure that beans would rise, senior traders at Cook Industries (until then a major commodity trading firm) were equally certain that beans were overpriced. Trading largely against the Hunts', Cook Industries assumed a substantial short position in beans. Losses resulting from persistent high prices eventually forced the firm to liquidate much of its assets. Ironically, soon after Cook covered its short positions, bean prices dropped below the level at which the Hunts began their buying. The Hunts, who were wrong on price-direction but right on timing, made money. Cook was right on price fundamentals but wrong on timing, and thus lost its shirt.[13]

The Hunts: Silver II

The latest and most publicized of the Hunts' commodity deals involved a second round with silver.[14] Believing that the sky was the limit, they bought large quantities of silver futures contracts in 1979 and into 1980. A group of Arab investors were brought into the Hunt's deal. As prices went up, they used the group's paper profits to support additional purchases. Silver ultimately rose from around $8 per ounce to over $50, causing many individuals to sell their silverware for its bullion content. This time the Hunts overreached themselves. Eventually both the CFTC and the commodity exchanges became alarmed. Very high margin percentages were established, and the Hunts were ordered to begin liquidating their positions. The subsequent silver price decline, coupled with the illiquidity of the vast majority of the Hunt's assets, made their situation precarious. The entire financial market briefly panicked on the rumor that the Hunt empire was about to collapse. Soon, however, a one-billion-dollar bank loan was arranged, collateralized by the Hunt-owned Placid Oil. The Hunts agreed not to speculate in commodities for ten years and were expected to begin selling their still substantial silver holdings. As of this writing (1984), however, they still held most of the silver and its price fell as low as $5 per ounce before rebounding somewhat. This deal caused Bunker (whose losses seemed astronomical) to quip that "a billion dollars just doesn't go as far as it used to."

The possibility of events such as these adds to the risk of commodity trading. Those who sleep with elephants, even very nice elephants, are bound to get squashed from time to time. The risks are equally great for those who trade in elephant pits.

TECHNICAL ANALYSIS APPLIED TO COMMODITIES

Chart reading is, if anything, more prevalent in commodity trading than in stocks. Given the short-term nature of futures contracts, coupled with the great difficulty of successfully applying fundamental analysis, traders not surprisingly seek out other approaches. Indeed some have gone so far as to program computers to perform technical analysis.[15]

The same *a priori* arguments against effective technical stock analysis apply to futures. If the charts provide useful signals, traders who act on the signals should affect their future usefulness. Even if nonrandom price movements are more common in commodities than securities markets, commissions and other trading costs may prevent their successful exploitation. Empirical work in the area is mixed. Some studies found dependencies while other work found none.[16]

FUNDAMENTAL ANALYSIS APPLIED TO COMMODITIES

Fundamental analysts evaluate changes in relevant underlying factors and equilibrium relationships. Such analysts may consider anything that affects the commodity's supply or demand including the weather, input costs, the price of related goods, the potential actions of national and international organizations, and the price relationships among different commodities.

An Example of Fundamental Analysis Applied to Commodities

Harlow and Teweles attempted to predict soybean prices by analyzing the relevant supply and demand.[17] They used exported and crushed soybeans as a measure of demand and stocks in position as supply. Their findings are represented in Figure 19.2. The ratio of supply to demand is taken as the explanatory variable (x), and the difference between the market price and the previous government-guaranteed price as the variable to be explained (y). The relationship between

Figure 19.2   Soybeans Supply (Stocks in All Positions, January 1) and Demand [October–December Crush Plus Exports (X)] Versus Price Highs (Y) in March–July for July Soybeans, 1952–1972

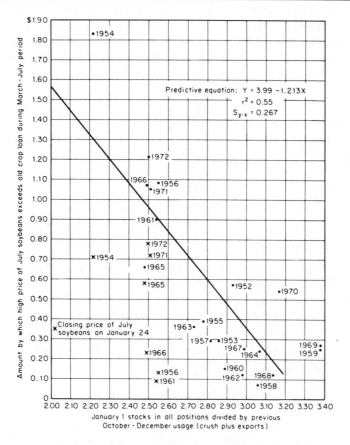

Source: R. Teweles, C. Harlow, and H. Stone, *The Commodities Futures Game.* Copyright 1974 by McGraw-Hill, Inc. Reprinted by permission of McGraw-Hill Book Company.

these two variables is estimated by regression analysis.

The authors calculated the possible gains from using an x of less than 2.60 as a buy signal. Seven of the twenty-one years studied had x values below 2.60. Long positions on January 24 (the first date on which one has enough information to make a decision) had at least a 95% chance of showing a profit. The model's profitability was tested with the same data that were used to form the relationship, however. A more convincing test using new data would be an interesting exercise for the reader.

Crop and Weather Forecasts

Agricultural products are the delivery instrument for many of the actively traded commodities including both old-line contracts on corn, wheat, and beans and some of the newer commodities such as live cattle and pork bellies. Accordingly, a solid understanding of crops, crop forecasts, the weather, and weather forecasts may help one trade such commodities.[18] While knowing what is generally known imparts no advantage, knowing less can be a substantial disadvantage. Only those who obtain the information early (unlikely and probably illegal) or analyze it in a superior manner (quite difficult at best) are likely to use crop and weather forecasts profitably.

The Basis, Basis Risk, and the Carry

While the possibility of delivery keeps futures and spot prices reasonably close, the difference or basis is usually nonzero and can vary over time. For example: on June 12, 1984, Corn (No. 2 yellow deliverable in Chicago) traded in the spot market for $3.42 1/2 per bushel. On the Chicago Board of Trade, July delivery contracts traded for $3.46 1/4 per bushel. Thus the futures contract traded at a 3 3/4¢ per bushel basis to the spot price. The risk of an adverse relative-price move is called basis risk. Suppose one is long spot corn and sells a futures contract for July delivery at the above prices. If basis narrows as delivery approaches, this hedged position will tend to show a profit regardless of the overall direction of prices. The basis has moved in a favorable direction. For the other side of the contract, the basis risk has been adverse. The size of the basis usually varies with the distance to delivery. Indeed, with agricultural commodities, the pattern made by the constellation of futures prices will vary with the product's current and expected future availability vis a vis current stocks and expected future harvests. This variation tends to reflect the cost of storage (the carry). In the above example, spot corn sold for about 4¢ less than contracts calling for delivery a month later. On a 3.43¢ bushel, this represents about 1.2%, which is probably not too far from one month's financing and storage cost (the carry). Since carrying a commodity in inventory has a cost, the price usually rises as the distance to delivery is increased. The market is, however, sometimes inverted (the price is lower for more distant deliveries) when supplies are short prior to a new harvest.

Combination Trades

An appreciable portion of commodity trading involves combination positions on similar futures contracts. Just as options are often "spread," commodity contracts can be used in hedged positions. One might, for example, buy a delivery month whose price is expected to rise relative to a short position in another delivery month. Such spreads avoid the risk of an adverse move in the constellation of commodity prices. Spreads may also involve different exchanges trading futures contracts on similar physicals. For example one might spread between Chicago and Kansas City wheat and indeed that of the Minneapolis Board of Trade as well.

Crushes and reverse crushes are relatively common types of combination trades. Most of the soybean crop is processed into soybean oil and meal. A given quantity of beans can be crushed into a predictable quantity of oil and meal at a known cost in a relatively short period.[19] A bean trader could actually purchase the beans, crush them, and sell the oil and meal. In futures terminology, a crush is a trade in which one buys bean futures and shorts equivalent amounts of their derivative products. Market forces are expected (although not necessarily depended upon) to drive them back into line with the technological and physical relationships. While the oil and the meal cannot be turned back into beans, market forces should also operate to restore the historical equilibrium when the beans are overpriced relative to their derivative products. A similar type of relationship, called a crack, exists between crude oil and gasoline and heating oil, all of which now have futures contracts.

Combination trades sometimes involve even more distantly related commodities. Since corn and wheat can both be used as feed grains, the prices of the two commodities should influence each other. Why feed corn to the cattle when wheat is cheaper? Or so the reasoning goes.

Combination Trade Recommendations

Two combination trades (a reverse crush and corn/wheat trade) recommended by Stanley Angrist, Forbes commodity columnist, were examined.[20] The investor was assumed to have entered the trades shortly after the Angrist recommendation and covered them near expiration. Angrist advised closing any position once its prices began to move adversely; the results reported below assume one stuck by the original recommendation through thick and thin (perhaps hoping against hope that all would eventually work out).

For the so-called relatively riskless corn-wheat trade, one could have bought the wheat contract in the 2.65 1/2 to 2.66 range and sold it at 2.73 1/2, for a gain of 7 3/4¢ per bushel. The corn contract would have been shorted at 2.49 to 2.48 1/2 and covered at 2.55 to 2.54 1/2, for a loss of 3 1/2¢. The net gain (ignoring commissions) would have equalled 4 1/2¢ per bushel.

As for the reverse crush, one would have paid 141.00 and 18.44 and received 5.23 to 5.22 for meal, oil, and beans respectively. Covering would have been at

149.40, 19.95, and 5.56 3/4 to 5.57, producing a net loss of 24.39¢ per bushel (plus commissions). Thus the reverse crush would have involved per-bushel losses of several times the gain on the "riskless trade." Clearly commodity spreads are not guaranteed to make money.

Commodity Analysts

Though fundamental commodity analysis is difficult to apply successfully, perhaps those who are paid to advise commodity traders generally recommend worthwhile trades. To shed some light on this issue, one of the present author's graduate students tested a series of Angrist recommendations, finding that one who followed them would have lost money. After receiving a copy of the term paper, Angrist discussed his performance in his column. According to Angrist, about half of his recommendations over the period studied by the student were profitable but the total profits outweighed the losses.[21] He followed this up with further tests of his recommendations. For the last half of 1977, he reported that his recommended trades approximately broke even. Of course many other commodity analysts' advice may work out better (or worse)[22] than Angrist's did for 1977. In 1979, for example, Angrist asserted that "traders who followed every recommendation had nothing to complain about, as once again I caught hold of a couple of nice winners that more than made up for the dogs."[23]

Diversification with Commodities

Since commodity price volatility (relative to the margin deposit) seems to be largely unrelated to fluctuations in other markets,[24] futures might serve as a useful diversification vehicle. Such diversification is, however, likely to be accompanied by a major increase in nonmarket risk. Thus commodities are probably not an ideal vehicle for diversifying portfolios of other types of investments.

SPECIALIZED COMMODITY MARKETS

Commodity futures have long been traded on agricultural and mineral physicals. The new types of commodity contracts have accounted for much of the market's growth, however. In particular, interest rate, currency, and, more recently, stock market futures have grabbed the spotlight. While as yet still minor factors, commodity options and commodity mutual funds also have substantial potentials. A variety of commodity-related investments also deserve mention.

Interest Rate Futures

Money lending has gone on about as long as trading in such futures-related items as wheat and gold, but no one gave much thought to a debt instruments futures market until the early 1970s. Many individuals and institutions do, however, have a stake in and/or opinion on the future level of interest rates. Just as similar circumstances have long fostered futures trading in other commodities, interest rate futures trading looked like a good bet.

Beginning with the Chicago Board of Trade's GNMA futures contracts and the Chicago Mercantile Exchange's T-bill contract, the market subsequently expanded to include long-term governments, CDs, and Eurodollars, with still more contracts promised eventually. Like all futures contracts, interest rate futures call for delivery of a specific amount of the relevant commodity at the contract's expiration. For example: the GNMA contract specifies the delivery of $100,000 face amount of 8% GNMA passthroughs. Price fluctuations in the contract reflect variations in the expected GNMA interest rate. Institutions who plan to borrow at some later time can use this market to hedge against adverse interest rate moves. Financial institutions with future sums to invest may use the market to establish the rate that they will earn on the investment. Those whose expectations differ from the market may speculate in interest rate futures.

Interest Futures Examples

Mortgage bankers can use the interest futures markets to hedge their expected mortgage production. Suppose that on June 1, such a banker expects to originate $10,000,000 in mortgages during the next quarter based on the FNMA market, which is then at 99-24 (99 and 24/32 which corresponds to a 7.989% yield). To hedge the expected mortgage originations, the banker can sell 100 GNMA December contracts at 99-00 (a yield of 8.092%). One possible result (ignoring transaction costs) from the hedge is illustrated below:

Hedging Expected Mortgage Production

Cash market	Futures market
June 1	June 1
Commits to originate $10 million of loans based on current FNMA price of 99-24 (yield of 7.989%)	Sells 100 December contracts at prevailing market price of 99-00 (yield of 8.092%)
September 15	September 15
Sells $10 million of Ginnie Mae 8s to permanent investors at market of 92-24 (current yield 8.992%)	Buys 100 December contracts at prevailing market price of 92-00 (yield of 9.105%)
loss of $700,000	gain of $700,000

The mortgage banker's position was protected. The loss in the cash market caused by an interest-rate rise was offset by a gain in the futures market. Had interest rates fallen, the loss in the futures market would largely have been offset by a gain in the cash market.

The above is an example of a short hedge in which the mortgage banker's expected long mortgage position was offset by a sale of futures contracts. A long hedge, in contrast, allows one who expects to be short in the future to cover that anticipated need. As an example of a long hedge, consider a money manager who buys $5 million in three-month T-bills. The manager will need to reinvest the funds at maturity. To assure a rate on the funds' rollover, he or she could buy December T-bill futures. One possible result from this hedge (again ignoring transaction costs) is illustrated below:

Hedging for the Reinvestment of Maturing T-bills

Cash Market		Futures Market	
September 15		September 15	
bought $5 million in T-bills @ 9%		Bought 5 Dec. contracts @ 9% (I.M.M. 91.00)	
Value	$4,886,250	Value	$4,887,500
December 10		December 10	
Sold over $5 million in T-bills @ 7%		Sold (offset) 5 Dec. contracts @ 7% (I.M.M. 93.00)	
Value	$4,911,528	Value	$4,912,500
loss of	$ 25,278	gain of	$ 25,000

As with the short-hedge example, the future's market profit has offset the opportunity loss in the spot-market. Had interest rates risen rather than fallen, the future's market loss would have been offset by a spot-market gain.

Stock Market Futures

The successful introduction of debt instrument futures spurred interest in equity futures. The Kansas City Board of Trade's (KBT) *Value Line* stock market index futures contract was followed by the Chicago Mercantile Exchange's (Merc) S&P 500 index and the New York Futures Exchange's (NYFE) NYSE Composite Index. The Chicago Board of Trade's (CBT) effort to list a Dow-Jones Industrial-type index was blocked (at least temporarily) by the opposition of Dow Jones Incorporated. The NYFE's NYSE financial index futures contract was the first of several specialized stock futures. The equity contracts offer a variety of new ways to speculate or hedge on the stock market's movement.[25] In particular, the contracts provide an ideal way for portfolio managers to hedge their anticipated funds needs.[26]

A Stock Index Futures Example

Suppose a large common stock portfolio manager anticipates a market decline. To liquidate and then later reinvest the portfolio would be costly (spreads, commissions, etc.). The stock index futures market provides a relatively simple way to neutralize the portfolio, however. First, the manager would determine his or her portfolio's beta and then use the following formula to determine the number of contracts to short:

$$\frac{\text{Portfolio Value}}{\text{Contract Value}} \times \frac{\text{Weight Average Beta}}{\text{of Portfolio}} = \frac{\text{Number of}}{\text{Contracts}}$$

Consider a portfolio with a weighted average beta of 1.142 and market value of $20,000,000. The S&P contract value is 500 times the S&P index value, which we shall assume is 115. Thus a contract would be worth $57,500. Accordingly:

$$\frac{20,000,000}{57,500} \times 1.142 = 397 \text{ contracts}$$

Thus selling 397 contracts should approximately neutralize the portfolio from market fluctuations. That is, 397 contracts should fluctuate proportionately with a $20,000,000 stock portfolio having an average beta of 1.142. If the portfolio's value declines, a short position in the S&P futures contracts should rise by an offsetting amount. Similarly, an increase in the portfolio's value should be offset by a fall in the futures position's value.

Commodity Options

A commodity option is an option on a futures contract. The mechanics are similar to those of puts and calls on stocks. If the underlying futures price rises sufficiently, the commodity call will also rise. A decline in the futures price will, at worst, only cost the call's purchase price. All of these relations are reversed for puts. With futures contracts, in contrast, the loss-liability may be much greater. Thus commodity options offer upside leverage and downside protection. A rather hefty premium is, however, required to induce option writers to assume the risks inherent in the contract's sell side. Moreover, listed option trading was prohibited in the U.S. in the 1930s. Accordingly, one had to seek a market outside the U.S. or trade in an over-the-counter market. In either case, up-to-date price quotes were difficult to obtain and the market was relatively imperfect. Two major commodity-option scandals occurred in the absence of an exchange market.

Commodity-Option Scams

In the early 1970s, the West Coast firm of Goldstein-Samuelson began selling over-the-counter commodity options at such attractive prices that their customer's-account values grew very rapidly. Because the options were underpriced, most "investors" made "profits," which encouraged them to purchase new options. In effect Goldstein-Samuelson was operating a Ponzi scheme. By the time the nature of the operation was exposed, losses exceeded $100,000,000.[27] This scandal slowed commodity-option trading for several years. Eventually, the industry revived by using the London options market. Most of the publicity centered around some very questionable selling tactics employed by fly-by-night commodity option firms. High-pressure telephone solicitations were employed to sell options at huge markups. Many relatively uninformed "investors" spent thousands of dollars on options that typically expired worthless. When too many option-positions showed a profit, the sellers usually disappeared.

Lloyd Carr, the largest of the new-wave commodity options houses, has an instructive history. Operating out of Boston, a man who gave his name as James Carr quickly established a thriving business. The firm maintained boiler rooms with huge banks of telephones. Salespeople were stimulated to ever higher sales by such devices as having their supervisor run down the aisles dressed in a Gorilla costume. Eventually several states began to investigate the numerous complaints and the CBS investigative reporting TV program *60 Minutes* broadcast an exposé on commodity-options firms and Lloyd Carr in particular.[28] Events moved quickly thereafter. Lloyd Carr was prohibited from doing business in several states. "Mr. Carr" was fingerprinted. The firm went bankrupt. "James Carr" was determined to be Alan Abraham, an escapee from a New Jersey prison. Mr. Abraham, who again became a fugitive, was ultimately apprehended in a Florida motel.

Goldstein-Samuelson and Lloyd Carr notwithstanding, the commodity option instrument itself has a legitimate role.[29] Indeed the commodity exchanges resumed listed commodity options trading in 1982.[30] Early commodity option listings include the Coffee, Sugar and Cocoa exchange's sugar option, the Comex's gold option, the CBT's Treasury Bond option, the Chicago Mercantile Exchange's S&P 500 option, and the NYFE's, CBOE's, and AMEX's stock index options. Both puts and calls are listed. Such trading and the increased flow of information that it generates may well reduce the abuses that have resulted from OTC commodity options trading. Figure 19.3 shows a typical futures option quotation.

Commodity Mutual Funds

Commodity funds appeal to those who are tempted to trade commodities on their own but fear their tremendous volatility. While such funds have generally been no more successful than individual commodity traders, they do diversify risk, and a few have done very well.[31]

COMMODITY-RELATED INVESTMENT AREAS

Puts, calls, convertibles, warrants, and mutual funds offer investment opportunities akin to, but different from, common stock. Similar investments are related to, but distinct from, commodity futures and options. The commodities on which futures contracts are listed also have active spot-markets that provide an alternative of sorts to futures trading. Most such spot-markets have relatively little speculative appeal, however. Leverage is greater and storage costs are avoided with a futures position in such physicals as corn, lumber, heating oil, and pork bellies. The spot-markets for precious and semi-precious metals, in contrast, offer

Figure 19.3 Typical Futures Options Quotation

Futures Options

Tuesday, June 12, 1984

Chicago Board of Trade

TREASURY BONDS–$100,000; points and 64ths of 100%

Strike Price	Calls–Last			Puts–Last		
	Sept	Dec	Mar	Sept	Dec	Mar
54	....	....	....	0-06	0-30	0-54
56	....	....	....	0-18	0-55	....
58	3-27	....	....	0-41	1-33	2-07
60	2-09	2-39	3-00	1-18	2-19	3-04
62	1-14	1-51	2-08	2-20	3-27	....
64	0-39	1-09	1-36	3-42	4-48	....
66	0-18	0-45	1-03	5-22	6-14	....
68	0-09	0-27	....	7-09	7-60	....
70	0-03	0-17	....	9-09	....	....
72	0-01	0-10	....	11-09	....	....
74	0-01	0-06	....	13-09	13-45	....
76	0-01	0-02	....	....	....	....
78	0-01	0-01	....	....	....	....
80	0-01	....	....	....	....	....

Est. total vol. 20,000
Calls: Monday vol. 8,461; open int. 164,901
Puts: Monday vol. 8,187; open int. 76,125

Comex, New York

GOLD–100 troy ounces; dollars per troy ounce.

Strike Price	Calls–Last			Puts–Last		
	Aug	Oct	Dec	Aug	Oct	Dec
340	....	....	....	.40	1.40	....
360	21.50	29.50	38.50	1.90	3.30	4.20
380	6.60	15.50	24.00	7.30	9.00	9.50
400	1.80	7.80	12.70	21.50	20.00	17.50
420	.50	3.90	7.20	41.00	34.50	30.50
440	.30	1.40	3.80	61.00	....	46.50
460	.10	....	2.40	....	....	65.00
480	.10	....	1.30	....	....	....
500	.10	....	....	....	....	....
530	.10	....	....	....	....	....

Est. total vol. 9,200
Calls: Mon vol. 5,199; open int. 46,705
Puts: Mon vol. 3,283; open int. 28,769

Chicago Mercantile Exchange

S&P 500 STOCK INDEX–Price = $500 times premium.

Strike Price	Calls–Settle			Puts–Settle		
	June	Sep	Dec	June	Sep	Dec
145	7.35	....	....	.002	.75	....
150	2.50	6.50	....	.15	1.90	2.55
155	.10	3.55	....	.25	3.80	4.25
160	.002	1.70	....	7.65	6.85	6.85
165	.002	.75	2.40	12.65	10.85	10.05
170	.002	.35	1.50	....	....	....
175	.002	.15	....	....	....	....
180	.002	.10	....	....	....	....
185	.002	....	....	....	....	....

Estimated total vol. 3,883
Calls: Mon vol. 718; open int. 15,195
Puts: Mon vol. 1,450; open int. 12,004

W. GERMAN MARK–125,000 marks, cents per mark

Strike Price	Calls–Settle		Puts–Settle	
	Sept	Dec	Sept	Dec
34	....	....	....	....
35	2.44	....	0.14	....
36	1.62	2.33	0.33	....
37	0.97	1.70	0.66	....
38	0.54	....	1.19	....
39	0.28	0.76	1.91	....
40	0.15	....	2.78	....
41	0.08	....	3.73	....
42	0.05	....	....	....

Estimated total vol. 2,731.
Calls: Mon vol. 114; open int. 13,380.
Puts: Mon vol. 376; open int. 4,830.

N.Y. Futures Exchange

NYSE Composite Index–Price = $500 times premium.

Strike Price	Calls–Settle			Puts–Settle		
	Jun	Sep	Dec	Jun	Sep	Dec
84	3.95	5.75	....	.05	.60	....
86	2.15	4.20	5.90	.25	1.05	1.50
88	.85	2.95	4.55	.95	1.80	2.15
90	.25	1.95	3.45	2.35	2.80	3.05
92	.05	1.30	2.60	4.10	4.50	4.20
94	.05	.75	1.90	6.10	5.60	5.15
96	.05	.40	1.40	8.10	7.25	7.00
98	.05	.25	.95	10.10	9.10	8.55
100	.05	.15	.65	12.10	11.00	10.25

Source: *Wall Street Journal.* Reprinted by permission of *Wall Street Journal,* © Dow Jones & Company, Inc., 1984. All Rights Reserved.

some advantages over the futures market. Storage costs are minimal and one can buy and trade them in very small quantities. Thus many investors do purchase physical (as opposed to futures contracts on) gold and other precious metals (silver, platinum, and palladium). Moreover, the absence of a futures market in strategic metals forces interested speculators to trade the physical.

Gold Bullion

After being an illegal substance for almost forty years, United States citizens were on December 31, 1974, again allowed to own gold bullion without special permission. A variety of outlets, including department stores, jewelers, banks, and brokerage houses set themselves up to sell gold. Citizens of other countries have long held gold as an inflation hedge. Some analysts also urge U.S. citizens to buy gold as a hedge against adverse economic fluctuations. While its appropriateness in investment portfolios is difficult to assess in the abstract, gold, like most other investments, does have some obvious drawbacks.[32] First, gold's price has exhibited considerable volatility. Soon after central banks stopped selling gold at $35 an ounce (the official price since the 1930s) the price rose to $200 per ounce (1974), only to fall back substantially once the U.S. market opened up. During the 1980 Afghan crisis, gold reached a high of $850 per ounce and then fell to less than half that level. Clearly the gold price can fall as easily as it rises. Second, gold yields no dividends, rents, interest, or other type of income except possible price appreciation, and that will be at least partially offset by insurance, storage, and financing costs. Third, gold's buying and selling prices can differ appreciably. Depending on the quantity purchased, one may pay as much as a 10 to 15% premium on a purchase and incur a similar discount when selling. Sales taxes may also be added to the price. Such transaction costs could easily absorb the gain from price appreciation. Fourth, fraud, counterfeiting, and short-weighing are potential problems for the unwary. Finally, investors may have to pay a fee to have their gold assayed when they try to sell.

In spite of its drawbacks, gold is often recommended to investors.[33] Thus we shall explore the various direct and indirect types of gold investing. Buying gold bullion is one way. The bullion investor should seek to minimize the markup and avoid potentially counterfeited or short-weight gold. The offering price should be compared with the price reported in the financial press (The Wall Street Journal, for example). The markup will vary both with the quantity purchased and with the seller. Weight and fineness (percentage of gold) are measured and stamped on bullion by refiners. A well-known stamp makes counterfeiting less likely and buyers more willing.

Gold Futures and Options
Gold futures are traded on the commodity exchanges; these, like any futures contract, allow one to trade on margin, go short, or hedge—options not easily accomplished through bullion ownership. On the other hand, the large risks inherent in other types of commodity trading are also present with gold futures contracts. Options on gold contracts reduce the downside risk but are costly.

Other Ways to Invest in Gold
Gold coins, gold mining stocks, and gold jewelry are all alternative ways of buying gold. Some gold coins only command a small and relatively stable premium over their bullion value. Moreover gold coins are more difficult to counterfeit and, in smaller quantities, may be marked up less than bullion. The Krugerrand, which contains exactly one ounce of gold, is designed for gold speculation. Fractional Krugerrands are available in 1/2-, 1/4-, and 1/10-ounce sizes. The U.S., Canadian, and various other public and private mints issue coins and metals that compete with the Krugerrand.

Gold mining company stock prices are closely related to gold's price. Gold that is unattractive to mine at $35 per ounce may be quite profitably extracted at $350 per ounce. Relatively small price changes can substantially affect mining profits. Leverage works in both directions, however—a fall in gold prices can greatly reduce mining profits. Several mutual funds specialize in gold mining shares.

Retail gold jewelry prices always substantially exceed bullion values. Buying jewelry at bullion prices from one who is in the business of trading scrap gold is one way of minimizing the markup. Such dealers may be willing to sell nice jewelry at slightly higher prices than the refiners would pay, which is usually a fraction of retail.

Institutions similar to mutual funds that would buy and sell gold bullion and have their shares fluctuate with the price of gold have been proposed. Such funds would offer small investors some of the advantages of large dealers. Fees and expenses would, however, be borne by the fundholders.

Another approach is the gold depository receipt, which is in essence a warehouse certificate for gold held in storage; it offers some convenience compared with holding physical gold. Having someone else hold one's gold is safe if the holder is well known and highly secure (Citibank, for example, will take phone orders and charge the bill to Visa or Master Card). On the other hand, a number of frauds have involved precious metal storage. The International Gold Bullion Exchange, for example, sold gold at the spot price, charging no fee for storage or trading. They even offered an interest return if the investor's gold was left on deposit. Their system seemed to work fine as long as more money was coming in than going out. Customers eventually discovered, however, that IGBE was running a Ponzi scheme when it ran out of money and gold.

Silver and Copper Bullion-Value Coins

Just as gold coins provide an alternative to gold futures, silver and copper coins serve as alternatives to silver and copper futures. While bullion-value coin investing is similar to precious metals trading, some important differences remain. Since coin values do not reflect bullion values precisely, an underlying move in the commodity price may lead to a greater or lesser move in coin prices. On the other hand, the coin's value cannot fall below its face value. Thus a $50 bag of pennies is worth $50 even if the value of copper falls to $30 or $10.

Since coin trading is much less active and more diverse than the commodities market, the buy/sell price difference for coins is usually much greater. Markups of 20 to 50% on coins are typical. The markup on large quantities of bullion-related coins, while low relative to that on some other kinds of coins, is still above that of most other investment types. A number of coin-investment brokerage firms, however, permit margin purchases and storage—especially for bags of silver coins (often at substantial costs). Margin buyers who only receive a warehouse receipt cannot be sure that the coins actually exist. In some cases, they have not, reminding one of the "bucket shop" operations common in earlier days of the stock market.[34]

Consider the following example of a silver coin transaction: on July 25,

1974, a New York coin dealer was selling $1,000 (face) bags of silver for $3,500 and buying for $3,400 (2.9% spread). Other dealers were quoting $3,350 bid and $3,550 asked (a 5.8% spread). New York residents would also incur a sales tax. Margin purchases required a 30% deposit and were charged an annual rate of 13 1/2% or $330 per year on the $2,450 borrowed. This particular dealer would absorb the storage charge. The buy-price would have to rise $430 (to $3,730) within a year for the investor to cover the $330 interest and $100 spread. This is equivalent to a percentage increase of 12.3% on the original price of $3,500. Thus after investing $1,050, the price would have to rise by over 12% before a profit could be realized.

In comparison: on July 25, 1974, New York Mercantile Exchange contracts to receive $1,000 bags of silver in July 1975 (one year from date of purchase) traded for $3,710 which was approximately the price that the coins needed to reach for the investor to profit ($3,730). The commodity trade had at least two advantages, however. First, the lower required margin on the futures contract meant that less interest was foregone on the amount invested. Second, the commodity contract commission would be much lower than the spread involved in an off-exchange transaction. Furthermore, as long as delivery is not taken, no sales tax is due on a commodity exchange transaction regardless of the buyer's residence.

While most bullion coin action is in gold and silver, copper could reach a level where a cent's bullion value exceeded its face value. In early 1974, this looked like a possibility; but by late 1974, the copper price had fallen enough to make pennies unattractive to copper speculators. Indeed pennies continued to be made of copper through 1981, although a shift to zinc occurred quietly in 1982.

Strategic Metals

While no futures markets yet exist in strategic metals such as titanium, antimony, beryllium, germanium, vandium, zirconium, cobalt, manganese and molybdenum, some investors have shown considerable interest. It is the old story of rapid price rises generating expectations of further rises. Unscrupulous promoters persuade investors to buy the metal for perhaps double the current wholesale price. Little is said about subsequent sales. No doubt strategic metals do offer some profitable opportunities, but unsophisticated investors are likely to learn of the problems the hard way.[35] Indeed most strategic metals seem quite unlikely to experience any serious shortages.[36]

Deferred-Delivery Foreign Exchange Contracts

Some foreign currencies are traded on futures exchanges, but the bulk of the market is in over-the-counter forward contracts not requiring margin. Otherwise the two types of contracts are quite similar.[37] Both envision future delivery at a price negotiated at the time of the trade. Both offer international traders an opportunity to hedge their foreign exchange risks.[38] Some spot-speculation in foreign exchange also utilizes travelers checks, foreign bank accounts, and securities denominated in foreign currencies. Still others trade options.[39]

Foreign exchange speculators bet on the relative movements in exchange rates. Thus one who expected the mark to appreciate relative to the dollar could buy marks or deferred-delivery marks (either futures or forward contracts) with dollars. If the investor's analysis is correct, the position can subsequently be covered at a profit. If exchange rates move adversely, however, the position will produce a loss. This is another huge market, but largely beyond the scope of this survey.[40]

SUMMARY AND CONCLUSIONS

A large dollar volume of futures trading takes place. Contracts standardized in grade, size, location, and delivery date facilitate substantial hedge and speculative trading. Relatively low-percentage margins mean profits and losses are greatly magnified by price moves. Commodity trading has grown rapidly because of the poor performance in alternative markets and the introduction of a variety of new types of contracts. Commodity contracts exist in agricultural, mineral and financial instruments. To succeed, a contract requires a physical with sufficient competition, standardization, storability, and price volatility.

Commodities differ from stocks in a number of ways, including: term, trading limits, delivery possibility, margin percentages, absence of short restrictions, no interest on unpaid margin balances, no specialists, commission structure, and the need to open and close positions with the same broker. Because of their relatively independent (not related to the stock market) volatility, commodity contracts may be useful in diversification, but their own volatility limits their appeal.

A variety of professional futures traders compete with the amateur speculator: scalpers trade on the floor of the exchange seeking very quick turns; day traders close their positions at the end of each day; position traders may hold for several days; arbitragers seek profits from disequilibrium price relations; firm representatives trade for the accounts of firms that deal in the underlying physical. A series of large disruptive trades have at times substantially altered price relationships.

Futures trades may be based on fundamental and technical analysis. Crop and weather forecasts play a large role in fundamental analysis of agriculture commodities. Combination trades involve offsetting positions in related contracts with the hope of profiting from relative price moves.

Specialized commodity instruments include interest and stock market futures, options on commodities, and commodity mutual funds. A number of commodity-related physicals also appeal to commodity speculators. Gold bullion, gold coins, mining companies, jewelry, and warehouse receipts facilitate trading in the precious metal. Similar alternatives are available in silver and copper. Finally, strategic metals without a futures market and currency with an active forward market both appeal to futures-oriented investors.

REVIEW QUESTIONS

1. What characteristics are needed for a commodity contract to be traded actively on a futures exchange?
2. What factors have led to the recent growth commodity futures markets?
3. Discuss the various types of professional commodity traders and the advantages possessed by each.
4. What is the relevance to small investors of the various examples of disruptive large futures trades?
5. Discuss the application of fundamental analysis to commodity trading. How do crop and weather forecasts fit in?
6. What are combination-commodity trades? Illustrate with some examples.
7. Discuss commodity analysts.
8. Compare commodity trading with stock market trading.
9. What are the pros and cons of commodity diversification?
10. How do interest rate futures work?
11. How do stock index futures work?
12. What is a commodity option? Discuss two major commodity-option scams.
13. What are the various ways of investing in gold? What are the pros and cons of each?
14. Discuss investing in silver and copper coins.
15. What are the drawbacks to investing in strategic metals?

REVIEW PROBLEMS

1. Apply the Harlow and Teweles soybean trading rule to the last five years. Now apply it to five years that were covered by their study. Compare the two performances. Write a report.
2. Assemble a list of five commodity-trade recommendations and track their performances. Write a report.
3. Select ten futures contracts that are near expiration. Compute the basis on each. Now compute the basis monthly for these same contracts going back one year. Plot each set of bases over time. Do you see any pattern? Explain.
4. Compute the carry for price constellations of three agricultural and three metals contracts. Estimate the actual carrying cost for holding

the physicals from one delivery period to the next. Compare the two "carrys." Repeat the computation for five prior periods.

5. Construct three combination trades and track their performances. Write a report.

6. Assume that a year ago you wished to hedge your $100,000,000 portfolio of government bonds. Half were coming due in six months and the other half in a year. Your goal was to lock in a two-year return (one year beyond the current date). What interest futures contracts would you have bought? Compute the end-period value of your portfolio, giving full effect to commissions, assign cost, and interest. Compare this result with what you would have achieved from unhedged portfolio.

7. Assume that one year ago you wished to hedge your $50,000,000 stock portfolio against an expected decline in the market. Assume that your portfolio's performance paralleled the S&P 500. How many S&P 500 contracts would you have traded to hedge your position? Would you have bought or sold? Compare the results of hedging and not hedging on your portfolio's current value.

8. Plot the various stock index futures relative to the performance of their underlying index for a year. How do the price constellations vary? Write a report.

9. Select five commodity options and compare the performance over the past year of long positions in the options versus the underlying futures contracts.

10. Track the history of five commodity funds for two years relative to a stock and a commodity index. Write a report.

11. Obtain gold quotes for bullion, futures, and Krugerands. Compare the prices and write a report.

12. Select five gold mining companies and plot their monthly performances relative to gold's price for two years. Compare the relative returns. Write a report.

13. Obtain current buy and sell quotes on five strategic metals. Compute the relative markups.

NOTES

1. C. Harlow and R. Teweles, *The Commodity Futures Trading Game*, McGraw-Hill, 1977; C. Huff and B. Marinacci, *Commodity Speculation for Beginners*, McGraw Hill, New York, 1980.

2. A. Peck, *Readings in Futures Markets: Views From the Trade*, Chicago Board of Trade, 1978.

3. L. Telsen, "Margins and Futures Contracts," *Journal of Futures Markets*, Summer 1981, pp. 225–253.

4. G. Taylor and R. Leuthold, "The Influence of Futures Trading on Cash Cattle Price Variations," *Food Research Institute Studies*, Vol. XIII, No. 1, pp. 85–96; S. Martin and R. Spahr, "Futures Market Efficiency as a Function of Market Speculations," *Review of Research in Futures Markets*, Volume 2, November 3, 1982, pp. 314–328.

5. K. Arrow, "Futures Markets: Some Theoretical Perspectives," *Journal of Futures Markets*, Summer 1981, pp. 109–115.

6. W. Silber, "Innovation, Competition and New Contract Design in Futures Markets," *Journal of Futures Markets*, Summer 1981, pp. 123–155; N. Kleinfield, "Birth of New Futures Contract," *New York Times*, January 26, 1984, pp. D1, D12; R. Sandor, "Innovation by An Exchange: A Case Study of the Development of the Plywood Futures Contract," *Journal of Law and Economics*, April 1973.

7. T. Petzinger, J. Zaslow and W. Wall, "Amateur Speculators in Commodities Face Pros Holding the Aces," *Wall Street Journal*, February 16, 1984, pp. 1, 21.

8. B. Stewart, *An Analysis of Speculative Trading Grain Futures*, Technical Bulletin, No. 10001, Washington, D.C., Department of Agriculture, Commodity Exchange Authority, October 1949.

9. K. Dusak, "Futures Trading and Investor Returns: An Investigation of Commodity Market Premiums," *Journal of Political Economy*, December 1973, pp. 1387–1406.

10. C. Rockwell, "Normal Backwardation, Forecasting, and the Returns to Commodity Futures Traders," *Proceedings of a Symposium on Price Effects of Speculation in Organized Commodity Markets*, Stanford University, Food Research Institute Studies, supplement to Vol. VIII, Stanford, Calif., 1967, pp. 107–130.

11. R. Gray, "The Futures Market for Maine Potatoes: An Appraisal," *Food Research Institute Studies*, No. 3, 1972.

12. S. Jackeewicz, "Big Flap About Potato Futures Defaults Isn't Over Despite Settlement-Price Move," *Wall Street Journal*, June 28, 1976, p. 16; *Wall Street Journal*, "U.S. Commodity Agency Brings Charges Against 14 in 1976 Potato Delivery Default," *Wall Street Journal*, June 20, 1977, p. 3.

13. J. Huey and J. Laing, "How Cook Industries Speculated and Lost Millions on Soybeans," *Wall Street Journal*, July 14, 1977, p. 1.

14. T. Barnhill and J. Powell, "Silver Price Volatility: A Perspective on the July 1979-April 1980 Period," *Journal of Futures Markets*, Winter 1981, pp. 619–647; Stephen Fry, *Beyond Greed*, Penguin Books, Middlesex, England, 1982; R. Hudson, "SEC Staff Blame '80 Silver Market Crisis on Easy Broker Credit, Big Board Laxity," *Wall Street Journal*, October 21, 1982, p. 3; G. Getschow and G. Hill, "Hunts Try to Sell Some Big Assets, Apparently to Pay Off Silver Loan," *Wall Street Journal*, February 11, 1982, p. 31.

15. C. Waterloo, "Rapidly Growing Use of Computers Brings Changes to Futures Trading," *Wall Street Journal*, October 19, 1982, p. 37.

16. S. Alexander, "Price Movements in Speculative Markets: Trends or Random Walks," *Industrial Management Review*, May 1961, pp. 7–26; R. Bear, "Martingale Movements in Commodity Futures," Ph.D. dissertation, University of Iowa, 1970; R. Gray, "Fundamental Price Behavior Characteristics in Commodity Futures," Paper presented at the Futures Trading Seminar of the Chicago Board of Trade, Chicago, Ill, April 28–30, 1965; T. Martell and G. Philippatos, "An Option, Information and Dependence in Commodities Markets," *Journal of Finance*, May 1974, pp. 493–498; G. Booth, F. Kaen and P. Koveos, "Persistent Dependence in Gold Prices," *Journal of Financial Research*, Spring 1982, pp. 85–94; S. Taylor, "Tests of the Random Walk Hypothesis Against Price-Trend Hypothesis," *Journal of Financial and Quantitative Analysis*, March 1982, pp. 37–59.

17. C. Harlow and R. Teweles, "Commodities and Securities Compared," *Financial Analysts Journal*, September/October 1972, pp. 64–70.

18. K. House and J. Winsk, "Estimating U.S. Crop in a Painstaking Job and an Important One," *Wall Street Journal*, August 11, 1975, p. 1; S. Synder, "The Weather and the Futures Markets," *Fortune*, April 1977, pp. 59–65.

19. R. Williams, "How a Soybean Processor Makes Use of Futures Markets," *Readings in Futures Markets*, Book III, 1978, pp. 173–176.

20. S. Angrist, "A Reverse Crush in Soybeans," *Forbes*, September 1, 1977, p. 78; S. Angrist, "A Relatively Riskless Trade," *Forbes*, December 1, 1976, pp. 102–103.

21. S. Angrist, "Seattle Slew I'm Not," *Forbes*, July 1, 1977.

22. A. Mackay-Smith, "Commodity Forecasting Off Target Last Time, Offer New Choices in Latest Investment Survey," *Wall Street Journal*, January 11, 1982, p. 56.

23. S. Angrist, "Profits Top Losses Again!" *Forbes*, July 9, 1979, p. 148.

24. A. Robicheck, K. Cohn, and J. Pringle, "Returns on Alternate Investment Media and Implications for Portfolio Construction," *Journal of Business*, July 1972, pp. 427–443; Z. Bodie, "An Innovation for Stable Real Retirement Income," *Journal of Portfolio Management*, Fall 1982, pp. 5–13.

25. *Business Week*, "How to Trade the New Stock-Index Futures," *Business Week*, June 7, 1982, pp. 126–129; D. Grant, "How to Optimize with Stock Index Futures," *Journal of Portfolio Management*, Spring 1982, pp. 32–36; P. Grossman, "Hard Look at Index Futures," *Financial World*, July 1–15, 1982, pp. 16–22; G. Gaotineau and A. Madarsky, "S&P 500 Stock Index Futures Evaluation Tables," *Financial Analysts Journal*, November/December 1983, pp. 68–76.

26. S. Figlewski and S. Kon, "Portfolio Management with Stock Index Futures," *Financial Analysts Journal*, January/February 1982, pp. 52–61; R. Zechauser and V. Niederhoffer, "The Performance of Market Index Futures Contracts," *Financial Analysts Journal*, January/February 1983, pp. 59–65.

27. B. Shakin, "Commodities Options," *Barron's*, January 27, 1975, pp. 11–12.

28. *Business Week*, "Finally a Crackdown on Commodity Options," *Business Week*, February 6, 1978, pp. 70–71.

29. C. Camarer, "The Pricing and Social Value of Commodity Options," *Financial Analysts Journal*, January/February 1982, pp. 62–67; M. Belongia, "Commodity Options: A New Risk Management Tool for Agricultural Markets," *Federal Reserve Bank of St. Louis Review*, June/July 1983, pp. 105–15.

30. A. Mackay-Smith, "Commodity-Futures Options Trading Resumes with Exchanges Hoping to Avoid Past Pitfalls," *Wall Street Journal*, October 4, 1982, p. 56; M. Belongia, "Commodity Options: A New Risk Management Tool for Agricultural Markets," *Federal Reserve Bank of St. Louis Review*, June/July 1983, p. 5–15.

31. H. Maidenberg, "Why Commodity Pools Keep Growing," *New York Times*, February 14, 1982, p. F13; H. Maidenberg, "Spreading Risk with Commodity Funds," *New York Times*, November 14, 1982, p. 17F; *Wall Street Journal* "As Commodity Funds Proliferate, Investors Have Ups and Downs," *Wall Street Journal*, September 27, 1976, p. 31; D. Moffitt, "Here's a Look at Costs, Risks and Rewards in Big New Publicly Offered Commodity Fund," *Wall Street Journal*, September 11, 1978, p. 44; *Business Week*, "Commodity Funds: A Safer Way to Play a Hot Market," *Business Week*, April 11, 1983, pp. 134–136; W. Baldwin, "Rags to Riches," *Forbes*, March 1, 1982, p. 144.

32. M. Slot and P. Swanson, "On the Efficiency of the Markets for Gold and Silver," *Journal of Business*, July 1981, pp. 453–478; A. Herbst, "Gold versus U.S. Common Stocks: Some Evidence on Inflation Hedge Performance and Cyclical Behavior," *Financial Analysts Journal*, January/February 1983, pp. 66–74; *Business Week*, "Economists Start to Take Gold Seriously," *Business Week*, May 23, 1983, pp. 118–122; E. Sherman, "A Gold Pricing Model," *Journal of Portfolio Management*, 1983, pgs. 68–70; A. Mackay-Smith, "Gold and Other Metals May be Bargains Now, But You need to Look Out for Shady Operators," *Wall Street Journal*, June 6, 1983, p. 56, A Mackay-Smith, "Commodity Funds Let Small Investors Partake with Limited Liability, but Risks are Sizable," *Wall Street Journal*, October 3, 1983, p. 60; R. Ricklefs, "Americans May Find Buying, Owning Gold a Bit of A Nuisance," *Wall Street Journal*, December 5, 1974, p. 1.

33. S. Angrist, "For the Gold Bugs," *Forbes*, April 1, 1977, pp. 92–93; E. Sherman, "Gold: A Conservative Prudent Diversifier," *Journal of Portfolio Management*, Spring 1982, pp. 21–27; A.

Renshaw, "Does Gold Have a role in Investment Portfolios?," *Journal of Portfolio Management*, Spring 1982, pp. 28–31; R. Stucky, "Gold Belongs in Your Portfolio," *American Association of Individual Investors Journal*, October 1983, pp. 30–34.

34. G. Hill, "An SEC Suit Marks the biggest Step Yet to Control Silver Coin Margin Contracts," *Wall Street Journal*, December 13, 1974, p. 32; D. Evans, "Here's Jonathan, But Where are his Customer's Gold Coins?," *Barron's*, January 3, 1983, pp. 14, 24, 26; L. Tell, "Revise Alchemy? Leveraged Contracts in Precious Metals Draw Regulatory Fire," *Barron's*, July 4, 1983, pp. 24, 26, 27.

35. *Business Week*, "Adventurous Investing in Strategic Metals," *Business Week*, October 12, 1981, pp. 170–174; B. Szuprowicz, "Mining Profits in Strategic Metals," *Fact*, April 1983, pp. 29–33; K. Moble, "The Risky World of Strategic Metals," *New York Times*, September 6, 1981, p. F11.

36. S. Cook, "The Crisis That Didn't Happen," *Forbes*, November 22, 1982, p. 91–94; W. Gibson, "Why Strategic Metals have Fallen From Favor," *Barron's*, October 3, 1983, pp. 8, 9, 38, 40.

37. J. Cox, J. Ingersoll and S. Ross, "The Relation Between Forward Prices and Futures Prices," *Journal of Financial Economics*, December 1981, pp. 321–346.

38. C. Dale, "The Hedging Effectiveness of Currency Futures Markets," *Journal of Futures Markets*, Spring 1981, pp. 77–88.

39. *Business Week*, "A Safer Hedge in Currencies," *Business Week*, January 17, 1983, p. 103; N. Biger and J. Hull, "The Valuation of Currency Options," *Financial Management*, 1983, p. 24–28.

40. *Business Week*, "Chartist's: The New Currency Gurus," *Business Week*, October 12, 1981, pp. 93–96; *Business Week*, "Getting into the Foreign Exchange Game," *Business Week*, May 25, 1981, pp. 182–184.

20 Real Estate and Real Estate Stocks

Finance department investment courses' frequent neglect of real estate investments seems unfortunate. Even investors who prefer other media need some exposure to the subject to decide. This chapter provides such an overview. First real estate's role in the economy is explored. Then we examine its investment suitability and discuss specific guidelines and parameters. Next, ten basic principles of real estate investing are considered, followed by illustrations of three approaches to real estate valuation (market, cost, and income). In the process, such topics as bargaining, loan negotiation, property management, and refinancing are explored. Then various types of real estate investments are considered, including: apartments, land, condominiums, recreational property, commercial property, franchises, and cemeteries. Finally, we examine the pros and cons of investing in different types of real estate companies and tax shelters.

Real Estate Ownership is a Large and Profitable Part of the Economy

The real estate market dwarfs the stock, bond, commodity, and option markets. Estimated U.S. real estate values are more than double those of corporate stocks and six times the value of all capital equipment. Moreover, two-thirds of all dwelling units are owner occupied. Average real estate returns have generally exceeded average stock returns by a wide margin.[1] Past average profitability is no guarantee of attractive subsequent returns on specific real estate, however.[2]

Who Should Invest in Real Estate?

In spite of the real estate market's large size and profitable history, far more people are well-positioned to invest in stocks or bonds (other than owning their own home). Serious beginning real estate investors should be able to answer yes to each of the following five questions.

1. Can at least several thousand dollars be tied up for a minimum of several years? Real estate is priced in the tens of thousands of dollars and typically requires at least 25% down. Furthermore, real estate is difficult to sell on short notice. Thus one should be prepared to hold properties for an appreciable period (perhaps several years).
2. Is the investor likely to remain in the same geographic area for the fore-

seeable future? Real estate investments usually require frequent attention. Thus investors should be near enough to supervise their properties
properly.

3. Does the investor have the time and talent to manage property effectively? Rental property often requires substantial maintenance. New
tenants must be found periodically. Rents must be collected. Records
must be kept and bills must be paid. Even if others are contracted to do
these tasks, someone still must hire the managers and monitor their
work. Investors who do the tasks themselves enhance their returns.

4. Can one assume the substantial risk inherent in real estate investing?
High leverage and low liquidity both add to real estate's risk.

5. Does the investor have the credit standing necessary to borrow at attractive interest rates? Most successful real estate investors use extensive leverage. One who is unable to borrow at attractive terms may find
real estate relatively unprofitable. Since real estate loans are usually secured by the property values themselves, most people can answer yes
to this question.

Only investors who can answer each of these questions affirmatively are
suited for real estate investing. Some who are not now positioned to invest in
real estate may eventually be better able to participate. Many of those not well-
situated for general real estate investing may still be prospective homeowners.
Still others may prefer the stocks of real estate-oriented companies. The following discussion is addressed to all such investors.

The Parameters of Different Types of Real Estate Investments

The minimum investment period, the amount of equity capital necessary, and
the leverage percentage usually employed differ with the type of real estate. The
following table represents one estimate of some of the typical parameters for
several types of real estate investments:[3]

Table 20.1   Real Estate Investment Parameters

Type	Minimum Investment Period (Years)	Maximum Leverage	Minimum Capital Requirement	Potential Holding Period Return
Raw Land	3 to 4	50%	$5,000 to $10,000	300%
2-6 Unit Apartments	5 to 10	75 to 80%	$7,500 to $20,000	300%
Shopping Centers	5 to 7	75 to 80%	$50,000	500%
Garden Apartments	8 to 12	75 to 80%	$50,000	300%
Office Building	8 to 12	75 to 80%	$100,000	500%
Highrise Apartments	8 to 12	75 to 80%	$250,000	400%
Commercial Space	3 to 4	75 to 80%	$10,000 to $20,000	300%
Industrial Space	3 to 4	75 to 80%	$50,000	400%

Table 20.1's entries differ substantially in reliability. The leverage numbers, derived from experience with banks and other lenders, are dependable estimates, as are the minimum capital requirement estimates, which reflect experience with current price-levels. The potential return and minimum-investment-period numbers are, in contrast, pure guesses.

While these entries only represent one opinion, they do provide some idea of the possible range of expectations. We see that expected minimum holding periods vary from 3 to 4 years in land to 8 to 12 years in various types of developed real estate. Minimum investment amounts range from $5,000 to $10,000 in land to $250,000 for highrise apartments. Expected holding-period returns range from 300% to 500% of the amount invested (the down payment).

REAL ESTATE INVESTING PRINCIPLES

The preceding discussion has introduced real estate investing, considered its investor suitability, and briefly explored some relevant parameters. Now we turn to some specific aspects of real estate investing, beginning with ten investment principles.

Principle 1: Real estate values are determined by their highest and best (i.e. most profitable) uses. Potatoes could be grown on midtown Manhattan land and a flea market operated on Miami beach-front property. Such locations could, however, almost certainly be put to much more profitable uses. For example, the Manhattan land would earn more as a site for office buildings, apartments, hotels, department stores, or even parking lots. The Miami beach-front parcel should yield a much higher return as a hotel-site. Investors have a strong incentive to acquire and upgrade underutilized property. Bidding prices up to their most-productive-use values tends to maximize each property's productivity. Potential buyers and sellers should always evaluate real estate in terms of its most productive use. While poorly informed sellers may sometimes price their property below its highest-use value, an efficient investment market should make such bargains relatively rare. On the other hand, one never wants to sell real estate for less than its most-productive-use value. Thus determining realistic values is a key aspect of real estate investing.

Principle 2: The supply of land is largely fixed, while demand tends to increase over time. Heretofore worthless land may sometimes be made useful by draining, clearing, grading, or irrigating. In rare instances, air rights may substitute for high-priced land. Increasing the supply of usable land is relatively expensive, however. Growing population and affluence have tended to raise land values while rising materials and labor prices have tended to increase construction costs. Since these trends seem likely to persist, real estate values should continue rising, at least in the long run.

Principle 3: As with almost any investment, short-run individual price moves may differ substantially from the long-run aggregate trend. During the 1930s, real estate values plunged along with almost every other asset price. Much of the property bought in the 1920s remained below its purchase price until well into the 1940s. Some property bought in the 1920s Florida land boom is still worth less than the inflated sums of the hysteria's peak. More recent boom-bust real estate cycles have involved such diverse areas as Hawaii, Hong Kong, Tuscon, Miami Beach, and Anchorage.[4]

Principle 4: Careful comparison shopping is a useful first step in identifying real estate values. As with all investing, shopping around and bargaining is advisable. Paying more than is necessary or selling for less than top dollar reduces returns. Comparative fundamental analysis of an assortment of available properties is an important aspect of real estate investing. Similarly, obtaining properties at attractive prices usually requires information on alternative real estate opportunities. Few fortunes have been made with hasty, half-baked decisions.

Principle 5: Effective real estate investing almost always involves careful but extensive use of leverage. Few investors have the resources to buy very much real estate for cash. Moreover, property that earns more than the cost of financing it yields a positive differential. Thus one should use a property's collateral value to borrow heavily whenever the projected return safely exceeds the borrowing cost. Banks, savings and loan associations, and other financial intermediaries are quite willing to lend a substantial percentage (usually up to 75% to 80%) of developed property's purchase price. The interest expense is tax-deductible while any unrealized price appreciation on the property is tax-deferred and when realized taxed as a long-term gain after the property is held more than one year. The lower a particular purchase's down payment, the more is available for other properties. Borrowers must normally make a large enough down payment to protect the lenders in case they default.

Principle 6: As with the purchase price, one should shop around and bargain for the best financing terms. While the amount borrowed, length of repayment, and interest rate (or formula) are all important, other factors such as repayment flexibility should not be overlooked. Since an interest rate decline may make refinancing attractive, the absence of a prepayment penalty is particularly desirable. Closing costs, insurance arrangements, and property-tax escrow accounts should all be considered in negotiating a loan. Closing costs include fees paid to the lender for granting the loan (points), lawyers' fees, title search expenses, etc. A point is 1% of the loan principal. Lawyers charge both for drawing up the purchase-and-sale agreement and for searching and guaranteeing the title. A number of loan provisions are designed to protect the lender from unexpected contingencies. For example, lenders will normally require fire and casualty insurance on any developed property, and perhaps borrower-life insurance equal to the outstanding loan principal. Any unpaid property taxes are assessed against the property. Thus the lender may require that the pro rata expected property taxes be added to the mortgage payment. Since property taxes are due at specific times (once or twice) during the year, borrowers who are not constrained with escrow payments have full use of the funds until the due date. Moreover, the escrow account may earn little or no interest.

At one time, almost all real estate mortgages had fixed terms and interest rates. Such loans' initial payments (usually monthly) are primarily interest with a small principal repayment component. Over time, however, the amount of the debt is reduced so that less of the fixed payment goes to interest and more to principal repayment. Economic uncertainty and increasingly volatile interest rates have more recently led most lenders to prefer variable or adjustable-rate mortgages (ARMs). Since ARMs terms can differ substantially, one still needs to shop around and negotiate. Many ARMs start with a set rate for the first year and have a limit to how much the rate can vary per period and how high it can go (a cap on the rate). Thus one lender might offer a 12% first-year rate and a rate which varies each year, with a 15% maximum. Another might start at 11% and change the rate each year with no cap on the rate. In some mortgages, the monthly payment is fixed, with the variation in the rate affecting the number of payments. In most cases, however, the payment rate fluctuates with the interest rate.

Several new financing methods reduce what would otherwise be a substantial interest burden on the buyer. One of these is the appreciation mortgage, which, in exchange for a lower interest rate, entitles the lender to receive a portion of the gain when the property is sold. The appreciation-mortgage lender, in effect, bets that the property will appreciate by more than enough to offset the difference in interest rates. Other types include the growing-equity and graduated-payment mortgages. Both types begin with relatively low mortgage payments that increase over time.

Knowledge of the available range of interest rates or rate formulas, minimum down payment percentages, point charges, escrow terms, available maturities, prepayment penalties and the like should help one select the most attractive place to begin negotiations.[5] Different lenders' terms will be more attractive in some respects than in others (e.g., a lower interest rate but a higher down-payment), so persistent negotiation with several lenders may afford the best of each world.

Principle 7: All improvement and maintenance spending should be cost effective. One should not automatically replace a deteriorating roof, repaint the exterior of a faded duplex, or remodel the interior of a now out-of-date office complex, as the additional rents may not be worth the higher costs. Maintenance and remodeling expenditures should be justified by the expected payback rather than the physical need. Rental rates that are depressed by rent control or a deteriorating neighborhood encourage one to realize what is possible with minimal maintenance and eventually abandon the property. On the other hand, perfectly functional structures may at times be substantially altered or torn down if a different structure would earn enough to justify the conversion.

Principle 8: Real estate should never be purchased without a careful on-site inspection and comparison with the relevant alternatives. Some companies use a free dinner and slide show to sell Sunbelt property to people living in other areas—especially the Snowbelt. An on-site inspection has no substitute, however. Such inspections may reveal a drainage problem; unpleasant odors from nearby factories, sewage treatment facilities, or garbage dumps; neighboring developments that limit land values; more attractively priced nearby property; and many other unexpected factors. One should only consider property that is near enough to inspect. The following list contains some relevant characteristics to consider in any proposed property purchase:

- *Location*—What changes are taking place? Will they work to the benefit of the property's owner? Consider road-access, utilities and services, and neighboring property development. If one is buying property for business purposes, do surrounding businesses complement it? Are suppliers nearby? Is parking adequate? Would the owner be able to expand to adjacent property if need be?
- *Competition*—What nearby properties have similar uses? Does this choice have any particular advantages or disadvantages? Will competitive moves in the area affect the owner?
- *Facilities and Maintenance*—Does the buildings' physical quality compare favorably with neighboring properties? Do the structures have multifaceted use? Are costly repairs likely? If so does the asking price reflect these projected costs?
- *Financing*—Can the property be financed both by the current buyer and a subsequent buyer? How committed is the original lender to financing the rest of the development? Would other area-lenders consider financing the property? If not, why not?
- *Operating Expenses*—How stable are the expenses for taxes, management, utilities, and insurance? Might they rise substantially? Will the owner be adversely affected by rising energy costs? Are the figures provided consistent with the experience of owners of similar

buildings? Do long-term leases provide sufficient additional revenues to cover these cost increases.

- *Income*—If the property provides rental income, can rents be increased? How do the rents compare with those for similar property?
Is the tenancy likely to be stable? Do government regulations allow
the landlord to choose tenants selectively? What lease terms can
the owner offer?

- *Price Asked*—How does the price compare with that paid by other
property buyers? Could the same dollar commitment buy attractively priced property in a more established area? If the property is
income producing, does the price permit a positive cash flow after
taxes and mortgage payments? How firm is the asking price?

Principle 9: Minimize the use of expensive professionals. Real estate investors often require the services of lawyers, real estate agents, appraisers, architects, accountants, contractors, property managers, and several other types
of professionals. While such professionals are sometimes well worth their
cost, at other times the owner may effectively perform the task and save
the fee. Since real estate commissions are normally 7% on developed property (10% or more for land), a $90,000 house sale would generate a $6,300
fee. A successful owner effort to sell directly by reducing the price $1,500
and spending $100 on classified advertising would save $4,700. Moreover,
investors who buy directly may obtain a better price, as owners who avoid
paying commissions can afford to sell for less. Most owners can also handle
such jobs as bookkeeping, appraising, and property managing.

Some professional services are very nearly unavoidable, however. For
example, few non-lawyers know how to search a title, and the lender is
unlikely to accept the work of those who do; few laypersons can design
and contract major construction; an independent appraisal of a very large
parcel might be well worth its cost; and large property holdings may benefit from professional management and accounting. The issue really boils
down to how much the investor values his or her time and talent.

Principle 10: Investors should continually keep abreast of relevant local,
state, and federal agency policies and proposed policies. For example, moving quickly to secure property near new government projects such as interstate highway exits or rapid transit terminals may yield large profits.
Other state or local government actions (e.g. rent control) can, in contrast,
appreciably depress some real estate values.

We shall now explore the impacts of such factors as major government and
nongovernment construction, permitting gambling, rent control, the environmental movement, national credit trends and property tax levels.

Major Government and Nongovernment Construction

Developable property near successful shopping centers usually appreciates. Since local zoning board approval is one key to shopping center development, real estate investors should keep abreast of the issues coming before such agencies. Federal installation contructions also offer profit opportunities. Private enterprise is expected to provide support services for the new facilities' employees. Since suppliers, restaurants, and shop owners will need space, nearby land will usually appreciate. Recreational land values near expanding government installations may also rise. For example, a planned dam that creates lakefront property, or a new access road to some scenic or recreational attraction, almost always increases nearby property values. To learn about proposed projects, one should follow the activities of the legislative agencies and their parks and public works committees. While many such proposals are easily approved, those for nuclear power plants, sewage treatment facilities, prisons, and airports may reduce nearby land values, and thus are likely to be hotly contested.

Permitting Gambling

Legalizing casino gambling caused Atlantic City real estate values to soar. Property suitable for hotel-casinos rose dramatically, but even many residential property values quadrupled. The Atlantic City example illustrates the profit potential of anticipating and taking quick advantage of an event. On the other hand, those who waited too long got hurt when property values declined appreciably as a result of overbuilding.

Rent Control

Since laws that constrain rent increases can appreciably reduce an investment's return, real estate investors should closely monitor rent control efforts. Local media generally report this issue thoroughly. Landlords may even take a leaf from the tenants' book and organize themselves.

The Environmental Movement

With the demise of the Indochina war issue and decline of the civil rights movement, the environment may have become the major social concern of the day. Controlling real estate development constitutes an important aspect of the environmental movement. Downie has articulately presented this movement's view of alleged real estate abuses.[6] He appears to be on firm ground in criticizing those who sell run-down inner-city houses to the poor at inflated prices. Usually the Federal Housing Administration (FHA) guarantees the loan. The FHA appraiser may be bribed to approve a loan at well above the property's market value. If, as often happens, the new owner is unable to keep up the payments, the FHA ends up with the overvalued property. Downie also justifiably criticizes developers who use bribes to obtain favorable zoning, or approval of clearly inadequate construction. Abuses of real estate sales companies are also effectively criticized. Not stopping here, however, Downie views with alarm the conversion of urban residential property to commercial use, the residential development of what had been agricultural land, the planned development of new towns, and even individual homeowners' preferences for dwellings with investment potential. His basic thesis seems to be that profit-oriented real estate development has led to the rape of America. He proposes that the government plan and control real estate development, thereby greatly restricting profit opportunities. Downies' controversial views involve many debatable value judgments. In effect, he questions the capitalistic approach to economic activity.

Regardless of one's own opinion, disregarding antidevelopment sentiment is hazardous. Views such as Downie's are popular. Land use and zoning regulation may require environmental impact findings, limit the owner's ability to subdivide property or convert apartments to condominiums, force expensive improvements such as buried telephone and transmission cables, and require that a major part of the land be left in its natural state. Vermont has even passed a special tax on land profits. These restrictions clearly limit the land's desirability and investment potential. Even if current legislation does not constrain development, restrictions may be imposed before the purchaser has time to realize a profit.

National Credit Trends

National credit trends also affect real estate investors. When the high cost of mortgage money threatens real estate profits, investors should beware but not overlook attractive opportunities. High interest rates burden real estate buyers, but burdensome carrying costs may force some property owners to sell at distress prices. Particularly well-positioned investors may find a tight, credit-weak real estate market an excellent time to buy.

Property Taxes

A shrinking tax base can adversely affect local real estate values. High real estate taxes may also reduce returns and thereby decrease potential price appreciation, so the investor should be cautious when taxes are high. On the other hand, a high level of government services may enhance property values sufficiently to offset the taxes required to provide them.

DETERMINING REAL ESTATE VALUES

The ten real estate investment principles enumerated below constitute a useful set of ad hoc advice for novice investors but do not come directly to grips with the basic issue of real estate valuation. Accordingly, we shall now explore three different ways of estimating real estate values.

1. A property's value is determined by its most profitable uses.
2. Land supply is fixed while prices may rise with population and affluence.

3. Real estate prices often fall in the short-run.
4. Shop around and bargain for the best price on property.
5. Use leverage where profitable.
6. Shop for attractive terms on interest, down payment, maturity, closing cost, insurance, points, escrow accounts, etc.
7. Justify all expenses by expected incremental returns.
8. Never buy property sight unseen.
9. Minimize the use of professionals.
10. Be mindful of the impacts of government actions.

The Market Approach

Most people would agree that an item is worth what it will sell for. Thus a particular property's value should not differ greatly from realistic asking prices and recent sale prices of similar real estate. No two properties are precisely equivalent, however. Location always differs and other characteristics (size, condition, etc.) will usually vary. Furthermore, a property's market value may differ appreciably from its worth to a particular investor. Thus the market approach should not be relied upon exclusively. On the other hand, a price that is above the comparable alternatives is surely too high, while a price that is below the competition is worth further consideration.

The Cost Approach

Values may also be based on the cost of equivalent land and construction (including the cost of funds tied up while the property is being built and allowing for the differential values of new versus used structures). Replacement costs below market prices encourage one to build rather than to buy. Developed property selling for less than its replacement cost may, depending on demand, be either a bargain or severely outdated or mislocated. Thus replacement-cost-based valuations provide a much better ceiling than a floor on true values.

The Income Approach

Just as common stock values are related to expected future dividend payments, real estate values are strongly influenced by their expected future rental (or other) income. Suppose an apartment building yields annual rentals of $10,000; is to be purchased for cash (no mortgage) and has expected annual expenses (maintenance, property taxes, insurance, etc.) of $3,000. Ignoring depreciation, income taxes, and resale-value changes, which may be offsetting, the property is expected to yield $7,000 annually. The present value of a constant income stream is simply $1/r$ times the income stream (where r is the appropriate discount rate). Thus, discounted at 20%, the property's expected income stream is worth $35,000.

This very rough-and-ready use of the income approach provides a cursory evaluation of a particular property. One simply estimates rental income and direct expenses (exclusive of mortgage payments and income taxes) to find the real estate's gross income. Dividing this sum by the appropriate discount rate produces a "first pass" value estimate. Such an approach can help separate obviously unattractive opportunities from those deserving further study. A much more detailed treatment is needed before a final decision is made, however. Specifically, one should consider the cash flows after mortgage payments and income taxes are paid, take account of the property's expected market-price change, and relate the return to the actual outlay (down payment) rather than the total cost.

Determining the Present Value of Income Real Estate

Valuing real estate by the income approach is just another application of capital budgeting—the cash flows now relate to real estate rather than, say, a piece of equipment or a new product. The following steps are involved:

1. Determine the appropriate discount rate r.
   a) First ascertain the current market cost of borrowing funds to finance the contemplated real estate purchase.
   b) Estimate the highest alternative low-risk return that might otherwise be earned on the down-payment funds.
   c) Determine the weighted-average cost of funds from these two sources by multiplying the percentage to be borrowed by the borrowing cost, and the percentage of the down payment by its alternative rate, and then summing.
   d) Add a risk premium to this weighted-average cost of funds. The premium might be 2%, but could be somewhat higher or lower, depending on the project's risk. Thus a very low-risk project might warrant a 1% premium, while a high-risk investment could deserve 4%.
2. Forecast future rental income. An established property's current rental rates are known. Otherwise one may start with rates on similar units. Forecasting future rates is more difficult. In some cases the future rates may be built into the lease. Rental rates on comparable property, vacancy rates, construction costs, and building activity are all relevant factors in rent determination. One should usually forecast rent increases conservatively.
3. Forecast the future expenses associated with maintaining the property including taxes, repairs, renovations, and management costs. A knowledge of the building's structural soundness should be helpful in estimating some of these costs. Current expenses might be projected to rise with inflation and be adjusted for anticipated needs (such as a new furnace). Note, however, that even experts have difficulty predicting future

inflation rates. Since inflation's effects on rents and maintenance costs tend to be offsetting, one can at least assume consistent increases for both. Mortgage payments should be added to the other expense estimates to forecast the before-tax cost of maintaining the property. The property's taxable income must be determined before income taxes can be calculated.

4. Forecast the property's holding period and value at time of sale. Again, one should try to be consistent. The property's sale price should not normally be expected to rise faster than its ability to produce income.

5. Use these figures to estimate the real estate's value.

   a) Subtract each year's expected costs from its anticipated revenues to obtain that year's expected net cash flow.

   b) Use a present value table or financial calculator to compute the discounted value of each year's expected net income for the selected r.

   c) In like manner, find the present value of the property's expected sale price.

   d) Add the present value of the expected net income and expected sale price to obtain the present value of the total.

6. Compare the present value of the expected income stream plus future sales price (the income-approach valuation) with the price of the property. The higher the income-approach valuation relative to the price, the more attractive is the potential investment.

The Income Approach: An Example

Now consider a brief application of the income approach procedure:

1. Determine r

   (a) Borrowing cost: 17%
   (b) Alternative yield on low-risk investment: 13%
   (c) Percent down payment required: 25%
   (d) Weighted-average cost of capital $.25 \times .13\% + .75 \times 17\% = 16\%$
   (e) Risk Premium: 4%
   (f) Total cost of capital (r): 20% = 16% + 4%

2. Estimate current and future rental income
   Current rental income: $1,000 per month or $12,000 per year
   To be conservative, use this amount for future years.

3. Estimate current and future property expenses

Property Taxes	$2,000 per year
Repairs	200 per year
Miscellaneous	300 per year
Total	$2,500 per year

4. Expected holding period and selling price
   Expected holding period: five years
   Expected selling price: $82,000 (a modest increase over the current asking price of $78,000)
5. Add figures
   (a) Net income per year: $12,000 − 2,500 = $9,500

	Net Yearly Income		Constant*			
Year 1	$9,500	×	.833	=		7,914.
Year 2	$9,500	×	.694	=		6,593.
Year 3	$9,500	×	.597	=		5,500.
Year 4	$9,500	×	.482	=		4,579.
Year 5	$9,500	×	.402	=		3,819.
					Total	$28,405.

*From 20% column in present value table.
(c) Present value of expected sales price: $82,000 × .402 = $32,964.
(d) $28,405 + $32,864 = $61,369.

Since the present value is appreciably less than the asking price ($61,369 versus $78,000), the property seems relatively unattractive. If we could justify a lower discount rate, however, the estimated value would increase. Moreover, the seller might accept a lower price.

Note that while we used greater detail than in the earlier simplified example, this procedure still focuses on the whole project's return. The return on the investor's contribution, a more meaningful figure, will be taken up in greater detail later in this chapter.

Combining the Three Valuation Approaches

Attractive real estate opportunities are priced below their market, cost, and income valuations (Table 20.2). Real estate priced above any one of these three "values," is probably an unwise investment. If, for example, the price is above either the market or replacement values, more attractively priced properties should be available elsewhere. A price that is high relative to the income approach valuation suggests that non-real-estate investments offer higher returns. An investment's attractiveness varies inversely with its price, however, and real estate asking prices are often flexible.

Table 20.2   Three Approaches to Valuing Real Estate

Market Approach	Base value on asking and sale prices of comparable properties
Cost Approach	Base value on cost of constructing equivalent property
Income Approach	Base value on present value of expected future net income stream

Bargaining

Unlike most other investments, real estate transactions often involve some bargaining. Thus investors should try to purchase potentially attractive investment possibilities as cheaply as possible. Sellers generally expect to receive less than their asking price. Investors should seek to buy at the lower end of the realistic range. One should begin with an offer high enough to be taken seriously but well below what is likely to be accepted. An offer of about 20% below the asking price (or 10% below a realistic market price) would normally be viewed as low but not ridiculously so. The appropriate level for an initial offer is difficult to prespecify in the abstract, however. Some properties are so overpriced that an offer of 2/3 or even 1/2 of the asking-price would be realistic. In other cases, 20% below the asking price might be insulting. The offer should be high enough to elicit a counteroffer while leaving the potential buyer maximum flexibility. Unless the market is particularly strong, the seller will usually counter a noninsulting offer. The seller might, for example, drop 5% off the price. Then the investor can come back with a proposal for an additional 5 to 10% decrease. Once the offer and asking price get close, one of the parties will usually suggest splitting the difference.

Uninformed sellers can pose both opportunities and difficulties: one who wants cash in a hurry or does not recognize his or her property's value may set too low a price. On the other hand, a seller who has an exaggerated vision of property values may try one's patience. Examples of uninformed sellers include an heir who needs to pay estate taxes or one who has lived in a building for many years without realizing that much greater rents could be charged were the property rehabilitated.

While some uninformed sellers may not know how much their property is worth, others may not know how little it should sell for. Some novice sellers may believe that the real estate market is so strong that eager buyers will meet almost any asking price. Perhaps having the property on the market for a few months will persuade such a seller to be reasonable. When an uninformed seller overestimates a property's value, the interested investor can look elsewhere or try a reasonable offer. One might, for example, offer 5 to 10% below the property's full market value and then not budge unless the seller gets reasonable. Alternatively, one might try out a very low price, say one-third below its market value. Who knows, the seller might just accept.

Seller-Financing

Real estate investors may also use the seller to help finance the purchase. For example, a seller desiring a steady income might take back a below-market-rate mortgage on the old property. Most people cannot earn investment returns as high as mortgage lenders, so a relatively low mortgage rate may still seem attractive to them. The seller who received a mortgage earns a steady monthly income, and qualifies the transaction as an installment sale, reducing taxes.

A buyer who knows the seller's circumstances may be able to work out financing that is beneficial to both. For example, the buyer might make a 20% down payment, assume the seller's existing low-interest mortgage and give the seller a five-year note for the remaining debt. Such a note's principal will, however, need to be refinanced or paid off well before a long-term mortgage. Interest rates may or may not then be lower. Thus the buyer who relies on seller-financing may only be postponing the inevitable. Seller-financing is helpful to buyers who need a few years to prepare for higher interest rates and mortgage payments, but should not be viewed as permanent financing. Indeed, borrowers frequently have difficulty paying off the short-term seller-financing.[8] Moreover, even first mortgage default rates have increased.[9]

The seller should also understand the advantages and disadvantages of entering into a financing arrangement. Seller-financing helps market the property and may reduce the seller's tax liability (installment sale). On the other hand, the buyer's note almost always bears a below-market interest rate. As a "second," it should yield more than first mortgages. Thus if first mortgage rates are 16%, second mortgages should yield 18% or more, and a lower rate is in effect a hidden price reduction. Moreover, a buyer who has difficulty paying off the note may pressure the seller into an extention. Clearly seller-financing is no panacea for either party.

Negotiation Through Intermediaries

Involving a third party such as a real estate broker or lawyer in real estate negotiations usually avoids potential personality conflicts from direct buyer-seller contact. The seller may become defensive if the buyer directly notes the property's negative factors. Since commissions are earned only if the buyer and seller come to terms, the agent has an incentive to convey in a tactful manner the buyer's concerns about the property's condition, location, and/or price relative to that of similar properties. While agents may pressure both the seller and the buyer to improve their offers, buyers usually have alternative investment opportunities. Sellers, in contrast, often have only one sale to make.

Buyers should never tell an agent their maximum possible offer until that offer is ready to be made. An intermediary who knows the top figure may not be sufficiently vigorous in seeking a still-better price. The negotiating agent should, however, be given some explanation for the offer, particularly if it is low. Experienced sellers know not to expect top dollar for second-rate property. Once the buyer's position is clarified, the seller will often make significant concessions.

Closing the Deal

If bargaining reaches an impasse, the would-be buyer should consider lowcost concessions that might push a close negotiation to a conclusion. Thus an early closing date might elicit additional flexibility from a seller who is concerned about timing. Similarly, relenting on some original demands, such as ignoring certain small problems, offering to buy some of the seller's personal property, or working out a payment plan suitable to the seller could all clinch a deal at minimum expense. If, however, negotiations proceed to differing figures that seem firm for both sides, the would-be buyer must decide whether to pay more or look elsewhere.

Negotiating the Loan

The next step after establishing a price is obtaining financing. One might begin by making preliminary inquiries at a local bank and/or thrift institution. Assume that the savings and loan is short of mortgage money, but since the buyer is a long-time depositor, the bank is willing to consider an application. The buyer then applies for a $50,000 loan (80% percent of the purchase price). The bank is willing to make a 20-year loan at 13%, plus two points. The bank had earlier quoted 12%, but now notes that the rate was a month-old figure which applied to loans with 25% down payments. The bank then offers a $47,000 20-year loan at 13% with no points. The borrower asks for and receives an option to repay any time after three years without penalty as well as the right to handle property tax payments without an escrow account. The borrower is required to purchase a term life insurance policy equal to the mortgage's face value, thereby providing effective low-cost family protection.

Completing the Transaction

Once the financing has been arranged, the present owner's clear title must be established (a title search). The transaction also needs to be registered and taxes paid in the proper locality. At the closing, the buyer, the seller, mortgage-granting institution, and their attorneys meet and pass the final papers and funds.

EXAMPLE: INVESTING IN A DUPLEX

Having discussed various aspects of real estate investing from a variety of viewpoints, an extended example is now in order. Suppose a duplex priced at $50,000 can (after negotiations) be acquired for $44,600. A 12% loan of $33,450 (75% of $44,600) is assumable. Payments on a 25-year loan of $33,450 would amount to $352.30 per month. Current monthly rentals are $300 for one side and $280 for the other (a total annual rental of $6,960). Current-year property taxes are $1,400; insurance, $400; repairs and upkeep, $500; and miscellaneous expenses, $200 ($2,500 total). Thus, gross annual income (ignoring interest, depreciation, and income taxes) amounts to $4,460 ($6,960 − $2,500).

Income and expense forecasts may be based on previous experience. Since rent schedules are known and verifiable, income is usually easier to project than expenses. Rents can generally be raised sufficiently to cover higher expenses. Moreover, proportional increases in rents and expenses should normally yield a positive incremental cash flow. A real estate broker or property manager may help one forecast future rental rates. Assume the following projection is made:

Year	1	2	3	4	5
Income	$7,260	$7,500	$7,740	$7,980	$8,220
Expense	2,600	2,700	2,800	2,900	3,000
Net Income	$4,660	$4,800	$4,940	$5,080	$5,220

The property is available at 10 times its current net annual rental, or $44,600. If this relation is maintained, the market value will rise to $52,200 in five years. The present values (using a 10% discount rate) of the net income and sale price are:

$$PV = 4,500\,(.909) + 4,800\,(.825) + 4,490\,(.751) + 5,080\,(.683)$$
$$+ 5,220\,(.621) + 52,200\,(.621) = \$51,033.78$$

If these expense and rent estimates are accurate, the property is a bargain at $44,600. Any price under $51,033.78 is expected to yield a 10% or greater return. Some additional factors should be considered, however.

First, are the revenue and expense estimates realistic? One should recompute the present value, reestimating revenues on the low side and expenses on the high side. While nothing may go wrong, a cushion would be helpful. Second, can the required sum be borrowed at the presumed rate? In this case a below-market-rate mortgage is assumable. Such deals are relatively rare. Also, any loan charges and fees should be considered. These expenses are added to the property's purchase price at the closing. The loan should not have a prepayment penalty. While one would like to cover monthly payments out of net income, a high-interest environment may make this impossible. Eventually, rental income may catch up with mortgage payments—but one should be prepared for several years of negative cash flows. Third, can the owner sell the property at the expected price without an agent? At least a modest amount of selling expenses should be anticipated. Fourth, are better deals available? Even though this property is attractively priced, other properties may be still better bargains. Since funds are limited, one may have to pass up some attractive properties. Fifth, will the owner accept a lower price? Sellers usually expect to bargain a bit over the price. How much can one reasonably expect to reduce the price through negotiation? Sixth, is the assumed 10% discount rate realistic in the current market? What is the property worth at a 15% discount rate, for example?

Cash Flow

Now consider this investment's cash flow. Current expected monthly rental income and expenses are $580 and $208.33 respectively. The difference of $371.67 should cover the assumable mortgage payments of $352.30. Before continuing this examination of cash flow, however, some important questions need addressing.

Improvements

Could additional revenue be generated without greatly increasing costs? One might for example, (1) turn the duplex into one large house, (2) divide the duplex into a four-bedroom rooming house, (3) remodel the existing units and raise the rents.

Checking comparable rents shows that converting the duplex into a single residence would reduce the return. The second possibility is also ruled out. The four bedrooms with joint use of two kitchens and living rooms should each rent for $175 per month, or $700, compared with the current $580. Alteration costs would be minor, but the area is not zoned for such usage and the neighbors fear that a zoning change would reduce their property values. Rather than anger them, rezoning is not attempted. Finally, the existing neighborhood, while fine for current tenants, would not justify sufficiently higher rents to make a major remodeling worthwhile.

Some minor changes might produce additional profits, however. First, a large garage in the rear is rented for $15 a month. Second, a tenant offers to repaint his unit's interior for the cost of the paint. His choice of colors is approved and durable paint is purchased. A new paint job should make the duplex easier to rent if the tenant leaves. Moreover, the tenant is likely to take better care of the unit after spending time improving it. Next, both tenants complain about their heating bills and ask for additional insulation. The insulation is added along with weatherstripping, caulking, storm windows, and doors, thereby yielding an energy tax credit. The insulation reduces the tenants' heating bills by more than enough to cover a monthly rent increase of $10. The tenant who has just repainted is agreeable to the increase. The other tenant, who had been commuting a long distance to her new job, gives notice.

Having a vacancy creates an opportunity. Both units are currently unfurnished. A furnished unit might rent for $320 a month, however. Since furniture could be bought for $500, the extra $30 a month would cover the cost in less than two years, while the furniture itself should last at least four years. A small advertisement in the local paper offers the furnished duplex for $320 a month. Prospective tenants are told that the unit will be available in 30 days. Before the 30 days are up, a tenant is found. Some of the previous tenant's furnishings are bought and the rest is picked up at a used furniture shop and a garage sale for slightly below the $500 estimate.

The conversion to a furnished apartment proved so profitable that a similar move is planned for the other unit. The current tenant has a lease that cannot be broken without refunding one month's rent, however. Since he takes good care of his unit and has just repainted its interior, asking him to leave seems unfair. As luck would have it, when the lease expires, he decides to move out. Furnishings costing $550 are moved in and a renter is quickly found at $350 per month. The rent on the other unit is increased to $325 a month.

The two units' second, third, fourth, and fifth year monthly rents are $360,

$370, $380, $390, and $335, $345, $350 and $365 respectively. The garage continues to rent for $15 a month. Expenses for the five years are: $2,600, $2,700, $2,800, $2,900 and $3,000. A cash-flow analysis reveals the following:

Year	1	2	3	4	5
Rental Income	$8,100	$8,340	$8,580	$8,760	$9,060
Expenses	2,600	2,700	2,800	2,900	3,000
Difference	5,500	5,660	5,780	5,880	6,060
Furnishing cost	500	550	0	0	0
Net	$5,000	$5,110	$5,780	$5,860	$6,060
Mortgage Payments	4,130	4,130	4,130	4,130	4,130
Net cash flow	$ 870	$ 980	$1,650	$1,730	$1,930

In just over four years, three quarters of the original investment is recovered, with a steady income payable thereafter. Let us now consider the return on the actual investment. To do this requires more information.

After-Tax Return

Since taxes are a critical part of the analysis, they should be incorporated into the assessment. This investment has earned much more than the original forecast. At the end of five years, net annual rents exceed expenses by $6,060, compared with the earlier estimate of $5,220. A sale at 10 times that amount ($60,600) would yield a substantial profit. Assume, however, that it sells for only $54,000 (about nine times net income) and that the owner's marginal tax rate is 30%. First, the property's taxable income is determined by subtracting all deductible expenses from rental income. While the amortization portion of the mortgage payment cannot be subtracted, depreciation, a non-cash expense, is deductible. If, for example, the house has a 25-year life remaining and the land is worth $6,525, an annual deduction of $1,527 can be taken ($38,175 divided by 25). Land is not depreciated. The furniture is assumed to last five years. Thus, the first year's depreciation is $100 and in subsequent years $210. Putting these figures together with the bank's computation of the annual interest portion of the mortgage-payments yields the following:

Year	1	2	3	4	5
Rental Income	$8,100	$8,340	$8,580	$8,760	$9,060
Expenses	2,600	2,700	2,800	2,900	3,000
Difference	$5,500	$5,660	$5,780	$5,860	$6,060
Depreciation	1,627	1,737	1,737	1,737	1,737
Operating Income	$3,873	$3,923	$4,043	$4,123	$4,323
Interest	3,996	3,984	3,972	3,848	3,936
Taxable income	(123)	(61)	71	175	387
Tax (assume a 20% rate)	0	0	21	53	116

*Actually the first two years' loss could be deducted against other income but to be conservative, we will ignore this option.

Adding non-cash expenses (in this case depreciation) to income produces net cash flows (before tax). Subtracting taxes from this figure produces net after-tax cash flow.

Year	1	2	3	4	5
Net cash flow	$1,504	$1,676	$1,808	$1,912	$2,124
Tax	0	0	21	53	116
Net after-tax cash flow	$1,504	$1,676	$1,787	$1,859	$2,008

Next, the gain on the unit's sale is computed. The costs of closing and the furniture are added to and depreciation deducted from the $44,600 purchase price to obtain a basis of $38,175. The basis is in turn subtracted from the expected net sale price of $54,000 (assume a direct sale, so no commissions are incurred), to produce a taxable gain of $15,825. Since the gain is long term, only 40%, or $6,330 is taxable. At 30%, taxes equal $1,899. Five years of amortization reduces the loan principal to $32,683. Subtracting the loan (assume no prepayment penalty) and taxes from the house's sale price yields the following:

Sale price	$54,000
Loan repayment	32,683
Gross profit	$21,317
Net Tax	1,889
Net Proceeds for Seller	$19,418

Thus the first-five-years' expected net after-tax cash flow on the original investment of $11,135 is $1,504, $1,676, $1,787, $1,858, $2,008, and $19,418. These flows represent an anticipated after-tax annual return of over 25%. That is, the present value of this projected income stream discounted at 25% is greater than the $11,135 original investment.

Assessment

While one could earn this much even with the high interest rates that now seem more or less permanent, the example does make some rather optimistic assumptions. For instance, occupancy is very unlikely to be 100%. In addition, the duplex might require a new roof, a new furnace, an outside paint job, or some other major unexpected expense. A tenant could leave owing back rent, taking some furniture, and/or seriously damaging the structure. Finally, part of the return is compensation for managing the property (collecting rents, making minor repairs, selling the property without a broker, etc.).

EXAMPLE: THE APARTMENT BUILDING OWNER

After some initial trial and error with duplexes and/or single-unit properties, the successful real estate investor with perhaps $80,000 to invest might next consider a 24-unit apartment building. Both the problems and the profit-potential increase with the scale of investment.

The investor might look for an old but solidly built structure in an established neighborhood close to transportation routes. Let us assume that a 10% minimum initial return is required. Note that the minimum acceptable return should vary with market interest rates. If, for example government bonds are yielding 12%, 10% would be too low.

Suppose that after reviewing the various possibilities, the investor chooses an established section in his or her locality. Real estate brokers are then contacted and objectives explained. Market conditions, while not ideal, are considered acceptable. Most available properties are either run down or high priced. After three months, however, a new listing looks promising. Since the property meets the desired physical objectives, its financial picture is carefully examined.

The seller's fact sheet shows gross income of $90,000, operating expenses of $70,000, and net cash flow of $20,000. A cash flow of 25% on the $80,000 down payment seems suspiciously high. In fact, it *is* too good. After careful examination, a more realistic picture emerges.

24-Unit Building - (2 bedrooms)

Financing
1st Mortgage—13% due 2002		$200,000
2nd Mortgage—15% due 1992 (10-year amount)		120,000
Down payment required		80,000
Total Price (after negotiations)		$400,000

Annual Results		Cash Flow
Gross Income		$ 90,000

Operating Expenses
Fuel	$ 2,870	
Utilities	1,070	
Taxes	10,400	
Insurance	275	
Maintenance	3,500	
Superintendent (part time)	2,580	
Management	12,500	
Vacancy (3%)	2,000	
Total operating expenses	35,195	
Interest 1st Mortgage	$25,869	
Interest 2nd Mortgage	17,625	
Principal 1st Mortgage	2,249	
Principal 2nd Mortgage	5,607	
Total Mortgage payments	$51,350	
Gross Cash Outflow		86,545
Cash Flow		$ 3,955
New Cash Flow		
Cash return on investment	4.9%	
Return prior to principal repayment (+ $7,856)	14.8%	

The first year's cash return is 4.9% instead of the claimed 25%. Clearly the potential buyer should always seek to determine the true story. Assume the buyer has decided to use a small local company to manage the property for 5% of gross income. Since the management company will look after the property's problems, why not get them into the act early? The buyer might well have them evaluate the building's price and general condition. Their fee should be modest compared to the purchase price.

Suppose that a price of $400,000 is eventually agreed to. The investor is now an apartment owner. What about the risks? What safeguards does the investor have? Any risks involved with the neighborhood and its environment should be considered. If the management company selects responsible tenants and maintains the property, the occupancy rate should be relatively high.

The building's superintendent is often given a rent-free apartment for doing odd jobs such as simple plumbing, carpentry, and electrical repairs. Perhaps a share of profits would increase the superintendent's interest. Beyond that, management problems belong to the management company. An occasional visit will reveal whether management is handled smoothly and show that the investor is not an absentee landowner.

If rents are reasonable for the area, turnover should be low and occupancy high. Tenants who offer to fix up their apartments should be encouraged. Their costs will be low (no labor) and they will be happier with units that they can alter to suit themselves.

How can profits be increased? Perhaps buying quality furnishings for some of the apartments would allow a $50-a-month rent increase. In two or three years, the furniture would be paid for but would probably last five or six years. Converting twelve of the apartments over several years could increase annual income by a few thousand dollars.

REFINANCING

Assume that an apartment building purchased five years ago for $200,000 with a $40,000 down payment has appreciated as amortization reduced the mortgage principal to $140,000. While a sale could realize a substantial gain, the owner may prefer to extract some funds by refinancing. If a reappraisal establishes $300,000 as a fair market value, the bank may be willing to increase the loan by $100,000 (to $240,000, or 80% of $300,000).

While refinancing may seem an attractive way to obtain additional funds, some pitfalls should be noted. An existing loan might have to be refinanced at a higher rate. Second, additional fees and penalties are associated with refinancing (e.g., a prepayment penalty, title search, and points). Third, the new loan will require larger mortgage payments.

Rather than a complete refinancing, the investor might take out a second mortgage, thereby retaining the existing mortgage while paying the new (higher) rate only on the new loan. Depending on the relative loan size and rates involved, obtaining a second may be a less costly and more flexible way of extracting additional principal.

OTHER INVESTMENTS

Condominiums

A substantial investment market has recently developed for condominiums. The rent on a unit will usually cover most of the costs while providing the owner with depreciation, interest, and property tax deductions. Condominium investments require only limited management, and maintenance is covered by a monthly assessment to the owner's association. Some parents even purchase condominiums for their children to live in while attending college.

Condominium investors have often earned high returns in the short period that the market has been active. Growth in the singles and older populations has helped boost condominium prices almost as rapidly as prices of single-family homes. Since the apartment shortage has added to the rental market's strength, condominium investors have frequently received excellent rents while they wait to sell their units at attractive prices. As with all investments, however, condominiums are far from a sure thing.[10]

While some financial institutions prefer borrowers who intend to live in their units, they will usually lend to condominium investors when money is less tight. On the other hand, many communities have strictly limited the conversion of existing apartments to condominiums. Thus potential government restrictions are one major factor to consider before buying an apartment building for condominium conversion.

Commercial Property

One could become a silent partner in a car wash, distributorship, or shopping center. That, in effect, is what commercial property investors are. Such investors do have the security of owning the property, however. If one tenant does poorly, perhaps another will be more successful. Since location is a very important aspect of profitable operations, potential investors should carefully evaluate main traffic arteries, exits, parking, and the proximity of competitors.

Investors can normally borrow up to 75% of a commercial property's price. A five- or ten-year lease is signed, obligating the tenant to pay all operating costs except for mortgage service, property insurance, and major renovations. The proposed tenant's credit-rating should be carefully examined before executing a lease. One should expect to earn at least several percentage points above the current inflation rate. Some owners charge a percentage of sales rather than a flat rental fee. Paying less in poor years provides renters with a bit of a cushion. They pay more in a good year when they can afford to. Assuming this added risk should generally increase the owner's return. Rents can also be structured as a flat amount plus a percentage of sales.

Franchises

Poor locations and inferior products often cause franchise investors to fail. Their high mortality rate makes gas stations and fast food operations a poor place to invest retirement money. Whether an investor should avoid franchises depends on his or her risk orientation. Many well-known franchises such as Baskin Robbins and McDonald's earn attractive returns. Investors should ask the franchiser to sign his or her lease. If the franchiser refuses, ask why. Don't they believe in their product? Additionally, many franchises will help secure the needed funds or offer a limited repayment-guarantee for the borrowed capital. Prospective investors should see if these options are available.

Land

Land ownership appeals to many investors both because of its high profit-potential and because in a sense land costs less than developed property.[11] Relatively large land parcels are often available for less than $50,000, while most developed real estate sells for far more.

Undeveloped real estate's attractiveness is increased if it yields a return. Some types of land are suitable for farming, grazing cattle, timber, hunting, or fishing. Thinning out woodlands allows the remaining trees to grow faster. Depending on the quality, the timber harvest might be sold for lumber, firewood, or Christmas trees.

While holding land for subsequent development is often profitable, years may go by before the growth of a city, the construction of a highway or shopping center, or some other nearby activity makes development attractive. Once such an event takes place, however, the land's value might multiply many times.

Unlike developed real estate, loans are generally limited to 50% of undeveloped land's value. Moreover, the taxes and mortgage payments will at best only be partially covered by the land's modest return (if any). Land investors must be prepared to service the loan and pay the property taxes largely from other sources.

Attractive parcels are likely to have one or more of the following characteristics.

1. The property is the next step or the second step beyond the area's most recent development.
2. The property is already zoned for development and the local government might allow even higher density residential, commercial, or industrial use.
3. A nearby property owner might soon want to add the land to his or her own parcel.

4. Developers or other knowledgeable real estate entrepreneurs are buying or about to start buying in the area.
5. A public or private development has been announced for the area.
6. The land is producing an attractive yield from farming, grazing, or some other activity, helping offset holding costs.

Note, however, that even under the most attractive circumstances, raw land is a relatively risky investment. As with other investments, largely overlooked land investments may be the most profitable.

Recreational Property

At one time, sites that offered recreational opportunities, especially those near water, were hotly sought after. More recently, gasoline's high price and occasional scarcity has hurt the recreational real estate market. Thus investors should consider how potential owners would reach their property. On the other hand, since many city dwellers still want to get away to fish, hunt, boat, hike, grow something, or just relax, well-located recreational properties continue to be attractive. Moreover, the transportation outlook can change, or a population-center might grow up near to a heretofore isolated area. As with other types of real estate investing, predictions and generalizations are hazardous. Isolated out-of-the-way spots might suddenly seem much closer to civilization if an interstate highway is built or oil is discovered nearby.

Cemeteries

Cemeteries are a potentially profitable form of land development.[12] Many states, particularly in the South and West, allow profit-making cemeteries. The economics are staggering. Depending on the configuration, between 1,000 and 1,500 graves may be obtained per acre. A successful cemetery will sell perhaps 500 to 800 graves per year, so 50 acres yields a 75-year supply. Grave sites may be priced for a few hundred to several thousand dollars. While some of this fee must be put in a maintenance trust, even at $100 per grave, an acre represents $100,000 of potential sales.

REAL ESTATE STOCKS AND TAX SHELTERS

Many investors are not well-situated to own, manage, and assume the risks involved with direct real estate ownership.[13] Yet past property returns are attractive. Perhaps such investors should consider other ways of investing in real estate. Commingled real estate funds, real estate investment trusts, real estate development companies, real estate tax shelters, real estate sales companies, and companies with substantial property holdings all represent indirect ways of investing in property. Each offers the opportunity to participate in the market without having a management involvement. Most of these investments are publicly traded companies that own, develop, manage, or sell real estate.

Commingled Real Estate Funds

Commingled real estate funds (CREF) are in essence self-liquidating unit investment trusts that assemble and manage real estate portfolios. Most are managed by large life insurance companies or commercial banks for their pension-fund clients. Others are available to trust-department clients. Still others are sold directly to the public. Though a relatively small industry, the funds have grown from $750 million in 1974 to $4 billion in 1979. According to Miles and Esty, the larger and older funds have tended to produce the highest returns.[14] Moreover the large funds are able to diversify more effectively.[15] The CREFs are, however, rather costly to buy and sell because secondary market trading in the units is very thin and initial sales to the public usually involve a substantial load.

Real Estate Investment Trusts

In 1961, Congress passed legislation permitting real estate investment trusts (REITs) to buy and manage portfolios of real estate and real estate loans. REITs are organized like and trade in the same markets as corporations, but are not assessed corporate profits taxes if their dividends equal 95% or more of their income. Many such firms were formed in the early 1970s, and most offered relatively attractive dividend yields. By mid-1974, however, overbuilding had begun to take its toll. Many real estate developers defaulted on their loans, forcing the REITs to foreclose on unfinished property that frequently bore no income. The REITs own debt continued to require servicing, however. In 1976, many REIT stocks sold for 5 to 10% of their original-issue prices. Some subsequently went bankrupt and others continued at the behest of their creditors. Eventually, however, most of the remaining REITs paid and/or swapped (for their own assets) their debts down to manageable levels. Many of the survivors now own both real estate, which has appreciated substantially, and have large tax-loss carryforwards.[16] Moreover Burns and Epley report that REITs provide excellent diversification for a stock and bond portfolio.[17]

Real Estate Development Companies

Real estate development companies own land, build on it, and then sell the developed property. They may construct apartments, office buildings, shopping centers, townhouses, single units, or practically any other type of structure. Often these projects are undertaken as joint ventures with other firms. Obviously, the development company hopes to build and resell the property at a substantial profit. Developers need large sums to finance their projects. If costs are higher or the market weaker than expected, the developer may incur a major loss. Thus these companies are quite risky, although as with firms in most industries, effectively managed companies often do well.

Real Estate Tax Shelters

Many companies make a business of selling tax shelters to people in high tax brackets. Tax shelters are often built around wildcat oil wells, cattle farms, equipment leases, and real estate.[18] Real estate tax shelter syndicates are generally formed to finance a construction project or the acquisition of existing properties. Subtracting depreciation, operating expenses, and interest from rental income produces a tax loss. Once rents rise sufficiently to generate a profit (in perhaps five years), the property is sold for a long-term gain (so the tax is relatively low, and deferred until the sale). Thus, the shelter produces tax losses for a number of years, and then when a taxable gain is realized, the applicable rate is substantially lower than that on ordinary income. To be an attractive investment, the capital gain needs to exceed the operating-loss total. Often, however, an investment that seems attractive on paper does not produce the desired results. Promoters sometimes organize these shelters to pay themselves unreasonably high sales and management fees. In other instances, inefficient management and real estate sales reduce the return. Inflated prices are frequently paid to acquire the shelter's property, reducing any chance for a gain. Most such shelters are not very marketable. Moreover, the IRS eventually disallows part or all of the tax-loss deduction, charging the investor interest and a penalty on the resulting tax underpayment. In other instances, tax laws are changed to eliminate or substantially reduce a particular type of deal's projected tax advantage.[19] While tax shelters are ill suited to most small investors, the wealthy may find the tax advantages well worth the effort.

Real Estate Sales Companies

Some companies sell retirement and investment homesites in Arizona, New Mexico, Florida, or even Australia through sales demonstrations coupled with a free dinner. The sales companies usually "promise" to install streets, recreation areas, and other improvements (swimming pools, tennis courts, golf courses, etc.). The property is offered for a minimum down payment, with principal to be repaid over an extended period. Slides, movies, and glossy brochures are used to show the property to its maximum advantage. Rarely if ever are these promotion-sales attractive to the buyer. Often the land is substantially overpriced and the promised improvements left undone. The stocks of most real estate sales companies are also very risky. At one time, such companies were reporting rapidly increasing earnings by claiming the full profit on a real estate sale in the year that they received the down payment. Since subsequent defaults were very common, such profit figures were misleading, to say the least. Now the firms must report income as payments are received.

Companies with Real Estate Holdings

In addition to the real estate related investments discussed above, a number of other types of companies have large property holdings. In most instances their properties are related to their primary business, while in others they just happen to own the real estate. Among the different types of real estate holders are:

Paper and Forest Products Companies—Such firms often have substantial land holdings from which they obtain their timber and wood-pulp needs. Some of this land may be worth far more as homesites, for example, while other property may be worth a good deal just as timberland.

Railroads—Many rails, particularly those located in the West, own substantial tracts, much of which goes back to nineteenth-century government land grants. Other rails own valuable downtown property near their terminals. Because of their poor prospects as transport companies, railroad stocks are often quite depressed. If their land holdings are ever liquidated, however, the profits should be substantial.

Ranch and Farm Companies—Some agricultural operations with substantial landholdings are organized as corporations. Frequently this property is carried on the books at very low historical costs. Such firms' liquidation values are often well above their stock's market prices.

Oil and Mining Companies—Generally, the most valuable holdings of these companies are their mineral resources, but often they, too, own some real estate. As with the other types of firms, the stock price often does not fully reflect the property's liquidation values.

Manufacturers—While most manufacturers only own the plants that they operate, some own valuable office buildings and attractive land holdings that are often overlooked by the market.

Insurance Companies—Life insurance companies have huge sums to invest. While most goes into bonds, mortgages, and other loans, some is invested in real estate. In many instances, the market seems to undervalue that property.

Movie Companies—While most have sold off their real estate, some still have valuable studio property in Hollywood. Such property may or may not be recognized in the stock's price.

The investment attractiveness of companies with substantial real estate holdings depends both on the extent to which their stock price reflects the holdings and the likelihood that the property will be sold in the relatively near future.

SUMMARY AND CONCLUSIONS

This chapter considered a number of aspects of real estate investing. A prospective real estate investor should first determine his or her suitability for such investing. Can sufficient funds be tied up for several years? Is the investor likely to remain in the same geographic area for the foreseeable future? Are the talents needed to manage real estate present? Is the investor willing and able to accept the risks? Next, certain principles of real estate investing were considered. These principles related to the determination of land price by its most valuable uses, the fixed supply of land, the possibility of adverse price moves, the importance of shopping around, the use of leverage, the control of expenses, the inspection of prospective real estate, the use of professionals, and the impact of government actions. Then three approaches to real estate valuation (market, cost, and income) were considered, followed by a detailed application of the income approach. Bargaining, loan-negotiation, property-management, and refinancing were examined along the way. Finally, various types of real estate investing and related investments (including duplexes, apartments, land, condominiums, recreational property, commercial property, franchises, cemeteries, and companies that own substantial amounts of real estate) were discussed.

REVIEW QUESTIONS

1. What type of investor is and is not suited for real estate investing?
2. Discuss the principles of real estate investment.
3. Compare the methods of valuing real estate, and discuss the uses of each.
4. Examine the advantages and disadvantages of investing in real estate compared with common stock.
5. Consider indirect real estate investing via REITs, development companies, tax shelters, etc.

REVIEW PROBLEMS

1. Ask three local bankers for their terms on rental property loans. Also determine closing costs. Compare the rates and write a report.
2. You are considering the purchase of a parcel of land for $15,000. You can borrow up to 50% of the purchase price at a rate of 16%. What rate of return on the investment is appropriate to make this offer attractive? Explain.
3. Ask a real estate agent to recommend three investments. Evaluate each investment's price using the income, market, and replacement cost approaches. Determine the highest price that should be paid for each property.
4. Evaluate the property where you now live. If you were the seller what

would you ask for it? What is the least you would take for it? If you were a prospective buyer, how would you proceed? What is the most you would pay? What would you try to buy it for?

5. An apartment building is offered for sale at $180,000. After expenses, it offers a net rental income of $28,000 per year. The rents, expenses, and market value of the property are expected to remain constant for the foreseeable future. The buyer may borrow up to 90 percent of the purchase price at 14 percent. The seller agrees to deduct any closing costs from the purchase price.

   (a) Should you buy it? Why or why not?

   (b) Assume you do buy it and borrow 90 percent on a 25-year loan and are in the 35-percent tax bracket. The apartment is depreciated over a 40-year period. Calculate after-tax cash flow for a 10-year period. Assume you sell for $180,000 at the end of the 10-year period. Interest on the loan is as follows:

Year	Interest	Principal	Principal Outstanding
1985	$22,631.97	$ 769.23	$161,230.77
1986	22,517.08	884.12	160,346.65
1987	22,385.06	1,016.14	159,370.51
1988	22,233.29	1,167.91	158,162.60
1989	22,058.89	1,342.31	156,820.29
1990	21,858.41	1,542.79	155,277.50
1991	21,628.02	1,773.18	153,504.32
1992	21,363.20	2,038.00	151,466.32
1993	21,058.85	2,342.35	148,123.97
1994	20,709.03	2,692.17	146,431.80

6. Assemble a list of companies with real estate holdings whose market values substantially exceed the values of their outstanding shares. Determine if a major shareholder group controls each company. Plot their performances over time. Write a report.

NOTES

1. J. Webb, C. Sirmans, "Yields and Risk Measures for Real Estate 1966–77," *Journal of Portfolio Management*, Fall 1980, pp. 14–20; T. Cayne, W. Goulet and M. Picconi, "Residential Real Estate versus Financial Assets," *Journal of Portfolio Management*, Fall 1980, pp. 20–24.

2. E. Paris, "Make Me an Offer: At last California Confirms that the Law of Gravity Applies to House Prices Too," *Forbes*, December 7, 1981, p. 128.

3. Hume Publishing, "Real Estate 1," *Successful Investing and Money Management*, Hume Publishing, 1981 pp. 175.

4. *Forbes*, "Real Estate: A Time to Beware," *Forbes*, June 11, 1979, pp. 53–61.

5. *Business Week*, "Nailing Down an Affordable Mortgage," *Business Week*, March 14, 1983, pp. 152–155.

6. L. Downie, *Mortgage on America*, Pareger, New York, 1974, pp. 135–152.

7. J. Webb and R. Curcio, "Interest Rate Illusions and Real Property Purchases," *Journal of Portfolio Management*, Summer 1982, pp. 67.

8. J. Andrews, "Creative Financing Ends in Foreclosure for More Home Buyers," *Wall Street Journal*, February 26, 1981, pp. 1, 19.

9. D. Rotbart and M. Yao, "Record Level of Home Foreclosures is Bringing Grief to Many Families," *Wall Street Journal*, June 19, 1982, p. 23.

10. R. Guenther, "South Florida's Condo Boom Cools as Speculator's Retreat," *Wall Street Journal*, November 20, 1981, p. 29; R. Smith, "Condo Market Turns Into 'Disaster' As Housing Slump Cools Demand," *Wall Street Journal*, July 2, 1982 p. 15.

11. *Business Week*, "Investing in Rural Land," *Business Week*, April 30, 1979, 106–108.

12. S. Reiher, "All Sales are Final," *Forbes*, October 30, 1978, pp. 106–108; A. Bagamery, "Death and Real Estate," *Forbes*, August 30, 1982, pp. 68–69; P. Engelmayer, "Cemetery Companies Aggressively Market Burial Plots as Costs Soar and Business Falls," *Wall Street Journal*, January 24, 1984, p. 35.

13. P. Miller, "Strategies for First-Time Property Investors," *Fact*, April 1983, pp. 55–57; N. Schloss, "Realty Reality, A Look at the Alternatives," *American Association of Individual Investors Journal*, April 1984, pp. 10–14.

14. M. Miles and A. Esty, "How Well Do Commingled Real Estate Funds Perform?," *Journal of Portfolio Management*, Winter 1982, pp. 62–68.

15. M. Miles and T. McCue, "Diversification in the Real Estate Portfolio," *Journal of Financial Research*, Spring 1984, pp. 57–68.

16. D. Nossiter, "Building Values, REITs Adapt to Changes in the Business Climate," *Barron's*, November, 1982, pp. 11, 34; L. Wayne, "The Return of the REIT's," *New York Times*, December 5, 1982, pp. 1F, 3F.

17. W. Burns and D. Epley, "The Performance of Portfolios of REITs & Stocks" *Journal of Portfolio Management*, Spring 1982, pp. 37–42.

18. *Business Week*, "Tax Shelters: The Action is in Oil and Real Estate," *Business Week*, December 22, 1973; M. Farrell, "Tax-Advantaged Oil and Gas Ventures," *American Association of Individual Investors Journal*, November 1983, pp. 29–33; M. Farrell, "Equipment Leasing," *American Association of Individual Investors Journal*, May 1984, pp. 11–17.

19. K. Slater, "Before Buying Tax Shelters Look at Moves in Congress to Limit Abuses, Change Rules," *Wall Street Journal*, April 9, 1984, p. 37.

Conclusion: Investing, an Overview

Investing is somewhat akin to a very special kind of boat race. Contestants are allowed to use a wide variety of vessels, including some expensive ships with well-trained crews in top condition. Others go out alone in dangerously unseaworthy crafts. The water is poorly charted. The current is constantly shifting and frequently changes. Several regulating groups have overlapping authorities. Some people cheat successfully. Those who offer assistance usually assist themselves more than they help their clients. The contestants watch each other closely, and once one finds a useful technique, the word usually spreads, thereby destroying its relative value. Clearly the race is difficult. On the other hand, most who play long enough receive small prizes, and some do very well indeed. At times, however, virtually no one wins, and many suffer substantial losses.

REALISTIC EXPECTATIONS

Like this hypothetical race, investing is difficult and can be filled with disappointments born of unrealistic expectations. Several years ago a professor in a major university asked his MBA students to estimate the average return each would expect to produce as portfolio managers. The answers averaged 35%. At 35%, $1,000 becomes a half million dollars in 20 years and a quarter billion dollars in 40 years. Clearly very few portfolios could consistently grow at such a rate, or much of the nation's wealth would soon be concentrated in a very few hands. In a given year, some portfolios increase by 35% or 50% or more, but consistent growth at even a 20% rate is unlikely. Investors would do well to content themselves with less lofty goals. Long-run performance may average 8 to 9%, and one who outperforms this by a few percent is clearly successful.

As important as setting realistic goals is, the realization that one's own judgment must be relied upon. As a group, investment analysts, brokers, and portfolio managers have yet to demonstrate above-average performance. Reliance on others is likely to produce random results. The judgments of such individuals will sometimes be accurate, but only perceptive investors are at all likely to discriminate between accurate and inaccurate advice.

The dynamic nature of the market should also be noted. Heretofore useful techniques that become well known tend to lose their values. Thus much of

528

the research discussed in this book will lose its value as it becomes more widely known.

SHOULD INVESTORS MANAGE THEIR OWN PORTFOLIOS?

Readers should now be prepared to decide whether or not they are willing to pit themselves against the market's collective wisdom. Those who are reluctant to test their skills can select one or several mutual funds to manage their wealth (Chapter 14); hire an investment manager (Chapter 3); or assemble their own portfolio of low-risk, fixed-income securities (Chapter 15). Each of these strategies requires considerably less skill than is needed to manage portfolios of equities or most other types of investments.

This book should help one reach a decision to manage or to let others manage. The material in Chapters 3 and 14 should help one decide how to select a manager. If the decision is to manage one's own portfolio, the investor will find a number of other chapters useful.

STEPS INVOLVED IN MANAGING A PORTFOLIO

Serious-minded investors will continually look for interesting investment opportunities (Chapter 9). They will read the financial press and keep up with business news (Chapter 10). They will be alert to the comments of friends and to observations that may have investment implications. They will even listen to their brokers (Chapter 3).

From these various sources they will accumulate a list of securities deserving further study. These securities, as well as those of other companies in similar industries, will be researched until some sort of preliminary decision is made. The most attractive investments will have a number of characteristics. For example, stocks of small firms neglected by analysts that have low PEs but deserve a higher multiple are particularly attractive candidates (Chapter 9). Similarly, potential takeover candidates (Chapter 9) and stocks with a story that has not yet caught on (Chapter 13) often do quite well.

Consistently high past earnings growth is a favorable sign (Chapter 4). Interim earnings and management forecasts should be considered (Chapter 4). One would also want to evaluate the potential of the firm's industry and the firm's position within the industry (Chapter 7) and the orientation of its management (Chapter 9). If the industry has plenty of growth potential with no apparent constraints on the horizon; if the firm appears well equipped to participate in the industry's success; and if management appears to be orientated toward the stockholders' welfares, the stock may well be attractive. One would want to check the firm's financial statements for any evidence of accounting gimmicks (Chapter 8) as well as to evaluate the firm's short- and long-term financial health (Chapter 7). If managers are purchasing stock in their firm, and if the firm is buying stock in itself, the stock may well be underpriced (Chapter 13). An R&D-oriented firm which has been successful in its past research (Chapter 9) is a plus.

If the stock looks attractive on the basis of considerations mentioned above, a further examination is indicated. First, one would want to investigate the various possible means of participation in the firm's success: common or preferred stock, convertible bonds, or convertible preferred stock, warrants, and options (Chapter 17 and 18). Each type of security has its own particular attractions and drawbacks. Investors should consider the relative prices of these securities and their own financial position and preferences (Chapter 1). Depending on one's attitude toward and ability to absorb risk, the investor may find convertibles, common, or warrants attractive. In particular circumstances, he or she may find the other securities either over- or underpriced relative to the common.

Assuming that the investor has found the company appealing, and has decided on a type of security that is most attractively priced relative to his or her needs, the investor should next consider the state of the market. Particular attention should be given to the relative (vis-a-vis interest rates) multiple of the popular averages (Chapter 12), the state of the economy and its prospects, and the likely future of fiscal, and especially monetary, policy (Chapter 11). Some attention may be given to some of the indicators of market strength such as the *Barron's* confidence index, specialists' short selling, liquidity of mutual funds, etc. (Chapter 12). If PE ratios are low relative to interest rates, if no downturn is on the horizon, if expansionary fiscal and monetary policies are likely, and if market conditions are otherwise favorable, it is probably a good time to buy.

Next the investor should examine his or her current portfolio and financial resources. Is the addition of this security likely to increase or decrease the portfolio's risk (Chapter 5)? Are liquid resources available to finance the purchase (Chapter 1)? If not, are some other securities ready to be sold?

After determining whether the firm has promising prospects and is favorably priced, which securities are best suited to the investor's needs, whether the market is at an attractive level, how buying the security would affect the total portfolio, and if resources are available to finance the purchase, the investor should consider how to acquire the security (Chapter 3). If the sums involved are appreciable and the investor simply wants to make trades, a discount broker should probably be used. If the stock is traded on an exchange, the investor should estimate the optimum limit-order buy price with reference to past volatility, tendency to cluster, and ex-dividend date (Chapter 3). He or she might also check prices on the third market and regional exchanges if applicable (Chapter 3). If the stock is traded OTC and considered attractive in spite of the spread, a market order could be entered at the current price or the investor could wait for a better price to appear and then buy.

Assuming the order is placed and executed, the investor should then follow the firm and any news on it. At a minimum he or she should read the annual and quarterly reports and check *Value Line* and Standard & Poor's commentaries on the firm (Chapter 10). The investor should be constantly aware of three options:

buy more, hold, or sell. If the firm does well but the market is slow to recognize its performance, a further purchase may be warranted. If nothing major happens for some time, the investor is urged to be patient. Rapid trading and turnover may be profitable for the broker, but probably not for the investor (Chapter 3). The firm and the market should be closely watched for any clouds. If a market downturn appears likely, some selling is probably advisable. Speculative high-multiple stocks are particularly vulnerable in a downturn (Chapter 12). Very few stocks are immune to a general market decline, however. Once a decline has begun, the investor is well-advised to let it run its course. Once the averages have fallen sufficiently and the market foresees a future economic expansion, a rise is likely (Chapter 12). Investors would like to time their re-entrance as close to the bottom as possible, although one should realize that to get relatively close is a real triumph (Chapter 12). A gradual re-entrance is usually advisable. At the bottom, the high-risk, low-quality speculative stocks are most attractive and have the greatest upside potential (Chapter 12).

The steps outlined above will be very difficult to follow fully. No doubt few trading opportunities will fit all the desirable characteristics mentioned. Seldom will the market be clearly in the buying area. Ambiguous firm and market characteristics are the rule, not the exception. To some extent, the investor can wait for attractive stocks and markets although he or she should not expect perfection in either. One must reach a compromise between attractive situations and truly outstanding but very rare opportunities. Like most worthwhile pursuits, investing involves many trade-offs and balancing of interest.

PERSPECTIVE ON THE EFFICIENT MARKET HYPOTHESIS

Will a faithful attempt to follow this outline ensure success? Nothing can ensure success in the stock market. Some people believe that the market is so efficient (Chapter 6), that any attempt to spot systematically mispriced securities is certain to fail. This book may be taken as a brief for the opposing view. While difficult, successful investing is not a hopeless dream. Turn the question around. Can one make mistakes by knowing too little? Obviously: rapid turnover (Chapter 14), buying front-end-loaded mutual funds (Chapter 14), believing the chartists (Chapter 12), using short interest as a timing signal (Chapter 12), paying a high premium for growth stocks (Chapter 9), ignoring tax considerations (Chapter 2), believing the market to be an effective inflation hedge (Chapter 11), ignoring third-market and regional exchange opportunities (Chapter 3), and paying substantial retail commissions are all examples. Surely the most dogmatic believer in market efficiency will concede that one who knows too little can do consistently worse than the market. The question that remains, then, is whether one can know enough to outperform the market consistently. That judgment is left to the reader.

Glossary of Investment Terms

absolute priority of claims principle
The bankruptcy principle that each class of liability claims is repaid in full before the next highest priority category can receive even a partial payment.

acceptance or bankers acceptance A money market instrument usually arising from international trade. A bank's guarantee or acceptance makes such issues highly marketable.

accelerated depreciation Writing off assets at a more rapid rate than proportional to their pro rata life expectancy.

accrued interest The pro rata interest obligation that has accumulated since the last payment date. Most bonds trade at a price which reflects their net market price plus accrued interest. Defaulted and certain other bonds, however, trade "flat," which means without any allowance for accrued interest.

acid test ratio *see* quick ratio

actuarial tables Tables reporting particular age group's probabilities of death. These tables are based on past experience with separate tables for men and women and certain hazard-ous occupations. Such a table might indicate that at age 25, a male would have 1 chance in 350 of dying within the next year and is expected to live 36 more years (to age 71). A 65-year-old male's chance of dying in the next year might be reported as 1 in 15 and his future life expectancy as ten years (to age 75).

ADR (American depository receipt) A United States-traded security representing stock in a foreign corporation.

Advisor's Sentiment Index A technical market indicator based on a composite of investment advisor's forecasts. Bullish advisor's sentiment is thought to forecast a market decline.

agency security A debt security issued by federal agencies such as GNMA or Freddie Mac.

air rights The right to build over someone else's property. For example, an office complex might be constructed above a downtown rail switching yard.

All-Savers Certificate A tax-exempt security offered by banks and thrifts; authority to issue these securities expired at the end of 1982.

all-or-nothing order An order which must be executed in its entirety or not at all.

alpha The intercept term in the market model; provides an estimate of a security's return for a zero market return.

amalgamation Combining more than two firms into a single firm.

AMEX (American Stock Exchange) The second largest U.S. stock exchange (after NYSE); occasionally abbreviated as ASE; listed firms tend to be medium size compared with the larger NYSE issues and the typically smaller OTC issues.

alternative minimum tax Tax which may be applicable to those with large amounts of otherwise sheltered income such as long-term capital gains on accelerated depreciation deductions.

American Association of Individual Investors Organization designed to help and promote the interests of small investors.

American Stock Exchange Index A value-weighted index of AMEX stocks.

amortization The writing off of an asset or liability particularly a paper asset or liability.

annuity An asset which usually promises to pay a fixed amount periodically for a predetermined period. Some annuities, however, pay a sum for an individual's lifetime and certain annuities' values are variable depending on the issuer's investment experience. Most annuities are sold by insurance companies.

annual report A yearly report to shareholders containing financial statements (balance sheets, income statement, source and application, and funds statement), auditor's statement, president's letter, and various other information.

antidilution clause A provision in a convertible bond or other security indenture restricting new share issues.

anxious-trader effects Short-run price distortions caused by sales or purchases of impatient large traders.

appreciation mortgage A mortgage in which the lender is given the rights to a percentage of any price appreciation derived when the property is sold. In exchange the borrower receives a more attractive loan rate.

arbitrage (pure) Simultaneously buying in one market and selling equivalent assets in another for a certain if modest profit. *See also* risk arbitrage.

arbitrage (risk) The taking of offsetting positions in the securities of an acquisition candidate and the would-be acquirer which should show a profit if the merger takes place.

arbitrage pricing model A competitor to the capital asset pricing model which introduces more than one index in place of (or in addition to) CAPM's market index.

ARM (adjustable rate mortgage) A type of mortgage in which the interest rate is periodically adjusted as market rates change.

Arnold Bernhard and Company The firm that owns Value Line and manages the Value Line mutual funds.

arrearage An overdue payment as in passed preferred dividends. If cumulative, arrearage must be made up before common dividends are resumed.

ask The lowest price at which a security is currently offered for sale; may emanate from a specialist (exchange), market maker (OTC), or unexercised limit order.

asset Any item of value; often income-producing; appears on left of balance sheet.

at-the-close order An order that must be executed near or at the daily close.

at-the-opening order An order that must be executed at the daily opening.

auditor's statement A letter from the auditor to the company and its shareholders in which the accounting firm certifies the propriety of the methods used to produce the firm's financial statements.

Auto Ex A division of Xerox which attempts to forecast large block trades for institutional clients.

balanced fund A mutual fund which invests in both stocks and bonds.

balance sheet A financial statement providing an instant picture of a firm's or individual's financial position; lists assets, liabilities, and net worth.

balloon payment A final large principal payment on a debt that is either incompletely amortized or not amortized.

Barron's A major weekly investment periodical published by Dow Jones, Inc.

Barron's Confidence Index A technical indicator based on the yield-differential between high-grade and average-grade corporate bonds. A small differential is a sign of confidence in the future. A large differential signifies a lack of confidence.

banker's acceptance *see* acceptance

bankruptcy proceeding A legal process for dealing formally with a defaulted obligation. May result in a liquidation or reorganization. *See also* Chapter X Bankruptcy and Chapter XI Bankruptcy.

basis (commodity) The difference between the spot and futures price.

basis (taxable) An asset's acquisition cost less any capital distributions. The taxable gain is the difference between the sale proceeds and the basis.

basis point One hundredth of one percentage point; primarily used with interest rates.

basis risk The risk that a commodity contract's basis will move adversely.

BCG or Boston Consulting Group A strategic planning consulting firm famous for its growth-share matrix.

bear One who expects a declining market.

bear market A declining market.

bear raid An attempt to drive prices down by selling short.

bearer bond An unregistered bond whose ownership is determined by possession.

Beta A parameter which relates stock performance to market performance. For a $z\%$ change in the market, a stock will tend to change by $\beta z\%$ where β is the stock's beta ratio.

bid The highest currently unexercised offer to buy a security; may emanate from a specialist (exchange), market maker (OTC), or limit order.

big board A popular term for the NYSE, the largest U.S. stock exchange.

bills Government debt securities issued on a discount basis by the U.S. Treasury for periods of less than one year.

Black Scholes Formula An option pricing formula based on the assumption that a riskless hedge between an option and its underlying stock should yield the riskless return. Asserts that option value is a function of the stock price, striking price, stock return volatility, riskless interest rate, and option term.

block trade A trade involving 10,000 shares or more; usually handled by a block trader.

block trader One who assembles the passive side of a block trade.

blue chip stock Shares of a large, mature company with a steady record of profits and dividends and a high probability of continued earnings.

blue sky laws State laws designed to protect investors from security frauds.

Blume Adjustment A method of adjusting estimated betas toward unity to improve their general accuracy.

bond A debt obligation (usually long-term) in which the borrower promises to pay a set coupon rate until the issue matures, at which time the principal is repaid. Some bond issues are secured by a mortgage on a specific property, plant, or piece of equipment. *See also* debenture, collateral trust bond, and equipment trust certificate.

bond rating An estimated index of a bond's quality/default risk.

bond swap A technique for managing a bond portfolio by selling some bonds and buying others; may be designed for taxes, yields, or trading profits.

book value of common shares The total assets of an enterprise minus its liabilities, minority interests, and preferred stock par, divided by the number of outstanding common shares.

borrower life insurance A life insurance policy on a borrower equal to the outstanding loan principal and naming the lender as the beneficiary.

broker An employee of a financial intermediary who acts as an agent in the buying and selling of securities. Unlike a dealer, a broker never owns the securities that he or she trades for his or her customers.

broker call-loan rate or call-loan rate The interest rate charged by banks for loans brokers use to support their margin loans to customers. The margin loan rate is usually scaled up from the broker call-loan rate.

brokerage firm A firm that offers various services such as access to the securities markets, managing accounts, margin loans, investment advice, underwriting, etc.

business cycle The pattern of fluctuations in the economy.

Business Week A major weekly business periodical published by Mc-Graw-Hill Inc.

bull One who expects a rising market.

bull market A rising market.

call An option to buy stock or some other asset at a prespecified price over a prespecified period.

call feature In bonds or preferred stock, an option of the issuing company to repurchase the securities at a set price over a prespecified period.

call-loan rate *see* broker call-loan rate

call price The price at which a bond, preferred, warrant, or other security may be redeemed prior to maturity. Also referred to as the redemption price.

call protection An indenture provision preventing a security (usually a bond or preferred stock) from being redeemed earlier than a certain time after its issue. Thus a twenty-year bond might not be callable for the first five years after its issue.

call risk The danger that a callable bond or preferred will be called.

callable The property of a security allowing the issuer to redeem it prior to maturity.

capital asset Virtually any investment asset. To qualify as a capital asset (and thus be subject to long-term capital gains treatment), an asset must be held as an investment rather than in inventory as an item of trade.

capital distribution A dividend paid out of capital rather than earnings. Such distributions are not taxed when received but do reduce the investment's basis.

capital gains (losses) The difference between the basis and sales price of an investment asset. A capital asset that is held more than one year is considered long-term, and only 40% of the gain is taxable. Only 50% of net long-term losses are deductible against income and only up to $3,000 annually.

capital market line The theoretical relation between an efficiently diversified portfolio's expected return and risk derived from the capital asset pricing model.

capitalizing of expenses Placing current business expenses on the balance sheet and writing them off over time.

CAPM (Capital Asset Pricing Model) The theoretical relationship that explains returns as a function of the riskfree rate and market risk.

capacity effect The tendency of inflationary pressures to accelerate when the economy approaches the full employment level.

carry The cost of holding a physical commodity until it is deliverable on a futures contract.

cash flow Reported profits plus depreciation, depletion, and amortization.

cash management account An individual financial account that combines checking, credit card, money fund, and margin accounts in order to maximize returns and minimize interest charges on transaction balances.

cash market A market where physical commodities (spot) are traded for cash.

cash surrender value The accumulated savings element of a life insurance policy that can be recovered by canceling the policy, or borrowed against at a specified interest rate.

CBOE (Chicago Board Options Exchange) The first and largest of the option exchanges.

CBT (Chicago Board of Trade) The largest of the commodity exchanges; lists futures in wheat, corn, oats, soybeans, plywood, silver, GNMA, and long-term bonds.

CD (certificate of deposit) Special redeemable debt obligations issued by banks and other depository institutions.

CEA (Commodity Exchange Authority) A defunct government agency that had regulatory authority over agricultural futures markets.

Central Certificate Service An organization that allows clearing firms to effect security deliveries with computerized bookkeeping entries.

central market A Congressionally mandated concept for a complete linkup of the various markets trading securities. As of 1984 the development process was underway but incomplete.

central unemployment rate The unemployment rate for males in the 25 to 45 age group.

CFTC (Commodity Futures Trading Commission) The federal regulator of the futures markets.

changes in financial position statement An accounting statement that reports on a firm's cash inflows and outflows.

Chapter X bankruptcy Formal, detailed, and usually time-consuming bankruptcy proceeding.

Chapter XI bankruptcy Informal, less costly, and quicker procedure than Chapter X; only allowable where creditors agree.

characteristic line The relationship between a security's expected return and the market return. The line is defined by the security's α (intercept) and β (slope parameter).

chart reading Attempting to forecast price changes from charts based on past price and volume data.

Chicago Mercantile Exchange (the Merc) The second largest of the commodity exchanges; lists futures in cattle, hogs, pork bellies, fresh broilers, and lumber.

churning Overactive trading of customer accounts designed to generate commisions for the manager/broker.

classified common stock Different categories of stock, some of which may be nonvoting and others non-dividend receiving.

clearing house An organization that guarantees fulfillment of futures contracts or options contracts.

Clifford trust A device for shifting tax liability on income, usually from parent to dependent child. The principal reverts to the parent (or the other person setting up the trust) at the trust's expiration. The trust must be irrevocable for at least ten years.

clipping coupons Claiming income on coupon bonds by detaching each physical coupon and presenting it for payment when due.

CLOB (consolidated limit order book) The central market concept of a composite book of limit orders which can be executed in any market where a security is traded. As of 1985, the proposed concept had not been implemented.

closed-end fund A type of investment company organized as a corporation with its stock traded in the same markets as other stocks. Its price may vary appreciably from fund's net asset value.

closing costs Costs associated with obtaining a real estate loan and completing the purchase. May include title search, points, transfer taxes, and various other fees.

Coffee, Sugar and Cocoa Exchange A commodity exchange located in New York City which lists futures contracts on coffee, sugar, and cocoa.

collateral Asset pledged to assure repayment of debt.

collateral trust bond Secured bonds such as equipment trust certificates which are secured by railroad rolling stock or airplanes.

combination security An asset combining characteristics of more than one type of security. Combination securities include convertible bonds, convertible preferred stocks, hybrid convertibles, equity notes, commodity-backed bonds, and stock-indexed bonds.

commercial paper or paper Short-term, usually low-risk debt issued by large corporations with very strong credit ratings.

commingled real estate fund or CREF In effect, a self-liquidating unit investment trust with a managed real estate portfolio.

commissions Fees charged by brokers for handling security trades.

commodity In general, any article of commerce. In investment terminology, any of a select group of items traded on one of the commodity exchanges. Such commodities are traded either spot (for immediate delivery) or in the futures market (for delivery at a prespecified future date.)

commodity board An electronic sign in the trading room of a commodity exchange that displays current market statistics.

commodity option A put or call on a futures contract.

common stock Represents proportional ownership of an incorporated enterprise. Common stockholders are the residual claimants for earnings and assets after all holders of debt and preferred stock have received their contractual payments.

compound interest Returns are compounded by reinvesting one period's income to earn additional income the following period. Thus at 9% compounded annually, $100 will yield $9 the first year. In the following year the 9% will be applied to $109, for a return of $9.81. In the third year the principal will have grown to $118.81 (100 + 9 + 9.81) and another 9% will add about $10.62. This process continues with the interest rate being applied to a larger and larger principal. Compounding may take place annually, as above, or more frequently.

compound value The end-period value of a sum earning a compounded return.

COMPUSTAT Data Tape A data source containing balance sheet, income statement, and other information on a substantial number of companies for the past 20 years.

conditional forecast A forecast based on some exogenous factor such as a stock performance forecast relative to market performance.

Conference Board An organization that compiles quarterly capital appropriations statistics and reports them in *Manufacturing Industrial Statistics.*

conglomerate A company with a diversified portfolio of business units; particularly one formed though a merger of a diverse array of formerly independent companies.

consumer credit Personal debt as represented by credit card loans, finance company loans, and similar debts.

consumer durables Long-life assets such as furniture or appliances.

Consumer Price Index (CPI) A monthly cost of living index prepared by the U.S. Government's Bureau of Labor Statistics.

Consumer Reports A periodical that frequently contains personal-finance-oriented articles.

consumption expenditures Spending by individual consumers on final goods and services.

convertible bond A bond that may be converted into common shares at some predetermined rate prior to its maturity.

consol A perpetual debt instrument that pays interest but never matures and thus never returns principal.

contrary-opinion An investment approach that concentrates on out-of-favor securities, asserting that what is not wanted today may be quite desirable in the future.

conversion A complicated maneuver involving purchasing options, shorting the underlying stock, and reinvesting the sale proceeds. Brokerage fims can use the technique to earn substantial returns when option and stock prices are appropriately related.

conversion price The face value of a convertible bond divided by the number of shares into which it is convertible.

conversion ratio The number of common shares into which a convertible bond or preferred may be converted.

conversion value The market price of a stock times the number of shares for which the convertible may be exchanged.

convertible A bond or preferred stock that may be exchanged for a specific number of common shares.

convertible debenture A debenture which may, for the bond's life, be exchanged for a specific number of shares of the issuing-firm's common stock.

convertible preferred A preferred stock that may be exchanged for a specific number of shares of the issuing-company's common stock.

corner A large, often controlling, interest in a security issue or other specific asset-type which pushes the market price to a very high level and restricts supply, especially to shorts who may need to cover.

corporates Corporate bonds.

corporate bond fund A mutual fund holding a diversified portfolio of corporate bonds.

correlation coefficient A measure of the comovement tendency of two variables.

coupon bond A bond with attached coupons which must be clipped and sent in to receive interest payments.

coupon effect The price impact of differential-yield components derived from coupon versus price appreciation as a bond moves toward maturity. Thus a deep-discount low-coupon bond will offer a yield-to-maturity that includes a substantial component of tax-sheltered capital gains. Such a bond's price will usually be affected favorably by the coupon effect.

coupon-equivalent yield Yield on an investment computed to correspond with a bond which pays a semiannual coupon.

coupon rate The stated dollar return of a fixed-income investment.

covariance The covariance of variables x and y is: $\text{Cov} = E[x-E(x)][y-E(y)]$ where $E(z)$ is the expected value of z. If x and y tend to be above their means simultaneously or below their means simultaneously, the covariance is positive. If one is above when the other tends to be below, the covariance is negative. If they are independent, the covariance is zero.

covered writing Writing options against existing stock holdings.

covering Repurchasing securities or other assets sold short.

crack Combination commodity trade in which one buys crude oil futures and sells corresponding amounts of heating oil and gasoline futures.

credit balance A positive balance, as in a brokerage account.

credit union A cooperative association where the members' pooled savings are available for loans to the membership.

CREF *see* commingled real estate fund

CRISPE Data Tape A data source containing daily stock price information.

crown jewel option Antitakeover defense in which the most sought-after subsidiary of a target firm is spun off.

Crown loan Interest-free loan, usually from parent to dependent child; designed to shift taxable income from high- to low-bracket individual.

crush A combination trade, especially a commodity trade, in which one buys soybean futures and shorts corresponding amounts of soybean oil and meal futures.

cumulative preferred A preferred stock for which dividends in arrears must be paid before common dividends can be resumed.

cumulative voting A method of voting for directors which allows minority shareholders to concentrate their votes on one or a few candidates and thereby elect at least their proportional share.

cum-rights period The time prior to the day-of-record that determines when shareholders receive a rights distribution.

Curb or Curb Exchange The New York Curb Exchange, which became the American Stock Exchange in 1953.

current assets Assets that are expected to be used up or converted to cash within the next year or next operating period, whichever is longer. Cash, accounts receivable, and inventory are the major types of current assets.

current liabilities Liabilities that will become due in the next year or the next operating cycle, whichever is longer. Current liabilities include accounts payable, short-term bank loans, the current portion of long-term debt, and taxes payable.

current ratio The ratio of current assets to current liabilities; a measure of short-term liquidity.

current yield A bond's coupon rate divided by its current market price, or a stock's indicated dividend rate divided by its per-share price.

day-of-record The date on which ownership is determined for that quarter's dividends or for the issuance of some other distributions such as rights.

day order An order that is cancelled if it is not executed on the day it is entered.

day trader A type of commodity trader who closes all positions by the end of the day.

dealer A security trader who acts as a principal rather than as an agent. Thus specialists and market makers are dealers, while brokers are agents.

debenture A long-term debt obligation which, unlike a collateralized bond, only gives the lender a general claim against the borrower's assets. In a default the debentureholder has no claim against any specific assets.

debit balance A negative balance in a margin account.

debt/equity ratio The ratio of total debt to total equity.

debt securities Bonds and similar securities that call for the payment of interest until maturity and principal at maturity. A firm that defaults on its interest or principal obligations may eventually be forced into bankruptcy.

decreasing term A type of term insurance in which protection decreases with the insured's age.

deep-discount bond A bond selling for substantially less than its par value.

default Failure to live up to any of the terms in a bond indenture or other credit agreement.

default risk The risk that a debt security's contractual interest or principal will not be paid when due.

deferred compensation plan A procedure whereby employees are permitted to set aside and defer the tax liability on a portion of their wages and salaries into approved deferred compensation plans.

deflation An increase in the purchasing power of the dollar or some other currency unit. Deflation is the opposite of inflation.

depletion The writing off of assets, particularly mineral assets such as oil or natural gas, as they are exploited.

Depository Trust Company A firm that facilitates exchange members' securities trading with each other, using bookkeeping entries rather than physical delivery of the stock certificates.

depreciation A deduction from income that allocates the cost of fixed assets over their useful lives.

depression An economic collapse with high unemployment and slow or negative economic growth.

dilution Issuing additional shares, thereby reducing proportional ownership of existing shareholders.

discount brokers Brokers who charge below-retail commission rates, usually coupled with more limited investment services.

discount loan A loan from the Fed to a member bank to cure a temporary reserve deficiency.

discount rate 1. The interest rate charged by the Fed on loans to member banks. 2. The interest rate applied to an income stream or expected income stream in estimating its present value.

discount yield A yield computation in which the return is based on the final value of the asset. A bill that sells for $100-x$ and matures in one year at 100 has a yield of $x\%$.

disintermediation The tendency of high interest rates to draw funds out of thrift institutions and therefore away from the mortgage market.

diversifiable risk Firm-specific or industry-specific risk that tends to average out in an efficiently diversified portfolio.

diversification The technique of spreading one's investment portfolio over different industries, companies, investment types, and risks. This technique is used to reduce risks by not having "all of your eggs in one basket."

dividends Payments made by companies to their stockholders; usually financed from profits.

dividend exclusion An amount of qualifying dividends which an individual may exclude from taxable income.

dividend reinvestment plan A company program that allows its dividends to be reinvested in additional shares. The shares are often newly issued and may be sold at a discount from the current market price.

divisor The number divided into the sum of Dow Jones Industrial Average to determine the average. The divisor is adjusted to preserve consistency when any of the components is split.

dollar averaging A formula-investment plan requiring periodic (such as monthly) fixed dollar amount investments. This practice tends to "average" the unit purchase cost of an investment made over time.

Dow Jones Inc. The firm that publishes the *Wall Street Journal* and *Barron's*. Also compiles Dow Jones stock indexes.

Dow or Dow Jones Industrial Average The most commonly referred-to index of stock prices. The index is computed as the sum of the prices of thirty leading industrial firms, divided by a divisor which is adjusted to reflect splits of its components. Dow Jones indexes are also computed for utilities and transportation companies.

Dow Theory A charting theory originated by Charles Dow (Dow Jones Inc.). According to Dow Theory a market uptrend is confirmed if the primary market index (such as the Dow Jones Industrial Average) hits a new high which is soon followed by a high in the secondary index (such as the Dow Jones Transportation Index).

draft A checklike instrument which calls for payment upon receipt.

dual fund A type of closed-end investment company that divides its returns between dividend-receiving fundholders and capital gains holders.

dual listing A security listed for trading on more than one exchange.

Dun and Bradstreet A firm that rates the creditworthiness of many borrowers and generates financial ratios on many industry groups.

Dupont Equation A profitability relationship that relates return on equity to several components; ROE = ROS × Sales/Assets × Assets/Equity.

duration The weighted average rate of return of a bond's principal and interest. A superior index of the payback rate compared to maturity, which ignores returns prior to principal repayment.

earnings per common share (EPS) The net income of a company—minus any preferred dividend requirements—divided by the number of outstanding common shares.

economic analysis An evaluation of a firm's investment potential within its economic setting.

econometrics The statistical analysis of economic data.

econometric model A model based on an analysis of economic data; particularly models of the economy.

efficient frontier A set of risk/return tradeoffs, each of which offers the highest expected return for a given risk.

Efficient Market Hypothesis The theory that the market correctly prices securities in light of the known relevant information. In its weak form the hypothesis implies that past price and volume data (technical analysis) cannot be profitably used in stock selection. The semistrong form implies that no superior manipulation of public data can improve stock selection.

In the hypothesis' strong form, even inside (nonpublic) information is thought to be reflected accurately in prices.

efficient portfolio Portfolio on the efficient frontier, offering the highest expected return for that risk level.

election-year cycle The alleged tendency for the stock market to reach a peak about seven months after a presidential election and then fall to a low about eleven months later.

equipment trust certificate A type of bond collateralized by equipment, particularly railroad rolling stock or airplanes.

equity Net worth; assets minus liabilities. The stockholder's residual ownership position.

equity kicker A sweetener designed to make a debt issue more attractive by giving its owner an opportunity to benefit from the borrower's success.

equity accounting Partially consolidating income and equity of affiliates which are 20% or more owned by the parent firm.

equity notes Debt securities which are automatically converted into stock on a prespecified date at a specific price or one based on a formula that is prespecified.

ERISA (Employee Retirement Income Security Act) A 1974 federal law that protects worker's pension funds.

escrow account In general, an account designed to hold a sum of money for a specific purpose. In real estate, the fund is normally set up for monthly deposits of the expected pro-rata real estate taxes.

ESOP (Employee Stock Ownership Plan) A program in which a corporation contributes newly issued company stock worth up to 15% of employee payrolls into what amounts to a tax-sheltered profit sharing plan.

estate tax A progressive tax on the assets left by deceased parties.

Eurobond A bond, denominated in dollars or other currency, that is traded internationally.

Eurodollars Dollar-denominated deposits held in banks based outside the U.S. Most Eurodollar deposits are held in Europe; some are in Asia and other areas.

ex-dividend date The day after the day-of-record. Purchases completed on or after the ex-dividend date do not receive that period's dividend even if the stock is held on the payment date.

ex-rights period The time subsequent to the day-of-record for a rights distribution.

exemption A sum (currently $1,000 per dependent) that an individual is permitted to deduct from his or her taxable income.

exercise value *see* intrinsic value

expected value The sum of the probabilities multiplied by their associated outcomes; the mean or average value.

expense deferral An accounting technique whereby expense recognitions are spread over time.

explanatory notes Letter-symbols attached to stock and bond quotations; they signal additional information.

extraordinary gain or loss An unusual nonrecurring gain or loss.

FASB (Financial Accounting Standards Board) An accounting organization which establishes rules for preparing financial statements.

face value The maturity value of a bond or other debt instrument; sometimes referred to as the bond's par value.

FDIC (Federal Insurance Deposit Corporation) A federal agency that insures deposits at commercial banks up to $100,000.

Fed (The Federal Reserve System) The federal government agency that exercises monetary policy through its control over banking system reserves.

Federal Reserve Board of Governors The governing body of the Federal Reserve System. The seven members are appointed by the President for long and staggered terms.

fixed-rate mortgage A mortgage having a constant interest rate for the life of the debt.

federal funds The market where banks and other financial institutions borrow and lend immediately-deliverable reserve-free funds, usually on a one-day basis.

FHA (Federal Housing Administration) A federal government agency that insures home mortgages.

FIFO (First In, First Out) An inventory valuation method whereby items taken out of inventory are assumed to have cost the amount paid for the earliest unused purchase.

fill-or-kill order An order that must be either immediately filled or canceled.

filter rules Any mechanical trading rule; for example, a rule to buy stocks when their PE ratio falls below some predetermined value or to trade whenever a particular price pattern is observed.

financial ratio A ratio, such as debt/equity or times-interest-earned, designed to reflect a firm's long-term financial strength.

fiscal policy Government tax and spending policy.

fiscalist A type of economist who believes that fiscal (not monetary) policy is the primary economic tool.

firm analysis Evaluating the strengths and weaknesses of a firm and its investment appeal vis a vis its markets and competitors.

Fitch [Francis Emory] Investors Service A bond rating service that is considerably less well known that Moody's and Standard & Poors.

fixed costs Costs that do not vary with output in the short-run.

fixed-income security Any security that promises to pay a periodic non-variable sum—such as a bond paying a fixed coupon amount per period.

flat Bonds which trade for a net price that does not reflect any accrued interest are said to trade "flat."

floating rate notes A type of debt security whose coupon rate varies with market interest rates.

floating rate preferred A type of preferred stock whose indicated dividend rate varies with market rates.

floor trader or registered competitive market maker (RCCM) One holding a seat on an exchange who trades for his or her own account.

Florida land boom A 1920s speculative real estate boom followed by a crash in the price of Florida property.

flower bonds Government bonds that may be used at par for estate tax payments.

flowthrough A method of handling investment tax credits in which benefits are taken into profit and loss statements as they are incurred rather than spread over the acquired asset's life (normalization).

FNMA (Federal National Mortgage Association) A previously government-owned, but now a privately owned, corporation which operates a secondary market in mortgages.

focal point A generally agreed-upon or recognized round number value.

footnotes to a financial statement An integral part of a financial statement; they explain or expand upon its entries.

Forbes A twice-monthly popular investment periodical. Famous for its *Forbes* lists, such as its list of loaded laggers.

Form 10K A detailed annual report that must be submitted to the SEC, listing exchange, and any shareholders who request it.

Form 10Q A detailed quarterly report that must be submitted to the SEC, listing exchange, and may be sent to shareholders who request it.

Form 13D A required SEC filing of any individual or group owning 5% or more of any public corporation. Form might disclose any relevant agreements of owners.

futures Deferred delivery commodities contracts.

Freddie Mac (The Federal Home Loan Mortgage Corporation) A government agency that assembles pools of conventional mortgages and sells participations in a secondary market.

front-end loading Taking a large portion of the sales fee from the early payments on a long-term purchase contract.

FSLIC (Federal Savings and Loan Insurance Corporation) A federal government agency which insures deposits at savings and loan associations up to $100,000.

full employment The unemployment rate which is thought to be the minimum level before inflationary pressures accelerate, and the maximum level the public will view as reasonable. Opinions on this level have over time varied from around 4% to 6%.

fundamental analysis The evaluation of firms and their investment attractiveness based on their financial, competitive, earning, and managerial position or similar evaluation of other investment types.

fourth market Direct trading of listed securities between institutions.

gambler's ruin The possibility that a series of adverse events may wipe out the individual's original capital.

Gamma factor The number of years of above-average growth at the recent past rate that is necessary to justify the current multiple on growth stocks.

GAAP (Generally Accepted Accounting Principles) A set of accounting principles that are supposed to be followed in preparing accounting statements.

general creditor A creditor whose loan is uncollateralized.

general mortgage bond A bond having a generalized claim against the issuing company's property.

general obligation A municipal bond secured by the issuer's full faith and credit.

gift tax A progressive tax on gifts; now incorporated with estate taxes.

gilt-edge security A very secure bond or other asset.

give-up A now-prohibited practice whereby brokers making trades for a mutual fund were directed to pay a portion of their commission fees to brokers who had sold the fund's shares.

GIC (guaranteed interest contract) An investment sold by insurance companies, it offers high yields plus the opportunity to earn similar returns on additions to plan.

Glass Steageall Act A 1933 federal act requiring the separation of commercial and investment banking.

GNMA (Government National Mortgage Association) A government agency that provides special assistance on selected types of home mortgages. Its securities are backed both by its mortgage portfolios and by the general credit of the government.

go-go fund A type of mutual fund popular in the late 1960s which sought short-term trading profits; also called a performance fund.

going public The process of a startup or heretofore-private firm selling its shares in a public offering.

golden parachute A very generous termination agreement for upper management; takes effect if control of the firm shifts.

good til canceled (GTC) order A type of order that remains in effect until executed or canceled.

goodwill The amount by which a firm's going concern value exceeds its book value.

governments U.S. Government bonds issued by the Treasury Department and backed by the full faith and credit of the government.

Graham or Graham and Dodd approach A type of securities analysis stressing fundamentals. Its originator, Benjamin Graham, coauthored the dominant investment text of the 1930s to 1950s.

Gray approach An investment timing device that seeks to identify over- and undervalued market phases on the basis of interest rates relative to PE ratios.

great crash 1929 stock market decline.

greater-fool theory The tongue-in-cheek view that a still "greater fool" will come along to bail out a foolish investment.

greenmail The practice of acquiring a large percentage of a firm's stock and then threatening to take over the firm unless management buys you out at a premium.

gross margin The net sales of an enterprise minus its cost of goods sold.

gross national product (GNP) The sum of the market values of all final goods and services produced annually in the country.

growth fund A common-stock mutual fund that seeks price appreciation by concentrating on growth stocks.

growth stock The shares of a company that is expected to achieve rapid growth; such shares often carry above-average risks and PE ratios.

guarantee bond or preferred A bond or preferred stock with a guarantee from a company other than the issuer.

head and shoulders price formation A technical pattern which looks like a head and shoulders and is said to forecast a price decline.

hedge fund A type of mutual fund that seeks to offset some of its long positions with short positions.

hedging Taking opposite positions in related securities, hoping to profit from relative price movements (risk hedging) or to reduce an existing risk (pure hedging).

histogram A discrete probability distribution display.

holding company A company set up to maintain voting control of other business enterprises.

holding period return The rate of return over some specific time.

horizontal spread Short and long option positions on the same security with the same strike price but different expirations.

Hulbert's Financial Digest A publication containing ratings of investment advisory services.

hypothecation The pledging of securities as loan collateral.

immunization The process of buying bonds with durations equal to one's investment horizon or using interest futures to accomplish the same purpose.

inactive post NYSE trading post for inactively traded securities.

in and out The purchase and sale of the same security within a short period.

income anticipation An accounting practice whereby a profit is reflected in the income statement before it is received.

income approach Valuing real estate or some other asset as the discounted value of its expected income stream.

income bond A bond on which interest is paid only if the issuer has sufficient earnings.

income fund A common stock mutual fund that concentrates on high-dividend-paying stocks.

income statement A financial statement of the firm's interim earnings; shows how revenues were spent and how much remains as net income.

income stock A stock with a high indicated dividend rate.

indenture of a bond The statement of promises the company makes to its bondholders. Among these is a commitment to pay a stated coupon amount periodically and return the face value (usually $1,000) at the end of a certain period (such as 20 years after issue). A trustee, such as a bank, is charged with overseeing the issuing-firm's commitments.

independence, statistical Two variables are independent if knowledge of one's value does not help explain the other's value. Thus, if IBM and AT&T stock returns are totally unrelated, knowing that AT&T stock returned X% over the most recent twelve months would not help explain IBM stock's return over the same period.

index fund A mutual fund that attempts to duplicate the performance of a market index such as the S&P 500.

industry analysis The evaluation of an industry's position and prospects as they relate to its component-firm's investment attractiveness.

inflation The rate of rise in the price level. If, on the average, $1.06 will buy what $1 would buy a year earlier, inflation has equaled 6%.

inflation hedge An asset whose value varies directly with the price level.

input/output model A model that relates various industries' outputs to their derived demands from other industries.

insider trading Buying or selling by persons having access to non public information relating to the company in question.

insolvency Insufficient liquid assets to meet currently due financial obligations.

installment sale In general, any sale that calls for payments to be made over time. In real estate transactions, an installment sale may reduce and postpone tax liability if the payments are stretched out over a sufficiently long period.

Instinet An automated communications network among block traders.

institutional investor An organization, such as a pension fund, mutual fund, bank trust department, insurance company or investment company, that invests the pooled assets of others.

intercorporate dividend Dividend payment from one corporation to another. Eighty-five percent of such dividends are not subject to the corporate income tax.

interest The amount a borrower pays for the use of a lender's funds; frequently expressed as an annual percentage of the principal balance outstanding and may be compounded on a monthly, quarterly, annual or some other periodic basis.

interest futures A commodity futures contract calling for delivery of a debt security such as a T-bill or long-term government bond.

interest-rate risk The risk that an interest rate rise will take place, thereby reducing the market value of fixed income securities.

international fund A mutual fund that invests in securities of firms based outside the fund's home country.

International Monetary Market A futures exchange associated with the Chicago Mercantile Exchange; trades futures contracts on gold, T-bills, Eurodollars, CDs, and several foreign currencies.

in-the-money option An option whose striking price is more favorable to option-holders than the current market price of the underlying security.

intraday dependencies Nonrandom price movements of transactions taking place over the course of a single day.

intrinsic value or exercise value That portion of an option's price which reflects its value if immediately executed. For a call, right or warrant, the market price of the underlying asset less the striking price, or zero if the difference is negative. For a put, the striking price less the stock price, or zero if the difference is negative.

investment Any asset expected to yield deferred benefits.

inverted market A futures market in which the futures price exceeds the spot.

investment banker Organizer of a syndicate to underwrite or market a new issue of securities.

Investment Companies Periodical reporting on mutual funds; published by Weisenberger.

investment company A company that manages pooled portfolios for a group of owners. The two types of investment companies are closed-end—whose fixed number of shares outstanding are traded like other shares—and open-end (mutual fund)—whose shares outstanding change by the amounts bought and sold.

Investment Company Institute Organization of mutual funds and other institutional investors; publishes *Mutual Fund Forum.*

investment manager One who manages an investment portfolio.

IRA (individual retirement account) A retirement plan which allows employees to set aside up to $2,000 annually in a tax-sheltered instrument.

January indicator A technical timing device holding that as January goes, so goes the year.

junk bonds High-risk bonds, usually promising a very high indicated return coupled with a substantial default risk.

Kansas City Board of Trade A futures exchange listing wheat and *Value Line* stock index futures.

Keogh account A retirement account that allows self-employed individuals to set aside (1984) up to $30,000 or 20% of their income into a tax-sheltered fund.

key person life insurance Life insurance on key employees with their employer as the beneficiary; designed to assure creditors and suppliers that the firm would survive the loss of the insured.

Krugerrand A South African gold coin containing one ounce of gold; often traded by gold speculators.

kurtosis The degree to which a distribution departs from normal. See also platakurtic and leptokurtic.

lagging indicators Government-compiled data series whose movements are identified as tending to follow turns in the overall economy.

law of one price Whenever two assets offer equivalent payoff matrices, their prices must be identical.

leading indicators Government-compiled data series whose movements are identified as tending to precede turns in the overall economy.

lettered stock Newly issued stock sold at a discount to large investors prior to a public offering of the same issue. Lettered stock buyers agree not to sell their shares for a prespecified period. SEC Rule 144 restricts such sales.

leakages In fiscal policy, stimulatory spending or tax-reduction impacts are reduced each round by funds that "leak" into savings, import purchases, or taxes.

legal lists Lists of stocks authorized by various states for fiduciary investing.

leg on The process of assembling a spread or other combination position one side at a time.

leptokurtosis The degree to which a distribution differs from the normal by having more probability in the peak and tails.

leverage Using borrowed funds or special types of securities (warrants, calls) to increase the potential return. Leverage usually increases both the risk and the expected return.

liabilities Debts; appear on right side of a balance sheet.

LIFO (Last In, First Out) An accounting method which for income reporting purposes values items taken out of inventory at the most recent unused invoice cost.

line of credit Prearranged agreement from a lender to supply up to some maximum loan at prespecified terms.

limited liability Property that under most circumstances limits shareholders' liabilities for their corporation's debts to their initial investments.

limit order An order to buy or sell at a prespecified price.

linear model A method of estimating portfolio risks which requires only α and β estimates of the components.

liquidation The process of selling all of a firm's assets and distributing the proceeds first to creditors and then any residual to shareholders.

liquidation value The value of a going concern's assets if sold piecemeal.

liquidity The ease with which an investment can be converted to cash for approximately its original cost plus its expected accrued interest.

Liquidity Preference Hypothesis The term-structure-of-interest-rates hypothesis; asserts that most borrowers prefer to borrow long and most lenders prefer to lend short, implying that long rates generally exceed short rates.

liquidity ratio A ratio (such as current and quick) of a firm's short-run financial situation.

liquidity risk The degree to which an asset's holding-period return varies with interest-rate moves.

listed stocks Stocks approved for trading by one or more of the stock exchanges.

listing The act of obtaining exchange approval for trading.

listing requirements The qualifications that a company must meet in order to be listed on an exchange.

load The selling fee applied to a load mutual fund purchase.

load fund A mutual fund type sold through agents who receive fees that are typically 8.5% on small purchases and somewhat less on above-$10,000 trades.

long-interest The number of outstanding futures or options contracts owned.

long position The ownership of stocks or other securities; opposed to a short position, where one has sold securities that are not owned.

long-term (fixed) assets Tangible assets with a relatively long expected life (greater than a year), which are not intended for resale and which are used in the operations of the business; includes plant and equipment but not inventories or accounts receivable.

long-term capital gain or loss Gain or loss on a capital asset held for at least six months.

long-term liabilities Liabilities that are not due in the next year or next operating period, whichever is shorter; usually includes outstanding bonds, debentures, mortgages, term loans, and similar types of debt.

low-PE stocks Stocks with low price/earnings ratios.

management control A situation in which no group owns enough of the firm's stock to exercise control, thereby abdicating control to the managers.

management-oriented company A firm run largely in the interest of management as opposed to that of the shareholders.

manufactured call A call-like position generated by a combination put and long position in the underlying stock.

margin Borrowing to finance a portion of a securities purchase. The Fed regulates the extent of margin borrowing by setting the margin rate. If a 60% rate is set, $10,000 worth of stock may be purchased with up to $4,000 of borrowed money. Only listed and some large OTC companies' securities qualify for margin loans.

margin call A demand by a brokerage firm for more collateral or cash to support existing margin debt; required when the borrower's equity position falls below a preset percentage (e.g. 35%) of the value of margined securities.

margin rate The percentage of the cost of a purchase of marginable securities which must be paid for with the investor's own money.

marginal tax rate The percentage that must be paid in taxes on the next income increment.

market approach Valuing properties (particularly real estate) relative to what similar properties are selling for.

marketability The ease with which an investment can be bought or sold without appreciably affecting its price. For example, "blue chip stocks" are usually highly marketable, since they are actively traded.

market indexes An average of security prices designed to reflect market performance. The Dow-Jones Industrial average is the best known and most closely followed of the market indexes. It is calculated by adding the market prices of 30 leading industrial companies and dividing by a divisor which is changed periodically to reflect stock splits. The Dow Jones Corporation also compiles averages for utility and transportation stocks. Standard & Poor's investor service, the NYSE, NASD, and AMEX all compute their own indexes. Indexes are also compiled for bonds, commodities, options, and various other investment types.

market (or technical) indicator A data series or combination of data series that is supposed to forecast the market's future direction.

market maker One who creates a market for a security by quoting a bid and asked price.

market model Relating the price of individual security returns to market returns with a linear equation of the form: $R_{it} = \alpha_i + \beta_i R_{mt}$ where R_{it} = return of security i for period t; R_{mt} = market return for period t and α_i and β_i are firm i parameters.

market order An order to buy or sell at the market price.

market portfolio A hypothetical portfolio representing each investment asset in proportion to its relative weight in the universe of investment assets.

market price The current price at which willing buyers and willing sellers will transact.

market or systematic risk The return variability associated with general market movements; not diversifiable within the market.

mark-to-market Practice of recomputing equity position in a margin account (stock or futures) on a daily basis.

matched and lost When two traders simultaneously arrive at the relevant trading post with equivalent orders, only one of which may be filled, they flip a coin to determine whose order is to be filled. The loser has "matched and lost."

maturity The length of time until a security must be redeemed by its issuer.

maturity date The date at which a security's principal must be redeemed.

mean The average or expected value of a sample or distribution.

me-first rules Restrictions in a bond's indenture that limit a firm's ability to take on additional debt with similar standing to that of the bonds in question.

merger The act of combining two firms into a single company.

MGIC (Mortgage Guarantee Insurance Corporation) A firm that guarantees timely payments of a portion of certain mortgages' obligations.

middle-of-the-road fund A mutual fund which invests in a balanced portfolio of stocks (some blue chips and some more speculative).

mode The high point or most likely outcome of a distribution. For a symmetrical distribution, the mode and mean (average value) are identical.

Monday-Friday stock pattern The observed tendency of stock prices to decline on Mondays and rise on Fridays.

monetarist One who emphasizes the powerful economic role of monetary (as opposed to fiscal) policy.

monetary asset An investment denominated in dollars.

monetary policy Government policy which utilizes the money supply to affect the economy. The Fed influences the money supply through its control of bank reserves and required reserves.

money fund or money market mutual fund A mutual fund which invests in short-term highly liquid securities.

money illusion Failure to take account of inflation's impact.

Money Magazine A monthly personal finance periodical published by Time Inc.

money market The market for high-quality short-term securities such as CDs, commercial paper, acceptances, Treasury bills, short-term tax-exempt notes, and Eurodollar loans.

money market account A type of bank or thrift institution account that offers unregulated money market rates; requires a minimum deposit of $2,500 and limits withdrawals to six per month, only three of which may be by check.

money multiplier The ratio of a change in reserves to the change in the money supply.

money supply The sum of all coin, currency (outside bank holdings), and deposits on which check-like instruments may be written.

mood indicators Technical market indicators designed to reflect the market's pessimism or optimism.

Moody's Industrial Manual An annual publication containing detailed historical information on most publicly traded firms.

Moody's Investor Service A firm which publishes manuals containing extensive historical data on a large number of publicly traded firms. Moody's also rates bonds.

mortgage A loan collateralized by property, particularly real estate. The lender is entitled to take possession of the property if the debt is not repaid in a timely manner.

mortgage-backed security A debt instrument representing a share of (e.g. GNMA pass throughs), or backed by (FNMA bonds), a pool of mortgages.

multiplier The ratio of the change in government spending to the resulting change in the GNP.

municipals Tax-free bonds issued by state and local governments.

municipal bond fund A mutual fund holding a portfolio of municipal bonds.

multi-index model A method of estimating portfolio risk; utilizes a market index and indexes for various market subcategories.

mutual fund A pooled investment in which managers buy and sell assets with the income and gains and losses accruing to the owners. May be either load (with sales fee) or no-load (no sales fee). In either case the fund stands ready to buy back its shares at their net asset value.

mutual fund cash position A technical indicator based on mutual fund liquidity. High fund liquidity is said to be associated with subsequent market rises.

Mutual Fund Forum Periodical featuring articles on mutual funds; published by Investment Company Institute

naked option writing Writing options without owning the underlying shares. If the option is exercised, the naked writer must buy the required shares on the market.

NASD (National Association of Security Dealers) The self-regulator of the OTC market.

NASDAQ (National Association of Security Dealers Automated Quotations) The name applied to stock quotation machines of NASD.

NASDAQ Composite Index A value-weighted index of OTC issues.

NASDAQ National List A second (after the National Market List) list of OTC stocks carried in most newspaper stock quotations. Membership is determined by criteria similar to AMEX listing.

NASDAQ National Market List A list of the most actively traded OTC stocks. Its newspaper quotations contain the same information as the NYSE and AMEX listings.

National Association of Investment Clubs Organization that fosters and assists in the setting up of investment clubs.

NAV (net asset value) The per-share market value of a mutual fund's portfolio.

NBER (National Bureau of Economic Research) A private nonprofit research foundation that dates business cycles and sponsors economic research.

near money Assets such as savings accounts and Treasury bills that can quickly and easily be converted into spendable form.

net worth *see* Equity

new issue An initial stock sale, usually of a company going public; also an initial sale of a bond issue.

new listing A stock recently listed on an exchange. The listing may be its first or it may have previously been listed on some other exchange.

New York Curb Exchange The former name for American Stock Exchange.

nifty fifty A list of about fifty companies with high multiples and rapid growth rates which are preferred by many institutional investors.

no-load fund or no-load mutual fund A fund whose shares are bought and sold directly at the fund's NAV. Unlike a load fund, no agent or sales fee is involved.

non-market or unsystematic risk Individual firm risk not related to general market movements.

non-normal distribution A distribution, such as a skewed distribution of returns, which differs from the normal shape.

nonparticipating insurance An insurance type sold by a (stock) company owned by the firm's shareholders, as opposed to participating insurance,

which is owned by its policyholders (mutual).

normal distribution A distribution corresponding to the normal shape.

normalization Spreading the benefits of investment tax credits across the life of an asset. *See also* flowthrough.

notes Intermediate-term debt securities issued with maturity dates of one to five years.

NOW (Negotiable Orders of Withdrawal) Accounts A special type of deposit account that draws interest and allows check-like instruments to be written against it.

NYFE (New York Futures Exchange) A futures exchange associated with the NYSE which lists a futures contract on the NYSE composite index.

NYSE (New York Stock Exchange) The largest U.S. stock exchange.

NYSE Composite Index A value-weighted index of all NYSE-listed securities.

odd-lot A transaction involving less than one round lot of stock. Most stock is traded in round lots of 100 shares. A few stocks are traded in 10-share round lots, however.

odd-lotter One who trades in odd-lots.

odd-lot short ratio A technical market indicator based on relative short trading by small investors. The market is said to be near a bottom when small investors are selling short in disproportionate numbers.

off-board trading Trading that takes place off an exchange, particularly OTC trading in NYSE-listed securities. NYSE rule 390 restricts such trading by NYSE member firms.

one-decision stocks A now largely discredited concept of the early 1970s that said certain high-quality growth stocks should be bought and held. Supposedly the only decision was to buy.

open-end investment company A mutual fund or other pooled portfolio of investments that stands ready to buy or sell its shares at their NAV or NAV plus load if the fund has a load.

open interest The number of option or commodity contracts outstanding. Analogous to shares outstanding for stock.

Open Market Committee The Federal Reserve Board committee that decides on open-market policy. The Committee consists of all seven of the Federal Reserve Board Governors plus five of the presidents of the regional Fed banks, including the president of the New York bank.

open market operations Fed transactions in the government bond market. Open market operations affect bank reserves and thereby influence the money supply, interest rates, and economic activity.

option A put, call, warrant, right, or other security giving the holder the right but not the obligation to purchase or sell a security at a set price for a specific period.

ordinary least squares A method of estimating regression parameters by choosing linear coefficients which minimize the square of the residuals.

organizational slack Wasted firm resources due to managerial deadwood, lack of aggressiveness, carelessness, etc.

OTC (Over the Counter) The market in unlisted securities and off-board trading in listed securities.

out-of-the-money option An option whose striking price is less attractive than the current market price of its underlying stock.

overbought An opinion that the market has risen too rapidly and is therefore poised for a downward correction.

oversold An opinion that the market has fallen too rapidly and is therefore poised for an upward correction.

Pac Man defense Tactic to avoid takeover by attempting to take over the attacking firm.

paper *see* commercial paper

paper loss An unrealized loss.

paper profit An unrealized gain.

par 1. The face value at which a bond issue matures. 2. A stated amount below which per-share equity (net worth) of a common stock may not fall without barring dividend payments. 3. The value on which a preferred stock's dividend and liquidation value is based.

par ROI equation An empirically estimated profitability equation of the Strategic Planning Institute.

participating bond Bond that may pay extra coupon increment if the issuing firm is especially profitable.

participating preferred Preferred stock that may pay an extra dividend increment if the issuing firm is especially profitable.

participating life insurance Life insurance sold by a mutual company owned by, and sharing its profits with, its policyholders.

passed dividend The omission of a regular dividend payment.

passthrough A share of a mortgage pool whose interest and principal payments are flowed through to the holders.

payback period The length of time until an original investment is recaptured.

payout ratio Dividends per share as a percentage of earnings per share.

penny stock market A market for low-priced stocks (under $1 per share), especially active in Denver, Colorado.

PE ratio The stock price relative to the most recent 12-month earnings per share.

PE ratio model A model designed to explain PE ratios.

percentage order A market or limit order which is entered once a certain amount of stock has traded.

performance fund A type of mutual fund popular in the late 1960s that primarily sought short-term trading profits.

physical The underlying physical delivery instrument for a particular futures contract.

pink sheets Quotation source for most publicly traded OTC issues.

pit The name of the physical location where specific commodity contracts are traded.

planning horizon The time-frame in which a portfolio is managed.

platakurosis The degree to which a distribution differs from the normal by having more of the distribution concentrated at the peaks and tails.

point Pricing units; for stocks, a point represents $1 per share; for bonds, a point is equivalent to $10.

point and figure chart A technical chart with no time dimension.

points A fee charged for granting a loan, especially for a mortgage on real estate.

poison pill Antitakeover defense in which a new diluting security is issued to existing shareholders if control of the firm is about to shift.

ponzi scheme An investment scam promising high returns, which are secretly paid out of investor capital. The scam is usually exposed when incoming funds are insufficient to cover promised outpayments.

pooling-of-interest accounting A type of merger accounting in which an acquired firm's assets and liabilities are transferred to the acquiring firm's balance sheet without any valuation adjustment.

portfolio A holding of one or more securities by a single owner (institution or individual).

portfolio risk Risk that takes account of the diversifying impact of portfolio components.

position trader A commodity trader who takes and holds futures positions for several days or more.

post or trading post One of eighteen horseshoe-shaped locations on the NYSE floor where securities are traded.

postponable expenditures Purchases of long-term assets such as consumer durables.

preemptive rights Shareholder rights to maintain their proportional share of their firm by subscribing proportionally to any new stock issue.

preferred stock Shares whose indicated dividends and liquidation values must be paid before common shareholders receive any dividends or liquidation payments.

premium (bond) 1. The amount by which a bond's price exceeds its par. 2. The market price of an option; confusingly, the term is also sometimes used to refer to time value.

premium-over-conversion value The amount by which a convertible's price exceeds its conversion value.

premium-over-straight-debt value The amount by which a convertible's price exceeds its value as a nonconvertible debt security.

present value The value of a future sum or sums discounted by the appropriate interest rate.

prepayment penalty The fee assessed for early liquidation of an outstanding debt.

price dependencies Price movements related to past price movements.

price floor The support level a convertible bond provides by its straight-debt value.

price stability The absence of inflation or deflation.

primary distribution The initial sale of a stock or bond (new issue).

primary market The market for initial sales of securities.

prime rate The loan rate banks advertise as their best (although some very secure borrowers may receive a still lower superprime rate).

principal 1. The person or institution for whom an agent acts in a trade. 2. The face value of a bond.

private placement A direct security sale to a small number of large buyers.

probability distribution A display of possible events along with their associated probabilities.

profit Net revenues minus costs.

profit and loss statement A financial accounting of revenues and expenses during a specified period, i.e., three months, one year, etc. *See also* income statement.

professional corporation pension plan Professionals such as doctors, lawyers, and architects may organize their businesses as corporations and then set up pension plans as a means to shelter income from taxes. The 1982 tax act severely limited the amount of tax-sheltered contributions that may be put into such plans.

profitability models Models designed to explain company profit rates.

profitability ratio A ratio, such as return on equity and return on sales, designed to reflect the firm's profit rates.

prospectus An official document that all companies offering new securities for public sale must file with the SEC; spells out in detail the financial position of the offering company, what the new funds will be used for, the qualifications of the corporate officers, and any other material information.

proxy A shareholder ballot.

proxy right A contest for control of a company.

proxy material A statement of relevant information which the firm must supply to shareholders when they solicit proxies.

public offering A security sale made through dealers to the general public and registered with the SEC.

purchase accounting A type of merger accounting in which the net assets of the merged firm are entered on the books of the acquiring firm at amounts that sum to the firm's acquisition price.

pure-risk premium The portion of the expected yield above the riskless rate that is due to pure risk aversion as opposed to the expected default loss.

put An option to sell a stock at a specified price over a specified period.

put bond A bond with an indenture provision allowing it to be sold back to the issuer at a prespecified price.

put/call parity A theoretical relation between the value of a put and call on the same underlying security with the same strike and expiration date.

quarterly report A report to shareholders containing three-month financial statements.

quick ratio or acid-test ratio Liquid assets (cash and receivables) divided by current liabilities.

rally A brisk general rise in security prices, usually following a decline.

random walk A process analogous to the movement of a drunk in the middle of a large field. At any time he or she is as likely to move in one direction as another. The random motion of stock prices implies that the next price change is as likely to be up as down, regardless of past price behavior. In the physical sciences this type of behavior is called *Brownian motion.*

rate of return A rate that takes into account both dividends and capital appreciation (increases in the price of the security). A 9% rate of return implies that one who owns $100 worth of stock will earn a total of $9 in dividends and capital appreciation over the forthcoming year.

rating on a bond A quality- or risk-evaluation assigned by a rating agency such as Standard & Poor's or Moody's.

ratio analysis Balance sheet and income statement analysis utilizing ratios of financial aggregates.

record date The shareholder registration date that determines the recipients for that period's dividends.

real estate sales company A firm that sells property, especially at complementary dinners. The property is often in a distant location and part of a projected retirement or vacation development.

real return A return adjusted for changes in the price level. If the nominal rate of return were 11%, a 3% inflation rate would reduce the real return to 8%.

recession An economic downturn. The National Bureau of Economic Research (NBER) informs the government and country when the economy is in a recession. In the past, two successive quarters of decline in real (in noninflationary dollars) GNP has signaled the start of a recession.

redemption fee A charge sometimes assessed against those who cash in their mutual fund shares.

redemption price The price at which a bond or preferred stock may be called prior to its maturity. Also referred to as the call price.

refinancing The selling of new securities to finance the retirement of others that are maturing or being called.

registered competitive market maker (RCCM) *see* floor trader

registered bond A bond whose ownership is determined by registration, as opposed to possession (bearer bond).

registered representative A full-time employee of a NYSE member firm who is qualified to serve as an account executive for the firm's customers.

registered trader An exchange member who trades stocks on the exchange floor for his or her own account (or account in which he or she is part owner).

registrar A company, such as a bank, which maintains the shareholder records.

registration statement A statement that must be filed with the SEC before a security is offered for sale. The statement must contain all materially relevant information relating to the offering. A similar type of statement is required when a firm's shares are listed.

regional exchange A U.S. stock exchange located outside of New York City.

regression An equation that is fitted to data by statistical techniques, with computers often used to perform the calculations. In the simplest case, a regression will have one variable to be explained (dependent variable) and one variable to explain it (independent variable); it takes the form: $x_t = a + by_t$ (where x_t = dependent variable; y_t = independent variable; and a and b are parameters selected by the computer that best fits the data). Graphically, one can envision a scatter diagram relating x_t and y_t with a line drawn through the points close to line on the average) as the regression line. The "a" is the intercept and "b" the slope coefficient of this line. More complicated regression equations of the form $x_t = a + by_t + cz_t + dw_t + ev_t \ldots$ containing more than one explanatory variable may also be estimated. Again the computer can be used to select the best values of a, b, c, etc.

regression toward the mean The tendency of many phenomena to migrate toward the average over time.

Regulation Q A Fed rule that limits interest rates that banks and thrifts can pay on certain types of deposits/ investments. Deregulation has largely eliminated the regulation's effect.

Regulation T A Fed rule that governs credit to brokers and dealers for security purchases.

Regulation U A Fed rule that governs margin credit limits.

reinvestment risk The risk associated with reinvesting coupon payments at unknown future interest rates.

REIT (real estate investment trust) Company that buys and/or manages rental properties and/or real estate mortgages and pays out more than 95% of its income as dividends; no corporate profit taxes are due on such income.

relative strength A technical analysis concept that stocks which have risen relative to the market exhibit "relative strength," which tends to carry them to still higher levels. Tests of the concept are largely negative.

reorganization Restructuring a firm's capital structure and operating facilities in the face of a default, near-default, or bankruptcy.

replacement cost approach The valuing of real estate or other assets on the basis of the cost of producing equivalent assets.

Repo (repurchase agreement) A type of investment in which a security is sold with a prearranged purchase price and date designed to produce a particular yield.

reserve requirement The percentage of reserves the Fed requires each bank to have on deposit for each increment of demand or time deposits.

resistance level A price range which, according to technical analysis, tends to block further price rises.

retained earnings That portion of profits not paid out in corporate profit taxes or dividends.

return on equity Profits after taxes, interest, and preferred dividends as a percent of common equity.

return on investment Profits before interest and taxes as a percent of total assets.

return on sales Profits as a percentage of sales

revenue bond A municipal bond backed by the revenues of the project that it finances.

reverse crush A commodity trade involving buying oil and meal and selling soybean futures.

reverse split A security exchange in which each shareholder receives a reduced number of shares but retains the same proportional ownership. Thus a ten-for-one reverse split would exchange ten new shares for each one hundred old shares.

retained earnings Annual after-tax profits less dividends paid (income statement) or the sum of annual retained earnings to date (balanced sheet).

riding the yield curve A bond portfolio management strategy taking advantage of an upward sloping yield curve by purchasing intermediate-term bonds, then selling them as they approach maturity.

right A security allowing shareholders to acquire new stock at a prespecified price over a prespecified period. Rights are generally issued proportional to the number of shares currently held and are normally exercisable at a specified price, usually below the current market. Rights usually trade in a secondary market after they are issued.

risk The variance of the expected return, i.e. the degree of certainty associated with the expected return.

risk arbitrage Taking offsetting positions in the securities of an acquisition candidate and its would-be acquirer.

risk-averse Preferring security and demonstrating a willingness to sacrifice return to achieve a more secure yield.

risk-neutral Preferring the highest return without regard to risk; indifference to risk.

riskfree rate The interest rate on a riskless investment such as a Treasury bill.

riskless investment An investment having an expected return which is certain: if a riskless asset is expected to yield 6%, the chance of a 6% return is 100%.

risk premium The return in excess of the riskfree rate reflecting the investment's risk.

risk/return tradeoff Tendency for more risky assets to be priced to yield higher expected returns.

Robert Morris Associates An organization of bankers that compiles averages of financial ratios for various industry groups.

round lot The basic unit in which securities are traded; 100 shares is a round lot for most stocks, although some trade in 10-unit lots.

Rule 144 An SEC rule restricting the sale of lettered stock.

Rule 390 An NYSE rule restricting members from off-board trading.

Rule 415 An SEC rule allowing shelf-registration of a security, which may then be sold periodically without separate registrations of each part.

rule of 20 Market timing rule holding that the Dow Jones Industrial Average's PE plus the inflation rate tend to 20. Thus departures in either direction tend to be followed by a reversal.

run An uninterrupted series of price increases or a similar uninterrupted series of price decreases.

Sallie Mae (Student Loan Market Association) A federal government agency which sells notes backed by government-guaranteed student loans.

saturation effect The impact on revenues and profits when a heretofore rapid-growth firm or industry largely satisfies its market's demand.

savings bonds Low-denomination Treasury issues designed to appeal to small investors.

scalper A commodity trader that seeks to profit from very short-run price changes.

seasoning The process of new issues acquiring market acceptance in after-issue trading.

seat A membership on an exchange.

SEC (Securities and Exchange Commission) The government agency with direct regulatory authority over the securities industry.

secondary distribution A large public securities offering made outside the usual exchange or OTC market. Those making the offering wish to sell more of the security than they believe can be easily absorbed by the market's usual channels. A secondary offering spreads out the period for absorption.

secondary market The market for already-issued securities; may take place on the exchanges or the OTC market.

second mortgage A mortgage debt secured by a property's equity after the first mortgage holders claim has been subtracted from the pledged asset's value.

securities Paper assets representing a claim on something of value, such as stocks, bonds, mortgages, warrants, rights, puts, calls, commodity contracts, or warehouse receipts.

Securities Amendment Act of 1970 An act that restricts front-end loading fees that mutual funds can charge.

security market line The theoretical relation between a security's market risk and its expected return.

segmented markets hypothesis A theory that explains the term structure of interest rates as due to the supply and demand of each maturity class.

self-tender A firm tendering for its own shares; often used as an antitakeover defense.

seller-financing A procedure using the real estate seller to finance part of purchase price.

selling short The act of selling a security that is not owned. Securities belonging to someone else are borrowed and sold. When the short-seller covers, equivalent securities are bought back and restored to the original owner.

semistrong form of the efficient market hypothesis The view that market prices quickly and accurately reflect all public information; implies that fundamental analysis applied to public data is useless.

semiweak form of the efficient market hypothesis The view that market prices cannot be successfully forecast with technical market indicators.

serial bond A bond issue, portions of which mature at stated intervals rather than all at once.

serial correlation Correlation between adjacent time series data.

shark repellant Action designed to prevent a hostile takeover.

shelf registration An SEC provision allowing preregistration of an amount of a security to be sold over time without specific registration of each sale. Permitted by SEC Rule 415.

short against the box The short-selling of stock which is owned; usually employed as a tax device for extending the date of realizing a gain.

short covering Buying an asset to offset an existing short position.

short-interest 1. The number of commodity futures or options contracts written and outstanding. 2. The number of shares of stock sold short.

short position To have sold an asset that is not owned in the hopes of repurchasing it later at a lower price.

short-squeeze The result of powerful forces driving up a stock's prices, thus squeezing a substantial short-interest.

short swing rule Rule requiring insiders (including holders of more than 10% of a firm's stock) to turn over any gains made on holdings that are sold less than six months after they were purchased.

short-term gains or losses Gains or losses on capital assets held less than one year. Such gains are fully taxable.

short-term trading index A technical market indicator based on the relative percent of advancing versus declining stocks.

short-term unit trust A unit investment trust made up of an unmanaged portfolio of short-term securities; usually self-liquidating within six months of issue.

single-index model A method of estimating portfolio risk which utilizes only the market index and market model, as opposed to the full variance/covariance matrix.

single-payment deferred-annuity contract An annuity with a defined future value; sold by an insurance company.

sinking fund An indenture provision requiring that a specific portion of a bond issue be redeemed periodically. Many bond indentures require sinking-fund provisions so that all of the debt will not come due simultaneously.

SIPC (Securities Investors Protection Corporation) A federal government agency which guarantees the safety of brokerage accounts up to $500,000, no more than $100,000 of which may be in cash.

skewed distribution A nonsymmetrical distribution which is more spread out on one side of its mode than the other.

skewness The degree to which a distribution is skewed.

Small-Savers Certificates A depository institution investment paying the 2 1/2 year Treasury rate on 2 1/2 year, $500 minimum certificates.

smokestack companies Basic-industry-type companies whose profits and sales are cyclical with the economy.

social responsibility fund A type of mutual fund that avoids investments in allegedly socially undesirable companies such as those involved with tobacco, alcohol, pollution, defense, South Africa, etc.

source and application of funds statement An accounting statement reporting a firm's cash inflows and outflows. Now called Changes in Financial Position Statement.

special offering or spot-secondary A large block of stock offered for sale on an exchange with special incentive fees paid to purchasing brokers.

specialized dependencies Predictable return patterns related to some specific type of event such as a new issue or tax-loss trading.

specialist An exchange member who makes a market in listed securities.

speculating The act of committing funds for a short period at high risk in the hopes of realizing a large gain.

SPI (Strategic Planning Institute) A strategic planning consulting firm that is famous for its Par ROI equation.

spot-market The market for immediate delivery (as opposed to futures market) of some item such as wheat or silver.

spot-secondary *see* special offering

S&P (Standard & Poor's Corporation) An important firm in the investment area that rates bonds, collects and reports data, and computes market indexes.

S&P 500 Index A value-weighted stock index based on 500 large firms' share prices.

split A security exchange whereby each shareholder ends up with more shares representing the same percentage of the firm. In a two-for-one split, a shareholder with 100 old shares would receive an additional 100 shares.

spread (bid/ask) The difference between the bid and ask price.

spread A type of hedge trade such as a vertical or horizontal spread (options) or some comparable combination trade in the futures market. The spreader takes offsetting positions in similar securities in the hopes of profiting from relative price moves.

Standard and Poor's Corporation Reports An investment periodical containing quarterly analysis of most publicly traded firms.

Standard and Poor's Encyclopedia A book containing analyses of S&P 500 stocks.

Standard and Poor's Stock Guide A monthly publication with a compact line of data on most publicly traded corporations.

Standard and Poor's Investor Service An important firm in the investment area; rates bonds, computes market indexes, and compiles investment information.

standard deviation A measure of the degree of compactness or spread of a distribution. In statistical terminology, one standard deviation is the square root of the variance. About two-thirds of the time, the actual value will be within one standard deviation on either side of the mean value. The chances are about 19 out of 20 that the actual value will be within two standard deviations of the mean. *See also* variance.

Stein estimators Statistical techniques for estimating a variable which assumes a regression toward the mean tendency.

Stock Clearing Corporation A NYSE subsidiary that clears transactions for member firms.

stock dividend A dividend paid in the form of additional stock. Similar to a stock split, but usually involves proportionately less new stock.

stock exchange An organization for trading a specific list of securities over specific trading hours, usually at a single location.

stockholder-oriented company A company whose management is particularly responsive to the interest of stockholders. A large ownership group may exercise effective control, or management itself may own a large block of the stock.

stock split The division of a company's existing stock into more shares (say, 2-for-1, or 3-for-1). Stock is usually split to reduce the price per share in the hopes of improving the shares' marketability

stop-limit order An order to implement a limit order when the market price reaches a certain level.

stop-loss order An order to sell or buy at market when a certain price is reached.

straddle 1. A combination put and call on the same stock at the same striking price. 2. Another name for a commodities spread where offsetting positions are taken in similar contracts, such as adjacent expirations of the same physical.

strap A combination of two calls and a put, each having the same strike and expiration date.

street name Securities held in customer accounts at brokerage houses, but registered in the firm's name.

straight-line depreciation A method of writing off assets at a constant dollar rate over their estimated lives.

straight-debt value The value of a convertible bond as a straight-debt (nonconvertible) bond.

striking price or strike The amount an optionholder has to pay (or will receive) to exercise an option.

strip A combination of two puts and a call, each having the same strike and expiration date.

strip bond A coupon bond with its coupons removed. Such a bond returns only principal at maturity, and thus is equivalent to a zero-coupon bond.

strong form of the efficient market hypothesis The view that market prices quickly and accurately reflect all public and nonpublic information; implies that inside information is useless in security selection.

subordination provisions Bond indenture provisions that give an issue a lower priority than other issues.

sum of the year's digits depreciation A method of accelerated depreciation which assigns depreciation equal to the ratio of the number of years remaining to the sum of the years in the asset's estimated life.

superNOW account An interest-bearing checking account with no set maximum interest rate; requires a $2,500 minimum balance.

support level A floor price which, according to technical analysis, tends to restrict downside price moves.

Survey Research Center Research institute at the University of Michigan that surveys and publishes statistics on consumer sentiments.

swap fund A type of mutual fund which allows purchases with shares of other companies at their market prices.

sweep account A type of bank account that daily sweeps the portion of the balance exceeding some pre-assigned minimum into a money fund, where rates are not limited by Fed restrictions.

syndicate A group of investment bankers organized to underwrite a new issue or secondary offering.

systematic risk *see* market risk

takeover bid A tender offer designed to acquire a sufficient number of shares to achieve working control of the target firm.

tax-loss carryforward Unutilized prior-period losses which may be employed to offset subsequent income.

tax-loss trading Year-end selling of depressed securities; designed to establish a tax-loss.

tax swap A type of bond swap in which an issue is sold to yield a tax loss and replaced with an equivalent issue.

tax-managed fund A type of investment company that seeks to convert dividend income into capital gains by organizing itself as a corporation rather than as a mutual fund and reinvesting its portfolio's dividends.

tax shelter An investment designed to yield tax-protected income for its owners, who are generally in high tax brackets.

TEBF (tax-exempt bond fund) A mutual fund that invests in municipal bonds, offering tax-free income to its holders.

technical analysis (narrow form) A method of evaluating securities based on past price and volume behavior. Largely debunked by evidence favorable to efficient market hypothesis.

technical analysis (broad form) A method of forecasting general market movements with technical market indicators.

technical indicator A data series said to be helpful in forecasting the market's future direction.

Templeton approach A fundamental approach to investment analysis which emphasizes a world view in finding undervalued issues; named after renowned mutual fund manager John Marks Templeton.

tender offer An offer to purchase a large block of securities made outside the general market in which the securities are traded (exchanges, OCT).

term insurance A life insurance type not having a savings feature. Rates rise with age to reflect the greater probability of death. *See also* whole life insurance.

term structure of interest rates A pattern of yields for differing maturities (risk controlled). *See also* segmented markets, unbiased expectations, and liquidity preference hypotheses.

term-to-maturity The length-to-maturity of a debt instrument.

thin market A market in which volume is low and transactions relatively infrequent.

thrifts Institutions other than commerial banks which accept savings deposits, especially savings and loan associations, mutual savings banks, and credit unions.

third market The over-the-counter market in listed securities.

tick The minimum-size price change on a futures contract.

ticker symbols Symbols for identifying securities on the ticker tape and quotation machines. Identifications are listed in *S&P Stock Guide* and several other publications.

ticker tape A device for displaying stock market trading.

Tigers (Treasury Investment Growth Receipts) Zero-coupon securities assembled by Merrill Lynch and backed by a portfolio of Treasury issues.

tight money Restrictive monetary policy.

times-interest-earned ratio Before-tax, before-interest profit relative to a firm's interest obligation.

time value 1. The value of a current, as opposed to a future, sum. 2. The excess of an option's market price over its intrinsic value.

title search A process whereby the validity of a title to a real estate parcel is evaluated.

TOLSR (Total Odd-Lot Short Ratio)
A technical market indicator that relates odd-lot short sales to total odd-lot trading.

top-tier stocks Established growth stocks preferred by many institutional investors.

total return Dividend return plus capital gains return.

total risk The sum of market and nonmarket risk.

trading post *see* post

transfer agent The agent who keeps track of changes in shareholder ownership.

transfer tax A New York state tax on the transfer of equity securities.

Treasury bills or T-bills Government debt securities issued on a discount basis by the U.S. Treasury.

Treasury stock Previously issued stock reacquired by the issuing company.

trustee A bank or other third party which administers the provisions of a bond indenture.

Turov's Formula A formula with which one computes the amount by which a stock price must change to produce equivalent returns on its options.

turnover Trading volume in a security or the market.

two-tier tender offer Takeover tactic in which one offer, usually for cash, is made for controlling interest in the target, and a second, less-attractive, offer is made for the remaining stock.

unbiased expectations hypothesis A theory explaining the term structure of interest rates as reflecting the market concensus of contiguous forthcoming short-rates.

underwriter An investment dealer who agrees to buy all or part of a new security issue from a company planning to sell the securities to the public at a slightly higher price.

unemployment The percentage of those actively seeking employment who are out of work.

universal life A type of life insurance in which the cash value varies with the policyholder's payments and the company's investment returns.

unit investment trust A self-liquidating unmanaged portfolio in which investors own shares.

Unlisted Market Guide An investment publication that periodically covers small companies not found in periodicals such as *Value Line* and *Standard and Poor's.*

unlisted security A security which only trades in the OTC market.

uptick A transaction that takes place at a higher price than the immediately preceding price.

unsystematic risk *see* nonmarket risk

urgent selling index A technical market indicator based on the relative volume in advancing and declining issues.

usable bond A bond that may be used at face to exercise corresponding warrants.

VA (Veterans Administration) A federal government agency which guarantees mortgage loans of veterans.

Value Line A firm which publishes quarterly analyses on about 1,700 firms and compiles the *Value Line Index*. Owned by Arnold Bernhard and Company.

Value Line Index An unweighted broadly based stock price index.

variable annuity An investment vehicle similar to mutual funds, but sold by insurance companies.

variable life A type of life insurance in which the cash value varies with the return of the policyholder's portfolio.

variable rate mortgage A mortgage in which the interest rate is allowed to vary with market rates.

variance The expected (average) value of the square of the deviation from the mean. Variance of $X = E(X-\bar{X})^2$ where $\bar{X}$ is X's mean and E is the expected value.

variance/covariance model A method of estimating portfolio risk which utilizes the variances and covariances of all the potential components.

Vasacheck adjustment A method of adjusting estimated betas based on the uncertainty of the mean and specific beta estimates.

venture capital Risk capital extended to start-up or small going concerns.

versus purchase order Sale order which specifies purchase date of securities to be delivered for sale.

vested benefits Pension benefits that are retained even if the individual leaves his or her employer.

vertical spread Short and long option positions on the same security with the same expiration but different striking prices.

volume The number of shares traded in a particular period.

Wall Street Journal A five-days-a-week business/investments newspaper published by Dow Jones Inc.

warrants Certificates offering the right to purchase stock in a company at a specified price over a specified period.

wash sale A sale and repurchase within 30 days that thereby fails to establish a taxable loss.

weak form of the efficient market hypothesis The view that market prices move randomly with respect to past price-return patterns; implies that the broad form of technical analysis is useless.

when issued Trading in as-yet-unissued securities which have a projected future issue date.

Weisenberger A major publisher of mutual fund investment information, including *Investment Companies*.

whole life insurance A type of policy that couples life insurance with a savings feature. Premiums are fixed and a surplus built up in the policy's early years meets claims that exceed premiums when the policyholders are older.

Wilshire 5000 Index A value-weighted stock index based on a large number of NYSE, AMEX and OTC stock.

wire house An exchange member electronically linked to an exchange.

working capital (gross) The sum of the values of a firm's short-term assets.

working capital (net) A firm's short-term assets minus its short-term liabilities.

working control The ownership of sufficient shares to elect a majority to the company's board of directors.

writer (of an option) One who assumes the short side of a put or call contract and therefore stands ready to satisfy the potential exercise of the long side.

yield The return of an investment expressed as a percentage of its market value.

yield (current) Current income (dividend, coupon, rent, etc.) divided by the price of the asset.

yield-to-earliest-call The holding-period return for the assumption that the issue is called as soon as the no-call provision expires.

yield-to-maturity The yield which takes account of both the coupon return and the principal repayment at maturity.

zero-coupon bond A bond issued at a discount to mature at its face value.

zero-tick A transaction immediately preceded by a transaction at the same price.

Index

Note: Entries in **boldface** indicate a table, chart, or graph.

Potatoes, on commodities market, 476–477

Preferred stock, 38, 50, 395–396
return on, 38
risk with, 38

Premium, defined, 427

Premiums and discounts on closed-end investment companies, 318

Premium over straight-debt value, 454

Present value:
applied to bonds, 94–95
applied to stocks, 100–101

Present-value equivalents, 93

Present-Value Tables, 96, 97
uses of, 96–98

Price/earnings ratio models, 217

Price/earnings ratios:
combined with other factors, 205–207
firm size, 206
research and development spending, 206–207
sales, 207
conflicting results with, 205
relative, 205
relative to inflation rates, 309–310
relative to interest rates (Gray approach), 308–309
use of in fundamental analysis, 202–207

Price floors and conversion premium, 456

Price/research and development ratio, 206–207

Price/sales ratio, 207

Primary market, 74–76, 78
going public in, 74–75
indirect stock sales: warrants and convertibles, 76
private placement in, 75, 78, 395
rights offerings in, 75–76

Private placement, 75, 78, 395

Probability distributions, 112–114

Probability Distribution of Returns, 113

Professional corporation pension plans, 15

Profitability, Key Determinants of, 174

Profitability models, 172–175
Boston Consulting Group (BCG) model, 172, 175
growth-share matrix, 172, 173
Strategic Planning Institute (SPI) model, 172–175

Profitability ratios, 168

Profit Impact of Marketing Strategies (PIMS), 172–173

Prospectus, 226–227

Proxy statements, 227

Psychological aspects of investing, 31–33
bias sources, 32

Pure option securities, 426–448
brokerage commission on, 444
put and call quotations, 429–432
terminology used, 427
trading. *See* Option trading strategies
Turov's formula, 432
valuation of, 432–434
See also Calls; Options; Puts; Rights; Warrants

Put and call quotations, 429–432

Put/call parity, 434

Put/Call Parity Formula, 449

Puts, 38
buying versus short-selling, 440
exercising versus selling in-the-money puts, 440
manufacturing, 440
trading strategies with, 439–440

Put terminology, 440

Quarterly earnings extrapolations, 106

Ratio analysis, 166–172
cash flow per share, 170
earnings per share, 170
efficiency ratios, 168
financial ratios, 166
illustrated, 168–170
liquidity ratios, 166
profitability ratios, 168
ratios summarized, 171
sources of ratios, 170